305.3896 Loughery, John.
LOU
     The other side of
     silence.

$35.00

DATE			

THE
OTHER SIDE
OF SILENCE

THE
OTHER SIDE
OF SILENCE

Men's Lives and Gay Identities:
A Twentieth-Century History

JOHN LOUGHERY

A JOHN MACRAE BOOK

Henry Holt and Company
New York

Henry Holt and Company, Inc.
Publishers since 1866
115 West 18th Street
New York, New York 10011

Henry Holt® is a registered trademark of
Henry Holt and Company, Inc.

Library of Congress Cataloging-in-Publication Data

Loughery, John.
The other side of silence : men's lives and gay identities :
a twentieth century history / John Loughery.—1st ed.
        p.   cm.
"A John Macrae book."
Includes bibliographical references (p.   ) and index.
ISBN 0-8050-3896-5 (HB : acid-free paper)
1. Gay men—United States—History—20th century. 2. Gay men—
United States—Social conditions. 3. Gays—United States—Identity. I. Title.
HQ76.2.U5L68   1998
305.38'9664—dc21   97-42575
                                                                        CIP

Henry Holt books are available for special promotions
and premiums. For details contact: Director, Special Markets.

First Edition 1998

Designed by Kelly Soong

Printed in the United States of America
All first editions are printed on acid-free paper.∞

3   5   7   9   10   8   6   4   2

Dedicated, once again,
to Tom

and to a few of the many men
who shared their vivid memories
of gay life before the 1960s:

Harry Adler

Bob Basker

Stephen Blair

Peter Conway

George Flemister

David L. Leavitt

Stuart Loomis

Jose Sarria

During the ride back Randall had his hand lying on mine, and a girl across the aisle made an audible remark about it to her companions. But Randall in his melodious voice said, "We should worry," and kept his hand on mine. He said, "Be glad she noticed, so she won't be shocked the next time she sees it."

—From *Jeb and Dash:*
A Diary of Gay Life, 1918–1945,
entry for 5 September 1920

Contents

Introduction

In his award-winning play *Clean*, produced just after his graduation from Yale Drama School in 1994, Edwin Sánchez wrote about a Puerto Rican family in New York City trying to understand their ten-year-old son's obsession with a handsome white parish priest and, as he grows into adolescence, his defiant acceptance of his own homosexuality. In roughest outline, *Clean* sounds like another coming-of-age tale, a staple of modern literature. Not so. Or, not exactly.

One of the interesting aspects of Sánchez's play, something that marks it as a work of the 1990s, is its slowly widening focus and the *unease* with which the young author views those discrete classifications of "old": homosexual and heterosexual. Gustavito, the boy filled with longing for a man he first sees as a father figure and then as a lover, is the protagonist, but the audience is also asked to consider, intimately and sympathetically, the dilemma of the priest who cannot contain his feelings for the boy; the frustrations of Gustavito's heterosexual brother; the confusion and rage of their father; and the surprise with which Norris, a black drag queen, confronts his own emerging passion for Gustavito's stepmother whom he has employed as his dressmaker. By the end of the play, "Miss Norry"—who has brought Gustavito to his first gay bar and offered to show him the ropes—is ready to see where his own unexpected love for a woman will take him, and the priest realizes that he cannot ignore the steadfast Gustavito indefinitely. Race, gender, sexuality, vocation, age, and even transvestism are seen as complications or impediments to love, but not—or not all of them—as fortress categories invulnerable to change or redefinition.

At any time before the 1960s, a play about a young man embracing his homosexual desires as fiercely as Gustavito does, and a priest owning to the same urges in himself, would have been shocking enough, and quite unstageable. But thirty years ago, as censorship barriers fell and the curiosity of mainstream audiences grew, many once-taboo subjects found their way into print or onto the stage or screen. The dimension of *Clean* that would have been troubling even into the 1970s and early 1980s has nothing to do with its honesty about gay passion and family dysfunction. Rather, it is Miss Norry's desire for Gustavito's stepmother that would have aroused an angry response. Fifteen or twenty years ago, a gay playwright writing about a gay male character (a screaming queen preoccupied with finding the perfect wedding gown, no less) who yearned for a woman was likely to be read as a betrayal of gay self-affirmation. A good woman might straighten a bent twig in the world of *Tea and Sympathy*, but by the 1960s, the boys in the band (so we were told) would always be the boys in the band and, in the late 1970s, the high-kicking drag queens of *La Cage aux Folles* would announce to thunderous applause, "I Am What I Am." A good deal of the gay movement even before Stonewall was predicated on the idea that sexual orientation is "fixed" early in life and, accordingly, no apologies were to be made for an alternative way of loving, an alternative form of lust, an alternative culture.

But Edwin Sánchez—and he is by no means alone in his generation—operates from a different self-affirming context than that of gay men of the 1970s. The old certainties and slogans are under attack. In the same vein, a nineties "queer" emphasis on the fluidity of sexual desire and disdain for "the clingy, cartoony embrace of 'gay pride' " (in the phrase of one gay commentator) is as unsettling to the Stonewall generation as radical gay liberation was to the men who "came out" in the 1940s and 1950s. Yet it is possible to see male homosexuality in America as a concept fashioned anew every twenty-five years or so, and the very adoption in some contemporary circles of the term *queer* (or *lesbigay*) in preference to *gay* marks another such shift.

The subject of this book is that still-unfolding process, whereby men who have made other men the focus of their romantic and erotic lives attempt to define themselves (to themselves and to society), wrestle with the narrow images society continues to foist on them, and decide to what extent they should view their sexuality as a defining characteristic of their lives.

The Other Side of Silence takes as its scope gay male life in the United States from the end of the First World War to the early 1990s. At the time of the 1919 scandal at the Newport Naval Station in Rhode Island, the topic of the first chapter, and throughout the twenties, a concept of a "homosexual identity" in America was in an early but dynamic stage. It was possible for a man like Harvard professor F. O. Matthiessen to write to his lover in 1925 about the "uncharted" land they were inhabiting, which (he nervously observed) called on them to "create everything for themselves." Yet other men had, even before this time, found tight circles of friends and extensive social networks to provide them with their bearings— and not only in the "fairy culture" that has been admirably charted in Jonathan Ned Katz's *Gay American History* (1976) and George Chauncey's *Gay New York* (1994). In fact, the tension between those men who embraced the label of "fairy" or "pansy" in the twenties and thirties and those who saw themselves as homosexuals but didn't wish to adopt the effeminacy of their more flamboyant peers was the first of the many conflicts that have characterized gay male life in twentieth-century America. Far from meaning one thing to all gay men, the import of their same-sex desires has varied enormously over the years, by region, color, and class as much as by personal circumstance and temperament.

It is doubtful, then, that any one book could do justice to this evolution, its range and permutations, and in no sense is the book in hand to be thought of as "definitive" or "comprehensive." Furthermore, there are good reasons why no single text should work toward that end. First, the necessary scholarship is in too rudimentary a stage. Over the last few years, excellent studies, oral histories, dissertations, and essays have appeared analyzing gay life in Manhattan (*Gay New York* and Charles Kaiser's *Gay Metropolis*), the rural Midwest (Will Fellows's *Farm Boys*), the South (James T. Sears's *Lonely Hunters*), San Francisco, Philadelphia, Seattle, and other cities (see, especially, Brett Beemyn's anthology *Creating a Place for Ourselves* and John Howard's *Carryin' on in the Lesbian and Gay South*). Barbara Smith's major study of the African-American gay and lesbian experience is in progress as I write, Latino- and Asian-American scholars are engaged in important research, and other books are forthcoming about the rise of the gay political movement and gay life in specific regions. But these explorations are only beginnings. Even more to the point, just as earlier summary statements about "the homosexual" have given way to a wider, deeper sense of the variety of gay lives, so the idea of a "gay community" or a "gay lifestyle" looks increasingly out-of-date. Most observations about gay Americans will apply to only a small segment of those men who identify as gay. That said, the corollary that gay men lack any version of a shared past, any cultural, psychological, and philosophical bonds spanning the decades, seems to me mistaken, and it is with those aspects of experience—of differing relevance to different groups—that this book deals. Even when told in a narrative style, such a history can only be fragmentary, highly subjective, and at points idiosyncratic, concerned as much with the symbolism of certain moments or the texture of certain lives as with anything more all-encompassing.

Gay history is also American history, though, and the widest possible context is desirable for understanding what it has meant to be gay in this country and in this century. The liberalized standards of public sexual expression (particularly in literature and film) and the gender-role anxieties of the 1920s; the impact of the Depression and the drive to demonize homosexuals as child molesters and Fascists; the turmoil of the Second World War and the divided character of the 1950s—McCarthyite repression amid an increasingly sexualized popular culture—as well as political activism and the rise of the counterculture in the 1960s, all play a crucial part in this endeavor. The famed Stonewall riot is set within its own context here as a culmination rather than an isolated uprising, just as the tenets of gay liberation and the bathhouse culture have to be considered against a backdrop of social criticism and anti-asceticism in society at large. Later chapters review the ensuing attempt to forge a gay culture that was more than social and sexual, the tensions between gay men of different colors, and of course the implications of the AIDS pandemic. *The Other Side of Silence* ends circa 1990, when new ambiguities about "gay" and "queer," about the fugitive status and impending assimilation of gay men, appeared to disrupt the clarity (and the neat battle lines) of the 1960s to the 1980s.

ANY WORK OF gay history, particularly a "popular history," is necessarily a chronicle of persecution and accomplishment. I do not share the belief that the injustices inflicted on homosexuals have been sufficiently documented and discussed so that all that is called for now are the higher reaches of theory or political predictions and strategizing for the next century. The extent of society's vilification of those men who are sexually different is a story that warrants further telling, not least because the daily and degrading injustices are still with us. The ways in which gay men have failed to respond to those attacks demand further attention, as does an appreciation of gay resistance and resilience. This chronicle ignores neither; there is reason to carp (and the 1990s have seen a number of stinging gay critiques of gay life) and there is reason to celebrate. Underlying all of these concerns, however, is the more pressing question of "gay identity" and the degree to which this is still a tenuous, ill-defined link between men who are primarily or exclusively homosexual.

When historian David Halperin writes that the modern practice of classifying human beings by their sexual preferences makes no more sense than would an attempt to classify them by their dietary preferences, anyone can nod in agreement. Who is so narrow as to project onto others, or to assume for oneself, a core identity as a salad lover or as a devout cake eater? Food choices might be important (they are to the dedicated vegetarian who distinguishes himself from the unrepentant carnivore), but they are not going to be the central facts of anyone's life. Gore Vidal has been sagely proselytizing on this theme for years: "Homosexual acts," yes. "A homosexual," no. What on earth, Vidal is fond of asking, do Roy Cohn and Eleanor Roosevelt have in common?

And yet when playwright Larry Kramer writes in his introduction to *The Destiny of Me* that his journey toward acceptance of his homosexuality, "from discovery through guilt to momentary joy and toward AIDS," has been more important than his life with his parents, his life as a writer, and his life as an activist, any gay man over thirty is likely to nod even more readily in agreement and understanding. "My homosexuality, as unsatisfying as so much of it was for so long," Kramer proclaims with typical bluntness, "has been the single most important defining characteristic of my life." We must choose between Vidal's appropriate but utopian sense that people are more complex beings than a simple designation like "gay man" or "lesbian" would imply and Kramer's insistence that there is no looking away from the unusual position homosexuals have been placed in by an intolerant culture, a position that asks homosexuals to confront and cope with a specific designation.

"The invocation of identity is always a risk," gender theorist Judith Butler has noted, referring to the dangers both of identity politics and the very act of self-naming and self-labeling. The caveat applies not only to the use of a single term—though it is doubtful that anyone has ever viewed himself or herself solely as a gay man, a lesbian, a Jew, an African-American, a southerner—but even to a multiplicity of labels. Yet there is an equivalent danger that the freedom of beyond-categorizing, never-to-be-summarized "personhood" carries with it a disconnectedness that is apt to fail us in critical moments. Nowhere was that more true than among those men who felt no particular ties to the gay world (especially as readers of the gay press) in the early 1980s. In many parts of the country, they were among the last to hear the warnings about the dangers of AIDS transmission and the least able to seek the support of other gay men and gay support structures in dealing with the illness. "Queer theory" makes salient observations about the ways in which language is a tool of the dominant order and identity politics confines its adherents, but most lives, it seems to me, take sustenance, periodically and to varying degrees, from concrete identifications that transcend uniqueness. The relevant questions are: What do these words ask of us in return for what they give? How long do they carry their invented meanings, and how easily and at what cost can they be discarded?

Growing up in an industrial town in central Connecticut in the 1960s, I knew and "placed" myself at fifteen, for instance, not only by the details of my personal history, the myriad quirks of my extended family, and my fantasies and aspirations, but by means of several nouns and adjectives—*Irish-Catholic, working-class, New Englander, homosexual,* even *future priest*: These were concepts that had a living meaning for me at the time. Rarely said aloud and not necessarily bound to any objective accuracy, they nonetheless provided certain things I needed: from a comfortable relation to the past of my immigrant relatives and the factory that employed so many of them, to the here-and-now of a particular landscape, climate, and cultural history I loved, which made me different (I imagined) from, say, southerners or farm boys; to a future that involved a form of service, but not a wife and children. By nineteen, that list had undergone some changes. *Gay* had replaced *homosexual* and meant something else (absurdly exciting rather than sadly narrow). *Irish-American* was now more applicable than *Irish-Catholic* even as I attended a Jesuit university in the Bronx but left the Church, and *New Yorker* and *would-be poet* became terms that distanced me from burdensome career expectations and the world of people who didn't spend all their time and money at plays and in coffee shops. Eventually, as my income ebbed and flowed and ebbed again, and as my ties to my family diminished, class and ethnicity gradually meant less as identifying markers. Those particular concepts acquired an ambiguity, a diffuseness, that they did not have earlier.

Everyone can offer his own version of these passages toward a never-finished self-determination. This book will argue, though, that homosexuals are in a peculiarly difficult situation in modern America in terms of their public *and* private identity and that that difficulty has to do with our inability to articulate to ourselves the potential value of those labels—and the history, bonds, and challenges that go with them. Few people regard a Jew's embrace of his religious and cultural background as a limitation on his individuality. No one sees an informed consciousness of "racial pride" as a ridiculous attribute for contemporary African-Americans or Latinos to cultivate. Many people—gay and straight—do indeed think it absurd or quaint that sexuality should be an issue of equivalent profundity. "I am not a 'professional gay,' " more than a few gay men interviewed for this book commented, and a standard heterosexual response has always been, "Why must you people make an issue of what you do in private? Why do you have to talk about it?" The naïveté of the heterosexual query means less, ultimately, than the defensiveness of the gay pronouncement, which is tied to several factors: principally, the lack of concreteness or lack of consensus that plagues the word *gay*, and fear of an openness from which there is no turning back.

How one reacts to loving or sexually desiring members of one's own sex does matter in twentieth-century America because society has made it matter by means of repressive laws, by condoning violence and discrimination, by its own incessant style of classifying and naming. It matters because we are all, always, ready to lose sight of the cultural and spiritual richness to which difference and uncertainty can lead. A more fully embraced gay identity—a question of nouns as much as adjectives—matters even if the homosexual impulse exists (as modern gender theory reminds us again and again) along a continuum and as a universal potentiality in a way that religion, race, or ethnicity does not. It matters today *even if it might be shed later*, in a less sexually divisive future in which homosexuals no longer feel the need to form social and political ties based solely on their same-sex orientation. The moments at which gay men have been cognizant of that truth, and the more frequent periods in which they have lost sight of it, are elements of this book.

Put another way, in the end even Roy Cohn and Eleanor Roosevelt—to borrow Vidal's too easy pairing—had a good deal in common. At some point in their lives (in the one case, much earlier than the other), they perceived a difference from their peers in their most fundamental yearnings, a difference so significant that it could not be voiced, so intense that it could not be ignored. Adulthood took them in opposite directions, to be sure: on the one hand, to work maniacally to achieve a place in a power structure that would keep victimhood at bay and, on the other, to change that power structure and speak on behalf of individuals who could not speak for themselves. Considered as adults, Cohn and Roosevelt would appear to verify the idea that entities such as "gay history," "gay identity," and "gay people" are chimerical or irrelevant. But it is with that earlier pained awareness that we might be more concerned, that experience shared by homosexual men and women, often in their youth—the universal starting point, the knowledge of a desire that must not be known, which initiates for many people a time of confusion and pretense that cannot plausibly be seen as a minor aspect of personality and outlook. Some men and women, we know, took their secret and their shame to their graves. Others acted on it (and still do) in self-destructive ways. A large number found their way to happiness and fulfillment. But still others chose to move beyond silence, to see what could be done, what humane capital could be made, out of that childhood or adolescent sense of otherness. We have yet to reap the full benefit of their daring, doubts, instructive failures, and hard-fought triumphs.

THE
OTHER SIDE
OF SILENCE

I. A New Order

1

Scandal in Newport

... thus the whirligig of war brings in its abrupt revenges.

—Radclyffe Hall,
The Well of Loneliness

In the spring and summer of 1919, only a few months after the Armistice was signed ending the war to end all wars, Franklin Delano Roosevelt, then assistant secretary of the Navy, found himself grappling with the embarrassing issue of homosexual sex in the military.

The problem originated with an investigation into "immoral conditions" in Newport, Rhode Island, but it might just as easily have started in Norfolk or San Francisco or any number of other cities where a lively local homosexual population and a naval installation full of young, sexually eager sailors came together. Its importance to later generations seeking to understand the development of sexual identity, the course of homophobia, or the urgent mainstream wish to ignore a gay presence in American society lies in the richness of its documentation (by way of the court transcripts) and the fascinating questions it suggests about how early twentieth-century men looked on the matter of enjoying sexual release and passionate attachments with other men. That the issue was bound to be brought into focus in a highly public way, given the social upheavals that America's involvement in the First World War precipitated, or accelerated, seems in retrospect almost inevitable.

For many Americans, the United States entry into the Great War in 1917 had promised to do more than defeat "the Hun," aid our embattled allies, and avenge the *Lusitania*. Their hope was that national virility would be reaffirmed and domestic uncertainties put to rest. In some concrete ways, the traditionalists were right—labor agitation and Progressive-era reform died with mobilization—but in others, particularly those having to do with mores and strict gender roles, a "return to normalcy" after Versailles was more wishful thinking than reality. Even for the victors, a world war brings in its wake "abrupt revenges," as Radclyffe Hall noted, and the nature of the ensuing turmoil, psychological as much as political, cannot always be anticipated. Many of the doughboys who returned from Europe were not the same innocents they had been before their time in the trenches and the brothels. Nor were their wives, daughters, and girlfriends, whose new ideas about suffrage, smoking, work, courtship, and attire presented formidable challenges to the patriarchal order. Nor, for that matter, were those men whose sexual urges were directed primarily, or exclusively, toward other men unaffected by the war years.

The existence in America of a large underground—and sometimes not so underground—world of men who violated society's codes of dress, deportment, and sexual desire was something residents of working-class neighborhoods had long been familiar with, but even the more sheltered urban middle class had been awakening to this truth for more than three decades. Reverend Charles Parkhurst's nocturnal tours of Manhattan's brothels in the early 1890s had brought him into contact with male prostitutes who wore makeup and used women's names—a particularly distressing revelation for the famous vice crusader—and the noted German sexologist Magnus Hirschfeld had been told upon visiting the United States in 1893 that, even if homosexual life in Boston and Philadelphia was not immediately apparent to him, its presence in those cities was nothing short of "colossal." A homosexual teacher in Denver, writing to Hirschfeld, seemed acquainted with the erotic possibilities of the Turkish bathhouses of New York, Boston, Philadelphia, Chicago, and "a small city in Ohio." The military base near Denver had been a source of good contacts as well, Hirschfeld's correspondent reported. A writer for the New Orleans *Times-Picayune* in 1895 was perceptive enough to see beyond the simple entertainment factor of Mardi Gras pageantry. "Carnival time suggests that all men and women are not what they seem," the reporter noted. "There are effeminate young men who like to parade in female attire."

These words allude to a subculture—frequently, but not entirely, defined by a male identification with traditionally female patterns of behavior—that many Americans preferred to know nothing about. But as the urban population grew, as the press became more vigorous and sensationalizing, and as the medical and legal authorities began to take notice, that blissful ignorance was coming to an end. In 1907 investigators in St. Louis had been shocked by the spectacle of a number of black men, many of them cooks, butlers, and chauffeurs from the better homes, carousing in drag with white men at a local dance hall, a discovery at least as unsettling for its violation of racial taboos as for what it suggested about erotic deviance in Missouri. (The names of the "negro perverts" were published in the newspaper, according to an area doctor, but "the names of the white degenerates consorting with them were not given.") A scandal in Portland, Oregon, in 1912 had led to the arrest of dozens of prominent citizens, including lawyers and Chamber of Commerce officials, who had been involved in a sex ring at the local YMCA. Vice commissions in the larger cities routinely noted the prevalence of male homosexuals, but smaller towns such as Lancaster, Pennsylvania, and Boise, Idaho, had to attend to the "problem" in their midst during the war years. A roundup of gay men in San Francisco in 1918, following a raid on the Baker Street Club, led to more than thirty arrests, an investigation that was called off only when the names of several well-connected individuals were mentioned in court.

"The world of sexual inverts is, indeed, a large one in any American city," Havelock Ellis observed, quoting an informed correspondent in the 1915 edition of *Sexual Inversion*, "and it is a community distinctly organized—[with] words, customs, traditions of its own," a widespread society known to the police and tolerated by them "for a consideration." In *Gay American History* and *Gay New York*, historians Jonathan Ned Katz and George Chauncey have verified the extent of the dynamic *public* homosexual presence in Manhattan well before the twenties, but even in Louisville, Kentucky, or New Haven, Connecticut, a man "coming out" before World War I could find a place in a loosely defined and supportive (if less visible) subculture. The "Ladies of Newport," as the resident sailors called themselves, were not quite the anomaly they seemed to some people at the time.

FOR A TOWN best known as the elegant summertime retreat for America's wealthiest families, site of a naval training station that had accommodated two thousand sailors in 1917 and twelve times that number a year later, Newport had managed the trauma of mobilization as well as could be expected. Complaints about the ease with which sailors came by liquor, cocaine, and the services of "women of the night" disturbed the straitlaced head of the Navy department, Josephus Daniels, but after a series of crackdowns and brothel closings, Newport's mayor insisted that his city was "as clean as any . . . in the United States." Yet, in the eyes of one new resident, Chief Machinist's Mate Ervin Arnold, recently transferred from San Francisco, the mayor's claim was far from the case (or, taken in another way, just true enough to cause concern).

Arnold was being treated for severe rheumatism in the naval training station's hospital in February 1919 when he became aware of the widespread homosexual activity occurring off base, involving both sailors and local men of varying ages and professions. His suspicions were first aroused by an effeminate young sailor in the hospital; conversations with others subsequently confirmed that Samuel Rogers was indeed known about town as a "pogue," or punk, a man who enjoyed receptive anal sex. A second patient Arnold met that week, Thomas Brunelle, mentioned the names of others he knew with similar tastes and implied that Newport was a great place for contacts and parties along that line. Arnold found this information troubling and, once his medical treatment was completed, set about collecting what data he could on the perversions the civil and military authorities had overlooked.

What Arnold discovered during the ensuing days was the eclectic world of fairies and trade, of cross-dressers and party-givers, cocaine addicts and heavy drinkers, for whom mobilization had been a wildly social experience. Thomas Brunelle's "steady," Billy Hughes, was nicknamed "Salome" and had recently appeared in drag as the female lead in a musical at the naval station. Military men in drag for theatrical purposes raised few eyebrows at the time (or even later, during World War II), but Brunelle boasted that Hughes paid him regularly for sex. Arnold also met "Theda Bara," as hospital corpsman Fred Hoage was known, and "Ruth" (John Gianelloni), who were both praised for their oral skills, much like their friend Jay "Beckie" Goldstein, who had, everyone agreed, "a nice chin to rest a pair of balls on." Frank Dye was so good, Arnold was told, that he could draw your brains out through your penis. The Ladies of Newport were often joined in their partying at apartments at Whitfield Court and on Golden Hill Street by an assortment of civilians that included waiters, an area librarian, and a salesman from Providence. As "fairies," or flamboyant or more obvious homosexuals, especially when they were among their own, they were always happy to find interested "trade," or those masculine men who saw themselves (and were seen by the fairies) as free from the stigma of effeminacy or perversion. Trade did the fucking; trade never sucked. Trade wasn't queer. Determined by demeanor and the role assumed during sex, rather than the gender of one's partner, these sexual demarcations remained in play to one degree or another until the eve of Stonewall.

Exactly why the machinist's mate became preoccupied with the homosexual scene in Newport so soon after his arrival is impossible to say, but Ervin Arnold gives every appearance of having been a homophobe in the truest sense of the word. He manifested not only a distaste for the practices homosexual men engaged in, but an anxiety bordering on obsession. In his forties, and therefore considerably older than most of the men he was insinuating himself with, Arnold was a fourteen-year veteran of the Navy by the time of the Armistice and, before enlistment, had worked for nine years as a detective in Connecticut (home state of the famous vice crusader Anthony Comstock), where "running down perverts" seems to have been for him a particularly important part of his job. Indeed, some recent evidence suggests that there existed before the war a class of detectives who specialized in homosexual hunting and plied their trade around the country. Whatever his motives, Arnold decided to report his findings to his superiors once he had ascertained the gravity of the situation. The downtown Army & Navy YMCA, not surprisingly, had become one of the key centers of assignation, and an Episcopal military chaplain, Reverend Samuel Neal Kent, was said to be one of the most notorious of the older men ready to pay sailors for their private companionship. The parish house on Spring Street had allegedly seen its share of overnight guests. All this was past tolerating, in Arnold's estimation.

Lieutenant Erastus Hudson of the training station's welfare office agreed with Arnold, and the two of them took the matter to the station commander. Within a short time a four-man court of inquiry under Lieutenant Commander Murphy Foster was established to study immoral conditions in Newport, and Assistant Secretary of the Navy Roosevelt, acting as head of his department in Secretary Josephus Daniels's absence, agreed that "a most searching and rigid investigation" needed to be conducted with the aim of prosecuting those individuals responsible for the spread of degeneracy. Roosevelt later claimed that the methods used to accomplish this goal were nothing he had had the time or inclination to oversee, though few people believed him when the entrapment scandal broke. Arnold and Hudson, however, were confident that they knew what tactics were called for and in fact had implemented them several days before the assistant secretary was briefed.

The ex-detective from Connecticut who boasted that he could pick out the "cruising" fairies on Manhattan's Riverside Drive with 90 percent accuracy—not a challenging task, given the blatant style of the area—convinced his superiors that an undercover operation was the only way to secure evidence that would stand up in court. Accordingly, he quietly enlisted a staff of Navy investigators "in the capacity of detectives" who would circulate among the suspected population of perverts at the YMCA or elsewhere, strike up friendships, and take careful note of all that transpired. He wanted no one over thirty, he said, on the well-known assumption that homosexuals never bothered with men that old. His ideal volunteer was in his late teens or early twenties, handsome, none too intellectually inclined (to judge by their later testimony in court), and willing to put himself in awkward situations for the good of the service. He found an ample number to take on the assignment, more than a dozen at first, and sought assurances that his men, if forced to break the law—that is, go the limit to complete their mission—would not themselves be subject to prosecution.

The specific duties the recruits were charged with fell into three areas: to gather information about "cocaine joints" and the sale of liquor; to gather information "pertaining to cocksuckers and rectum receivers" and any network of "said fairies"; and to gather information about prostitutes in the area. In reality, once their project hit its stride, Arnold's band of investigators showed no interest to speak of in the "fallen women" of Newport and only minimal concern with the illegal drug traffic. What went on behind closed doors at the YMCA or in the romantic shadows of Cliff Walk was another matter. In their pursuit of the "cocksuckers" Arnold had charged them to find—and in the fairly staggering amount of oral sex they enjoyed in the line of duty—this group of young men was all but tireless. In fact, their assiduous performance was to become by the end of the summer a profound humiliation to the Department of the Navy and its leadership.

From the night of March 17 and into April when the arrests began and then on through the summer, the sailors loitered at the YMCA, made dates, attended parties, went strolling with new acquaintances after dark by the beach and in the cemetery, and dined at the Tokio Restaurant on Thames Street (where waiter Eddy Harrington was known to be partial to beefy seamen whose muscles he liked to squeeze while taking their orders). The files on the men who succumbed to the charms of Arnold's entrappers grew at a frantic pace, to Arnold's delight, typed up by his assistants in exacting and colloquial detail.

From the perspective of the 1990s, the unnerving aspect of the Newport undercover operation isn't the risks taken by the Salomes and the Theda Baras, who had no reason to assume that their "dates" weren't what they pretended to be, but the amount of consummated sex that seems to have taken place between these self-identified homosexual men and the partners who would have emphatically rejected such a label for themselves. Yet from the outset it was clear, or strongly implied, that the "operatives," as they were called, weren't being relieved of their other duties merely to document immoral propositions and lewd gestures; they were being sent by the Navy's own Comstock to record the nitty-gritty, complete to climax, and that they did. If Arnold and Hudson never felt uneasy about their squad's professionalism under these strange circumstances, they should have. In at least two instances, operatives later admitted to having had anal sex to orgasm with their delighted partners. Transcripts indicate that others slept the night through in the same bed once the deed was done, with one operative even paying for his room with "Beckie" Goldstein. (The only aversion that remained an absolute for the sailors was kissing, something that trade could never engage in without jeopardizing the distinction between him and his queer partner.) James Goggins, a new recruit in the summer—when the number of operatives swelled to over forty—and one of Arnold's busiest young men, acknowledged a midnight tryst on the grass near Forty Steps on Cliff Walk in which he was fellated but then failed to get the name of the sailor who "did" him. They met again. A second time Goggins neglected to return with a name for the record. Many of the operatives, when recounting their pre- or postcoital conversations, also seemed especially gratified at being told by the fairies that they had large penises. The screen of disinterest grew rather thin at times.

The first of the Ladies of Newport to be brought in was Fred Hoage, a bit-part silent-screen actor before the war and—ironically—one of the more discreet members of his circle. Nervous and confused, he professed to be willing to tell whatever he knew about gay life in Newport, as did many of the men rounded up in the coming weeks. By the time five men were sitting in the brig five days later, a panic had set in among the potential suspects. Men who were arrested began implicating others whom the operatives had never met. With more than a dozen in detention by the end of the next week, and the number scheduled to rise, Lieutenant Commander Foster (head of the court of inquiry) began to wonder if the Navy was going to be able to contain Ervin Arnold's one-man purity crusade. The brig aboard the USS *Constellation* was full; if Arnold wasn't put in check soon, he'd hang the whole state of Rhode Island, Foster complained to another officer.

On May 1, 1919, the Foster court of inquiry announced its findings and declared that sufficient evidence had been gathered to court-martial fifteen of the arrested sailors. They remained behind bars all summer and were tried in the fall, at which time some were released and others sentenced to varying prison terms. And there the matter might have ended, had not Arnold, Hudson, and a few other equally zealous officers wished to press on with the investigation even before the first court-martials began, expanding their field of operations beyond downtown Newport and encompassing the arrest of civilian homosexuals as well. Roosevelt gave his permission and allotted the needed funds, displaying what was later felt to be a dismaying lack of concern over the ethics of entrapment and the welfare of sailors, some still in their teens, who were being allowed— encouraged, really—to participate in illegal sex acts. But even then the repercussions of the investigation might not have been so dramatic had Arnold been more selective in his quarry. It was one thing to go after "Duke" Hawkins, the handsome young black man who waited tables at the Y restaurant. It was quite another to want to bring down an Episcopal minister with a solid reputation among the church hierarchy and citizenry of Newport.

When Reverend Samuel Neal Kent was arrested in midsummer, the investigation officially ended and the troublesome publicity began. His trial brought to the fore two different kinds of innocence about sexuality and sexual issues—both of which are still part of the debate today, though to a much less striking degree. On the one hand, the church fathers of Rhode Island seemed quite sure, at least in their public statements, that the forty-six-year-old chaplain, graduate of the renowned Latin School of Boston and a man who had devoted his life to good works, was not guilty of the eleven counts of "lewd and scandalous" behavior with which he was charged. Known to his men as "Pop" Kent, he was clearly a decent fellow and an effective professional who took his spiritual duties seriously. That a minister who had risked his life the year before tending to the sick during the dread influenza epidemic could also be the same man who liked to masturbate sailors bordered on the incomprehensible to Rhode Island Bishop James DeWolf Perry and his colleagues, or so they intimated. He couldn't have anything in common with a Fred Hoage or a Beckie Goldstein. On the other hand, the government and prosecuting attorney had no problem believing that Kent was guilty, but were—at first—oblivious to the import of their own methods. They were naively unprepared for the fact that a judge or a jury would be equally outraged by the story behind the indictment.

Kent's trial necessarily brought out all that Arnold had labored to keep secret. Young men of seventeen had been sent out into the night like street-walkers, taught to dissemble, paid to spend their time in rooms where liquor and drugs were available. Men in their late twenties, who could certainly have declined the assignment, had allowed their bodies to be used "in unspeakable ways." When one befuddled operative left the stand, having acknowledged that he understood his instructions were to let the minister "play with my penis and to allow it until [I] had an emission," reaction in town set in against the Navy and its tactics: Kent was found innocent. Stung by the verdict, the government wasn't ready to let the matter rest.

Under a recent war statute that prohibited conduct leading to "moral con-tamination" within a ten-mile zone of any military installation, plans were made to try Kent a second time in a federal court. He was hunted down like a fugitive while recuperating at the Battle Creek Sanitorium in Michigan and brought back to Providence.

Embarrassing as the ordeal was for Samuel Neal Kent, the second trial in January 1920 was no less a rejection of the Navy's approach and values than the first. The highly capable defense attorney humiliated Arnold's operatives, hammering away at their inexact memories and dwelling on the extent to which they had solicited and enjoyed the attentions of the many men they reported on. By this strategy, the debauched nature of the operatives—or, just as frightening a thought, the debauching of these boys by a government into whose care their parents had entrusted them—became a more pressing concern than the supposed lust of Newport's homosexual crowd. Fourteen clergymen, business leaders, and prominent socialite friends of Kent's testified on his behalf, and Kent was found inno-cent a second time. At this point the *Providence Journal*, a newspaper long antagonistic to Secretary Daniels and the Wilson administration, went on the attack, and publisher John Rathom did his best to inflame public opinion and widen the scandal to a national level. He was eminently suc-cessful. Fearing catastrophic effects on enlistment, Daniels was forced to call for a high-level naval investigation of the matter. Two months later that commission issued what was essentially a whitewash of the Navy (not a surprising development to anyone following the proceedings), which in turn led to a more aggressive, independent-minded Senate investigation.

Homosexual acts were hardly within the range of traditional senatorial experience, and there is the quality of a turning point in American sexual history in the image of the three senators who composed the committee reading the explicit testimony of the Newport and Providence court tran-scripts and journeying to Portsmouth, New Hampshire, to interview the defeated sailors at the naval prison. There Fred Hoage told them of Lieu-tenant Hudson's threat to "make it hard" for a friend of his unless he testi-fied that he had slept with Kent, and others insisted that they had been denied counsel, were beaten under interrogation, and coached in their self-incriminating testimony. The committee members also met with Franklin Roosevelt, the now-indignant Arnold and Hudson, and as many of the pan-icked operatives they could locate, several of whom were suddenly develop-ing what one senator described as suspiciously convenient memory lapses. The committee's report was made public after Roosevelt had left office and well after the 1920 election in which he ran as the Democratic candidate for the vice presidency, but it was nonetheless a galling moment for him.

His part in the entrapment, any specific knowledge of which he continued furiously to deny, had been characterized by the naval investigators as "ill-advised." The Senate committee went much further, declaring Roosevelt's actions "reprehensible." Senator Henry Keyes, Republican of Vermont, urged the release of all the men held at Portsmouth in the light of the government's contempt for due process. LAY NAVY SCANDAL TO F. D. ROOSEVELT, ran the *New York Times* headline, DETAILS ARE UNPRINTABLE.

Two of the investigating senators also had something to say on the subject of the government's policy toward homosexuals in general. If the medical and scientific community was now suggesting that sexual deviance was a mental illness rather than a crime, it should be treated as such, they argued. The recommendation was made that anyone in the armed forces suspected of homosexuality be dishonorably discharged and referred for medical care rather than tried and imprisoned. "Perversion is not a crime," Senator Keyes maintained, "but a disease that should be properly treated in a hospital." Edwin Denby, Josephus Daniels's successor in the new administration of Warren Harding, dismissed the proposal out of hand for two reasons, one enlightened and one vindictive. He wisely noted that innocent men might be affected by unfounded malicious gossip. Suspicion of homosexuality was too vague a charge. The sterner aspect of Denby's reasoning, though, was that the true perverts would be getting off too lightly if they were simply slapped on their limp wrists and released from the service. The Navy would become a refuge for the sexually maladjusted, and that must never be allowed to happen.

THE NEWPORT SCANDAL faded rather quickly from the national news—it was not the kind of occurrence the public enjoyed hearing about—and by the time FDR ran for the governorship of New York in 1928 and then for the presidency four years later, the sad fate of the Newport men and their sexually active entrappers and Roosevelt's part in the affair were ancient history. Interestingly, we may never know if the thirty-second president was aware of the complex nature of the relationship between his wife and Lorena Hickock, the lesbian journalist who moved into the White House with the Roosevelts in 1941, but we do know that Roosevelt came to see that homosexuality was not necessarily an impediment to effective government service. During World War II he protected Sumner Welles, his undersecretary of state, as long as he could, until Welles's indiscretions passed all acceptable bounds. Only with great reluctance did Roosevelt ask for his advisor's resignation.

The traumatic events of 1919 and 1920 were probably never forgotten, however, by three groups of people: the men who stood trial or were court-martialed, the operatives who were initially billed as guardians of morality and later portrayed as victims or potential degenerates themselves, and the shaken clergy of Newport. The ministers, led by Bishop Perry, had been forced to cope with some disturbing ambiguities. They had insisted throughout the ordeal, and especially after the second acquittal, that the Navy owed Reverend Kent an apology. (Convinced to the last that Kent had had sex with the men who testified against him, Daniels and Roosevelt swore they would never apologize.) Yet the ministers were equally vocal in their demand that the government agree never again to press young men into this kind of unsavory covert operation. The paradox of their position wasn't lost on the Navy's lawyers when the ministers were questioned during the naval court of inquiry's hearings in early 1920: the ministers wanted an apology made to Kent—implying that the operatives were perjurors and that no illegal sex had occurred—yet they also wanted an end to the entrapment practices, which supposedly hadn't amounted to anything if the operatives were fabricating their stories and Kent was innocent. The government was within its rights when it said to the complainants, in effect: Which is it? But by the time the dust had settled, the clergy of Rhode Island and the leaders of the American Episcopal Church had had to come to terms, in private, with the inadequacy of their notions of male sexual expression and sociability. At some point they realized that the "Christian brotherhood" Kent professed as his principal feeling toward the sailors, however genuine, was complicated by other factors. Arnold's net hadn't brought to the fore a world divided, neatly and absolutely, into pogues and cross-dressers on the one hand and older men of fatherly mien and pastoral tenderness on the other. The lines were blurred, and the weight of the testimony left its mark. After 1921, Samuel Neal Kent was quietly disqualified from performing religious duties and, except for a brief stint as a chaplain aboard a cruise ship in the 1930s, worked in secular positions until his death in Florida in 1943.

(The bishops, especially Kent's friend and best character witness, Philip Rhinelander of Pennsylvania, would have been mindful of the sex scandal that had rocked the Episcopal Church only several years earlier. During Christmas week in 1912, Alfred Garnett Mortimer, the sixty-four-year-old rector of Philadelphia's most affluent parish and a leader of the American High Church movement, was dismissed from his post by Bishop Rhinelander and then defrocked. He left the country on New Year's Day 1913. The bishop refused to discuss the case, despite a public outcry for information, but rumors about a homosexual ring at St. Mary's were widespread, and some of Mortimer's curates were dismissed a few weeks later. Only a short time before, an elderly Episcopal minister in a nearby suburb had resigned under a similar cloud, and in the same embarrassing month of Mortimer's departure—January 1913—an Episcopal pastor in Westfield, New Jersey, was reported by his teenage choir boys for "familiarities" and vanished overnight. In sum, a moral and public relations debacle for the Episcopal Church that threatened to tar the whole profession.)

Nothing of any detail is known about the later lives of the young operatives, but they were left in the most curious position of all. They had agreed to join Ervin Arnold's squad of their own free will and had assumed their roles without complaint. They had been told that they were ridding Newport of degenerates who, left to their own devices, would entice innocent sailors into sexual relationships. None questioned the logic of preventing that end by proceeding to have sex with those same suspects. More important, none felt he was descending to the level of a homosexual simply by engaging in sex with homosexuals because they weren't—in their chief's phrasing—the "cocksuckers and rectum receivers." The operatives lived by the unwritten codes of their day and their class; they knew that society was more interested in, and repulsed by, the effeminacy and gender confusion the fairy represented than anything that these masculine decoys adopting a non-oral or active anal role did. Their tragedy resulted from the clash of values that occurred when the normal practices of trade were scrutinized in too public a forum by the military hierarchy, the clergy, the press and its middle-class readership. What was accepted among working-class youth in most parts of America was intolerable debasement, if widely known and discussed, to other classes of society. In that light, their leader was transformed from a psychosexual expert and moral watchdog to a pimp. They were seen as dupes.

Finally, what of the Ladies of Newport? By the early 1920s, it appears, all those who were in prison had been released and allowed to resume their civilian lives. If they had come from big cities and returned there, they were probably aware that what had happened to them was not unique. They weren't the first and they wouldn't be the last homosexuals made to pay for their mannerisms, cross-dressing, and sexual dalliances conducted in private or otherwise. Resuming an old life in a small town would have been well-nigh impossible: a Wing Biddlebaum run out of town at night, seeking anonymity in Winesburg, Ohio, was nothing compared to this antic group with its relish for feminine names, gay argot, cosmetics, and boisterous sex parties. For them, a more plausible home would be the gay subculture of New York and San Francisco, Philadelphia and St. Louis, New Orleans and Baltimore, Boston and Chicago.

Yet the very existence in Newport in 1919 of a robust circle of fairies—self-identified gay men who, before their persecution, felt surprisingly little need to disguise their adopted feminine attributes—prompts speculation about their lives before they joined the Navy. It strains credibility to think of them meeting one another aboard ship and only then evolving the styles with which they were comfortable. Their flagrant use of the YMCA lobby as a pickup area, their willingness to talk with Arnold in the naval hospital even though he must have appeared an outsider, their gait on the street, and their success in impersonating women in the Navy's theatrical revues, which carried over into their private parties, is evidence that implies they had long since formed their ideas about what they wanted and what they thought they could get away with. They weren't inventing a way of life in the nineteen months of the American involvement in the war; they were more likely bringing it, ready-formed, into a new community from the disparate cities and towns they came from. What the war provided for them was what large-scale military conflicts often provide: a sense that their number was larger than they thought, that their sexual and social world was not a small one.

That world was as rigid as it was convivial. The fairies' testimony in court hints at some well-established rules. Those among them who took on the role of "husbands," who were scarcely regarded as homosexual, were expected to remain the dominant partners; everyone was expected to have a sexual specialty—pogue or cocksucker, active or passive; a true fairy was locked into his femininity as securely as a husband was locked out of it. But their position also involved an astonishing bravado, the savvy and pluck of a survivor. (It was a boldness only the exceptional outsider could appreciate. Moving to Chicago in the late 1890s, Sherwood Anderson was shocked by his first sight of men with painted faces, but gradually came to feel a troubled fascination with their ability to handle the abuse they endured in the rough-and-tumble of the warehouse district.)

The assumptions at the end of the century—our assumptions, our stereotypes—about gay life in America at the beginning of the century have been so governed by the concept of "the closet" and related notions of invisibility, as George Chauncey has persuasively argued, that we are apt to lose sight of an important element of gay history and, indeed, of American history. The sexual world of our grandfathers was never as simple as ours is alleged to be complex, nor was any thinking person's experience of public social life as tidy or narrow as the high school texts and the television documentaries would make it. Life in 1920 *was* perilous for a gay man, to be sure, and potentially isolating for anyone who was not inclined to bond with the overtly homosexual, convention-defying fairies. Most men who wanted to have a sexual relationship with another man were well advised to keep their interests or activities a secret from family and heterosexual friends. The price to pay for deviating from masculine traditions was high. Proclaim it from the rooftops, as F. O. Matthiessen wrote to his lover, the painter Russell Cheney, and you must live with the consequences "for it is an anomaly the world as a whole does not understand." But the public life of the fairies in Newport and elsewhere, the forging of so many happy private unions (like Matthiessen's and Cheney's), and the increasing concern with limiting homosexual activity after World War I (in the form of bathhouse raids, police "sweeps" of movie houses, and censorship in the theater) tell us something vital, namely that the old social order with its strict gender roles was being questioned long before Stonewall and the counterculture of the 1960s appeared. That process was also under way prior to the upheavals wrought by the Second World War and the Great Depression. In fact, the first traces we are able to perceive at this moment of ongoing research assume a discernible outline even before the highly eroticized decade of the screen idol, the speakeasy, and the flapper.

2

IMAGINING THE TWENTIES

Before the War we used to consider homosexuality as a more or less foreign importation. We regarded ourselves as true exponents of the sane and uncompromising traditions of our pioneer ancestors. The dross of abnormal desire [in our immigrants]—assuming that they may have been thus infested when they landed in this country—was burned away in the melting pot of our staunch masculine or commendably feminine characteristics. This is what we thought.

—Dr. La Forrest Potter,
*Strange Loves: A Study in
Sexual Abnormalities*, 1933

With near-perfect timing, F. Scott Fitzgerald published his first novel on March 26, 1920, only three months into the roaring new decade. *This Side of Paradise* was advertised by Scribners, at its twenty-three-year-old author's suggestion, as "A Novel About Flappers Written for Philosophers." The newly liberated American woman—hair bobbed and hemline raised, forsaking her mother's prudishness about sex and eager to flout the Volstead Act—and the men who contemplated her, their own recklessness and cynicism, and the failure of the old ways of living were Fitzgerald's heady concerns in his debut work. The story of the hard-drinking, gone-to-hell Amory Blaine, as a Fitzgerald biographer recently noted, "both baptized the Jazz Age and glorified its fashionable hedonism."

Yet limits were carefully set to the extent and the nature of the questioning that Gertrude Stein's "lost generation" embarked on in their time of postwar gloom and revelry. These were men and women "lost" to certain of the old values but firmly bound to others, and the result is a strange lacuna in the ample portrait of a decade provided by Fitzgerald and Hemingway, Dos Passos and Faulkner, Dorothy Parker and the Algonquin circle, the Village poets, the new dramatists, and the Harlem Renaissance novelists. The modern woman—a Daisy Buchanan or a Fran Dodsworth—was a fair theme, or target. Satirical attacks on Harding and Bryan, George Babbitt and Billy Sunday, or anyone who believed Wilson's jingoistic cant about the war, found an enthusiastic audience. Racial identity, miscegenation, divorce, alcoholism, family strife, and varieties of erotic experience from Oedipal confusion to sexual dysfunction: the range of topics explored in the imaginative literature of the 1920s in America is nothing short of extraordinary, given the timidity of readers and publishers only a few years earlier. A nation, or a significant part of it, was choosing to see itself in a new light, and it had little use for heroic gestures and sexual reserve. But despite all those daughters petting in all those roadsters out past curfew—the image of which Fitzgerald loved to use in tweaking middle-class mothers—the younger generation proposed to take their much-lauded rebellion only so far. More sex between men and women, and the right to talk about it, was a central goal; breaking down stereotypes or renegotiating time-honored gender roles was not.

Even more baldly put, then, it comes down to the question: Just where were the homosexuals in this pageant of the new America? Not entirely effaced, they seemed to be defined by appearances that are brief, infrequent, foreign, sometimes coded, almost always steeped in acceptable prejudice. Several men with "white hands, wavy hair, white faces" come simpering into the *bal musette* with Brett Ashley, largely so that Jake Barnes (of the defective equipment) can tell us how much he wants to "swing on one" lest he throw up. A handful of fairies make a flit-through cameo in *Tender Is the Night*, a twenties book regardless of its publication date in the early thirties. With Grecian lips and amber curls, Erik Valborg—a suspicious 4-F during the war—is too expressive and artistically inclined for Gopher Prairie; an "Oh, dear" at the wrong moment and the girls of *Main Street* roll their eyes. Wing Biddlebaum is a sweet soul, "forever frightened," in Sherwood Anderson's elegant, mournful "Hands," while Waldo Frank's visiting New Yorker in *The Dark Mother* is a potential corrupter of a small-town innocent. *The New Yorker* critic and screenwriter Charles Brackett displayed his worldliness in his French Riviera novel *American*

Colony with an expatriate homosexual whose tastes run to drunken alter-cations, facial creams, and straight friends who call him a pervert behind his back. And when Eugene O'Neill looked to his two homosexual painter friends Charles Demuth and Marsden Hartley for a mother-obsessed com-posite in *Strange Interlude*, not much about the reality of their lives ended up in the play beyond a merging of their first names. Despite the suspicion that writers of this stature must have been aware of many men and women who were homosexual whose experience was infinitely richer than that of an Erik Valborg or a Charlie Marsden, the gallery of Jazz Age gay portraits we are left with is frustratingly meager. No criminal masterminds or eager young men from the provinces, ninety years after Balzac's *Lost Illusions*; no Billy Budds, no Dorian Grays, no Aschenbach and Tadzio on the beach.

Yet even when the writers were probably homosexual themselves, the nature of their fiction wasn't likely to unsettle contemporary opinion or rouse the censorship leagues to action. *Bertram Cope's Year,* Henry Fuller's 1920 novel, which has been called by one critic "the first truly modern gay novel in American literature," is a guarded tale of a bachelor's longings and loneliness set in the Midwest in the decade after the Civil War. The gay men of Carl Van Vechten's novels are emblems of frivolity and not much more. (The sissy hero of Van Vechten's *The Blind Bow-Boy* takes up with the jaded Duke of Middlebottom, whose stationery carries the motto, "A thing of beauty is a boy forever.") Novelist Wallace Thurman was particularly ambivalent and sometimes downright nasty in his depictions of gay life in Harlem. Censorship was a factor, to be sure. Not too many years before, realists like Theodore Dreiser were challenged for writing honestly about heterosexual promiscuity in books like *The "Genius,"* and H. L. Mencken was still battling the guardians of public morality as late as 1926 in the famous "Hatrack" case. But the problem goes beyond what was officially allowable or, for a publisher, worth a legal contest. Treatment of male homosexual life had to do with what was acceptable to the postwar public, not only as a fact of life to be accommodated by rational people, but as an object of private musings, social debate, and cultural spectacle.

Two men expressing, or hinting at, their mutual love or lust continued to be a painful subject in the 1920s, no matter what other changes in mores the decade witnessed. The needs of randy youth, as in the case of the Newport naval operatives or the red-blooded trade of any American city or small town, had to be met, but that was a different, more understandable matter. Homosexuals were marked, in the first place, by their desire for *men*, not women substitutes—for male penetration, not mere sexual release. They were also, often, presumed to be effeminate, sometimes ashamedly and sometimes defiantly so. They were easily identified and therefore easily shunned. (The trend-setting Fitzgeralds were especially repelled by most of the gay men they met in their travels. Visiting Capri in 1925, Fitzgerald took one look at Somerset Maugham, E. F. Benson, and their companions and expressed his profound distaste at finding the island's writers' colony so "full of fairies." Their response to the homosexuals they saw in Paris and New York was no different.) The smug sense that one could spot "them" quickly was, indeed, vitally reassuring; "they" were so noticeable, so obviously repulsive, these misfits, that no one need fear their power. Anxieties about an escalating, or at least bolder deviant presence in twentieth-century America were containable precisely so long as those who didn't conform to type remained invisible, leaving the field to the detectable "fairy," not the disguised but possibly ubiquitous "homosexual."

Interestingly, the nervous concern that male same-sex involvements still prompted in the twenties was not matched by an equivalent anxiety about lesbianism. The man who had abandoned his masculinity by allowing another man to touch him in certain ways and on certain parts of his body was a much more degraded figure than the "unnatural woman." It was possible to contemplate lesbian desire because the topic, however offensive to society at large, was both slightly less threatening to the prerogatives of manhood and (as always) rife with fantasy material for heterosexual males. Lurking condescension played its part—after all, a woman gone astray could be recovered by the right virile man, her erring ways need not preclude marriage and childbearing, her sexual acts were not generally recognized under the legal definition of sodomy. The Sapphist might even have an element of glamour about her.

"Lesbian chic" in the postwar years took a variety of forms. When in his silent film *Wings* director William Wellman wanted to suggest the exciting decadence of Europe that the doughboys encountered in 1918, he devised a spectacular entry shot into a Parisian nightclub that includes a close-up of two young women in masculine attire staring into each other's eyes. A similar scene between men would have registered a different condition—moral filth—but continental lesbianism suggested multiple truths to urbane audiences in 1927: the modern abandonment of normal values, the strangeness of the world "over there," unexpected styles of erotic allure. The same ambiguity allowed for the *succès de scandale* of the 1926–1927 Broadway season, *The Captive*. Edouard Bourdet's play dealt with a lesbian's obsessive love for a married woman whom she gradually woos away from her husband to the world of "shadows." *The Captive* had to be closed and the cast arrested—"Some tragedies cannot be viewed without disgust," one reviewer observed—but, with a wink and a nod, Mayor Jimmy Walker sent his own car and chauffeur to take actress Helen Menken (Humphrey Bogart's first wife) to the stationhouse for a perfunctory booking. By the time the paddy wagons came around that night of February 9, 1927, the raid had been discussed in the press and over 75,000 New Yorkers had paid unheard-of prices, filling the Empire Theater to capacity for most of the play's four-month run. Similar titillation was felt a few years later when Eva Le Gallienne, rising star of the American theater, was "outed" in the tabloids in the wake of a scandal that actually followed the plot of *The Captive*, with Le Gallienne named as the third party in a divorce action. Notoriety that would have ended any actor's career had the advantage of adding to Le Gallienne's mystique. Nor did Ma Rainey's arrest in 1925 on the charge of staging a lesbian orgy in her Harlem apartment alienate many of her fans, of either race or proclivity.

The most decisive example of the era's willingness to make allowances in this realm is seen in the legal and literary fortunes of Radclyffe Hall's *The Well of Loneliness*, a book (or phenomenon, really) for which there has never been an equivalent in gay male life. E. M. Forster shelved *Maurice* to be published posthumously, and the appearance in America of an English translation of Marcel Proust had an impact limited to a highly elite audience. The agents of the Society for the Suppression of Vice weren't the kinds of readers to make their way through the dense, page-long paragraphs of *The Cities of the Plain* to find the sensational bits, any more than the average gay reader. But Hall was determined, as she told her lover Una Troubridge, to write an honest book "on sexual inversion, a novel that would be accessible to the general public who did not have access to technical treatises." The time was ripe, she felt. Despite its war propaganda and painstaking detail (and despite its less than agreeable ending, by contemporary standards), her project bore fruit in a most remarkable way. Banned as pornography and then dropped by Knopf, its first American publisher, *The Well of Loneliness* was eventually published by the more intrepid firm of Covici-Friede and became the subject of landmark obscenity trials on both sides of the Atlantic. It achieved its vindication in court in New York in April 1929, became a bestseller in the United States immediately thereafter, and is still in print today.

Stephen Gordon, Hall's Edwardian protagonist, struggles throughout most of the story to understand the nature of her difference from other young women, when no one she knows even has a term for her desires, and gradually learns to deal with the prejudices of others. But the heroine of *The Well of Loneliness* is also clever and independently wealthy, like Hall herself. A novel about a working-class lesbian (no English country houses, no Parisian restaurants) would not have interested either Alfred Knopf or Pascal Covici. How much more arduous, then, was the process of forging a sense of self and developing protective armor for a homosexual man in America, whose existence didn't give rise to fashionable plays or literary causes, whose life involved punching a time clock and dealing with judgmental relatives. How much more uncertain was the task of deciding what part his sexual urges should play in his image of his life when the common "line" was that only a few men anywhere shared those feelings. Yet adopting their own argot and, among the more audacious, their own sartorial clues to recognize one another—a red tie was a great favorite in the twenties—meeting at the cafeterias and nightspots where their presence was tolerated, enjoying abundant though furtive sex in the YMCAs and bathhouses of the larger cities, homosexuals of all temperaments managed to form sustaining social ties and relationships. Recent oral histories and archival evidence suggest that this was as true in Tampa, Florida, or Long Beach, California, as it was in New York, Chicago, or St. Louis.

"Certainly a great deal of it depended on where you lived *and* what line of work you went into," one man remarked in 1994 about his experience of gay life in the 1920s and 1930s. "My lover came from Pittsburgh. He had seen homosexuals, men who were identified that way, when he was growing up. He knew what was what, early on." Some of those men were the so-called fairies, and some were men just thought to be "odd," loners who never went with girls. "In Iowa, I can't say that I ever heard the words [fairy or homosexual]. . . . Then [my lover] went into banking, there was no question about *not* covering it up—'passing.' I went into theater . . . and then I worked in a department store in Philadelphia for ten years, so it was pretty obvious to me that there were legions of us out there, not all of them so obvious."

Though some segments of the rest of society also knew or suspected those "legions," a determined effort was made to prevent any legitimizing of that information. The arrest of a man in drag or the outcome of a sodomy trial was printable news in many papers by the early 1920s, but an unbiased journalistic account of the subject was as rare as a nuanced depiction of a gay character in fiction, theater, or film. The norm was George K. Arthur's catty dress designer in *Irene* (1926), the lisping queen of vaudeville stock in trade, or the tortured artist who pines for his young model in Carl Dreyer's *Chained: The Story of the Third Sex*, a European "art" film that briefly played in a few American cities in 1926 and 1927. The paradigm of a "real man" was a Charles Lindbergh, a Douglas Fairbanks, a Jack Dempsey, or the square-shouldered Arrow shirt model of J. C. Leyendecker's ads who had become popular among style-conscious young businessmen—an image drawn from life, though few people knew that the healthy, well-scrubbed "Arrow man," Charles Pearce, was in fact the illustrator's lover. "Big Bill" Tilden dominated tennis in the 1920s and was popular enough to play an exhibition match on the White House lawn for President Harding, but no one openly questioned his bachelorhood or the presence of so many attractive young men in his life. Sportswriters' hints on the subject were sufficiently vague to keep Tilden's image intact for another two decades, which is just how the public wanted it.

The very narrowness of popular conceptions about what it meant to be a homosexual could sometimes be as significant a problem as a family's bitter reactions or the fear of losing a job. The diaries of Richard Cowan, who committed suicide in 1939 at the age of thirty, record Cowan's active gay sex life in his student days at Cornell in the late 1920s and in Boston in the 1930s. Yet Cowan never seems to have made a workable life for himself as a gay man who was not a fairy or to have enjoyed his homosexual relationships without an edge of guilt. Jeb Alexander, a government clerk in Washington, D.C., from the early twenties until his retirement four decades later, was another man ultimately defeated by his own sense of how others viewed him. His diary, edited in 1993 by his niece from fifty volumes into one, chronicles the busy cruising scene in Lafayette Square across the street from the White House, the clumsy police surveillance of the area, and the roller-coaster friendships and affairs of his circle, many of whom lived at the YMCA. One of the earliest diary entries records the suicide of a homosexual classmate at Washington and Lee in 1921. Another, for August 21, 1920, remarks on his discovery of two men masturbating each other at dusk near Baron Von Steuben's statue in Lafayette Square. Numerous entries refer to his almost lifelong unrequited infatuation with his gay college friend, the moody and attractive "Dash."

But Jeb Alexander's diary, which constitutes a priceless window on his times, proved to be more than just an opportunity to sketch in the details of gay life in the nation's capital between the wars. Piecemeal, the entries create a portrait of a middle-class man, unexceptional in every respect but for his diary-keeping, worn down by a self-consciousness about his outcast status. Neither a true fairy ready to take on the world nor a man masculine enough to "pass," he was caught in what felt like a limbo that would never allow for any real happiness or peace. "You're morbid on the subject," a heterosexual character in Charles Brackett's *American Colony* says to his gay houseguest. "Nobody cares nowadays." But that was evidently not the case for a Richard Cowan or a Jeb Alexander, who worried the issue no end. The suggestion or the style of homosexuality, in certain circles, was one thing—urbane, in-the-know, enjoyable to the degree that it irked stodgier souls—but at home the mundane reality was quite another.

THE "FEEL" OF homosexual experience and identity in the 1920s, especially for boys or men just coming to terms with their desires, is difficult to re-create today. We grasp that world by means of tantalizing fragments, scattered or random memories. Police and court records tell us that there were significant numbers of men who acted on their sexual urges and were arrested or harassed for their desires, but official documents tend to say little beyond that. Published accounts of drag balls indicate that thousands of men were self-confident enough to flaunt their disdain for a manly affect, but these rebels constitute only the smallest fraction of the total population who were drawn toward members of their own sex. We do know enough now, however, to appreciate that the responses of gay men to their differentness were as varied, as individually determined by factors of personality, family circumstances, and social background as they are seventy years later. Blanket projections about naive or tormented young men, unbreakable walls of silence, sexual frustration, and bitter loneliness need to be put to rest. From simple acceptance and curious, even eager experimentation to self-doubt and suicidal anguish, men reacted to their homosexuality—as always—in disparate ways.

In *Chapters from an Autobiography* (1981), short-story writer, English professor, and onetime tattoo artist Samuel Steward wrote of his high school years in southeastern Ohio in the mid-1920s and the gradual dawning of what he really wanted. An older boy had just returned from Buckeye Lake with a report about a fairy at the summer resort who had given him a "tongue bath." This was exciting information, and a school fullback proved ready to let Steward do his own exploring with his mouth in the attic of Steward's grandmother's boardinghouse. "And there on a sheeted mattress amidst the dust and cobwebs," he wrote fifty-five years later, "the morning stars sang together for the first time for me—for a period of about two minutes, since the football hero was very quick on the trigger." Not long after, Steward had the good luck to make a discovery that placed his introductory frolic in a larger context. One of Grandma Morris's tenants, a traveling salesman, moved and left under his bed a copy of a book stolen from the restricted shelf of the Columbus Public Library. If Samuel Steward felt any uncertainty before beginning the book, the purpose of Havelock Ellis's *Studies in the Psychology of Sex*, he decided, was to assure him that he wasn't insane or alone in his new interests.

To anyone who still thinks of American society before the Second World War as lacking the erotic charge of our own day, the telling feature of Steward's experience is how extensive, lively, and guilt-free his ensuing activities with his male classmates were. Even the youthful adventurer and later author, reflecting on his situation in old age, thought it curious that no one called him a queer or threatened to beat him up. As "healthy young Ohio animals," his seventeen- and eighteen-year-old peers accepted his services as a pleasure for them and a mild eccentricity on his part. Steward was alert enough, however, to know that the adults in the community had other ideas on the subject. When his father cornered him one day after having seen an ill-placed love note, distraught at the possibility that his son was the "town cocksucker," Steward was able to dissemble and avoid the charge. "Schooled in duplicity," he knew what his father really wanted to hear. It was, after all, only a short wait until college and a final leavetaking from the confines of Woodsfield, Ohio.

Samuel Steward, who went on to befriend Gertrude Stein and Thornton Wilder in the 1930s and to write the "Phil Andros" stories in the 1960s, is scarcely to be taken as typical or representative of anything, though he himself felt that his experiences were not out of step with his time in one key respect. Homosexuality as a way of life in the 1920s, by virtue of how little public discussion it elicited, was considered by middle-class Americans—or was fervently hoped to be—a rare phenomenon peculiar to big cities and nonexistent in many parts of God's Country, an aberration without any wider meaning. As one of the less astute officers prosecuting the Newport homosexuals in 1919 observed, a singular tragedy of the war was that innocent boys from the Midwest, where such deviance was unknown, were now being exposed to corruption in the East. The result of this "quaint" thinking, Steward believed, was a greater latitude for young men like himself to romp at will—and so he did, in his college days at Ohio State and while teaching in Montana and later while traveling in Europe and living in Chicago. (Steward's tour-de-force seduction was his afternoon tryst with the elderly Lord Alfred Douglas in the late 1930s, an effort to forge a mystical bond with Oscar Wilde "by placing my lips where Oscar's had been." Bosie later informed his astonished guest that he had gone to rather more trouble than Wilde ever did as their relations had been more masturbatory than anything else.)

A contemporary of Steward's had a more difficult time finding willing partners in late adolescence in New Hampshire, but affirms the notion that the publicity of a later age necessarily led to a stricter scrutiny and the closing-off of certain kinds of expression. "Before I left home to go to college in Boston, I had 'slept with' three or four boys my age quite happily,"

Albert Munro noted in an interview in 1994. "One of these fellows went on to marry a girl I dated in high school, but the other was at least as queer as I was. I always wondered what became of him. But I doubt anyone suspected anything about us. We weren't obvious, and it wasn't in my parents' vocabulary. It wasn't in my vocabulary, either, not in 1927. Think of it! As I think back, I *like* that aspect of it. The vagueness served a purpose—like a wonderful secret. I just knew I was different and that the city was probably going to be the answer for me. I was uncomfortable about it at times, but not distressed."

The potential "distress" started for Munro—as it would for other men like him who weren't inclined to ignore their drives, stay home, and marry—when he arrived in the nearest big city and discovered that the Boston police did indeed have a vocabulary and a way of dealing with young men who seemed too familiar with each other on the Common (an approach that grew increasingly aggressive over the years), and that the gay men he met lived by some equally firm concepts. "If you weren't a fairy, what was your place in the whole thing? I don't think I figured that out until [World War II], and by then it was a different situation entirely. *They* were after all of us then. *They* knew how many of us there were, fairies or not."

The "protective umbrella" of society's ignorance, which Samuel Steward speaks of in his autobiography, could also work the other way, making it difficult for young gay men to understand who they were and to realize that they were not alone. Richmond Morrell Purinton of Augusta, Maine, confided to his own teenage diary his "adoration" for a handsome high school friend, Murray. The happiness of each day was measured by how much he saw his eighteen-year-old chum, how pleasant their walks were, how carefully he could observe the boy's "graceful movements and persuading smile." Murray's interest in girls and Purinton's vague sense that he himself was a freak of nature were sources of discomfort. "I read and reread *The Sheik*," Purinton wrote on February 12, 1922. "It is a wonderful book. I wish I could be the heroine with Murray as the Sheik, but God wished it otherwise and by accident made me a boy." Sensitive to his perilous position at age seventeen, Purinton was caught in a bind of long standing. Where were the men—the gay men—to suggest that his wasn't "the heart and soul of a girl" (as he phrased it) but something different, the heart and soul of a young man who loved men?

Paul Phillips, a middle-class African-American man who was just slightly older than Richmond Morrell Purinton, grew up in the Midwest oblivious even to the strangeness of his affect and desires. The son of a black lawyer with a white clientele, Paul was in an odd position to begin with. His father's services were in demand, but the family lived a mile out of town in what were still highly segregated circumstances. When rumors about his son being "that way" reached Mr. Phillips, he approached Paul and explained the situation, as society saw it, of a young man who didn't date girls or evince any interest in them. He informed Paul that his was an "unnatural" condition and that they would have to see what could be done about it. The family had enough money to afford a trip to the Mayo Clinic in Rochester, Minnesota, camping out en route as they couldn't stay in the whites-only hotels along the way. There Paul spent several terrified days being interviewed and examined. At the end of that time, the doctors had nothing more to report to Mr. and Mrs. Phillips other than that their son was a homosexual and would probably be one all his days. According to the criminal code of Minnesota, they were then supposed to report Paul to the Rochester police but graciously announced that they would overlook the law in this case. After taking a while to get used to the idea, Paul's father came to a judicious conclusion. If his son suffered from an illness that couldn't be cured by the best doctors in the country, then he'd lead his life as he had to—but lead it with caution and dignity. "Find yourself a friend you can trust," Mr. Phillips said, "and bring him home." Hanging out on the streets or fooling around on country roads was dangerous "because you never know who's going to step up behind you. . . . What you do in your own room is your business." As Phillips told interviewer Eric Marcus in the eighties, it took him many years, until he was a lawyer himself, to find a congenial lover, but at college in Topeka in the mid-1920s he befriended another gay black man, a musician who played the organ for the churches near school, forging a comradely bond that eased the loneliness and confusion.

The Phillips family at least had the wit to acknowledge their son's sexuality; they never fully understood it, but they were willing to stand by their child. In those homes where ignorance and anxiety about sex was the rule, the difficulties a young gay man faced could be excruciating. Even heterosexual sex was, to his family, "as fearful as black magic," the playwright William Inge remembered about his childhood in the twenties. For a borderline sissy, "getting by" in high school in southeastern Kansas meant success in drama-class productions while keeping as low a profile as possible. Freshman year at his frat house at the University of Kansas in 1930 allowed for some "tentative, groping, unfulfilled experiences," but Inge knew that he had to avoid associating with any effeminate men on campus as he feared the "effeminate element in myself that might classify me as *one of them.*" The boy he bunked with at the fraternity would pretend that his own arousal occurred while he was dreaming, and Inge was sufficiently nervous, even hysterical, in this mock-cowboy climate to participate in a gang-bang with a willing girl from the college. Joining a line of naked "brothers" in the basement of the frat house to take his turn between her legs, he felt more uncertain than ever that sex was something that could be integrated into a happy life.

Earlier in the decade, Julian Green had grappled with the same questions that worried William Inge and Paul Phillips—what role was sex to play in his life and what was he to make of these strange, intense sensations he had in the presence of handsome classmates? But Green's dilemma was complicated by his religious fervor. In the third volume of his autobiography, *Love in America* (1994), published in the United States in his ninety-fourth year, he wrote in uncanny detail of the "lunacy of a male virgin," trapped between the dictates of his church—the Roman Catholic Church—and the clear values of society and, on the other side, the maddening impulses of nature. When Dr. Fitzhugh of the Classics department was blunt enough to inform his students that the troubling passage in Virgil that no one could explicate dealt with nothing less than "the shame of Antiquity, by which I mean boy-love," Julian Green was rendered as speechless as everyone else in the class at the University of Virginia. "A blinding flash had clarified my entire life," he wrote. And a sorry revelation it was because he knew no other boy-lovers in Charlottesville in 1920 (or so it seemed that day), and that must mean he alone had carried the "shame of Antiquity" into the modern age, a feat of staggering ill luck. It took some time for common sense to reassert itself. A lingering glance in the dark from a sailor in Savannah, a few more knowing and helpful friends on campus (at twenty, Green was still convinced that masturbation was a sin until an amazed classmate, holding in his laughter, advised him that he had been reading the wrong books on the subject), an encounter with Edward Carpenter's *Love's Coming of Age* and, even more momentously, with the same Havelock Ellis text that Samuel Steward had found, and Green was on his way toward a more cosmopolitan view of his situation.

For intellectually inclined young men and for those who lived in areas remote from large, relatively visible gay groups (Julian Green walking Jefferson's colonnade to his classes in 1920 fit snugly into both categories), the importance of the few books that dealt with homosexuality is manifest. Ellis could be dreary, Green thought, as love was reduced to the level of a case history and the sex was described too graphically, but he also provided Green with that crucial feeling that he "was not some monster from another age." Triumphantly, he realized that his prison was so much mist, that his "attraction toward masculine beauty was something that may well fill the hearts of many young men" alive right then, in the here and now. Always a naïf, Green then began to look differently at the student who commemorated Oscar Wilde's death date each November clad in a head-band and Greek robe, and even came to talk with sufficient openness that one faculty member felt impelled to warn him to be more discreet. "I don't, but there are some people who consider that sort of thing very wicked," the professor told him meaningfully, tipping the ash "from his long jade-green cigarette holder."

As tortuous and cerebral—and retrospectively entertaining—as Julian Green's road to self-knowledge was, other gay men of the era have recounted awakenings of a more aggressively experiential nature. In Los Angeles, eleven-year-old Harry Hay had been precocious enough to take a peek into Edward Carpenter's *The Intermediate Sex* in 1923 when the local librarian was away from her desk, but an equally important event occurred when he was fourteen. At 175 pounds and well over six feet tall, Hay passed for eighteen with no trouble and had already lived away from home and worked with the Wobblies. A night of lovemaking—his first—on the beach at Santa Barbara with a gentle, handsome twenty-five-year-old mer-chant seaman named Matt was as thrilling for him imaginatively as it was erotically. After the sex, Matt panicked at learning Hay's real age. But he stayed with him to tell Hay about the other men like them whom he had met on his journeys around the world. It was a "silent brotherhood" that they were a part of, Matt said, a hidden society of kindred spirits he could count on, made up of men who were always able to recognize one another. "As a child," Harry Hay liked to say in old age, "I molested an adult until I found out what I needed to know." He and Matt spent the night together in a lifeboat onboard the tramp steamer in the harbor and never saw one another again.

Hay's parents would have been appalled had they known what their inquisitive son was up to while supposedly working with laborers who would "make a man" of him. Some families were more willing to take stock of the truth right under their noses, both because it was harder to avoid than not and because they saw themselves as less provincial, or more offbeat, than their neighbors. Gene Berton, a brilliant musician in a family that doted on music, didn't need to worry about his mannerisms or his place in the Windy City's gay party circuit in the twenties. Berton was secure enough about his campy friends and his parents' esteem to invite his much younger teenage brother to join him at a party in an apartment near the University of Chicago. Ralph Berton and the pal he brought with him were more intrigued than shocked at the "boyish girls and girlish boys" they met amid the Turkish screens and the burning incense, "smoking, sipping wine, necking, wooing, or just chatting." There seemed to Ralph to be two camps at this lively affair: the intellectual gays who "haunted the Dill Pickle Club, the Art Institute . . . the Chicago Opera" and those "plain Janes" who worked as stockroom help or shipping clerks at Marshall Fields, "and whose only common bond with the other guests was their homosexuality—a rather firm bond, in those illiberal days." A number of his brother's friends, including a well-known Chicago photographer, were in drag that night. The only comment offered by Ralph's companion, a young jazz musician from Iowa, Bix Beiderbecke, was characteristically terse: "Shit, Davenport was never like this." Ralph took some pleasure in explaining the ways of his brother's bizarre social circle to Bix. He had long since been taught by Gene to be ready with "The List" (Michelangelo, da Vinci, Tchaikovsky, Wilde) should any philistines venture a rude opinion.

Few gay men were as brazen as the teenage Harry Hay, whose night under the open sky has a mythic stature that fits with his later role in gay political life, or as lucky as Gene Berton in having so charming and supportive a brother. More typical, perhaps, was John Calder's haphazard sense of his place in the scheme of things in Tennessee in the late 1920s. "I was just effeminate enough to have a hard time of it in school," he recalled, "and just manly enough so that my parents didn't notice anything too strange." The eldest son of one of the town's most prominent families, Calder felt he was expected to marry as soon as he finished college, though there was the encouraging example of a maternal uncle in Memphis who traveled frequently to Chicago and New Orleans, lived alone in high style, and seemed (to his nephew's eye) to employ remarkably good-looking male hired help. "Yet I would no more have dropped a hint to my uncle than I would have written to President Hoover. A hint about what? I wasn't clear what I was feeling then, not really. I just knew . . . that *you did not talk about it*, not where I lived. That was the rule of the day." Calder married in 1930 and, after five childless years, he and his wife separated in 1935, by which time he had had several affairs with other professional men, one of whom was also married.

That "rule of the day" could prompt a terrible sense of alienation and leave a man confronting a host of awkward questions: Am I sick, curable, capable of adjustment? Is my sexuality a moral weakness? Can I hope to meet enough other like-minded men, people I will be comfortable with? And who can I trust to help me sort this out? "It seemed to take me forever to put the pieces together," Calder marveled in an interview in 1995. "The doctor I consulted was vague. He was discreet. He was so discreet that I wasn't sure for the longest time if he knew what I was trying to discuss with him. Eventually he talked us both into a corner, but he did give me some books and said he found my case absorbing. I don't know what struck me more, that I was a 'case' or that I was 'absorbing.' "

ON MANY FRONTS, the medical and psychiatric community was beginning to find the whole subject absorbing, and that interest, for better or worse, was a factor in altering, albeit slowly, the terms of gay life in America. Gone were the days when a member of the profession could assert, as George J. Monroe had in 1899, that the habits of "perverts" were too revolting even for doctors to write about. A decade of vice commission studies, the popularized and often misread ideas of Freud, the disruptions of the war, new mores, new affluence, and (not least by any means) a sense of a burgeoning, lucrative market for the troubled and the curious had changed all that; doctors and psychiatrists were often only too willing to issue pronouncements and theories. Much of their counsel was grim and demeaning, if not vicious, and we will never know how many men and women were committed to asylums or became the objects of appalling surgical trials. Yet some medical opinion in the 1920s aimed—or pretended—to be better informed and more broad-minded than its prewar or more conservative counterparts. Not every man of science shared Dr. Joseph Tennebaum's addled conviction in *The Riddle of Sex* (1929) that "the origin of the perversity lies in middle Asia, whence it was introduced into Crete" or that homosexuals could be identified by their insane jealousy and "feline ferocity." The alarmist tone of Dr. Don McCowan's *Love and Life: The Sex Urge and Its Consequences* (1928) or the hysteria of Dr. Meyrick Booth's *Youth and Sex* (1933) was something most author-practitioners avoided, and Dr. James Segall was hardly speaking for the whole profession in *Sex Life in America* (1934) when he railed against society's moral laxity and complained that if Oscar Wilde were to return from the dead and visit New York City, he would be received as an honored guest.

The Doctor Looks at Life and Love, published in 1926 by Dr. Joseph Collins, tried to deflate the hysteria the subject always provoked by calmly observing that homosexuality had been with us for all of recorded history, that homosexuals came in every size, shape, and style, and that only the hidebound older generation would consider the topic literally unmentionable. Even more remarkably, Collins chided those of his colleagues who declared all homosexuals to be neurotic or psychotic and insisted that in his private practice he had known many healthy, productive homosexuals of both sexes. He further deplored the tradition of urging homosexuals to marry as a means of overcoming their wayward drives. Writing his best-selling tract as part of a series designed for a lay audience, Collins wasn't about to risk criticism or limited sales by straying too far from conventional wisdom, however. Homosexuality was still a sorrowful condition in his allegedly liberal view, one that science (specifically, endocrinology) would someday be able to eradicate for the benefit of all. Collins also made a careful distinction between those well-bred homosexuals who stayed celibate and those who would turn from God and "forsake their souls" by actually engaging in sex with their own kind.

In no more helpful a vein, the prominent Boston neurologist whom the architect Philip Johnson consulted while a student at Harvard in 1925 prescribed, above all else, rest. Homosexuality was not necessarily an impediment to a successful life, especially in the arts, the doctor told Johnson, who had come to him worried that his depression and difficulties in school were caused by his sexual desires. Surely this was more intelligent information than Johnson's father was able to offer. ("Boys don't fall in love with boys," he told his son. "Find something to take your mind off it.") But Johnson's need for therapy and guidance was hardly met by being told not to overtax himself. A contemporary of Johnson's was referred to a psychiatrist in his hometown, but his Philadelphia doctor spent most of their sessions probing the young man about his willingness to try dating girls and masturbating to images of male-female coupling. "I was looking to adjust to my situation, not change it," the patient noted, "but I don't think that view counted for much."

The trouble was, and would continue to be so for several decades, that the men of science who ventured into the area of gender study and sexual health were anything but dispassionate investigators. They operated from an Olympian height, and they knew it. In 1922, Samuel Kahn was serving as a psychiatrist for the Department of Corrections in New York City and was sufficiently interested in the sizable male and female homosexual population of the Blackwell's Island penitentiary to undertake a four-year study of those inmates. His initial findings became the subject of his master's thesis at NYU in 1923, while the complete study was published long after the fact, in 1937, as *Mentality and Homosexuality* "by Samuel Kahn, B.S., M.A., Ph.D., M.D." Unfortunately, Dr. Kahn, a sort of rudimentary Freudian, was for all his degrees and licenses no more sophisticated an investigator than he was a writer—Freud would have cringed at the brutality of his patient-interview style, which seemed to take on in most cases a threatening aspect of "All right, we know you're queer so you might as well tell us about it," quickly followed by friendly overtures to inspire cooperation—and a golden opportunity was lost in the compiling of his many case studies. The people he talked with never became complex human beings for him, and their experience was never analyzed with any great skill or insight. Kahn acknowledged that the time would probably come when society no longer viewed homosexuality as pure degeneracy, but he was unable to get beyond some fairly elementary stereotypes and condescended to the inmates in a manner that must have been tormentingly obvious to most of them. His prose is so slapdash that a modern reader can't be entirely sure if, when Kahn writes that "most homosexuals are drug addicts," the doctor is referring to the men and women he is studying or slipping into a generalization about all homosexuals.

Yet what Kahn did hear from his five hundred subjects, seventy-five of whom he concentrated on, spoke volumes about homosexual life beyond the confines of the prison. The subjects attested to the extent of homosexual activity not only in large urban areas but in the smaller cities and towns they had grown up in, and to the fact that homosexuality was by no means an essentially middle- or upper-class phenomenon. Indeed, not surprisingly given his subject pool, Kahn was corroborating a theory that later historians would verify in other contexts, namely that conditions for homosexual sex were often more agreeable in working-class environments in American society than among the more inhibited but allegedly less prejudiced higher social classes.

A great many of the men interviewed in Kahn's study had been employed before their arrest as cooks, waiters, elevator operators, launderers, hospital orderlies, or stagehands and had found their sexual partners in the lobbies of metropolitan hotels, in the theatrical touring companies they joined, and among those who shared their problems with liquor and drugs. One man told of losing his virginity in the bushes of Central Park—a stretch of which was already known in the 1920s as "the fruited plain"—and another of being seduced in his teens by a priest while working as a bellhop in Fall River, Massachusetts. Stories of broken homes, alcoholic parents, widespread adolescent sexual initiations, and transient employment patterns were common (as they would have been among the heterosexual prison population), but the study also hinted at a variety of background and a range of experience that Americans would be reluctant to acknowledge for many years. Kahn's group included natives of New York, Nova Scotia, and the Midwest, Italian immigrants, blacks from the Deep South, an actor from London, veterans of the Great War, drag queens, farmhands, and men with the self-education to have read

Shakespeare and Ibsen. (The man who had read *A Doll's House* strongly suspected Ibsen of being a member of the tribe, plausibly observing that most heterosexual men he knew had no interest in women's rights or their personal growth.) Kahn thought the homosexuals he interviewed necessarily overestimated their number at 10 percent of the city's population, but was willing to concede that the figure in New York was probably 100,000 or more. Joseph Collins had estimated the total homosexual population of the United States at 3 percent, or between 3.3 and 3.7 million.

For all their limitations, Samuel Kahn and Joseph Collins were probably no better or worse than many of their peers. Sex research in America was in its infancy, and the medical and psychiatric profession, which saw itself as more intellectually advanced (or at least more reasoned in its judgments) than the mass of society, was in reality simply pursuing the same divided goals it had been committed to since the mid-nineteenth century. Having replaced religion as a final authority for many people, science had been called on (in the words of historian Vern Bullough) "to give a new foundation to traditional morality." In this endeavor, true disinterest was rare; value-laden judgments were common. Reacting to an a priori standard of moral right and mental health based on Judeo-Christian tenets, rather than listening to and learning from their patients, the science professionals were in effect holding the line against dangerous new ideas and impending threats to the social fabric.

Yet it is not as if the doctors and psychiatrists of the 1920s, any more than the sociologists and lawmakers, lacked for opportunity to observe the diversity of real life around them—both gender-role deviant behavior among the so-called fairies and the bonding of more masculine homosexuals. In the Southwest at that time, anthropologist Ruth Benedict was studying the Native American phenomenon of the *berdache*, the cross-dressing members of the Zuni tribe (which, in fact, corresponds to neither of the above designations). Chicago sociologist Nels Anderson had already written with remarkable sensitivity in his 1923 book *The Hobo* about the extent of same-sex activity and affection among the vagrant male population. The lumber camps of the Northwest had been well-known in this respect since before the war. James Fishman, a federal prison inspector, was only one of several penologists coming to the conclusion that it was time to examine on a national scale the issue of homosexual relations, coercive or otherwise, in the American prison system. Certain places of business—big-city department stores and hotels, for instance—were notorious for the number of homosexual men they employed. Greenwich Village was already a tourist stop for those who wanted to see "the horticultural lads" (that is, the pansies) in their milieu, and Harlem was renowned for its gay-friendly nightclubs and annual drag balls. But the *berdache*, the hobo, the logger, the convict, the ribbon clerk, the artiste, and the black queen defined the social fringe, and the social fringe was not presumed to have any lessons to impart to the wider world.

Not surprisingly, those who constructed and articulated the definitions of mental health and moral respectability weren't aiming to open new frontiers of thought. In an era whose spirit is as aptly symbolized by Henry Ford's assembly lines and Klan marches down Pennsylvania Avenue as by Algonquin witticisms and nightlife glamour, any such new ground was looked upon skeptically. It was enough, most educated men felt, that the subject of deviant behavior should be broached at all and treated with a modern sense of proportion. William Sadler, a Chicago doctor, wrote in *Piloting Modern Youth* (1931) that "every father should instruct his adolescent sons regarding homosexuality"—not a statement that would have found its way into the literature of family life ten years earlier. But Sadler was a firm believer in a new, calculated openness: "Young men should be told frankly that they will come into contact with men who are a bit queer sexually . . . who want to fondle [them], who seek to make social contacts." As a result of this honesty, "many regrettable experiences may easily be prevented." No mention is made in the book of dealing with a son's desires should he be the one who wants to fondle his male friends. The deviance is "out there," like the lesbian lovemaking in the Paris nightclub in *Wings*, not within the homes of the God-fearing middle class. Yet at least as interesting as anything else in this passage from Dr. Sandler's respected guide to proper parenting is his wording about the fact that American boys "*will* come into contact" with those men, or other boys, who desire more intimate contact. By the late 1920s, in the minds of the professionals, it is not a question of *may* but of *will*: homosexuals exist in larger numbers than we had realized, the doctors and psychiatrists were implying, and their increasingly active presence must, in some form, be acknowledged.

3

DEFIANCE, PAGEANTRY, POLITICS

You don't understand. I've got seventeen real live fairies on stage!

—Mae West explaining the idea behind
her new play *The Drag*, 1926

On the night the police closed *The Captive*, to the dismay of New Yorkers who hadn't been able to get tickets to the first lesbian drama on Broadway, two other plays were also shut down. One, *The Virgin Man*, was innocuous boulevard fare about a woman's efforts to seduce her younger brother-in-law. The other, a considerably more salacious production, was the bluntly titled *Sex*, written by and starring as the "whore with a heart of gold" the thirty-four-year-old Mae West.

Sex wasn't a play about homosexuality, but the significance of its demise for gay men lay in its impact on the play West was hoping to bring to New York later that season. Ever on the lookout for more sensational material to fuel a career that hadn't yet lived up to her ambitions, she had concocted the potboiler of all time, a three-act play about gay life designed to make Edouard Bourdet's *Captive* look like *Abie's Irish Rose*. Though she fancifully claimed to have read Freud, Jung, and Havelock Ellis before beginning *The Drag* (an amusing notion to anyone who knew her), West was simply interested in claiming some of the profits and publicity that *The Captive* had reaped while sharing with the world her own impressions of the "third sex." Those impressions were a tad muddled. Her protagonist is a young man, the son of a judge known to have sentenced many homosexuals to prison, who has never consummated his marriage and is attracted to one of his male employees. Though he lives a suffocating double life, he shows no restraint in exhibiting his real feelings to the straight man he loves and regularly invites his gay friends, principally a crowd of drag queens, to come to his home when his wife is away. Between the reactionary judge and a more liberal doctor (the main character's father-in-law), the audience is treated to the range of modern opinion on the issue. The high point of the play, far and away surpassing the protagonist's murder, is a third-act drag party, with "seventeen real-life fairies" onstage for the first time, as West ecstatically put it, wearing wigs and dresses and camping it up. Shock value, a plea for tolerance, mild disdain at the vapid, bitchy nature of the queens, sympathy for the wife who has unknowingly married a pervert: the jumble of *The Drag* was vintage West.

In its tryouts in Connecticut and New Jersey, *The Drag* was wildly successful. Gay men from New York who doubted from the start that the exotic patchwork of a play would ever make it to Manhattan hurried out to Bridgeport or Paterson to see it, but a significant portion of the audience in both cities seems to have been local. Dismissed by *Variety* as "a revel on the garbage heap," it inspired considerably less venom from other reviewers than might have been expected, but the February 9, 1927, theater raids in New York pretty much sealed its fate. The police promised that they would arrest the cast and padlock the theater if *The Drag* ever opened on Broadway. Mayor Jimmy Walker and Governor Al Smith were opposed to the precedent of official intervention, but the furious pressure brought to bear by the Catholic Church hierarchy, groups like the Society for the Suppression of Vice, and William Randolph Hearst (who had been waging his own circulation-boosting morality crusade in his newspapers) didn't leave them any choice. Worse still, in the wake of the controversy, the New York state legislature passed what became known as the Wales Padlock Bill, banning the dramatization of any form of "sex degeneracy, or sex perversion" from New York's theaters. The law would remain on the books for the next forty years. "*The Drag* brought on the crisis," as one producer summarized the situation, and so the state's resistance to homosexuality as a legitimate topic for a public art form like theater was codified. For West, the matter didn't end there, however, and the transvestite party scene was resurrected for *The Pleasure Man*, another hack play she wrote on the heels of her success with *Diamond Lil* in 1928. That sassy, belligerent act led to her arrest and trial, by which time her attention was directed elsewhere. The point had been made. Americans were just "too childlike to face like grown-ups the problem of homosexuality," West complained.

Mae West as an early spokesperson for gay rights is a dubious proposition, as her own comments on the subject (and on all other subjects, for that matter) varied from year to year and according to what she assumed the interviewer of the moment wanted to hear. She used the word *fag* rather freely and was partial to the notion of gay men as "women trapped in men's bodies," though it could be argued that that line of thought simply aligned her to one old-fashioned element of the 1920s medical establishment. In the 1960s she maintained that she had written *The Drag* to warn the public about the dangers to children and wives posed by the gay minority, but by the 1970s she would take credit for having glorified "the boys," especially the campy crowd around whom she was most comfortable. While masculine homosexuals oblivious to her charms made West uneasy, even angry, fairies elicited her interest and compassion. She professed to have known many who had been manhandled by the police and felt a measure of indignation for their plight. Bert Savoy, one of the most talented drag performers of the day, supposedly served as West's model for the brassy persona and gait she developed as a sex star of the thirties. But much more to the point is West's usefulness in defining the boundaries of what was acceptable for public presentation in 1927 and in calling attention to the shifting interests of contemporary urban culture. That fairies were now a hot topic, she had no doubt. Implicitly questioning the "natural," unbridgeable chasm between the masculine and the feminine, they touched something in the postwar national psyche. West was only wrong about one thing, the openness of Broadway and the politicians to that fascination.

The tradition of non-gay—or ostensibly non-gay—female impersonation on the American stage was a long and rich one. Vaudeville drag acts were acceptable family entertainment in the 1890s, at least for those families who didn't object to vaudeville itself as tawdry or sinful, and many men—gay and straight—made a nice living out of singing in dresses, wigs, and makeup. The question of perversion, of the lives these actors led offstage, was distant or irrelevant. They played their parts as refined or uproarious pretend-women, not as perverts, and that made all the difference. Fatty Arbuckle, Charlie Chaplin, and Harold Lloyd put on women's clothes for early silent-comedy roles—Arbuckle even making a specialty of Miss Fatty in her bathing suit at the seaside, a frequent object of male attentions. A greater verisimilitude was achieved in 1919 when Mack Sennett cast Bothwell Browne, a well-known theatrical female impersonator, to play the part of an American aviator who goes behind enemy lines in drag to rescue the heroine of *Yankee Doodle in Berlin*. Even the Kaiser is enticed by Browne's femme fatale.

By degrees, though, an uneasiness about the implications of cross-dressing came to the fore. Browne had been the subject of nasty innuendos long before his movie debut. James Cagney's first stage job, in 1919, was as a member of a female chorus line, a role he could assume only by reminding himself that even the Navy approved of sailors-as-women for the purpose of entertaining the troops (the "Ladies of Newport" scandal was just unfolding). Julian Eltinge probably *was* gay, but anxiously sought to portray himself as a "real man" to his many interviewers. He knew what people thought—flawlessly delicate in his act, popular enough to appear before royalty on his European tour and to get away with lending his name for a corset ad, he was too good at what he did. With Karyl Norman (born George Paduzzi), the tacit understanding that spectators were applauding a normal man acting as a woman for simple comic effect was also stretched to the breaking point. "The Creole Fashion Plate," *Variety* noted, could switch from "a male [baritone] to a female falsetto with the agility of a Flatbush commuter changing trolleys." Even more openly gay than Norman, Bert Savoy was as campy on the street as he was in the theater. He was, possibly, the most uncloseted homosexual in vaudeville, a fact that did nothing to diminish his appeal at the box office. When he was struck by lightning in 1923 during a storm at the beach in New Jersey—reportedly having just remarked, "Mercy, ain't Miss God cutting up something awful?"—his death was mourned even in the highbrow pages of *The Dial*, where Edmund Wilson eulogized the deceased as "the vast vulgarity of New York incarnate and made heroic."

The post-*Captive*, post-*Drag* developments of the late 1920s only took matters to the logical next step. An aspect of what came to be called "the pansy craze," this shift involved the inclusion of more specifically homosexual references in popular entertainment acts and the appearance in nightclubs of effeminate gay men, in or out of drag, acting explicitly as homosexuals.

Managers of vaudeville houses in many towns carefully monitored the content of the acts they booked right up to the last days of vaudeville. They knew better than anyone what the locals would and wouldn't tolerate. But in the bigger cities, there was less concern for the usual limits of propriety, and the existence, the vast number, and the fashion codes of gay men were no longer a secret. As one contemporary writer summarized the change in 1928: "The comedians of the musical revues can hardly escape wearing a red necktie in some skit or other, with the broadest hints of its acquired significance." "Respectable" content was even less of an issue for nightclub owners and their jaded patrons, especially after the Crash of 1929 when business was tight and a new angle was desirable. A club like the Rubaiyat in Greenwich Village with a largely gay clientele was vulnerable to police raids, but when its star performer relocated to a more established venue in midtown with a principally straight crowd of patrons, the result was mainstream success and notices in *Vanity Fair*. The brazen Jean Malin was the talk of the town in 1930 and 1931 when he took over as the Club Abbey's gay master of ceremonies, introducing the singers and answering the catcalls of straight men spoiling for a fight. He later relocated to Hollywood where he had a club in his own name.

Karyl Norman lived on the cutting edge with the same fearless energy. He appeared in an act at the Palace in 1930 entitled "The Glorification of the American Boy-Girl" and, that same year, was the headline performer in a new club on 48th Street and Broadway that did away with all pretense and simply called itself the Pansy Club. Dick Barrows, "the sepia Mae West," had a serious following, as did Francis Renault and Rae Bourbon. In Atlantic City, Boston, Chicago, San Francisco, and numerous other towns and resorts, gay entertainers found a variety of clubs to employ them, some short-lived and others more established. Far from William Inge's Kansas and John Calder's Tennessee, "Scythian madness" took hold for a time. (The idea that sexual or gender-role deviance had roots in Asia enjoyed a brief reign circa 1928—hence the phrase "Scythian madness," used by several cultural critics of the day. The 1927 edition of Krafft-Ebing's *Psychopathia Sexualis* repeated Hippocrates' story of the debilitation of their manhood suffered by Scythian warriors whose bareback horse-riding allegedly caused their testes to shrink, followed by a desire to dress and act like women.)

The sight of gay men putting on a show for straight audiences—the "pansies on parade" motif—drove some gay men to distraction. "I hated it, just hated it," one Californian who moved to New York in the early 1930s commented. "They had the same kind of thing going on in the clubs in [Los Angeles, Hollywood, etc.]. Queens prancing around on the street was bad enough, I always thought. No discretion. No dignity. Before a crowd of straight men in a cabaret, being laughed at—I mean, what good did that do us?" A twenty-five-year-old artist interviewed by a New York psychiatrist in the mid-1930s said that he thought "a good deal of harm [had] been done on the stage by talking about pansies." Slightly effeminate himself, Gene S. detested flamboyant types and told Dr. George Henry that he didn't even "begrudge normal people their feeling against homosexuality." But other gay men admired the daring of the performers, appreciated the rare honesty of openly pitting one mode of life against another, and marveled at the interest heterosexual audiences showed in the flowering of camp. Certainly, it appeared to a great many mainstream observers that straight men were playing with fire by demonstrating *any* tolerance for freakish sexual displays. Whether it was the advent of the wristwatch during the war (more practical than the pocketwatch, but thought to look suspiciously like a bracelet) or the fad for silk undershorts or the whispers about Valentino, conservative social critics believed that they had ample evidence that the "vogue for effeminacy" was undermining the American character. Pope Pius XI had expressed his alarm in 1928, warning that male youth was being led astray by feminizing influences in postwar Europe and the United States. The implications went beyond indecent new dances, bawdy films, birth-control agitation, and a rising divorce rate. Unstated but never far from anyone's mind in these commentaries was the dread fear of men kissing other men, men sucking other men, men loving other men.

In one sense, the 1920s fascination with effeminate behavior could be taken as just another example of the era's compulsive need for novelty, a fever allied to a self-conscious rejection of the *Main Street* way of life. The silent majority had been made uneasy about the more tumultuous features of urbanization and the trend toward hedonism, but a vocal, visible minority delighted in making fun of prudishness in any form. Earnest disapproval was enough to ignite a fashion, from bobbed hair to the college man's hip flask. Historians of the decade have also analyzed the voracious nature of 1920s consumerism and the destabilizing effects of Prohibition, as law-abiding citizens who wanted to drink were made into criminals and brought into contact in speakeasies with a rowdier social element. These are both relevant, if more subtle, pieces of the puzzle. An ethos based on disdain for the standards of the recent past, a view of law and leadership as comically antiquated, a need to feel au courant, and a restless craving for amusement will yield all manner of explorations into previously forbidden areas of life. In the time of "Flaming Youth," manic gratification and earnest rebellion proved to be equally potent, unpredictable social forces.

The tendency of all sexualized entertainment to lose its edge played a part as well. More and more blatant manifestations of heterosexual desire—the provocative atmosphere of the jazz club, the strident figure of the vamp, the bared breasts and exposed bottoms (male and female) of silent films—were linked to the ensuing search for unconventional forms of erotic expression, the inevitable refueling that titillation demands. "The revolt of the virgins," as one wag termed the upheaval in values, led some of its participants through uncharted byways of modern sexuality. Out of this flux emerged an eager audience for *Diamond Lil*, a vast readership (not exclusively gay) for *The Well of Loneliness*, and a spectator's interest in men who bleached their hair, wiggled their hips, and answered to feminine names. In *Call Her Savage* (1932), Clara Bow has money, appetite, and a ferocious will. Her tour of New York necessarily includes a stop at a Village club peopled by anarchists, bohemians, women in ties, and waiters who sing soprano, dance in aprons, and wave their feather dusters about.

Smugness and control were other, more obvious factors. In the time of Paul Robeson and Duke Ellington, white condescension to African-Americans in the form of blackface routines and coon jokes was beginning to wane. The flapper and the Nineteenth Amendment had relegated caricatures of cigar-smoking women and marching suffragettes to the dustbin. Jews were harder to mock openly as they became powers on Wall Street, on Broadway, and in Hollywood. Pansies, however, were an ideal target. They were asserting themselves in a public forum, and middle-class or well-to-do men and women could declare the superiority of their lives by smiling and shaking their heads at pathetic, nervy half-men like Jean Malin and Karyl Norman. Furthermore, they could tell themselves that there was such an entity as a "typical homosexual," now that the word was coming into wider use, and that Malin and Norman were the classic examples. For anyone troubled by the thought that sexuality was indeed the labyrinthine force Freud wrote about, with bisexual instincts to be found among all manner of men—among husbands and fathers, soldiers and athletes—what better way to quiet that fear than to reiterate and exalt the evidence to the contrary? Pansy performers were well paid to enter the nightclub arena. A focus on derided effeminacy was also an excellent means of keeping in place the unstereotypical homosexual (the queer, rather than the fairy or pansy, in the language of the day). Announce yourself as a deviant, and this travesty is what you will universally be perceived to be. For the next fifty years, an expectation of effeminacy would continue to be the portal through which young gay men had to pass as they worked their way toward a sense of the style of homosexuality that was right for them.

The popularity of pansy acts and vaudevillians in red neckties hinted at even more momentous changes, or anxieties, in the culture. No one laughs at the inconsequential, or the unthreatening; our sources of entertainment give us away. In the 1920s, femininity in men was out in the open, as a cover for pondering same-sex urges and, in its own right, as the most visible sign of a nervous curiosity about gender-role transgression. If many middle-class women were voting and working outside the home before marriage, and a number were claiming their right to take a lover (just as working-class women had done all along), everyone had cause to wonder which of the old beliefs would be challenged next and, more personally, which still made sense to them. Men who came of age in the 1890s were expected to dress soberly, work hard, and exhibit some degree of fortitude and thrift; their sons balked at these restraints. Their sons also had to contend with something their fathers had taken care to ignore or censor—the reality of women's sexual responsiveness, a fact of life that provided new opportunities for mutual delight, and a troubling potential for "performance anxiety." Douglas Fairbanks and John Gilbert set a high standard for amatory skill, and the risks and competitive demands of "dating" had little in common with the late-nineteenth-century notion of "calling on" a young woman. ("Do You Have What It Takes?" asked the 1920s ads for cologne, close-shaving razors, and countless other products that implied one might be found wanting. "Are American Men Too Lazy to Be Good Lovers?" Bernarr MacFadden, the Jack LaLanne of the era, liked to challenge his male readers in the pages of *Physical Culture*. These aren't questions that would have meant much to Sister Carrie, but they did to the women of Fitzgerald and Hemingway and the men who courted them.) Yet by gently sliding the scale that defined acceptable modes of masculine demeanor, behavior, and success—sliding it so as to bring into wider consciousness a level of male-femininity ignored twenty years earlier—middle-class heterosexual men effectively kept their place in an evolving gender hierarchy. The man who wore a soft-collared shirt and studied the toiletry ads was a bit fey by the standards of 1900 to 1910. Now, on a spectrum that included men who were practically women, he was as masculine, as normal and secure, as any "man's man" of his father's day.

Even more critical, perhaps, was the memory, the bitter residue, of President Wilson's crusade. Worship at the altar of old-style manliness had led to some of the unforgivable traumas of modern life: Verdun, Belleau Wood—where a thousand U.S. marines fell in a single day. To many Americans, World War I was a bracing test of the national mettle. To smarter souls, it had been a charade and the cost had been borne by those young men who refused to question their faith in patriotism, authority, and masculinity. Hurried into the jaws of war, as John Dos Passos wrote, they discovered that rugged individualism meant nothing in the mud of the trenches. Old men sent young men to confront the new weapons of destruction in foreign lands, while women waved flags and handkerchiefs. There was a distasteful quality to the pansy, but it was a distaste mixed with faint stirrings of doubt about the rigidity of its polar opposite. For many, the mythology of San Juan Hill was as dead as the Rough Rider who had inspired and shaped it.

In certain contexts, effeminacy offered a playful allure even for a mass audience, male and female, who would never have set foot in a Hollywood nightclub or a Times Square theater. The travel writer Edward Halliburton made the rounds of the lecture circuit in the twenties and knew enough to hide his homosexuality behind the mask of the dashing, unattached adventurer. Real-life heroes didn't bed their mates or act fairyish, not if they wanted to make a lot of money. But when Willard Huntington Wright, a notorious homophobe, created the Philo Vance detective series, beginning with *The Benson Murder Case* in 1926, he pressed in the opposite direction as hard as he reasonably could. As "S. S. Van Dine," he concocted a bachelor sleuth—uninterested in women, indifferent to masculine pursuits, affected in his speech, pampered and bookish—to drive the gender traditionalists mad. The plots of the Philo Vance stories are never very compelling; it was the amoral dandy at the heart of the books who captivated the popular imagination. By 1930, S. S. Van Dine's novels had sold more than a million copies, and Scribner's credited Van Dine with seeing the company through the first rough months of the Depression. In a fantasy context, it would appear, a hint of willful deviance was exciting, and the ever-calculating Wright took some pleasure in seeing how far he could push the public tolerance for that hint, all the while hoping to avoid the charge that he had actually created a limp-wristed protagonist. Americans in the 1930s wanted a Sam Spade or a Philip Marlowe to protect them from treacherous wrongdoers. Americans in the 1920s embraced Philo Vance, whose usual response to a discovery was a terse "Oh, my aunt!"

THE WAY IN which the pansy craze lodged itself in late-1920s, early-1930s American culture—as an implicit means of acknowledging, exploring, and yet containing the specter of homosexuality—was mirrored even more dynamically in the position gay men and lesbians created for themselves in enclaves like the Vieux Carré in New Orleans, the Near North neighborhood and Jackson Park area of Chicago, the blocks around St. Botolph's Street in Boston and Rittenhouse Square in Philadelphia, or Greenwich Village and Harlem in New York. Living in the midst of one's own kind could be a fortifying experience, yet it was also the means by which society came to identify, categorize, and more aggressively stigmatize members of the group.

Pre-Depression Harlem is especially rich terrain for learning about the possibilities and tribulations facing gay men in a period of rapid social change and the inconsistent level of acceptance they were afforded. A surge of high-profile literary talent, giving rise to the Harlem Renaissance, came into being in tandem with a transformation of the area's nightlife, as cafes and speakeasies north of 125th Street accommodated revelers of every race, gender, and sexual persuasion. A section of Manhattan that hadn't even existed as a primarily black neighborhood two decades earlier and, once established as such in the 1910s, never anticipated a nocturnal white influx, found itself during Prohibition at the center of a cultural whirlwind.

For blacks, Harlem was the place where people of all classes and tastes lived side by side. It was home to churchwomen, laborers, Garveyites, poets, shopkeepers, domestics, doctors, and drag queens. For whites, it was a slummer's paradise. Many of the whites who came to the area by taxi or in their chauffeur-driven cars no doubt genuinely appreciated their experience of the blues, with its more unrestrained acceptance of sexuality than white music provided, and found in the rhythms of jazz something that was lacking in their downtown lives. On the other hand, white racism had rarely assumed a form so patronizing. The Cotton Club, where Duke Ellington and Cab Calloway performed amid the jungle decor, was for a whites-only audience (which was fine by its patrons who didn't want to go so far as to *sit* with blacks), and according to some sources Cole Porter and his Yale buddy Monty Woolley found plenty of dark young men to choose from, for a fee, at Clint Moore's or Caska Bond's. Charlotte Mason, the Park Avenue "angel" for several Renaissance notables, was a master of dictatorial philanthropy, and even the first important novel to examine the aura of Jazz Age Harlem was published by a white author, complete with a glossary at the back of "Negro Words and Phrases." Carl Van Vechten's *Nigger Heaven* opened the floodgates in 1926, alerting thrill-seekers and would-be bohemians that uptown at night was the place to be. Van Vechten's book dodges the issue, but "faggots and bulldaggers," as gay men and lesbians were called in Harlemese, also found a place for themselves in this chaotic milieu, in a much more public fashion than white areas allowed. As George Chauncey has written in the most extensive study of the place and the period, "The Village's most flamboyant homosexuals wore long hair; Harlem's wore long dresses. The Village had cafes where poets read their verse and drag queens performed; Harlem had speakeasies where men danced together and drag queens were regular customers."

The gentry of Harlem wanted no part of a rude social scene that tolerated homosexuals any more than bootleggers or prostitutes, but in the salons of an arriviste like A'lelia Walker, the "mahogany millionairess" whose mother had made a fortune with her hair-straightening product, or Alexander Gumby, an affable postal clerk known for his excellent library, gay men and lesbians had no need to hide their sexuality. Of equal importance, black and white homosexuals were provided the opportunity to mingle at private gatherings and dinner parties in Harlem, making possible more than a few interracial love affairs and relationships of long standing. "I never met a professional black man in the neighborhood I grew up in

[New Jersey], and that's the way my parents wanted it," one gay white man in his late eighties said in a recent conversation. At a sedate, largely gay dinner party a friend took him to on Edgecombe Avenue a few weeks before the stock market crash, Gerald R. met an older black homosexual, a teacher with whom he became happily involved for several months. "I learned a good deal more from him than I did at [Columbia]," he remembered. Amid the later chronicling of dusk-to-dawn bacchanals, the middle-class dimension of Harlem's gay social life is often lost to sight. Alexander Gumby's comfortable studio came to him by way of the young white stock-broker with whom he enjoyed a decade-long relationship, and Philip Johnson commented about his two-year affair with entertainer Jimmy Daniels that "it could only have happened uptown." The papers of Glenn Carrington at the Schomburg Center for Black Culture in Harlem are yet another reminder—a rare documentary chronicle—of this aspect of gay life in northern Manhattan. An African-American sociologist and parole officer, Carrington came to Harlem in 1926 to find a job, make friends, and have lovers, black and white, which he did, and, not long after settling in, was inspired to write a blunt "coming out" letter to his family back in Virginia. To young men of all races who were uneasy about their homosexuality, he was, even in his early twenties, a level-headed friend and a supportive correspondent.

Hospitality farther down the social ladder came in diverse styles. The Garden of Joy, an open-air dance pavilion, catered to a mixed crowd. Edmond's Cellar was a basement dive with a heavy transvestite clientele, while the Hot Cha was a convivial place for more upwardly mobile black gay men. "Jungle Alley," the stretch of 133rd Street between Seventh and Lenox Avenues known as the center of Harlem's "sporting life" ("the real swing street," Billie Holliday said), was by the late 1920s the site of one of the city's best-known gay nightspots. The Clam House was "not for the innocent young," *Vanity Fair* advised, but sophisticates who wanted their entertainment as ribald as possible couldn't do better, especially during the heyday of Gladys Bentley. Bessie Smith, Ethel Waters, and Alberta Hunter were all known to have had their flings with women as well as men; "La Bentley" was alone, though, in the way she advertised and capitalized on her same-sex interests. At an ample two-hundred-and-fifty pounds, dressed in her trademark white tuxedo and top hat, she sat through the night at the piano, delighting patrons with an incandescent smile, a high-energy performance, and her own mischievous parody versions of current popular songs. Eminently comfortable being known as a bulldagger, "she could be seen any day marching down Seventh Avenue in men's clothes," one writer observed, and her Atlantic City "wedding" to a white lesbian was a hot gossip item for months. Bentley also starred at the nearby Ubangi Club, where the renowned female impersonator "Gloria Swanson" had been a hit, and began a recording career in 1928. To men and women of a more circumspect temperament, she was a rare model of what was possible outside the mainstream. She was unapologetic, she had fun—and, for a few years, she made rebellion pay.

Speakeasies, cafes, bathhouses, and even brothels where homosexuals could relax, enjoy themselves, meet friends, or have sex were common to many American cities by the end of the 1920s. The somewhat different phenomenon of the "buffet flats" was probably a little more freewheeling than most neighborhoods, or cities, could tolerate. But in the ghettos of New York, Chicago, Detroit, Philadelphia, and Washington, D.C., they flourished and were another highly indiscreet, highly libidinous means by which gay life might assert itself. A buffet flat was, as its name implies, a pick-and-choose arrangement. Tenants of an apartment who had trouble making the rent would open their doors to paying guests (originally, to blacks who couldn't get a bed in a segregated hotel), to gambling parties, to prostitutes and exhibitionists and drunken partygoers. When inhibitions were at their lowest, guests might wander from bedroom to bedroom watching a kind of erotic circus, sometimes of an interracial character. Americans were reluctant to admit how much sex had taken place, and continued to take place, between white men and black women, but sex between white and black *men* was still an unthinkable prospect in most quarters. In Harlem and a few other locales, the sex tableaux of the buffet flats openly broke even that taboo forty years before the orgy rooms of the post-Stonewall bathhouses.

The one legal means by which gay men got together in large numbers had to do, paradoxically, with that most arrogant affront to gender codes: full, glorious drag. In every state, a male caught in women's clothing outside a theater was subject to arrest or harassment. The true drag artist might be lucky enough, on occasion, to elicit a more tempered response. The *New York World* seemed to think that bobbed-haired, twenty-six-year-old Raymond Stanley was worthy of a flattering photo in the March 2, 1924, edition. The detectives who booked him for shoplifting from Orbach's were unaware of his gender when they arrested him and later doffed their hats to him as the "rival of Julian Eltinge." But patently obvious or badly made-up transvestites almost always paid a high price for their cross-dressing. Someone like Al Williams, who in his own view made a pretty unconvincing female in his drag period after high school in 1929, was frequently beat up by the police and neighborhood thugs in his native Philadelphia. It all depended on how you carried it off; "If you don't make yourself obnoxious, nobody notices," another of Dr. George Henry's patients, a married cross-dresser, told him. But at regular intervals, transvestite balls were held in several cities with licenses granted by the police, allowing the participants—literally, thousands—to dress as women for that one evening. Again, several strands come together in this phenomenon: a fierce drive on the part of some gay men to express themselves as they chose; a fluctuating but emphatic measure of heterosexual curiosity; and a sense—or hope—by those in power that tolerance for *some* displays of unconventional behavior would serve the purpose of a safety valve, preventing a wider breakdown. "Allowing the 'freaks' their night out made sense for everybody," one participant of the balls in the 1930s acidly commented. No doubt the police made money by this arrangement, as those affairs that were launched without official approval were subject to raids in which the queens were insulted, arrested, and often brutally manhandled.

By 1924, Baltimore had its first public ball, and Chicago not long after was holding two a year at the Coliseum Annex. In New Orleans, Mardi Gras in the Jazz Age was a natural time for drag pageantry, though community historian Roberts Batson reports on a rollicking costume gala in a male brothel on Barrone Street as far back as the turn of the century. In the twenties, the "Million Dollar Dolls," a black transvestite group, were parading their talent at carnival time to wild applause, dressed in huge wigs and leotards decorated with hundreds of dollar bills. In New York, where the tradition of lavish masquerades predated the war by two decades or more, the Astor Hotel and Madison Square Garden were the sites of well-attended balls in the 1920s. Like the similar events at the Liberal Club and Webster Hall in Greenwich Village, they were not exclusively gay-transvestite showcases so much as opportunities for gay men to join in a frolic involving women and heterosexual men who dressed in all sorts of colorful outfits.

The biggest and flashiest ball of all, though, was very much a gay drag enterprise by 1926, and that took place in Harlem at the Manhattan Casino, later called the Rockland Palace, at Eighth Avenue and 155th Street. Sponsored by the Hamilton Lodge, a chapter of the Oddfellows, it brought together in one location the cream of the crop, with men coming to Harlem from as far away as Boston and Pittsburgh. Two thousand participants, mostly black, and two thousand spectators of all races were not uncommon figures; the numbers climbed even higher by the mid-1930s. Planning their costumes months in advance, anyone with the figure and an interest in sartorial experimentation wanted to compete for awards, make dates, observe the creations of their friends and rivals, and be seen—ogled or applauded—by a balcony jammed with gay and straight "tourists," including frequently a celebrity contingent. One aspect of the night rarely noted, but discussed by Langston Hughes in his memoir *The Big Sea* (1940), was the presence of the aging queens on the sidelines, still dressed in the costumes they had worn in years past for their turn in the spotlight. Hughes saw them as cast-offs, unbearably sad, and perhaps they were the relics he thought they were; the notion of the older homosexual as a pitiful creature was scarcely questioned before the 1970s. What we lack is a first-hand account of what *they* felt, these black men of another time, sons of Reconstruction and the Gilded Age alive to see the triumph of jazz and the splendor of Gladys Bentley.

Descriptions of drag balls crop up in only a handful of novels, suggesting that many fiction writers of the time were less determined to *épater les bourgeois* than legend has it, or at least less inclined to dramatize interracial events. Blair Niles was one exception. The protagonist of her 1931 novel *Strange Brother*, published by Liveright, attends a Harlem drag ball and sits in her box mesmerized by the spectacle of men "in all sorts of women's fancy dress, in elaborate wigs . . . from the towering curled and powdered head-dresses of the Marie Antoinette period to the close marcelled bobs of 1930 . . . in the voluminous costumes that go with powdered wigs and in the long sheath-like evening gowns of the mode of 1930." The middle-class gay man who serves as June Westwood's guide through the subculture is mortified by the display—Mark Thornton is a suicide by the end of Mrs. Niles's fairly heavy-handed novel—but June is sensitive enough to find interest in the ball as a challenge to women ("They make us see ourselves! Do we look that way, I wonder . . . to men?") and to notice her ex-husband in the crowd of dancers, a discovery that helps to explain a great deal about their brief, tepid union several years earlier.

Despite the fact that the visitors' presence had the effect of turning the balls' participants into bizarre objects of study, and despite the likelihood that drag in the 1920s spoke to no larger a segment of the gay population than it does today, the balls served a crucial purpose. As queens from several states laughed, danced, and dished the competition at the Rockland Palace, they came to see that the boundaries of their outsider's world were not as narrow, nor its character so dour, as might have appeared to be the case when they were growing up. Great fun was to be had, after all. Solidarity of a kind was possible, and strength in numbers did mean something, at least for the night. Even class barriers were momentarily lifted. The singer Taylor Gordon wrote in 1929 of the drag ball he attended at the Savoy Ballroom on Lenox Avenue that it was "packed with people from bootblacks to New York's rarest bluebloods." True enough, this did no immediate or discernible good for the great mass of homosexuals, black or white, who didn't identify—or want to—with gender-rebellious spectacle, but public awareness of any radical idea (as homosexuality was, and still is) inevitably begins in America with a focus on the more newsworthy, and paradoxically less frightening, extremes. The extensive, sarcastic, but not always hostile coverage the balls received in the black press was a step down a long road, and in that vital process Harlem led the way.

Yet it is easy in hindsight to overstate the freedom that men had to flourish "in the life," as the gay world was called in black circles. The tricks of memory are always going to create conflicting guides to the past, and some men who lived in Harlem in the 1920s remembered the era as tolerant to a degree that sounds implausible today. "You did just what you wanted to do," the artist Richard Bruce Nugent told an interviewer in his old age. "Nobody was in the closet. There wasn't any closet." But, on the contrary, many African-Americans were uneasy about their sexual proclivities in the midst of an overwhelmingly heterosexual community. Black Baptist ministers often spoke from the pulpit about the evils of homosexuality, and black-owned newspapers were capable of the usual vindictiveness in printing gossip about "roommates" and publishing the names and addresses of men arrested for solicitation. When the respected NAACP member Augustus Granville Dill was picked up by police in a subway bathroom in 1928, W. E. B. DuBois immediately fired him as business manager of *The Crisis*. The readership of *The Crisis* wasn't to be expected to deal with the taint of "vice" in DuBois's sober, politically oriented "Record of the Darker Races." And when Nugent himself published a stunning homoerotic prose poem in 1926 in the one-issue avant-garde journal *Fire!!*, he identified himself by his first and middle name only so as to spare his mother any embarrassment.

Nugent's blend of self-knowledge and intermittent discretion was shared by many of his contemporaries. The joy of acting on one's homosexuality *and* a simultaneous discomfort with its social implications is, if anything, more vividly exemplified by the lives of Harlem Renaissance men than by any other source of the time. (Not that this is a fact many literary or historical studies of the movement dwell on—homosexuality is a suffocatingly genteel presence even in the best of these books.) Claude McKay, for instance, seems to have been at ease in his relationships with other males. He had no problem approaching men he was attracted to, gay or straight, black or white—though he had been married for several months after college to a childhood sweetheart. Introduced in adolescence in Jamaica to the books of Wilde, Whitman, and Edward Carpenter (by his white British mentor), McKay had as sure a grasp of the modern homosexual literary tradition as anyone. After his divorce, he enjoyed affairs with men and women, including an unlikely relationship with a young Irishman who made his living as a blackmailer of "respectable" gay men caught in compromising situations. Yet his vernacular novels of Harlem life steer clear of anything more than a fleeting reference to a delicate Pullman car waiter or "pansies and dandies" mingling in area cabarets. McKay's most extensive, favorable depiction of gay men appears in *Return to Marseilles*, a novel (unfortunately never published) based on his time in the south of France.

Like McKay, Wallace Thurman and Countee Cullen also felt the pressure to marry in their twenties, and their unions were just as short-lived. Thurman had the bad luck to get arrested in a subway men's room on a morals charge within a week of his arrival in New York, only to be bailed out by a friendly minister who expected a sexual favor in return. A troubled man and a hard drinker, he never made peace with any of his attributes as an outcast intellectual or found sufficient solace with his white lover. *The Blacker the Berry . . .*, his 1929 novel about a dark-skinned woman's search for her place among black peers who prize lighter complexions, includes a sinister lesbian landlady and the heroine's manipulative bisexual boyfriend. Alva is ultimately caught by Emma Lou with a male partner in a "vile embrace." But everyone, gay or straight, comes under harsh scrutiny in Wallace Thurman's arid fictional domain. As Ann Douglas observed in *Terrible Honesty: Mongrel Manhattan in the 1920s*, Thurman's most famous novel *Infants of the Spring* is "a bitter reworking of the *Waste Land* theme," but Thurman's despair admitted of even less possibility for change or growth than Eliot's.

If Thurman was Harlem's greatest misanthrope, Countee Cullen was its genial prodigy, and his sexual ambivalence was played out on a painfully public stage—on one level in the elegant ache of much of his poetry and more visibly in the debacle of his 1928 marriage to Yolande DuBois. At the wedding of the decade in Harlem, W. E. B. DuBois's daughter was a pawn in a game that fooled few people beyond her domineering father, who was glad to see his child make an alliance with the most promising poet of his generation. When Cullen left for Europe two months later with his handsome friend Harold Jackman, an item in one of the black papers reported the news with appropriate sarcasm: GROOM SAILS WITH BEST MAN. In contrast, Cullen's good friend Langston Hughes chose to stay unmarried and avoid the mistakes made by Cullen, Thurman, and McKay. His tragedy, however, involved a chilling asexual affect that forestalls any pat identification of him as "gay" but also made him a lonely man in flight from intimacy, an anomaly to his friends. Not until the early 1960s did Hughes write his first story with a gay character. "Blessed Assurance," about a talented young man, a "brilliant queer" whose father cannot accept his effeminacy, was one of his few explicit comments on the subject.

Someone who gave the impression of not being tormented or hobbled by his sexuality, however, was Alain Locke, "the Proust of Lenox Avenue." The exemplar of a certain style of gayness—hypercultured, hyperaesthetic, mannered, and controlling—he was one of the key figures of Harlem's "Talented Tenth" and a dynamic sponsor of its young male writers. (With the exception of Zora Neale Hurston, he was callously indifferent to women and didn't care who knew it.) Recipient of a Harvard doctorate in philosophy and the first black Rhodes scholar, Locke was a professor at Howard University, though not by any stretch of the imagination a run-of-the-mill academic. The man who edited the groundbreaking literary anthology *The New Negro* in 1925 was as familiar with Europe's art galleries as any white connoisseur, had hopes of founding an African art museum in America, and exhibited the last word in mother obsession when he held his mother's wake in his apartment, serving tea to his guests and referring to her in the present tense while she sat upright, embalmed, in her favorite lounge chair. ("A possible explanation for such peculiar behavior," writes one explicator of Locke's philosophical texts, "is that Locke was disaffected from the tenets of his family's Episcopalian background." Indeed.) He pursued Langston Hughes with calculated ardor and had an almost classical Greek conception of the role he was best suited for, as a mentor-lover to younger intellectual men.

Fastidious, cosmopolitan, competitive, and opinionated, Locke is sometimes taken to task today for his innocent faith in culture as the means by which advancement would finally come to his people. To be sure, he was a bossy cheerleader for the Harlem Renaissance as well as a probing critic. But this steamroller passion for the arts wasn't entirely apolitical, in that he wanted the writers he valued to show a distinct consciousness of race, and it is an impulse that makes sense in light of his homosexuality. Locke accepted the terms white European society promoted. Sensibility, wit, Eurocentric erudition, artistic accomplishment, and a rich literary tradition were the hallmarks of "civilization." Moreover, they were the characteristics of any gay man educated at Harvard and Oxford in the Edwardian era who felt an affinity for Pater and Santayana and was most fully alive in the world of books and pictures. In latching on to aestheticism as a means to power in a world of hearty philistines, in cultivating an air of learned preciosity, Alain Locke was speaking as a fin de siècle homosexual as much as a value-theory philosopher or a New Negro. As such, he remains a singular and fascinating figure in American cultural history.

Locke also had a keen if rarely expressed sense of his own evolution, quirks and accomplishments both. In an unpublished essay on psychological disturbances, he articulated the belief that "an antagonistic social reality" could lie at the root of an individual's neurotic behavior as much as the childhood family traumas that Freud delineated. Homosexuals often acted in conflicted or antisocial ways, he mused, but this was no different from the behavior of equivalently disturbed Negroes, Jews, or women who suffered in relation to a dominant group that wished to keep them in their place. Society's enforcement of restrictive values made for twisted personalities as readily as a father's abuse or a mother's neglect. Pondering Wallace Thurman's suicidal pain or Langston Hughes's reticence, or the erotic excesses of his neighbors that sometimes had an aspect of desperation more than pleasure, or even his own cranky need to dominate others, Locke was wise enough to understand the importance of an oppressive social context. This was not a way of thinking that would be shared by many people in the next three decades.

FOR ALL THE good accomplished by the elaborate social networks of the drag balls and the gay nightclubs, or by the examples of men as different as Bert Savoy and Alain Locke, one element conspicuously lacking for homosexual men in America in the 1920s—in sharp contrast to Europe—was any movement toward political organization or open intellectual exchange on the subject. Homosexuality, male or female, languished in the category of moral turpitude, medical anomaly, or sheer exotica. The sole exception to this lack of vision that has come to light is the ill-fated Society for Human Rights, founded in Chicago in December 1924 by a thirty-two-year-old postal clerk. Henry Gerber, who was born Josef Dittmar in Bavaria and changed his name upon emigrating to America in 1913, had been interned during the war as an enemy alien but served for three years with the Allied Army of Occupation in Europe in the early 1920s. During his time in Germany, he had been impressed by the seriousness with which gay life and problems could be treated. After examining some of the early homophile publications and learning about the pioneering work being done by Magnus Hirschfeld at his Institute for Sex Research and his recently formed World League for Sexual Reform, he returned to the United States preoccupied with the notion of introducing that level of discourse to the topic of same-sex love. From sober debate and better public relations (he was not a devotee of camp or drag), Gerber was hopeful that understanding, tolerance, and legal reform would follow. An admirer of H. L. Mencken and a man every bit as irascible as his literary hero, he was perhaps the wrong individual to lead a movement. But the problems went far beyond Gerber's personality.

Most gay men in Chicago whom Gerber approached assured him that his project was sheer folly. Their view of themselves and their situation was set in stone: the dangers of independent action were too great; the idea of the "double life" and the "forbidden fruit" was not without its charm; and homosexuals were well-known to be fun-loving and apolitical, even militantly antiorganizational. Undeterred, Gerber eventually found six other men willing to put their names on articles of nonprofit incorporation for a group whose purpose would be "to promote and protect the interests of people who by reasons of mental and physical abnormalities are abused and hindered in the legal pursuit of happiness which is guaranteed by the Declaration of Independence." By specifying its aim as combating prejudice by the "dissemination of facts according to modern science among intellectuals of mature age," the Society for Human Rights further emphasized its character as a discussion group, not a proselytizing or social body and not a group that would have anything to do with minors. Like the later Mattachine Society, it would advance its program by means of lectures and a publication, to be entitled *Friendship and Freedom*. John Graves, an indigent preacher, agreed to be the group's president, in name anyway; Al Meininger ("a laundry queen," in Gerber's words) became the vice president; Gerber was to serve as secretary.

Application to the state for a charter for the group went smoothly enough. "No one seemed to have bothered to investigate our purpose," Gerber noted. But any progress thereafter was thwarted by the usual obstacles: lack of funding, lack of grass-roots appeal, the fear prominent and respected men felt about lending their names to so radical an endeavor. The two issues of *Friendship and Freedom* that did appear were written and financed by Gerber himself, his comrades proving to be largely "illiterate and penniless." According to a secondhand source, the first issue contained an essay on self-control, a poem by Whitman, and an article on Oscar Wilde and the wearing of green carnations as a gay code.

The actual defeat of the Society for Human Rights was the result of a betrayal from within. Having decided to restrict membership solely to homosexuals—feeling that bisexual men would lack the commitment they wanted—the members were unaware of the fact that their laundry queen–vice president was married with two small children. His wife, distressed by her husband's associations, called a social worker, who in turn reported the case to the Chicago police department. At two in the morning one Sunday in the summer of 1925, Henry Gerber was awakened by a city detective and a reporter who searched the apartment for incriminating evidence and, without bothering to have obtained a warrant, arrested him. Arraigned at the Chicago Avenue Police Court, he found that Graves and

Meininger had also been brought in. STRANGE SEX CULT EXPOSED was the headline of the article in one paper that day, alerting readers to the danger of a sinister band of deviants who had "urged men to leave their wives and children."

Henry Gerber paid a high price for his boldness, but not as high as the police and the district attorney's office wanted. His own lawyer arranged the appropriate payoffs and the presiding judge in his trial then set him free, even going so far as to reprimand the police for arresting a man without a warrant. The postal service, however, was not as obliging. Gerber's superiors threatened to prosecute him on an obscenity charge for sending his perverted magazine through the U.S. mail but ultimately accepted a bribe, settling for Gerber's dismissal for "conduct unbecoming a postal worker." Forty years later, Gerber still remembered as he left the courtroom the parting taunt of the detective who had arrested him: "What was the idea of the Society of Human Rights, anyway? Was it to give you birds the legal right to rape every boy on the street?" In another version of this tense moment, confided by Gerber in a private letter, the language of his questioner was more aggressive still: "Did you think you'd be given the right to fuck boys up the ass?" The dismal experience taught him, Gerber wrote, "that we were up against a solid wall of ignorance, hypocrisy, meanness, and corruption," and in 1925, for the moment, "the wall had won."

4

Days of the Code

When I was a kid, I listened to a network radio soap opera called *Myrt and Marge*, sponsored by Wrigley-Spearmint gum. They were Follies girls, a mother and daughter, Myrtle Spear and Margery Minter. It was called the Hayfield Follies and the show was a lot of life-backstage episodes. The costume designer was Clarence. Clarence was a screaming queen. Clarence was always having snits. . . . This was my introduction to [gay men]. Screamers having snits.

—Peter Conway, on growing up gay in
Bethesda, Maryland, in the 1930s

The cataclysm of 1929 altered the sexual landscape of America much as it affected every other aspect of society. Yet the changes in the area of public sexuality brought on by the collapse of the economy were necessarily more gradual and less immediately obvious. In 1930 and 1931, the pansy craze was at its height, though a crackdown on homosexual nightclub and vaudeville fare was imminent. Inspired by Radclyffe Hall's vindication in court a few months before the stock market crash, publishers for a while showed an unheard-of interest in books with gay themes, and Hollywood explored the subject as well in a variety of modes, both subtle and shocking. By mid-decade, however, tolerance for these developments had peaked, and a fierce, moralizing reaction set in. Curiosity about sexual expression and sexual differences remained as strong as it had ever been in postwar years, but with traditional values threatened by devastating unemployment rates, radical political agitation, and strained family relations, new ideas about gender-role freedom and same-sex love were shunted aside. Earl Hamner may have convinced a generation of television viewers that the Depression brought families closer together, but the anguished fear of splintering suffered by the Joads was closer to the mark than the good cheer and stability of the Waltons. The divorce rate declined significantly in the 1930s, it is true, for the good reason that fewer couples could afford to separate and maintain two households.

The attack on American homosexuals in the interest of protecting "wholesome" ideals was by no means unique to the dark years of catastrophe. The visibility of gay men had provoked strong responses even in more settled days. The last months of 1929 saw a police raid on New York City's popular Village bathhouse, the Lafayette, in which patrons were savagely beaten; Communist Mike Gold's vitriolic denunciation of Thornton Wilder as an "art pansy" writer of unmanly literature in the pages of *The New Masses*; and Reverend Adam Clayton Powell's heated warnings about the danger to the black race posed by gay men and lesbians. For black homosexuals, a campaign for "decency" led by as influential a man as the leader of Harlem's Abyssinian Baptist Church was an unpleasant reminder that there were limits to acceptance in Jazz Age Harlem. Not everyone saw "Gloria Swanson" and the Ubangi Club as emblems of liberation. Yet the fears for the future unleashed by the Depression were singularly powerful motivations in accelerating an ugly process. Herbert Hoover stood firm for a modified laissez-faire approach to the crisis, insisting that the government had to avoid direct action in managing the economy, but America's social critics were not as hesitant about the need to influence the course of events in other areas.

Judicial rulings were beginning to lean toward greater freedom for serious novelists, but protection of the supposedly more impressionable, less literate masses was easier to arrange. Public obscenity was still a viable concept, and politicians and businessmen were sensitive to the new mood. In 1931, as New York authorities were beginning to reevaluate their acceptance of the gender-rebellious spectacles taking place in the midtown clubs, the RKO vaudeville circuit management called a nationwide halt to the use of the words *pansy* and *fairy* by any of their performers. Atlantic City's mayor banned all pansy acts in January 1933 and, not long after, the police in San Francisco raided Tati's Cafe to put a quick end to that city's first pansy show in the form of Rae Bourbon's "Boys Will Be Girls." The flouting of the law that Prohibition had made into a middle-class art form had gone too far, many people argued, and a new rigor and clarity were called for. By the end of the decade, ordinances against cross-dressing were being so strictly enforced in Los Angeles that the great Julian Eltinge was reduced to performing there in a small, run-down club dressed in male attire, with his elegant female garb on hangers behind him. The forces of social order were inclined to work the situation both ways, however, making motions toward banning any reference to degeneracy while using horrified curiosity to their advantage. Sexual deviance was useful now as a smear tactic in the political arena. "It might or might not interest you to know," a Chicago friend wrote to Leo Adams in New York City in 1931, "that homosexuality was quite an issue in the almost unbelievably abusive [mayoral] primary campaign." According to Adams's informant, Big Bill Thompson had effectively undercut his challenger, Judge Lyle, by charging that he was a "homo" and "even had women-only meetings for the purpose of having women speakers explain to women voters just what kind of a horrible thing a 'homo' is." (As Lyle lost despite his vigorous protestations of innocence, he should have given in and "gone after the 'Michigan Avenue vote' " anyway, Adams's gay friend decided.)

The end of Prohibition in 1933 did not benefit gay men and lesbians, either. One means of appeasing the "drys" who still supported the Volstead Act lay in an inventive policy of state regulation, of both the liquor to be consumed *and* the space in which it would be served. "The return of the saloon either in its old form or some modern disguise," President Roosevelt reassured the country, was not the aim of Repeal. The new discretionary power of individual state agencies ensured that abuses of alcohol and the congregation of undesirable elements, whether working-class roughs or blatant homosexuals, could be controlled. Overnight, state liquor authorities and alcoholic beverage commissions, whose job it was to issue and renew licenses for establishments serving alcohol, became the arbiters of respectability. As a result, not only were those places where gay men or lesbians gathered in large numbers vulnerable to the loss of their permits, but so were those bars where *any* homosexuals disported themselves in a manner deemed offensive or too open. The institution of the "gay bar" was born of this confusion, as bar owners who had previously ignored the mix of their clientele became nervous about the loss of their livelihood if they failed to keep the queers away. At the same time the all-gay bars became targets of constant surveillance and persecution and a bottomless trough for payoffs to police and state inspectors. "There was a lot of backroom activity in those days, cops getting special favors [financial and sexual] from business people and others," recalled one longtime resident of Seattle. The custom then, gay men who were on the scene agree, was for a bar to open as discreetly as possible, submit to the payments and abuse that were demanded for as long as it was practical to do so, and close with the hope of reopening at a later time.

Indeed, a system evolved in the 1930s that allowed for a fair amount of outrageous behavior—perhaps no more or less than had taken place in the previous decade—but with a new twist: now that the novelty was gone, the only heterosexuals who were supposed to know about gay sex and gay society were those who could profit by it. The problem with the exhibition of Paul Cadmus's painting *The Fleet's In!* at a 1934 Works Progress Administration art show at the Corcoran Gallery next door to the White House was precisely its violation of that assumption. Cadmus's hectic record of shore-leave debauchery shows six servicemen, all but one drunk, gathered on Riverside Drive in New York with six women of equally relaxed natures, whose dresses fit as snugly around their bottoms as the sailors' pants do around their backsides and plump crotches. Only three figures are not immediately involved in the strutting and groping—an old woman who has wandered into this crowd while walking her dog, one still-sober sailor, and a local on the prowl for trade, who knows that his success requires a little more subtlety than the women are displaying. The Navy's indignant removal of the painting from the walls of the Corcoran and the attention the episode received in the press had three results: Paul Cadmus, who was gay, became a much-discussed artist at the age of twenty-nine; the War Department demonstrated how touchy it was about the image of its recruits fifteen years after the Newport scandal; and the painting reached a larger audience than it would have otherwise. "For every individual who might have seen the original," a writer for *Esquire* maintained, "at least one thousand have seen it in black and white reproduction."

What people saw, however, was different from what they read. As art historian Jonathan Weinberg observed in *Speaking for Vice*, none of the newspaper accounts of the controversy mentions the homosexual pickup as a factor in the government's decision to suppress the painting, which was kept from public view for the next fifty years. But that omission doesn't imply ignorance: the effeminate features of the civilian offering the sailor a cigarette, his calculating stare, his two rings, his red necktie (*the* gay symbol of the day), all denote him as unmistakably degenerate. What's more, the sailor accepting the cigarette is hardly an innocent. Male-female raucousness in *The Fleet's In!* was distressing enough to anyone who felt that the

U.S. Navy's reputation was on the line. There was no point in referring to the insult that had been added to injury. In fact, good taste *required* that the gay man and his would-be partner not be alluded to. Heterosexual issues overshadowed gay realities; bluntness about the one eliminated, for a time, the need to affirm even the existence of the other.

NIGHTCLUBS, VAUDEVILLE THEATERS, bars, art museums—for millions of Americans, these cultural battlefronts represented foreign territory. The more profound, all-encompassing statement of the national desire to push sexual variance back into the shadows took place in movie houses, specifically at the time of the renewal of the Hollywood Code in 1934. The Code has been a fruitful area of study for modern film scholars, though the emphasis has largely been on the means by which illicit heterosexual passion and nudity on screen were curbed in the 1930s. Seventy years ago, those who bristled at Hollywood's pre-1934 willingness to depict homosexuals understood the reach of the new medium (unprecedented in the history of entertainment) and, just as critically, knew that Hollywood had always had a fondness for this uniquely offensive subject matter. Unlike novels or plays, which may or may not have a direct link to everyday life (and, in a Modernist context, could often assume a fanciful or elite character), movies were the true barometer, the young person's mirror, of evolving social norms. If they weren't creating trends in sex and relationships, as the more irate commentators implied, they were certainly validating perceptions most people shared. And what "most people" knew was that all men were not alike in their affect or desires.

The sissy as a neat, recognizable point of contrast to the "real men" of the far West made his debut as early as 1909 in D. W. Griffith's *The Renunciation*. By 1923, in Stan Laurel's *The Soilers*, which also had a cowboyish setting, he was a pert thing evincing a real interest in other men. Four years later, he was bold enough to ask for a date. (Clarence in the 1927 *Wanderer of the West* is "one of Nature's mistakes in a country where men were men.") Nor was it a closely guarded secret that the studios knew the type firsthand. About an early Adolph Menjou silent film, in 1916, *Variety* commented that the extras must have "been selected by someone who is guilty of a dash of lavender," and Alla Nazimova's florid version of *Salome* (1923) was reputed to have an all-gay cast. First World War–era audiences had opportunities to witness playful gender-role reversals—and the dismayed reactions they could inspire—in *Algie the Miner* (1912), *A Florida Enchantment* (1914), and Charlie Chaplin's *Behind the Screen* (1916). By the time Garbo's bachelor Queen Christina and Dietrich's tuxedo-clad Amy

Jolly in *Morocco* planted kisses on the lips of other women in 1933, abnormal sexuality was not a new topic.

Throughout the 1920s, the studios had to contend with local and state censorship boards, women's groups, and religious leaders who complained about the perverts and prostitutes, gangster violence, lascivious dancing, and pre- and extramarital sex that the movies brought to their neighborhood theaters. Will Hays, a respected member of Warren Harding's cabinet, was enlisted as head of a trade association whose main purpose was to reassure the public that the industry was sensitive to the problem. He was on hand to set up some general guidelines for writers and directors (known as the "Don'ts and Be Carefuls" list) and later, in 1930, to approve the Motion Picture Production Code, which sought to expand and formalize the earlier list of acceptable values and taboo subjects. But Hays's best efforts weren't of much use to anyone. A code with no enforcement muscle behind it was seldom honored in practice, and as profits declined after the Crash and a mad scramble began to keep the customers happy, some of Hollywood's raciest products appeared between 1930 and 1933. The titles tell the story: *Passion Lady, My Sin, Hot Stuff, Call Me Savage*. "Art houses" showing foreign films offered Hedy Lamarr nude and orgasmic in *Ecstasy*, a lesbian schoolgirl in love with her teacher in *Mädchen in Uniform*, and a revival of Carl Dreyer's *Chained* ("An Astounding Tale of Unnatural Loves!"). Charles Laughton as Nero feasts his eyes on his slave boy in Cecil B. De Mille's *The Sign of the Cross* (1932).

Even the most innocent-seeming fare could energetically mock the Code. In 1932 Hal Roach directed Laurel and Hardy in what is widely regarded as a prolonged and uproarious gag about homosexual coupling. In *Their First Mistake*, Ollie sets up housekeeping with Stan after his wife has stormed out. She claims, rightly, that Stan has alienated her husband's affections. Despite Stan's fear that people will talk, the two men stay together to watch over Ollie's newly adopted baby and share a bed—a happy threesome. Milk plays a coyly lascivious part in a story full of erotic subtexts, as Ollie squeezes the baby's bottle between his thighs, making a nice sticky mess of his pajamas and later, assuming he is feeding the child, holds the same bottle to Stan's lips for a good long sleepy suck. Yet, Oliver Hardy's viscous squirter notwithstanding, there came a point when self-censorship on the male-male theme began to seem more politic. Busby Berkeley's 1933 musical *42nd Street* dropped a character's homosexuality, which was apparent in the novel it was based on, and even Mae West's Bowery tale, *Diamond Lil*, drew the line at serious deviance. In the play, Lil speculates that an unmarried crony might be homosexual. (Don't be misled by Dan Flynn's masculine ways, she tells a friend; he's just the type to hang out down the street at Paresis Hall with the fairies.) In the 1933 film, retitled *She Done Him Wrong*, Flynn wants the buxom Mae.

On all counts, too little, too late. By the beginning of 1934, the Catholic hierarchy in America was ready to show the Jewish moguls that they could supply the backbone Hollywood lacked. Confronted with the Legion of Decency's rating system ("Acceptable," "Morally Objectionable," "Condemned") and the threat of a Church-led boycott, studio executives agreed to revivify the Code and establish sanctions against those who violated it. The blue pencil reigned. Failure to secure the new Motion Picture Production Code seal of approval meant a fine and near-insurmountable obstacles in obtaining bookings, regardless of the interest moviegoers in a given area might have in the picture. The consequences of this development for gay men and lesbians were quite specific. The Code did not—and never had—regarded all immorality as cut from the same cloth. There was, so to speak, the unavoidable immorality of life: such as murder, theft, drug trafficking, rape, and prostitution. These were activities the Code defined as criminal or "repellant," and no one imagined filmmakers would forgo all mention of them in their screenplays. Even adultery was labeled as "sometimes necessary plot material." What was required as of 1934 was that such moral failings be treated with discretion, never glamorized, always punished. "Sex perversion *or any inference of it*," on the other hand, was forbidden, rendered nonexistent. Like miscegenation and venereal disease, homosexuality was declared beyond the needs of any reasonable film story, beyond the bounds of what decent people should have to hear about, beyond the parameters of social breakdown marked by shootings, bank robberies, and infidelity. The lisping bathhouse attendant in Raoul Walsh's *Sailor's Luck* (1933), Franklin Pangborn's "high society" decorator in *Only Yesterday* (1933), the two male dancing partners in *Wonder Bar* (1934)—it didn't matter that the homosexuals in recent films were achingly thin characters, usually cameos provided for the sake of low comedy. The new rules called for their exclusion as well.

The men and women who made movies weren't inclined to take the Legion of Decency criteria to heart any more than they had to. Wide-appeal entertainment and moral purity were not only different but often contradictory goals. The way around the Code was to soft-pedal the stereotype; he couldn't be the vile, omnipotent Nero anymore, he couldn't even be the cowboy fairy in *The Soilers* or *Wanderer of the West* who is clear about what he wants—but he could be an effete half-man, the asexual buddy or acquaintance, a prissy type made famous in the 1930s by Edward Everett Horton, Franklin Pangborn, and Grady Sutton. The key was that the sex drive of these characters had to remain obscured, even neutered, and no man was allowed to hint at his passion for another. In this reading, as far as the censors were concerned, a sissified man was *not* necessarily a pervert—contrary to all the propaganda of the last decade—but simply an amusing fugitive from virility. Gay men could also be remade as highly symbolic figures (for example, the outcasts of horror-movie director James Whale have been read as gay stand-ins) or simply a different kind of mammal. A wet smack on the lips between two men would have rendered Will Hays or his "chief censor" Joe Breen apoplectic, but the Code said nothing about a man and a rabbit. Not only does Bugs Bunny kiss Elmer Fudd in a very un-storybook way when he wants to, but he camps it up, as seductress or in Carmen Miranda–style, with all the élan of one of the great pansy performers. It wasn't much, but between 1935 and 1945, the Legion of Decency and its allies were dictating the terms.

IN SOME QUARTERS, more scholarly ones than those in which the Motion Picture Production Code was hammered out, the drive to categorize experience according to its relation to absolute, allegedly timeless moral principles was being challenged. The challenges were necessarily small-scale. There were few ideas Western society was less interested in hearing about at this juncture than sexual and ethical relativism and the utility of a multi-cultural perspective. At the University of Chicago, sociologist Ernest Burgess and his graduate students were going out onto the streets of that city to learn firsthand about Chicago's gay men, their haunts and habits. The very act of interviewing homosexuals on their own turf, and asking questions to which one didn't already have the answers (in sharp contrast to the psychiatric approach), was more than unusual. It was revolutionary. Burgess's project didn't lead to publication, unfortunately, but the notes he and his students left behind document several corners of a thriving subculture. A more direct assault on homophobia was anthropologist Ruth Benedict's landmark *Patterns of Culture*. As her biographer, Margaret M. Caffrey, has explained, Benedict's much-admired book about the Zuni of the American Southwest, the Dobu of Melanesia, and the Kwakiutl of the Pacific Northwest was conceived as a response "to questions asked in anthropology, the other social sciences, and society in general concerning the importance of biology vs. culture, chaos vs. order, the individual and society, especially the role of the misfit." It was written out of a desire to change the ideas of normal and abnormal in American society, particularly rising out of the experience of her married life. (Though married, Benedict did not hide from herself her socially unacceptable feelings for women and had a romantic relationship with Margaret Mead in the 1920s, when Mead was a student at Barnard.) Not unlike Margaret Mead's *Coming of Age in*

Samoa, Patterns of Culture examined the role that cultural factors, rather than biological imperatives, played in determining relations between sexes or generations or classes in other parts of the world. From this perspective, antihomosexual belligerence was no more "natural," inevitable, or eternal than patrilineal inheritance or the morality of celibacy or premarital virginity. These were invented concepts, perhaps useful, perhaps outdated—certainly not "fixed" laws of life. About homosexuality as it was known in America, Benedict implicitly lashed out at the Freudians and argued that guilt and self-loathing were caused by "the disrepute which social tradition visits upon [gay men and lesbians]," not anything inherent in that sexual choice itself.

Bold words to be published in the same year in which the Hollywood Code was newly triumphant. Yet, with sexuality now perceived as a dangerous topic even in academic circles, the work of intellectuals like Ruth Benedict or Ernest Burgess could have only a limited influence in its day. Henry Gerber's 1932 article, "In Defense of Homosexuality," published in the magazine *The Modern Thinker* under the pseudonym "Parisex," was one of the few pro-gay arguments that might have reached a large general audience in various parts of the country. (A society led by "normal" men that was in "such chaotic condition" must have better ways to spend its time, Gerber wrote, than to castigate homosexuals for their neurotic private behavior, so much of which was aggravated by heterosexual persecution.) For the most part, young men or women who longed to know something of the gay world, especially in the early 1930s, were left to flounder. A philosophy of "the less said, the better" was fast taking hold. Every schoolboy knows what a pansy is nowadays, Dr. La Forrest Potter had remarked in his book *Strange Loves* (1933). Just so, parents and educators believed, and it was time to restore a climate of innocence to American youth. Once in a great while, a combination of uncanny luck and personal initiative might overcome the obstacles this anti-information outlook fostered. As a teenager, Elver Barker and his boyfriend had no trouble learning what they wanted to about homosexuality. The mass-market monthly *Sexology* was sold on one newsstand in their hometown in Wyoming, and they secured a copy that discussed Magnus Hirschfeld's recent efforts on behalf of gay men. They also found the spot at the town dump where unsold copies were thrown and regularly scavenged about for other relevant issues of the magazine. (Barker later put his determination to good use when, in 1956, he founded the Denver chapter of the Mattachine Society.) Such opportunities for uncensored reading, though, were few and far between.

(*Sexology* wasn't a bad find for Barker or any other gay teenager, relative to what else they might have come across. From its first issue in 1933 and throughout the rest of the decade, this illustrated, easy-to-read magazine—a sort of forerunner of *Psychology Today*—mixed old prejudices with progressive thinking about sexuality. The editors were careful to avoid language that might be construed as approval of gay sex and repeated the statement that homosexuality was *not* a happy or desirable way of life, but they decried mean-spirited bigotry and gave space to some fairly liberal doctors. "Normal is a relative term," George B. Lake noted in "Sex 'Inversion' " in the March 1934 issue, while James Winsco reminded his readers in "The Real Homosexual" in the June 1935 issue that homosexuals saw themselves as perfectly natural and were hardly susceptible to "cures." The gay young men from Alabama, Florida, and Texas who wrote letters to the editor were treated with the same dignity accorded letter-writers who were inquiring about contraception, menstruation, or pregnancy. The letters also served to alert homosexual readers that others were "out there," waiting to be found and helped by their own kind. The four-page letter, "In Defense of Sappho," in the May 1937 issue surely achieved its strong-willed purpose in spite of the editor's rebuttal.)

The more typical experience than Barker's in Wyoming involved a frustrating absence of recognition. "I knew I liked men, I knew I liked penises, long before puberty," Peter Conway said, summarizing the dilemma. "But I didn't know what this was going to *mean*. I thought, 'Does this make me like Walter the ballet dancer who lived down the street? Do I *have* to be one of the other effeminate types I was seeing at the movies, the Franklin Pangborns?' " Before older men started showing an interest in Conway as an adolescent, the connection between "liking penises" and maleness, relationships, or one's place in the world was obscure. "I would have killed for one glimpse of a gay couple or even one single individual I could identify as a gay adult," another man remembered about his childhood in West Virginia in the 1930s. For Austin Wade, a sheltered life in a suburb of Newark, New Jersey, meant never a whisper of the subject of homosexuality at home or at school, never a clue as to whether any other boys or men shared his sexual urges. That torturous uncertainty ended abruptly one summer evening in 1934, when Wade overheard his father talking about the day's headlines. Eric Röhm and his cadre of brownshirts had been murdered in Hitler's Night of the Long Knives purge of the Nazi Party. Wade caught the drift about Röhm's interests. There was some relief to be felt in knowing that his desires were familiar to others, somehow truly *existed* in the world. But that event suggested a new problem: he may not be "the only one" after all, Wade concluded, but it was sadly apparent that he was the only one from a decent family.

• • •

"WAS I THE only one?" is a question that echoes down the corridor of the years from the 1920s to Stonewall and beyond. How to assimilate that query fully and honestly is a complex business, especially as one considers that it would not have had exactly the same meaning in 1935 that it had in 1920, or in 1955 and again in 1970. The possibilities for acquiring some information, some clue, about the life one might lead as a homosexual changed every few years, just as the life itself was subject to new influences and accordingly reinvented. The image of gay life in America in the 1930s that has long held sway is bound to the image of straight life *in response to homosexuality*. That approach usually works out as a negative proposition: heterosexual society was oppressive; as a result, there wasn't a "gay world" of any consequence and so homosexuals waited, miserably, for better times. Certainly the path for a gay man was not easy. Finding an apartment or buying a house with a lover, explaining away bachelorhood to colleagues and family, and coping with the fear of blackmail or entrapment were only a few of the obstacles daily life presented. None of these trials, however, meant that gay men as a whole were any less resilient, searching, or creative than other groups.

More an "aggregate of cliques," in activist Harry Hay's words, than a tightly knit community, the social world gay men had constructed for themselves by the 1930s was as divided along lines of race, class, profession, and regional differences as the rest of America. Some heterosexual observers, alarmed that homosexuals had formed any connections at all, claimed to see a monolithic brotherhood. "They are a tribe," a reporter for a Los Angeles newspaper wrote in 1937, "with incantations and grapevines of their own. They know each other by secret signs even when their tragedy is hidden from the multitude." The truth was a little more mundane, a little less Masonic.

If you were one of the young men who wore makeup and cruised the burlesque houses of Seattle, avoiding the cops on Pioneer Square and never knowing where your next meal was coming from, you had more in common in many ways with other Depression-era adventurers than with the well-fed, well-bred homosexual men who lived discreetly and comfortably on Beacon Hill or Park Avenue. (To wit: "Mother Red was a mean cop," "Vilma" told the authors of *An Evening at the Garden of Allah* about Seattle street life in the 1930s. "We'd see him coming and we'd cross the street to another cop's beat. When Mother Red left, we'd go back to the totem pole and cruise again.") If you were a black lawyer in the Midwest sensitive to your reputation with your churchgoing clients (such as Paul Phillips, mentioned in chapter 2), you and your lover cultivated a different manner and circle of friends from those of the gay men who frequented or performed at the drag Canine Club on Chicago's South Side or at Finocchio's in San Francisco. The latest Noel Coward play or the rumors about Cole Porter meant nothing to the working-class homosexuals who gathered at a gay bar like Tommy's in San Jose, a place one patron recalled as "seedier than seedy, smellier than smelly . . . where the wino scene and the gay scene were forced together" and where the available trade pickups were generally Okies and Arkies, refugees from the Dust Bowl. A banker or an accountant might have no chance to meet other "temperamentals" on the job in comparison, say, to a man working in fashion or the theater—yet even in the theater, as Alfred Lunt sternly warned the young Montgomery Clift, no one was going to tolerate an openly, admittedly gay actor. Some writers have speculated that life for gay men in rural black America involved a measure of look-the-other-way tolerance; other writers have narrated tales from small-town white America that have described a living hell of bigots and busybodies. For a ship's cook like the protagonist of William Faulkner's story "Equinox," a middle-aged man in love with a messboy, the act of placing himself in relation to his fellows means almost nothing. His romantic attachment doesn't faze his shipmates, and the affection and jealousy of the moment are all that matter. Varied factors were involved in the creation of numerous, overlapping gay identities of many styles, of many homosexualities (some more tautly self-defined than others)—not at all the uniform entity some observers thought they saw.

Geography was never incidental either, and many young gay men heard from friends about the different, often better lives they had made for themselves upon relocating to New York, Chicago, or Los Angeles. Yet the distinction between the smaller city (a site of limited possibilities) and the larger metropolis (a place of wider freedom) was not always the "constant" it was presumed to be. In Savannah, "Things went on, things happened, though everything was pretty quiet," one man remarked about the gay social and sexual activity in the black community there, and it was not until he moved to Manhattan in the late 1930s that Fred Stevens came to know the more ebullient world of Harlem's parties and clubs. But, in contrast, Stuart Loomis found an ample field of exploration in his hometown in Nebraska during the same period. Plenty of adolescent sex play and a wide-ranging "library curiosity" initiated a process of self-examination, which was helped along by two fellow students at North High School in Omaha who were contentedly homosexual ("Norman was a poet . . . David served tea in his attic bedroom and talked about Asian art"), by the many men Loomis met hanging out in a downtown restroom, and then by a professor who lectured on André Gide's life and novels to Loomis's freshman class at the University of Omaha. Soon after, Loomis discovered that many of the men he had been cruised by on the street "had a full social aspect to their lives, too." One man gave cocktail parties in his apartment at which Loomis served as bartender, an out-of-towner used his hotel room for regular gatherings, and "Mother Mocha," bedecked with amber beads, threw parties for his white friends at his bungalow on the edge of the black section of town. For those men who were able to make sufficient contacts in less bustling areas—and many did in cities such as Tulsa, Tampa, Ann Arbor, Providence, and Albuquerque—migration to one of the country's major urban centers wasn't the only, or the automatic, route. (For that matter, even in a city as large as San Francisco, a teenager of exceptional determination and eagerness could have a hard time locating anything that approximated a gay community. "Before the start of the war," Jose Sarria maintained, "it did not exist in San Francisco. There may have been a 'subculture' of some kind, if you like that word so much, but there was not what I would call a gay society. I know. I looked!")

The advanced state of gay argot in the 1930s also points toward the existence of some form of self-conscious, self-directed social world, a milieu with its own codes, its own history, its own issues to contend with. A list of gay slang vocabulary compiled by a sociologist at the end of the decade, by no means complete, includes more than three hundred words and terms pertaining to male homosexual or lesbian identity and activity. It was a language richly textured, humorous, alternately self-deprecating and self-glorifying, and marked both by devious double entendre and breathtaking honesty. Gay slang also embodied a sense of comprehensiveness more than isolation, of energy and choice. The fact that gay men spoke of "R.F.D. queens"—rural homosexuals who weren't as knowing as their urban cousins—signals their awareness that not all gay men moved to the big city; "temperamentals" were to be found everywhere. Sexual strategies had long since been refined to the point of acquiring their own language as well: one "cruised" the streets for sex, "played checkers" in a darkened movie house (moved from seat to seat until finally landing next to an interested party), or simply "basketeered" (visually appraised the crotch, or "basket," or "eggs in the basket," of men walking by).

For obvious reasons, secrecy and disclosure were themes that required their own linguistic flourishes. The now universal trope of "the closet," as George Chauncey has pointed out, was not the common symbol of the hidden life in the 1930s—and was rarely, if ever, used before the 1960s. The image of self-protection from pre-liberation days had to do, instead, with hair and its proper arrangement. A cautious man "let his hair down" only among those who could be trusted (other homosexuals or liberal straight friends). "Dropping hairpins" or bobby pins gave away crucial information, leading others to discover that a man was gay. Just as vivid was the manner in which gay slang commented on the dichotomy between the high-brow and the low. To one another, gay men were known as "Presbyterians" or as members of the "fraternity," the "cognoscenti," or the "twilight aristocracy." A young man might be a "belle," an elderly man a "dowager," and any homosexual would earn the royal appellation "queen" by virtue of his good taste in wanting a real man. ("Straight" and "trade," on the other hand, were prosaic terms, suitable for those not among the cognoscenti. In the same derisive spirit, sailors became objectified as "seafood.") Public lavatories were quaintly called "tearooms," and when a tearoom queen was made to vacate a stall by an attendant, he was said to be "dethroned" or forced to "abdicate." Yet a noneuphemistic directness was sometimes appealing. Anal sex, which might reasonably have been masked by a particularly discreet code phrase, was labeled in such a way—"browning"—as to be unmistakable, even rude and defiant.

Interestingly, the two words most familiar to the post-Stonewall generation were already established sixty years ago, one with a different meaning and one essentially unchanged. "Coming out" was an important concept for gay men in the 1930s, with its satiric connotations of a debutante's rite of passage. But before the 1960s, a gay man did not "come out" to the world—family, neighbors, colleagues. He "came out" *to the life*, meaning that he went to bed with a man and so became progressively more experienced as a homosexual. The difference is vast. A need to tell heterosexuals who might be unsympathetic, especially relatives, would have struck most gay men of an earlier day as a bit odd. All well and good, for anyone who was lucky or bold, but by no means a political or psychological necessity. Yet there was a need, everyone recognized, to make a definite decision eventually about one's own sexuality, which might lead to a "coming out" with other men.

"Gay," however, made its first appearance in the late 1920s and, among homosexuals, had secured its meaning as we know it long before the beginning of World War II. The purposes the word served were many, its value inestimable. Straight society had plenty of terms to describe men who liked men, either emphasizing their gender-role deviance (birdie, buttercup, fairy, flit, flutterer, nance, pansy, yoo-hoo) or aiming to be more general in its characterization and disgust (faggot, homo, queer). Homosexuals used some of these words themselves, particularly faggot, pansy, and queer. The advent of "gay" was a step in a new direction. Homosexuals had appropriated an existent word that had proved especially malleable over the last hundred years. The "gay" women of the nineteenth century were the fancy women, the fallen women, the terrors of the virtuous middle class. By the early 1920s, "gay" had evolved into a less charged adjective. Any fun-loving person might have a gay time at a party or on vacation. ("Gay" tenaciously retained its sexual edge in other forms—falsies were "gay deceivers" and a "gay cat" was a ladies' man.) Conscious of their status as fallen men, of the view of their lives as barren and joyless, of the stereotype of flippancy and silliness that attached to pansy culture, homosexuals latched on to a word that played off all of these different ideas and the word's own sly history. Best of all, it could pass undetected in its double meaning among heterosexuals. "Is he gay?" or "Did you have a gay time?" sounded like innocent questions to much of America before 1960. To homosexuals, they epitomized the power of coded language and effectively, or intermittently, moved away from the belligerence of "faggot" and "queer."

A social system so new, and one that operated in such a hostile climate, could not have sustained itself without a foundation in camaraderie and without a willingness on the part of older homosexuals to act as mentors. To heterosexuals who think of gay sexuality as originating in the seduction of adolescents, this concept bogs down (despite all evidence to the contrary) in the propaganda of the molester/predator. But whatever sex did take place between older and younger men, it was not the sex alone that mattered to the inexperienced. Bedmates could be found among their own age group. What a gay man in his teens or twenties couldn't often get from his peers was a feeling for the ways in which his sexuality might take on the dimensions of a full life outside the mainstream. In this realm, the "aunties" were indispensable. The term itself implies a brutal age-consciousness (one could pass from the "belle" to the "auntie" stage by thirty or thirty-five), but the reality is that most gay men approaching, or well into, middle age during the pre–World War II period did not consider themselves out of the running. The first blush of youth might have passed, but not the urge to party, advise, camp, cruise, take a lover, find a mate. And the knowledge and encouragement they had to offer younger homosexual men were valued by many of their charges.

Some of what older gay men had to teach was tied to the gender-role polarization that still dominated gay life—a state of mind that would be challenged on a large scale by gay participation in World War II—and was, at heart, a routinized mimicking of straight society. Are you butch or are you femme? Are you active or passive in bed? Are you a queer or a fairy? The distinctions might not actually have been observed under the sheets (where taking turns at being the "top" or the "bottom" in anal intercourse was not unheard of, and where "sixty-nine" threw all categories to the wind), but they mattered in public life among homosexuals. The labels were a security blanket as much as a straight jacket, accepted as plausible by some men and deeply resented by others. Also essential was a camp name for use in private. "That was lesson one," many men remember about their introductions to gay life. An approximation of a masculine first name was best (John could become "Johanna," Morris could become "Mona"), an inversion that played neatly on the idea of gayness as an identification with womanly traits rather than a question of sexual-object choice. Sometimes the selection of a name was more imaginative and particular to the individual: "I was 'Edith' for a quite a while because everyone knew how much I liked Edith Wharton's novels," a Baltimore teacher recalled, "but I settled on 'Lily' for the long run because of one of her characters." Dressing in full or partial drag at a private party, a frequent occurrence before the 1940s, was part of the same endeavor, a simultaneous assault on the premise of natural/unnatural gender distinctions in attire and an implicit agreement that gay men had more in common with women than with straight men.

If some aspects of what young men were taught was a parody of conservative thinking about womanliness and manliness, other lessons were more original. Straight life was focused—in theory—on marriage, monogamy, a tightening up of a man's social circle, and a winding down from wilder experiences after the all-important pairing off. Gay men, however, looked to pride themselves on what their freedom might bring. Without children or status in the community, they could enjoy their independence, their more numerous friendships, and, if money wasn't a problem, their more extensive travels and evenings on the town. Talk about relationships, though, brought most homosexuals back to the old stereotypes. Homosexuals were psychologically incapable of long-term intimate bonds, the "authorities" on the subject said. The male sex drive warred against monogamy, the biologists insisted—it was hard enough for women to tame men, they pointed out. Two men together could never approximate a true marriage. So one was apt to hear a line from other homosexuals on the subject that went in one of two possible directions, both of which were variations on the straight world's skepticism about male-male unions. Accept that all romances are doomed to end, many young men were told by those who had taken them under their wing, and live for the moment: "And when you leave—and you will—take everything that's yours." In another vein, common wisdom suggested that two men might well live all their days together and even remain in love, *if* both partners understood that love and sexual fidelity were not synonymous. It was for the two individuals to decide between themselves what was workable. The quick anonymous encounter, the weekend tryst, the full-scale affair: the possibilities for sex outside the home—furtive or open, frequent or rare—covered a wide ground. That gay relationships would ape straight marriages by their faith in the "higher" love of monogamy was only rarely, it seems, a serious consideration. Call it cynicism, call it joie de vivre. Most older gay men called it facing reality.

Perhaps the best, certainly the most generous, feature of the "wisdom of the aunties" (to use Stuart Loomis's phrase) was its implicit nod to the future. Intergenerational parties and friendships—not a common feature of gay life in the 1980s and 1990s—provided for homosexuals in the 1930s a sense that they were part of a continuum, a social order with a meaningful life that would outlive its participants. This vital cultural transmission often included a bit of instruction about responsibilities in the decades to come. In other words, how nice to be young, but of course time moves on, and the help you receive today is to be extended to others in later years. The comely twenty-year-old taken out to dinner by his friend of forty-five or sixty, introduced to other gay men (thus easing his fear of isolation, of freakishness), brought to the theater, or taught how to camp or deal with the police or employers or how not to drop hairpins, was made aware that he, in turn, should "give something back" when the time came. The older man paid the bill at the restaurant, made the introductions, provided the useful tips—in what might have been a sexual or a platonic relationship, or something in-between—in a manner fundamentally different, in this instance, from the male-female pattern. Part of the younger man's repayment to the aunties was tied to the notion that he would someday assume the same role for others. "It was very much drilled into me," one gay man commented about his coming-out period in the 1930s, "that this is how things are done. We show each other the ropes." The bitchiness that was a dramatic, undeniable aspect of gay life has in many retrospective accounts overshadowed a more big-hearted form of exchange: the support men knew then through their buddies, patrons, and guides.

THE "WISDOM OF the aunties" (the rich aunties, anyway) also suggested that it made sense, when possible, to seek out one's own kind in a pampered environment that could be a form of sanctuary. An enclave for homosexuals beyond the usual metropolitan neighborhoods was a rarity, and not without its problems. Taking up residence in such a place sometimes left gay men, in the words of anthropologist Esther Newman, "caught in midflight between escape and nesting, between voluntary exile and the longing to belong." But there is no doubt that a "gay space," exclusively homosexual or merely protected, afforded some men the psychological respite they needed, even as it emphasized their separation from other gay men (those who couldn't afford the luxury of leaving their workplace and the larger heterosexual world) and aggravated class and racial divisions. The Cherry Grove section of New York's Fire Island, for instance, saw an influx of gay theater people before the Second World War. The waterfront parking lot in the town of Sayville, the ferry stop to the Grove, was "full of cars, all with gay people," Stephan Cole recalled to Newman when discussing the summer of 1938. In her history of this community, Newman reports that the arrival of *New Yorker* critic John Mosher and his lover to stay for the summer, not as renters but as owners of their own house, completed in 1939, signified the arrival of an acknowledged gay presence on this thin stretch of beach forty miles from Manhattan. On the other side of the country, Santa Fe had an appeal for some of the same reasons Cherry Grove had: the beauty of the terrain, the sun, the quiet, the indifference of the locals, the cosmopolitan seasonal visitors who allowed gay men to feel less like an endangered minority. One of the most famous of the eastern emigrés who chose in the 1930s to relocate to New Mexico on a year-round basis was the poet Witter Bynner. In New York, Bynner had once been the victim of a physical assault by the editor of a prestigious magazine that published his poetry, *The Smart Set,* when the editor decided Bynner was "coming on" to him. In Santa Fe, that kind of nuttiness was left behind.

The biggest enclave of all was Hollywood, though as usual there were unspoken rules to be followed. George Cukor, *Grand Hotel* director Edmund Goulding, Tyrone Power, Cesar Romero, Charles Laughton, Ramon Navarro, Clifton Webb, and Monty Woolley—not to mention countless set and costume designers, cinematographers, writers, dancers, bit players, extras, and office personnel—understood these principles for the most part and benefited accordingly. "Roommates" Cary Grant and Randolph Scott chafed at the restrictions the studio placed on them in their younger days in the early 1930s, but got used to the situation and the money. Director Mitchell Leisen kept some people guessing (he was married for many years and had affairs with men and women), while William Haines brought an end to his acting career by his flagrant—and, to the studio heads, entirely unacceptable—behavior in local YMCAs. At a certain point, *Frankenstein* director James Whale, who lived with producer David Lewis, also decided that the cost of discretion was higher than he was willing to pay and retired early. With her brush-cut hair and custom-tailored suits, director Dorothy Arzner had relatively little trouble fitting in (aspiring to be "one of the

boys" was a goal the men at Paramount could understand), while the virility of Errol Flynn was sufficiently impressive to most people that rumors of
an occasional romp on the other side of the line were not regarded as particularly noteworthy. In many ways, Hollywood truly was a microcosm:
men who were exclusively homosexual knew to keep a low profile if they
wanted to enjoy the good life; open displays were quickly and ruthlessly
dealt with; hints of lesbianism excited comparatively little hysteria (Arzner
in a suit and Cukor in a kimono would not have been identical problems);
and a charismatic "he-man" style forgave a multitude of sins.

In the view of some observers, the interesting differences were between
those talents who were "passing through" the movie capital and those who
planned to stay, between the men who felt they had less to lose and those
who were acutely aware of the dictates of studio image-making. Barely out
of his teens, Tyrone Power arrived in Hollywood in 1932 and, for a short
time, became a member of lyricist Lorenz Hart's circle. The notoriety Hart
courted, like his raucous gay one-upsmanship with Cole Porter when he
was in residence, was distressing to Power. Lorenz Hart and Cole Porter
had made their reputations already and, in any case, they weren't entirely
dependent on the approval of the moguls. For an up-and-coming screen
idol, revelations about varied sexual escapades would have spelled a professional dead-end. His affair with Robin Thomas, John Barrymore's stepson
and one of the great beauties of the age, was conducted in strict secrecy.
Nor did the situation change much from Tyrone Power's day to the time of
Rock Hudson and Anthony Perkins twenty-five years later: the psychological pressure of a highly public life based on falsehood and an element of
derision (the secret kept from fans was never a secret from the smirking
publicists and gossip columnists who perpetuated the fable of normality)
was torturous. In this sense, the creation of a precious enclave, a world-
within-the-world of Hollywood, was both a credible defensive measure and
an unfortunate means of ensuring the system's control, which remains in
place even in the 1990s. Screenwriter Frank Mankiewicz noted that "homosexuals would call George [Cukor] as soon as they arrived in Hollywood,
and if he liked them, he would introduce them to other members of the
elite." Almost as important as career advancement, the social life to be
found at Cukor's house became over the years an important feature of gay
life in southern California. "George created a civilized gay society,"
another writer commented. "You could always meet intelligent gay men at
his house." There one ate and talked with kindred spirits, convinced oneself that the world was perhaps not so unkind after all, and learned to play
the game now that the Production Code really meant something.

George Cukor knew the game as well as anyone. Stuck early in his career with the telling label "a woman's director," he had even fewer chances than other directors to explore sexual themes in his work, especially after the walloping critical and commercial failure of the picaresque *Sylvia Scarlett*. At a preview of the film in January 1936, moviegoers walked out despite the presence of Cukor and his star in the theater. A film in which a rakish, cross-dressing Katharine Hepburn puts on the affect of a male or a female as if it were a learned routine rather than a natural, immutable condition seemed inexplicable and annoying at the time. (In the age of gender studies, *Sylvia Scarlett* has acquired a following.) What fun Cukor must have had, though, in directing Cary Grant to remark about the "queer feeling" he gets whenever he looks at Hepburn's androgynous young man and to invite "Sylvia" (pretending to be "Sidney") to keep him warm in bed on their travels, titillating an audience that "knows" what Grant doesn't about Hepburn's sex. All very amusing in a more innocent age, but surely "a 'jolly' relished by everyone in the studio according to his respective sexual lights," as Parker Tyler once commented. Grant's real interests weren't the best-kept secret, and the element of masquerade in the story extended beyond the screen.

Poolside brunch at a gay director's or a weekend at a Fire Island beach house (in 1935 or, for that matter, in 1975) was a comfortable but limited experience—limited in the range of people one was apt to meet, limited by the emphasis on tone and style. College campuses and college towns were often settings for the more varied, venturesome opportunities that arose out of the mixing of hundreds, or thousands, of middle-class eighteen- to twenty-two-year-olds with a profession that numbered many gay men, amid heterosexuals who might be inclined, sometimes, to look the other way. At the University of Colorado in the late 1930s, an important figure in the music department entertained in a grandly uninhibited style, never hiding his affairs and offering his house as an unofficial social center for gay faculty and undergraduates. (The administration ignored the gossip. In the different climate of the postwar years, though, the man lost his job.) Denver attorney William Reynard, a student in Boulder before the war, enjoyed his first romantic relationship with another member of the same department and met other gay students and future boyfriends through these two teachers. "It was a funny situation," he thought, "in that it was both 'kept quiet' and 'known.' " There was a sense, a mid-1930s graduate of a New England college felt about this period, in which certain homosexual professors were comfortable introducing their students to the gay world around them—socially or even sexually—in the same manner in which they had introduced them to Virginia Woolf, Stravinsky, or Picasso. "They were opening doors that weren't so easily opened then, playing on our eagerness.

It didn't always have the same meaning [of impropriety, presumably] that it would have had twenty or thirty years later," he insisted.

At other schools, the initiative—and the subsequent initiations—had to come from the students themselves. At Texas Christian University in San Antonio, according to Morris Kight, those developments took the form of the Oscar Wilde Study Group. Every Thursday night, interested students met on their own in a classroom on campus to discuss another of Wilde's essays or plays, with never a mention, even in a strictly literary context, of the author's homosexuality, the troublesome Bosie, or the trials. Afterward, the Wildeans quietly paired off and returned to their dorm rooms and off-campus apartments. They all regarded a scrupulous, but not overly subtle "cover" as their one essential safeguard. In his published diaries, Donald Vining testified to the relative ease with which he formed friendships in the 1930s with gay peers. At West Chester State Teachers College in Pennsylvania and later at Yale Drama School, Vining cultivated the image of a "homosexual roué," though he actually had no experience. After going to bed with another student in New Haven in the fall of 1939, he wrote in his diary that it was encouraging to meet someone admittedly homosexual who strongly attracted him. "Now, tho, I'm a little embarrassed at not being more homosexual myself." At Swarthmore, Bertram Schaffner found it difficult to meet other gay men on campus, in part because he was three years younger than most of his classmates (having started college at fifteen), but he had no trouble meeting his lover of the next five years, an older man, at the college president's tea for prospective Rhodes Scholars. Friends of Jim Kepner, America's first gay archivist and an early activist, told him of covert homosexual societies, based on Cambridge's "Apostles," that had been formed at Iowa State and other colleges during the middle and late 1930s.

At the same time, in Lincoln, Nebraska, a positively ribald social scene took place under the auspices of two local men, a printer and a pastry chef at the Cornhusker Hotel. Walter and Emmett were in their thirties and lived together near the campus of the University of Nebraska (as room-mates, not lovers) in an unpretentious house they had dubbed "Sagamore Manor." Gay men and lesbians newly arrived to begin their studies soon learned that Sagamore Manor was *the* place in Lincoln for dancing, drinking, drag revelry, and relaxing with one's new boyfriend or girlfriend. They performed skits Walter and Emmett had written, and one weekend helped orchestrate a drag wedding for Emmett and his lover. Twice Walter and Emmett moved when neighbors began to speculate about the crowd of co-eds arriving after dark; the police suspected a male-female brothel. But at their second home—Volga Villa, or Vulgar Villa in the Russian section of town—and at their third, Radclyffe Hall, even farther out of town, the good times continued for the students until their hosts eventually departed for California.

For a student like David L. Leavitt, son of a minister, who arrived at the University of Nebraska in 1937 well aware of his interests, such hospitality nicely confirmed his belief that being gay was going to be something of an adventure. As a first-semester freshman, he explored the school's library and found the sexuality shelves remarkably well-stocked, enough so to suggest the hand of a gay librarian at work. A friend brought him to the Manor, where he became a delighted regular. "Walter and Emmett just loved to have young people swirling about," Leavitt remembered. "Dressing up was a fun part of it," he added. "You could just let your hair down and do whatever you wanted to. It was a classic small-town gay experience." These gatherings for the college crowd were not exactly a secret confined to the gay circles on campus or the immediate neighborhood. Stuart Loomis and his friends made trips from Omaha a hundred miles away for the parties they had heard about, and a graduate student later gave a short report on the Manor in a paper for a psychology class at the university.

The blending of lesbian and gay male social life—an integration in sharp contrast to the separatism of the 1960s to 1990s—served a tactical end, often helping to prevent the police raids or harassment to which gay parties were subject. Walter and Emmett's guests came as male-female couples or in mixed groups, and no one arrived in drag. To prying eyes, they were kids out on the town on a Saturday night; nothing more normal. The same practice was considered a wise strategy in larger cities. The all-gay Nucleus Club organized by Gean Harwood and Bruhs Mero in 1939 in their studio at 52 West Tenth Street in Manhattan was a highly structured undertaking, with membership cards and a limit on the number of non-members who could be brought as guests to the Saturday night gatherings throughout the club's three-year existence. Most important, everyone arrived and departed on the arm of a member of the opposite sex. Even in "Gay New York," caution was desirable. An East Coast black social organization that went by the name JUGGS (as in "Just Us Guys and Gals") was to all intents and purposes a convivial, congenial group of professional black men and women, including more than a few prominent ministers, who held formal-dress events from time to time. Only those "in the life" were alert to its true makeup: gay men and lesbians who used one another as "covers," even to the point of marrying to satisfy the demands of family and career.

The private party circuit mattered—and thrived—in the 1930s because the bar and club scene was so unstable. A missed payoff, a reform-minded mayor (such as Fiorello LaGuardia in New York), a neighborhood protest, and overnight the police made life impossible for bar owners with a same-sex clientele. Coverage in the black press of these shifts in tolerance suggests that gay clubs sometimes fared better in black neighborhoods. ("Is the Reign of Harlem's Twilight Men at an End?" asked the *Baltimore Afro-American* in October 1935—quite some time after the pansies had been swept out of white midtown. "Chicago Has Pansies on the Run," the same paper noted two months later, concluding that the Windy City, especially the black South Side, was belatedly going "goody-goody.") Finocchio's, the Black Cat, the White Horse, and Mona's were all in operation in San Francisco by the middle of the decade, but their appeal was to that part of the tourist trade that wanted an outré experience and didn't mind sharing space with obvious homosexuals. "I would call them 'bohemian bars' rather than 'gay bars,' as we use the term," said one Californian who frequented them. The Showboat and Carroll's in Washington, D.C., appear to have been bona fide gay bars, tolerated by the authorities for the ample payoffs they provided and frequented by locals under forty and servicemen passing through town. (The elderly bartender and the two waitresses at Carroll's, Haviland Ferris remembered, were "affectionate intermediaries" between the gay men and the soldiers and sailors, maintaining good relations with the District police and the shore patrol.) Stella's in Pittsburgh, in the memory of a Carnegie Tech student who went there, also managed without much trouble for a variety of reasons. The four-story building (one floor for drinking, one for dancing, one for "come what may," and one for Stella herself) was in a decrepit part of town; Stella had friends at City Hall and delivered the vote in her ward; Stella took care of her poorer neighbors and the cops on the beat. The result was a place "more open and wilder than anything in New York at the time." Yet Finocchio's, Carroll's, and Stella's are known today precisely because they were *not* typical and managed to remain open for more than a few weeks or months.

At times, an extraordinary inventiveness was called for. One California gossip columnist reported in the summer of 1935 that New Yorkers were outwitting the police in ways that harkened back to the era of the speakeasy: "One of the Broadway theaters which hasn't housed a show in six months has plenty of backstage activity, we discovered." At four each morning the watchman allegedly unlocked the doors, turning the building into a private nightclub. The columnist added: "The place is frequented, we judge from the high squeals we hear in passing, by a flock of androgynes."

WRITING ABOUT FEMALE homosexuality in this era, the historian Lillian Faderman observed that "to live as a lesbian in the 1930s was not a choice for the faint-hearted." For men, the word *choice* has never seemed fully applicable, but the mutual experience of lesbians and gay men in confronting intolerable prejudice is obvious. Yet there is a danger in perceiving experience so removed from ours as uniform, stripped of nuance or specificity—a leveling tendency that is always stymied (happily) by encounters with gay men in their eighties who have few horror stories, or sometimes none at all, to tell about their families and their own evolving self-image. The common thread among these individuals often has to do with one of two factors. The most significant probably is the level of openness or acceptance they were able to achieve, in the midst of an increasingly belligerent society, with their parents or siblings.

"Coming out" to their family in the 1930s was not a realistic option for the vast majority of gay men. "Always, always . . . life demanded secrecy and silence," a gay character reflects in the 1933 novel *Better Angel* as he acknowledges in his college days the great divide that must exist between him and his parents from that time on. But for those few men who did take the risk—and still enjoyed the respect and love of their parents, brothers, or sisters after their revelation—the difference, then as now, was momentous. "There's an annoying stereotype about [those of us] who were young and gay before the war, before the sixties, way back when," one Philadelphia man in his late seventies recently argued. That stereotype usually involves furtiveness, depression, self-loathing. "But I never had any major problem with it and my parents didn't, either. It was awkward, that was the problem. I always felt that they accepted me and loved me. My father never pretended to understand it, but that's another matter. The police and the job problems [were] another matter. I mean, I was their only son. It wouldn't have occurred to them to tell me to go away." Telling his family about his sexuality in 1937, Harold McNulty soon found his lover accepted into the family as readily as he was accepted into his lover's, once the decision was made to be honest with them as well. "You didn't shout it from the rooftops, and my father was very uneasy about the neighbors knowing," he insisted, but neither was parental rejection automatic, particularly in McNulty's case where his mother appeared relieved not to have to deal with a daughter-in-law and had never evinced any interest in grandchildren. Indeed, an unconditionally loving mother, Oedipally inclined or otherwise, was often a gay man's best support in dealing with the wider world of bigotry and derision.

A second factor that made a difference had to do, not surprisingly, with sex and attractiveness. A refrain runs through many interviews with older gay men who remember their twenties and thirties with more pleasure than anguish, and that refrain has to do with how social, popular, or erotically satisfied they became once they had navigated their way, under the guidance of an "auntie" or not, into the field. Or, more bluntly put by one California man: "I was good-looking. I liked sex. I had a lot of it. That's what mattered at the time. It's hard to be depressed when you're twenty-two and lots of people want you in that way. Men were always buying me drinks." Striking even at eighty, he astutely commented after a moment's pause: "Not that my brother was much different, chasing girls, running around like crazy before he got married. Young and queer, young and straight. . . ." Far from verifying the shibboleth about a uniquely gay obsession with youth and sex, remarks such as these address the similarity between heterosexual and homosexual teenagers and young adults. A consciousness of one's place in the world and fears about the future can be troubling but, at least for a time, bountiful erotic opportunities will overshadow a great deal.

Still and all, the ego-building love of a mother, the supportiveness of a father, the affection of siblings and boyfriends, the uninhibited pleasures of sex with another man: when these could be called upon and maintained, they were at best an oasis (albeit sometimes a large one) in a world that was crystal clear in its thinking about gay life. Americans during the Depression years urgently wanted to limit or erase homosexual experience in the public sphere, rendering it unmentionable outside of specialized contexts and therefore almost unthinkable. It was a naive, wasteful, and life-denying enterprise, but no less vigorously prosecuted for that.

5

A LITERATURE OF SEXUALITY: I

I'd rather have negative than nothing.

—Harvey Fierstein, in
The Celluloid Closet

The overturning of the obscenity conviction against *The Well of Loneliness* in 1929 was hailed far and wide as a victory for free speech. For homosexuals, it meant a good deal more. The novel seemed to be in every drawing room in San Francisco, a California teacher wrote to a friend abroad, and he predicted that if Radclyffe Hall were to visit the West Coast, she would be welcomed as quite the celebrity. In print and onstage, the 1930s saw lesbians derided, pitied, or meeting a just and terrible fate (Lillian Hellman's 1934 play *The Children's Hour* is the most famous example), but Hall had cleared a path of sorts: books such as Elisabeth Craigin's *Either Is Love* (1937) and Diana Frederic's *Diana* (1939) told of the self-affirming aspects of lesbianism. Sinclair Lewis's *Ann Vickers*, a phenomenal bestseller in 1933, was, in its early college scenes, middle-class America's real introduction to "unnatural" desire. To his credit—and, according to her biographers, to his wife Dorothy Thompson's credit—Lewis portrayed his lesbian characters with a rare matter-of-factness.

Gay men were less fortunate. A fair number of literary works about male homosexual life appeared in the 1930s, principally between 1931 and 1934, but they distressed and angered gay readers as often as not, and, perhaps mercifully, attracted a small heterosexual audience. Any publishing breakthrough at this time should have been a positive development—and it was, in one light—but the new literature also inevitably reflected the crassness of the fashionable interest in deviance and the hatred of homosexuals felt by society at large. Seen from a distance of more than sixty years, however, these books chart a distinctive territory. The "gay world" that emerges in this collective portrait is a well-populated place, and its construction isn't even especially recent. "Vine-Streeting" in Philadelphia, frolics with sailors on Manhattan's Riverside Drive, pageants in Atlantic City, gay parties in Pittsburgh and Boston, and elaborate bicoastal networks all predate the war. The brotherhood (or sisterhood, to be precise) isn't only something to "come out" into—a person becomes *immersed* in it, educated by its codes, changed forever by its nerve and irreverence. Sex is plentiful and hedonistic. Parties are wild. The early-1930s gay novels also have something to say about the degree to which gay men saw themselves as molders of their own destiny, given certain limits in a stigmatizing culture, and in that regard, there was a difference worth noting between the fictional perspective of interested heterosexuals and the view of those who were "in the life."

The depiction of gay men as fundamentally passive, existing under a cloud that encouraged victimization rather than choice, rebellion, or accommodation, came naturally to heterosexuals. Journalist Blair Niles had good intentions, one supposes, when she explored the gay scene of Manhattan in *Strange Brother*, which the always adventurous firm of Horace Liveright brought out in 1931. She was a travel writer, the exotic was her specialty, and no one had "done" the drag balls before. But the result of her plodding research and earnest prose was a narrow view of life's possibilities for her decent, unimaginative protagonist. Mark Thornton is dismayed by the campiness of most homosexuals he knows, overwhelmed by the prejudice of society, and in the end blows his brains out when forced to deal with a neighborhood blackmailer. Andre Tellier's novel of the same year, *Twilight Men*, also entailed a gay suicide (two, actually) and a number of other horrors. Making use of a French-born protagonist to give his story an unearned Proustian feel, Tellier leads the effeminate Armand—who, even for a none-too-bright child of the leisure class, takes an unconscionable amount of time to figure out he is queer—from Paris to London to Washington Square on a downward spiral of drink, drugs, meaningless attachments, patricide, and ultimately his own death in an Eleventh Avenue flophouse. (Tellier's nasty little book, which was republished in the late 1940s during the second gay book boom and again as an illustrated paperback in the late 1950s, was the product of a less distinguished house than Liveright. Greenberg Publishers seems to have been a small and undiscriminating firm, but its editors knew a trend when they saw one.) For readers worn down by characters with so little backbone, a homosexual villain could be refreshing. Joel Cairo in *The Maltese Falcon* (1930), even with his "plump hips" and "mincing, bobbing steps" (and every other stereotypical attribute Dashiell Hammett could think of), has an unflappable quality. Decked by Sam Spade, he rouses himself to fight again, single-mindedly pursuing his quarry. He plays with the big boys.

Hammett's homosexual gangster, immortalized by Peter Lorre in the John Huston film, was quite the lone wolf in the landscape of successful popular fiction in the 1930s. Gay writers, necessarily out of the mainstream, had less trouble imagining their characters as strong personalities, even when they also saw them as pathetic or tragic. *Goldie* (1933) and *Butterfly Man* (1934) are as badly written and one-dimensional as *Strange Brother* and *Twilight Men*, but they acknowledge some level of decisiveness, or at least willfulness, in the "adherents of Limbo." "Goldie" is Paul Kameron, who leaves the Midwest to join the Royal Air Corps during the war and returns from a German POW camp a confirmed invert. After pandering to the longtime notion of Europe as the birthplace of all corruption, author Kennilworth Bruce then pastes together every other slice of hokum he can: Paul becomes a platinum blond, can't keep his fly zipped, hustles for a while, and ends his days on the gallows for murdering a young bed partner whom he discovers to be his own illegitimate son. Passive, inactive, Goldie is not. Along the way to Death Row, he is privy to a different kind of busyness. New York friends talk about forming an organization to petition the state to end discrimination. "We want the same protection that the law gives everyone else," one character argues. "I'm telling you here and now, fairies have just as much right to live as everyone else." The Twilight League quickly founders, but in 1933 who knew any homosexuals who thought they had civil rights to agitate for?

No one in *Butterfly Man* is as politically astute as the League queens, yet there is a similar hustle and bustle. Lew Levenson's central character, Ken Gracey, a Texas farm boy turned star pansy-performer, exhibits a healthy nerve and anger before his alcoholic demise—an ending that was near-essential to get into print. The hero's wanderings take him to Malibu, Tiajuana, New York, Boston, Philadelphia, and Atlantic City, during which time he learns the value of a slim, youthful body and has affairs with an older man, an older woman, and an assortment of chorus boys. In Chicago, he catches the eye of one of Al Capone's rivals; in Pittsburgh, he wakes to find a thousand dollars tucked in his shoe after an all-night orgy with a secret society of elderly millionaires. Levenson's encouragement to his readers is roundabout: even as happiness eludes most of the novel's gay characters, a guest at a party waxes philosophical about the beauties of male-male love, and one of Ken Gracey's acquaintances looks to settle down with someone he cares for.

Goldie and *Butterfly Man* were dreary books on the whole, but *A Scarlet Pansy* had the advantage of being hilariously campy. The 1932 novel by "Robert Scully" is a deft parody of that much-beloved American genre, the innocent abroad story. Fay Etrange, whom the reader recognizes by the second chapter is not a girl but a highly effeminate boy, is the classic country bumpkin gone to the big city to see the world and make something of herself. Good intentions fall comically by the wayside as successive men in Baltimore, Philadelphia, New York, and San Francisco teach the pretty young thing about sex, trade, the varied needs of aging married men, and pansy culture. The "pleasantly rounded and winsomely lovely" teenager, an embarrassment to her macho brother, becomes in time a very naughty, very funny, tough-as-nails queen who also earns a medical degree and serves on the front lines in Europe. The book's exaltation, or at least its breezy acceptance, of the camp life—drag parties, feminine names, easy sex (" 'Oh, the fleet's in! The fleet's in!' joyously caroled Fay, as what girl wouldn't. . . .")—was anathema to those gay readers who saw girlish flamboyance as part of their public relations problem. Henry Gerber, for one, strongly disliked the novel. But what the cranky Gerber failed to appreciate about Fay is just what most people were slow in granting gay men in general: the intensity of their friendships; the way in which their humor is not just a shield ("the defensive wit of homosexuals" is the hoariest of backhanded compliments), but a robust, sustaining force; and the advantage that could be made of having dealt with adversity from an early age. As a medic in the trenches, Fay is unfazed by the blood and gore. The he-men she ministers to have a more difficult time of it. Her voice may be high-pitched and her wrist limp, but she has a self-sacrificing grit.

The archetype of the tough fairy wasn't destined to find a niche in American culture in a decade of suffering that placed a premium on masculine values, or in the two succeeding decades when manhood was defined by a neutral gray-flannel-suit style and a rejection of anything fey. There was a place in the scheme of things for the suicidal homosexual (Mark Thornton, Armand de Rasbon, Ken Gracey) and for the family misfit— Uncle Harry looks at his nephew too longingly in the 1932 novel *This Man Is My Brother* and is obliged to die in a swimming accident; Edward Everett Horton plays with dolls in the movie *The Gay Divorcee* and does his best to avoid the marriage trap for as long as possible—but there was no room for the clever, effervescent Fay Etrange. A third image, though, just as acceptable to society at large and just as problematic for gay men themselves, was a residue from the era of the Wilde trials, the myth of the affluent gay man with designs on innocent and less affluent youth. (That there have always been rich homosexual men who paid working-class or middle-class men or teenagers to have sex with them goes without saying; the extent to which this represents a corruption of unwilling heterosexuals is the more complicated question.) The ghoulish Mr. Lowell who transports Ken Gracey, future "Butterfly Man," from Texas poverty to the lap of luxury in his California mansion is pure predator and dies a brutal death years later, strangled with a woman's stocking.

A less far-fetched and more vivid expression of this scenario in the early 1930s came in the form of a play rather than a novel. *The Green Bay Tree* opened in New York in the fall of 1933 after a successful run in London. The schoolmaster-author of the popular drama, Mordaunt Shairp, managed to do something that hadn't been attempted by many writers for the stage since the 1890s—dramatize the seductive power of male homosexual decadence.

Without actually invoking the dread word itself, Shairp told a story about a middle-aged man of great wealth and affectation who takes a working-class boy under his wing and now has to face the threat of the young man's marriage to a woman his own age. The notable twist to the story is the ambiguous sexuality and character of Julian, the ward, who has been raised to enjoy the good life and refrain from any work or self-scrutiny. Dulcimer, who might have wandered in from *An Ideal Husband*, has a pleasing honesty to him as he reminds Julian that the world of marriage and heterosexual responsibility and the world of all-male companionship in a rich setting are mutually exclusive. ("But life with me and life with [Leonora] are two very different things. You can't expect them to overlap.") A slow learner by training, Julian wants his woman *and* his allowance and travels abroad with Dulcimer. Leonora more quickly sizes up the situation and sees in Julian's guardian a formidable adversary, even questioning the extent of Julian's passion for her. When she accuses her fiancé of not being a man at all, but merely a "bundle of sensations," Julian resists that thorny self-image, though it is clear that that is exactly what he has been groomed to be. Dulcimer himself makes no bones about it: "I am a materialist and I glory in it." The homosexual lives for his food, his fabrics, his clothes, his wine. In the end, following a melodramatic third-act resolution, Julian is left in peace to lead the dilettante's life he craves, spared both his mentor's suffocating presence and Leonora's crushing expectations. With a shrewd eye on the box office, Mordaunt Shairp concocted a morality tale about the sordid influence of an unnamed evil and to the delight of his gay audience, fearful of the sound of churchbells, sent the woman packing, leaving the young wastrel to be tended to by Dulcimer's butler, himself a "poofter" of the old school.

Director Jed Harris's casting of the popular James Dale as the older gay man and the young Laurence Olivier as his eminently seduceable ward involved its own level of gender-role provocation. As one Olivier biographer tells it, Harris "thought it would be very clever to have such masculine types as Olivier and Dale cavorting on the stage as a couple of classy queens." He made it clear to the actors that he wasn't looking for anything "swish in the performances . . . but the suspicion had to be there." No one in the audience was going to miss the point, though James Dale had strong reservations about his co-star's ability to convey the edge of softness, the veiled effeminacy, that was crucial to Julian's character. Olivier himself later admitted that he detested the role and the whole experience of working with the notoriously bitchy Jed Harris. A further complication to the production was the casting of Olivier's new wife as Leonora. A recent biography reports that Jill Olivier was just coming to terms with her own lesbianism at the time she appeared as the aggrieved heterosexual in *The Green Bay Tree* in New York. The Oliviers separated the following year.

As usual, gay theatergoers turned out in force to see a play that dealt, ostensibly, with their lives. ("The gay bars must all be empty tonight," one man commented after surveying the balcony of the Cort Theater during the twenty-two-week run of the play.) That their lives in 1933 had little to do with holdovers from the time of Oscar Wilde, the godsend of a sympathetic butler, or the freshness of the tulips in the drawing room would also not have been lost on a homosexual audience in the fourth year of the Depression, but there are times when any public image is preferable to none, and Dulcimer's almost diabolical hold over Julian makes a point that cuts both ways. Rich, older homosexuals are a dangerous breed, Shairp was reminding his heterosexual audience. But to a gay viewer, this thought translates in a different vein: we are hated because we are, covertly, powerful. Our life has its allure, it seems. Not all young men will choose the path of heterosexual marriage, given an alternative. The fantasy world of the stage could, at moments, provide its own unintended sustenance. "I'd read about it in the papers," Floyd Clement remembered, "and I knew I had to see it. I didn't tell anyone I was going"—Shairp's play was not a topic a twenty-one-year-old black man was going to talk about on his job as a shipping clerk or to his fervently religious parents in Queens—"but I thought, oh, this *is* exciting."

Certainly no one on either side of the issue in the 1930s was interested in the homosexual as a mundane, tax-paying laborer or professional man interchangeable with his neighbors. That idea was much more dangerous than the hothouse threat of *The Green Bay Tree*. Wallace Thurman's *Infants of the Spring* (1932), another example of the same premise, is a morose account of the Harlem Renaissance more interesting for its homosexual undercurrent than its snide portrayals of Zora Neale Hurston, Countee Cullen, and Alain Locke. But even in a novel about Harlem before the Crash, the gay men are self-absorbed aesthetes. The protagonist of the story may not even be fully aware of his attraction to men, one of the unspoken causes of his discontent and lack of will, but the character based on Richard Bruce Nugent is more forthright about his homosexual dreams and experience. Paul Arbian spends his days "courting the bizarre," longing for "notoriety à la Oscar Wilde," and writing mash notes to Gabriele D'Annunzio in Paris.

The emphasis on the exotic in 1930s gay fiction—"As if we weren't people who got up and went to work every morning," one gay man said—irritated some homosexual readers. Yet at a certain point, the outlandish does take on a larger meaning, becomes more than "bohemian," particularly when an inventive style matches inventive content. Such is the case with the book Louis Kronenberger called in the *New Republic* in 1933 "the first candid, gloves-off account of more or less professional young homosexuals." (This was the novel's only review in America.) The professional homosexuals in question, Charles Henri Ford and Parker Tyler, were destitute Greenwich Village writers with strong Modernist connections. *The Young and Evil* earned praise from Gertrude Stein and Djuna Barnes and much talk among the avant-garde literati. Unfortunately, it was far too unsentimental, independent, and cocky (in all senses) for native readers who still thought of Hemingway, Mencken, and Lewis as iconoclasts. Published by Obelisk Press in Paris and judged to be pornographic by customs officials, it only trickled its way back into the country over the next few decades. By the time it was reissued by an American press in 1960, *The Young and Evil* was a cult classic.

Whatever attributes impoverished poets may share the world over, Charles Henri Ford and Parker Tyler were sui generis. They were the pansy poets even liberals disparaged but, blessed with unusual talents, they made no apologies for their manner. Ford had endured the cultural confines of San Antonio as long as he could, leaving Texas before the end of high school, later to meet Parker Tyler, already a mascara-decorated dandy, in New York. If their collaboration is taken as autobiography, which Ford insisted it was, their forays in Gotham circa 1930 were unrestrained and unabashed. They also suggest a valuable attitude toward life. Adventure, "lush expectancy," is what counts, and the opinions of others can be as meaningless as the rules of punctuation the authors jettisoned in their episodic antinarrative. It's a matter of "proud rumps" and fresh poems. Posturing and name-dropping aside, the novel also offered some much-needed clarity.

The clarity had to do with sex. Conservatives have always been leery of any mention in print of homosexual acts on the accurate assumption that the demonizing process requires distance; that which becomes known, then plausible, then familiar, is harder to stigmatize. By the same token, there have always been enlightened souls in twentieth-century America who could see that some men were not made for marriage with women. The state of mind of these men who are different from their peers, their alleged wit and aestheticism, their problems with the law, their role in high society were all topics within the pale, even if many educated heterosexuals didn't care to read about them. Charles Henri Ford and Parker Tyler approached the matter from a different angle, claiming a place for mouths, genitals, and torsos along with psychology, temperament, social history, and good table manners.

In "Cruise," a late chapter of *The Young and Evil*, Karel (Parker Tyler) and a friend, Frederick, are horny. They decide to see what's available on Riverside Drive. Julian (Charles Henri Ford) elects not to join them. They leave a gay nightspot on Forty-sixth Street and, like expeditioners, take a bus sixty blocks north and then begin a promenade southward. Instead of finding the agreeable trade they want ("I'm dying for it," Frederick wails), they are assaulted by some sailors. And what audacity, what cussedness, Karel thinks: one of the sailors had his fly open only a minute before. The police arrive to break up the melee and haul everyone down to the station house. In the car, Karel uses his handkerchief to wipe off his mascara. The desk sergeant tries to get the facts, while the arresting cop spits out his understanding of the row: "thissailorsaidhefuckedhiminthemouthbutthere'snocomplaintsoit'sdisorderlyconductforall." No undue surprise on anybody's part. This is the big city, the real world. The police aren't amazed that a sailor would have used his penis in that fashion, or that the boys from the Village would have wanted it, and the "disorderly conduct" charge has a ring of "What else is new?" The only recrimination is about the homosexuals' having left their true, accepted playing field: "If you stayed on Broadway this wouldna happened." Best of all, after a night in the slammer in which they make up with the sailor who hit them, the pair are brought before an elderly magistrate of a sympathetic nature. Impressed by Karel's publishing credentials and Frederick's good looks, he lets them off with a wink and a sweet reminder to be more careful next time. They debate whether to kiss the sailor on the street afterward, but settle for ice-cream sodas instead.

The following for *The Young and Evil* was always rather select, though its admirers grew in number as the obscenity barriers came tumbling down in the 1950s. *Better Angel*, on the other hand, seems to have found numerous fans right away. In the midst of so many madcap queens, effete artists, anguished suicides, and sad, aging (but rich) homosexuals, the appearance of Forman Brown's novel in 1933 was something of a miracle. Published by Greenberg, the book went into a second printing, though exact sales figures are impossible to come by. (In 1995, in his ninety-fourth year, Brown did recall receiving letters in 1933 from older gay men, commenting on the difference such a book would have made to them in their youth in the 1880s, and from younger gay men expressing their appreciation.) Writing under the pseudonym Richard Meeker, Brown knew the European fiction that dealt with the subject—Gide, Cocteau, the extravagant portrayals of Baron Charlus and his circle in Proust—and was well aware of how sorry the American literary record was in this area. With *Better Angel*, his only novel, he made a serious effort to fill the gap.

What Brown produced was a curious, capable combination of Sherwood Anderson–style realism and, in the latter part of the book, a scene-shifting pace and a spirit of intelligent yearning and inner exploration out of Fitzgerald. From his early, difficult days in Barton, Michigan, to his coming out in college, where he learns that he is far from alone in his sexual interest (and also notes that gay men run the range from the unthinking and "straight-seeming" to the "arty" and self-conscious), through his time in Europe and New York before he takes a job at a New England boarding school, Brown's protagonist is both a young man trying to make a life for himself as a self-recognized homosexual and a person with other facets to his life. Family, school, work, travel, other friends matter in *Better Angel* in a way they don't in many gay novels. Most important, Kurt Gray is a successful literary character—credible, appealing, varied in his reactions to different situations, a figure who changes in small ways over the ten-year span of the story. He isn't the generic fairy, despite his sensitivity and interest in music, nor does he have much use, when he first encounters him, for the young man he later falls in love with. Kurt comes rather slowly to learn *who* he wants, though he has always known *what* he wants. And he has fallen for someone who, in his early twenties, already has a history of white lies and philandering that is not likely to end. What some readers still take for a perfectly happy ending to the book is in fact a little more ambiguous: Kurt's life with David is not going to give him the "pure" faithful passion he is looking for, but something more earthbound, and Kurt has cause to know that. The whole concluding third of the novel, once he returns from Europe, is about Kurt's education in the hard, "impure" facts of life. A friend is arrested in a Connecticut movie theater by a cop out to entrap homosexuals, Kurt longs to help one of his students accept his own differentness without incriminating himself, and the lure of a fast, rich gay life remains a problem for the man Kurt wants to settle down with. Gently, but honestly, the book questions how effectively settling down for gay men can ever mirror the settling down their parents and grandparents took for granted.

The ultimate effect of *Better Angel* is to leave the reader with a sense of how layered and intricate homosexual experience can be—a lot in life that is inherently unfair under present circumstances but never uninteresting or without its compensations, a situation offering plenty of opportunity to be miserable but one that also calls upon an individual's creative potential, insight, trust, and tenacity. To be homosexual, in Forman Brown's story, is to worry and question, love and deceive, aspire and fail, much like any other civilized human being. In the stark climate of the 1930s, that was saying a great deal. The authenticity of *Better Angel* was hardly the norm, and even its few reviewers conceded as much. If not "within the zone of popular fiction," a *Minneapolis Journal* critic wrote, the book was executed "with restraint" and its protagonist "traced with admirable candor." The reviewer of the *Herald-Sun* of Durham, North Carolina, agreed that Kurt Gray was looking for a "true, honest love."

The importance to gay men of this hodgepodge of writing about homosexuality is impossible to chart with any precision. Yet it is hard to believe that it wasn't, in toto, a significant part of the changes in consciousness that took place in the period between the Crash and Pearl Harbor. Sexual energy has a role to play in fiction that goes well beyond how darkly a given story ends, how unkind an author's caricatures are, how slight the work may be as literature. In *Strange Brother, Twilight Men, Goldie, Butterfly Man, A Scarlet Pansy, The Young and Evil, Better Angel,* and assorted short stories of the day (such as James Farrell's "Just Boys"), readers were told in one way or another that the characters were having homosexual sex. Wing Biddlebaum sleeps alone, and Willa Cather's young fugitive in "Paul's Case" (1905) dies a sensitive virgin, but in the early 1930s such reserve was past enduring. Heterosexual passion had long been subject to censorship as well, of course, but the ramifications were different. Straight adults didn't need to read Zola or D. H. Lawrence to know that men and women fucking was a good thing. Gay men did need to see that acknowledgment, however oblique, *in print.* In a print-oriented culture, words on paper had almost the same value that film and television images have assumed in the post–World War II video-oriented culture. Raw experience or individual truth becomes more than a personal reality when it finally appears in the defining medium—it becomes part of a collective reality, of everyone's life, and there is no stepping back from that enlargement. Lugubrious, exploitative, brazen, or doggedly sincere, the least of these writers put the gay man's erotic and romantic nature on the map of modern life. The best of them made those yearnings seem dynamic and credible.

It also matters that this wedge into a closed system was attempted by storytellers, for it is through stories rather than argument that the deepest changes in perception are made, or at least most accurately charted. By the end of the 1930s, sociologists and psychologists had written at great length about the homosexual as a threat to the young or a paradigm of maladjustment in need of sympathy and study. Before this mountain of grim prose, the few articles or essays that talked sense weren't of much use, and the artistic record is not much more brilliant. But it was a start, and it was taking place just as the film world was closing its doors to homosexual experience. A literary line that runs from Gore Vidal's *The City and the Pillar* and James Baldwin's *Giovanni's Room* to Mart Crowley's *The Boys in the Band* and later to the books of Paul Monette, Armistead Maupin, E. Lyn Harris, and Christopher Bram actually begins much earlier, with writers unknown today but valuable in their time.

6

FROM PANSY TO
PUBLIC MENACE

We have talked too long about homosexuality in hushed whispers, thinking of it purely as a problem in morality when it is in reality a disease. It needs to be cured. To be sure, that cure may be difficult. When the tendency to homosexuality does not seriously menace society, we may not have to worry overmuch. But when it leads to crimes against defenseless children, we must deal with it.

—"The Sex Criminal,"
The Christian Century,
10 November 1937

When a man like Dr. Joseph Collins, who before the Great War had scoffed at the Freudian emphasis on sex as pornographic, told his readers in 1926 about the many homosexuals he had treated in his private practice, he was playing to an audience that yearned to view itself as more sophisticated than the previous generation. Collins's book, *The Doctor Looks at Love and Life*, sold nicely. But how many readers believed the author's statement that homosexual men came from all walks of life, worked in every profession, and might be indistinguishable from the most masculine men they knew? No doubt many people found that a questionable insight; the stereotypes of the day—the swishy waiter, the overwrought decorator, the gossipy hairdresser—were firmly in place and loudly trumpeted. By the end of the next decade, however, the image of the sexual deviant was undergoing a modification. The awareness, restricted but growing, of the diverse nature of homosexual life and the nature of sexuality itself, especially of the fact that male homosexuals were not universally weak or effeminate, meant that a new stereotype had to be fashioned and widely broadcast. While still loosely defined as pansies by much of society, gay men also came to be seen as dangerous—dangerous in ways that had not been a significant part of the public discourse before the 1930s. This change presented new obstacles for men attempting to form an identity based on their sexual activities, love affairs, and social life, even as it prepared the ground for larger possibilities of self-definition.

That men who love men might also love women, or at least be able to perform as husbands (whatever their real desires), is a profoundly disturbing reality for some people. Many societies have managed to accommodate themselves to that truth, from Periclean Athens to the England of James I, but the late-Victorian drive to analyze, differentiate, and classify had brought a more rigid perspective to bear on the matter. It was part of the culturally knowing aura the 1920s had trafficked in that such facts of life should once again be accepted by the worldly. So *Dangerous Corner* (1932) didn't create shock waves on Broadway or anywhere else it played with a married homosexual as one of its central characters, but J. B. Priestley's murder mystery did indicate where the loopholes in the state censorship laws were to be found: a pervert worth banning was a coarse Mae West drag queen, not simply an effete upper-middle-class gay man (British, to boot) with a wife on his arm. Noel Coward, who could do no wrong in the decade before the war, invested the two men–one woman ménage à trois with prolix wit in *Design for Living* (1933) and had audiences in New York, Washington, Pittsburgh, Cleveland, and elsewhere applauding a comedy that was recognizably "tinged with lavender." Laurel and Hardy made a grand and timely joke about the subject in *Their First Mistake* (1932) and blues artists such as George Hannah sang of the susceptibility of all men ("You run around with funny people, you'll get a streak of it up your back") in *Freakish Man Blues* (1930).

The transition in this regard between the early 1920s and the late 1930s was strikingly apparent in criminal contexts. The Walter Ward case, for example, was a lurid headline grabber in 1923. Scion of a wealthy family and a father of two little children, Ward had been arrested in New York's Westchester County for the murder of an ex-marine who was purportedly blackmailing him for his "sexually degenerate" practices. So evident was his guilt—and so far-fetched his story of how he happened to be alone with his blackmailer—that Ward's father (allegedly approached for the money) did not appear in court on his son's behalf and the press treated a guilty verdict as a foregone conclusion. The defense lawyer didn't call any witnesses and rested his case after parading Ward's young wife and a photograph of his children before the jury. Ward was found innocent. A decade later, that same verdict, based on the assumption that family men didn't meet working-class toughs on country roads after dark for illicit purposes, might not have been so easily reached. By then, journalists had been reporting on too many stories of married men whose interests had strayed from hearth and home, to girls, boys, or other men. The topic was broached even in the religious press. In November 1937 a minister told the far-flung readership of *The Christian Century*, a nondenominational weekly, of having performed the wedding rites for a man he later learned was homosexual. (He blamed the groom's mother for pushing her son into marriage, knowing full well he wasn't attracted to women.) The young man was eventually imprisoned for the murder and attempted sodomy of two boys, leaving behind a pregnant wife and a humiliated mother. Americans had been complacent in their thinking (and too focused on punishment instead of treatment), the minister's editorial implied; the deviant had many faces, not all of them powdered and rouged. His argument was made to a receptive audience. By the time of the more famous Wayne Lonergan case in the early 1940s, shock at the notion of virile men of multifarious erotic interests wasn't universal.

Doctors and psychiatrists had been assiduously promoting this wider view for some time, often with an air of amazement that their observations hadn't been more promptly heeded by society. Only the most old-fashioned authorities still insisted on femininity in men as the key, or only, marker. One of the "progressives" (a relative term here), George W. Henry of New York's Payne Whitney Clinic, had worked with the Committee for the Study of Sex Variants since its founding in 1935, interviewing gay men and lesbians who volunteered to be examined. The inquiry's results were published as *Sex Variants* in 1941, and several of the forty men profiled in the two-volume book, at least as Dr. Henry described them, could have "passed" without much effort. One of his bisexual interviewees, a man who had been courted by various officers in Europe during the war and was a devotee of bathhouse sex, "might easily be mistaken for a day laborer," he wrote. Another, Leonard R., was a small-time gangster, with "broad shoulders, heavy muscles . . . large, powerful hands" and a deep attraction to men. Peter R., an athletic blond with a forthright manner, was insistent that numerous policemen he had met were hot for sex with men, especially if they had just arrested them. Many of the experiences Antonio L. recounted were with older married men who appreciated his Italian prizefighter's build. Malcolm E., an exclusive homosexual who disliked effeminacy, was square-jawed and muscular, indistinguishable from other athletic twenty-four-year-olds. Norman T. had spent three years fighting with the Chinese Nationals against the Japanese forces in China. George W. Henry was not the objective analyst he pretended to be and his distaste for the men and women he studied in the five years he labored on *Sex Variants* was thinly veiled, but his message was an apposite one: the image of the sissy repelled by, or incapable of, vaginal sex, manual labor, street brawling, or service on the front lines did not apply to all those individuals who might be called, or might call themselves, homosexual.

THE REPRESSIVE CHARACTER of the 1930s makes it difficult to develop a sense of the true visibility of sexual difference at the time. The fact that a given type of behavior was not depicted regularly in the movies or on the stage, or was not considered by the *New York Times* to be part of that selective category "All the news that's fit to print," does not mean that it wasn't alive in the consciousness of astute adults, or even adolescents. When fuller histories of the Depression are written in the years ahead—treating the state of the family, changes in mores, and the social life of minority groups as of equal moment with New Deal strategies and employment figures—more will be known about how America was altered *in its totality* by the rapid collapse of the economy, a totality that included millions of gay men and lesbians. By degrees, the picture is being enlarged. In a particularly promising vein, historian Allan Bérubé's ongoing research into the operation of the Marine Cooks and Stewards Union, which provided the workforce for the Pacific luxury liners of the day, has uncovered an organization full of working-class gay men—black and white, queens and roughnecks, and, more remarkably, some dynamic homosexual labor activists who enjoyed a wide respect among their peers. (The union's motto was "No red-baiting! No race-baiting! No queen-baiting!") Other historians are currently investigating different branches of the labor movement from the same angle.

The communities of homeless men that had long been a feature of both urban and rural life along the nation's railroad lines grew to astronomical proportions after the Crash. Estimates are that as many as two million men of widely varying ages were wandering the countryside in 1932. Here, too, the implications of this cross-class, interracial, intergenerational arrangement are significant. The hobo's world, in Eric Sevareid's phrase "a vast, submerged, secondary United States" that is still being delineated by historians today, was a place where the teenage sons of bankrupt businessmen encountered aggressive vagrants who wanted their bodies—this was Sevareid's own experience, as he took to the road and left middle-class security behind—and where male bonding became something closer to marriage. For those who were able to recover their economic stability after the Depression as much as for the men who remained outside the ordinary structures of society, the nature of male life on the road suggested a range of intimate human needs, not all of them traditional. "There was a tremendous amount of homosexuality among the hoboes," one of Dr. Henry's subjects told him from firsthand knowledge, "and generally a great deal of affection."

Gay veterans of the Civilian Conservation Corps, or C.C.C., camps, in which the hard-core unemployed were housed and put to work in the nation's woodlands, remember the ease with which a pair of men might disappear for a few hours on their own after a day's labor. The camps "were staffed by Army personnel and a certain amount of discretion was needed," Warren James of Portland, Oregon, has noted in talks to gay groups in the 1990s, "but it wasn't hard to find a place to go in private with the forests and the parks all around you." Here, perhaps more than anywhere else, the view of the homosexual as necessarily giving himself away by his delicacy meant nothing. "The C.C.C. wasn't an environment where a pansy would have lasted two minutes," Roger Cyr, who spent a year in a camp in California, remarked. "So I went in thinking, all right, watch yourself and you'll get by. No problem." The pleasant surprise for Cyr was the possibility—albeit never as frequent as he would have liked—of a ferocious coupling in the woods with another man who was as masculine, as "dirt poor and streetwise," as Cyr himself.

Documents in the Kinsey Institute for Sex Research in Indiana, located by historian Martin Duberman in the 1970s, touch on the extent of homosexuality that could be found in the camps and the likelihood that this situation was taken in stride, if the participants were not too brazen about it. A married man known by the code name "BA," who had had ample experience with other men and boys in his life, kept a record for the Institute of his sexual activities. In a camp (apparently in Texas) that housed just under two hundred men between the ages of eighteen and twenty-six, almost a third of them enjoyed masturbation and fellatio with BA over a six-month period. At another, the sixty-year-old superintendent had a similarly busy time of it with his charges. At a third, the owner of a rental-cabin unit near the camp—a forty-year-old camp foreman, married with several children—made use of the cabins to establish relations with "nine boys, ages 17–21."

Given the age, energy, and geographical isolation of those who took part in Roosevelt's Civilian Conservation Corps, no one is going to be thunderstruck by any amount of same-sex carrying-on. Take several hundred thousand young men, all under the age of twenty-six (the cutoff point for the program) and most between seventeen and twenty years old, and remove them from female companionship to spend their days planting trees, building roads, and laboring on water-conservation projects, and a release of tension will take whatever form it must. But we shouldn't be too ready to peg this aspect of Depression life as simple expediency, divorcing it entirely from more self-defined, self-accepting homosexual contexts. As the experience of C.C.C. veteran Warren James implied, some participants became aware in the camps that this was exactly the kind of intimacy that would always be most important to them and knew others who came to feel the same way. Not all of the shirtless, hardworking C.C.C. men were examples of trade, scrupulously refusing to find their pleasure by kneeling down or bending over themselves—or simply hugging or kissing another man.

Public acknowledgments of scrappy, rough-hewn, or working-class homosexuality were few and far between in the 1930s, but the ones that do exist provide some tantalizing suggestions of the truths that Americans were aware of but were reluctant to discuss. *This Finer Shadow*, written in the early 1930s but not published until 1941 after the author's suicide, experienced a vogue among gay readers, especially those who had been dismayed by the manic camp of *Goldie* and *A Scarlet Pansy*. A seafarer himself in his youth and a married man, Harlan McIntosh offered an unusual character for the time: a tough, muscular, educated seaman who is physically drawn to both men and women and yet not fully comfortable with either. Employed on a tramp steamer at the start of the book, the protagonist Martin Devaud might just as easily have worked in a C.C.C. camp or in one of the Bowery kitchens he visits on leave.

Harlan McIntosh understood the ubiquitous nature of same-sex desire, but his take on the subject was edgy and ambivalent. Rex Stout, on the eve of his great Nero Wolfe success, produced a realist novel in 1933 that found a wider audience and treated "abnormal" sexual feelings with an honesty and clarity few other literary works of the decade approached in America. Set in Montana, in a community that has never heard of drag balls or pansy nightclubs, *Forest Fire* is the story of Stan Durham, a forest ranger, a husband and father (though now grown indifferent to the conjugal side of married life), a dour, rugged man who has always been self-sufficient, businesslike, unreflective. A sexy twenty-year-old who works for him provokes a crisis in Stan, who analyzes the intense emotions Harry

Fallon arouses and tries to fit them into all the categories he knows. But he can only manage a few "bewildered guesses." Is he seeking in his good-looking employee another son? The brother or buddy he never had? A friendship that would be "a new soft thing for his middle age, a new soft warm thing"? When Harry touches his knee or boyishly cajoles him into ignoring some infraction, Stan is bewitched. Finally, Harry's involvement with a woman vacationing in the West precipitates a kind of madness in Stan, which leads to the novel's brutal, not entirely surprising climax. In trying to sort out his feelings, Stan decides that the term *homosexuality* is inappropriate, but not irrelevant: "He was no cross-eyed bull. He shied away from that, but pulled himself back to it again. . . . He had heard many of the forest and prairie epithets and phrases and jokes regarding intimate physical relations between men, or between men and boys, but he knew nothing whatever of the actual facts on which they were based. He was aware that to most men there was something both shameful and funny about it, but to him it was neither one nor the other." A lifetime of purposeful, masculine labor and a carefully constructed asexuality are undermined by sensations that are simultaneously erotic and fraternal, romantic and protective. Stout dramatized a state of mind in *Forest Fire* that dodges the labels but also resists a characterization of same-sex impulses as discrete, fringe aspects of experience. It was precisely this awareness that the interior life of any man or woman might not always be bound to imaginary absolutes of "normal" sexuality and "natural" gender roles that Depression-era Americans were eager to contain. It was more than weak dialogue and a meandering plot that killed *Sylvia Scarlett*.

Such knowledge had to be contained because it carried within it the seeds of an unwanted revolution in perception. Consider the life and fabulous career of J. Edgar Hoover in the 1930s. We can discount the claim made by Anthony Summers in *Official and Confidential* (1993), the most freewheeling of recent Hoover biographies, that the FBI director was seen in drag in the 1950s. (Summers's lone eyewitness is a dubious source with an ax to grind, and the practice of cross-dressing is not synonymous with homosexuality, anyway.) We can put aside the statements about his homosexuality made after Hoover's death by friends like Ethel Merman—how well she, or any of his public life friends, really knew him is open to question. Hoover's evident lack of sexual interest in women may not mean much, either, nor has any of the alleged Mafia blackmail evidence come to light. What we cannot ignore is the cache of private photographs found in Hoover's home after his death, hundreds of pictures taken over several years, which he meant to be destroyed. The photographs he took of his friend, traveling companion, and assistant director Clyde Tolson (particularly those of Tolson sleeping, or in his bathing suit or bathrobe) situate Hoover for us—not necessarily as "gay," perhaps not even as "a homosexual," but certainly as a man (very like Rex Stout's protagonist) whose affections and erotic drive were far removed from the heterosexual norm. Hoover was no more exempt from romantic longings than any other human being.

But the question is: To what degree was J. Edgar Hoover, creator of the G-man mythology and head of America's most admired crime force, perceived by others to be sexually different in the decade he turned forty? The rumor was brought to President Truman's attention, and by the Kennedy years it provided the material for a good many jokes within the government. Yet to believe that an awareness of this aspect of Hoover dates only from the postwar period is to reinforce the most shopworn of stereotypes about heterosexuals: before the 1940s, adults were sexual innocents, lacking the sophistication of our own time. Indeed, Hoover was a source of speculation for many years precisely because he embodied so many paradoxes. He was the man who went after queers wherever they could be found but felt no need to marry for a "cover" or to explain away handsome Clyde Tolson's meteoric rise in the Bureau; he was the tireless compiler of sexual dossiers who rebuked his agents for off-color jokes, the anti-smut crusader who made sure that FDR knew in prurient detail about Sumner Welles's tomcatting or that Ike's staff heard all about Joe Alsop's misdeeds with a male Soviet agent on a trip abroad in the 1950s. With breathtaking nerve, Hoover lived out his life confident that he would be protected by his files on his adversaries, by his own brand of discretion, and by the fact that most Americans did not want to accept that a man in his position would have more-than-friendly feelings for another man.

In response to the sensationalism of *Official and Confidential*, a number of Hoover allies have made their way into print to insist that the scandalous charges could not have any basis in reality. Cartha DeLoach's *Hoover's FBI* (1995) is the most indignant of the lot, and the most useful in illustrating how vital the stereotypes still are in some quarters. DeLoach knew the director: he was a gruff, manly sort. Clyde Tolson was a "healthy, strapping fellow in his youth" who played on the FBI baseball team. Homosexuals aren't gruff, they aren't strapping, they hate sports. Neither man acted like a fairy, and so neither was homosexual. DeLoach, a thirty-year veteran of the Bureau, is sure that he would have been able to detect it. That others did, and were quite willing to drop a broad hint, is made plain in an article about Hoover, which appeared five months after FDR took office, in *Collier's*, as wholesome and unscandalous a weekly as one could find on the newsstands in the 1930s. Ray Tucker, a frank journalist, sounded the alarm about the "miniature American Cheka" Hoover was forming in the hope that the new president would put a stop to it. He characterized J. Edgar Hoover in terms no one was apt to mistake. The unmarried FBI head was a fastidious dresser, always careful to color coordinate. (His favorite color: "Eleanor blue.") He would "quiver with excitement" when following a lead. He was known to walk "with a mincing step." For giving life to the whispers in 1933, Tucker earned a permanent place on Hoover's enemies list.

Out of the limelight, the same conditions could prevail. Many gay men who were of marrying age in the 1930s knew the terms of the social contract and counted on the timidity and willful ignorance of their peers and elders to shield them. Frank Carlson, an Ohio lawyer, walked a fine line in his younger and middle-aged years, relishing a homosexual life in private but, like Hoover, refusing to go out of his way to pretend he was heterosexual by marrying or socializing with women except in a perfunctory way. "I lived those years," he ably summarized in his late eighties, "with a sense that the unsophisticated people around me, my older relatives or some of my employees, probably assumed I was asexual or I was undersexed or some kind of sadsack who never found the right woman, and it was a little irritating that people viewed me that way. Because I dated very rarely and I never talked about women and, obviously, I wasn't inclined toward marriage or children." But Carlson also found it hard to believe that everyone was in the dark. "On some level, they knew." The "they," in his estimation, might have included his younger law partners, the more urbane people in his family's social circle, his nieces and nephews. "It didn't matter that I had a gun collection, I hunted, or that I was a lawyer. Not everyone bought into that. They would never have said anything because I didn't fit the run-of-the-mill image. It was an image they cultivated." And, it could be argued, any image that requires cultivating is not one that all of society readily accepts, or comes by naturally.

Celibacy, real or feigned, allowed people to give men such as Hoover and Carlson the benefit of the doubt. A passionate demeanor could be more problematic. If two good-looking eligible men weren't involved with women, rumors were inevitable. Randolph Scott and Cary Grant, who set up housekeeping together in Hollywood in 1932, took an almost devilish pleasure—certainly it seemed devilish to the studio publicists—in teasing out a reaction to the great unmentionable. While alert to the career necessity that they marry eventually (which they both did, more than once), they attended parties and premieres as a couple in the early 1930s until executives at Paramount demanded they show up in public with "beards" (dates of the right gender). Columnists, most notably Edith Gwynne of *The*

Hollywood Reporter, dropped hints right and left about the unusually devoted pair. The movie-magazine spread in 1933 of Scott and Grant at home in aprons or sitting down to a cozy meal alone elicited the snide, knowing comment from one male reporter that they were "carrying the buddy business too far." The best the studio could manage was a statement that the highly paid stars were attempting to save on rent by living under one roof and splitting expenses.

At times, Cary Grant acted as if he were both fascinated and horrified by the position in which he found himself—on his way to being rich, already famous, in love with Scott, not uninterested in women, talked about in Hollywood as a queer, but being groomed to play a man devastatingly attractive to women who would no more believe the rumors of his desire for men than they would believe J. Edgar Hoover's. The brutality Grant exhibited toward his first wife, Virginia Cherrill, in their short-lived union (February 1934 to March 1935) suggests that he wasn't ready for the leap into respectability, but at the same time he could make sport of the restrictions his life as a screen idol had placed on him. The famous ad lib in *Bringing Up Baby* (1938)—asked why he is wearing Katharine Hepburn's nightgown, Grant retorts on camera, "I've just gone gay, all of a sudden!"—was unthinkable from Tyrone Power or any other actor in the closet. (The cozily domestic photo layout he and Randolph Scott posed for earlier in the decade was in the same spirit of make-of-this-what-you-will.) But that daring quality in Cary Grant isn't completely surprising: his mentor was a professional in the gender-war trenches. A close friend and possible lover from his Greenwich Village period in the 1920s was Francis Renault, the female impersonator known as "the last of the red hot papas," a man, as one Grant biographer put it, both virile and "unabashedly gay."

The virile homosexual was a concept to be resisted because it was a new, looming, complicating reality. Glenn Carrington, born in Richmond in 1904, told his parents about his homosexuality after he moved to Harlem following his graduation from Howard University, where he had studied under Alain Locke. As one of New York State's first black parole officers, Carrington could hardly have managed to retain his position in the criminal justice system if he had been effeminate or blatantly homosexual. Yet he appears not to have been unduly preoccupied with hiding his interests and strongly advised friends against the practice of marrying for the purposes of a cover. People could think whatever they wanted to. Carrington, who died in 1975, might be the paradigm of the man—a not uncommon type—about whom colleagues and neighbors drew their own conclusions but said nothing, thereby furthering that healthy sense that gay men were a varied, ultimately uncategorizeable group. His extensive correspondence gives the impression of an individual who hadn't limited himself in any way or seen his sexuality as a obstacle. Friends and correspondents ran the gamut: academics and political figures, prison convicts and boys in the C.C.C. camps, people he met on his trips to Scandinavia and Africa, a black musician who toured the country with his jazz band, a gay math teacher in North Carolina, a nudist camp owner in Michigan. A number of these men had been his sex partners at one time or another, including many who later married and had children.

Carrington was evidently a desirable lover. One of his many boyfriends in the 1930s wrote to him, "I was extremely happy to learn that you wanted me to be, or should I say, prefer me to be, the more 'feminine' side of our 'marriage.' This joy justified my attraction to your masculinity, which I had doubted once." The "once" is telling: in a still role-rigid subculture, Carrington's masculinity meant that he was locked into the position of the sexual aggressor as firmly as any heterosexual man. Much praised for his "wolfy" ways, he was a catch for effeminate gay men who didn't want to sleep with other effeminate men.

THE MOST BLATANT exploration of aggressive, stereotype-defying homosexuality in the 1930s—a link, in its way, to the idea of the sex criminal whose nature and actions jeopardized all of society—evolved out of the growing concern with the inadequacies of the American prison system. Men behind bars have raped other men, slept with other men, and formed deep emotional attachments throughout the ages, just as women inmates have. Few people saw this as a fit subject for study or discussion, though, prior to the early twentieth century. In 1920 Kate Richards O'Hare, a Socialist activist, published *In Prison*, which described "the thorough education in sex perversions" that her year in the Missouri State Penitentiary had provided. Eight years before, Alexander Berkman's *Prison Memoirs of an Anarchist* dealt with the same theme in Pennsylvania's Western Penitentiary, where Berkman spent several years. (An interesting contrast is that O'Hare's view of the lesbianism she encountered is one of unrelieved sorrow while Berkman stressed the tenderness as well as the coercion of prison relationships.) Nonetheless, even by the standards of the "new penologists" of the 1930s, Joseph Fishman, a former federal inspector of prisons, was going out on a limb when he devoted himself to a blunt study of the extent of homosexuality permitted and even encouraged by American prisons. Funded by the Guggenheim Foundation, *Sex in Prison* (1934) was an indictment of a system that left men sitting in their cells all day with nothing constructive to do (Fishman regarded the obsessive masturbation that resulted to be a mental illness in itself), that refused to institute conjugal visits, and that pretended homosexual sex, both forcible and consenting, wasn't a common occurrence.

On the public's blindness, or pretense of blindness, about the true nature of gay men, Fishman was admirably forthright. He lectured his readers as if what he had to say could hardly be taken as new information by anyone with two eyes. "The mere fact that they are homosexuals no more makes them all similar than the fact that men who smoke or play the piano are similar. Homosexuality is but one phase of their personalities just as heterosexuality is but one phase of the personality of a normal person." Homosexuals, he affirmed, were not only to be found hanging about public bathrooms and lurking behind bushes. Some people believed they were capable of a pure love no different from heterosexual love. They often held "responsible, high-salaried positions" and were "prevalent in almost all industries and professions." None of these comments were to be mistaken for unqualified approval. Rather, Fishman was advocating clear-eyed realism. Looking the other way, either within the prison or on the streets of America, did not make the problem disappear. Hence, Fishman's belief that work and recreation were crucial and that conjugal visits were an idea worth considering. The underpinning of his argument was part Freudian doctrine, part criminological reform: anyone, even the burliest mobster, was capable of a sexual drive toward another man or boy, and left unchecked the male libido was bound to run amok, breaking down all social norms.

His liberalism notwithstanding, Joseph Fishman was also a man of his times. He was of the opinion that the figures cited by Havelock Ellis and others—that as many as 80 percent of the modern prison population practiced homosexual sex—were inflated, and he was skeptical of the claim that prison guards took their pleasure with the male inmates just as the "wolfy" inmates did with the "punks." His attention to an unusual incident at the U.S. Penitentiary in Atlanta, however, provides an invaluable record of an early, highly public protest against sexual abuse by authority figures. As Fishman relates the episode, a group of prisoners, some avowedly homosexual and others not, brought charges against a number of uniformed guards and civilians who worked in the prison. "They produced numerous affidavits signed by prisoners, some of them reciting in great detail, alleging that the officials indulged in homosexual union with the inmates, and demanding that an investigation be made." The district attorney of Atlanta felt there was a case and prosecuted. The trial was short. All of the accused state employees were acquitted without the jury even leaving the box. To Fishman, this was right and proper; the trial was an example of prisoners' rights taken too far. The sexuality he observed in prisons and worried about was on the other side of the locked door, among the inmates themselves. To readers sixty years later, the accusations, especially those brought by the inmates who claimed to be heterosexual, men who would not want to talk in open court about being sexually "used" by another man, have a different feel, and it is hard not to wonder if everyone in Georgia who read of this trial was equally confident that the charges were false.

Fishman's book, published by the National Library Press, was intended for a select readership, but mainstream publishers were alert to the growing curiosity, even titillation, of a nonprofessional audience. Little, Brown brought out *Prison Days and Nights* (1933) by Victor Nelson, a highly articulate ex-convict, which spoke directly to the interested "general public" and went far beyond the passing acknowledgment of homosexual sex to which other prison memoirs of the day were confined. Heterosexual himself, Nelson appraised the idea that incarcerated men temporarily sought relief with other men, happily returning to their women in due course, as a short-sighted version of a complex reality. From all perspectives, he believed, every man was changed by the experience of raping a man or being raped, sharing a bunk or acquiring a "wife." Not as despised in prison as he was in society at large, the "natural" homosexual was free to be himself, and in the resulting encounters and relationships lay "a major factor in bringing out and strengthening the latent homosexual tendencies of [the homosexual's] new associates." These tendencies were not always disowned, Nelson insisted, when the inmate was finally released. An "unpremeditated" decline into homosexuality by a masculine heterosexual was always a possibility, and *Prison Days and Nights* recounted some credible examples from the author's circle of acquaintances.

Victor Nelson also provided a discussion of the common terms that defined the sexual topography of the prison and, in turn, alluded to the working-class world from which many of the inmates came. Jockers and daddies were the men who took the active, or insertive, role in sex—often aware that they were engaged in a degenerate act, Nelson noted, but still glad to retain their status as men. Muzzlers, fairies, and fags serviced their jockers orally; punks, gonsils, and mustard pots were on the receiving end in anal sex. Nelson's most troubling point, however, was that the jockers were by no means as secure in their heterosexual identity as they, or society, assumed. Lust—and love—asserted its own unpredictable hold on "manly men."

As social criticism, both *Sex in Prison* and *Prison Days and Nights* were ahead of their time, though a January 1934 clean-up raid on the New York City jail on Welfare Island called attention to "pansy degeneracy" in prisons for a few days as local newspapers described the segregated quarters and easy tasks assigned to the queens who promenaded through the corridors, some in rouge with shoulder-length hair, "in most cases hips swinging and hands fluttering." The death of Richard Loeb in an Illinois prison in January 1936 was a more nationally covered and more relevant event, verifying Fishman's and Nelson's contention that homosexuality went beyond giddy spectacle and gender inversion. Leopold and Loeb, the two most famous homosexual criminals of their day, had been in prison for twelve years for the "lark killing" of fourteen-year-old Bobby Franks. When Loeb was slashed to death in the shower by a fellow inmate whose advances he resisted, no one other than Leopold mourned the loss. James Day, the murderer, was found not guilty after claiming that Loeb had tried to force himself on him, an assertion that neither the warden nor the prison's chaplain believed. "Nobody liked a queer, a homo, or a lesbian," one of the jurors in the trial commented almost forty years later, "so it was a good thing to get rid of such people." The irony that one homosexual was getting rid of another homosexual, with the murderer-homosexual allowed to go unpunished, didn't seem to matter to the judge or the prosecutor. The warden was not allowed to offer his views of James Day's veracity or his homosexual inclinations. Given the amoral character of both the victim and his attacker, fine distinctions were hardly worth the trouble.

A report that same year from the Prison Advisory Committee in Kentucky, where inmates convicted of sexual offenses had one side of their heads shaved to identify them at all times, suggested that such men were even more dangerous than heterosexual prisoners. The number of degenerates in prison was "disgustingly large," the report commented, and many of them were unstable and beyond rehabilitation. The only murders committed in the Frankfort Reformatory in recent years, according to state officials, had involved "sex struggles"—knifings by jealous lovers and spurned wolves. Prison officials were uncertain what course to follow in the future, but the article in the *Louisville Herald Post* discussing the committee's work was titled "Reform By Surgery?"

Not a topic for dinnertable conversation, to be sure: Mae West's acknowledgment of the Cherry Sisters, an arm-in-arm tough-guy couple she greets on a visit to the "pen" in *She Done Him Wrong*, was closer to the line. The popular interest in crime, gangsters, and prison life was more readily satisfied by the movies of James Cagney and Edward G. Robinson and the new school of hard-boiled detective fiction. Close to home, the homosexual thug was too disturbing to be a source of humor. But as news from abroad, the concept had a market. One of the best ways to characterize the vileness of Nazism before the war, writers and cartoonists found out, was to equate it with sexual perversion. Bolsheviks were a threat to be fought by every means necessary, but they represented an enemy perceived as masculine—dour, determined, pragmatic. National Socialism with its florid pageantry, its leader's histrionics (not to say hysterics), its cult of blond youth, and its self-conscious joy in male bonding lent itself to a different approach. The Nazi was not only an anti-Semite and a bully; he was that lowest of men, the sexual degenerate. As Neal Gabler observed in *Winchell: Gossip, Power, and the Culture of Celebrity*, Walter Winchell rarely introduced the distasteful subject of "homosexualism" in his widely syndicated columns in the 1930s. With "Adele Hitler," he made a strident exception. By 1938 theater censorship wasn't even an issue during the short Broadway run of *Waltz in Goose Step*; playwright Oliver Garrett's Nazi homosexuals were acceptably diabolical and lecherous.

Hitler's purge of Eric Röhm and dozens of his storm troopers in July 1934 had confirmed the impression that the rise of Nazism did have something to do with homosexuals (even the German government, in its statement about his death, couldn't escape mentioning Röhm's "unfortunate characteristic"), but the Night of the Long Knives was almost incidental for those anti-Fascists who wanted an effective smear tactic. In fact, the caricaturing of Hitler as queer was under way long before the summer of 1934, despite the fact that everyone who followed the news out of Germany knew that the party's policies toward gay men and lesbians had always been fiercely negative. No matter. *Americana*, a magazine of satirical drawings and sketches, was the most unsparing with its cartoons in 1933. In one issue, it was Hitler as a limp-wrister directing his goose-stepping hordes as a corps de ballet; three issues later, it was Hitler and Mussolini in bras and girdles; in another issue, it was Der Führer as a testy bitch on Hindenburg's leash. A cartoon in the *Broadway Tattler* of January 1934 depicted Hitler announcing that the purity of the race required the castration of all pansies, at which point Goering carts off Hitler to the hospital with instructions to Herr Doktor to "giff him der vorks." In the next frame he is crying out in a falsetto wail. The oily effeminacy of the Great Dictator was a given in popular culture by the time Chaplin's film was made during World War II, as were the corresponding ideas that homosexuality was no longer to be associated only with effeminacy and, in any event, that effeminacy itself was no longer to be seen as inherently weak or harmless. Queer wolf or pansy, storm trooper or hairdresser: they were all warped, they were all dangerous.

The face of evil was not always so lurid, though, and that was the real problem, gradually giving rise during the later years of the Depression to concerns of a different kind. By the middle of the decade, large-circulation newspapers began to report stories that would had been ignored or played down in years past. In 1935, for instance, Henry Wadsworth Longfellow Dana—who, as the scholarly grandson of both the poet Longfellow and the novelist Charles Henry Dana, had a Boston lineage as impeccable as any— was arrested at the family estate on Brattle Street in Cambridge. His accuser was a sixteen-year-old student from the Latin School, who seems not to have been of an especially victimized nature. He had been involved with three other young men in stealing the Dana family car and, presumably because he knew Dana had something to hide, expected the theft to go unprosecuted. The horror of this episode for the residents of Massachusetts was threefold: an illustrious name had been sullied; deviant sexuality was now shown to thrive beyond the seedier fringes of Boston (in the very temple to the memory of *Hiawatha*'s creator); and a courtly middle-aged man had reminded the citizenry that no one was safe if predators like Dana weren't identified. Several weeks later Dana was acquitted in court, but the damage had been done. The trial made the wire services. The murder the year before in a suburb of Pittsburgh of a female impersonator who had been blackmailing the head of the athletic department at Washington and Jefferson College—a father of three children—was another flagrant example of the same theme. It was one thing for George Cukor to be picked up by police cruising for trade in Long Beach in 1936, and quite another for Boston Brahmins and married gym teachers to be caught with high school sophomores and drag queens.

Journalists understood that there was a viable middle ground between complete discretion, which meant never mentioning sexual deviance, and the crassest sensationalism, and throughout the 1930s reporters became adept at hinting at the pervasiveness of homosexuality and, more dramatically, in painting for their readers a picture of a world governed by dark, illicit forces. If a charge was made in open court, there was no need to beat around the bush; so when two counselors at a city-run summer camp in Philadelphia—one a gymnast in the 1936 Olympics—were accused of lesbian activity during an investigation into the death of a five-year-old girl camper, the charges made all the major papers in the fall of 1937. But when the sexual aspect of the story was more opaque, both the tabloids and the more mainstream papers knew to offer enough information to fill in the gaps. Claude Kennan, a forty-six-year-old New York publisher, was found beaten to death in his room at the Madison Hotel in November 1937. With no comment or interpretation, press reports noted the elevator operator's statement about admitting Kennan in the wee hours of the morning with a young man he had evidently just met. Friends remarked on Kennan's sociability, but readers could put the pieces together without much difficulty.

The issue mattered because it addressed the growing fear that in the area of sexual health America was out of control, as out of control as it was in its economic and political health. Beginning in late 1936, a "sex crimes panic" gripped the country that lasted for almost three years. More a foreshadowing of what was to come in the late 1940s and early 1950s than a phenomenon that spent itself with full force before the war, this concern that the nation's children were suddenly in danger of sexual attack while playing in the street or on their way to school became a very real anxiety during the last years of the decade. There is some question now—as there was even at the time—whether the number of assaults on minors and women was actually on the rise or whether it was the reporting, and subsequent publicizing, of the attacks that was increasing. Whatever the truth of the matter, by early 1937, the alarm had been sounded. The district attorney of Brooklyn, worried that molestation was underreported for fear of embarrassing the victims, acknowledged that a citywide drive "against sex crimes involving children" was needed in his community. The cooperation of parents would be vital, he announced, in rounding up degenerates. The governor of Michigan hosted a high-level conference on the emergency situation in his state (the *Detroit Free Press* had covered numerous cases of sexual assault on both boys and girls in a two-month period in 1937), and in Philadelphia, Chicago, Los Angeles, and dozens of smaller cities, parent groups, politicians, and sex hygiene experts met to debate the problem. Advocates of sex-education courses in high schools saw this as yet another compelling reason to implement their new programs.

Since the Lindbergh tragedy, kidnappings were a significant news item and had become a dramatic element in the sex crimes panic. Even when the names were not prominent, papers from one end of the country to the other recounted the abductions of children and adolescents, the ransom demands, the family's anguish, the joyful release of the victim, or the terrifying discovery of the body. Painful as any child's abduction was, the crime had a special horror when it involved a boy and the possibility of homosexual lust. This was not something Americans were used to. The kidnapping of Charles Mattson, ten-year-old son of a Tacoma, Washington, doctor, took front-page space for more than a month between Christmas 1936 and February 1937, even in the usually circumspect *New York Times*. The criminals' failure to finalize the arrangements to collect the money they demanded and the boy's savage murder—his nude body was found in the woods near Everett—led to speculation that the kidnappers were homosexual. The coroner would neither confirm nor deny that the boy had been molested, though J. Edgar Hoover expressed the view that the FBI was most likely dealing with a "sexual degenerate." Homosexuals were picked up for questioning in several states, and hobo camps were raided for men fitting the criminals' descriptions. Landladies were told to be on the look-out for single men acting suspiciously. By the end of the 1930s, after enough of these stories with gay subtexts, it was harder than ever to see the homosexual as an object of amusement, pure and simple. He was a man capable of Nazi inhumanities, the deception of his parents and neighbors (even his wife), the stripping and abusing of innocent boys like Charles Mattson.

In April 1932, Dr. W. Beran Wolfe had written in *The Modern Thinker*, a popularizing intellectual journal, about homosexuality as a sickness that was "not only a flight from [normal] sex but also frequently an active aggression against society." It was a condition "*on the borderland between neurosis and crime.*" Within a few years, worried parents felt that they had been provided with concrete evidence to verify that thesis. Nor did one have to look too far from home: "Sometimes [the pervert] is a prominent or trusted person, sometimes a leader in boys' welfare work," the author of *New Patterns in Sex Teaching* (1938) reminded her readers. The older, grandfatherly molester was no different from his younger counterpart; he beguiles his prey, Frances Strain wrote, "through offers of candy, money, trinkets, movie shows, picnics, rides."

Reactions to the crime wave ranged from the prudent to the nutty. Following a Boston man's confession in September 1937 to the rape and murder of a ten-year-old Brighton boy the year before, the Boston district attorney loudly demanded that the state's criminal code be revised. Longer prison terms were needed, and psychiatrists had to be brought into the process of evaluating the accused. That same week, the molestation of a brother and sister in Fairmount Park led the mayor of Philadelphia to urge the sterilization of all convicted sex offenders. A doctor in Detroit offered the opinion that a ban on female impersonation would go a long way toward ending sexual abuse in his city. At no time in these public discussions did anyone articulate—let alone stress—the fact that most homosexuals were uninterested in sex with children, that the homosexual child molester constituted the same unfortunate aberration among gay men that the heterosexual child molester did among heterosexuals. That observation would have been seen as fastidious and inappropriate to the gravity of the topic.

Yet it is not as if official recognition of a sex crimes problem was needed to grant the police or vigilantes license to abuse gay men during the 1930s. It happened with depressing regularity. In his introduction to *Sex Variants*, George W. Henry relates the story of "T., a middle-aged man . . . wealthy and socially prominent" who returned to the United States with his wife and four children after a long trip to South America. In his absence, a vice crusade had started in his hometown and when T. was asked to come to the police station for questioning, he obliged without any suspicion of what was in store for him. His name had been given to the police by another man and, after a long interrogation, he was duped into signing "confidential" statements about his private homosexual involvements over the years. He was then held in jail for five days before his hearing while the roundups continued and the local paper listed the names of those men charged with being "idle, lewd, and dissolute persons," the common euphemism of the time. Eventually thirty men were arrested, T. was sentenced to six months' hard labor in a road camp (he managed to be placed in a sanitarium instead), and a leading physician in the community committed suicide while on bail.

Vigilante action was yet more terrifying in that it negated even the remote possibility that a lawyer or a psychiatrist could come to one's aid. In June 1936, acting in response to a rumor (never substantiated) that a man staying at William Haines's weekend house near Manhattan Beach in southern California had made an advance on a neighborhood boy, local men severely beat Haines, his companion Jimmie Shields, and three other guests. The men were forced to their cars, which were pelted with tomatoes, and told never to return to the area. The attackers then moved down the road to invade another secluded beach house shared by several gay men, assaulted them, and forced them to their cars with the same warning. Any enclave, as the gay residents of Fire Island and Provincetown would later learn, afforded only limited protection, and police investigation of anti-gay violence tended to be perfunctory at best.

THE ATTEMPT TO stigmatize homosexuals as a menace to children and as men whose lives were necessarily furtive and violent, a drive that reached its zenith in America in the years 1935 to 1960, was the work of a society that was awakening to the fragility of its own dichotomies: healthy/sick, married/promiscuous, masculine/feminine, active/passive, heterosexual/ homosexual. An attitude of "live and let live" would only move things in one, probably irreversible, direction: toward the diverse and the makeshift, toward an easing of the assigned roles, toward a skepticism about many of the edicts whose authority came from the Old Testament, the state, and one's elders. Accepting that human sexual drives were not uniform, but were shaped by changing cultural conditions and individual needs, would also mean accepting that the guardians of public welfare—FBI directors, parole officers, or lawyers like J. Edgar Hoover, Glenn Carrington, or Frank Carlson—might well love other men, and that the actors who represented the best of heterosexual passion on the screen—Cary Grant and

Tyrone Power—might play very different parts in the privacy of their homes. It would also mean accepting that none of these alleged contradictions really mattered. "Sex criminal" was a label to effect the containment that "pansy" had not fully, or even satisfactorily, accomplished.

The use of derogatory new terms and the promotion of unsavory myths made public life more difficult for gay men. The "umbrella of ignorance" that Samuel Steward felt had long guarded the homosexually inclined from nosey speculation was fast giving way to an inquisitorial atmosphere. Silence and cunning became more important. Yet the development of the concept of the homosexual predator had one inadvertently positive effect, in a quite different arena. Unlike the image of the fairy, which was to some homosexual men a celebration of gender-role freedom and to others a brutal accusation of impaired manhood, the image of the molester was too far-fetched to take hold as an assault on the gay male ego. Even the most masculine homosexual might harbor nagging doubts about his true relationship to the fairy, secretly asking himself if those who shunned or challenged him might not be right in their belief that gay men were damaged, malformed beings—frustrated women at heart. But no gay man assumed that a homosexual urge to seduce, rape, or murder children was anything but the fantasy of people who were nervous about the extent, perhaps even the appeal, of same-sex romance and eroticism. There was a form of liberation to be found in the 1930s to 1950s campaign against "dangerous" homosexuals, one man commented, "because you said to yourself, 'If they're this far off on this, how right can they be about anything else about me and my life?' " The distance between an uncertain, evolving sense of self and a fabrication as threadbare as the Nazi/kidnapper/pedophile charge provided a rare psychological space for evaluating society's faulty definitions and its means of keeping certain groups in line.

In such a climate, the real danger was to be found elsewhere, among those who claimed to have an objective, even humane interest in homosexuality and who stood by ready to "help." From this allegedly enlightened community, which was expanding its influence each year during the middle third of the century, came a more corrosive threat to gay identity in America, one that sought to replace criminal prosecution with what amounted to an attack on homosexual relationships and self-esteem in the name of progress and compassion.

7

FREUDIAN AMERICA

"I don't like that word [homosexual]."

"It's highly scientific."

"Oh, I know that, but it makes me sound like a biological freak of some sort—to be classed with morons and cretins and paranoiacs."

"And that's probably just what the jolly little scientists would think about it."

—Richard Meeker, *Better Angel*, 1933

The transformation of America between the wars into a nation with a more psychological perspective on human behavior was a fast-paced, highly political, and variously motivated enterprise, and its implications for homosexuals were—and are—enormous. The consequences of the belief that sexuality could be scientifically studied, its manifestations cataloged, and its causes named (and, just possibly, its painful dimensions alleviated), dealt a critical blow to the late-nineteenth-century view of the world that focused more exclusively on character, restraint, free will, and moral choice. By midcentury, the concepts of sexual development articulated by Sigmund Freud had become something close to articles of faith for a great many people, and Freudianism a veritable religion. But the ironies involved in this cultural shift form an edifice of their own. As homosexuality was redefined as a psychosocial issue rather than a moral lapse, it took on the qualities of a discrete category, rather than an *aspect*, of life—quite the opposite conclusion the founder of psychoanalysis had intended his adherents to reach. As analysts won over the educated public and a skeptical medical community and consolidated their power in America, an interest in "cures" supplanted the traditional faith in punishment, a development that complicated and in some ways worsened for gay men and lesbians an already grim situation. Again, not an outcome anticipated by Freud or his closest followers. Nor did matters improve much as the generation after Freud worked with more homosexuals in their private practices. Seeing what they wished to see, the professionals shaped new stereotypes scarcely less blinkered than the old. Finally, disastrously, the acceptance of Freud's assertion that homosexual desire was an innate capacity shared by all men and women led not to the encouragement of tolerance or benign neglect, but to the alarmist notion that greater vigilance was the answer. Beware the dominant mother, take heed of the passive father: perversion begins at home.

Nothing illustrates how great the distance grew between Freud and the Americans who treated sexual deviance and wrote about the subject than two contemporaneous events. In September of 1935, Louis W. Max of New York University spoke to the American Psychological Association about recent efforts to "disconnect the emotional aura" of a patient's "fetishistic stimulus" and consequent homosexual behavior by means of electric shock—the first documented use of aversion therapy on a homosexual, as historian Jonathan Ned Katz reports. The patient admitted to some "backsliding" at first but, after three months of escalating shock treatments, the "desensitizing" was judged to be 95 percent complete.

From the same year we have Freud's now-famous correspondence with an American woman who was worried about her son. Freud's response to her query (unpublished until many years after his death, unfortunately) reveals a man at odds with Dr. Max and the advocates of aversion therapy. "I gather from your letter that your son is a homosexual," Freud wrote to the woman in English. "I am most impressed by the fact that you do not mention this term yourself. May I question you why you avoid it? . . . Homosexuality is assuredly no advantage, but it is nothing to be ashamed of, no vice, no degradation, it cannot be classified as an illness; we consider it to be a variation of the sexual function, produced by an arrest of sexual development." A productive and harmonious life might well await her son, he observed, whether he remained a homosexual or not. Freud was doubtful of the possibility of change, but confident that condemnation and persecution were the responses of cruel and ignorant minds.

THE SCIENTIFIC, OR quasi-scientific, investigation of homosexuality predates Freud by a good many years. Karl Heinrich Ulrichs, a nineteenth-century prophet of the "coming out" experience, had advanced the proposition of a third sex during his futile campaign in the 1860s to convince the German government to remodel its laws along the lines of the more tolerant Napoleonic Code. The alienist Richard von Krafft-Ebing had presented dozens of lurid case histories in his *Psychopathia Sexualis,* dispelling some myths and inventing others, while making use of the term *homosexuality* coined by a Hungarian writer, Karoly Maria Kertbeny, in 1868. Several American doctors had offered their impressions of the phenomenon in articles for medical journals in the 1880s (a few extolling the benefits of castration) and, in a different spirit entirely, Albert Moll had taken issue with the more hysterical reactions to aberrant desire in *Perversions of the Sex Instinct* (1893). John Addington Symonds and Havelock Ellis had collaborated on the most compassionate and intelligent book on the subject, *Sexual Inversion,* the first volume of *Studies in the Psychology of Sex,* in 1897. But none of these men were to have anything like the influence Freud did, an influence only slightly diminished by the fracturing of his original discipleships into the competing schools of Alfred Adler and Carl Jung or, later, Karen Horney and Melanie Klein.

So the selective use of Freud's ideas, and the hardening into dogma among both American psychoanalysts and psychiatrists of Freudian insights and creative speculations about sexuality, are topics of more than academic importance: they say a great deal about the climate homosexuals had to confront from the 1920s through the 1960s. The voice of authority in the form of oppressive legislation and religious intolerance was painful to deal with, but the more articulate "wisdom" of modern science proved to be an almost unstoppable force. How and why was this force turned against homosexuals, which was never really Freud's intention?

Freud never wrote extensively about male homosexuality, but his views were articulated early in his career in the first several pages of *Three Essays on the Theory of Sexuality,* published in 1905 and revised many times thereafter. The concepts of infantile sexuality and polymorphous perversity addressed in the second essay of the book proved to be so provocative and far-reaching that Freud's equally acute observations about "inverts"—using the term favored by Symonds and Ellis—were scarcely afforded their share of attention over the years. But what he had to say and the tone in which he said it were no less important and no less relevant to the new theory of human development he was propounding.

First, Freud expressed his doubts about the value of the medical diagnosis of homosexuality as a sign of nervous degeneracy; too many inverts were perfectly functional members of society and, he observed, the "extreme," or lifelong, invert was apt to feel "at one with his peculiarity." He also set himself in opposition to the recent trend toward viewing same-sex desire as a separate realm of experience that had nothing to do with "normal" people and "normal" drives. Concerning the debate over the causes of homosexuality, he initially steered clear of both extremes. Those who characterized homosexuality as innate might be correct in certain (rarer) instances, while those who argued that it was acquired were likely to be proved right in others. In truth, Freud's bias at this point in his thinking was with the latter camp, though he didn't envision the process of "acquiring" specific sexual desires as a passive or involuntary one. Rather, Freud maintained that an individual's family history and his or her unpredictable, self-protective—even creative—responses to that history were the telling factors. Freud's given was that a bisexual drive was shared by all human beings; the idea "that everyone is born with his sexual instinct attached to a particular sexual object" was, for him, a "crude" elementary notion. What interested him was why certain men and women formed themselves so as to act out their "sexual aim" toward one "sexual object-choice" rather than another, and the extent to which this development brought satisfaction or discontent into their lives. It was the underlying "aim" forged in childhood that offered the clues that determined "sexual object-choice." The distinction, for Freud, was crucial, as he was well aware that on this topic most educated people missed the forest for the trees. Religion, law, and popular prejudice had had rather too much to say about the trees.

The most astonishing fact about Freud's comments on homosexuality in this short essay was revealed by the author, almost offhandedly, in the essay's first footnote: in 1905, Freud had yet to analyze a single homosexual patient. His information was taken from the writings of Krafft-Ebing, Moll, Symonds, Ellis, and other pioneer sexologists such as Ivan Bloch and Magnus Hirschfeld. This in itself separates Freud from those who followed him, in two radically different ways. Many postwar psychoanalysts and psychiatrists in major cities in America and Europe worked extensively with homosexual patients or, in the case of prison employees, with homosexual inmates who were "available" for study. But these men, who saw themselves as laboring on the cutting edge of science, assumed very different truths about homosexuals from those Freud did, even when they had read the same early texts as the author of *Three Essays on the*

Theory of Sexuality. Absolutist notions of sickness and health, even moral right and moral weakness, often form an intrusive part of their commentaries. Rare was the practitioner, for all of his clinical experience, who could write with Freud's lack of nervousness about fellatio and anal arousal. Few are the books between 1905 and the 1960s—academic, popular, or otherwise—that treat variant sexual expressions with anything approaching clinical objectivity or suggest, as Freud did, that exclusive heterosexual desire "is also a problem that needs elucidating and . . . not a self-evident fact based upon an attraction that is ultimately of a chemical nature."

But Freud was never destined to be a heroic figure to gay men—and even less to lesbians—in twentieth-century America. For all his doubt about labeling homosexuality as an inherently pathological condition, he never achieved a consistently wide or deep view of the individuals he was referring to, and he was capable of repeating some dubious statements from his varied sources—for example, that many inverts have a lessened sexual drive and a "slight atrophy of the [sexual] organs" (this from Havelock Ellis). Most important, he accepted without question the Judeo-Christian view that the highest aim of the sexual urge was procreation, thereby establishing a hierarchy of development with heterosexual married life at the peak and homosexuality placed anywhere from a well-adjusted middle to a self-destructive lower level. Such a limning of "sexual maturity" was necessarily a slap at even the most contented, fulfilled, stable homosexuals, and American psychoanalysts and psychiatrists during the 1930s were all but unanimous in their acceptance of this approach. Yet "immaturity" and "pathology" are radically different notions, the one condescending and the other vehemently aggressive—as far apart as a belief in the efficacy of analysis to probe an Oedipus complex and the use of electric shock treatment to recondition a sexual object-choice. The sorrow, even the tragedy, of this drama is that Freud saw the ways in which his theory of the unresolved Oedipus complex and the mother fixation of the homosexual was being used to castigate gay men as sick and dangerous without ever once addressing the issue in public. A patrician disdain for the New World—Americans were not a people to appreciate subtlety and complexity anyway, so what was the point of reproach?—freed Freud in his own mind from worrying about the slanted interpretations and the different, more ruthless emphases his books and case studies inspired.

A fair amount of early damage was done by Freud's legendary study of Leonardo da Vinci of 1910. Earnest and reductive, imaginative and probing, this biographical sketch and analysis of a childhood memory offered, and still does perhaps, something for everyone—sexual progressives and homophobic reactionaries alike. Disconcerting is Freud's assumption that da Vinci was immune to the "stormy passions" of life simply because we have no evidence of what he did, or how often he did it, with the handsome boys whose company he enjoyed. But a de-sexed genius suits the purposes of the venture; a man of appetites, serenely untroubled by his erotic drives and prudently discreet, would be a different protagonist altogether, and not one suited to the matter at hand, which had to do with sublimation, mother obsessions, distant fathers, and oral needs ungratified from infancy. For a generation of American Freudians, this short essay was rich in suggestive detail, however flawed the biographical premises, and prominent analysts of varying temperaments mined these ideas for all they were worth. Healthy men—heterosexuals—had enjoyed good breast-feeding, proper weaning, and a father's timely presence. Homosexuals were the victims of the opposite conditions. Never was Freud so indifferent to the uses to which his explorations would be put.

On the other hand, Freud's relentless pursuit of a homosexual motif in da Vinci's supposed childhood memory of a vulture's tail penetrating his mouth furthered the principles established by the sexuality essays of 1905: the multifaceted drives of the body had to be understood separate from the dictates of culture and religion; civilized people should be able to talk about sexual variations without undue fuss; sexual awakening long predated adolescence; orality and anality were key sexual features of childhood; and homosexuals were more likely to be made than born and were as capable of significant achievement as heterosexuals. Freud's insistence that fellatio was being practiced "with great frequency among women today" was a daring comment intended to restructure the debate about acceptable erotic practices, and he was able to look on sexual variants as more than a catalog of their habits in the bedroom. "What decides whether we describe someone as an invert is not his actual behavior," Freud wrote in a moment of true sensitivity, "but his emotional attitude."

A case could be made for the view that no intellectual leader can be held responsible for the form his ideas later assume in other hands. On occasion, Freud said as much. He would have preferred worldwide unquestioning acceptance of his methods and conclusions and, when that degree of fealty was not forthcoming, was apt to bristle and turn away. But there is, still and all, a remarkable quality to the speed with which Freud's way of perceiving reality was accepted in America (much more rapidly than in Europe)—and how completely he lost control of its articulation and dissemination in the matter of sexual differences. A country proud of its independence from European political systems and proud of its role in "saving"

Europe from the Hun ironically saw in Freud a means of understanding the postwar social changes that American philosophers and psychologists hadn't provided. Americans weren't, however, about to swallow the message whole, least of all when it strayed too far from, or explicitly contradicted, religious teachings or existent legal codes. The id, the ego, repression, and sublimation were concepts the church and the state could live with; any hint of finding a place for the invert in a continuum of plausible human behavior was more revolutionary and offensive.

The fascination with Freud was, from the beginning, as crassly popular as it was specialized (a fact noted by American Freudians in need of a market), and it was fueled by secondhand accounts as much as it was by American analysands returning from Vienna or the professionals who spread the gospel at conferences and lectures. Middle-class matrons heard of psychoanalysis, "whispering hope to millions of nervous invalids," in the pages of *Good Housekeeping* as early as 1915. In 1925 Louis B. Mayer tried to get Freud to write a screenplay—for good money, he told reporters. The testimony of Dr. William Alanson White at the Leopold and Loeb trial in 1924 was a milestone (though in some press accounts the public had to read between the lines to know that homosexuality was at the root of the disturbance White was analyzing), and dozens of Jazz Age novels made use of the new terminology or introduced psychiatrists as characters. "You could not go out to buy a bun without hearing of someone's complexes," the playwright Susan Glaspell remarked about her life in New York in the 1920s. Eugene O'Neill's *Strange Interlude* was more part of a growing bandwagon in 1927 than a breakthrough with its interior monologues and mother-obsessed, latently homosexual Charles Marsden. Some of this attention was satiric—the bearded analyst called in to assist the police in the movie *The Front Page* (1931) is criminally and comically inept, a buffoon who gets himself shot by the suspect—but the caricatures only underscored how well established the prestige of the "mind doctor" was becoming.

The number of Americans who had been in analysis or actually read Freud's books was presumably quite small, but a literate adult had to be rather out of touch not to know the elements of the story by the mid-1930s. Journalists Dorothy Bromley and F. H. Britten weren't surprised to discover in their extensive survey of the sexual attitudes and practices of young men on campus that undergraduates reacted negatively to questions about homosexuality. (What is your frank opinion of it? Do you know any homosexuals? Have you had any homosexual experience yourself?) They were intrigued, though, by the willingness of some of their interviewees to frame their responses in more modern terms than those of simple moral disapproval. "Before Freud's theories became common knowledge," Bromley and Britten wrote in *Youth and Sex: A Survey of 1,300 College Students* (1938), "it is doubtful whether any member of a happy-go-lucky student community would have stopped to analyze causes and classify this way of life as 'a psychological maladjustment.' "

The exact nature of that "common knowledge," however, had taken a slightly different shape in its transatlantic crossing, retaining elements of Freud, Ellis, Moll, and others, but evolving away from its sources—generous, ambivalent, or narrow—into what psychologist Kenneth Lewes has bluntly described as an authoritarian framework that allowed some analysts "to engage in rather sadistic abuse and ridicule at the expense of their homosexual patients." In essence, the perspective on homosexuality offered to the college-age generation of the 1930s—or the teachers who instructed them, the law enforcement officials who wanted to bring psychiatry into alliance with criminology, or any interested parent, cleric, or social worker—was not one to inspire the tolerance toward gay men or lesbians that Freud believed to be a hallmark of a civilized society. It assuredly wasn't anything to bolster the self-image of those gay men and lesbians who took the experts to heart.

The language the subject was couched in was the first hurdle. Phrases like "the problem of the homosexual" suggested a closed inquiry right from the start. In content, too, the literature assumed a numbing uniformity. Readers were informed that a man's sexual attraction to another man was a misstep on the path of adulthood, attributable to the dominant influence of his mother and his failure to establish a proper identification with his father and the masculine role in sex, a bond that would have enabled him as a child to deal with his desire to sexually possess his mother. Certain theorists, looking for causation prior to the Oedipal period, were particularly taken with the idea of an unresolved oral need from the time of breastfeeding. In Melanie Klein, this avenue of thought found an influential and sometimes cogent spokesperson; in Edmund Bergler, an Austrian emigré to the United States, a less reasoned advocate. (Indeed, anything to do with sucking eventually became almost a monomania with Bergler, who in his later writings made no effort to disguise his horror at the practice of fellatio and even heterosexual cunnilingus, which he likened to "sucking on a wound." About the "hyper-masochistic act" of swallowing semen, Bergler verged on the rabid.)

Some—but not all—psychoanalysts and psychiatrists were happy to nod in the direction of the bisexual premise, one of the more durable Victorian intellectual legacies. The lesson, as they saw it, however, was that greater care was needed in childrearing as it meant that anyone inadvertently "mismanaged" in infancy could grow up to be a sexual deviant. And who more qualified to provide that guidance than the modern mental health professional? By 1940, though, Sandor Rado was winning converts to his critique of the idea of an innate bisexual drive, arguing that the urge to couple with a member of the opposite sex was biologically determined, with postadolescent homosexuality a sign of a profound disturbance. In this schema, homosexuality was caused by a trauma of great magnitude. The "natural" process was derailed by a child's response to a formidable inner crisis.

Karen Horney, an early Freudian turned breakaway critic, advanced the idea throughout the 1930s of homosexuality as an aspect of a universal male "dread of women," an anxiety focused on female genitalia that was particularly intense among, though by no means confined to, homosexual men. This angle appealed to several groups, including those who worried about the male chauvinism of the "penis envy" tenet of psychoanalysis and those who questioned patients' claims that they could be equally aroused by both men and women. "No man can dance at two weddings, not even the wizard of the homosexual," Edmund Bergler liked to say in his frequent dismissals of bisexuality. Others went much further. In a 1938 article in *Psychiatry*, William V. Silverberg speculated that the passive male homosexual's need to be used like a woman by a masculine man was triggered by his desire to keep the man (his father) from sexual union with the woman (his mother), having despaired in childhood of winning the woman himself. From this starting point, the next step was distressingly clear: passive male homosexuals were, at least in principle, a menace to society. They had "infantile ideas of pleasure" (oral and anal rather than properly phallic) and longed to keep *all* men and women apart. They did so by interposing their bodies between the manly male and the woman. They obliterated the woman by becoming her substitute. Their condition was more than not-heterosexual—it was anti-heterosexual. Therefore it was possible, Silverberg wrote in "The Personal and Social Significance of Passive Male Homosexuality," that the ancient taboos against same-sex lust existed for a valid reason, warding off race or tribal extinction.

The emphasis on misogyny, vagina anxiety, and a failure to assume the father's role served a useful end. Indeed, if male homosexuality was a flight *from* women and heterosexual responsibility, rather than an attraction *to* something reasonable and desirable in itself, then it followed, given the nature of Western society, that the young man who persisted in gratifying his unnatural urges was doomed to a life of unhappiness. Promiscuity, sexually transmitted diseases, empty relationships, suicidal depression, and ostracism were his natural lot. The doctors weren't inventing this sad scenario, they wanted everyone to realize. They saw it and heard about it from their patients. Evidently the number of patients they learned from, or how large a cross-section of the homosexual population they knew, counted for little. *Psychoanalytic Review* had no qualms about printing an article in 1943, "Psychological Implications of the Male Homosexual 'Marriage' " by Bernard S. Robbins, that characterized gay unions as "the parasitic boring of one member into the other," grounded as they were in the emotional sadism of the homosexual and so leading inevitably to discord and separation. Dr. Robbins based his presentation on his recent treatment of four homosexual men—a grand total of two couples.

Despite the nastiness inherent in this kind of science, which was really no more than the legitimization of prejudice, the doctors saw themselves as light-years removed from the primitive character of the vice cop, the backwoods preacher, and the town councilman who wanted the full weight of the law exercised against the pervert. The doctors spoke out frequently and even eloquently against the imprisonment of homosexuals for acts committed with other consenting adults. They offered, instead, what they felt was a more intelligent response to the problem: a search for a cure. Freud was horrified when he learned of former pupil Otto Rank's claims in New York in the late 1920s of a high success rate in changing homosexuals into heterosexuals. A few years later, Freudian doubts about the possibility of altering an established sexual orientation had given way in America to the can-do spirit of a people who still believed modern science could accomplish almost anything, or should try. Until a congenital cause was proven, Ervin Wexberg argued in *The Psychology of Sex* (1931), the assumption that homosexuality was a developmental issue made sense; only then could men of goodwill, like Wexberg and his colleagues, roll up their sleeves and do their best.

SPEAKING AT A gathering of the Southern Psychiatric Association in Jacksonville, Florida, in October 1940, Dr. Newdigate Owensby of Atlanta presented some hopeful findings from his recent work on the "correction of homosexuality." The cause was an urgent one, Owensby reminded his listeners. Homosexuality in the United States was increasing with "unparalleled rapidity" and was "no respecter of race, creed, sex, or social milieu." Having seen the diversity of the afflicted population "from farm laborers to financiers," he knew two things for certain: the myth that homosexuals could always be distinguished from the normal population belonged to another era, and no homosexual, at least none he had met, wanted to change. The latter statement did not mean that the sickness approach needed to be rethought (not all people who are ill want to be cured) but suggested to Owensby that the "hanging judges" in his state were on the right track. Social disgrace and legal penalties were the motivation the troubled homosexual needed.

In his lecture in Jacksonville, as in an earlier article in the *Journal of Nervous and Mental Disease*, Owensby recounted his success using the drug metrazol in shock treatments. Now that castration, hypnosis, and other turn-of-the-century procedures were being viewed with skepticism by reputable medical authorities, many professionals were eager to learn about more sophisticated methods. Owensby was proceeding, he wrote, "on the assumption that homosexuality and lesbianism [were] symptoms of an underdeveloped schizophrenia." The metrazol "liberated" the previous fixation of the libido and "the psychosexual energy [became] free once more to flow through the regular physiological channels." One case study he offered involved a nineteen-year-old in Georgia who had been arrested for violating the state's sodomy law and was sentenced to a jail term. The judge promised a pardon "if his perversion was corrected." The patient accepted fifteen shock treatments in all; by the ninth, his homosexual desires were supposedly gone "but treatment was continued until all feminine mannerisms were removed." He was pardoned and had been enjoying "normal sex relations" for the last eighteen months. (Presumably Dr. Owensby occupied an adjoining room for that year and a half.) In fact, Owensby proudly claimed to know of only two relapses out of the fifteen homosexuals he had treated since 1937.

Owensby's cautious optimism wasn't shared by everyone in the field. Others expressed hope that hormone medications might be effective, though as one ghastly experiment after another was tried in that area in the 1940s, the results were no more positive or conclusive. Most psychiatrists still shared the belief that in the realm of sexual maladjustment, traditional therapies were the suitable course of action. The patient needed to be guided through the psychosexual labyrinth of his early family life, his unconscious fears and desires made conscious, his sense of himself rebuilt in the light of his new knowledge and a heightened sense of possibility. He needed to be weaned away from the self-destructive motives governing the choices he made as an adult, most of which he masked from himself. He needed to be separated from the sordid influences of the gay world. An integral part of the odyssey, naturally, was the patient's acceptance of himself as a person suffering from a neurosis that had left him crippled or at least painfully handicapped. Using the more abstruse tools of classic psychoanalysis or the more conscious goal-focused means of psychotherapy, the men and women who saw homosexual patients in the years before World War II, and for some time after, were especially talented at achieving this end. They had less success in leading their maladjusted charges to forsake their crippling if sensually charged condition for the higher plain of heterosexual bliss.

The frustrating aspect of any nonpharmacological treatment of homosexuals was just that: the failure rate was sky-high and, in those rare instances when a gay man would finally evince some sexual interest in a woman, there was no way of knowing how long his newly freed heterosexual drive would last. More remarkable to the professionals was how obstinate their patients could be once the analysis or therapy was under way. Gay resistance was wondrously protean. "But I enjoy the kind of sex I have," some men would tell their analysts, recounting in unabashed detail the pleasures of sucking a big penis or being sucked to orgasm or having one's prostate massaged as another man skillfully entered him. We come from a long line of magnificent people, others insisted, running through the ever-growing famous persons list, from Alexander the Great to Whitman, Wilde, and Proust. (The warriors-to-great-writers litany seems to have been especially galling to many doctors.) Patients complained that no outsider could appreciate the mystique of the "twilight world" or the fun a gay man could have with coded language and role-playing. Our sensitivity and powers of observation have been expanded by virtue of our outcast status, ran another common line. And, men repeatedly asked—in a more legitimate challenge—what do you think would be left of theater and dance, fashion and interior decoration, without us, just as we are? In one commentary after another, the professionals' sense of amazement, defeat, and anger at these strategies is palpable: many gay men don't want to be helped, they glory in their degradation, their resistances are too well established to break down. And so the myth that homosexuality was treatable continued to hold its own in the public sphere, yet any legion of "recovered homosexuals" was mysteriously hard to find.

A true scientist acknowledges a dead end when he comes upon one, but the stakes for American psychoanalysts and psychiatrists were high and, especially in the period just prior to the war, there was much to be lost in the admission that they could not work the wonders that had been claimed for their profession. In implying that they could do what a generation of lawmakers, religious leaders, sociologists, and criminologists had been unable to do—make sense of the chaos of modern sexuality, interpret (if not stem) the tide of dysfunction, deviance, and sexual crime—they were making a perfectly plausible bid to be the new authority figures, the moral guides and social managers, of the "American century."

More specifically, those men and women who brought the ideas of Freud, Horney, Klein, Rado, Bergler, and others into the intellectual mainstream of American life were in the unique position of being able to offer credible support to a gender system that was still reeling from the shock of the 1920s even as it coped with the different repercussions of the 1930s. Massive unemployment and the inability to provide for a family were exacerbating tensions long since set in motion by industrialization and the corporate nature of the workplace (where fewer men could be said to be their own boss or to see the product of their labor) and then aggravated by women's suffrage, the bitter debate over contraception, and more widespread female sexual aggressiveness. Modern life made it difficult for men to know any longer what it meant to be "a man," and not all women were comfortable with the new world in which their roles had shifted, either. In the face of this dilemma, "psychology offered some solace," as Michael Kimmel summarized the situation in *Manhood in America: A Cultural History*. If paychecks, property, and your place at the head of the table meant less and less, the whole notion of traditional manliness based on accomplishment and awe needn't be scrapped; it could be "reconceived as the exterior manifestation of a certain inner sense of oneself. Masculinity could be observed in specific traits and attitudes, specific behaviors and perspectives"—exactly the sort of thing the specialists were trained to evaluate. Kimmel's book offers a trenchant analysis of the all-time classic example: the famous M/F scale created by Stanford University psychologist Lewis Terman and his colleague Catherine Miles and published in *Sex and Personality* (1936). Regularly used by educational counselors for the next two decades, the Terman-Miles test measured degrees of acceptable masculinity and femininity in adolescents based on state-of-the-art techniques ranging from Rorschach ink-blot studies to questions about interests, general knowledge, and reactions to hypothetical situations, all of which (as Kimmel and other contemporary sociologists have shown) are scandalously stereotypical. The girl who knew too much about ships or cars, and the boy who enjoyed his nightly bath or kept a diary, could be watched for future signs of continuing gender-inappropriate traits. It was healthy for a girl to check the box indicating that she aspired to be a librarian or music teacher, for a boy to dream of a career as a soldier or a forest ranger—Rex Stout notwithstanding. With his highly regarded test, Lewis Terman (creator of the equally influential Stanford-Binet IQ test) was joining the ranks of those who maintained that there still was such an entity as a properly nurtured, clearly defined Masculine Male Heterosexual, free from contradictions and conflicting urges, and that weaknesses in the construction of that cherished identity could be quickly spotted and treated. The M/F scale came out of the same frame of mind that shaped the theories of Sandor Rado and Edmund Bergler and guided innumerable private practices across the country.

In effect, for all their differences, American psychoanalysts, psychiatrists, and psychologists were engaged in a common pursuit. They were cementing their power base in a time of dwindling faith in heroic figures by an implicit strategy of some cleverness. The professional in these fields was skilled in diagnosing unseen ills, dysfunctions threatening to all of society. He investigated a territory of mind and culture that more timorous souls ignored. But unlike the revolutionary who gave voice to truths people adamantly did not wish to hear (in the manner of, say, Darwin, Strindberg, Nietzsche, Veblen, Symonds, and Ellis), the psychologist of deviance was telling people *exactly* what they wanted to hear. Men and women of wealth, education, and power weren't countenancing the torture of disturbed souls; they were modern, they weren't the kind of people to spend a Sunday at Bedlam. They wanted the sexually twisted brought back into the fold, shamed but cured. Freud's renegade offspring understood their mission. They would not have been respected and applauded, consulted by lawmakers and fairly remunerated, had they acted otherwise. The true disturber of the peace, Freud himself, could say what he wanted about the great difference between "neurosis" and "inferiority": the Berglers, the Rados, the Termans and their followers knew differently and were prized for saying so. A. A. Brill's reminder in 1913 that many inverts neither needed nor wanted the help of the psychoanalyst was a quaintly liberal sentiment by 1940. The new ideal was not the restlessly questioning Freud of the later years, who argued in 1933 that a "single standard for sexual life for everyone disregards the dissimilarities, whether innate or acquired, in the sexual constitution of human beings," but something more like Bette Davis's pipe-smoking savior in Now, Voyager (1942)—paternal but friendly, omniscient, conventional, and effective.

For the victims of this monumental smugness, the scars could be permanent. "I would never in a million years have told my parents I was a homosexual," one man in Virginia, now approaching eighty, recalled in the 1990s. But, caught in bed with another student in his college dormitory during his freshman year, the situation quickly passed out of his control. From a recent interview: "I had no say about staying in school. Word got around pretty fast. It was a disgrace. I never did find out what became of my friend, but I was told by my father that there was one condition to my returning to college, not the same college obviously, and to remaining in the house for the time being, where I had two younger brothers. I had to see a psychiatrist in Richmond and do whatever he told me. And I had to agree to pay my father back *every single fucking penny* that the psychiatrist cost him." Interestingly, there was no question in anyone's mind in this middle-class family that, even during the middle of the Depression, the psychiatrist wouldn't be worth the money, either in effecting a cure or in containing the problem. The result of two years of therapy for "Allen" was a crushing financial burden and no change in his sexual urges "but a strong feeling that I should be ashamed of myself for what I wanted to do in bed and for my [effeminate] mannerisms."

The mental-health profession in its many guises was not, of course, a monolithic entity. Those who addressed the subject of sexuality ranged from specialists presenting their research in academic journals to populariz-ers whose work was in the hearty spirit of anything-to-make-a-buck. In 1969 Dr. David Reuben's *Everything You Always Wanted to Know About Sex, But Were Afraid to Ask* broke all records in the latter category, making 1930s books like LaForrest Potter's *Strange Loves* or James Segall's *Sex Life in America* look small-time indeed. In so vast a territory, then, it wasn't absolutely impossible to find reasoned judgments. The tragedy was that, in the larger scheme of things, those judgments counted for very little.

In 1931 an American publisher brought out a translation of *The Perver-sion of the Sex Instinct* by Albert Moll, the German physician who had been one of Freud's early sources. Moll's book was a pleasingly strange 1890s tract that took aim at the more extreme charges against homosexu-als while it repeated some of Ulrichs's bizarre generalizations (for example, homosexuals can't whistle). Moll was a bit of a provocateur—he went out of his way to mention "the frequency of pederasty among the Catholic clergy"—and, contrary to his fellow scientists, believed that the recorded past had to count for something in this area. "The history of ancient Greece," Moll wrote, "proves to us that a nation does not endanger its foundations because its people do not hold homosexual love in contempt." An admirable thought (even if scholars today question the exact appli-cability of twentieth-century concepts of "homosexual love" to the prac-tices of earlier civilizations), but by the 1930s it hardly mattered one way or the other: Moll was just another late Victorian, a spokesman from the day of horsehair sofas and gimcrackery.

One of the only contemporary researchers to address the possibility that the anxiety the subject inspired among adults might be linked to a repres-sion of homosexual desire, or discomfort at remembering the pleasure same-sex play had brought in adolescence, was New York psychiatrist Gilbert Hamilton. His 1929 study focused on one hundred male-female couples he had been seeing in his private practice. Fifty-six percent of the men Hamilton interviewed for his book *A Research in Marriage* acknowledged having had homosexual experiences at some time in their lives, 17 percent of them after the age of eighteen. Seventy-five percent of these married men insisted that, even if all considerations of conscience and public opinion were cast aside, they would not be attracted to members of the same sex. Kevin White reads this survey astutely in *The First Sexual Revolution* when he points out that Hamilton's clientele was essentially a professional theater group and so its statistics are less confused than they might seem at first (so many men admitting to homosexual sex but so many disclaiming interest in it); the figures reflect both the "accelerated homo-phobia" of the late 1920s, when pansies became more visible, and an "incipient liberalism" in theater people. What fascinated Dr. Hamilton more than his data, however, was the tone of the response his questions elicited. Men didn't become uncomfortable when asked if they were klepto-maniacs or bigamists. They simply said that they were not and gave the question no further thought. That was never the case with homosexuality, Hamilton observed, and there was apt to be a compelling reason for that level of uneasiness. Hamilton's speculation was just the sort that the psychi-atric establishment had less use for as 1920s openness gave way to 1930s conservatism: "The majority of American adult males probably fear their own homosexual impulses," he wrote, "more than they fear all the other tabooed components of the human reactive equipment taken together."

Hamilton's perspective, which implied some skepticism about the validity of the taboo, put him in a minority. In private practice, a few therapists made an effort to help their patients to deal with their family's rejection, their relationship or job-related difficulties, and the internalized guilt that was often a feature of life in a society that insisted homosexuals were peo-ple of defective upbringing and repugnant habits. One of Joseph Collins's patients, as reported in *The Doctor Looks at Love and Life*, had told him of a psychiatrist he consulted who urged him to "lose [his] shame" of the sexual instincts that came naturally to him and "seek the company of men where perhaps [he] might find love." Hamilton later wrote, not disapprov-ingly, of a woman he had treated for incapacitating depression in the 1930s who was cured after she established a lesbian relationship with her nurse. At the University of Chicago in the early 1940s, Stuart Loomis spoke about his homosexuality to one of his professors, the psychiatrist Mandel Sher-man, who observed that Loomis's own value as a psychologist might even be enhanced by his outsider's viewpoint. But, to judge by the available testimony, the calm clarity and fellow-feeling of these examples were rare.

THE MAIN PROBLEM with a clinical understanding of homosexuality had always been that the pool of subjects from whom the doctors might learn something was small and narrow. Gay men and lesbians who were emotionally and professionally fulfilled had no reason to consult a psychiatrist, and those who chose to—or were forced to—were usually troubled or atypical individuals. (An obscure professor of zoology at Indiana University, Alfred C. Kinsey, was already attempting to redress this imbalance in his own way. By 1941, he noted in an article in the *Journal of Clinical Endocrinology*, he and his team of researchers had already interviewed 1,600 men about their sexual practices, 354 of whom had been "involved in homosexual behavior.")

Not surprisingly, the few firsthand accounts of homosexual experience intended to be read by the medical profession in America were records of disconcerting self-hate and remorse. Claude Hartland's *The Story of a Life* (1901) was privately published in St. Louis "for the consideration of the medical fraternity." A patient of Dr. Charles Hughes, a renowned turn-of-the-century alienist and proponent of surgery to "relieve" the homosexual's sex drive, Hartland narrated a tale—in florid, lachrymose prose—of a sissy childhood, an unhappy adult life, and unending subterfuge. (Despite his negative view of his effeminacy, it is interesting that Hartland seems to have done rather well picking men up on the streets of St. Louis.) Earl Lind's *Autobiography of an Androgyne* was written at about the same time but not published until 1918; it was announced as "for sale only by mail order" and was intended "for doctors." The author depicts himself as a virtual slave to his need for regular oral sex, a compulsion that led to many episodes of abuse at the hands of soldiers and Bowery toughs, and saw himself as a woman trapped in a man's body. Nature's trick had been to create him "*puellam sine vagina.*" Lind had himself castrated in 1901 at the age of twenty-seven, a step that did nothing to ease his "paroxysms of melancholia" and "seasons of anguish."

Self-deprecation in print didn't disappear with the fin de siècle nor was it confined to tortured, pseudonymous writers such as Hartland and Lind. Even as gifted a man as Somerset Maugham at the height of his fame was disturbed by the conviction that he would have been a greater novelist had he not been gay. In one of his few published remarks on the subject (in a 1935 essay on El Greco), he generalized in a vein that seems today appallingly sad, given the light it casts on his own achievements. In a passage much favored over the years by anti-gay psychiatrists and journalists,

Maugham wrote that the homosexual "is emotional, but fantastic. He is vain, loquacious, witty, and theatrical. With his keen insight and quick sensibility he can pierce the depths, but in his innate frivolity he fetches up from them not a priceless jewel but a tinsel ornament. He has small power of invention, but a wonderful gift for delightful embroidery. He has vitality, brilliance, but seldom strength. He stands on the bank, aloof and ironical, and watches the river of life flow on." "Innate frivolity" and a "small power of invention" would hardly seem to apply to the artist who wrote *Cakes and Ale* and *Of Human Bondage*, but that sense of standing on the riverbank while the real business of life—family and children, apparently—passed one by was something many gay men, and many unmarried men and women who aren't homosexual, have had to grapple with.

The pain heard in the words of Hartland, Lind, and Maugham was fuel for the Great Crusade, the mission to redefine life as a matter of proper and improper adjustment, but even when homosexuals wanted to speak up in a less programmatic spirit—to articulate to the "experts" the particularity and texture of their own lived experience—they weren't able to change the script. In 1934, a few individuals in New York were willing to try and approached a group of interested medical professionals. Jan Goldburg, a lesbian journalist and writer of children's travel books, had been collecting case histories of her own since the early 1920s. Thomas Painter, a gay man and a recent graduate of Union Theological Seminary, had embarked on a similar examination of male prostitutes. In Robert Latou Dickinson, a respected gynecologist and leader in the birth-control movement, Goldburg believed she had the right man to bridge the gap between the medical community and the homosexual world.

Early in 1935, the Committee for the Study of Sex Variants was founded by Dickinson "to undertake, support, and promote investigations and scientific research . . . of variations from normal sexual behavior" and to disseminate that information. "Miss Jan Gay" (Jan Goldburg) and Thomas Painter provided volunteers for study, and over the next five years two hundred gay men and lesbians took part in this unusual educational enterprise. Under the direction of Dr. George W. Henry, the procedure was earnest, thorough, and pedestrian. It involved one or more interviews to learn about the subject's family background and personal history, with the emphasis placed heavily on sexual acts—and the completion, some time later, of a lengthy questionnaire. Case studies of forty men and forty women were then selected for use in what became the committee's only publication, *Sex Variants: A Study of Homosexual Patterns*. All of these subjects were given a physical examination, including X rays of the head and pelvis. A third agreed to be photographed nude, with a number of the men providing samples of semen and the women permitting gynecological exams. Everyone took the Terman-Miles M/F test, and a few of the men agreed to try hormone therapy—"on a purely experimental basis," Henry casually noted.

The volunteers brought to George W. Henry, and the friends they in turn enlisted, were a motley group, but they had in common a certain pluck, an uninhibited nature, and an innocent's faith that in telling their stories—and in the more extreme cases, undressing for the camera or sharing their semen—they would be advancing the cause of knowledge and tolerance. Even Henry agreed that it took a great deal of courage to speak as openly as he wanted them to about the details of sexual experience from childhood sex play, masturbation, and incestuous relations to the specifics of their current fantasies, habits, and sex roles. Should anyone have had doubts about the seriousness of the endeavor, though, the roster of names and affiliations would have been daunting: committee members included psychiatrists and psychologists from Yale, Harvard, Johns Hopkins, and several other major universities, as well as Lewis Terman of Stanford and the respected director of the Psychiatric Division of Bellevue Hospital, Karl Bowman. Henry's demeanor, implying that he was there to learn, not to judge, was sufficiently cool to provoke one interviewee to explode in anger at his lack of any response to the intimate confessions he was listening to.

George W. Henry's impassivity was purely for show. The man was loaded with opinions. When *Sex Variants* was published by the medical books division of Harper & Bros. in 1941 in a two-volume edition with numerous appendices (pages of nude photographs, the M/F test scores, an essay on "the gynecology of homosexuality," an essay on gay argot), the prejudices of its author were readily apparent. First, there was his definition in the negative: "The sexual variant," Henry wrote, "is a person who has failed to achieve and maintain adult heterosexual modes of sexual expression." After hundreds of hours of listening to dozens of men and women describe their passion for members of their own sex, Henry was still conceiving homosexuality as fear and flight, rather than desire and difference. Other views were similarly archaic. Society had a vested interest in protecting itself, and the classification of sex variants was the most expeditious way to do that. It was doubtful that society would ever tolerate complete openness in this area, Henry believed, and homosexuals would be well advised to accept that premise.

Numerous interviewees had made statements indicating that they were at peace with their sexual orientation: "I don't want to be normal" (Gene S.); "Homosexuality is natural to me" (Walter R.); "Homosexuality is my normal" (Eric D.). A remarkable number of the lesbians Henry met saw their sexuality as a positive good in their lives, the reason they had been able to achieve the independence or career goals they had always wanted. These personal truths were related without comment, as if to say, what could one expect from people so psychologically damaged? Recriminations and anxiety often elicited Henry's approval throughout the text: "With much justification Nathan regards himself as a grotesque"; "Reginald correctly visualized his future—it looks empty"; "When [Moses' wife] leaves him, he will have no other recourse than that of self-destruction." Like any good American Freudian, Henry knew the goals healthy people should aspire to and he applauded those same realizations in the people he studied ("Michael is aware that many homosexuals are dependent on physical charm in the gratification of their desires and that there is no adequate substitute for the satisfaction derived from a home with children"). Those who did not connect in some way to the world of Henry's values were slightly contemptible. The remarks about Walter R. (who was actually Caska Bonds, a flamboyant Harlem personality) have a racist quality, and the summary of Rudolph von H.—an aging, nearly blind transvestite and father of three—is openly derisive. The narrative of Howard N. suggested to the doctor that his quest was "pathetic and at times desperate." Thomas Painter (Will G.) found himself described in the text as frustrated, bitter, and defiant.

Despite its paucity of insights about the etiology, development, or treatment of homosexuality, and the wildly random nature of its subject pool, *Sex Variants* wasn't dismissed by the profession. Just how noteworthy an occurrence it was in the 1930s for homosexuals to be heard in even a weak approximation of their own voices is illustrated by Ashley Montagu's review of the book in *Psychiatry*. Montagu, who had no patience for anti-gay bigotry, described *Sex Variants* as an important contribution to the field and praised Henry especially for having "kept his own views entirely out of the picture." Fifty years after its publication, *Sex Variants* reveals to us something quite different—an intellectual and emotional rigidity in its author and medical sponsors that is a source of marvel. How far sexology had declined from its origins with Havelock Ellis, who (while no less unscientific, haphazard, and impressionistic than the Bergler-Terman-Henry camp) was at least a man who was "full, eager, open-minded" in the view of John Addington Symonds, a man who knew homosexuals, an individualist who was excited by the example of Hardy and Ibsen. So, too, the tentative quality of Freud on the subject of homosexuals and the honest curiosity of Moll were nowhere to be found in Dr. Henry's tome. The appendices, with their pelvic measurement charts and drawings of erectile areolae, might have been borrowed from the racial science programs being touted in Berlin.

The reaction to *Sex Variants* from the gay men and lesbians who had trusted their interviewer to deal fairly and sensitively with their life stories was sharply negative. They felt belittled and betrayed—and properly indignant about a process that had reduced them to caricatures in the name of science. When Alfred Kinsey met some of them later in the 1940s, "it took extra tact and persuasion," he told a colleague, to get them to participate in his own more searching, less judgmental project. Degraded by George Henry, they were understandably wary of repeating the experience.

Is it a coincidence that the most forceful, humane, and consistent spokesman for a view of the profession that transcended *Sex Variants*, Bergler's manias, and Owensby's "cures" was a gay psychiatrist? Respected, influential, humorous, sometimes unpredictable and abrasive, Harry Stack Sullivan was in a difficult position in the 1930s. As the founder of the interpersonal theory of psychiatry, he was an important player in the reevaluation of Freudian doctrine—and, some people felt, the key player. An eager audience attended to his thoughtful criticism of the "childhood sexuality" model as a concept that was too rigid with its implication that aspects of personality were fixed in one's earliest years and forever dominated by the shadow of the original parent-child bond. The "fields" of interaction Sullivan lectured about at the Washington School of Psychiatry, his own institution, posited a view of identity that emphasized flux, growth, needs that changed after childhood, and self-creation wrought by myriad factors, particularly the sexual struggles of early adolescence. About his colleagues' fascination with lobotomies, metrazol, and electric shock, he was skeptical and sometimes indignant. Sullivan's bachelorhood and his quiet life in suburban Bethesda with an adopted "son" and amanuensis twenty years his junior prompted gossip about his own sexuality. "It was known but not openly discussed," psychiatrist Bertram Schaffner remembered. "The feeling was, he doesn't talk about it, we don't know for certain, and it isn't relevant to his ideas." Accordingly, Sullivan had to tread carefully when addressing the topic of homosexuality in his work and, as a founding editor of *Psychiatry*, he was forced to watch his coeditors select for publication articles he no doubt found repugnant.

In discreet ways, Sullivan attempted to steer his students and colleagues back to the one Freudian model he did believe in, in which sexuality was seen as more than a matter of the normal/biologically natural versus the abnormal/biologically unnatural. "To talk about homosexuality being a problem really means as much as to talk about humanity being a problem," he noted in one of his lectures in the 1940s. It was also crucial, he felt, for the psychiatrist to be anthropologically minded, to be alert to cultural differences and to the relativity of values that only seemed fixed and universal. "In this culture," he told his students, "the ultimate test of whether you can get on or not is whether you can do something satisfactory with your genitals or somebody else's genitals without undue anxiety and loss of self-esteem." A subtly broad statement on all fronts, despite the characteristically jocular tone; that is, other cultures may have better gauges of success than "genital activity," so let us not think that ours necessarily represents the wisdom of nature; perhaps many people make use of their genitals in ways displeasing to the majority, but suffer no anxiety or loss of self-esteem in doing so; anxiety and self-esteem are influenced by society, but ultimately determined by the individual. Not surprisingly, Sullivan was a friend and sympathetic reader of Margaret Mead and Ruth Benedict.

Perhaps as important as any oblique efforts to educate his charges to be large-minded about the homosexuals they might treat in their future practices was Sullivan's insistence that the psychiatrist's omniscient affect—perhaps even his actual conception of himself in that hallowed light—was injurious to the patient and detrimental to the profession. The process should be thought of as another field of interaction, a creative encounter, more than a treatment. "Attend closely to the ways in which you manifest prejudices and preconceptions about what is 'right' and important in understanding and influencing other people," he liked to tell his students at the Washington School of Psychiatry. The psychiatrist who was sure he had all the answers, who was convinced that he knew more than his patient about life and happiness and so existed on a plane far removed from the patient's distress, was apt to do more harm than good. With a position of national importance to consider, Sullivan had to let it go at that. He understood the tide of opinion and the power of homophobia. He knew that the best that could be done under the circumstances was limited to reminders of what should have been obvious from the start.

III. An Emergent Minority

8

On the Homefront

I was arrested last night. I am in the barracks under guard . . . Mother of God! I don't know what to do or say . . . I destroyed all my letters and flushed my address book down the latrine, so no one else needs worry . . . don't write.

> —An Army friend writing to
> Sgt. Jon H—— at Camp Polk,
> Louisiana, 2 November 1944

Gawd, the place is mad. Drink, eats, song, apartments, cars, girls, boys, boy-girls, girl-boys, bitch, butch—heavenly days, McGee!

> —Another friend writing to Sgt. Jon H——
> describing a New York City furlough,
> 11 November 1944

Nothing did so much to advance the new model of homosexuality as an illness requiring treatment, and "the homosexual" as a supposedly identifiable, even self-proclaimed type, as America's entry into the war. "If psychiatry had been the Cinderella of medicine in World War I, ignored by her sister specialties," as William Menninger phrased it, "she was the queen of the ball in the early 1940s." Unlikely as such a line of questioning would have been during the mobilization twenty-four years earlier, the induction process this time involved an effort, albeit a crude one, to determine each man's sexual nature with an eye to labeling and weeding out those with undesirable histories and tendencies. "Deciding in advance how I was going to answer 'that question' caused more soul-searching than I can describe," one 1942 draftee commented. "But you knew it was part of the deal."

The dilemma for gay men in the wake of Pearl Harbor was acute. Most wanted to serve their country; participation in the war effort was both an appealing moral imperative, given the brutal nature of the enemy, and a chance to confirm to oneself that being gay wasn't a bar to meaningful action. For once, a gay man could be just like all the other guys. "A lot of us at that time had to prove our manhood," George Buse said in the documentary *Before Stonewall*, explaining his decision to join the Marines and, in his own mind, flout the stereotype of weakness and effeminacy. The alternative—announcing a sexual preference—involved a measure of public shame, and the 4-F deferment that resulted from that admission could be hard to explain back home in the absence of any obvious physical disabilities.

Yet to take a place in the ranks could be done only by lying, outright or implicitly, and the consequences of being discovered in that lie were worse than anything the deferment might entail. "We all knew what happened to queers caught doing something once they were in," a gay Coast Guard veteran remarked. "It was on everybody's mind, I'm sure." Thus the induction process in the early 1940s presented hundreds of thousands of young American homosexuals with the starkest reminder of society's growing interest in seeing its citizens, especially men, declare themselves as belonging to one group or another.

Most gay men went into the military assuming they would have to make use of all the skills at dissembling they had acquired and honed through childhood and adolescence. For some, it was a pleasant surprise to come upon a more live-and-let-live atmosphere, particularly in combat zones, than they had expected. "Ask anyone who served in World War II in any branch of the service," Dan Murphy of the Florida Gay Veterans maintained, "and they will tell you they knew someone who was gay then and it didn't bother them. Getting caught [in a homosexual sex act] was the problem, but if you were just known to be gay and did your job well and acted like a real sailor, you were left alone." Allan Bérubé's definitive study of the subject, *Coming Out Under Fire*, recounts numerous episodes of soldiers and sailors finding the time and the privacy for intimate moments, of officers looking the other way, of men who harbored suspicions about a comrade but ultimately respected his contributions to the unit and let him be. In contrast, Bob Kohler, a founder of the Gay Liberation Front in 1969 and still in his teens when he was a sailor based in San Francisco at the end of the war, was among those more impressed by the need for extreme caution. "I met my first gay friends in the war and, yes, there was a great deal going on," Kohler agreed, "but you didn't really come out. Or, let's say you came out, but you stayed in at the same time. The homophobia was just taken for granted, and you had to be very careful who you opened up to. On leave in San Francisco, that was one thing, but when you got back on ship, that was another. You kept it quiet. It was just too dangerous."

Individual experiences varied enormously, then, but one fact that was clear from the start was that the induction process itself wasn't a serious obstacle to anyone desperate to serve. Many of the examiners were military personnel who had been put through a slapdash three-month training program in the elements of psychiatry—the "90-day wonders," as they were known—and hadn't a clue how to detect sexual deviance in a man who looked pretty much like his peers. In 1940 Harry Stack Sullivan and several colleagues made progress in convincing the War Department that a more systematic, truly professional mental-health screening process, with limited attention to sexual issues, would be needed if the government wanted to avoid, in the coming conflict, the billion-dollar cost of treating the psychological casualties that the short-term American involvement in World War I had wrought. But Selective Service Director Lewis Hershey, always antagonistic to psychiatry, put a stop to any ambitious plans in that area by the end of 1941. So the questions directed at inductees tended to be juvenile or transparent (Do you date girls? Have you ever had sex with a man? Do you like to take a shower or a bath?) and, as the need to fill quotas grew, draft boards were willing to turn a blind eye to almost anyone who was willing to put up the right front for the three minutes or less that the standard interview took. Scarcely less helpful was the 1942 revised regulation listing a "patulous rectum" as one of the sure signs of the pervert a doctor could look for, along with physical delicacy and an effeminate manner, a notion based on the quaint assumption that all male homosexuals regularly assumed a passive role in anal intercourse. Indeed, to some gay draftees, the whole process was a charade that simply served to underscore the government's hypocrisy on the subject—pretending that sexual orientation mattered by asking about it and threatening a reprisal in the form of an undesirable deferment, but quietly acknowledging that no one cared in a time of crisis.

The figures support that impression: almost eighteen million men were examined at 6,400 draft boards and 108 induction centers around the country between 1941 and 1945, but not quite 5,000 were rejected on the grounds of homosexuality. If Kinsey's estimate of 4 percent of the population as "exclusively homosexual" is accepted, over 700,000 of those men were gay. If his figure of 10 percent as having had significant homosexual experience is true, then the number the military would have wanted to exclude by its own guidelines would be closer to 1.8 million.

Some veterans recall the psychiatrists they faced at the time as dour, judgmental professionals, but on occasion these men could be reassuring and even solicitous. At the induction center in Camden, New Jersey, Donald Vining found to his great relief that his declaration of his sexual preference was accepted "without shock and without condescension." Dr. Bertram Schaffner, gay himself, did his best to determine whether the gay men before him really wanted to serve and could handle military life, and processed their papers accordingly. George Flemister, a native of Tennessee, was a particularly innocent, pretty twenty-one-year-old when he reported for his physical on Governors Island not long after Pearl Harbor. Despite a pleasant sexual initiation two years earlier while visiting New York to see the 1939 World's Fair (the shower room at the Sloane House YMCA was the happy setting) and a job at Macy's—"Oh, in 1940, such a gay place to work!"—George had no clear sense of himself as "a homosexual," as a part of a discrete group. The examining psychiatrist, however, quickly sized up the thin, high-strung young man as a plausible 4-F and gently told him that it would be better for everyone concerned if George returned to his job at the store in Manhattan. It was a suggestion George resisted with the unassailable logic that, while he might indeed be frail, he could take a bullet for his country as well as the next man. The psychiatrist tried to get closer to his point by looking meaningfully at George and asking him who he liked better, girls or boys? "Why, I love everybody!" George exclaimed. After a few more fruitless questions, the psychiatrist disappeared for several minutes and returned with a colleague. They stared at George, sitting there in his underwear. "Now, isn't he as attractive as I said he was?" the original examiner asked his friend. Fifty years later, George was still unclear as to whether he had been paid a surprise compliment by two gay psychiatrists or been "set up" to react to their comment, affirming his sexuality one way or another. As it turned out, George was eventually steered into accepting his deferment and took the ferry back to Manhattan. Before his release, the psychiatrist saw to it that he was spared the indignity of being corralled with the raucous queens who had been segregated from the rest of the inductees.

Other men, even some as obviously gay as George Flemister, looked upon a 4-F as a stigma that would be impossible to live with. "I truthfully wasn't sure about going in," Adam Wright remembered, "but I couldn't figure out how I would explain it to my father, how it would affect my chances of getting a good job, the whole bit. So I lied and said I was engaged. I'm positive [the psychiatrist] didn't believe me for a minute, but the right answer to the question was all that mattered. He just nodded and smiled. If you could walk on two legs, you had blood flowing, you were in." (Wright later served aboard an LST in the Pacific.) Many men who accepted their homosexuality as a legitimate reason to stay home did in fact find themselves newly outed in their communities and now more closely associated with, or thrown into, a distinct subculture of their own kind. At best, an able-bodied gay man out of uniform was the object of unpleasant suspicions.

ONCE IN THE service, a gay serviceman's lot in life was determined by myriad factors, not the least of which was luck. But self-image, masculine social skills, and experiences before the war (sexual and otherwise) played a part. For a young man who knew his desires but didn't have the vocabulary or even a rudimentary concept of homosexuality, the first weeks of military life were apt to be unnerving. "It was a shock to me from the minute I got on the troop train to San Diego," Jerry Bowen of Texas remembered, "a rude shock." Raised as a self-described "floppy-eared country boy" in a small town near Odessa, Bowen had "messed around" with other boys since the onset of puberty. "But they didn't have a word for it then, where I came from," he explained. There weren't any strange men in town branded as "queer," or labels that meant anything, or clues pointing to a whole subculture in distant Houston or Santa Fe. But on the train west in 1943, thrown in with rough young men from the bigger cities, Bowen heard vivid, frightening stories about "cocksuckers" back home who had the life knocked out of them by the boastful recruits. He was also informed that homosexuals had an extra hole in the back of their mouths where they took their partner's penis, a fact that momentarily reassured the seventeen-year-old Bowen that he couldn't have anything in common with the degenerates who got beat up.

Bowen's arrival at the naval training base in California brought more revelations about sex as well as some mixed messages about allowable sexual conduct. On the one hand, there were the rumors of kaya parties, so called because of the brand name of the stiff brushes the sailors were given to clean their clothes: sex offenders were stripped and scrubbed by their heterosexual bunkmates until they bled, before being turned over to their commanding officers for arrest. And then there were the detentions themselves; it was Bowen's bad luck to be assigned to guard a group of ostentatious gay men "who had been caught doing something or other" and were awaiting discharge or court-martial. "It was upsetting. They were very nelly and they had nothing left to lose. They were offering to give blowjobs to the guards. I was becoming more aware of my own feelings, but I didn't connect—I certainly didn't want to connect—to the guys I was guarding." Even more complicating was the way some of the better-endowed straight men, often (it seemed to Bowen) the rural southern boys, carried on off-duty, spending an inordinate amount of time in the shower, strutting around the barracks nude, making it clear that they liked being looked at, but—should they be propositioned—were ready "to kill a queer for Christ," as one of Bowen's Baptist fellow sailors put it.

Only when he was stationed in Alaska later in the war did Bowen, then nineteen, have his first prolonged sensuous encounter with another adult. That experience also carried a weighty lesson: in order to preserve his view of himself as "not a queer," a man will devise and enforce carefully set limits on his homoerotic activity. Bowen's strapping partner, attractive to women and clearly interested in the opposite sex himself, liked to kiss and hold hands on long romantic walks in the dark. The one time Bowen talked him into something more—anal sex—was the last time they were together as a couple. Even as the active party in the enterprise, Bowen's friend wasn't prepared for the implications of that level of intimacy. ("I overstepped," Bowen concluded.) Not until he became friendly with a gay black man in his outfit, an unexpected development for a man from southwest Texas in 1945, did Jerry Bowen begin to see homosexuality as having a social and emotional as well as a sexual dimension.

At the other end of this vast spectrum, a man like Bob Basker, who was twenty-three when he enlisted in 1941, had long since made a successful life for himself as a gay man. While stationed in England, he sought out kindred spirits (who seemed to him "very uptight" in comparison to their American counterparts) and had a long, tumultuous relationship with an older Belgian man when his unit was moved to Antwerp. With his Army buddies, he maintained, he was never singled out as queer. "Sex was on an individual basis, in the shower room, in different ways. There were a few gay ones among them, but most of them were straight but willing to play. How it worked was you'd get in the shower, around one o'clock in the morning after you'd been out on the town, taking a shower before you went to bed. My technique was to say to the guy next to me, 'Hey, would you do me a favor and soap my back?' And the guy would soap my back and I'd say, 'Thanks,' and then I'd say, 'Here, let me do your back.' I wouldn't ask, I'd just assume, and start to soap his back. If he didn't flinch, I'd start soaping his chest, and if he didn't flinch then, I'd start soaping his stomach. Then I would do one leg, then the other, then start soaping his balls, then maybe his ass. Generally, by this time, they'd have a hard-on. If they flinched anywhere along the line, they'd say 'Thanks,' and move away. Only one time did someone come to me who must have heard something from someone else and approached me to have sex. Other than that, I never had any problems."

The fact that normally heterosexual males were also capable of enjoying sex with men wasn't news to most gay people. The psychiatrists liked the term "situational homosexuality," and the military leadership had always known what resulted in the barracks or in the field from a prolonged lack of female contact. The draconian treatment of sodomists was meant to be a deterrent, and the distribution of condoms was a way of telling the men that, despite the warnings about "Victory girls," everyone expected them to sleep with prostitutes or at least have a frisky date while on leave. But to the gay servicemen who did go to bed with their straight comrades, or play in the shower or embrace in the dark, the message conveyed by these experiences went beyond the limits set by a tidy concept like situational homosexuality with its air of "making do," of a substitute gratification. They often intuited something more profound, about the human capacity for emotional and erotic expression that transcended customary boundaries or definitions. In effect, if men who loved women and lived by society's codes could thrill to the touch of other men, whatever the circumstances, such desires couldn't be all that strange, repellent, or immoral.

But much more important than seeing their straight buddies open themselves to homoerotic feelings, gay men in World War II—and lesbians in equal measure—were heartened by a new sense of how large and varied their numbers were. Careful as they had to be not to expose themselves to the wrong people, the right people always found a way of recognizing one another. The young man from a small town defeated by the fear that he was "the only one," the member of a clique of gay friends who assumed they constituted a minuscule, freakish minority, the gay man from New York, Chicago, or Los Angeles who had come to think that all homosexuals were urban-based and identical in style and family history—for all these people, the war brought revelations about the size, heritage, and diversity of one of America's least talked-about minorities.

"None of it was the way I had been told it was," a chaplain's assistant from Richmond said. "I was brought up by my family, who knew about me, and even by my older gay friends to think that I was part of this very small, very unfortunate . . . odd, chi-chi group. I suppose that's the way it looked in Virginia." During training at Camp Gordon in Georgia and later with the Army of Occupation in Japan, he acquired a radically different perspective. If it is true that approximately one million men who self-identified as gay served in World War II, they necessarily filled every conceivable role—infantryman in the trenches, gunner on deck, stenographer, pilot, medic, mechanic, instructor, quartermaster—held every rank, and came from every walk of life. Chuck Rowland was amazed to discover that most of the officers running the induction station at Fort Snelling where he worked were familiar faces from the gay bars of Minneapolis-St. Paul. Alan Phelps was thrilled to come upon a much-admired, heavily decorated lieutenant from his company at the bar of the Royal Hawaiian Hotel in Honolulu ("a good pickup spot," he noted), obviously infatuated with the man he was drinking with and whom he later learned to be the officer's longtime lover. Luis Rabell's life as a gay man in northern New Mexico had been confined to anonymous, furtive encounters before the war; that changed after a lengthy, affectionate affair with a Navy doctor who insisted on taking him to a movie or a good restaurant before or after their trysts. The notion of two men "dating" was completely new to Rabell.

On Guam, Ensign David L. Leavitt and his newfound gay buddies constituted a large enough group to establish their own beach. Purple Beach Number 2 was on a remote part of the island; the only men who made their way there through the jungle were "in the life" or, at the very least, friendly and in the know. Seaman David Bowling slept for the first time with another man at a hotel while on leave in Washington, D.C., and was struck by the sailor's tenderness and solicitude the next morning as he explained to Bowling that he was probably going to torment himself later about their night of passion. "You're going to try to rationalize what you've done," he told Bowling, and urged him instead to accept it and think no more about it. In a 1943 letter to a friend in Louisiana, a sergeant at Camp Roberts in California described with delight a bus ride he had taken on a recent furlough: he had sensed "in the very black dim-out area that hands were rather busy," and when the bus arrived in Santa Barbara and the lights suddenly came on, "there was a very touching scene with a younger sailor asleep with his head on the big one's shoulder and the big one had the most terrific hard-on, which his navy blues did nothing to hide." The sergeant added that "they practically had to drag me off the bus."

Such awakenings went beyond sex, which in every instance was affected by the danger of discovery. Friendships were formed that lasted decades beyond the war. Lovers who accepted the imminence of parting and wanted to make the most of what time they had together found that a midnight walk on a deserted beach, arm in arm, was the height of pleasure. Younger gay men were initiated into the argot, the folklore, and the rich variety of the gay life by older men, in this case thirty or thirty-five. The sense of isolation, of spiritual aloneness, had always been the big problem. "Finding out that while I was dealing with everything I had to deal with growing up, that other guys were going through the same thing in Oregon or Connecticut or wherever the hell they lived, made a huge difference," one sailor from Illinois remembered. For many, this newly acquired view of the world prompted thoughts about a different kind of future. Tales of the romance, sex, relative freedom, and conviviality to be found on the two coasts or in larger cities could make going back to a hometown look like a foolish retreat.

There was also the matter of capability, toughness, and commitment. Whether the label of "sissy" had been applied to them or not, many gay men had grown up troubled by the thought that their different sexual desires necessarily implied other, more consequential differences from their peers. Were they, at heart, as "manly" as their straight comrades? Could they be as rugged, tenacious, and stoical? Four years of war, from the challenges of boot camp to the trial by fire of combat, answered those questions. Not only did gay servicemen acquit themselves honorably in the jungles of Guadalcanal and on the beaches of Normandy, but they bore as heroically as anyone else the psychological toll that constant uncertainty, loss of individuality, and the omnipresence of death necessarily entail. At times they were forced to endure a kind of pain never asked or expected of heterosexual servicemen. The grief a straight man could openly express at the loss of his spouse, or even the emotional support he could count on in coping with his separation from his wife, fiancée, or girlfriend, was seldom a possibility for the gay man who felt lonely or who had just learned that his lover was a casualty of war. Far from seeing themselves as easily traumatized or unable to carry their weight, the generation of gay men who served in World War II had an experience denied to the next generation. They *knew* that their capacity to survive and function—and, for some, to excel—was in no way impaired by their sexual life. On the contrary, their position in a society that disapproved of their desires and tormented or ostracized them had on occasion prepared them for the struggle and the sacrifice.

The parallel lessons of these years, however, were just as distressing as the gay camaraderie and sense of accomplishment were sustaining. Estimates are that nine thousand servicemen and women were discharged during the war on the basis of their sexual orientation, and only gradually and in limited instances had liberal members of the medical profession been able to convince skeptics that the situation was more complex than the hardliners pretended it was. The randomness of anti-gay harassment in civilian life or in prewar days was replaced by a much more nervous approach, casting a wider net based on the fear that gay men would weaken the fighting capacity of any group to which they were attached.

If a serviceman was caught in flagrante delicto, on base or off, his fate was apt to be determined by the temperament of the officer in charge. At Fort Meade in Maryland early in the war, one young soldier had acquired a fairly outlandish reputation. After dark, the man was reputedly "doing" everyone in the barracks, the captain complained to one of his staff sergeants, Arthur Maule. Rather than have the offender arrested, the captain called him into his office for a frank, fatherly conversation in the best Judge Hardy vein. Couldn't he just control his urges until he was on leave, the boy was asked—make some effort to be patient and discreet, for his own good? The captain knew full well there were other men under his command who were "that way," he explained, but they had the good sense to wait until they got into Baltimore or Washington for the weekend where they were less likely to be noticed. (This was indeed what Sergeant Maule was doing.) But the young man would have none of it; one hand on his hip, eyebrows raised, he shot back at the captain, "Sir, let me put it this way. If you were in a harem of beautiful women, what would you do?" A quiet discharge was arranged.

While his understanding captain at Fort Meade was hardly typical, Arthur Maule had noticed in his five years in the Army from early 1941 through late 1945 that discretion and a straight affect covered for a multitude of sins. Shipped overseas after Pearl Habor, he learned that being gay under General MacArthur in New Caledonia didn't have to mean much. Two sergeants who had been caught in the act were simply transferred without much ado to different islands. With the expanding Japanese offensive on their minds, no one in the unit seemed particularly shocked. What did constitute an intolerable violation of the military order, however, was sex across the ranks. When an officer of Maule's acquaintance was caught in bed with an enlisted man, both were arrested, publicly humiliated, and ultimately sent home with less than honorable discharges.

Most officers, like most enlisted men, were firmly of the opinion that homosexuals had no place in the military—notwithstanding the obvious fact that most of them served effectively, even in the most stressful combat situations. A strong antipathy was felt toward the new leniency, such as it was, that the psychiatrists and some War Department personnel had been pushing. A no-nonsense interrogation, a court-martial, and imprisonment seemed to them an appropriate response to what the laws in most states still referred to as a heinous "crime against nature." Anything less, the opponents of change argued, would encourage shirkers to declare themselves homosexual to avoid the burdens and risks of service. But by the end of 1942, the number of court-martials had become a costly drain on time and manpower, at least in the view of Army Chief of Staff George C. Marshall, and the pressure was on to make use of the alternatives. The next January, Secretary of War Henry Stimson altered his belligerent 1941 "Sodomists" directive, which had condemned the lenient suggestion that homosexuals be discharged without trial, observing that the time had come to pay heed to the medical approach. Secretary of the Navy Frank Knox had already suggested a similar rethinking of the old guidelines to his officers. Henceforth, the "blue discharge," known by the color of the paper it was printed on, would become a more common end of the line for most gay men and women drummed out of the military, linking them with alcoholics, drug addicts, social misfits, and other Section Eights.

The growing influence of the psychiatric community was a mixed blessing for men in uniform. Probably nothing was worse than a lengthy sentence in the hell of Fort Leavenworth or Portsmouth Naval Prison, and so the 1943 directives to allow more gays to be hospitalized and later discharged was a step forward. But a different set of problems emerged that went to the heart of the dilemma of being gay in midcentury America. First, the gradual acceptance of a new method of dealing with homosexuality meant a new understanding of the terms in which it would be couched. The act of sodomy or the demeanor of a fairy was no longer the only focus of attention, but shared the spotlight with the murkier matter of tendencies and suspiciously homosocial rather than strictly homosexual conduct. Servicemen who might have been left alone in earlier days because they hadn't actually been arrested for having sex with another man were now fair game. In this sense, the scientists were implying that the War Department had been too narrow in its approach in the past; it wasn't only those men who indulged in homosexual practices who posed a threat, but those who were homosexual in their outlook and nature. "Latency" was beyond detection for the untrained, but here the astute professional could lead the way.

For those unlucky men caught in the showers or in bed, or implicated by an arrested friend or an incriminating letter, who were then placed in hospitals for observation while their fate was being decided in this climate of conflicting beliefs, everything hinged on the sophistication and compassion of the doctors in charge of their ward. Those were qualities in short supply. "You got used to being patronized after a while," one veteran who was given a blue discharge said of his months under study. Homosexual soldiers and sailors awaiting termination routinely became the objects of belittling clinical studies, the most ridiculous of which was probably the tongue depressor test administered to over one thousand patients by Dr. Nicolai Gioscia to gauge a man's gag reflex to determine whether he was a practiced fellator or merely a malingerer pretending to be homosexual. In a few instances, veterans reported that the psychiatrists they met while in the hospital appeared sympathetic to their plight and intimated that they believed an honorable medical discharge was called for. More objective researchers, confronted for once with a true cross-section of the population (in contrast to the disturbed men they saw in private practice in civilian life), began to note the ways in which homosexuals did not differ significantly from the mentally healthy heterosexual population.

No matter what the psychiatrists had to say, the military knew how to get its own way in the long run. The periodic witch-hunts, like the one in New Orleans in 1944 that purged forty-seven officers and enlisted men from the Army and the Navy or the ruthless investigation of lesbian activity at Fort Oglethorpe the same year, terrified gay servicemen and women who heard about it. And that was how the military wanted it. Fear was an important tool. So, too, was entrapment. Not all gay soldiers or sailors could be counted on to be in the wrong place at the wrong time. The ONI, or Office of Naval Intelligence, was well-known for its use of spectacularly built young Marines to do the work of luring susceptible men into compromising situations. (At the time the Marine Corps was a part of the Navy, just as the Air Corps was a part of the Army.) They would turn up not only in the barracks or in a secluded area of the base, but in the off-base apartments and boardinghouses where officers lived, arriving to introduce themselves as friends of a friend, make idle conversation, drop hints about how sexually frustrated they were, and wait for an advance to be made. A visit from the MPs would follow a short time later.

The most heartrending parts of Bérubé's *Coming Out Under Fire* and Arthur Dong's film of the same title deal with the "queer stockades," the detention areas where gay men were housed while awaiting discharge or transport home. Every effort was made to break the spirits of the men, kept behind barbed wire and treated with considerably less respect than German prisoners of war. Taunted, paraded as freaks before other servicemen, and sometimes sexually abused by their guards, they survived in an atmosphere of ritualized humiliation. New Caledonia, where Arthur Maule felt safe in the early weeks of the war, was the site of one of the principal queer stockades, and even MacArthur's staff was allegedly subject to an investigation and a purge.

The viciousness of the punishment, and being brought before their commanding officers and told to name names, was often a shock because it contrasted so completely to the loose style to which those men had grown accustomed. Drafted in December 1942, Marvin Liebman was first stationed in Fresno and took his furloughs in Los Angeles where he watched the nighttime crowds of sailors and soldiers on Hollywood Boulevard cruising for men. Aboard the SS *General Meigs* bound for Naples, he found the area of the upper deck where the gay men congregated during the blackout, laughing and gossiping or crawling into the far corners for "sexual encounters that were far less secretive than anything I expected." A circle of tight buddies evolved, all fans of Dorothy Parker, who after reassignment stayed in touch by mail. Liebman and his best friend began their letters with the endearment "Darling" and always signed off with a campy line from a Parker story.

Nothing seemed more innocent to Liebman, whose sex had been restricted to a few quiet encounters, but those giddy letters precipitated a nightmare that ended with his blue discharge. One day Captain Ripley, "a short, fat, and very red-faced Texan," had the unsuspecting private brought to squadron headquarters outside Cairo where he confronted him with his intercepted mail and demanded to know, in front of ten or fifteen men working in the office, if he sucked cock "like all those other New York Jew faggots." Ripley proceeded to torment Liebman every day he remained under his command by having him drill alone in the desert heat in front of the entire squadron while he barked orders at the "New York Jew faggot," all to the great amusement of the onlookers. "I obeyed his orders," Liebman wrote in his autobiography, *Coming Out Conservative*, "and with each step I lost more of my self-worth. . . . I became a pariah, bitterly lonely and desperately unhappy." The Catholic chaplain he turned to in his pain spoke only about the gravity of Liebman's mortal sin. A psychiatrist finally arranged for his discharge, and he was sent home like a convict under guard.

It was never enough just to acknowledge that a crime had been committed or a standard violated, with a penalty to be paid for the wrongdoing. That mode was suitable for a host of other offenses, but for men who had had sex with other men, the military tended toward more vehement expressions of disdain. *Gay men had to be made to squirm.* John Hall told interviewer Keith Vach in the 1980s about his discharge, brought about by the actions of an alcoholic sergeant who wanted his sexual favors. Hall, not the sergeant, ended up before a panel of officers and a doctor, who fired embarrassing questions at him in front of a female stenographer and badgered him until he let loose with a furious torrent of self-deprecation. That, Hall felt, was exactly what his interrogators were waiting for.

The feeling of betrayal that afflicted men in Hall and Liebman's situation—the sense that they had served their country and the Allied cause in good faith only to be treated in an unspeakable fashion—was bad enough. But the feeling of anger toward other gay men was a reaction with potentially more damaging effects. "I was turned in by someone who gave a list of names, a gay guy I had never even had sex with," recalled a midshipman who fought his blue discharge throughout the 1940s. "Can I be sure I'd have been some kind of hero under the gun? No, but that didn't do anything to make me feel less like I'd been royally screwed. I thought I'll never trust the government again, and I'll never trust another fucking queer." The conviction that gay men weren't to be relied on in a tight spot was a specter that haunted him for decades. Other men were caught in the bind of asking over and over again, "Why me? Why not someone else?" Usually that "someone else" was a more flamboyant type, a queen who "deserved" to get hauled before a roomful of intelligence officers or a hospital disquisition board but never did. The war had also managed to widen the gap between masculine homosexuals and unrepentant fairies. Loren Wahl accurately touched on that long-standing prejudice in his war novel *The Invisible Glass* (1950). Watching two soldiers camp it up at a gay bar in Italy, a tech sergeant shares his annoyance with Lieutenant LaCava, the hero of the book: "They're so damn nellie, those two. Don't give a hoot who sees them. They're the kind who make it so rough on the rest of us."

Yet even in the area of proper gender roles, military life during World War II sent confused signals to gay men. A masculine demeanor was crucial for survival, some veterans will say, while others tell stories of campy officers and wildly effeminate marksmen or medics who were respected for their skills. The drag shows approved by the War Department for the entertainment of the troops, stateside and abroad, were an obvious haven for gay men, further complicating the issue. The Special Services production of Irving Berlin's *This Is the Army*, with its high-kicking chorus lines of men in skirts, "female" singers, and celebrity impersonators, played on Broadway, went on extended tour, and was made into a popular movie. President Roosevelt heartily applauded the show and received the cast at the White House. Black servicemen had their own all-male pageants in the still-segregated Army. Imitations of Carmen Miranda, the Andrews Sisters, and Gypsy Rose Lee were especially popular. Not every performer was homosexual, but for those who were, the role-defying costumes, jokes, campy antics, seductive glances, and double entendres were a means of fostering a gay identity under trying circumstances and in an oblique way communicating to the gay part of their audience. As usual, gay men knew how to interpret the leeway that officially sanctioned drag shows provided. When bound to a large purpose, an individual's sexuality and even his demeanor were of less consequence than on other occasions, provided the obvious was left unstated.

Leaving unstated the truths no one wanted to hear was, in the long run, the name of the game. The priest Marvin Liebman spoke to made that clear when he implied that he hoped the charges weren't true, as did the Presbyterian minister Robert Peters went to see during basic training at Fort Jackson in South Carolina. Peters, a shy eighteen-year-old and a devout Lutheran, wanted to talk about the conflict between his soldierly duty and the commandment "Thou shalt not kill." Chaplain Crutchfield quickly let him know he had come to the wrong place if he wanted to confess any sexual problems or uncertainties. "I'm under oath to transmit all such information to the battalion commander . . . Know what I mean?" If Peters was queer, he should have stayed home "wearing dresses and baking cookies." Fifty years later, writing *For You, Lili Marlene*, his memoir of World War II, Robert Peters could still remember the minister's "stolid mouth, the eyes luring me without a hint of compassion."

THE MOBILIZATION OF sixteen million men and women had an impact that reached far beyond the military, of course, and the carryover to civilian life was dramatic in its own right. Millions of Americans were living away from their parents or spouses for the first time, making decisions colored by a plausible sense of fatality and some very stimulating temptations. Restraint often seemed pointless in the face of contemporary upheavals and an uncertain future. Despite the periodic cleanup campaigns, big cities became a playground. "If life becomes any more fun," Donald Vining wrote in his diary in 1943, reflecting on all that went on at the Sloane House YMCA in New York City where he worked, "it will be more than a mortal can stand." British journalist and member of Parliament Tom Driberg found California every bit as uninhibited as Manhattan: the sailors he met were "ready and willing for everything," he observed. "Spreading goodwill toward Britain in the U.S. Navy" was a desirable goal, in Driberg's estimation, and he happily paid a visit to a male brothel in San Francisco that was staffed by off-duty Marines "and other delights of the 'butch' sort." For Bob Milne, just out of college (Dartmouth, Class of '42), Boston was a sexual wonderland during these years. The gay bar scene, in his recollection, was "booming" by the mid-1940s—a far cry from the more tentative atmosphere of the late 1930s when the few dingy bars in

Scollay Square represented the only sure, if furtive, points of contact with one's own kind.

Having lost his right arm in an auto accident at the age of twelve, Milne hadn't been called up for active duty. Instead, he lived on the top floor of his family's townhouse on tree-lined Commonwealth Avenue, managing the ten rental apartments in the building for his parents. The Milne flat was somewhat notorious by 1945 for its hospitality to groups of soldiers and sailors on furlough. It was finally, inevitably, raided by the Boston police. Ironically, that particular evening Milne was throwing a party for the touring company of *The Merry Widow*, which included a number of heterosexual women, who were then dragged off to the station along with their unflappable host and his friends in uniform. Police cars lined Commonwealth Avenue for the raid, much to the horror of the neighborhood busybodies, and the elderly Mrs. Milne, who lived in the townhouse next door and was apprised of her son's situation by one of the arresting officers, immediately posted bail. (A proper Yankee, Mrs. Milne was nevertheless not easily shocked. "I can understand loving a man, Robert," she remarked as they were leaving the police station, "but so many of them!")

The kind of open house that Milne offered to servicemen wasn't unique. In Louisville, Biloxi, Madison, Baltimore, and San Diego, men on leave found similar hosts and similarly relaxed establishments. Sometimes the ambience might be more sedate: a safe place to relax, talk, grab a free meal or a drink, or attend a more formal dinner party, under the watchful eye of an older gay man who was happy his name and address had made their way along the grapevine. Other houses were known for their available bedrooms or simply as a place where the host was amorous, affluent, and willing to accommodate diverse temporary arrangements. The strangest wartime stop-off point was probably Frank Hill's Barn, actually a dairy farm, midway between Akron and Youngstown. On Saturday nights, Frank hosted lively all-male parties in his barn, drawing in visitors from as far away as Cleveland and Pittsburgh.

The world of the serviceman, uprooted from his home and willing to experiment, and the world of the gay civilian also overlapped in the hotels and the bathhouses and, most exuberantly, in the bars of the major cities. Finocchio's, the Black Cat, and Li-Po's in San Francisco, Mary's Tavern in Denver, the Double Header in Seattle, the Beau Brummel in Louisville, Dirty Helen's in Milwaukee, Danny's Jewel Box in Tampa, the Pink Elephant in Houston, the Green Tree in El Paso, Pearl's in Oakland, Carroll's in Washington, D.C., Lucky's Rendezvous in Harlem—the range of watering holes, mixed or all-gay, from the nightclubish to the down and dirty, was considerable, and a uniform well filled was all but a guarantee of some interaction, though it also meant having to keep an eye out for the MPs and local vice squad. Nominally straight bars were safer and often had sections that were gay, or became gay at certain times of day. At the bar of the Astor Hotel in New York, the Statler in Boston and in Cleveland, the Palmer House in Chicago, the Biltmore in Los Angeles, and at the famed Top of the Mark in San Francisco, white gay men congregated in unprecedented numbers without harassment unless someone of their group became too loud, campy, affectionate, or blatant in his cruising. Philadelphia, Chicago, and New Orleans had lively arenas for gay socializing before Pearl Harbor, equal to those in New York and San Francisco; the significant change was that places like Miami, Kansas City, San Antonio, and Charleston were now hospitable in their own way.

But Washington, D.C., was "the ideal place to be during World War II," one resident of the capital in his teenage years insisted, and many gay men have echoed that claim. Jack Kersey, who was fourteen in 1944, came out early, felt no ambivalence about his interests, and met a wide range of men before the end of the war, some of them only four or five years older than himself. "There were something like seven men to every woman in Washington then, all these servicemen away from home, worried about being shipped out and getting killed, all these new people from every part of the country working for the government . . . plenty of opportunities," he said. But even for older men who had lived and worked in the capital since the 1920s, the difference seemed profound and delightful beyond anyone's expectations. "I made more new friends, had more sex, and thought less about the stigma of being queer between Pearl Harbor and V-J Day than at any time in my life," a War Department employee remembered. "Thousands of sailors and marines were on the loose with cameras strapped to their shoulders," John Horne Burns wrote in *The Gallery* (1947). "Everybody beamed at everybody else, particularly on Pennsylvania Avenue after dark" in an atmosphere, Burns knowingly punned, that was "united, proud, and rather gay." Henry Gerber, living in Washington at the time, felt that the police had momentarily given up trying to control the pickup scene in Lafayettte Square, but for those servicemen or civilians who didn't like the park, the bar at the Mayflower Hotel only a few blocks away was considered a discreet, surefire, risk-free setting.

Like Kersey, many gay men who are now in their sixties had their first dates or their first sexual encounters when they were teenagers, often under circumstances that hadn't existed in peacetime. Harvey Milk, fourteen years old the summer of D-Day, recalled the pleasures of an active sex life for a teenager who wasn't afraid to make the train trip into New York from Long Island every Saturday: Manhattan was overrun with servicemen not so much older than Milk, hot for a little action in the park. (Not that Central Park in the early 1940s was always the best place for assignations. Gay-bashing was a problem, and the poet Harold Norse told of being raped by two British sailors there.) At sixteen, Tim Connelly, also from Long Island, discovered that the plaza by Rockefeller Center was a surefire pickup area, though he didn't need to leave home if he wanted sex. At the railroad station near his house in Long Beach, he had been meeting sailors from the Lido Beach naval station after dark for the better part of two years. In Philadelphia, "I got taken out to some very nice restaurants," Michael Spano noted in discussing the officer, probably in his mid-twenties, who picked him up in the fall of 1943 and was later killed in action in Germany. "I was seventeen. . . . [He] liked ethnic, I think. Italians. He wasn't afraid of someone figuring out what was going on, which is surprising to me today, especially when I think about us checking into a hotel. He'd tell me to say we were cousins if anybody asked. But we didn't look related in the least. He was pure Alabama gentleman and very romantic."

Even some rather notable people who might have acted with great discretion in prewar days were more casual about their proclivities now. Cardinal Francis Spellman, an archbishop in 1942 and one of the Catholic Church's most outspoken critics of modern sexual immorality, regularly sent the archdiocesan limousine to pick up his boyfriend at the stage door of the theater where the young man was dancing in the chorus of the aptly named Broadway revue *One Touch of Venus*. C. A. Tripp, a prominent psychotherapist in the 1970s, was acquainted with the dancer and asked him—in some amazement on learning of their relationship—if his mentor wasn't afraid of their not-so-secret affair becoming common knowledge. Already most of the cast seemed to know where the limousine came from each night. Eventually the dancer put Tripp's question to Spellman, who responded with a cavalier, "Oh, who would believe *that?*"

Luckily for Spellman and the other clerics in similar situations, the press in the 1940s still took a protective approach toward America's religious leaders. Government officials no longer enjoyed quite the same protection. Early in 1942, the FBI began watching a house on Pacific Street in Brooklyn, the site of a male brothel with purported ties to German agents in search of blackmail targets and military secrets. A raid on the house ensued and, under threat of a lengthy prison sentence, the manager gave the names of his regular patrons, most notably a United States senator. The *Times* printed the story without identifying him. Walter Winchell dropped sufficient hints in his column to satisfy the curious, but it was left to the rowdy *New York Post* to go all the way and, in blazing headlines on May 6, named the guilty party as Senator David I. Walsh, Democrat of Massachusetts and chairman of the Naval Affairs Committee. According to other sources, the composer Virgil Thomson was arrested in the March raid, but an avant-garde artist and a senator were not in the same league as far as the government and the press were concerned. Isolationists protested that Walsh was being smeared for his antiadministration politics and, after a lengthy interrogation by FBI agents, the brothel manager agreed to say he was mistaken. But the damage had been done. For the first time, the wayward sexual practices of a bachelor member of Congress had been the focus of widespread discussion.

Much more upsetting to Roosevelt—because the rumors were indisputably true and involved his own circle—was the conduct of his trusted foreign-policy advisor, Undersecretary of State Sumner Welles. Long touted by Walter Lippmann and others as an effective administrator who might replace the ailing Cordell Hull as secretary of state, making him next in line to the presidency after the vice president (according to the succession law of the time), Welles had been out of control for years. A fair number of people in and out of government knew about the 1940 episode in which he had propositioned several black porters on a train trip from Alabama to Washington. Neighbors wouldn't let their sons anywhere near the grounds of his estate. By the middle of the war, Hull was referring in irritation to his second-in-command as "my fairy," and the director of the FBI had a thick file on Welles's activities, which he showed to the president. Despite his abhorrence of homosexuality, Roosevelt resisted for as long as he could the counsel of J. Edgar Hoover, Ambassador William Bullitt, and others to dismiss Welles. But a year after the Walsh incident, with Drew Pearson on the verge of telling all in his column and the Republicans threatening to take the matter up in committee, Sumner Welles was forced to resign. There were altogether too many homosexuals in the State Department and the diplomatic corps to begin with, most observers felt. The "cookie pushers" were taking over.

By degrees, the blackout on any open discussion of the subject that certain segments of society had pushed for in the 1930s was ending. The arrest of Wayne Lonergan in October 1943, though, brought a different slant to the public perception of homosexuality. Lonergan, described by *Time* magazine as a "handsome, six-foot, crop-headed Royal Canadian Air Force aircraftman," had brutally murdered his American socialite wife. The details were lurid even by tabloid standards: Lonergan had been "kept" by an older gay man all the time he was married to the beautiful Patricia Burton. Worse yet, before his marriage, he had been involved with his future father-in-law, who, investigators discovered, had been divorced in 1926 when his own wife came to suspect him of clandestine involvements with young men. (A joke that made the rounds in gay circles that year asked what Patricia Burton Lonergan had said about her intended on the eve of their wedding. Answer: "If he's good enough for Daddy, he's good enough for me.") The homosexual-as-psychotic-murderer was one thread of the fabric of Depression-era social mythology. The queer killer might be many things, in this scenario, even married with a child, but he wasn't supposed to be dashingly good-looking and athletically muscular. The Lonergan case served to fuel the wish to see gay men as crafty and dangerous, even as it further challenged stereotypes about weak homosexuals—and stirred the interest of young gay men combing the books and magazines of the day for any mention of the topic.

Lonergan's attorney initially angled for an insanity plea as his only hope of keeping his client out of the electric chair and questioned prospective jurors about their prejudices regarding "sex variations." He then brought in his own psychiatrists to evaluate the mental health of the man who was probably America's most notorious bisexual that year. Even the press turned to the experts for commentary. *Time* quoted two doctors on the causes of this sad condition—the most common of which, they said, was seduction in childhood—and the slim likelihood of any cure. The woman-trapped-in-the-body-of-a-man prototype so fashionable earlier in the century was of no use to anybody, considering the defendant's physical stature. Even the military, looking at many of the servicemen it had discharged, was by this time acknowledging that homosexuals were often physically indistinguishable from the most masculine heterosexuals. The one point of agreement among the commentators about Wayne Lonergan was that his "emotional shallowness" pegged him as a deviant. Financially as well as sexually promiscuous throughout his adult life, he exhibited none of the characteristics of the stable, loving, thrifty male.

"It was a very scandalous episode," one New Yorker recalled. "If you were gay, you wanted to know every last juicy detail." Those details, for men and boys who yearned to see the word *homosexual* in print, naturally had a different meaning from the one the journalists wrote about, a subtext dealing with sexual dishonesty and societal pressure. James Baldwin was nineteen at the time of the Lonergan murder; five years later, he was still preoccupied with the story and attempted a novel based on the case, which he called *Ignorant Armies*. The book floundered, though it played its part, he later said, in the evolution of *Giovanni's Room* and *Another Country*. According to one Baldwin biographer, the Lucien Carr murder case was also an event that stirred the budding novelist's imagination. Carr, a breathtakingly handsome man from St. Louis, was a student at Columbia during the war and a drinking buddy of Jack Kerouac's. He had been followed to New York City from St. Louis by David Kammerer, a childhood friend of William Burroughs and a former teacher who was obsessed with Carr's beauty. Though heterosexual himself, Carr was evidently not above leading his worshiper on, before he went too far and started trailing the young man at his every turn. Their strange bond reached its crisis point on the night of August 13, 1944, when Kammerer accosted Carr in Riverside Park and demanded that he finally go to bed with him. Frightened and angry, Carr stabbed Kammerer and dumped the body in the Hudson River. His light prison sentence was connected to his ability to prove that he himself was not gay. Some of the initial newspaper accounts, looking for a lover's quarrel angle, took a dim view of Carr's heterosexuality. He had, after all, been seen entering the police station carrying a book of poetry.

Given the dearth of readily available information, it is not surprising that younger gay men in the early 1940s devoured the bits and pieces that came their way in the form of crime tales and lurid headlines. Hollywood was still maintaining its high-minded ban on depictions of perversion, though at least in comic ways the movie world alluded to the widespread fear that military life could lead to something deeper than male bonding. When Dana Andrews and Danny Kaye played two sailors on leave in the 1944 film *Up in Arms*, their love patter drives the passengers on a crowded bus to distraction; the joke is they're really speaking to their dates behind them, who aren't visible in the rush-hour throng. Billy Wilder's 1945 screen version of *The Lost Weekend* expunged the homosexual dimension of Charles Jackson's novel (Ray Milland's problem was now writer's block rather than a confused sexuality), and the censors deleted any references to the obvious homosexuality of Waldo Lydecker in Otto Preminger's *Laura* (1944). It was bad enough, studio executives felt, that Preminger wanted Webb for the part. One of his early roles in pre-talkie days was playing an "amateur director à la 'nance' " in *New Toys* (1925), and Webb had always been a little too convincing in these unmanly parts for some tastes. Broadway had become slightly more audacious, whittling away at the authority of the Wales Padlock Law of 1926, with a few plays that contained gay characters. The most explicit, *Outrageous Fortune* in 1943 and *Trio* in 1945, were dramas of little insight or wit, but producers and playwrights understood that theatergoers were not about to tolerate being told what adult fare they could and could not see as they had twenty years earlier. For men and women born at the time of the First World War, the watchdogs could never mean what they had to their parents' generation. Danny Kaye as the swish magazine photographer in *Lady in the Dark* (1941), a musical written and directed by Moss Hart, and Carol Channing as a lesbian nurse in the play *Proof Through the Night* (1942) didn't provoke much comment, let alone anger or indignation.

One clever civilian who was banking on the hope that times were changing was Bob Mizer, a California aircraft factory worker and amateur photographer in his early twenties. In the decade before World War II, gay men who wanted to look at photographs of naked or scantily clad males had to subscribe to the few available nudist periodicals or physical-culture magazines. *True Vim, Tomorrow's Man,* and *Strength and Health* had a homosexual edge—some even ran ads for pen pals on occasion—but they existed essentially to provide tips on bodybuilding, transforming the ninety-eight-pound weakling into a he-man of the Bernarr MacFadden and Charles Atlas school. Mizer, who since his teenage years had been photographing naked men in the privacy of his parents' house and using his bedroom closet as a darkroom, was of the opinion that postwar society was going to be considerably more interested in the male figure, beyond the context of health or sports. He had witnessed plenty of sexual traffic in his native Los Angeles since the start of the war and, more important, an emboldened attitude on the part of gay men.

In 1945 Mizer founded the Athletic Model Guild, an undertaking that had little to do with athletics and everything to do with exposed flesh. In his family garage, he set up a studio to take full-length pictures of men, partially undressed or nude (seen from the back or the side), or costumed as farmers or gladiators. Four-by-five inches in size, the pictures sold for a nickel each, and Mizer quickly developed a 5,000-name mailing list. "Everyone was doing clandestine pictures," he later said, "but they wouldn't come out in the open and do physique pictures." Mizer felt the need for a certain amount of pretense and referred to AMG as a modeling agency, though it was unlikely that the street kids, weight lifters, and ex-convicts who flocked to his studio—there to strip or put on a revealing outfit, their vital statistics duly recorded by Mizer's mother—would ever have found work of a more professional nature. Mizer's company went through various transformations over the decades, bringing him into trouble with the law and making him a great deal of money. Its premise, however, originating in its owner's unabashed avocation, was simple. Gay men were ready to seek their own equivalent of pinup girls, their own license to savor the male body.

Bob Mizer was right, in essence. The genie was not going to be forced back into the bottle. "We met a lot of people. We became aware of our own kind, our own society," Johnnie Phelps, a lesbian WAC summarized the war years. "And I think that had a lot to do with the increase in population for the gay community in . . . metropolitan areas." Sergeant Phelps estimated that over 90 percent of her battalion was gay. If that figure seems suspiciously high, some corroboration is offered by the fact that she was the person General Eisenhower turned to when he wanted a report on the number (and names) of lesbians under his immediate command, a report that would then be used, he told Phelps, to clean house. In a now-famous exchange, Phelps told Ike that she would be pleased to complete the task as ordered, but that the general should know that her name would be the first on the list and that the ranks of the battalion's nine hundred women— drivers, file clerks, section commanders—would pretty much be emptied. The general's secretary then stepped forward and indicated her name would have to be on the list as well. Eisenhower told Phelps to disregard the order.

Ten years later, as president, Eisenhower would initiate the most sweeping purge to date of homosexuals in government service. What a society at war had had to tolerate, haphazardly and unwillingly, was far less acceptable in peacetime. But the changes in gay life in America were not to be so easily stemmed, nor gay men and lesbians so easily thwarted.

9

THE POSTWAR SCENE

There was no future in being gay.

—A Mobile, Alabama, man discussing
his decision to marry in 1951

I well remember the first time I went there, I stood outside for three-quarters of an hour, afraid to go in. Finally I realized that all these people were going in looking happy and coming out looking happier. I didn't see the roof falling in on anybody or anybody getting carried out dead, and this was just plain silly. So I walked in, took one look around, and said to myself, "This is for you. You've come home."

—Frank Kameny, on his first visit to a
gay bar in Tucson, Arizona, in 1954

Majorities create minorites, social theorists have long argued, and the conceptualizing of any people into a group or category different from others in some fundamental way is a process that rarely bodes well for the minority. Because skin color, genitalia, and the uses made of those genitals still matter to enough people who collectively determine the values of society, race, gender, and sexual orientation remain defining categories, part of the currency of modern thought. Food preferences count for little today ("vegetarian" was once a vivid, even confrontational label); hair color or handwriting, not at all. As a result, there is no division into conflicting states of dark-haired vs. light-haired, no reward or penalty (any longer) for being right-handed or left-handed.

For men who wished to live with or make love to other men, the late 1940s and 1950s was a watershed period in this regard. The social engineers of mobilization and military life repeatedly insisted that there was a useful homosexual-heterosexual dichotomy and that, moreover, every man should know which group he belonged to, accepting the benefits of the one choice or taking the consequences of the other. This line of thought, percolating for more than two decades, had one meaning for those individuals who knew from adolescence that they were not going to follow their father's lead or for those who had discovered during the war that a workable life was to be found among the "cognoscenti." They knew they were going to have to band together more energetically than they had before, to expand the territory in which they felt safe, and forge their own definitions of their experience to counteract the more shameful attributes others were publicizing. Many of these men understood that the nature of the animus against them was no more rational than a prejudice based on skin or hair color or tastes in food, but the time for discretion or vagueness about sexual matters was past. A spotlight was being turned their way. "Gay identity"—like the later "gay pride"—was born of heterosexual focus and vilification.

But to men who weren't prepared to invest their sexual interests with the power of an identity or status, the postwar situation held a different meaning. In earlier years, it had been possible for a man whose drives were essentially homosexual to wed and father children without feeling he had betrayed his "true self" or his spouse. His homosexuality was a component of his nature (troublesome, to be sure), but a readily accessible alternative life wasn't always to be found or embraced. In the more sexualized postwar era, even bachelorhood was suspect, and marriage became more than an emotional, economic, and procreative arrangement. It became proof that one was with the approved side, a desirable position to be in even if it entailed some hypocrisy. In this context, the married man with a homosexual past or an ongoing "double life" was in an absurd bind, if he chose to think about his position. He was a victim of misguided expectations or a "user" of his poor wife, depending on which psychiatrist he believed; he was living proof that deviants could force themselves to act as proper heterosexuals if they wished, according to some critics; or he lacked courage and self-awareness, in the eyes of the more independent gay men he slept with. He was also part of a vastly more numerous group than anyone before Kinsey suspected.

The pressure to marry after the war affected everyone and served multiple purposes. The job market purportedly required women to leave the workforce in large numbers to make way for demobilized veterans, and "settling down" signified to many people the creation of a more stable America. (Not, it should be emphasized, the *return* to a more stable America, but the *invention* of a more stable America: the 1930s had been a period of tumult that fractured old ideas about family and security as effectively as Pearl Harbor.) The need to stigmatize the bachelor and the career woman, then, was especially important and, within the wide bounds of public civility, especially ruthless. The problem, acknowledged by society now in myriad ways, was that the ability to bed a woman didn't certify a man's unblemished "normality." The 1946 movie *Gilda*, for example, was shockingly honest for Hollywood. Glenn Ford and George Macready are manifestly more interested in each other than in Rita Hayworth, whom they each marry in turn for different reasons. ("The most curious love-hate pattern I've ever seen," one character remarks of Ford's sexually tormenting relationship with Hayworth.) Glenn Ford later commented that he and Macready were well aware they were supposed to play their friendship as a homosexual bond, no matter what disclaimers director Charles Vidor cared to make on the subject. Two novels that year turned to the same theme of the married homosexual, *The Dazzling Crystal* by Janet Shane and *The Fall of Valor* by the popular writer Charles Jackson. No one thought of these stories as originating in twisted flights of fancy. Reality was providing abundant hints that the homosexual-as-screamer was a cliché of rapidly diminishing value. New York attorney Wilbur Stammler's murder of his lover, an Air Force pilot he had adopted at the end of the war, was only one of several crime sensations circa 1946 that called attention to men in love with men and women victimized by their abnormality. In the Stammler incident, newspaper accounts tiptoed around the obvious and simply remarked on the strangeness of an unmarried thirty-eight-year-old lawyer's adoption of a married twenty-five-year-old pilot. Washington's gay community became particularly nervous about the publicity—Stammler shot George Leist and then himself at the Wardman Park Hotel in Washington, D.C., on March 4, 1946. Psychiatrists in the late 1940s, some of whom were publishing in mass-market journals to reach the general public, vociferously repeated the warnings they had been sounding for twenty years about the danger of urging homosexual men to marry in order to change or "fit in."

But marry they did, by the tens of thousands. Some of these unions lasted for decades, grounded in the plausible assumption that spouses don't have to know absolutely everything about one another. Others ended in amicable understandings or in recrimination, sexual estrangement, divorce. When things went wrong, a toll was taken on others besides the man and wife—the children or, from a different angle, the men who had been dumped in their lovers' pursuit of social approval. In *Young Man from the Provinces: A Gay Life Before Stonewall* (1995), Alan Helms wrote of the heartbreak in 1958 of meeting a college lover at Grand Central Station after a summer apart only to be told, "It's over between us. I'm going straight." The blazing passion and deep affection between the two Columbia University students had been transforming experiences for Helms, but his lover's decision to marry and avoid a gay life at all costs was irrevocable, leaving Helms feeling more alone, more freakish and repellent, than he had felt before the relationship.

In September 1945, Leo Adams, a forty-year-old New Yorker, placed a notice for a pen pal in the back pages of the *Saturday Review*. (Coded pen-pal messages in reputable magazines had been a standard means of gay communication at least since the early 1930s). A three-year correspondence ensued between Adams and a man in Missouri sixteen years his junior. Eventually, gingerly, their letters worked their way toward the topic of settling down, of final choices. "I've filled my spare moments with every conceivable hobby and occupation, but that doesn't always help," Adams's long-distance friend wrote in 1946. "Marriage should at least keep me well enough satisfied along that line to minimize the enlarged outlook, and to partially remove the abnormal view, which I attribute somewhat to my stretch overseas." His fiancée had agreed that he could go to New York alone from time to time. Adams responded with clarity and eloquence, urging his pen pal to visit New York before getting married. He wanted him to see the vitality and fullness of gay life, and he urged him to reject the myth of the eternal outcast. His neighbors in Sedalia weren't the whole world. "When I was your age," Adams wrote, "it was quite a discovery to realize that there are heterosexuals who do not look askance to homosexuality."

Even men and women who had been ostentatiously comfortable with their homosexuality in a less repressive age drifted into marriage in the 1950s, including veterans of the Harlem Renaissance. Richard Bruce Nugent, Langston Hughes's friend and a contentedly gay artist in the 1920s, married in the Eisenhower years, as did that great "bulldagger who sang the blues," Gladys Bentley. Bentley's renunciation of her lesbianism was sadly thorough. Watching her fame and money slip away, and well aware that her notoriety as one of America's most famous Jazz Age rebels spelled doom in the new order, Bentley went so far as to offer a public mea culpa. Her autobiographical sketch in *Ebony*, "I Am a Woman Again," described her life as a lesbian in disparaging terms and lashed out at those who defended homosexuality. Abandoned by her husband (who claimed they had never actually been married), Bentley lived out her remaining days in southern California with her mother and died in 1960 on the eve of her ordination as a minister in the Temple of Love in Christ, Inc. Holdouts against the wedded-bliss ideal could find themselves in very awkward positions. In 1948 *Ebony* listed playwright Owen Dodson as one of the year's most eligible bachelors. Artist Charles Sebree tweaked his friend: "I knew you were a bachelor, but I never guessed you were eligible." In 1949 entertainer Jimmie Daniels was likewise named a "choice candidate for the altar."

THE DEMORALIZING DRIVE to conform played havoc with the lives of many gay men and lesbians, but American psychiatrists knew a golden opportunity when they saw one. As antipathy toward homosexuals grew and the esteem the psychiatric profession enjoyed reached its peak, incentives were in place for serious "curing"—incentives for the healer (money, kudos) and for the healed (social and family acceptance). "If you heard that a gay man was seeing a shrink" in the 1950s, Alan Helms wrote, "it meant only one thing: he was trying to go straight." The postwar triumph in America of Sandor Rado's critique of Freud and the tenet of universal bisexuality fostered a conviction that if only more were known about these unfortunates, a great deal could be done to relieve their misery. Indeed, the distaste many doctors felt about taking on homosexual patients in the 1930s was quickly giving way to a macabre fascination.

Psychotherapist George Weinberg, heterosexual himself, was at Columbia University in the 1950s and marveled at the approach taken to gay men seeking help. "When I was getting my doctorate in psychology, working with a homosexual was considered quite exciting. He was the model of a certain kind of sickness, a perfect field for study. He was the one 'from whom we have much to learn,' as Freud said." But how much did his peers and advisors really learn from their patients, Weinberg wondered at the time. While in training, he knew enough to turn off the tape recorder when he wanted to be encouraging to a gay patient about his life as a homosexual. Two men consulted him during a rough patch in their thirteen-year union, for instance. To tell them that it would be a mistake to break up over the minor issues they were squabbling about was a dangerous thing to do—on tape. Those who monitored Weinberg's progress as a psychotherapist would accuse him of validating a condition that the American Psychiatric Association, in its first official listing of mental disorders in 1952, had unequivocally defined as an illness. Even when Weinberg tried to bring together his psychiatrist friends and his gay friends, the results were dismal. The young psychiatrists he knew were impeccably polite when socializing but never forgot that, in terms of mental health, they were on a different plane from the homosexuals.

In Weinberg's estimation, the gulf was widened by the nature of the education mental health professionals received. They saw themselves as scientists, on one level or another, but their business took them into realms that were creative, imaginative, and often better charted by literature than science. They understood the worldview of their instructors, but not the worldview of Balzac, Dostoevsky, Ibsen, Yeats, Wilde, or Whitman. ("What good is an analyst or a therapist who doesn't have culture, have metaphor, love the arts?" Weinberg liked to say.) About his own background and sympathies, Weinberg noted in 1994: "I didn't know my father, he left before I was born, and I took solace from writers. I had no idea they were homosexuals, they didn't let you know that in school in those days, whether it was Housman or Proust or Shakespeare himself. So I found myself being whispered to by gay men in my early life."

(The author, in 1972, of the groundbreaking *Society and the Healthy Homosexual*, Weinberg even in the 1990s is a man of many passions and strong opinions, and time hasn't softened his memory of the profession as he first knew it in the 1950s: "The men in the analyst crowd were mostly miserable, unhappy, condescending toward their wives . . . pinched, trying to get their kids into the best schools, acting as if the secret of life was pleasing other people. These were men who should be helping people get their lives together?" Told that it was unwise to take on so many homosexual patients—Weinberg's practice was often one-third gay throughout the late 1950s and 1960s—and that it would be professional suicide to publish articles approving of homosexual sex, Weinberg lived to prove his critics wrong. Again, the literary element comes into play, in his view: "I was reading Gide and Baudelaire and Housman. They were reading Edmund Bergler.")

The nature of the proffered help that so rankled Weinberg and other critics of the psychiatric establishment reflected the biases and training of the individual doctors. Emetic aversion therapy, a procedure that involved showing the patient slides of naked men and then chemically inducing nausea, was popular in some quarters. Many psychiatrists held fast to the idea of "excavating" the buried Oedipus complex and attendant gynophobia. Two doctors at the Langley Porter Clinic in San Francisco wrote an article in the *Journal of Social Hygiene* in 1953 arguing that, despite the adverse opinion of the medical community, "therapeutic castration" was a promising avenue for research, especially for those homosexuals interested in minors. At the suggestion of a patient, a New York doctor organized a gay version of Alcoholics Anonymous that year (Homo-Anonymous had a short life), and other analysts reported progress with traditional group therapy for deviants, who were "poorly socialized" to begin with and benefited from controlled interactions. Whatever the method, pursuing the phantom of sexual normality was an expensive undertaking. In *Familiar Faces, Hidden Lives* (1976), Howard Brown, New York City's health commissioner under Mayor John V. Lindsay, described his excruciating experience with "one of the best psychoanalysts in the Midwest." Brown saw his analyst four times a week at $20 an hour for four years in the early 1950s, spending more on his analysis (which eventually totaled $15,000) than on all his other living expenses combined. The few insights he gained along the way, Brown wrote, "were nothing compared to [the] overriding message— that I was inherently impaired because of my sexual orientation and that if I could not change it, I was doubly a failure." For $15,000, Brown acquired a more troubled self-image than he had before analysis.

The inquiry into the causation and treatment of homosexuality assumed its most earnest guise in the form of a study undertaken in 1952 by the New York Society of Medical Psychoanalysts, in which seventy-seven psychoanalysts compiled comprehensive data on 106 predominantly homosexual and 100 exclusively heterosexual men, the latter serving as controls. Published in 1962 under the authorship of Dr. Irving Bieber with the simple title *Homosexuality: A Psychoanalytic Study of Male Homosexuals*, the book became what many doctors and counselors had long wanted, an authoritative scientific text—consulted by practitioners, stocked by reference libraries everywhere, quoted by *Time* and *Newsweek*. With its heavy emphasis on dysfunctional family patterns and its relatively small subject pool, *Homosexuality* did not offer any strikingly original conclusions, but it did aim to give the final, affirmative word on the "cure" debate. Of the seventy-two men Bieber & Co. worked with who were exclusively homosexual, fourteen, or 19 percent, "became" heterosexual after sufficient time in therapy and fourteen "became" bisexual. The unchanged (read: obstinate) 62 percent of this group didn't dampen the enthusiasm of the researchers one whit. In the face of the analysts' dubious conclusions about treatment based on their own modest numbers, reviewers opted for myopia as well: *Scientific American* hailed the text as a welcome contribution "to social responsibility and enlightenment" and the London *Times Literary Supplement* announced that it was especially impressed by the fact that the evidence had been collected "in such a way that subjective bias is excluded as far as possible."

For the parent who wanted to learn something about a homosexual son or daughter and needed the advice of an expert, just as for any homosexual who was beset by doubts about his own mental health, the available literature between the mid-1940s and the mid-1960s was thematically all of a piece, though there were differences in tone. By virtue of his prolific output, Edmund Bergler made sure that at least one of the books consulted would have to be his, and he had no use for Bieber's colorless, measured prose. In *The Basic Neurosis: Oral Regression and Psychic Masochism* (1949), he gave the fullest expression to date of his belief that homosexuality was necessarily incompatible with happiness ("A man who unconsciously runs after disappointment cannot be consciously happy"); that the worst heterosexual marriage was preferable to the best homosexual union; and that gay men were—in a phrase Bergler relished—"injustice collectors." *Fashion and the Unconscious* (1953) ranted about the pernicious gay influence in dressing modern women to look their worst. *Homosexuality: Disease or Way of Life?* (1956) ended its wide-ranging survey of current thought on the subject with the observation that the time had come for society to stop displaying sympathy for the homosexual, given what modern psychiatrists had proven about the ability to change one's orientation. "Homosexuality may have been tragic in the past," Bergler wrote, "before therapeutic methods were worked out; today, the only tragedy is ignorance, and—sometimes—lack of funds for treatment." Homosexuals were in need of treatment because they are "essentially disagreeable people, regardless of their pleasant or unpleasant manner . . . subservient when confronted with a stronger person, merciless when in power, unscrupulous about trampling on a weaker person." *Neurotic Counterfeit-Sex* (1958) reviewed all of the perversions in short-essay form, placing homosexuality in a wider context that included impotence, frigidity, and voyeurism.

All of these books, however, were mere prologue. With *1,000 Homosexuals* (1959), Bergler took off the gloves: homosexuality, part conspiracy and part masochism, had to be stripped of "its aura of false allure" before it claimed any more victims. This book is a milestone in many ways, a psychiatrist's version of the Nixon tapes. For Bergler was so taken with his skills that he devoted the bulk of the text to excerpts from his own cases. Whether the extensive dialogue in *1,000 Homosexuals* came from his tape recordings of the sessions or were re-creations from memory hardly matters. The evidence is his, and it reveals the true Bergler—his need to label and belittle his patients, his love of sarcasm and sparring, his belief that guiding the patient to a realization was a waste of time when one could "talk turkey" instead. (At some point in the process, usually early on, Bergler loved to ask the patient, "May I be frank?" A nod would do, and he was off and running: "You impress me as a fading, aging homosexual who pretends to be happy. . . . I know from other cases the tragedy of the homosexual who has reached middle age." One patient had the temerity to ask, "Who gave you the right to sit in judgment?" Bergler's response to the man: "Isn't it amusing when a cynic becomes indignant?") Even after the publication of these case histories, no peer review board sought to query Bergler about the appropriateness of his therapeutic techniques.

In his lack of reserve and dignity, Edmund Bergler is sometimes referred to today as if he were an extreme, isolated case, but his well-known snideness had an unfortunate way of filtering down to private practices in the smallest cities. The one psychiatrist in the town George Handler lived in in Pennsylvania in the mid-1950s told him that success in the form of a heterosexual life was a possibility if he worked long and hard, but failure was a certainty if he remained as willful "as you people often are." At their first session, his doctor made it clear to Handler, a college freshman, that he regarded his delicate mannerisms as a form of passive-aggression and that he expected him to show up for appointments "dressed appropriately" (i.e., more conservatively). In Meriden, Connecticut, in 1952, sixteen-year-old Rick Colantino found a haven from abusive peers and relatives in a circle of equally bold, sexually active gay students at the local high school. Unapologetic about his effeminacy and his campy friends, he was forced into therapy by his parents. "I can't do anything with him," the psychiatrist told his mother after a few sessions. He then dismissed his patient with no effort to hide his disdain: "Let him go to New York City and live with the rest of them."

Serious intellectual challenges to the dominant view were presented in these years by Alfred Kinsey (discussed in chapter 10) and by Evelyn Hooker (discussed in chapter 12). But as Kenneth Lewes noted in *The Psychoanalytic Theory of Male Homosexuality* (1988), Kinsey's research had little immediate influence on the therapeutic approach to gay men. Dr. Hooker's valuable work had still less. Few ideas were so entrenched by midcentury as those governing proper sexual choices and gender roles.

CONCERN OVER "POORLY socialized" free spirits such as Rick Colantino (who went on to become a noted drag artist in the late 1950s and early 1960s) and George Handler (who became a high school teacher) was part and parcel of a concern about social breakdown on a wider scale. In 1946 Attorney General Tom Clark warned of an "orgy of crime" overtaking the

United States, and in the same year the FBI announced that murder, assault, and larceny had increased by 12.3 percent in the preceding twenty-four months, while juvenile delinquency was "sweeping the nation like a plague," the director of the Secret Service told a parents' group. Against a backdrop of fears of another war in Europe, this time against the Communists, these were unsettling bulletins, and the news only got worse. Popular magazines of the time offered a strangely polarized view of the world: images of doting parents and two happy children, one of each sex, gathered around the kitchen table were interspersed with articles about the rise of hoodlum gangs and night-prowling psychopaths.

Throughout the late 1940s and early 1950s, a new sex crimes panic raised tensions far beyond those provoked by the same kind of crisis in the late 1930s. It is possible that the postwar panic would not have achieved the awesome momentum it did had the ground not been so well prepared by the same defensive excitement ten years earlier and the massive psychiatric call-to-arms against deviance, but other contemporary factors were at work. The suburban thrust of American life after the war represented a turning against not only the cities themselves, transformed by the black migration from the rural South and urban decay, but a turning against the *idea* of the city, as a place of stimulation, unpredictability, and robustly conflicting values. The safer, more uniform, and more knowable the suburbs seemed, the darker and more unnatural the city became. And in the minds of many Americans, urban life came to mean several not unrelated things: it meant black, it meant Hispanic, it meant unmarried, it meant crime-ridden, it meant beatnik, and it meant queer. When *Collier's* ran its sensationalizing series entitled "Terror in Our Cities" from 1949 to 1951, describing rampant crime in Detroit, Philadelphia, St. Louis, Cleveland, San Francisco, Boston, and seven other cities, readers naturally believed the worst, with little concern for whether these reports signaled an unprecedented, statistically verified breakdown of law and order or a new kind of attention to an old problem.

Journalist Howard Whitman painted a broad picture in his down-and-out travelogue, linking drug addiction, poverty, racist police brutality, and sexual license as part of the tapestry of American moral decline. "Dirty" art photos, twenty-four-hour movie houses where men gathered in back rows, and "strip" theaters should share in the blame, Whitman approvingly quoted the vice experts in his article on Detroit. Two years before his "Cities" assignment, this same writer had been the first to sound the alarm about sex crimes. "The Biggest Taboo" in the February 1947 issue of *Collier's* offered some hair-raising true stories and a reminder that "not a day goes by that aggrieved parents don't huddle in the waiting room [of the

Society of the Prevention of Cruelty to Children] with boys and girls of five, eight, or fourteen who have been lured into alleys or rooming houses and mistreated." In July 1947, J. Edgar Hoover stirred the pot with "How Safe is Your Daughter?" in *American Magazine* (answer: not at all, as "depraved human beings, more savage than beasts, are permitted to roam America almost at will"), and over the next few years newspapers and periodicals ran pieces with blunt, attention-grabbing titles such as "What Can We Do About Sex Crimes?" (*Saturday Evening Post*), "To Protect Your Child from Sex Offenders" (*Better Homes & Gardens*), "Murder as a Sex Practice" (*American Mercury*), and "Michigan's Most Revolting Sex Crimes in Words and Photos" (*Detroit News*). The nature of the 1947-to-1955 press coverage, compared to its prewar counterpart, was both tirelessly inventive and uninhibited.

The bulk of the attention was given to assaults against women and to the molestation of little girls, but the harm done by homosexual pedophiles was amply chronicled. Seymour Levin's trial in Philadelphia in 1949 for the rape and murder of a neighborhood boy was a major news story, and the arrest of former tennis champion Bill Tilden on charges of having had sex with a fifteen-year-old boy disturbed parents who remembered him as one of the most revered sports figures of the 1920s. (Similar episodes involving Cary Grant in Los Angeles during World War II and Montgomery Clift on Times Square in the late 1940s were quietly taken care of, according to their biographers; the Tilden case would have paled before either of those revelations.) One of the points made by historians Estelle Freedman and George Chauncey in their insightful essays on the panics is that while awful crimes were indeed taking place in these years, the press had adopted a calculated, inflammatory stance out of proportion to any known facts about modern levels of crime. Even more important, they note, the terms sexual psychopath, sex criminal, deviant, and homosexual came to be used almost interchangeably in discussing the situation. Many psychiatrists were unhappy about the confusion in definition, just as some were critical of the tough new laws against sex offenders that focused on longer prison time rather than better methods of treatment. However, no one voice, or group of voices, was strong enough to contain a crisis mentality arising from anxieties that weren't entirely bound to reason or fact.

Anxieties about sex are among the most intractable, and in this regard it is worth comparing the role of the black press in the panic to that of mainstream white journalism. Tabloid enthusiasm for tales of lust and violence isn't surprising, but the decision by magazines like *Collier's*, *Better Homes & Gardens*, and *Ladies' Home Journal* to publish articles about sex criminals preying on women, girls, and boys is exceptional. In black neighborhoods, rape and child molestation continued to be a threat—a much more real one than white middle-class areas would ever know—yet the major national black newspapers such as the *Baltimore Afro-American* and the *Pittsburgh Courier* never joined the sex-crimes bandwagon. Quite the contrary. It could be argued that they had more pressing battles of equality and self-definition to wage and no need to fabricate a grimmer reality than actually existed, and both of those observations are true. But on a more fundamental level, black journalists often evinced a different outlook on sexual topics. The *Pittsburgh Courier*'s campaign on behalf of World War II veterans saddled with the blue discharge (discussed in chapter 11), is a rare example of courage in postwar journalism. No news magazine with a white readership would have touched that subject. What happened to homosexuals forced out of the military was their own business.

Ebony, started in 1945 as a black equivalent of *Life*, naturally gave space to Gladys Bentley's 1952 shocker about finding her way to heterosexuality and to Adam Clayton Powell's worries about how numerous and bold "the boys with a swish and the girls with a swagger" were becoming and about the alarming number of black ministers who were gay (his theme since 1929). But Powell's remarks were in the context of a 1951 article on the benefits of liberal sex education for the young, a cause heartily backed by the magazine. What's more, a feature the next month on Lucky's Rendezvous in Harlem noted the cafe's gay clientele in the same even tone it described its celebrity patrons, and the coverage—in 1948, 1952, and 1953—of female impersonation clubs and the annual drag balls that had resumed in New York and Chicago was downright matter-of-fact. (Some readers thought the subject too gutter-minded for a black middle-class periodical and wrote to the editors to say so, but their indignation didn't have much effect.) Even when reporting on a gay crime situation in "Some Sex Clubs Practice Perversion, Are Interracial" (April 1952), *Ebony* avoided J. Edgar Hoover's purple prose ("depraved human beings, more savage than beasts") and any hint that such "love dens" were a common occurrence.

Ebony was also responsible for the most sensible and emotionally stirring mass-market article on gender affect and sexuality in the period. "The Man Who Lived as a Woman" concerned the death of elderly Georgia Black in Sanford, Florida. "By every law of society," the article began, "Georgia Black should have died in disgrace and humiliation and been remembered as a sex pervert, a 'fairy' or a 'freak.'" But the discovery on her deathbed that this wife and adoptive mother of two was in fact a man didn't lead to anger or epithets. George Cantey, a rural South Carolina farm child, had run away to Charleston in his youth and lived with a male lover before beginning his new life attired as a woman, marrying (twice) and raising his children. So loved and respected was Georgia Black that the only response to the news was genuine grief at her passing. From the pastor of her church to her black neighbors to the white people she was employed by, the "deviant" aspect of her doctor's disclosure seemed irrelevant to the larger matter of her sincerity and kindness. When her son published "My Mother Was a Man" in *Ebony* two years later, in June 1953, it was a testament in the same spirit. Willie Sabb had been shocked to learn that his mother was a biological male, but it didn't actually change anything. Despite publisher John Johnson's conservative politics and *Ebony*'s mania for "respectable" images of black life, his magazine was a radical one in this area—it ignored distinctions with which the rest of the country was becoming obsessed.

In white America, the whirlwind of public opinion militated against an outlook that honored a George Cantey/Georgia Black or thought the blue discharge a terrible injustice. White America was still reeling from the lessons of 1941 to 1945—the lurking potential for violence everywhere, the power of unrestrained sex, the "masculine" capabilities of women in times of crisis—and wanted its old pieties restored, its children guarded (which women in the workplace could not do), its deviants watched.

Those who were concerned had no trouble getting the men in power (governors, mayors, police chiefs) to pay heed. Both the Depression and World War II encouraged citizens—or, more accurately, voters—to think of their government as an active, responsive body, however ineffective or mismanaged its responses might be. A smart elected official didn't ignore the fears of his constituents, least of all when they pertained to family or public safety and when the only responses called for were moral outrage, a cry for greater vigilance, and a summoning of the "experts" to give counsel. The government-sponsored panels and commissions that were established around the country in reaction to demands from PTA and church groups, a demand that reached a hysterical peak in 1949 and 1950, frequently offered an analysis that served three goals at once. They bolstered the prestige of the psychiatric profession by introducing the concept of the "indeterminant sentence," making room for the psychiatrist in what had formerly been the judge's province alone; they tacitly validated the more aggressive posture of local police departments and vice squads; and they affirmed the idea that *any* variation from a socially approved sexual norm could indicate a hidden, or evolving, pathology. The latter notion was vital in keeping the nonconformist in line. "The sex pervert," a *Newsweek* writer commented in a review of J. Paul De River's screed *The Sexual Criminal* (1949), "whether a homosexual, an exhibitionist, or even a dangerous sadist, is too often regarded merely as a 'queer' person who never hurts anyone but himself." Not so, the cumulative evidence of the panic implied.

The ramifications of the panic extended well beyond protecting children in the schoolyard. It was suddenly open season on homosexuals. Philadelphia's vice squad created a backlog in the judicial calendar by dragging two hundred gay men a month into court in 1950. The *Denver Post* warned Coloradans in the spring of 1949 that homosexuality had reached an "all-time high" in their capital city, a threat that would have to be met head-on. A general cleanup campaign in San Francisco that summer won citywide approval. The police raid at the Black Cat led to ten arrests, with the names and addresses of the men printed in the papers, while a star performer at Finocchio's was taken in on lewdness and vagrancy charges. Nightspots in the North Beach area were warned to "dispose of obnoxious clientele or face closing." In the modern era, the public wanted the police to go after those men who broke the law, but also, as a San Francisco newspaper phrased it, those "characters who frequent certain types of cafes and bars." When the sex crimes panic eventually faded from the scene, a potent residue of suspicion and hostility was left to torment openly gay men for years to come.

As ALWAYS, THE fervor with which homosexuality was attacked had to do with the fear that it was on the rise—and would, in consequence, become more acceptable. The mix of sexually eager twenty-year-old college students and World War II veterans several years older than the rest of the student body, who were receiving their higher education courtesy of the government, created just that kind of circumstance and gave cause for just that kind of worry. In the midst of a growing macho fraternity house ethic on campuses, a hidden dimension of male-male sexual life was detectable. A Swarthmore freshman in 1947 analyzed the situation: "There were two factors at work"—liquor and a more virginity-conscious generation of women. "Though Swarthmore was supposedly a dry college then and you had to get rid of your bottles in town, there were a lot of beer parties and that meant a lot of guys who weren't too interested in gay or straight after a certain hour." Inhibitions lowered, they wanted sex, and the girls they knew were less inclined to go to bed with them than their counterparts of the 1960s would be. "The arboretum," he remembered, "saw a lot of activity." He also recalled the role his roommate's experiences with the Army of Occupation in Germany played in their semester-long romance. "He would tell me about the prostitutes in Berlin, implying that he wasn't used to going for long periods of time without sex, which was exciting to me, and I would give him my copy of *The Tropic of Cancer* to read, and we were all set." A freshman at the University of Illinois at Champaign-Urbana that same year, Harris Kimball, was amazed at how much sex was possible in the fraternity circles. "I wouldn't say they were all gay. Most of them went on to get married and have kids, so we're not going to call that 'gay,' and they were very nervous that no one should find out. But *my* part in it was gay and the more sex I had with other guys on campus, the better *I* felt about being gay. Which I was then, and I knew it."

Entering the University of Michigan in 1949, Jack Campbell found an atmosphere pleasingly "rampant with gay activity." On some nights, the swimming pool area at the Men's Union was "almost as wild as a bathhouse." (A relevant image, given Campbell's career as a founder of the Club Baths chain in the 1960s.) Angel Hall was "a wonderful meeting place," worth Campbell's revisiting on postgraduation car trips from his new home in Cleveland. "James," a more reserved gay man at college in Maryland in this period, who later entered the priesthood, was aroused but shocked by his roommate's bold advances. "Steven had been [in the Marines] in Europe at the end of the war; he was at least five or six years older than I was, and he loved 'the buddy thing.' " James had fantasized about having sex with Steven, he said in a 1994 interview, but was too nervous to follow through on the invitation. "He didn't lose any time in finding a lover elsewhere in the dorm," James added. Quipped another gay man about his senior year at UCLA in the early 1950s, "I owe my coming out to the G.I. Bill."

This clandestine activity didn't go entirely unnoticed by the professionals who tended to the students. Benjamin Glover's "Observations on Homosexuality Among University Students" in the *Journal of Nervous and Medical Diseases* in 1951 reported on his experiences working at the University of Wisconsin's Health Department. Dr. Glover wrote that since the war there had been a "noticeable increase in cases of homosexuality as well as other socially offending sex cases" among the student population; a majority of those cases had been veterans. Of fifty-two sexually troubled men who came to his office, ranging in age from seventeen to forty-two, twenty-nine were homosexual—twelve "real," in his estimation, and seventeen "latent." (Voyeurism, exhibitionism, and homosexuality were in the same general category, as Glover defined sexual dysfunction.) With one of the "real" homosexuals, he claimed some progress. The others manifested the usual problems of gay men in therapy—a lack of commitment to change, a disturbing "lassitude and inertia."

Attention to same-sex relations between students, or even between students and teachers, wasn't new in the late 1940s. Earlier examples come from all parts of the country. At Amherst in 1913, Robert Frost complained to the dean about a homosexual colleague in the English department, Stark Young, who had become, in Frost's eyes, too familiar with his students, and in 1922 future chef James Beard was asked to leave Reed College in Oregon for his dalliances with fellow students and an instructor. During World War II, a homosexual scandal rocked the University of Texas at Austin and led to the dismissal of several teachers and a report in *Time*. But it wasn't until the postwar era that college administrations perceived the situation as an impending crisis. Their responses varied, from a frustrated sense that there was little they could do (that was the view of the president of the University of Florida, though the laissez-faire approach in Gainesville would be drastically revised by the end of the 1950s) to the patrolling of men's rooms by campus security and the use of informers and local police. At the University of Missouri in Columbia in 1949, an investigation took an especially vicious turn when the dean of men decided that the school was becoming a "homosexual breeding ground . . . a base" for homosexuals around the country. A police raid on a private party in nearby Salem netted E. K. Johnson, the head of the famous journalism program, and numerous students, who were brutally beaten with truncheons, arrested, and then dismissed from the university. A line on the students' transcripts indicated that they had been expelled because of "charges relating to homosexual activity," a note intended to keep them out of almost any other college. One of the students committed suicide. Over the next few years, gay parties on or off campus were monitored, and the simple presence of a student at a social gathering that included "known homosexuals" was grounds for expulsion. For one man, interviewed by Jim Duggins for the "Uncles Project" in San Francisco, this expulsion came only *days* before his graduation and led to a profoundly humiliating situation with his father. In his recollection, hundreds of students at the University of Missouri were ultimately affected by the school's draconian policies.

Far more noticeable in the 1940s and 1950s, and much more bitterly warred against, was the bustling world of men's rest room activity. In his 1970 book *Tearoom Trade: Impersonal Sex in Public Places*, Laud Humphreys delineated the history and the complex sociology of these places of "controlled interaction." Wisely noting that he was not studying homosexuals, but rather "participants in homosexual acts," Humphreys was careful not to lump in one category the participants he observed. As court records throughout the century have verified, many men who frequent "tearooms" are husbands and fathers whose homosexual experiences are limited to infrequent excursions—they would never consider going to a gay bar or having a relationship with another man, and ten minutes of oral sex in an anonymous setting is all they want of gay life. For them, the men's room scene has always been an expedient, if risky, choice. (The most famous example is Walter Jenkins, a family man and White House aide to Lyndon Johnson, arrested in 1964 in a Washington, D.C., rest room.) Other participants include the bisexual and the merely curious or titillated, gay men who are uneasy or uninformed about the other avenues they might take to find sex partners, or gay men who are fully integrated into homosexual life but relish the atmosphere and the chance to have sex with straight men, keeping alive the gay-trade patterns of old.

"I suppose there has been such activity since the invention of plumbing," Humphreys quoted one man he interviewed. "I first started out in one of those pavilion places [the kind of public rest room built in the 1920s]. But the real fun began during the Depression. There were all those new buildings, easy to reach, and the automobile was really getting popular about then. . . . Suddenly, it just seemed like half the men in town met in tearooms." The WPA construction of public facilities throughout the nation's parks, many with heavy wooden doors screened from public view by a latticework partition, meant that men in smaller towns now had the same opportunities that urban men had been exploiting since the 1890s in subway or train station bathrooms. By the late 1940s, the extent of the sexual activities and pickups taking place in these settings was a major law enforcement concern. But its scope extended beyond downtowns, parks, and roadside stops; officers on military bases and administration officials on university campuses regularly had to deal with rest room "loitering" and the existence of "glory holes" (another stellar piece of 1930s argot), which were holes cut into the partitions between stalls for viewing of one's masturbating neighbor or for oral sex of a highly focused nature. These were not problems the military or the academic world was eager to have aired in public, any more than the Metropolitan Opera board wanted to face facts about some of their patrons. (The joke in the 1940s about the standing-room section at the Met was that it was harder to know which was the louder sound when the lights went up, the applause of the audience or the noise of zippers being yanked back in place.)

Legal commentators were freer to address the topic. "Sexual perverts, because of lack of control, [have] become very bold and are using public toilets and other public buildings as meeting places," a Pennsylvania judge wrote in a 1950 article addressing the need for tougher morals squads and greater latitude in sentencing sex offenders. Judge Crumlish's view was shared by many. Men hanging out in public bathrooms, either to lure innocent boys to their doom (in sex crimes panic fantasy) or (in reality) to suck each other off—what could be more revolting? It was a perfect image for those who wanted to proselytize about the inherent baseness of male homosexuality, and it was a stereotype that made many gay men uncomfortable and angry. (Gay critics of the tearoom trade grew in number as time passed and more gay bars and bathhouses opened and harassment declined. By the late 1960s, spending a great deal of time in rest rooms was looked upon by a new generation of gay men as a little odd when so many other ways to have sex or meet people were available. This outlook, however, ignored the fact that bar and bathhouse patrons and tearoom regulars are often part of very different groups, both in lifestyle and in the psychology of their sexual arousal.) Certainly to gay men who came of age in the 1920s and 1930s, the criticisms couldn't mean very much. Mocked, assaulted, or denied their basic rights if they indicated their love for another man (not to mention simple lust), they made do as they saw fit. They went where they knew men with similar sexual appetites went—and, in a crucial point Laud Humphreys makes about tearooms, where they were least likely to encounter unwilling witnesses (women, children) or unwilling participants (straight men). The tawdriness of the setting was a by-product that could in time become part of the erotic thrill or was simply ignored as best one could. In a society that said one penis in a man's mouth or rectum— wherever, whenever—had exceeded the limits of any moral person's lifetime, it could hardly matter what other fastidious pronouncements or conditions heterosexuals wanted to dwell on.

What mattered was the kind of internalization involved. The tearoom practice was unfortunate if a man viewed his experiences as a degradation appropriate to his station in life as a "deviant" (a great danger for those who became addicted to the setting, effectively divorcing sex and emotion), but not every man looked on it that way. In *Quiet Fire*, Keith Vach's book of interviews with older gay men, Bob Basker spoke of his many episodes, circa 1932 to 1934, as a teenage aggressor in a New York City subway bathroom: "I met some really nice people who were afraid of being involved [with someone my age], but I did manage to go home with some of them. . . . I got to learn something about classical music, ballet, opera. My cultural life began with these men, at the 110th Street and Lexington station john." Far from being ruined for life by his initiation, Basker became a successful businessman in the 1950s, took an active part in the black civil rights movement, and helped lead the campaign against Anita Bryant in Florida in the 1970s.

Two other examples from different parts of the country, separated by twenty years, indicate how little had changed in two decades, especially when public space was apt to be the only space. In the spring of 1934, Arthur Maule (who in the late 1950s would serve as president of the New York Mattachine Society) was a twenty-two-year-old who was, in his own words, "extremely unsophisticated." Having grown up in a small town in eastern Pennsylvania, a product of a Quaker-Presbyterian family, he had never come upon the term *homosexual* and hadn't a clue to the fact that there were other adults who felt as he did. One afternoon he went into the Broad Street station rest room in downtown Philadelphia to use the urinal and happened upon a strange scene. A dozen men were lingering about, "obviously not relieving themselves." Maule had stumbled upon "one of the most notorious tearooms in the city." He was picked up for the first time in his life and soon thereafter introduced into an ever-widening circle of gay friends. In the summer of 1954, in an almost equally naive spirit, nineteen-year-old John Halbach followed a much older man who had caught his eye through the park near his parents' house in Los Angeles. They made their way behind the shrubbery to the men's room. "I was desperate to meet someone and I was sure I was originating some very bold, crazy thing, following a guy into a bathroom." Halbach's tactic worked, though he was promptly disabused of the notion that there was anything original to the manner of his meeting the fellow he did in the stall, who soon became a close friend. "More than just a friend, though. [He] took me under his wing. The language, the better cruising spots, the different types of sex you could have, the way the police did business, I got all that from him. The idea that a cop could have been in the next stall and arrested us— my God, that was startling to me. That was news to me." Halbach's contact, a native of New Orleans and a World War I veteran, also gave him an appealing sense of being part of a group with a long underground history and a social code of its own.

Like Harry Hay's encounter with his sailor-lover in his teens, a moment that began as a purely sexual frolic could quickly take on a larger significance. The functions of the gay press in a later day, of providing information and a much-needed sense of the past, took place in postcoital conversations in hotel beds, in darkened movie houses while pants were being pulled up, in bathroom stalls, under trees and bridges. "If we are going to start apologizing for our history of public sex," as one septuagenarian veteran of decades of rest room activity summarized the matter in the 1990s, "someone is going to have to tell me how and where I would have met anyone and learned anything when I was a kid. I didn't make the rules." Or, with a little more drollery, as the lavatory-haunting doctor in Djuna Barnes's *Nightwood* asks: "Is it my fault that my only fireside is the outhouse?"

The furtiveness of a quick coupling in a park or a tearoom particularly suited the needs of men who were either married or unable to mingle in other ways with gay men, but the atmosphere could lend itself to epic proportions of self-hate and depression. "It was not an experience for the genteel," commented one man whose first sexual encounters—and many succeeding ones from the late 1940s through the early 1960s—took place in men's rooms in Cleveland and Chicago. The grubbiness and the element of danger inherent in the setting were aphrodisiacs for some men; for others, it was more a matter of compulsion than pleasure. But what of the bars and clubs, which were spaces of open declaration yet, at times, equivalent risk? To what extent did they contribute to, or impede, a sense of self-affirmation and conviviality?

One of the important topics in gay history today is the explosive growth, or presumed growth, of gay bars after World War II. The weight of anecdotal evidence suggests that the postwar period was the first real "boom" time, but this won't be known for certain until much more research is conducted in many cities—less atypical, perhaps, than New York or San Francisco—to determine what organized social opportunities existed for gay men before 1941 and then again, in those same locales, after 1945. As noted earlier, the fluctuating definition of a gay bar rightly and inevitably complicates the search. Bars in hotels or bars that were only partly gay, or gay at certain times of the day or days of the week, are fairly counted as havens for gay men in the 1930s, but by the 1950s, a gay bar or club, to most homosexuals, was either an all-gay establishment, a place no one would mistake for anything else, or one that was so hospitable it might as well have been.

Don Paulson's *An Evening at the Garden of Allah: A Gay Cabaret in Seattle*, published by Columbia University Press in 1996, is an example of a valuable local-history contribution to this picture of gay life pre– and post–World War II. Before the war, according to the many gay men of the region with whom Paulson spoke, the Casino in the basement of the Double Header was a decent place to go for an evening, but the significant activity was more scattered, located on the streets, in apartments, in the burlesque-house balconies. In 1946, the Garden of Allah was opened by two gay entrepreneurs in a ramshackle nineteenth-century hotel in the downtown area. Modeled on San Francisco's Finocchio's, it was intended to showcase drag entertainment for a mixed audience, but its open-door policy for the city's homosexuals made it, in the minds of Paulson's sources, a secure gay space for both men and women. (One man commented emphatically about the number of lesbians who frequented the Garden: "It was their place, too." This is in marked contrast to other cities, where lesbian–gay male socializing was becoming less common throughout the 1950s.) The draw was a melange of national and local female impersonation talent: Rae Bourbon, Jackie Starr, Skippy LaRue, Billy Devoe, Francis Blair, Ricky

Reynolds, Robin Raye, Hotcha Hinton. "The Garden was very earthy, a real underground decadent cabaret out of Toulouse Lautrec," another man said. Ignoring the seediness, he reiterated the common feeling: "It was our place." A University of Washington student, who discovered the Garden in 1956, recognized the setting as one that wasn't "all that attractive," but felt he had found a refuge where he could make friends and be as campy as he wanted to be, free from stares and judgments. Many Seattle gays wouldn't have been caught dead in the Garden of Allah, but Paulson nonetheless credits the cabaret (quite plausibly, given all the testimony he gathered) with "shaping the consciousness" of those who did go. "Being 'out' at the Garden of Allah in an oppressive time for gays and lesbians," he wrote, "was a giant step toward having the confidence to form political groups, challenge police authority, and pound on the doors at City Hall." Heterosexual commentary about gay bars and cabarets, written by men who rarely or never went to them, stressed the dark or shabby elements. Gay recollections are more varied.

Seattle wasn't unique in this respect. In those cities that had most benefited from a gay influx during the war, there was no reason to expect the momentum to subside. Gay archivists Eric Garber and Bill Walker compiled an annotated list of "San Francisco Resorts for Sex Perverts, Pre-1950" that includes more than thirty places in that city (some gay and some mixed) where homosexuals could meet in the late 1940s, and in Chicago, Boston, and Philadelphia, the bars and bathhouses did a brisk business. In New York, the difference in gay nightlife between 1939 and 1948, Leo Adams told a friend, was "unbelievable." Third Avenue, with its famed "bird circuit" of bars (the Blue Parrot, the Faison D'Or, etc.) was at "the height of gaiety" then, he said. Harlem entertainer Phil Black began his long-lived tradition of a Thanksgiving Day drag ball in 1945, and within a few years male couples at Lucky's Rendezvous were taken by Harlemites as a commonplace sight. Donald Vining concluded, in a Christmas Eve diary entry for 1950, that there had never been "a more suitable time to be homosexual," though he rightly concluded that his experiences in New York were not typical "because I reek so of self-respect." He did, however, find the "belles" who flocked in summer to the gay section of Long Island's Long Beach to be as "flagrant and unashamed" as he had been told they were, and the gay influx to Fire Island and Provincetown continued apace.

Yet even in areas where gay men who wanted to socialize or find sex partners might have had a difficult time earlier, new possibilities presented themselves. Trade Winds was a going concern in the Roanoke Valley by the late 1940s (according to area residents, the first openly or definably gay bar in Virginia); Cleveland had three or four bars then, though they tended to be "dark and cheaply furnished . . . little more than cleared-out storage rooms"; and the New Yorker, later known as the Ports O' Call, provided the gay men of Worcester, Massachusetts, with a focus for their cruising. (Well-off homosexuals "went somewhere else for their fun," a local man observed, "so that Worcester's gay community was made up mainly of machinists, textile workers, kitchen helpers, hairdressers and, on weekends, farmhands.") There were three gay bars in Albuquerque after the war, Morris Kight recalled, and by 1949 the Entre Nous in St. Louis was particularly well spoken of among East Coast gay men who traveled to the Midwest. When George Flemister moved from New York City to Florida shortly after V-J Day, he feared he was headed for a social wasteland, but that proved to be far from true. He soon met his lover of the next fifty years at the Singing Bar, one of several gay nightspots in Miami. As another Floridian commented, "It was a little easier in 1950 to think, 'Oh, we're really all over the place' than it had been in 1940." Frank Kameny's coming out in a Tucson, Arizona, gay bar was, he recalled forty years later, pure delight, while visitors to Columbus, Ohio, remembered the bar of the Neal House as a "great pickup spot."

The 1949 *Gay Girl's Guide*, a limited edition, privately printed "networking" booklet with construction-paper covers (subtitled "A Primer for Novices, A Review for Roués"), gave lengthy descriptions of the social possibilities in New York City that year, but also compiled a list of gay bars and known cruising spots, often in hotel bars, in more than thirty other cities from Boston to San Diego. The anonymous editors requested feedback from their readers, and the 1950 edition of the *Guide* offered updates and new suggestions in cities such as Atlanta, Hartford, Omaha, Pittsburgh, and Louisville and Lexington, Kentucky.

In the absence of bar guides or knowledgeable friends, gay haunts were not always easy to locate (especially for younger gay men) and, in some cases, diligent personal research preceded experience. For months, James Baird, a law school student at Stanford, had been picking up whatever odd bits of information about gay bars he could find in the few books or newspaper articles that touched on the existence of such depraved places. The problem was that none of the sources mentioned where to find these bars or clubs. Finally, one night in the fall of 1950, Baird and four friends—all straight—were driving back to Palo Alto from a football game in Oakland when they stopped for a drink in San Francisco. They spent an agreeable hour at the Golden Nugget on Market Street. Slowly, Baird came to the conclusion that a few of the other patrons, all of whom were men, looked gay—that, indeed, the whole place seemed to fit the description he had been studying of homosexual gathering places—though none of his classmates noticed anything out of the ordinary. On his first free evening, Baird raced back to the bar alone and his suspicions, or hopes, were confirmed. A man bought him a drink and, after a little conversation, asked if he wanted to join him to "cruise baskets at Keno's," another nearby bar; Baird was quickly introduced to the world of "cruising," "baskets," gay sex, and, in the case of his new acquaintance, friends willing to lend out their apartments to students in need of a place to bring a "trick."

In towns where the existence of openly or exclusively gay bars was still impossible after the war, social life in private homes continued to compensate. Tulsa in the late 1940s and early 1950s was "a great subterranean party town," a student at the university there remembered. The frequent gatherings tended to divide along rigid class and racial lines, as they did in most other metropolitan areas. The gay men from the well-to-do part of town—"the piss-elegant queens of Oklahoma, very snobbish"—kept to themselves, though there was always room for the attractive new arrival from the college. The middle-class and working-class gay men had their own busy social circles and were never, or rarely, invited to the better homes. The only bar within city limits where homosexuals congregated was the Cheyenne, a blue-collar dive (serving 3-2 beer only in this dry state) in which the straight customers kept to one part of the room and the gays, including some classic nellies, kept to the other. The bar patrons remained for the most part unharassed. Tulsa gays had more to fear from the police, who were known to demand "certain oral intimacies" (as one resident put it) as readily as cash in a shakedown.

The police everywhere were a problem. They seemed, sometimes, to exist to remind gay men and lesbians of two facts of modern life—first, that society did not merely disapprove of their orientation, but actively hated them; second, that their normal human needs for sex and sociability would, if acted upon, be turned to "useful" account. That usefulness was itself manifested in two ways: in its most elementary sense, it had to do with bolstering the ego of anyone who was *not* a homosexual. In the mid-twentieth-century pecking order, nothing was lower than a self-confessed faggot. No conscience-stricken liberals, no legal-aid societies, no civil rights advocates or ACLU boards stood ready to defend him, and few criminals brought before the bench were subject to the particular kind of humiliation and scorn visited upon homosexuals, whose families were often ready to disown them after their public disgrace. The laziest, most ignorant and corrupt cop knew that he enjoyed greater esteem than any of the queers he was given permission to beat or blackmail.

The second way in which homosexuals were brought into a pernicious, useful relationship with those who abused them was financial. When pressed, gay men paid. In the 1940s and 1950s, law enforcement officials must have found it hard to imagine how their predecessors got by without such a lucrative source of unreported income. (The advent of the tearoom scene and the gay bar are milestones of their own in the history of police work in America.) To be caught in a men's room or a park—as a victim of entrapment by a vice squad decoy, as an innocent bystander, or as a "criminal" engaged in sex—meant handing over a sizable sum to avoid arrest. Taken in a raid on a gay bar or followed out of the bar on his way home, a gay man knew the consequences that would follow from his exposure if he were unable to negotiate a quick cash arrangement. And, from all sides, the advice was the same: give them what they want. When a lawyer had to be used as an intermediary to keep the case off the docket, the under-the-table "extras" could easily cost the defendant a month's salary or more.

Watching the police come by a bar to collect their payoff money from the owner or the bartender was an experience nothing short of infuriating for the gay men present. But it was a mild irritation compared to the indignities, and the relish with which they were inflicted, when the police decided to intimidate a bar owner behind in his payments, placate a vice-crusading politician, or just "have some fun" by going after the patrons. A favorite tactic of the day, particularly popular with the Los Angeles police department, was to impress upon the nervous gays a sense of the randomness of their persecution. The police would stroll in, IDs would be checked, and everyone told to form two lines, after which several men would be selected and taken away for no other reason than their unlucky place in a given line. The others would be threatened, belittled, and then released to go home. The specialty of the Washington, D.C., police force was long assumed to be its comprehensive compilation of names and addresses of area gay men who had been stopped on the street, in parks, or outside bars, a list made available to the FBI. In every major city in the 1990s, there are gay men in their seventies and eighties who have stories to relate of sexual humiliation at the hands of the police who arrested them as they left a gay bar or a bathhouse. In the words of one California man, "Being forced to give some fat cop a blow-job in the back of his car is about as degrading an experience as you can imagine."

The wonder is that anyone ventured into this dangerous territory at all. The defensive posture a gay man could assume by leading a quiet, professional life (that one's homosexuality didn't have to mean that much, that one could "get by") was meaningless in a gay bar. A strong statement was being made—about need and nerve, vulnerability and identity—upon entering. It would also have been too much to expect that the enmity from outside wouldn't sometimes poison the atmosphere within. Pecking orders reproduce themselves endlessly, and camp behavior had its dark side. "It was very fashionable to be a super-bitch" in the 1950s, Rick Colantino admitted. "We honed it to an art." Cruising could become brutally competitive, a cynical affect was almost a grand tradition, and alcoholism among gay men was fast becoming a serious problem. Yet, throughout the postwar years, especially among white men, the gay bar continued to be an important focus of homosexual life in America, for the practical purposes of seeing new faces and old friends and as an emblem of cultural survival. Gay bars were often financed by the mob, on the East Coast particularly, and they were tolerated by society because policemen and politicians made money off them, but as an institution, they came into being and lasted because gay men and lesbians wanted them and were willing to run risks and suffer to keep them alive in one form or another.

10

A LITERATURE OF
SEXUALITY: II

I hope that Radclyffe Hall will one day write about a lesbian who is not tragic, as I hope to do a portrait of a man homo who is perfectly, or at least fairly, well adjusted to life. Don't you think the tragic and lonely aspects have been too much emphasized? Soon there will be no question about normal or abnormal people. One will merely write of individuals who fall in love in different ways, and the rigid conception of man and woman will melt away into something more fluid.

> —Clarkson Crane, a California teacher
> and novelist, writing to Elsa Gidlow,
> a lesbian friend, 11 April 1929

As many cultural critics have observed, the role of books and writing in the development of an identity—prior to the age of television, at any rate—has often been of special significance to marginalized groups. Denied access in their daily lives or in public forums to any kind of validation, or even a knowledge of their history and the diversity of their contemporary experience, such groups will look to writers to fill that gap. For homosexuals, whose families and teachers are not likely to have much to say to them on the subject, the gay novels and plays encountered in adolescence and early adulthood can be vitally important and long remembered. In a survey conducted in 1971 by sociologist Barry M. Dank, 50 percent of the gay men questioned said they came to develop their ideas of what it means to be gay through contacts with other gay men, and 15 percent developed their ideas through reading. The latter is an astonishingly high figure, as David Bergman pointed out in *Gaiety Transfigured*, considering how few Americans buy serious books or regard them as life-altering. In the 1940s and 1950s, this figure might well have been higher; conversations or interviews with educated gay men in their seventies and eighties invariably come around to tales of scouring public library shelves in their youth for relevant texts, the delight at coming upon any one of a dozen key novels from the time, the comfort provided by Donald Webster Cory's *The Homosexual in America* (1951).

In the years following World War II, libraries finally had something the troubled and the curious might hunt for and read, surrepetitiously or otherwise. College professors in many parts of the country in the 1930s had raised the issues of Whitman's "Calamus" poems, of Proust's inversions of his characters' gender, of Wilde's "Bunburying" jokes. After the war, however, the professorial campaign on behalf of European literature was all the more eager and respectable. Reading lists expanded to include *The Immoralist*, Cocteau, Isherwood. André Gide's Socratic defense of homosexuality, *Corydon*, came out in a widely available edition in America in 1950, complete with a few pages by a prominent Yale psychologist arguing that exclusive heterosexuality was not "an immutable biological law." A Broadway adaptation of *The Immoralist* in 1954 seemed, at long last, to spell the end of the prohibitions dating from the furor over *The Captive*. America's own writers took advantage of the new freedom, to varying degrees. When Blanche DuBois tells Mitch about the suicide of her homosexual husband, a boy too sensitive for this world, Tennessee Williams was reinforcing a cliché—loving and well-meant, but nonetheless a cliché. In his short stories, though, he moved without apology into uncharted territory, as mournful and eerie as his beloved Vieux Carré. In his "One Arm" (1948) and "Hard Candy" (1954), Gore Vidal's *The City and the Pillar* (1948), love stories like the soft-core soap operas of Jay Little, "Quatrefoil" (1950) and "Finistere" (1951), gay men had opportunities to read about themselves that were unimaginable by the standards of the 1930s. On occasion, those opportunities were guardedly affirming. "Love can happen like that. For one night only," Williams's narrator reflects in "The Angel in the Alcove," his watchful apparition neither approving nor condemning what has transpired in his rooming-house bed.

Objections of one sort or another quickly followed. In *After the Lost Generation*, a highly regarded study of the new fiction, John Aldridge expressed the opinion that homosexual talent was by definition narrow, "of one special kind," leading to an inevitable grotesquerie. Malcolm Cowley brooded about "fairy-Freudian" novels that lacked "ordinary human warmth." A more probing concern came from one of the post–Lost Generation principals. Then a twenty-five-year-old unknown, James Baldwin published an essay in 1949, "Preservation of Innocence," which questioned the appropriateness of any distinctions based on sexual acts, in fiction or in life. "It is quite impossible to write a worthwhile novel about a Jew or a Gentile or a Homosexual," he wrote, "for people refuse, happily, to function in so neat and one-dimensional a fashion." Moreover, Baldwin implied, a genre such as the "gay novel" was no less dangerous than the individual appellation "gay man" or "lesbian" because it served to divide people *and* strengthen the hand of those already in power, who always benefit from stressing differences and denying commonality. With *Giovanni's Room* (1956), Baldwin created a parable about the consequences of the polarities and the naming. Giovanni, an Italian, accepts his affair with David as an expression of his ardor for another human being. David, fiercely American, cannot see beyond "normal" and "abnormal," "heterosexual" and "homosexual," and abandons Giovanni to the waiting predators.

Baldwin's musings in "Preservation of Innocence" were, as usual in his writing, far ahead of their time. That homosexuality was becoming a more visible phenomenon in American life, and therefore a specialized, clearly defined topic of interest to more people, is evident from the attention it gained from the publishing world. Many of the Depression-era gay novels were products of small presses with a limited readership. In the next decade, big New York publishing houses, always a gauge of sorts, took stock of a changing market. What ensued was not exactly a wave, but more a steady stream of novels with gay themes or overtones. None of these books had the happy ending E. M. Forster believed was so necessary for gay readers (which he provided in *Maurice*, though that novel was to remain on his desk for the next twenty-five years), and not all were even written by gay authors, but for those homosexual men starved for acknowledgment of their existence and the variety and reality of their lives, a significant cultural change was in the making. Harper & Bros. brought out William Maxwell's *The Folded Leaf* the summer the war ended and then followed that subtle coming-of-age tale two years later with an even more audacious novel, *The Gallery* by John Horne Burns. In that same period, Dutton, Dial, Rinehart, Farrar, Straus, and Houghton Mifflin all tested the waters with their own gay titles.

One notable aspect of these books is their exploration of same-sex attachments in less Eastern-urban circumstances and locales: in Chicago and on a college campus in Illinois in *The Folded Leaf*; at the Citadel in Calder Willingham's *End As a Man* (1947); in Mississippi in Hugh Creekmore's *The Welcome* (1948); in Virginia in Gore Vidal's *The City and the Pillar*; in a New England prep school in John Horne Burns's *Lucifer with a Book* (1949). Even in novels not about homosexuality, gay men as minor characters appear as part of established subcultures all over the map—for example, in Honolulu in James Jones's baggy war opus, *From Here to Eternity*—or as part of a sensibility that is manifestly gay—the best example being *Other Voices, Other Rooms* by Truman Capote, who came out as much by way of his sultry Henri Cartier-Bresson dust-jacket photo as by anything overt in the novella itself. And just as Greenwich Village and its equivalents in other cities were no longer presumed to be the sole areas where gay life existed, the notion of the easily identified bachelor as the "regulation queer" was also reconsidered. Charles Jackson's married protagonist in *The Fall of Valor* (1946) awakens to his desires for young men while on vacation with his wife on Nantucket, and both men in *The Welcome* who shared a homosexual idyll in their teenage years later marry, though neither of them can quite forget "the close perfection of those days." Indeed, Gore Vidal's principal intention with *The City and the Pillar*, he wrote, was to shatter that romantic fallacy of the lost golden moment of homosexual grace and to situate homosexuality in the realm of ordinary masculine experience, in the here and now.

The man who slept with other men as a Regular Guy—not a subculture habitué, a trashy queen, or a dandy—was a hard sell at the time, but in the decade between *The Fall of Valor* and *Giovanni's Room*, the reach of novels about same-sex desire moved well beyond the formulae of the early 1930s' books, which had emphasized immersion and segregation in the "twilight world," the traditions of pansy culture, the argot, and the drag balls. With a few exceptions, the postwar writers labored to create a less exotic milieu for their characters, and that shift involved exploring some previously neglected themes. One was the impact of the war on bringing men out; no longer could the evil city, the funny uncle, or the man in the park be held to blame. A second was the dilemma of the women who were in love with or married to men who wanted more than a monogamous heterosexual union. The hurt, horror, insight, and confusion of these female characters was—rightly, finally—taken to be an integral part of the story. Ethel in *The Fall of Valor* and Hella in *Giovanni's Room*, for instance, respond bitterly to having been "used." Isabel in *The Welcome*, after the first shock, intimates to her fiancé that what she doesn't know about his extramarital life probably won't hurt her. Also of importance now was the frustration men felt at being defined by their sexual choices, as the time of official silence was drawing to a close—and the equally intense realization that, at least for the foreseeable future, society was going to insist on just that narrow arrangement.

The resulting problem for homosexual writers was that in the end they were likely to be squeezed into one of three grooves. They were "pleading" for a dubious minority cause. They were "chronicling" small-town oppression or a tawdry (and now topical) subculture. Or, on a higher but more perverse level, they were dramatizing their own misfortune, their exquisite pain, their Otherness. The one thing they weren't doing, apparently, was writing stories about people and relationships in the world as we all know it.

THE FIRST POSTWAR gay writer to command respect on the national level from the literary establishment and to give promise of surmounting those designations is relatively unknown today. John Horne Burns, a veteran from Massachusetts living as an expatriate in Italy after the war, was considered one of the bright lights of American fiction. *The Gallery* found passionate readers, both gay and straight, in 1947—and, fifty years later, still seems a tour de force. A series of portraits and vignettes set in occupied Naples and Algiers near the close of the war, it effectively evoked the culture shock and anomie that Americans encountered on liberating the Old World. The officers and GIs, chaplains and Red Cross women, fearful or feisty civilians, and sex-starved (and sex-glutted) multitudes who people the novel want consolation and connection, physical and spiritual, anywhere at all—in the streets, in dark corners and palazzi, in the land of "Queen Penicillin" in the VD ward. In the monstrous climate of Italy circa 1944, Burns's homosexual characters are not exactly integrated into the larger social fabric, but their needs are no more bizarre, or less crazed, than anyone else's.

The most appealing aspect of *The Gallery* for gay men was its extended treatment of a gay bar—the first, and still the best, in American literature. The bar is the domain of Momma—jokingly known as the "Napoli Milionaria"—the gray eminence who fought her way up from nothing to a secure position in the post-Mussolini era and lavishes attention on "her boys" that was once reserved for Poppa. Like most such places, her bar on the Galleria Umberto Primo is a theater and a playing field, crossing lines of rank and nationality, a haven that allows for low-key cruising, confessional drama, hilarious chitchat and, finally, a kind of "acid tenderness." "Magda" and "Esther," two British sergeants, serve as a queenly chorus; a token lesbian WAC observes from the end of the bar ("It's just like a salon"); and gender rituals are played out afresh each time the straights wander in slumming or by accident.

With a style that darts from the naturalistic to the surreal, Burns does justice to his material with the quick character sketches that give the entire book its weight and an unusual inclusiveness. It's all there, or close enough—the inexhaustible camp, the sentimentality, the posing, the good fellowship, and those moments, most acutely felt just before closing time or a raid by the MPs, when the air is filled with "a presentiment of possibilities, of hectic enchantments, of the fleeting moment that never could be again because it was too preposterous and frantic and keyed-up." Momma's patrons are from all over the globe, including decorated officers, and express their love as freely as their disdain or self-hate. Finally, and not coincidentally (at least as far as the editors at Harper were concerned), this gay bar is not in America. In certain ways, "over there" was still a nice idea.

After publishing two more books far below the quality of *The Gallery*, Burns died a quick, early death several years later, victim of a cerebral hemorrhage—or, as his friend and fellow expatriate Gore Vidal surmised, of too much Italian brandy and Italian sun. Vidal had more of the survivor in him. He was also more of a risk-taker. After publishing two novels in his early twenties, he was well on his way toward establishing a solid, if conventional, literary career. *The City and the Pillar* put an end to its conventional aspect and looked at first as if it would jeopardize its solidity as well. "Bored with playing it safe," Vidal said, he wanted to try something new.

"New" in 1948 did not mean writing a novel about homosexuals, obviously; it meant eschewing the outlandish elements, the egregious local color previous writers had exploited. To that end, Vidal wanted something akin to James Farrell's style and, for his early chapters, a Nick Adams setting. Jim Willard and Bob Ford, athletic high school students in Virginia, make love in the woods one spring vacation. They do this without guilt or recriminations. For Bob, this is a pleasant, fleeting episode of late adolescence and he eventually settles down to married bliss. For Jim, more attracted to men, their frolic is the signal moment of his life, a joyous coupling he invests with mythic qualities. Like Lot's wife in the story the book's title alludes to, Vidal's young man cannot refrain from the dangerous backward glance. As a result, his homosexual life away from home is unsatisfying and peripatetic. He crosses paths with a Hollywood star, a failed writer, a cloying sergeant in the Army, none of them likeable gay men. His later revenge against Bob is a Pyrrhic victory.

Critical response to the novel was mixed, though nowhere near as ill-tempered as might have been expected. Sales in the United States and

Europe were good. A 1965 revision provided a slightly less melodramatic ending, replacing the murder with a more plausible sexual assault. In either version, *The City and the Pillar* long remained a favorite with gay readers, its popularity surpassed only by *Giovanni's Room*. The lean, warts-and-all depiction of the gay scene that Jim Willard explores in California and New York was preferable to anything campier, more lurid, or more sugar-coated. Both the characters' intermittent philosophizing about society's bigotry and the forthright dialogue (how gay men love to bitch the nelly queens) struck a chord. The *New York Times* may have refused advertising space, but *The City and the Pillar* brought novels about gay men into the mainstream.

In the two years following Vidal's book two other important publishers made further, if very different, additions to the growing body of gay American fiction. These novels are pertinent here because they are the most sharply focused examples of a mid-twentieth-century perspective on male sexual bonds. *Stranger in the Land* is a novel set in a small New England town during World War II. The book was completed by 1946, but Ward Thomas was unable to find a publisher for three years, which suggests both the uncertainty with which publishers still regarded the topic and the lackluster quality of the prose. Thomas Hal Phillips's *The Bitterweed Path*, published by Rinehart in early 1950, had a good deal more to recommend it on several counts.

Stranger in the Land, published by Houghton Mifflin, is a book whose purpose, probably intentionally so, is hard to determine. If the author was a homosexual, he had an unremittingly bleak view of life's possibilities for a gay man and may have been making an awkward plea for sympathy; if not, he might have been asking that society reconsider its brutality toward homosexuals, though the book also comes perilously close to confirming the view of homosexuality as a socially menacing force. Raymond Manton, a prissy high school teacher, an embarrassed 4-F, takes care of his sickly mother and, at twenty-eight, acts as if middle age were about to overtake him. He has no friends, no sense of humor, no hope for a better life. Stuck in Chatford, a town that makes Winesburg, Ohio, look like a center of culture and intellect, he becomes enamored of a local Irish hood several years his junior and watches in horror as a police roundup drags rich, elderly Orville Finch and his friends off to jail for having enticed local youth into sex-for-hire. Manton's cock-teasing protégé takes advantage of the situation by blackmailing the frightened teacher, who at the end of the novel drowns his blackmailer during a midnight swim at a deserted lake. For a man whose goal was to achieve a "painless celibacy" and saw his life as "barren sorrow, egocentric and self-indulgent . . . a hopeless estrangement," the killing of Terry Devine was the only solution to his dilemma. A contemporary reader of this novel is apt to feel glad that the stud-punk gets what he deserves, but may be just as ready to see Raymond Manton come to a bad end if he snidely corrects the boy's grammar one more time. Please remember you are speaking the language of Shelley and Byron, he lectures Terry while they sit in the corner of a local dive, Manton paying for the beers and hiding his erections.

The unpleasantness of Ward Thomas's novel has to do with the ambiguity of the author's point of view. Were readers being asked to see Manton as a product of a twisted culture, or is Thomas's protagonist himself "naturally" twisted, one of those unfortunates on whom nature has played a dirty trick? The timing of the book's publication was another problem: for all its pretend-sympathy for the excruciating loneliness Raymond Manton endures, the novel plays a little too neatly into the new stereotype of the homosexual as a threat to the young. The Orville Finches of Chatford pay teenage boys to have sex with them; the Raymond Mantons of the world debase themselves in loveless relationships and act out a murderous rage. And that's all there is to gay men and gay life in New England in the early 1940s.

In contrast to the darkness and immaturity of *Stranger in the Land*, Thomas Hal Phillips's *The Bitterweed Path* was something rare in the literature of sexuality in America and mightily refreshing to any gay reader in the year Senator McCarthy went on the warpath. This was a book that not only refrained from clichés about horny, lonely men growing old before their time, but depicted romantic and erotic love as pleasingly ungovernable, impervious to categories, and natural in whatever forms it ultimately took. Set in Vicksburg in the early years of the century, the novel is about two bright, rugged boys who are quietly but strongly attracted to each other, and the father of one who is equally drawn—both emotionally and physically—to his son's best friend. Both young men eventually marry and feel toward their wives a legitimate passion, but it never occurs to them that the one impulse necessarily negates the others.

Phillips's material was of a highly sensational nature, obviously, and all the more remarkable given the fact that he wrote the book as his master's thesis at the University of Alabama. The wonder is that he was able to make of it something plausible and almost lyrical rather than crude or bizarre. When, on a riverboat trip, adolescent Darrell Barclay curls up in bed with his friend's father, Malcolm Pitt, with their hands resting lightly together, he feels happily "bound forever to the great strength against him." When, as a married man, he enjoys a night of "wild tenderness" with Roger, Malcolm's son, he knows he has more definitively crossed a line— "reached the just-beyond"—but acts as if he has been right not to deny this other, more intense part of his natural self. Interestingly, and a reason the author has set his novel more than forty years in the past, no one uses or even hints at the words or concepts of the Kinsey era. The divisions and the labeling, like the self-torture, belong to another age. Had they decided to stay together, Darrell and Roger might have been a version of the two unmarried plantation owners we hear about in *Cat on a Hot Tin Roof*, a haunting pair, the one unwilling to outlive the other, his bedmate for forty years—a kind of devotion, Big Daddy tells Brick, that any worldly man should be able to understand. Mendacity be damned.

The journey from *Strange Brother* and *Twilight Men* to *The City and the Pillar* and *The Bitterweed Path* is considerable and important. The latter books were not written for therapeutic purposes, as tidy little exercises in making oppressed people feel better about themselves, but they did help create a sense that male homosexual experience was more than a source of freakish entertainment, that it was as inherently interesting, as variously motivated, as tender or aggressive, as any other mode of life regarded as a fit subject for literature. How many of these late-1940s books dealing with same-sex desire were purchased or actually made their way into libraries across the heartland of America is, of course, another matter. "Certainly I knew about them," one gay librarian in the Midwest (now retired) commented in an interview. "I read them all myself. Vidal, Baldwin, Capote. *The Gallery* got a lot of attention. I remember thinking at the time that *The Bitterweed Path* ... was something that was not sensationalized, it was nicely written, made us look like human beings. But would we have ordered it for the library? Or, would *I* have ordered it for the library? In [our small town], I might as well have taken out an ad [about myself] in the paper." His point is not far-fetched. For the new literature to find a place, enough librarians, booksellers, and reviewers had to put themselves on the line. *Library Journal* offered the squeamish complaint about Thomas Hal Phillips's gentle story that "unfortunately there is no better word than homosexuality to describe the basic theme of this unusual novel."

THE TWO BOOKS that many librarians were comfortable ordering, and that might have had a more immediate impact on the lives of literate gay men, weren't novels at all. One was an 800-page scientific study replete with graphs and charts, Alfred Kinsey's *Sexual Behavior in the Human Male*, and the other, Donald Webster Cory's *The Homosexual in America: A Subjective Approach*, a treatise whose style was calmly pedagogical and whose message was progress through "minority" awareness.

Kinsey's work was the true landmark, both in its scope and its conclusions, and the fame it brought its author marked a new era in the history of sex research. An entomologist at Indiana University whose specialty was the North American gall wasp, Kinsey began his study in the 1930s. While teaching an undergraduate course on marriage and the family, he complained about how little accurate, detailed, and nonjudgmental information on sex was available. As a result, funded by a Rockefeller Foundation grant, he and his assistants ultimately met with tens of thousands of volunteers, using an elaborate interview system of 350 to 500 questions, designed, Kinsey believed, to detect inconsistencies in an individual's account of his sex life. Between 1938 and 1956, 18,000 men and women reportedly went through the process, 8,000 of them questioned by the ever-sympathetic Kinsey. The volunteers of the 1930s were indeed pioneers; by the 1950s, after *Sexual Behavior in the Human Male* had sold a quarter of a million copies and Kinsey had been on the cover of *Time*, it was a status symbol to claim to have been interviewed by him. He found his contacts and referrals everywhere: on college campuses and in prisons (the usual routes), but also on trains and in gay bars, amid church groups and PTAs, through marriage counselors and museum personnel, in hitchhikers, journalists, nurses, doctors, social workers, farmers, pimps, homemakers, and underworld hoods.

The loud criticisms heaped upon *Sexual Behavior in the Human Male*, heard from the moment of its publication in January 1948, focused on two areas. There were those who questioned Kinsey's methods in principle. They were uneasy with his implicit distancing of sex from emotion or any social or spiritual context, his reduction of his subject to the level of orgasm counting. Never seen as a thinker, like Freud or Ellis, Kinsey was relegated by many, as Paul Robinson wrote in *The Modernization of Sex*, "to the role of enterprising empiricist, a George Gallup of sexologists." Others argued with more credibility about the accuracy of his methods, believing that a reliance on volunteer interviewees necessarily gathered stories from an atypically active, even exhibitionistic group of people and that the whole study was skewed toward the white middle-class of the Midwest and Northeast: Indiana, Illinois, Ohio, Pennsylvania, New Jersey, New York, and Massachusetts were much more heavily represented than the South or the West. This objection had some validity and suggests that his exact figures on any topic should not be taken as holy writ applicable to the entire nation. Even if he had lived to complete the 100,000 interviews he hoped to do, numerical certainty about "the human male" (or even the white middle-class human male of Indiana) would have eluded him. What did not elude Kinsey was the big picture.

Sexual Behavior in the Human Male said a great many startling things about the frequency of pre- and extramarital intercourse in America, about the healthiness and near-universality of masturbation, about nocturnal emissions and prostitution. (The statistic that seems most alien to readers of the 1990s is Kinsey's contention that 69 percent of the white male population had had at least one experience with a prostitute. The Pill and post-1960s attitudes toward dating and virginity have obviously wrought an enormous change in the need or desire to pay for sex.) But the shock provoked by Kinsey's findings about homosexual sex was something else again. These findings confirmed the worst postwar suspicions about bachelorhood—of single men between thirty-six and forty years of age in Kinsey's pool, 35.7 percent had had some homosexual experience since adolescence and half of the unmarried fifty-year-olds "are so involved"—and offered new information about its prevalence everywhere, from the 60 percent of preadolescent boys who engaged in homosexual behavior to the 37 percent of all men who had had at least one homosexual experience in their lives between adolescence and old age.

Kinsey had a healthy skepticism about the standard "either/or" approach to sexual issues and realized that one or two homosexual experiences do not "make one a homosexual" any more than one or two heterosexual experiences "make one a heterosexual." In his interviews, he relied instead on a 0–6 continuum scale, which, as his associate Wardell Pomeroy said, was of use "in breaking away from the confines of classifying homosexual and heterosexual behavior as two separate, compartmentalized types." The scale rated an exclusively homosexual orientation as a 6, an equally homosexual-heterosexual sexual history as a 3, and an exclusively heterosexual orientation as a 0, with the appropriate gradations in between. On this basis, Kinsey found that 4 percent of men were unambiguously situated in the 6 range as exclusively homosexual throughout their entire lives; 8 percent were exclusively homosexual for a period of at least three years between the ages of sixteen and fifty-five; 10 percent were "more or less exclusively homosexual" for at least three years between the ages of sixteen and fifty-five. Thirteen percent were "more homosexual than heterosexual" for the same period in the same age range, and 18 percent were "as much homosexual as heterosexual" for the same period in the same age range. To Kinsey, these percentages meant, above all, that the old bigotry, scientific or religious, was a pitiful anachronism. "It is one thing," he wrote, "if we are dealing with a type of activity that is unusual, without precedent among other animals, and restricted to peculiar types of individuals within the human population." It was quite another if the frequency of such activity, and the variety of men who enjoyed it, was as vast as Kinsey believed it to be. In *Sexual Behavior in the Human Male*, a scientist—a married man with three children—was attempting to "prove" that homosexuality had been "a significant part of human sexual activity since the dawn of history, primarily because it is an expression of capacities that are basic in the human animal."

Kinsey took issue with other notions about homosexual sex that were then current, some of which were slowly being rethought after the war—most significantly, the practice of labeling as homosexual one man, the so-called passive partner, for his role in a male-male sex act, while considering the active partner (the one being sucked or the one doing the fucking) unde-filed trade. "Even clinicians have allowed themselves to be diverted by such pretensions," he marveled. He also made a point of observing that educational and occupational differences figured in the acceptance of homosexual sex as a viable form of release, meaning that working-class men with less education were more apt to have sex with other men, and think less of it, than middle-class or professional college-educated men. Most vigorously, Kinsey disputed the modern concept of a sexual identity. It was clear to him that "the homosexual" was an artificial creation in the making, that homosexuals had nothing in common beyond their choice of another male as their sex partner, and that the identification of certain attributes to homosexuals, such as effeminacy or a love of the arts, was a false impression. Even their sexual practices were not to be taken as uniquely "homosexual." For someone to refer to a male who "had sexual relations with his wife in a homosexual way" was, to Kinsey, illogical. Oral-genital or anal-genital contact was homosexual if performed between two men (or two women); it was heterosexual if performed between a man and a woman. In a society eager to believe that homosexuals were a type, and therefore definable and detectable—how else to keep homosexual desire in check?—Kinsey's arguments on this point were as repugnant as his high percentages.

Those numbers were what mattered most to gay men, naturally, and thereafter they were invoked time and again to refute the popular characterization of homosexuals as a minuscule minority of warped minds. (The erroneous assumption that Kinsey had shown that 10 percent of the population was gay, a myth well entrenched by the 1960s, served a political purpose for homosexuals campaigning for their rights, but as can be seen from the figures cited, that is not what Kinsey actually said or implied. The 10 percent who were "more or less exclusively homosexual for at least three years between the ages of sixteen and fifty-five" might have been having an extraordinary amount of heterosexual sex during the rest of that time.) Kinsey was respected because he provided ammunition with which to attack the repellent sexual orthodoxy of organized religion and the psychiatric establishment, because he spoke with confidence and independence,

and (not least by any means) because he became a somewhat notorious figure on the gay bar circuit—the willing listener, the never-fearful explorer.
According to one source, a North Beach bar in San Francisco in the late
1950s devised its own tribute to the Kinsey Report, as the book was called.
The walls of the men's room at the Anxious Asp were papered with pages
from the relevant chapters.

Three years after Kinsey's bombshell, another book appeared that in
some ways grew out of Kinsey's efforts to talk sense and elevate concrete
experience, but sharply diverged from Kinsey's view that *homosexual* was a
word more properly used as an adjective than a noun. That publication was
The Homosexual in America: A Subjective Approach. Its author, Edward
Sagarin, a New York teacher in his late forties, wrote under the pseudonym
"Donald Webster Cory." Published by Greenberg, the firm responsible for
those polar opposites of gay fiction in the 1930s, *Twilight Men* and *Better
Angel*, and more recently Nial Kent's popular *The Divided Path* (1949),
Cory's work was, in his words, a "spiritual autobiography." After twenty-
five years' "participation in American life as a homosexual," Cory thought
it high time that gay men said something on the subject that could be
regarded with the same weight given to the views of the psychiatrist, the
jurist, or the churchman. In the space of three hundred pages, he offered
that weightiness in a form that mixed sincere memoir, literary history, and
sociological analysis and provided a review of anti-gay hostility and discrimination right up to the McCarthy-inspired State Department firings of
that year, chronicles of the variety of gay life, a critique of the "cure" idea,
and a vision of a future of greater tolerance and understanding. Cory was
of a more psychological than political bent, and that suited the needs of his
readers as well. He preached the gospel of self-knowledge, of the overriding
need to perceive the ways in which society inculcated guilt or shame and
the need to divest one's self of those handicaps. Toward the latter goal, he
raised the possibility of support groups for homosexuals, and he urged
homosexuals to begin to think of themselves as part of an "unrecognized
minority." Kinsey believed that men who enjoyed sex with other men
should not be thought of as a distinct class of people, any more than vege-
tarians or left-handed writers should be so named and identified—it made
no sense. They were simply acting on an unexceptional capacity every
human shared. Cory asserted that an end to their persecution would come
only when homosexuals saw themselves as the equivalent of Negroes
or Jews.

The appeal of Cory's thinking was partly in its audacity and partly in its
timeliness. Between 1920 and 1950, men who loved other men had formed

increasingly tight subcultural bonds in their own defense. (Kinsey was perhaps not fully appreciative of the way in which oppression can have an effect on selfhood and will encourage people to feel or pretend that they have more in common than their simple status as outcasts.) To be sure, many men weren't looking for any alliances with other homosexuals: wealthy gay men insisted that they had less in common with street queens than with their affluent neighbors, masculine gay men disdained the campy crowd, and the gay aesthete and the gay ranch hand lived in distant worlds much as the straight aesthete and the straight ranch hand did. Men who "passed" with their heterosexual friends and colleagues didn't believe they had anything to gain from a politicized approach to their sexuality; the racial divide among homosexuals was also profound in these years. But many readers were of the opinion that Cory was on to something interesting. "No one had ever said anything like this before, about our being a minority group, not as far as I knew. It was a revolutionary book," one gay man who read it at the time commented. "I thought," said another contemporary, "when I came upon this book, finally, somebody is pointing us in the right direction."

Alas, Cory was not a simple hero. Everything about him was complicated, even "schizoid," as one of his lovers remarked: he was married with two young children, labored long and hard to keep the two halves of his life separate, was glad to be revered by those gay men in the 1950s who were thinking hopefully about organization, and turned on the gay movement in the mid-1960s—furiously—when homosexuals began insisting that they should agitate for their rights and confront the psychiatric profession. Something of this lurking ambivalence, or contrariness, is actually foreshadowed in the book's temporizing subtitle and, more seriously, in its first pages. Either on his own initiative or (more likely) at the suggestion of his publisher who wanted an establishment "name" to lend legitimacy to the project, Cory asked his friend, psychologist Albert Ellis, to write an introduction to *The Homosexual in America*. In doing so, Ellis offered some obligatory praise about the quality of the text, but noted that he was as prejudiced by his heterosexuality as Cory was by his homosexuality, meaning that no one should forget that homosexuals could be led "to more heterosexual modes of living," if they really tried. Ellis's words made for a strange introduction to a venture whose spirit was more daring and clearsighted. Yet in the light of Cory's later actions, Ellis's opinions might not have been completely distasteful to him. Quite a few gay men believed that they should be allowed to live in peace and dignity, but did not see themselves as the equal in every way of their heterosexual relatives and neighbors. Many of the gay activists who would challenge the American

Psychiatric Association on this point in the early 1970s were still in their adolescence when Cory was writing.

The Homosexual in America went through several printings and had a decent library sale, though it often ended up in some major universities in a special collection or rare book division, necessitating a specific and possibly embarrassing request. Nevertheless, a significant number of homosexuals who were looking for some kind of intellectual study or guide in the 1950s felt that Cory's was the work they had been waiting for. It appeared, however, at the beginning of a peak time for another kind of book that also served an educational purpose, in a roundabout way. From the early 1950s through the mid-1960s, a small mountain of undistinguished books saw their way into print (many as part of the paperback boom) with an aim to document or dramatize gay life, gay psychology, gay degradation. Fiction, sociology, or journalism, they usually had the same negative approach, and their tone often harked back to *Broadway Brevities*—lurid, mock-indignant, and informational. (*Broadway Brevities*, which was published in New York in the 1920s as a monthly and in the early 1930s as a weekly, was a small-circulation tabloid that ran articles such as its lengthy 1924 "Nights in Fairyland" series and dozens of cartoons about swish pickup artists on Riverside Drive. Yet, despite a malicious spirit, the paper provided so much detail about the best gay bars and cruising spots that it might well have been intended as a sly means of communication with other gay men. The writers' pen names are similarly telling: Buddy Browning, Stephen O'Toole, John Swallow Martin.)

Whether the readers of *The Twisted Heart*, *Shadows of Shame*, and *Oh, Dear* (about a window dresser who doesn't quite have the energy to kill himself) were heterosexuals who wanted to keep abreast of the newest indecencies or gays who were willing to read anything at all on the topic didn't matter to the publishers, but the curious end result of this trend was not without value for gay men. In a sense, the late-1930s attempt to control homosexuality by means of public invisibility—restricting discussion of it in books and newspapers and eliminating it entirely from moviemaking—was a much smarter strategy. Effacement can be harder to cope with than aggression or disdain. When the books and articles on the sexual tragedy of the American homosexual population began to proliferate, the field was once again open for gay men and lesbians to take note of their own numbers and cultural markers. A tittering description of a gay bar in a pulp paperback meant, for the uninformed young man who bought the book, that there *was* such a place as a gay bar. Nasty accounts of the cruising spots and pickup techniques used by deviants meant that there were so many others out there who wanted the same thing that the means to get it had evolved into longtime traditions. *Naked to the Night* might have been about a "descent into a personal hell," as its preface indicated, but it made gay sex sound pretty hot.

Perhaps the richest vignette on this theme—almost a backhanded homage to the anti-gay propagandists—comes from William B. Kelley, one of Chicago's gay activists in the 1960s. Curious to know more about homosexuality when he was a teenager in the 1950s (not an easy task growing up in a small town in southeastern Missouri), he came upon a copy of *Washington Confidential* in the Kennett Public Library. Published by Crown in 1951, the book was one of a series of cheap but popular exposés of modern city life written by Hearst columnists Lee Mortimer and Jack Lait. Its fiercest chapter, "Garden of Pansies," was about the large number of "fags" to be found in the nation's capital (a dull bunch, Mortimer and Lait noted, because the more talented homos tended to "drift to Broadway and to Hollywood"), the State Department's tolerance of perversions, and the police department's futile efforts to keep the "twisted twerps" in line. Of vital interest to Kelley was the information about where these disgusting people tended to congregate in Washington: "Their chief meeting place is in leafy Lafayette Square, across Pennsylvania Avenue from the White House. They make love under the equestrian statue of rugged Andrew Jackson, who must be whirling on his heavenly horse every time he sees what is going on around his monument."

In Washington a short time later for the National Spelling Bee, Kelley managed to leave his parents behind at their hotel for a few hours and promptly headed for Lafayette Square. "I wasn't taking any chances of being misunderstood," he remembered. He picked up a physique magazine at a nearby newsstand, held on to it rather visibly, and took a seat on one of the park's benches. He was not alone for long, a happy circumstance that can be attributed to the scurrilous Mortimer and Lait and the postwar need when writing about sexual life to be indignant, insulting—and highly explicit.

11

"PURGE OF THE PERVERTS"

It is disturbing to read of the retrenchment and the heads that seem to be following, and I can appreciate your comments that it seems like 1930 again. . . . I dread the thought of the early thirties repeating themselves. Equally disturbing is all the to-do in Washington about the homos. . . . Sounds like the days of the old Salem witch-hunts may be upon us.

—Jesse Malo of New Bedford, Massachusetts,
in a letter to Leo Adams of New York City,
24 May 1950

The causes of the anxieties that beset America in the 1930s—economic devastation and, later in the decade, the shadow of war—were based on unambiguous realities. The nervous preoccupations of the postwar world, which lasted from the late 1940s through the early 1960s, were in some strange way more intractable and pernicious. Was Communism the real and present danger it appeared to be: the forces of right on the one side, the forces of evil on the other, and so many dominoes in between? Was the security of the United States jeopardized by an expansionist foreign ideology? The nature of the earlier threats had prompted responses that were comparatively focused, though the effectiveness of those responses differed (ending the Depression proved to be a more elusive goal than combating Fascism). The nature of the new threat inspired myriad conflicting responses; forging overseas military alliances and inflating the defense budget to proportions that would have rendered prewar lawmakers speechless was, depending on one's politics, either an inappropriate response or simply an insufficient response. But few events indicate how psychologically wracked America was becoming in the 1950s, despite a strong consumer economy, than the presumed overlap of the Communist and the homosexual menace.

The federal government became involved in the issue only reluctantly, having spent most of the late 1940s trying to keep the topic of its homosexual employees in perspective. The memory of the Sumner Welles scandal died hard, not least because there actually were a large number of gay men in the State Department, as there often are in professions involving time spent abroad, away from home and family. The capital had also acquired a reputation during the war as a sympathetic home base. A young gay man in the Caribbean Affairs office at Foggy Bottom wrote to a friend in 1946, only half-jokingly, that it was "most fashionable" in Washington just then to be "sponsored by a rather aging person who desires that you do nothing but keep him company." Affairs between coworkers were not uncommon. Nelson Rockefeller had come to the department following Welles's departure and noticed that there were "a hell of lot of [homosexuals] there," whom he energetically tried to weed out. Most gay men, whether diplomats or office personnel, assumed that competence in the job and the right demeanor at work would suffice, so they understandably cringed when the topic made the news. Attorney Wilbur Stammler's murder of his lover and suicide in a posh Washington hotel caused "great excitement and caution in our little circles," one gay man noted, as did a "sweep" of Lafayette Park in 1947 that led to the arrest of sixty-five men. When *Time* reported in 1949 on a visa bribery scandal at the U.S. consulate in Hong Kong and the dismissal of four homosexual employees (only one of whom was accused of taking bribes), others felt nervous. But few gay men anticipated what lay ahead.

A foreshadowing of the mean-spiritedness to come was evident in the 1945 Veterans Administration ruling on the ineligibility of "blue discharge" veterans for the munificent benefits of the recently enacted G.I. Bill. Their cause was taken up by various legislators, labor leaders, and journalists not because it implied a defense of homosexuality, but because of the vagueness of the servicemen's status at the time they were relieved of duty; blue discharge veterans were people of allegedly "undesirable traits"—alcoholics as well as sexual deviants, men with drug, emotional, or general attitude problems—who had not been court-martialed or dishonorably discharged and yet were being penalized for life. The blue discharge made getting a job in civilian life difficult, and to the editors of the *Pitts-*

burgh Courier, the nation's largest African-American newspaper, it didn't seem coincidental that almost a quarter of those caught in this bind were black. The *Pittsburgh Courier*'s campaign for the rights of blue-discharge veterans, then, benefited both black and white soldiers, straight and gay. It had its effect: Congress leaned on the VA to reconsider its hard-line policy, ushering in what Allan Berube has called "a tense period of tolerance" between late 1945 and early 1947. In May 1947, however, the Army did away entirely with the blue discharge, replacing it with a general discharge for unsuitability, and established regulations to see that this category would not apply to homosexuals. Whatever compassion Congress and the press wanted to expend on alcoholics and troublemakers, under no circumstances, the new system made clear, would gay men and lesbians be welcome in the military or ever entitled to its benefits.

In February 1950, only several days after Senator Joseph McCarthy delivered his famous speech in Wheeling, West Virginia, waving his laundry list high in the air to announce that he had before him the names of 205 protected Communists in the State Department, the subject of homosexuals in government service came up in Congress, almost by accident. Testifying before the Senate Appropriations Committee about State Department employees who had been dismissed from their jobs in recent years, Undersecretary of State John Peurifoy volunteered more information than the situation required. Most of the ninety-one men who had been let go as security risks, he allowed, were sexual deviants. In the wake of the anger directed at Dean Acheson and his diplomats for the "loss" of China to the Communists the previous year and only four months before the start of hostilities in Korea, this was an unsettling piece of news. McCarthy was otherwise occupied with his own finger-pointing at Acheson and Truman, but Clyde Hoey, a Democrat from North Carolina, and Kenneth Wherry, a Republican from Nebraska, claimed to be aghast. By May, Wherry was charging that he had learned from reliable police sources that as many as 3,750 homosexuals held federal jobs. How had so many degenerates gained a foothold within the government, he wanted to know. Of what use was the State Department's elimination of a few dozen homosexuals if their numbers were so vast? (Wherry, a licensed embalmer known as the "merry mortician," was also the Capitol Hill king of the malapropism, who spoke about the "Chief Joints of Staff" and the problems in "Indigo China.") A month later, a full-scale investigation was authorized by the Senate, the first such inquiry in the nation's history.

Many people wondered if the "pervert inquiry," as it became known, was going to have any more substance to it in the long run than the wild accusations McCarthy was trafficking in. But the topic was not one with which most heterosexuals were at ease. During the war, Dwight MacDonald had given space in his magazine *Politics* to poet Robert Duncan's moving coming-out essay, "The Homosexual in Society," and diplomat George Kennan let it be known that he regarded Senator Wherry's fishing expedition as a profound waste of time. Few journalists would have considered doing the legwork or voicing the skepticism that characterized Max Lerner's eleven-part series in the *New York Post*, "The Washington Sex Storm," in July of 1950. The "purge of the perverts," Lerner discovered, was being "carried on hit-or-miss, without definition or standards of judging 'guilt.' " No one responsible for the probe seemed to have grasped Kinsey's most elementary arguments about the continuum; men who had sex with other men every day in the park, men who had had a homosexual relationship twenty years ago, and men of vague homosexual leanings were lumped together as one entity, the "moral degenerate" and the "security risk." The statistics the committee was given by the Washington police force, which employed four full-time officers to "deal with" homosexuals in the District, proved to be more guesswork than arithmetic. Lerner announced that he was unable to track down one verified case of a government worker having been blackmailed by a foreign agent because of his sexual orientation and could scarcely mask his horror at the shallowness of Senator Wherry and Lieutenant Roy Blick of the police department. "Mind you," Wherry told Lerner, "I don't say every homosexual is a subversive, and I don't say every subversive is a homosexual. But a man of low morality is a menace in the government, whatever he is, and they are all tied together." The "homosexual panic train," Lerner wrote, was racing through the capital at its own unstoppable pace. Throughout the summer and fall, amid mounting U.S. casualties in Korea and concern that Russia was soon to have its own nuclear arsenal, the committee conducted its investigation, hearing testimony and reading police reports.

The results of the "pervert inquiry" were made public in December. The timing could not have been worse. This was the same month that saw President Truman declare a state of national emergency, Governor Dewey argue for complete mobilization and the registering of all seventeen-year-olds (male and female), and New York's Mayor Impellitteri promise the Senate Armed Services Committee that his city's residents, determined to stand by their posts, would not evacuate in the event of a nuclear attack. Red China moved deeper into Tibet, and the Civil Defense Office renewed its drive to interest homeowners in backyard bomb shelters. CBS announced that loyalty oaths would now be required of its 2,500 employees and that armed guards would be placed at transmitter sites and in master control rooms. Twenty years later, a view of the early 1950s as a daffy, paranoid time took on humorous dimensions (the movie *Atomic Cafe* had great fun with the Civil Defense program for America's schools—"Duck and cover!"), but the flavor of the era was anything but slapstick. Midcentury in America had assumed in a relatively short time an almost poignant doomsday quality, and the fact that homosexuals were singled out as part of the larger problem isn't surprising—or retrospectively quaint, or even totally irrational. World War II had been fought to purge the world of two monolithic evils, but the fall of Nazi Germany and Imperial Japan did not restore to the victors a sense of safety and well-being. If anything, life seemed more treacherous and unfathomable than it did in 1939, and the problems were beyond juvenile delinquency and allegedly unrestrained sex offenders. A bitter irony for ex-servicemen, in the last weeks of 1950, was to hear many legislators urge the rearmament of Germany and Japan as crucial to the containment of Communism in Europe and Asia. Old enemies were now needed allies, and the face of the new enemy was often obscured.

The evolution of a "safe inside/dangerous outside" view of modern life—an "us versus them" frame of mind—need not have had any significant consequences for American homosexuals. Deviance as a foreign importation unknown to the natives of a New World free of sexual taint was an idea long out of circulation; every thinking person knew that "us" included homosexuals. The problem for gay men and lesbians arose out of the widespread fear that the ideological dangers from abroad had already infiltrated the country, fostering doubt and discord. The Popular Front alliances of fifteen years earlier, with Communists and New Deal liberals finding common cause in the fight against Fascism and social injustice, were no longer seen as examples of robust political pluralism. They were proof that our adversaries were among us, a part of the national fabric. The "enemy within" represented a small fraction of the population, but the potential for harm was immeasurable. Intercontinental ballistic missiles meant that two wide oceans didn't offer the protection they did in 1940, and the perjury conviction of Alger Hiss and the arrest of the Rosenbergs in 1950 fueled the fire. Who could be trusted? Surely the least trustworthy of our own people at this moment of crisis were the "perverts" coddled in high places.

This perception of a nation divided in its resolve, its security undermined from within and its own cities vulnerable to attack, established a climate in which even men of good faith were not inclined to question the link between disloyalty and weakness, on the one hand, and aberrant sexual proclivities on the other—any more than they questioned where, in the event of war, Mayor Impellettiri's six million residents would go if they wanted to evacuate New York City or how long the backyard bomb shelters were supposed to sustain their terrified occupants. The givens that made existence bearable in a time when a third world war seemed imminent were rather too easily agreed upon: salvation lay in order, vigilance, strength, and unity. Ambiguity, skepticism, and diversity spelled ruin. If the world beyond America's borders was no longer recognizable, everything had to be done to maintain *within those borders* elements of life that were safe, knowable, and morally clear-cut. Ex-President Hoover's suggestion that America consider Japan, the Philippines, and Britain as its "frontier" points of defense was dismissed by many as a modern version of isolationism, but Hoover's speech nonetheless acknowledged some disagreeable popular beliefs—that the course of events was out of our control, that America's survival was far from guaranteed, and that the best that could be hoped for was to hold the line against alien ways of thinking. What was manageable, presumably, were internal values, standards, and policies.

In that domain, three decades of thought about Reds and three decades of thought about sexual dissidents had at last dovetailed, leaving Americans with some remarkably clear and consistent generalizations. Both groups, Reds and homosexuals, were antifamily, antireligion, scornful of bourgeois morality, devious, manipulative, cynical, loyal only to one another and their cause, abhorrent to God, eager to convert the young and remake America. As historian John D'Emilio aptly summarized the situation, "The congruence between the stereotype of Communists and homosexuals made the scapegoating of gay men and women a simple matter." Even Hollywood understood the overlap. Helen Hayes dramatized every mother's worst fear in the cold war potboiler *My Son John* (1951): a traitor to sound values raised by well-meaning parents, one's flesh and blood suddenly revealed as a Party member, a stranger in the land. Sneaky and unrepentant, John might as well have been coming out to his parents as a queer.

The Senate report of December 1950 certainly suggested that the problem was not imaginary, that it was urgent and growing. The Truman administration was charged with an appalling indifference to the danger of homosexuals in government. With the Soviets on the lookout for new agents, the "lack of emotional stability" that homosexuals were known for as well as the "weakness of their moral fiber" made them obvious targets, or suspects. The committee also released the figures it had compiled on the number of degenerates fired between April and November of that year. Interestingly, three times as many homosexuals were ferreted out of the Veterans Administration as the State Department, but the image of the State Department as the focus of the trouble—bastion of liberalism and, therefore, "nest of pansies"—held firm because it was of greater use in attacking the administration and those effete men who had lost China for us. (Ninety-seven homosexuals were detected in those eight months at the VA, forty-nine at the Commerce Department, thirty-seven at State, fifteen at the Library of Congress, and three or four among congressional aides.) Earlier in the year, the House of Representatives had rejected an amendment to a foreign aid bill that would have barred homosexuals from federal employment, making a de facto situation a matter of law rather than policy. The momentum on the issue shifted in the other direction by December.

The change was immediately apparent in the numbers of dismissals. Between 1947 and 1950, approximately sixty civilian federal employees were fired each year and approximately one thousand servicemen and women discharged each year after an investigation of their sexual history. By 1951, the figure rose to sixty a month among federal workers and two thousand a year in the military. At the same time, the FBI established liaisons with local police departments to better coordinate efforts to keep records on deviants, and the Postal Service began monitoring deliveries to single men on the police lists.

The energy of this new wave of repression meant that the lightheartedness some gay men and lesbians felt during World War II about meeting their own kind was less applicable during the Korean action. The mood was different. Heightened anxiety, though, didn't necessarily translate into less sex. Peter Conway, who served in the Army in the early 1950s, recalled the panic that overtook him as a twenty-two-year-old when he received his draft notice. After numerous sexual relationships with peers throughout high school and college, he assumed that induction would mark an end to his sexual freedom. "But I wasn't in basic training three days," he later remarked, "before I realized how widespread gay life in the military was going to be. I went in with fear and trepidation, but it didn't turn out to be that way at all." At Fort Jackson in North Carolina, and later as a student in the signal corps school at Camp Gordon in Georgia, Conway not only had abundant opportunity for sexual activity but had his first experience of a glory hole in a men's room there. (The glory holes at Camp Gordon seem to have been notorious for their size and number; several gay veterans, unknown to each other and from different parts of the country, who served there in the early 1950s, commented on them in interviews.) Another veteran from Camp Gordon remembered a bar in nearby Augusta—or "Disgusta," as the gay GIs called it—that was straight during the afternoon and gay in the evening, but he agreed that by and large opportunities on the base were more than plentiful. James Montanile, stationed at Keesler Air Field in Alabama, was dumbstruck by the risks his officer-lover was willing to take. The lieutenant, who was married but whose wife resided back in their home state, would regularly take Montanile into New Orleans for the weekend, show him the sights, find a motel where they could make love undisturbed, and have them both back in Biloxi Sunday afternoon acting as if nothing out of the ordinary had transpired. "The difference," said one man who served in both World War II and Korea, "was that you looked over your shoulder more in the 1950s. You couldn't count on the brass looking the other way. This wasn't a world war. [Homosexuality] counted for more, somehow."

Another factor gay men had to deal with was that the military had gotten much better at the hunt in the intervening years. When *Quatrefoil*, James Barr's popular novel about two gay naval officers, was published in 1950, the Office of Naval Intelligence tried to learn from the publisher and other gay sources the author's real name. By the time James Fugate made the mistake of reenlisting in 1952 as a reserve officer—against the advice of his lawyer, his psychiatrist, the woman he was planning to marry, and a retired admiral who knew his story—his investigators were more adept, and he was soon confronted with their knowledge that "Barr" and "Fugate" were one and the same person. He was left to the mercy of the "experts," as he wrote, the "men who have been trained to dispatch his kind with a minimum of time and effort." With an elective in Russian on his college transcript and novels by Turgenev and Gorky in his possession, he was also forced to defend himself against charges that he was a Communist sympathizer.

The fact that the government, especially the Defense Department, had finally acknowledged the ubiquitous nature of homosexuality also worked in its favor. "In the 1950s," as one Florida writer phrased it, "homosexual activity in Pensacola was as rampant as it was repressed and oppressed." A large naval base was especially important to gay life in this Gulf Coast city of sixty thousand, both in the quick trade possibilities it encouraged at Wayside Park and in the active party scene it allowed for in the private homes in the North Hill end of town. The appeal of Pensacola wasn't strictly local, by any means. Gay men from Mobile, Birmingham, and New Orleans regularly made the trip, attracted to the area's white beaches and the infamous Navy "meat rack." The disadvantage for these civilians in making friends with gay, or simply horny, sailors was that the military police would sometimes tail their own men on their assignations, corner them later, and present them with a tidy plea-bargain deal: give us the names of the gay men you met and you will be dealt with more leniently yourself.

As a military leader in the 1940s, Dwight Eisenhower had been made aware—reluctantly—of the contributions of gay men and lesbians (particularly the WACs, in his experience) to the war effort. As president, though, he expressed his displeasure with the Truman administration's loyalty-security program and the hiring and firing leeway it allowed individual supervisors. Executive Order 10450, issued three months after his inauguration, explicitly listed homosexuality as a reason for denial of, or mandatory dismissal from, a government job. In theory, this order marked an end to the discretionary powers department heads might exercise and, if any further incentives for the watchdogs were needed, Eisenhower's executive order provided it. At the time of the congressional investigation of the Newport scandal in 1920, some senators had expressed their repugnance at the Navy's entrapment tactics—a repugnance equal to that which they felt toward sexual perversion itself. In the early 1950s, the feeling of both the executive and the legislative branches of government was less delicate: eliminate these people by any means necessary.

Government investigators took pleasure in pointing out how readily gay men incriminated not only themselves but their friends. "The sources of our information generally came from a co-participant," Paul Clarke of the State Department's Office of Security commented about his work in the 1950s in weeding out security risks. "We were fortunate in that when we interviewed some of the people before they left the department . . . they furnished us with a long list of names." Clarke's account makes naming names sound vaguely serendipitous, almost voluntary. Given the consequences of not cooperating with their interrogators, many men felt they had little choice. Sometimes the interview had a businesslike veneer. As Clarke admitted, almost everyone who was accused of homosexual conduct agreed to resign immediately, putting an end to the matter then and there. ("I doubt there were ten out of a thousand" who wanted to go for a full board hearing.) But for the man who didn't want to give up his job and his pension, or who didn't trust the promises made to him of confidentiality, the implications of what would ensue from a board hearing were dire. Robert L. had worked for the State Department since graduating from an Ivy League school in 1933 and had just marked his twentieth year in government service when he was called in. Reluctant to go without a fight, he was told that if he elected to have a hearing, he could expect that his father (a career Army officer stationed in Texas) would be notified and that everyone at his base would be made aware that he had a son who was a "homo Communist security risk." The investigators would be obliged, they added, to make explicit inquiries about him in his hometown in Oregon, where he had lived before college and where all of his mother's family still resided. In the end, Robert agreed to go quietly and provided the requisite names.

As rigorous as the surveillance and the list-making became during the Eisenhower years, not everyone who was under investigation was actually forced out of government service, even when his or her homosexuality had been well established. From time to time, a certain amount of expedient hypocrisy was called for. Thirty-year-old Captain Charles Gruenberger, for instance, worked as a much-valued dentist at the Pentagon from 1952 to 1954. Not long after the issue of Executive Order 10450 in April 1953, intelligence officers showed up at his apartment when he was out. Jack Kersey, his lover of six years, admitted the men. (Kersey and Gruenberger met at a party in Washington in 1947, when Kersey was only seventeen and Gruenberger twenty-four; they remained together for the next fifty years.) What followed was a lengthy, nerve-wracking cat-and-mouse session. The word *homosexual* was never used, but questions about the well-decorated apartment and the nature of Kersey's feelings for his friend and roommate made it crystal clear that Gruenberger's name was now on the government's list. Yet the boom was never lowered. As an endodontist, Gruenberger had a highly specialized skill and clientele: he performed root-canal surgery on the top brass at the Pentagon, serving directly under the president's military dentist. The security officer in charge of the case was content to let Gruenberger sweat it out, living in fear of a dishonorable discharge that would ruin his medical career, and there the matter ended.

Most men and women employed by the government were not so well positioned. The exact number of those whose careers were ended and whose post-government lives were marred by the exposure and degradation they endured is impossible to ascertain; records of sudden resignations for mysterious health or family reasons obscure as much as they reveal. But two facts do stand out that never seem to find their way into histories of the Cold War or books about America in the 1950s. The first is that, for all the concern about leftists undermining American security from within, the number of men and women dismissed for sexual reasons far exceeds—by any estimates—the number dismissed for real or alleged involvement with the Communist Party. The "purge of the perverts" was more productive than the hunt for Stalinists. The second fact about the early 1950s speaks to an even larger reality and affected every American, including those who never dreamed of a civil service job: for the first time, the federal government had addressed itself to the place of the homosexual in American society and concurred with those who argued that gay men and lesbians were not like other people and should not be trusted.

A paradox lies at the heart of the intense anti-gay sentiment of the 1950s. For the Communist-homosexual link was only one aspect of the problem, only one of the dangers that required purging if America were to remain free. A way in which Communists and homosexuals were not at all alike argued against tolerance for gay men from a different angle.

"One homosexual can pollute a government office," the 1950 Senate report claimed in an implicit assertion of homosexual strength and influence. Like the Reds who stopped at nothing to achieve their goals, the gay men whom Senators Hoey, Wherry, and McCarthy spoke of were serious and aggressive. Yet many Americans took the opposite approach—at the same time approving of the efforts to keep government offices uncontaminated—and nervously watched their sons for signs of girlish interests and unmanly traits. It was a lack of seriousness and aggression they worried about. Was Johnny a little too taken with show tunes and movie stars? Did Tommy walk funny, throw a ball like a girl? Did Bobby play with dolls and avoid the rough-and-tumble of contact sports? These were crucial matters, bordering on a mania, in the day of "butch" haircuts and kill-to-win Little League and midget football teams. "Paul spends too much time being silly with his day student playmates. It's not healthy. He's got a lot of growing up to do if he wants to be a man," wrote Paul Monette's high school advisor at Andover in an end-of-term report to his parents. Silly, not healthy, if he wants to be a man. Vital coded language, Monette realized, that in the 1950s meant one thing: your kid is becoming a fairy. Irresponsible, uncompetitive, weak. A sissy. A woman.

This attempt to renew the equation of homosexuality with giddiness, ineptitude, and lack of strength should have been an intellectual tightrope act. It necessitated forgetting any more worldly impressions acquired during the chaos of the war; overlooking the skill and nerve a "subversive" would presumably have to demonstrate; disputing Kinsey; and ignoring the all-important fact that urban homosexuality was not in timid retreat (as the press kept warning it wasn't) in the face of increased police action and psychiatric belligerence. But America had no trouble investing outworn images with new life, in part because a fairy was a more believable domestic type and in part because the usable evidence came from less elite, more mundane and effective sources. There was Christine Jorgenson to suggest that the distance between the sexes was dismayingly close thanks to modern surgery (the new medium of television offered a bombardment of "knowing" Denmark jokes on variety shows in 1953 and 1954). There were the lurid cover stories in *Confidential* and other rags that made money breaking new ground in scandalous innuendo: "Marlon [Brando] and Wally [Cox]'s Bedroom," "The Untold Story of Rock Hudson," "Why Liberace's Theme Song Should be 'Mad About the Boy!'" There were the caricatures of "Adelaide" Stevenson with his "teacup words" and "fruity" voice, the magazine articles on the "horror of seeing your son a pantywaist" (this from a *Better Homes & Gardens* piece on absent fathers), and the admonitions of Jack LaLanne to toughen up our candy-ass youth.

Again, the concern about boys growing up to be frail and affected wasn't entirely unrelated to the political climate. One of the people Max Lerner interviewed in 1950 for his *New York Post* series, an unnamed Harvard professor, offered a tidy summary when he remarked that in such dangerous times a more *virile* diplomacy was called for. We needed real men negotiating with the Communists, he told Lerner. (In this scenario, Sumner Welles's kind weren't wily double agents; they simply lacked sufficient testosterone.) Grit was all "the other side" understood. The world had to know, and we had to know, that we were ready to draw a line and stick by it. So Marion Morrison was reinvented as John Wayne, the cowboy's triumph over the Native American became the smash box-office genre, and the Allied commander—too nervous to take on McCarthy, whom he loathed, but no "teacup" wordsmith—defeated the Illinois intellectual in two battles for the White House. Yet postwar sociologists, like gender historians three decades later, knew to look to the home and the workplace for other explanations. It seemed to them that many men were ambivalent or insecure about their newly masculinized, nonmilitary role in life—which was characterized less by inventiveness, quiet confidence, camaraderie, humor, and an acceptance of painful changes such as the war had called forth, and more by routine, the stress of the office, conspicuous consumption, and a highly artificial swagger. Why did so many displays of American manhood seem to be based on envy and a fear of humiliation, Margaret Mead asked. What social and psychological factors accounted for the rising rate of coronaries among forty- and fifty-year-old American men, cardiologists wanted to know. Was the American male being emasculated by conformist pressures and "outer-directedness," David Reisman wondered in *The Lonely Crowd* (1950), his best-selling meditation on loss of self. And why, feminists later asked, had "the battle of the sexes" become such a monotonous motif, with marriage depicted as a process by which a woman "caught" a man and delivered him to the altar? The Organization Man, the Man in the Gray Flannel Suit, was evidently a bundle of discontent. Adjustment to civilian life hadn't gone smoothly. Three "demonized" figures, however, reinforced a now imperiled superiority. Those targets were the political or cultural radical, the woman who didn't know her place (sexually or professionally), and the man who wasn't a man in lockstep with all other men.

One of the best-known reflections of the sheer intensity of mid-1950s gender anxiety is Robert Anderson's story of Tommy Lee, a prep school student tormented for his unmasculine sensitivities and "rescued" from self-doubt by the sexual attentions of his housemaster's wife. *Tea and Sympathy* as a 1953 play was able to be more explicit about the homosexual subtext than Vincent Minnelli's 1956 film; the Production Code administration let Minnelli know that if Tommy was anything other than refined and artistic, the movie would never be released. The idea was to convey an impeccably liberal message—a male should be able to be "different" without being called a homo—while keeping clear of the perversion theme. But Minnelli was able to work in some of the real-life ambiguity of adolescent and adult sexuality. Tommy's attraction to the Deborah Kerr figure is legitimate puppy love, though his response to kissing the local waitress/slut in an effort to prove his manhood is excessive even for a fastidious heterosexual (for a minute, it looks as if the boy is about to vomit on her floor). Deborah Kerr's husband is still the hang-around-with-the-boys, bicep-grabbing closet case of the Broadway version, but the filming of the bonfire hazing scene, in which the underclassmen are chased and stripped of their pajamas, skillfully plays on the male need to touch other males in intimate ways while pretending that these contacts are rigorously asexual. What was described onstage becomes faintly homo-sensual on screen. Most remarkably, Tommy's father embodies a crossover potential, too. As he chortles over what he hopes is his son's loss of his virginity with the waitress, Minnelli shoots him in a peculiar manner—ensconced on the seat of a bay window, legs crossed in the "wrong," girlish way, wrist momentarily limp. Even a middle-aged businessman lapses from the approved style in an unguarded moment.

Despite the movie's supposed affirmation of Tommy Lee's "normal" sexuality, the Catholic clergymen consulted by the Production Code administration were far from happy with the ending of *Tea and Sympathy*. A married woman giving herself to a teenager in a misty glade transgressed other important boundaries. So an epilogue was devised to take up the story years after the "When you speak of this . . . be kind" moment, in which the audience learns that Tommy is married, but that Deborah Kerr's union foundered on the moral wrong she committed that day. Fate is cruel: she now lives in Chicago. The tendentious epilogue was forced on Anderson and Minnelli, but they managed to turn it to their own subtler purposes. Remaining behind in the idyllic garden house on campus is Kerr's husband, alone with his memories, his boys, and—of all things—a classical record collection. A taste for "long-haired music" has already been posited in the movie as one of the attributes of deviance, along with a fondness for solitary walks and taking girls' parts in school plays. The black-and-white, good-and-evil, heterosexual-and-unnamed-horror world that the Production Code assumed it was delineating does not really exist in *Tea and Sympathy*.

Tennessee Williams approached the same situation from another and more sophisticated perspective in *Cat on a Hot Tin Roof* (1953). Brick is not like Blanche's poet husband or Sebastian Venable, rapacious and doomed, of the author's later, more macabre *Suddenly, Last Summer* (1959). An over-the-hill athlete in a wealthy southern family, he wants to be Big Daddy's heir, Maggie's properly functioning husband (whose broken leg would then be his only obstacle to bedding his voluptuous wife), leaving his avaricious brother and sister-in-law and their "no-neck monster" children in the dust. But Brick's alcoholism and the unexplained suicide of his cherished friend, Skipper, have cast a shadow over the family. As well as anyone ever has, Williams in *Cat on a Hot Tin Roof* dramatized the panic that the suspicion of deviance will inspire in an American male in the 1950s. "Is that what you think?" Brick whines at Big Daddy. "That Skipper and me did sodomy?" The odd syntax is as plaintive as the look on Paul Newman's face in the movie version of the play.

In the face of the juggernaut of 1950s gender conformity, most gay men were neither saints nor martyrs. One response to the terror of being branded one of "them," the sodomites and the nancy boys, was to tie one's fortunes all the more vehemently to the power structure. Columnist Joe Alsop, for example, was known to use the words *fairy* and *queer* as a strategic—and usually successful—deflection of curiosity about his bachelorhood and wasn't above responding to a statement about another man, "Oh, is he one of those?" (Alsop knew enough about how the system worked, though, to swallow his pride and tell the FBI, upon his return from a 1957 trip to the USSR, of the KGB's blackmail attempt; he had been photographed in bed with a Soviet agent.) A less genteel Tommy Lee would have found some more delicate boy at boarding school to call a "homo" in front of the other students, and a Brick without crutches and a hangover would have led the bubbas on gay-bashing expeditions against the local decorators. Thousands of men with homosexual feelings did, hoping that their willingess to hit or hurl epithets would fool their peers.

On a grandly Hooveresque scale, the life of Roy Cohn was proof that modern America was enamored of nothing so much as an iron will and combative success. More than that, Cohn demonstrated that the simpering shallowness of homosexuality could be neutralized by an acceptance—an exhaustive embrace—of those values. Joe McCarthy limited his attacks on homosexuals in government service for three good reasons. He found red-baiting more useful (you could accuse George Marshall of being a Communist sympathizer, but not a sexual deviant); he had colleagues who were willing to take the lead in that area; and he felt vulnerable to the whispers about his own sexuality, whether or not there was any truth to the rumors. Drew Pearson had a fat dossier on the senator, still a bachelor at forty-three, and the *Las Vegas Sun* published a few blunt articles in 1952, one of which even named a man McCarthy allegedly went to bed with. (It is odd that McCarthy did not sue the paper and demand a retraction.) Cohn, however, was gay—later in life, ostentatiously so—and yet he understood from the moment he entered public life that if he wanted the privileges establishment success could offer, he would have to play the game with unmatched ruthlessness. His genuine anti-Communism aside, he was known as a man with few principles and as a lawyer no sane person would want as an enemy. Wide-eyed, he sweats on camera at the Army-McCarthy hearings when Joseph Welch, the Army's lawyer, makes his famous allusion to "pixies" and "fairies" at work for the senator, but that was the last time anyone would ever see Roy Cohn ill at ease. He steamrolled opponents for the next thirty years, threw professional ethics to the wind, and was disbarred only on his deathbed in 1986. (Biographers are still divided about his involvement in the suicide of Senator Lester Hunt of Wyoming, a staunch anti-McCarthyite. Hunt's son had been arrested for soliciting an undercover policeman in Washington, D.C., and Hunt was informed that everyone in his home state would know about his son if he ran for reelection in 1954. He shot himself instead.) In *Angels in America* (1992), Tony Kushner provided the best summary of Cohn's attitude toward gay men and the issue of their weakness when Cohn explains to his doctor, who is trying to tell Cohn that he knows he is a homosexual and that it doesn't matter, why he couldn't possibly be gay. Homosexuals are people without respect in this society, Cohn bellows. They lack the muscle to get a simple civil rights bill past the city council. What could he, the most powerful lawyer in New York, have in common with people so pathetic, so ludicrous, so victimized. Roy Cohn will not be a victim, no matter how intimate he must become with those in power who would make him one.

Gender-role polarities based on active/passive, manly/womanly distinctions had been a feature of gay life in America since the beginning of what could be called, as an organized entity, "a gay life." Fairies went looking for husbands—men to care for them, protect them, and fuck them—in a reductive simulation of the straight world. 1930s street language provided a term for the homosexual, neither butch nor femme, who resisted taking one path or the other—the "kiki" (by the 1950s, a predominantly lesbian term) was uncommitted and annoyingly vague, in the opinion of those who liked the traditional demarcations. But the rigidity of this gender system was on the wane by the end of the 1930s, and the early 1940s provided plenty of reasons to question the exactness of the self-labeling. Fairies or husbands, too many homosexuals had suffered, struggled, fought, and died in the war.

Yet the strident projections about a natural chasm between masculine and feminine styles and essences that informed 1950s culture in the United States were hardly irrelevant to gay men. Many shared the same biases. Androgynous beauty was not a much sought-after ideal at the time, and the glorification of brawn, like the denigration of femininity in males, became a new element of what some gay men wanted to be, as well as what they wanted to fantasize about. Looking back on the 1950s in *The Homosexual and His Society* (1963), Donald Webster Cory, who had expressed his discomfort with camp and effeminacy in 1951 in *The Homosexual in America*, and co-author John LeRoy took note of a new type emerging to rival the queen of old: "the muscle man, the weight lifter, the barbell collector, the body-worshiping physical culturist who haunts the gym as surely as his effeminate counterpart haunts the drags." With swaggering replacing swishing, the macho homosexual wore his muscular build, Cory and LeRoy wrote, "the same way the drag queen wore her dress." From this angle, homosexuality was less a challenge to ideas about rugged manhood than an acceptance of society's terms. One didn't have to be Roy Cohn to see how much could be gained by altering the line, "I'm a gay man and I camp and I swish, and so what?" to "I'm a gay man, but I'm as butch as any of you."

The beefcake magazines made vast fortunes for their owners by tapping into the increasingly overt fantasies of a tough, muscle-bound ideal. Bob Mizer discovered a market the scope of which he'd never imagined when he made his first forays into the business at the end of World War II; *Physique Pictorial* required a larger print run with each issue in the early 1950s, quickly reaching the 40,000 mark. *Vim, Trim, Grecian Guild Pictorial, Adonis, Body Beautiful*, and *Tomorrow's Man* were serious competition, and illustrators George Quaintance, Tom of Finland, and Etienne were known in their prime to more gay men than had ever heard of Charles Demuth, Paul Cadmus, or George Platt Lynes. A minimum of body hair, well-defined pectorals, taut thighs, big biceps, good teeth, a "basket" that bulged through a pouch, a vacant stare, nothing fey, nothing complicated: drawing or photograph, the attributes were always the same, as were the models' poses, youth, and race (almost always white). Not so very different, on the whole, from the appetites heterosexual society encouraged with Jayne Mansfield parodying Marilyn Monroe parodying female sexual beauty—lips thicker and redder, busts bigger and pointier, hair blonder than any man ever saw in daily life.

A more creative and dramatic gay exploration of hypermasculinity—or antifemininity—and the erotic dimensions of that state of mind came in the same period with the rise of the S&M scene. Compared to its blossoming and legitimization in the 1960s and 1970s, the world of arousal by way of masters, slaves, whips, chains, paddles, tough talk, and black leather was in its infancy in the 1950s, but the networks were there, operating effectively, and cruising spots to make S&M pickups were established in many cities. At least one bar in New York City was known to let patrons change into their leather outfits in the back after six P.M. A man in leather on the streets was sure to be stopped by the police.

It was no simple matter to be involved in sadomasochism on an elaborate scale; one had to want to take the trouble. The drive behind S&M was anything but casual. "We had no Pleasure Chest [to buy our wares], but we used our imaginations," a participant remarked at a panel in the 1970s about the early days of S&M in New York. Chains could be purchased in hardware stores, and a hose covered with black electrical tape and a condom served as a dildo. More specialized items were trickier to find. Uncle Sam's Umbrella Shop off Times Square, for instance, sold whips and paddles because it was a theatrical supply store in the theater district, though many an Uncle Sam customer never acted in a play. (The drawback was that the merchandise was designed for stage use. "The paddles fell apart on the third whack!" lamented one veteran.) Finding new members for a private-party group required some cleverness, too. The real estate section of the Sunday *Times* might advertise a rental share for a man who "collects flags"—that is, is interested in flagellation. "And there seemed to be a lot of 'Greek professors' wanting roommates then," joked another panelist. "We did somehow make a kind of society," remembered a longtime S&M advocate, a man who had been searching for just such a set of like-minded partners since the war. "I don't know how widely known or accepted it was, but we were there. The rough-sex crowd. Nothing Mamie would have approved of."

Not that Mamie Eisenhower would have had kind words for those on the other side of the line—the many gay men, young or old, who didn't want to relinquish their identification with the feminine. Swishy homosexuals knew perfectly well what less swishy homosexuals thought of them now that the pansy was a suspect figure. "If I wanted to have sex with a woman, I'd be straight" was a rote response from more masculine gay men that lasted well into the 1970s, as if the "choice" were that simple or the nelly queen's status as a woman that clear. Drag at parties became a subject of more criticism, the drag queen (in some circles) cut a less impressive figure in 1960 than she did in 1950, and the bullyboys weren't the only ones spending time at the gym. Yet the advantages of holding on to whatever degree of femininity felt comfortable were real—or, put another way, gay identification with stereotypical masculinity was potentially dangerous. For one thing, holding on to femininity was the surest way by which young men who didn't have the option of bars, baths, tearooms, or parks could find other young men. The isolation of the gay jock, the boy well on his way to becoming the "man's man" his parents wanted, was total and complete. The high school gang of peers Rick Colantino gathered around him in Connecticut spotted one another pretty quickly because they were all campier than their parents could stand. The tight circle of friends Benjamin Walker knew in the 1950s through his black Baptist church in South Carolina formed a kind of club, deciding to tone down their mannerisms (which had brought them together in the first place) in public in return for more spectacle and revelry in private among themselves. The members of the group Laurie Chilcote met while he was at Roosevelt High School in Portland, Oregon, in the late 1940s were all classic fairies. They carved out their turf at Bare-Ass Beach on Hayden Island unmolested, separate from the trade section ("horny boys from the north end") and the adult queers who came to make it with the straight guys. Tormented as sissies or ignored as beneath contempt, Colantino, Walker, and Chilcote turned the very mark of their perversion, their refusal to be a "man's man," into the means by which they developed a makeshift community before they were old enough to look for it elsewhere.

Or consider the crusade of Jose Sarria in San Francisco. A precocious child and a bit of a dandy, Sarria breezed through World War II as a colonel's orderly and returned to San Francisco after a tour of duty in Europe and a stay in New York. He started hanging out at the Black Cat Cafe, later covering for his boyfriend, a waiter there. (Sol Stouman's bar on Montgomery Street had known its share of harassment during the war from the city vice squad and the military police, and by the late 1940s became the focus of a milestone battle against the California Alcoholic Beverage Commission, which attempted to close the place as a "meeting ground" for persons "of known homosexual tendencies." In 1951 the State Supreme Court ruled unanimously that a tavern or cafe could not be denied a liquor license simply because its clientele was gay. Allen Ginsberg called it "the greatest gay bar in America," a gathering place for "screaming queens . . . heterosexual gray flannel suit types, longshoremen . . . poets.") The management quickly judged Sarria to be more valuable for his repartee and musical parodies of evangelist Aimee Semple McPherson ("I will save you girls from the evil that walks in the parks at night!") and assorted opera divas than for his services bringing customers their drinks. Arrested on a morals charge that forced him to drop his plans to be a teacher, he angrily changed course, becoming less discreet than ever. "I decided then," he said, "to be the most notorious impersonator or homosexual or fairy or whatever you wanted to call me—and you would pay for it." His acts at the Black Cat became more theatrical and Sarria was soon in makeup in broad daylight on errands around town. By the late 1950s, he was one of the most popular attractions of San Francisco's nightlife and took pleasure in sticking it to the police ("the blue fungus") in the lyrics he created for his songs.

Bitter and brash, Sarria was every homophobe's nightmare. The fear that limp wrists and a camp flair might not imply confusion and self-hate, that effeminacy might be as resolute, competitive, even willful—might, in fact, be as strong—as any masculinity was demonstrated each and every time Sarria performed at the cafe, walked the streets of San Francisco in mascara, or strode into I. Magnin's for a fitting in the lingerie department. He also insisted that the cafe's patrons stand, clasp hands, and join him in a song every Sunday afternoon. "God Save Us Nelly Queens," sung to the tune of "My Country 'Tis of Thee," was an anthem of resistance, to gay prejudice as well as straight tyranny. Not many gay men in America would have been happy to acknowledge it as such in the 1950s. But Sarria knew what he was doing. "Music leads people to war," he liked to say. In that sense, the Roy Cohns and the Jose Sarrias of the gay world had one thing in common—a hatred of polite submission, a kick-ass taste for life. They saw themselves as fighters and understood that postwar society was indeed a battleground. The difference was that Cohn existed only for Cohn, the butch lawyer; Sarria stood for queens everywhere, ballsy rather than butch, and militantly unapologetic.

12

VISIONARIES

Great perils have this beauty, that they bring to light the fraternity of strangers.

—Victor Hugo

In the late 1940s, Jim Kepner, a Californian living at the time in New York City, participated each year in the May Day parade. Walking down Lexington Avenue in 1948, surveying a crowd of thousands of marchers sympathetic to the Marxist cause, he turned to a friend—a man he knew was gay, though neither of them had ever discussed his sexuality with the other— and said, "Do you think, someday, our people . . . ?" His friend understood, without any further exchange, that Kepner was voicing a fantasy that, in some distant age, thousands of homosexuals might parade down the thoroughfare of a major city, as openly gay as the present marchers were openly Red. The man responded emphatically, *"Not in a thousand years."*

The concept of an organization of homosexuals who would meet for the purposes of defining their lives in relation to a discriminatory society and planning for a radically different future was hard for anyone to imagine in the postwar years, and Kepner's musings about gay marches were in the realm of comic speculation. Since the days of Henry Gerber's attempt in 1924 to interest the gay men of Chicago in such a group, the idea had surfaced from time to time in different areas, but never came to fruition. During the war, Kepner had been told of a clandestine body formed in the early 1930s that went by the name "the Sons of Hamidy" and included prominent political and military figures. He eventually decided that the group was a figment of his informant's overheated imagination. At approximately the same time, Gerber (then living in Washington, D.C.) was pondering a revival of his venture, though the experiences of his arrest and humiliation had made him wary and defensive. "Formal agitation is not effectual," Gerber wrote to his friend Manuel Boyfrank in 1944. "I have never entertained the idea that one could stand in Union Square and shout the gospel. That would be freedom of speech, and there ain't no such animal." He and Boyfrank had fun debating names—Band of Brothers, Band of Sisters, Children of Light—but concluded that their goal was unrealistic.

The Veterans' Benevolent Association, formed in New York City immediately after the war, was more social than political, though its parties—sometimes numbering hundreds of guests, according to Jules Elphant, a participant—provided its members with a much-needed esprit de corps. A Philadelphian, Jan Kingma, organized a short-lived group in 1947, with ties to a few sympathetic Pennsylvania clergymen, and in Los Angeles in 1950, a black lawyer, Merton Bird, had slightly more success with the Knights of the Clock, a society that took as its aims the promotion of interracial harmony (many of its members were black men with white lovers) and "outreach" to the families of gay men. However, no one was so taken with the idea of a gay organization, or so tenacious in pursuing that idea, as Harry Hay. A resident of Los Angeles, Hay was thirty-five in 1948, a member of the American Communist Party, and a married man with two adopted daughters. But Hay's marriage was on the verge of collapse and his political outlook was impelling him to look for new connections beyond the merely social or sexual. At an all-male party he attended the summer before the presidential election, discussion among the guests turned to Henry Wallace's candidacy. Hay touted the notion of a group that would support the Progressive Party's challenge to Truman and Dewey and lobby for a "right to privacy" plank in the party's platform: "Bachelors for Wallace." The talk that evening was lively, but no one really thought that Harry Hay's excitement was anything more than idle banter. When Hay went home to write what he termed "The Call," a five-page proposal for an organization that would bring gay men together and convince the world of their common humanity, he was fired with a missionary fervor that arose out of, but surpassed, the Bachelors for Wallace idea. The men he showed it to over the next few days were both shocked and indignant. No one was going to risk exposure and the loss of his job in pursuit of a misguided fantasy. What of the interest expressed at the party, such as it was? "Honey, that was the beer talking" was a kind response. The man who had hosted the party reacted with what Hay described as "self-destructive and withering cynicism."

And so it went for the better part of the next two years. Hay couldn't let go, but his passion and pleading fell on deaf ears. The refrain hadn't changed much since Henry Gerber had tested the same waters: gay men didn't constitute an entity with enough in common to rally behind any kind of homosexual banner. Gay men weren't political creatures—they could get by rather nicely by keeping a low profile and having a good time. The odds of a gay group surviving to achieve anything worthwhile were laughably slim. The benefits and the dangers weren't commensurate. Only when Hay met and became lovers with Rudy Gernreich, in later years a noted fashion designer (1960s creator of the topless bathing suit and the unisex look), did he find an ally who shared his nerve and interest in social change. From the minute he read "The Call," the twenty-eight-year-old Gernreich was ready to join his lover in trying to make the prospectus ("the most dangerous thing I've ever seen," he told Hay) a reality. Two midwesterners who had recently moved to California, Chuck Rowland and Bob Hull, were the next converts to the cause, and Hull in turn brought in his current amour, Dale Jennings. A short time later, in the spring of 1951, James Gruber and Konrad Stevens heard about this small, intense group meeting each week to discuss homosexual issues and were invited to join what was now called the steering committee, or Fifth Order, of the as yet unnamed body.

Gruber and Stevens were the only two of the original seven without strong left-wing ties or sympathies (Hay, Rowland, and Hull had actually been Communist Party members), but their physical charm, youth, and eagerness made them highly desirable additions and a speedy and significant difference in attracting new members. But they were also serious about the subject at hand; others had come and gone during the winter of 1950–1951, and Hay had started to worry that their dream might never grow beyond the five stalwarts.

The earliest gatherings of Hay's brainchild took the form of discussion groups, conducted in a clandestine manner. Rowland recalled putting a pillow over the phone to thwart wiretappers. Blinds were drawn, departures were staggered so as not to arouse the suspicions of neighbors, and outsiders expressing interest were carefully screened. Even to gather in a private apartment for the purpose of *talking* about their personal experiences as homosexuals, or their need for community or desire to live in a more tolerant society, seemed to these men a dangerous act. The medieval French name they finally settled on, a choice attributed to Bob Hull, reflected that dramatic outsider's stance as well: the "mattachine" was, according to one source, the folk dance performed by the masked figures who were part of the "Societies of Fools" in France and Italy. The esoteric term (from the Arabic for "mask") was a far cry from the whimsical Bachelors for Wallace, but then Hay's thinking had advanced from that earlier, simpler concept. A political push for the "right to privacy" was a laudable end, but Hay had hopes by 1951 that the Mattachine Society would grapple with more ambitious and more theoretical aims.

Steeped in Marxism, Hay and his friends—especially Rowland and Hull—wanted to explore the possibility that gay men and women might come to think of themselves in a radical new light: as a cultural minority, a self-defined group with its own history, psychological makeup, and identifying characteristics, capable of unified action to advance its collective goals. This was an outlook that, in one sense, ironically linked these pioneers of the gay movement to the psychiatrists who believed that homosexuals should be seen as fundamentally different from "normal" people, though of course for the mental health authorities "different" necessarily meant damaged or crippled. To Hay and his circle, "different" carried no such weight of judgment. But in all other respects, the Mattachine proposition that homosexuals had anything special to learn, or to gain, from group talks that stressed their role as part of an "oppressed people" was seen as unique, if not preposterous. In retrospect, the discussions were clearly the right means by which to aim—to grope—toward an understanding of homosexuals as a true minority (which was always Hay's purpose), and the credit must go to his, and Rowland's, experience with the Communist Party and its tradition of social theorizing, consciousness-raising forums, and self-examination. The last point was critical. "Homosexuals do not understand themselves and thus it is not surprising that heterosexuals do not understand them either," Hay wrote in notes for an October 1951 meeting.

Ken Burns, an early participant, remembered the discussion-group topics as ranging from the abstract ("what gayness was") to the more psychodynamic ("acceptance of ourselves, acknowledging our pain") to the more nitty-gritty troublesome issue of how and when to tell one's parents. Others recalled debating attitudes toward nellies (should effeminacy be accepted or discouraged?), the value or harm of the bar scene, the sickness doctrine, the best ways to find a lover, and the role of monogamy in gay relationships. For many people, it was helpful to know, simply, that the fact of parental anger, job discrimination, and police brutality wasn't their nightmare alone. Beginning in 1953, Hay would occasionally present papers on research he was conducting into the history of homosexuality.

Unanimity, particularly on the question of how to effect change and how strong a sense of solidarity could and *should* be expected of homosexuals, was never a common feature of the discussions. Martin Block was in his early thirties when he joined the Mattachine Society and, from his first session, found plenty to disagree with. On that evening Chuck Rowland devoted himself to a lengthy analogy of the gay struggle with the labor movement, a parallel Block found wide of the mark. Indeed, many participants were uneasy with the prospect of seeing themselves as significantly different from, or more progressive or revolutionary than, their heterosexual neighbors. Working-class agitation called for a rethinking of the nature of capitalist society, while gay men and lesbians were, presumably, asking for something simpler—to be left alone, to be free from interference in a private area of their lives that had little to do with larger policies or structures. On that basis, they could never constitute a unified movement, Block and others felt, and homosexuals would always resist a group identity.

Part of the problem originated in this genuine difference of opinion, but another part grew out of the stridency with which the "cultural minority" faction sometimes expressed itself. Harry Hay tended to come on strong— "like a bulldozer," Konrad Stevens told interviewer John D'Emilio in the 1970s—and his impatience and self-confidence alienated many prospective allies. Rowland, on the other hand, was no less a true believer but managed to project a less threatening image. "Chuck was an affectionate person, the most loving of them all," Stevens felt; Rowland was the member of the steering committee who really understood how vital it was to nurture "a sense of belonging," especially in newcomers. About two matters, though, everyone seems to have been in agreement: the rightness of the approach, implicitly Marxist, which Hay advocated—that the individual had to know himself and explore his condition before attempting to change society—and the fact that they were all engaged in something frightening, but very special. Never before, to anyone's knowledge, had homosexuals come together to debate these questions in a systematic way.

The sense of specialness had not been left to chance. The Mattachine Society at its inception displayed aspects that evoked the spirit of the Masons, an element of Alcoholics Anonymous, and most noticeably the hierarchical cell structure of the Communist Party. The Mason-like dimension had to with the secrecy and fraternity Hay felt were essential to the organization's life. Everyone had to pledge not to reveal the names of anyone else involved without his or her permission. (Though Hay, Rowland, and Hull were no longer members of the Party, they were fully aware of the need to keep that fact from becoming too widely known, given the political climate of the 1950s.) An initiation ceremony in a candle-lit room added to the mystery and expectancy. The A.A. aspect was seen in the verbal scrutiny of inner demons and a reliance on group support for encouragement and self-understanding. Far from having a perfectly integrated view of his sexuality, even Hay had doubts and tensions to work out. It was precisely because of the instability and sexual compulsiveness gay men manifested, Hay believed, that a fraternity and a minority identification were needed. Hay's Party ties were suggested in the pyramidal cell structure of Mattachine: public discussion groups, known as guilds, were the entry-level "order" of membership. A Second, Third, and Fourth Order reflected higher, more exclusive levels of authority and responsibility; those individuals were in charge of creating new cells and running the discussions. The founders of Mattachine made up the Fifth Order, an anonymous, self-appointed centralized leadership.

Growth was agonizingly slow, however (the Third and Fourth Orders never even came into being), and it wasn't until February 1952, four months after the first meeting, that the arrest of one of the group's original members provided an unexpected push. Dale Jennings was jailed for "lewd and lascivious behavior" in a Los Angeles park; the arresting officer claimed that Jennings had approached him, while Jennings insisted that the policeman, in a classic case of entrapment, had come over to him. After some disagreement, Jennings and the other members of the Fifth Order decided to fight the charge, acknowledging Jennings's homosexuality but disputing the accusation that he had broken the law in the park. Not yet ready to publicize the society's existence too openly, the Mattachine leadership acted under the guise of the Citizens Committee to Outlaw Entrapment, distributing leaflets and spreading the news that a gay man was going to fight back in court. When the Jennings case was dismissed (the hung jury voted eleven-to-one for acquittal), "overnight the word was all over town," Jim Kepner noted. "Legions of eager gays," Chuck Rowland said, wanted to know who was behind the action of challenging a policeman's word in court and convincing eleven jurors that the rights of a gay man had been violated. Over the next several months, membership in Mattachine, both male and female, soared. By the end of 1952, discussion groups were meeting up and down the California coast. A group of Los Angeles members had decided to bring out a small periodical, which debuted in January 1953 as *ONE Magazine: The Homosexual Viewpoint.* "It was an electric moment," one participant exclaimed, and that enthusiasm was widely shared, despite the increasingly unwieldy nature of an organization that was growing too quickly to allow its leaders to maintain full control, despite the astonishing, discordant variety of people and opinions that was emerging, and despite the unease some members felt about not knowing the identity of the men behind the whole thing. Rowland, among others, sensed trouble, but Hay was optimistic and excited.

THE INDIVIDUAL RESPONSIBLE for the genesis of the Mattachine Society was a perfect example of the archetype of "the man and the moment," though his time at center stage of the early gay movement was destined to be much shorter than he could have realized in 1950. Born to American parents living in England in 1912, Harry Hay was the product of an unusual family. Hay Senior was a mining engineer for the Guggenheims who had also worked for Cecil Rhodes in South Africa. His career was curtailed by an accident that cost him one leg and led to the family's relocation in California. Talking to his elderly mother in 1951 about his decision to be an open homosexual, Hay wondered how his late father would have reacted; his mother's only comment was, "Your father knew Cecil Rhodes."

Mrs. Hay's observation was deceptive. Accepting the homosexuality of a world-famous financier and empire builder was one thing—a sign of a worldly nature—but tolerating it in a blood relation was quite another. Hay's earliest recollections are of a self-assured, dictatorial father who wanted to beat any traces of effeminacy out of his eldest son and of a mother who countered this aggression by doting on her firstborn and dismissing as "those little peasants" his two younger, less precocious siblings. Uncle Jack, his mother's brother who lived with the Hays in Los Angeles for a while, was a bachelor with a dandy's wardrobe and an interest in theater. In his father's mind, Harry would be raised in a way to mitigate against such questionable influences. But the patriarchal decision to deny Harry an allowance and force him to labor at working-class jobs during his school vacations backfired in a serious way: his ranch-hand partners taught Harry about union organizing and Socialism, and alerted him to the existence of men who liked to have sex with boys. Harry's loss of his virginity with Matt, a merchant seaman he met on the beach one night in 1926, was a turning point, especially as Matt assured his eager bedmate that there were many others like them in the wide world, that they in fact formed a far-flung secret brotherhood.

It is possible that Harry Hay would have come to a benevolent view of his sexual nature without the experience of the night with Matt, an event that took on a grandly romantic aura for him as time passed. For Hay was by nature impressionable, curious, strong-willed, and sometimes brazen. Vivid memories from early adolescence included the time he and his father were forced to the side of the road by local Ku Klux Klan members to watch a cross burning, the way the Jewish families in the neighborhood were ostracized, his mother's edict not to play with a Negro boy he had befriended. His furtive examination of the local library's copy of *The Inter-mediate Sex*, Edward Carpenter's progressive study of "homogenic attach-ments," had the force of an "earthshaking revelation" as Hay evolved into a studious teenager who questioned the values most of his peers took for granted.

During his sophomore year at Stanford in 1931, Hay came out to his friends. Responses to his announcement were not especially dramatic, and the fraternity rejection that ensued wasn't too unsettling for a nineteen-year-old in the process of discovering how many other "temperamentals" were available if one knew where to look. Pershing Square in Los Angeles was a wonderful meeting ground, and a thirtyish boyfriend picked up there told Hay not only about the equivalent opportunities in Cheseman Park in Denver and on the streets of San Francisco, but also of his former lover's involvement with Henry Gerber's Society for Human Rights venture in Chicago.

One exploration followed upon another. New Year's Eve in 1930 was spent dancing and necking at a gay speakeasy, Jimmy's Back Yard near Hollywood Boulevard, and the following year brought a first visit to the bars of the Bay Area and several more exciting, short-lived affairs. A brutal sinus infection early in 1932 ended Hay's academic career, though not everyone then or now was convinced that the sources of his decision to leave Stanford were entirely physical. As Hay's biographer Stuart Timmons wrote, the gap between the pressure to please, or even answer to, a conser-vative, impossibly demanding father and the thrill of an immersion in the "twilight world" made a psychological crisis of some kind almost inevitable.

Hay made the acquaintance of Will Geer, a genteely impoverished actor (known forty years later to television viewers as Grandpa Walton), who became his lover as well as his means of introduction to the radical left. By 1938, Hay was committed to the Party and caught in the bind created by the Soviet government's reversal of its liberal policies toward homosexu-ality in the early 1920s. As a man preoccupied with economic and racial equality, Hay was sure he had made the right political choice; as a homo-sexual, he was under enormous strain to deny a part of himself he knew had nothing to do with a capitalist upbringing or "bourgeois decadence." A psychiatrist advised him to look for a boyish girl rather than a girl-ish boy, and in fellow Party member Anita Platky he found that person. The result of their union was a troubled thirteen-year life as a "pseudo-heterosexual," raising two adopted girls with his wife and meeting men for sex on the side in anonymous settings. The marriage ended in 1951, when Hay finally decided to tell Anita about his Mattachine activities. That frankness earned him the enmity of his in-laws, his straight friends, and Party members throughout Los Angeles, but one person stood by him. Hay's mother was supportive and ready to meet her son's new friends and even allowed her name and address to be used (a fact recorded in her FBI file) when Hay sought to establish the Mattachine Foundation as a state-registered, nonprofit research corporation separate from the Mattachine Society.

Coming out after marriage for Harry Hay—coming out not only in the old-time sense of admitting homosexuality to gay peers, but coming out to all the world—was supposed to be the beginning of a new life, and it was in many respects. But it was not the life he envisioned, of gay activism and leadership. Intimations of just how difficult a task he had set himself were apparent even in so simple a matter as the setting up of a board for the foundation that would include a few prominent names. Hay found Christopher Isherwood's refusal high-handed and irritating. Evelyn Hooker, a psychologist who was studying male homosexuals with an eye toward verifying Kinsey's assumptions of their mental health parity with heterosexual males, declined on the assumption that she would be compromising her standing as an unbiased researcher, and Kinsey himself, though he had interviewed Hay for his book, never met with the Fifth Order. Hay had to settle for a Universalist minister and a San Bernardino physician. Then, in March 1953, came the Paul Coates debacle.

Though its papers had not yet been processed by the state, the Mattachine Foundation was off and running and had sent a letter to the candidates for the Los Angeles City Council, querying them on their stand on police harassment of gays and sex education in public schools. Paul Coates, a reporter for the *Los Angeles Daily Mirror*, saw the letter and published a column about it. The state had no record of any such foundation, he accurately pointed out. The man named as their lawyer had recently been called before the House Un-American Activities Committee, where he refused to answer questions. No one seemed to know who the leaders of this Mattachine outfit were. Were they sincere Americans, or were they subversives taking their orders from Moscow? He ended with some friendly advice: "If I belonged to that club, I'd worry."

Nothing could have frightened Mattachine's rank and file more than Coates's inflammatory last line. Of the two thousand men and women who had participated in the discussion groups, only a tiny number could actually have named the people behind the idea or knew much about the other guilds in other towns. The whole structure began to feel suspiciously foreign, undemocratic, needlessly mysterious. Given the hysteria emanating from Washington, the panic that set in among First Order members was unstoppable. "It was a natural thing born out of fear," Konrad Stevens remembered. Not many people cared about the issue of the foundation's delayed paperwork. What mattered was the possibility that the police would be barging in at the next meeting, that hundreds of California homosexuals would be exposed as dupes of the Soviet Union, proving Senators Wherry and McCarthy right.

Never the most flexible of men, Hay was loath to give up the cell idea and the oath of secrecy. What he was especially worried about was losing the almost mystical bonding behind his notion of Mattachine. But a complete revision of the organization was essential to its survival, Rowland and the other founders insisted, and Hay reluctantly agreed that a convention had to be called for guild representatives to draft a constitution and air the grievances that the Coates article had brought to the surface.

In one respect, the Mattachine Society could be seen as a victim of its own rapid success, but the events of the spring of 1953 also indicate how passionately Hay believed in his conception of homosexuality, forever touched by that night on the beach with Matt, and how little he saw the people around him. For every brother-in-arms like Rowland or Hull he had brought into the fold, for every bookish radical he had befriended like Jim Kepner, for every bright, apolitical eccentric he had attracted like Dorr Legg or Martin Block, there were dozens more in the guilds who didn't want to live life in a mythic, questing spirit, who thought that HUAC was asking some fair questions and that the fight against Communism in Korea made sense, and who liked Ike just fine. Men like Ken Burns of Los Angeles and Hal Call of San Francisco were staunchly conservative. These people had to be taken into account at some point. They wanted to feel better as gay people, they wanted gay rights, but they wanted no part of an assault on American political or spiritual values.

The Mattachine convention was held on two weekends in April and May in 1953 at the Universalist Church whose pastor was on the Mattachine board. Even before the speeches and parliamentary wrangling over bylaws and new membership rules began, minor disputes erupted. Dale Jennings committed the faux pas of showing up with a gay friend who was not a member, a serviceman whose appearance in uniform rattled some of the delegates who then demanded his and Jennings's eviction. Others wanted to discuss the rumor that a leader of the Oakland group was involved with a seventeen-year-old and the damage this revelation would do to the society's image. In his keynote address, Chuck Rowland tried to sweep away all of the divisiveness with an appeal to an overarching philosophy of gayness. "We must disenthrall ourselves of the idea that we differ only in our sexual directions," he urged. Heterosexual society had long excluded homosexuals and that exclusion necessarily resulted in a separate development, a different consciousness. No one doubted that there was such a thing as a Jewish culture or an American black culture, and by the same reasoning gays might look to define gay culture. The intelligent goal was pride in a distinctive identity and the creation of an "ethical homosexual culture." Rowland's speech was certainly one of the most remarkable demonstrations of oratory by a gay man in America speaking on gay issues, not least for its prediction that "the time will come when we will march down Hollywood Boulevard arm in arm, proclaiming our pride in our homosexuality." Harry Hay's speech astutely defended the right of Mattachine's lawyer not to testify before the Senate's Red-baiters, observing that political dissidents and homosexuals had, in principle, much in common in a time of witch-hunts and coercive loyalty oaths.

Response to the two speeches, Rowland's in particular, was not uniformly positive. Many of those in attendance, most vocally Ken Burns and his Los Angeles guild and Hal Call and his northern California contingent, were adamantly opposed to the idea of political activism, a distinct gay identity, and any celebration of a militant or separatist subculture. They didn't want to march down Hollywood Boulevard advertising their difference or be linked with unfriendly HUAC witnesses. The goal of a homosexual organization, they argued, should be the integration of gay men and lesbians into mainstream society, and Rowland's philosophy implied the opposite intentions. Call's suspicions about Rowland's Communist background only aggravated the situation. "We were none of us," Call insisted to historian John D'Emilio in the 1970s, "going to lay ourselves open and let a person we regarded as a half-assed prick lead us by the nose and manipulate and use us to some advantage that we didn't know about." Marilyn Rieger contended more gently in a well-received speech at the second session of the convention that only by convincing the world that their homosexuality was irrelevant to their complete or larger selves could homosexuals rid the world of its misconceptions and prejudices: "We know we are the same, no different from anyone else." In this view, hope for middle-class gay people in 1953 came from the prospect of eventual acceptance, not separation in any form—as a cultural minority or a political force.

The actual downfall of the Fifth Order at the end of the May session of the convention is a curious matter. Call wanted the Mattachine constitution to clarify the group's opposition to "subversive elements." (At a follow-up convention in November, David Finn, a friend of Call's, went so far as to threaten to turn over the Mattachine membership lists to the FBI if the delegates did not explicitly repudiate any hint of left-wing sympathy, a violation of the oath of secrecy that disturbed everyone who heard the threat.) Other resolutions in November called for members to sign oaths pledging their allegiance to "the American creed," the flag, and the country's laws (the strangest of all suggestions in that those laws made criminals of every Mattachine member each time he or she made love to another gay man or lesbian). The delegates showed little or no interest in proving their patriotism to anyone. Yet Hay and his friends were uneasy about their future in the organization now that the touchy issue of their past political affiliations was out in the open; the inevitable FBI snooping and the dismay of those members who felt betrayed by the earlier code of silence would run them to ground. In the hope of keeping the dream alive, in May the founders identified themselves to the convention delegates and announced they would not run for office in the newly constituted, open-membership Mattachine Society. Many delegates were shocked and displeased by that announcement, but the opposition was primed to fill the void. Call, Burns, Rieger, and Finn, despite their failure to persuade their peers to affirm their Americanism and opposition to Communism, were elected to positions of responsibility. The decision to step down was a gamble, Rowland felt, that soon turned into a catastrophic mistake.

THE SHIFT IN power, which meant a shift in style as well as philosophy, had an immediate impact on the growth and even the existence of the discussion groups across the state. Within a few months, many died out, including most of those in the Los Angeles area. The number of lesbians, never great to begin with, dwindled. (The one advantage of this development was that it paved the way for Del Martin and Phyllis Lyon to found the first lesbian organization in America, the Daughters of Bilitis, in San Francisco in 1955.) Veterans of labor battles from the 1930s, or anyone who might have an FBI file, knew they were not welcome. To Burns and Call, this was not necessarily a bad development, however heartbreaking it seemed to Hay and Rowland. Too many firebrands, too much publicity, too many radical ideas would bring down upon them the wrath of the establishment.

The new strategy, especially when Hal Call succeeded Ken Burns as the organization's head and later moved the main office to San Francisco, was to work within the system in an impeccably respectable manner. In that sense, a small, unified, middle-of-the-road membership would be more effective. But effective for what end, the members of what Hay now called "First Mattachine" wanted to know. Forsaking the original plans for grassroots activism and identity building, Second Mattachine questioned how much gay people could accomplish on their own, or even how much they could understand about their own sexuality. Speakers at the Mattachine forums in the mid- and late-1950s in San Francisco, and in the several other cities outside California where small chapters were opened, sometimes included legal authorities, professors, doctors, and psychiatrists who did *not* believe homosexuals were healthy or responsible people and who advised their listeners to change their lifestyle. This fact, more than any other, has dogged the memory of the 1950s "homophile movement," as it was then called, and contributed to later derision of its efforts. We did not fully trust our own judgment at the time, a New York Mattachine member acknowledged, nor did we assume that we could explain our situation and our needs to the rest of society. "We wanted to ride on the shirttails of [the lawyers, psychiatrists, academics]," Hal Call agreed. At one point, Call remembered, the Mattachine Society used "the sop, the palliative" that it was not even an exclusively homosexual group, that it included heterosexual members (for example, Call's mother) who were interested in the topic as a social issue. The leadership under Burns and Call made it clear that taking on entrapment cases in the manner of the Dale Jennings cause célèbre or arguing with legislators about sodomy law repeal were not on the agenda; research projects, polite dialogue with professionals, and goodwill charity acts, such as contributing to local blood drives, were more the order of the day.

Though the total membership of the Mattachine Society in all of the chapters it was able to establish throughout California, and in New York, Boston, Philadelphia, Denver, Chicago, and Detroit, had not exceeded three hundred by 1960, it would be a mistake to characterize the group's efforts as utterly futile or retrograde. (With the same thoroughness that Second Mattachine rewrote history to expunge the memory of Hay and Rowland, so did the more radical gay political groups of the 1970s efface their predecessors, never alluding to the earlier work of Mattachine or attempting to understand it in the context of its times.) Some of the professional alliances the post-Hay Mattachine forged were vitally important. Blanche Baker, a San Francisco psychiatrist, was a consistent ally and often spoke to the membership—and her colleagues—about the need for gay men and lesbians to ignore society's messages and cultivate their own perceptions of mental health, dignity, and self-worth. "Learn to take out your resentments on those who are responsible for them," she preached to her gay audiences. Psychologist Evelyn Hooker had been encouraged by a gay friend in the late 1940s to embark on a study that would take the latest research on homosexuality to the next level.

In *Sexual Behavior in the Human Male*, Kinsey declared that same-sex orgasms were much more prevalent than most Americans believed. In *Patterns of Sexual Behavior* (1951), Cleland Ford and Frank Beach analyzed nearly eighty cultures as well as the behavior of nonhuman primates to suggest the universality of same-sex desire and the lack of a worldwide adult heterosexual "norm." By finding thirty well-adjusted gay men and thirty well-adjusted straight men to take the Rorschach and other personality tests, Evelyn Hooker wanted to see if a panel of nationally renowned experts could do what her profession had always taken for granted could be done: identify "maladjusted" or "psychopathological" men solely on the basis of their test results, without meeting them and knowing in advance which were homosexual. She found some of her volunteers among the ranks of Mattachine. Her findings, presented to the American Psychological Association in 1956 and at several Mattachine forums, proved that there was no greater pathology inherent in men who enjoyed sex with other men compared to men who enjoyed sex with women. The test evaluators judged many of the gay men, before knowing they were gay, to be well-balanced individuals. As Richard Bayer wrote in *Homosexuality and American Psychiatry* (1981), Hooker's research "provided the richest source of material for those who challenged the assumptions that homosexuality was a pathological condition."

In this same period, Call and a friend, Don Lucas, formed the Pan-Graphic Press and published *The Mattachine Review*. From January 1956 until 1964, when it began appearing only sporadically, the monthly *Review* served its two thousand readers "as an educational and informational tool," Call told journalist Eric Marcus. "The idea was to spread the word about what we thought was the reality of homosexual behavior." This is an accurate appraisal from every angle; "the reality of homosexual behavior" included activities and attributes that the more conservative members of the Mattachine Society did not approve of themselves, and more than a few articles in Call's periodical were about the need for homosexuals to institute some "personal reform." Yet *The Mattachine Review* was by no means as reactionary as later commentators have suggested. Reprints of the liberal Wolfenden Report from England and articles from more outspoken European gay journals ("Let Us Be Proud!" from *Der Kreis* in October 1957) served a dynamic purpose. Reviews of dozens of books with gay themes provided readers in smaller cities with intellectual connections they might not otherwise have had. In all of this, the word-of-mouth factor is incalculable, as copies were passed from friend to friend, rendering the actual circulation figures meaningless. Even gay men who were still struggling with their own doubts about the liabilities of a gay life, such as Elver Barker, inched their way toward a new perspective in *The Mattachine Review*. Writing as "Carl Harding," he pointed out in "Whom Should We Tell?" (August 1956) that if every gay man simply told one heterosexual he

232 • AN EMERGENT MINORITY

trusted about his sexuality, the perception of several million straight people would be changed. The homosexual as a person actually known to straight people, rather than as a symbol of alienation and furtiveness, would be harder to stigmatize. Bob Bishop in "Discard the Mask" (April 1958) and John LeRoy in "Defeating Fear" (September 1958) proselytized in the same vein.

Some of the books reviewed in the magazine were available through Call's mail-order catalogue, such as André Gide's *Corydon* or Jeanette Foster's important early study of lesbian writers, *Sex Variant Women in Literature*, or came off the presses of Pan-Graphic itself. One of the oddest of Pan-Graphic's own publications was also its first, *Gay Bar* (1957) by Helen Branson, the owner of a Los Angeles bar. Even here, the need for a medical or scientific seal of approval to treat homosexual life as a serious subject was an unchallenged notion. Blanche Baker was called into service for a liberal preface on the "problem" and a few tidbits of bibliographic information, a counterpoint to Ms. Branson's lightweight but more interesting reminiscence of her years as "mother hen" to "the boys" of southern California. Other Pan-Graphic publications in the late 1950s and early 1960s included the first national gay bar directory, transcripts of radio broadcasts discussing homosexuality, and *The Circle of Sex*, a slightly daffy classification of sexual types by Gavin Arthur, the wealthy grandson of President Chester Arthur and an openly gay San Francisco bohemian.

Elsewhere in the country, the sometimes timid, sometimes bold approach of the West Coast organizers replicated itself in a handful of cities. In New York, the Mattachine Society was the offshoot of a discussion group known simply as "The League," which had picked up members from the defunct Veterans Benevolent Association. Under the direction of Sam Morford and Tony Segura, who credited his awakening to reading Cory's *The Homosexual in America* in 1954, New York Mattachine met for the first time in January 1956 with about thirty men in attendance. Little had changed since 1950: "We were quite certain that we'd have trouble if anyone knew what we were meeting in this hotel to talk about," one man recalled, "and it was the same later when we rented a loft." To avoid any taint that might draw the vice squad down upon them, members were repeatedly reminded not to refer to Mattachine as a social club or an activist organization. It was an educational and research endeavor, first and last. But phone numbers were exchanged and friendships started, and many men were struck by what these meetings represented in the larger scheme of things: an implicit attack on the conspiracy of silence *within the group*. Homosexuals were coming together in a nonsexual setting to talk about their lives and the injustices they were forced to deal with every day. This was an unprecedented development for some of them. "When you lived in the world of Oscar Wilde, so to speak," said one highly educated and closeted participant, "it is an experience impossible to describe, coming into a room with fifteen or twenty people who think and feel as you do." The guest lectures by professionals like doctors Albert Ellis or Richard Robertiello, who touted the sickness-and-cure theory, were questionable exercises in rebuilding shattered egos, but the temperament of those who showed up for the New York meetings was no different from that of their San Francisco counterparts. They were not politically radical or willing to risk their careers for an idealistic cause, but neither were they lacking in curiosity about their situation and how others, gay and straight, interpreted it. They did what they felt they could do. Yet better to do nothing at all, was the argument of younger men, who'd be damned if they would ever sit through a talk by one of the enemy and hope for a pat on the head.

But then one never knew when an unexpected show of nerve was going to manifest itself. In Colorado, Barry Sheer, a college student from New York and a member of the newer Denver Mattachine, tried to find more liberal speakers, such as the Colorado judge who made the point at one session that homosexuals did in fact have some legal rights and should make it their business to know what they were. "In fact," Sheer said, "the idea of Mattachine appealed to the rebellious spirit in me. It was not a conservative thing in Denver then to get together in this capacity." Nor was it timorous of Elver Barker, who founded the chapter in 1956, to offer to host the annual Mattachine convention in Denver in 1959. Barker arranged for a member of the Colorado state assembly to speak (who questioned the level of education of the state's vice squads), as well as William Reynard of the state's ACLU board. (Reynard was actually gay himself, but as a lawyer thought it best to work behind the scenes for Mattachine. "I was a fellow traveler" was how he put it in 1996.) The *Denver Post* covered the convention, as Barker hoped it would, providing some of the most serious and extended coverage of the movement from the mainstream press up to that time. How many Denver gay men and lesbians read the three lengthy articles on September 4–6, 1959, and first learned of the homophile movement and its efforts to make their lives something more than a joke and a whisper? Such publicity was not gained without paying a high price. The police later went after Barker and two other Mattachine members, raiding their homes and arresting one of them for possession of nude male photographs. The man spent sixty days in jail and lost his job.

Boston Mattachine had Prescott Townsend, a renegade Brahmin who attended the Society's first meetings at the Parker House in 1957 and wanted to agitate for the repeal of the sodomy laws two years later—an idea whose time had not come, the officers of Mattachine in both New York and San Francisco explained to him. But Townsend, eccentric and self-absorbed, was also an example of one reason why men who might have shown interest in the cause did not. The type of person to question authority and instigate change was the type most middle-class men were afraid to be associated with. Charisma and diplomacy were in short supply in the early days of the gay movement. Quirkiness and irascibility were not.

THE STANDARDS AND hopes of Harry Hay and Chuck Rowland had raised expectations among the charter members of the Mattachine Society, yet there was no question that the fire dimmed after 1953. The people who saw themselves as keeping alive the more aggressive spirit of the founders, offering an alternative vision to the less self-confident style of the new leadership, were the men and women who had started publishing ONE Magazine: The Homosexual Viewpoint in January 1953. "They were always trying to be conciliatory," Dorr Legg said of Hal Call and his followers, "and we said to hell with conciliation."

Taking its title from Carlyle—"A mystic bond of brotherhood makes all men one"—the magazine was never intended to be an arm of Hay's Mattachine, though many of its first editors and writers (Legg, Dale Jennings, Martin Block, Don Slater, Ann Carll Reid, Jim Kepner) were Mattachine members. With the rapid change in the society's makeup only months after ONE's first issue, the editorial board was aware from the start of the need to be as iconoclastic as possible. No talk of "cures" or "passing." They knew they were the experts on their own experience, not the heterosexual doctors and lawyers, Legg maintained. "The whole thing was so contemptible . . . the absurdity, the complete mythology you were reading." By 1955, ONE claimed a circulation of almost two thousand and defined itself as the watchdog of establishment illegality ("Miami Junks the Constitution" was the cover title of the January 1954 issue about mass arrests in Florida) and the occasional critic of what Jim Kepner called the "schizoid" philosophy of Hal Call's Mattachine. Kepner, writing as "Lynn Pedersen" (one of numerous pseudonyms he used to give the illusion of a large staff at the magazine) staked out this territory with "The Importance of Being Different" in the March 1954 issue. The coup of ONE's early years, however, was getting Norman Mailer to contribute to the January 1955 issue. Though he later repudiated "The Homosexual Villain" as a lapse on his part into liberal sentimentality, gay readers were impressed at the time by the novelist's admission of his own homophobia and use of gay men as cardboard bad guys in his fiction, and his remarks about the more humane outlook Donald Webster Cory's book had inspired in him. There were occasional complaints about Kepner's regular "Tangents" column, which solicited clippings from around the country and acted as a kind of news service about police harassment and local anti-gay campaigns (too grim, too unrelenting, some men felt). More realistic readers understood Kepner's patchwork portrait of the times as both valuable and unique. No one else was attempting a similar comprehensive look at the injustices homosexuals were enduring in midcentury America now that the hunt was on.

The hunt inevitably turned against *ONE* itself. The October 1954 issue was selected as the target by the FBI and the postal service, which ignored any number of articles about gay marriage and promiscuity and focused on two innocuous stories as examples of obscene literature suitable for prosecution. The local ACLU board told the lawyer that *ONE*'s editors hired to represent them, "We don't handle things like that." "They were actually offended," attorney Eric Julber recalled, but Julber, who was not gay, took the case on its merits as a clear-cut censorship fight. The federal district court judge in the first trial pronounced the magazine obscene simply because the stories were about homosexuals—"A former USC football player," Julber described him, "not a guy known for great intellectual powers"—but the Ninth Circuit Court of Appeals judges who heard the appeal proved to be no more sophisticated and a good deal more hostile. *ONE*, in their opinion, was "dirty, vulgar, and offensive to the moral senses." Though Legg and Slater, who were now the powers behind the magazine, continued publishing and getting the magazine to its subscribers, it was not until January 1958 that Earl Warren's Supreme Court reversed the lower court rulings without comment. The justices did not want to make a momentous statement on the subject, but the point was clear. Henceforth, gay and lesbian publications were not to be considered obscene per se and had to be delivered by the post office. Don Slater boasted in the next issue, grandiloquently but not unfairly, "*ONE* magazine has changed the future for all U.S. homosexuals."

The name *ONE* quickly took on more than journalistic significance in southern California. As a nonprofit incorporated body, ONE Inc. had a life separate from the magazine, and that life in many ways reflected its principal financial backer. As sure of himself as Harry Hay or Hal Call, and no more diplomatic, Dorr Legg was a man with a scholarly rather than an overtly political mission, and his book collecting became, like Jim Kepner's, the basis for one of the country's major gay libraries. Legg was the son of Progressive-era Ann Arbor parents who raised him in an enlightened manner (it was a "Hawthorne-Emerson experience . . . a plain-living, high-thinking atmosphere," he said), though their liberalism did not extend to accepting their son's black lover. In the late 1940s the two men relocated from Detroit to Los Angeles, where they became involved in an active gay life. Reflecting on Legg's imperious, well-bred style, Harry Hay once quipped, "I could never look at Dorr without thinking of the carved wooden handle of my grandmother's umbrella." Yet for all his Victorian hauteur, Legg had an unambiguously positive attitude about being a homophile (his preferred term), a state of mind he credited to a happy coming out in 1927 on a trip to Florida, where he stumbled upon a delightful community of gay men of varying ages in Tampa. His vision for ONE Inc. was multifaceted and community-oriented.

Harry Hay dropped out of the movement not long after the convention fiasco—though he was to be heard from again, even more inspirationally, in the 1970s—but Chuck Rowland hung on a while longer, and looked to ONE as the indirect means to reinvent his call for a "homosexual culture." For almost a year, he worked at ONE's informal counseling center, where despondent gay men or confused boys just off the bus would stop by the office to talk about the mess of their lives. Rowland "was extremely good at taking kids who were essentially unhireable," Legg said, and training them to get jobs. Having known despair himself and having worked with the American Veterans Committee after his service in World War II, Rowland was a natural counselor.

The idea of a gay organization providing concrete social-services help to gay men was at least as revolutionary and risky a project in the climate of the 1950s as any other homosexual endeavor of the time. More controversial among ONE's inner circle was the short-lived First Church of ONE Brotherhood, which Rowland led for several months in 1956. That gay men were alienated from traditional religious institutions, that they had been scarred by society's insistence that their physical needs were at war with their spiritual needs, that many of them wanted to talk about religion when they came for counseling had been evident for some time. (In 1968, an ordained minister, Troy Perry, acted on the basis of the same realizations to found the first Metropolitan Community Church.) Rowland's makeshift ceremonies, held in his own home, were from the point of view of the skeptics either a poor substitute for the real thing—robes, candles, music, and poetic recitations notwithstanding—or a reinforcement of a crutch gay men were better advised to do without. It was news to most people that Rowland, a 1930s Party member and always an activist at heart, believed in a Supreme Being in the first place. Some ends justify quite a few different means, Rowland observed at a ONE board meeting. A man of heart more than faith, he was interested in "filling existing needs" above all else. He also had an eye on the "freedom of religion" angle, should ONE come under attack for more than its magazine.

Dorr Legg's commitment to education came to the fore when the organization, as ONE Institute, began offering courses, seminars, and lectures. It was these kinds of services for which the Institute was ultimately best known. Serenely indifferent to how many people would attend a talk on "Anthropology Looks at the Homophile" or a nine-week course on the gay novel, he forged ahead, recruiting volunteer teachers and guest lecturers whenever he could over the next few years, and brought out a journal that reprinted some of these lectures. Beginning in 1958, *ONE Institute Quarterly: Homophile Studies* pursued the academic approach to homosexuality with numbing earnestness, but gradually found its way toward articles with wider appeal. "The Moral Climate of Ancient Canaan," a two-part essay by Harry Hay at his most esoteric, was meat and potatoes for Legg, but Jim Kepner's dissection of Albert Ellis, Evelyn Hooker's summary of her research, Henry Gerber's translations of Magnus Hirschfeld, and appreciations of Gertrude Stein and Walt Whitman probably better served the quarterly's readership. In any event, by 1963, ONE Inc. recorded that it had offered 705 classes, lectures, and symposia over the course of its ten-year existence, which had been attended by 6,793 people, with attendance rising by 200 to 300 every year. Legg was notorious for doctoring his figures, but the exact numbers hardly matter. Gay studies was born and the credit goes to Legg, Kepner, and their colleagues. The incongruity of this development—homophile studies and ponderously erudite journals in the midst of the worst crackdown on gay men and lesbians in the country's history—still carries an edge. But if the Mattachine experience and its aftermath had proved nothing else, it showed that those individuals who were considering the ways in which life might be changed for the benefit of gay people were unexpectedly diverse and were not going to agree on many of the big issues.

Hay, Rowland, Legg, Kepner, and their allies had attempted, in one of the least visionary periods of American life, to articulate an idea of gay people as something more than the sum of their sexual appetites. The problem was not only that homosexuals were not ready in any significant number to rally to that banner, but that the idealists were not yet clear or specific enough, even in their own minds, about what they meant. The conceptualizing, no less than the articulation of the concepts, was still in its infancy.

13

HUNTED

You see, I'm always one of three things to most people who know about me: I'm a curiosity—a sort of sideshow—or I'm a joke, or a horror. Often people who don't know I am different will say to me that the whole tribe of us ought to be run in, locked up, or maybe put out of the way altogether. We are the modern witches—that's what we are!

—Mark Thornton in
Blair Niles's *Strange Brother*, 1931

In the spring of 1955, Harris Kimball, a talented twenty-nine-year-old lawyer from the North, had been living in central Florida for three years and practicing law there for a year. For a good-looking, masculine man who liked to golf and swim, opportunities for a vigorous if discreet sex life were abundant (with other gay men or, in rural areas, with good old boys who liked variety), but Orange County was also a region whose intense conservatism—Klan meetings, a White Citizens Council Kimball was advised to join, a judicial system that played by its own rules—was shocking to someone brought up in Oak Park, Illinois. It wasn't long before Kimball ran afoul of the district attorney in Orlando by treating local black men too deferentially on the witness stand and by agreeing to take the case of a young man who had been beaten to the point of disfigurement by an Air Force officer after the two men had sex together. The latter troubling event was exactly the kind of case the district attorney was loath to act on:

justice for a fag attacked following the commission of sodomy, involving two consenting adults or otherwise, was not a big priority in Orange County, and no one in the 1950s wanted to air the issue of deranged closet cases in the military.

Harris Kimball, however, never had the chance to pursue the case. On the night of May 12, 1955, he was having a drink in an area bar when he was abrasively approached by Gerald Sweat, a maintenance worker in the local school system. After much prodding, Kimball reluctantly agreed to give Sweat a ride home; he had seen him in the bar before and had always felt uncomfortable around him. Once in the car, Sweat insisted that the two drive out to nearby Lake Lorna Doone. There, in a secluded area, he undressed and went for a midnight swim and urged Kimball to join him, which he did. At some point, Kimball noticed that Sweat had gone back to shore and disappeared. Suddenly he was back on the dock, telling Kimball he wanted to fuck him then and there. No one was around. They were in the dark. Then he'd be ready to go home. Kimball resisted and, in the hope of bringing to a quick conclusion an episode he hadn't initiated, got down on his knees facing Sweat. At that instant the bright lights of a squad car illuminated a scene of two nude, wet men in a public place, one of them engaging in, or about to engage in, an act of oral sex. Kimball's impression, confirmed by subsequent events, was that Sweat had been in some kind of trouble of his own with the police; the arrest and humiliation of Harris Kimball was Sweat's part of the deal.

His would-be seducer on the dock wasn't arrested, but Kimball was. His boss from the law firm bailed him out in the middle of the night, and a quick, embarrassing negotiation ensued. The district attorney agreed to lower the charge to "indecent exposure" if Kimball would forfeit his bond and quietly leave Orlando, and he did so the next day. He was surprised to discover, though, that his seemingly reasonable adversary had no intention of keeping to the terms of their agreement. Kimball was reported in due course to his new employer in Miami as a homosexual who had been arrested for sodomy. The Florida Bar Association was similarly informed of his misconduct and, after lengthy proceedings in which he attempted to clear his name, Kimball was disbarred early in 1957. Stuart Clapper, the young man brutally beaten by the Air Force officer, told Kimball years later that the district attorney had called on him after his lawyer's arrest to imply that all had worked out for the best and that, if Clapper were sensible, charges could now be dropped against the serviceman and the unsavory matter put behind them. Clapper felt he had no choice.

At about the same time that Harris Kimball was grappling with the intricacies of his disbarment proceedings in Florida, Bob Milne, who had relocated to New York City in 1950 after no end of police harassment in Boston, was facing a different kind of problem with the authorities. Milne had a large collection of photographs of nude men and a friend unwise enough to talk about this cache of "physique" pictures in the bars of Manhattan. The friend, Ray, happened to bring the subject up one night at Mary's on West Eighth Street. His interested listener, a Catholic priest who was a regular at the bar, seemed to have no difficulty reconciling his religious vows with his homosexual social life but evidently drew the line at nude models. He in turn alerted a friend at the police department.

Shortly after, Milne began receiving calls from men who identified themselves as "friends of Ray's" and expressed an eagerness to see his photographs. They never wanted to take no for a final answer. Eventually, two men—one quite young and handsome, the traditional vice squad giveaway—showed up at Milne's apartment on Broadway and Tenth Street and, when they couldn't cajole their reluctant host into showing them what they wanted, savagely knocked him about and ransacked the bedroom. The result: arrest for possession of pornography. Represented by Enid Gerling, a lawyer well versed in the ways of the entrapment game, Milne had to pay $300 to the two detectives to see the charges dropped and a whopping $500 to Ms. Gerling, who was not in the business of keeping gay men at liberty as a charitable enterprise. When the pictures were returned to him, though, Milne noticed that several were missing. Rightly suspecting that he was by no means in the clear, he left New York to stay with a relative in Rhode Island as soon as he could pack his belongings. Milne's roommate in New York confirmed his suspicions the next time they spoke. The two detectives had, in fact, paid another aggressive late-night visit to the apartment within ten days of their first, prepared to "discover" more compromising pictures and earn another payoff.

The troubles Harris Kimball and Bob Milne confronted in the 1950s were hardly unique; similar examples can be cited from around the country. Those were the kinds of risks to be faced by any man who was out or simply known to be gay and sexually active. Kimball and Milne were unusual in one respect, however—they fought back. Kimball refused to reconcile himself to the antihomosexual code of the bar and eventually practiced law again, following an important court decision in the 1970s, and Milne joined the Mattachine Society. In an equally feisty spirit, Frank Kameny, an employee in the Army map service with a doctorate from Harvard, was fired from his job in Arizona in 1957 after refusing to deny his homosexuality in the face of his superior's nebulous allegations and became the first man to contest his dismissal from a government position, an ordeal as costly and almost as prolonged as Kimball's.

The distinctive temperament of these man played a key role in their refusal to burrow back into the closet (all three are self-confident, determined, and untroubled about their sexuality), but it is just as true that an isolated individual, especially when pushed to the point of assuming he has nothing left to lose, is more likely to explore his options and demand his rights than the victim who is part of a larger, more chaotic attack. When the net is cast for a wider haul, someone stands a chance of slipping away to safety if he keeps his mouth shut, and the power of the police never seems more forbidding than when there is a diabolical randomnness to it. The authorities understood this point and, in the most concentrated period of anti-gay persecution during the supposedly idyllic Eisenhower years, made full use of that knowledge. Hence, the vice-squad style of arrests in some bars and bathhouses in the 1950s: "You, you, and you, get lost; you, you, and you, come with us." In a mass action or a true witch-hunt, heroic defiance can quickly begin to look futile, even ridiculous.

What transpired in Boise, Idaho, beginning in the autumn of 1955 was a classic witch-hunt. An entire city was roused to fever pitch when the *Idaho Daily Statesman* warned of a "cancerous growth" taking root in the Gem State, and by the time the nightmare ended, nearly 1,500 men had been questioned about their sexuality. Many were forced to flee the area. Sixteen were ultimately arrested and ten sent to prison, some for having had sex with other consenting adults, not minors. As pieced together in the 1960s in *The Boys of Boise* by John Gerassi, an editor at *Time* and *Newsweek*, a fair amount of the drama and the tragedy was manufactured by a small group of men out to consolidate their power and topple their political opponents.

The hysteria about homosexuality that overtook Boise needs to be understood in both its local and its national contexts. On a national scale, the climate for gay men and lesbians was steadily darkening in 1955. A raid on Baltimore's Pepper Hill Club in October by police eager to stop Washington, D.C., gay men from flocking to their city on weekends led to the arrest of 162 people, an illegal sweep even some Maryland judges took issue with. The murder of three Chicago boys by two men in November kept alive the fear of networks of homosexual sex offenders, while in Sioux City, Iowa, a police roundup of alleged homosexuals followed the unsolved kidnap-murder of a boy there. Several of the men were detained for three-year treatments at a Mount Pleasant sanitorium. On Cape Cod, police promised to "make every effort to drive undesirables out of Provincetown" after raids on Atlantic House resulted in twenty arrests. It was, not surprisingly, so much easier and so much more fun to go after homosexuals than Communists. The field was rife. (A gay man from North Carolina joked that in the men's room of the Proctor Hotel in Greenville, the plainclothes cops always outnumbered the gay men.) At odd moments, the new disgruntled consciousness about the extent of homosexuality in America took on a bizarrely comic quality. When officials announced in December that a bridge under construction in Philadelphia was to be named after Walt Whitman, the Catholic Church and assorted women's groups went into action, attacking the degenerate poet of nearby Camden and calling on the public, schoolchildren especially, to offer more suitable names. Among the popular alternatives were the Ike and Mamie Bridge, the Penjerdel Bridge (as it connected *Pen*nsylvania, New *Jer*sey, and *Dela*ware), and the James Buchanan Bridge—the latter suggestion obviously made by someone not familiar with the rumors about America's bachelor fifteenth president.

Closer to home, a social reality and a political power play were coming together. The social reality was that, indeed, Boise had a homosexual population, of single men who had sex with other men (often in the rest rooms of a few of the grubbier downtown bars) and of married men who paid to fellate teenage boys. A shoe repairman taken into custody on that charge wouldn't ordinarily have occasioned much comment; Ralph Cooper was not represented by counsel at his trial and was sentenced to life imprisonment. But the arrest of a prominent banker, a married man with children, for having sex with the same young man suggested that another scenario was at work, as did the fact that these revelations were credited not to the police, but to a private investigator. Later, the Allied Civic Group, a conservative Mormon organization, paid Howard Dice to continue his work in ferreting out evildoers in Boise, but some people wondered how and why he happened to be on the case. Most later accounts point to his presence as part of a plan by several local businessmen to embarrass the reform-minded administration at City Hall, especially a councilman whose wealthy gay brother was known as "the Queen" and who had appeared untouchable up to that time. An old but serviceable strategy: Bring down all the deviants of Boise and the Queen will have to fall and, with her, her brother and anyone else who poses a threat.

The image fed to the newspapers, and promptly broadcast to an outraged public, was that the investigation, which the police and the district attorney had no choice now but to pursue, had uncovered widespread deviant sexual activity. Hundreds of adolescents had been enticed into illicit relations with adults from all walks of life, and they passed on the names of available boys to other homosexuals. It was a sordid business, every parent's worst fear come true. John Gerassi's conclusions ten years later were slightly different. There were "hundreds" of teenagers in the city involved in homosexual acts, he wrote in *The Boys of Boise*, only if you counted all of the local boys who engaged in mutual masturbation. The number who were orally serviced by adult men for money was probably under fifty, and many of them were members of gangs who were fully aware of what they were doing. Once the story hit the wire service, though, no one was interested in modest estimates or hair-splitting about consenting sixteen-year-olds.

Time fanned the flames with its December 12 issue, reporting (without any fact-checking) on a "widespread homosexual underworld" in Boise that involved some of the city's most respected citizens who had preyed on hundreds of teenage boys over a ten-year period. More arrests followed as nervous gay men were told to come by "to talk" with the special investigator the district attorney had hired and to provide the names of other men in the area they knew to be gay. Those who could afford to leave the state did so as quickly as possible, though some were rounded up in California and brought back anyway. For weeks, the police department was inundated with calls about suspicious men hanging around schoolyards, most of which turned out to be imaginary. "People were hysterical. They were getting frantic," recalled one resident, himself a victim of the investigation who was eventually sentenced to seven years in prison.

The big town meeting held in one of Boise's junior high schools on December 15 did nothing to calm irate parents. The speakers were a warden from the penitentiary, a school counselor, a young lawyer named Frank Church (Idaho's future senator), and a young psychiatrist who quoted Kinsey, disputed any talk of cures, and suggested that the problem with discontented teenagers who hung around men who paid them for sex might rest with the parents themselves and the kind of life they were offering their children. The latter point was not appreciated. In a state with a significant Mormon population, any effort to bring a psychological perspective to bear on the discussion—or any effort to see homosexuality as an illness rather than a moral lapse—was rejected, and the psychiatrists who testified in court on behalf of the gay men had little impact on the proceedings. The ground had been too well prepared, especially in the national tabloids, whose readership was at an all-time high. The supposedly well-bankrolled Mattachine Society had been the subject of a *Confidential* exposé the year before ("America, on Guard! HOMOSEXUALS, INC."), and in November 1955, just as the Boise scandal was breaking, *Coronet* was reminding its readers in "Third Sex—Guilt or Illness?" that sympathy for perverts was usually misplaced. "They" knew what they were doing. "They" wanted our children. Fresh in everyone's minds, also, was a similar scandal in Portland, Oregon, only four years earlier.

The City Council of Boise issued its own statement soon after, promising

to beef up law enforcement, establish juvenile courts, hire someone full-
time to deal with the homosexual menace in town, work for the segregation
of gay men in prisons, and vigilantly watch "all those who live outside the
law." The latter phrase was meant to apply to those deviants who had sex
with minors *and* to those who had sex exclusively with other gay adults. By
the time the last of the cases was tried, tens of thousands of tax dollars and
thousands of hours of state employees' time had been wasted, and hundreds of men's lives had been ruined, by innuendo if not by accusation.
Several of the defendants received five- or seven-year terms, and one man
who had turned state's evidence against his friends was rewarded with a
commutation of his five-year term to a sentence of six months. "The
Queen" was never implicated.

READING ABOUT EVENTS in Boise in 1955, some gay men were astute
enough to know that such craziness was possible at any time in any corner
of America. They could see that gay-baiting had passed all rational bounds.
Yet others looked on the tragedy in Idaho as a distinctly small-town, redneck phenomenon. The insularity of university life, for instance, had convinced more than a few professors—despite the evidence to the contrary
provided by the McCarthy steamroller and the loyalty oath controversy—
that they had less to worry about. In 1958 that complacency was shattered
when the faculty and staff of the University of Florida in Gainesville discovered that they were as vulnerable as anyone.

Two years earlier, the Florida Legislative Investigative Committee had
been formed—otherwise known as the Johns Committee, named after its
reactionary first chairman, state senator and former governor Charley
Johns—to probe illegal and antisocial activities in the state. What that
meant originally to this conservative body was an investigation of the presence in their midst of real or alleged Communists, integrationists, and bootleggers. It soon became apparent to the committee members, however, that
they had another inflammatory topic to deal with in the "sex perverts"
who, they were told by local police chiefs, had been flocking to the
Sunshine State in greater numbers since the war. (After 1961, homosexuality became even more of a focus for Johns and his colleagues as
worry about infiltration by Reds became a less fashionable issue and the
segregationists were forced to conclude that their days were numbered on
the race question.)

The Johns Committee first approached the homosexual problem by
pursuing some rumors about gay and lesbian high school teachers in central Florida and, in 1957, running a check on the employees of the state TB
hospital in Tampa, which was alleged (accurately, as it turned out) to have

a large number of gay men on its payroll. Surveillance of these men was authorized, and several low-level staffers were brought in to name names in private. One doctor in particular aroused the ire of the committee sufficiently to provoke a full-scale investigation. When he took his vacation in the Virgin Islands, the police there were notified that Florida officials would be grateful for information on his activities and associations during his stay. Eastern Airlines agreed to inform the committee about the doctor's flight plans and traveling companions, though a nervous Eastern official begged the committee not to make public the fact that the airline had provided this service as the company was well aware that releasing such information without a subpoena was illegal and unethical. By the time the committee turned its attention to the University of Florida, it already had considerable experience in the area of compiling dossiers about "degenerates," and chief investigator R. J. Strickland had honed his interrogation skills.

Like all state-funded institutions of higher learning, the University of Florida was an easy target in the 1950s. Professors were supposedly "eggheads," Stevenson supporters, individuals of doubtful patriotism who resisted the idea of loyalty oaths and protected Communists and integrationists when they weren't out-and-out radicals themselves. Any excuse to clean house would do. Moreover, some of the sexually active members of the faculty in Gainesville had been none too discreet. One instructor, returning to Florida after an absence of a few years, thought the scene had gotten out of hand. Tearoom activity at the local courthouse and on campus had been abundant right after the war, he said, but in the late 1950s, it was thriving on another, more elaborate scale.

Word got around about the English professor who tutored football players who were in academic trouble in exchange for being allowed to perform oral sex on them. Everyone seemed to know about the men's room in the school's library. In fact, the president of the university was later to admit to committee members that a few years earlier a meeting had been held in his office to discuss just this embarrassing situation, and a student reporter for the *Alligator* had even considered writing an article on the subject of homosexuality on campus. In the course of his research, "Dave" had pretended to be gay and made friends with several gay students (and possibly some teachers) but ultimately decided to abandon the piece for fear of incriminating innocent people. He also decided that the gay men he met tended to stay to themselves and that the whole "recruitment myth" was pretty much just that.

By the summer of 1958, chief investigator Strickland had been charged with the task of giving a full report on the matter, paying special attention to the role of faculty in homosexual activities in the Gainesville area. A judge, returning to the courthouse one August night after dark, came upon two men embracing in the hallway. He wanted something done about it, and that same month a student at the university complained that a professor had invited him to dinner at his home where—though nothing occurred—he was sure "an approach was in the making." The governor agreed that an undercover operation was needed. On August 18, Strickland probably assumed he had his first "break" when the police arrested an alumnus who worked in the university library on charges of solicitation in the courthouse men's room. The young librarian stunned his interviewers by declining their offer to show his goodwill by providing the names of homosexual professors he knew. "Oh, I know a great many and could certainly identify them by name," the man assured Strickland and his assistant, "but I am too much of a man to do that." His wasn't the last example of dignity under pressure over the next few months.

Inevitably, there were those among the many arrested in the stakeout at the courthouse, and later on campus at the library men's room, who were willing to turn others in when taken to the hotel room Strickland had set up as his headquarters. Some of the younger men who identified themselves as trade were eager to help. "Trade" was a creaky notion by this time, but one that Strickland, the police, and the committee evidently wanted to keep alive (as in the idea that some boys were just being boys, what with women so hard to get, and the oral-sex givers were the true queers). A few instructors and professors were sufficiently scared to discuss their colleagues as well. (A Presbyterian minister from McIntosh, Florida, arrested downtown in December, didn't know anyone on campus as he wasn't from the area; all he knew was the reputation of the courthouse lavatory.) The pretense that, if one talked honestly and assisted the investigation, no charges would be filed or jobs jeopardized naturally lulled some men into trusting the seemingly earnest Strickland and his handsome partner, a university policeman who served as the sexual decoy. But a wave of anxiety was felt across the campus in the fall and winter of 1958–1959 as the now not-so-secret list of homosexuals was drawn up.

In time, even the student who had once gone undercover himself for the school paper was brought in. Strickland was sure that this fellow's list was going to be a great help and was taken aback by the fact that he wasn't given so much as one name. Perfectly able to see through the ruse, the student calmly explained that if he identified even one person and turned out to be wrong, he couldn't live with the thought of having libeled someone. Certainly the state senators would understand that. He wasn't quite sure that the homosexuals posed a threat to anybody, anyway. More to the point, he told Strickland, the school paper had decided to drop the article because casting aspersions on men who devoted their lives to educating the students of the University of Florida could be seen as a threat to the faculty as a whole and would pose "too great a danger to academic freedom," an embattled idea as it was.

An even braver interviewee tried in his deposition to discuss the subject with Strickland on a more complex level. You want the names of homosexuals, he said, but just what does that noun mean? "I don't think that necessarily every man who participates in a homosexual act is a homosexual," he offered. There were questions of self-definition and social identity to be considered. When chided because he refused to name names, the man repeated again and again that he wasn't "refusing" to do anything; he "preferred" not to give names and saw no legal necessity that compelled him to do so. When the details of sexual experience were discussed, he was equally unflappable. Before authority figures who seemed titillated or unnerved (not to say, obsessed) with the idea of one man putting another man's penis in his mouth—the defining act of the pervert, apparently—he sat calmly and talked about the pleasures of "sixty-nine," a concept that did damage to the fairy/trade, passive/active distinctions that were being bandied about.

The men whose lives were to be affected by this six-month fishing expedition were a varied group. Some did hang out in the men's rooms in town and on campus, and a few might well have propositioned students. One professor was known to hug the frat boys at parties a little too affectionately. The members of the student body, with the exception of one young man who transferred to Emory because of a teacher's excessive attentions, didn't seem to think all that much about it. The Burger House on the edge of campus was a well-known hangout for gay teachers and students, and people adopted a live-and-let-live approach to those cliques. (There were exceptions: a young man who worked there enjoyed his share of attention as well-serviced trade and then indicated to Strickland that he would be glad to help clean out the trash. In spirit he was a close relative of the Newport operatives of 1919. Other teachers were guilty not as a result of their tearoom proclivities but as a result of their homosexuality per se. Married or single, members of the English, speech, music, education, and science departments, they were as different as any such group would be, ranging in age from their thirties to their late fifties. Several had published significantly in their fields, and almost all were tenured. Two, including an assistant dean, were recent Fulbright scholars and, to judge from the recently opened records in the Florida State Archives, every one of the sixteen who was later fired had been evaluated as a capable, even outstanding teacher.

But it was obvious to everyone involved that the scope of the Johns

Committee's work belied its alleged purpose of dealing with illegal activities on campus and in public facilities in town. Too many questions dealt with a farmhouse thirty miles outside of Gainesville where two gay men were known to live, one a writer affiliated with the university. Strickland wanted to know who went to their parties, what went on at the farmhouse, what other names their guests mentioned. Lists of gay bars from Tampa to Jacksonville were put together after questioning men about their socializing in other parts of the state. What the committee was after was a complete picture of gay life in the region, with documentation about the private lives of as many gay men as they could locate. The professors were merely a satisfying early target. By the time they issued a final report six years later, Florida's legislators were ready to decry the contamination of their state by a growing, increasingly militant group of deviants that they were willing to estimate at over sixty thousand.

Despite Charley Johns's desire to keep the story from the press for fear of losing their "cover," the labors of R. J. Strickland and his assistant were known to everyone on campus when the new semester began in January 1959. One by one various teachers disappeared that winter, having been told to go quickly and quietly, their careers at an end. By the time the *Gainesville Sun* got wind of the purge, an editorial could only lament the fact that the offenders had been let off so easily, without any criminal prosecution. That they had lost their pensions and would never again be able to work as teachers, and that those approaching sixty would have trouble finding any job at all, didn't seem to matter. In the words of one Florida educator who lived near Gainesville at the time (not a teacher at the University of Florida), "It was a black period. If I had ever thought of the academic life as being somehow removed from the rest of society in certain ways, I said to myself then, forget it. There's no haven here anymore. But there wasn't any alternative. There I was in [north Florida] and I had to keep my job, no matter what. So I hunkered down. I had no choices and really, truthfully, not much hope of things getting any better."

IN AN AGE that has witnessed the street demonstrations of ACT-UP and the court battles fought by the Lambda Legal Defense Fund, the imaginative leap to a time, more distant emotionally than chronologically, of "no choices and no hope" can be hard to make. But the lack of gay resistance to the witch-hunts in Boise and Gainesville, or dozens of other cities where less publicized or dramatic purges took place, was based on several compelling realities. First, with few exceptions, gay men and lesbians in the 1950s were restricted by the plausible belief that the opposition was monolithic and well-nigh unbeatable—all of heterosexual society argued the same point, that homosexuality had no legitimate place in the scheme of things and represented a threat to every time-honored value—and few allies were to be found in liberal or radical circles. "The ACLU just plain wasn't interested in us," one Mattachine Society member commented about the issue of gay civil liberties at the time. An Evelyn Hooker or an Eric Julber was a rarity. The voice of Senator Wherry or Edmund Bergler or Charley Johns was the voice of America.

Another significant problem was the dearth of ideas about tactics. Even if a group of homosexuals had wanted to fight back, no one was sure what strategies they might employ to make themselves heard. Mattachine and ONE Inc. did not exist for activist purposes. Simply gathering in private groups to discuss their mental health and political status, or fighting the postal service to see that *ONE* magazine reached its subscribers, was daring enough. The thought of gays picketing, the concept of organizing a boycott to suggest that gays had some economic clout worth attending to, the possibility of a "backstairs" influence at City Hall—all of these alternatives, whose effectiveness was just being tested by the black civil rights movement, seemed far-fetched in the dark days of Boise and the Johns Committee. Struggles for unionization, racial equality, or religious tolerance were predicated on the fact that many people were ready to demonstrate explicitly as laborers, blacks, or Jews. Without significant numbers of men or women willing to identify publicly as gay, protest remained something of a fantasy, vague and pointless.

Beyond anything else, though, lay the more troubling question of worthiness, or pride. The situation was dire in the late 1950s precisely because so much attention had been focused on homosexuality, the vast preponderance of it negative to a degree that necessarily inflicted psychological damage. Much had changed since the heady days of raucous socializing and heartfelt camaraderie during the war. In a draining climate of "terminal self-punishment" (novelist Michael Rumaker's apt phrase in *My First Satyrnalia*), gay men often questioned their right to do battle with their adversaries and implicitly faulted the victim as much as the victimizer. Discreet gay men don't get into trouble, went this line of thought. Those who ran afoul of "Lilly Law" had only themselves to blame; you knew the rules of the game and you took your chances. In any event, making waves only exacerbated an already delicate situation, causing problems for those who had engineered a successful life of "passing" or managed to accommodate themselves to the roles and the costs society demanded of them. "You seem set on stirring up a lot of trouble," a wealthy gentleman who has been paying off his blackmailer tells Dirk Bogarde in the groundbreaking British film *Victim* (1960) when Bogarde's character suggests a united front against the blackmailer. That tradition of hunkering down to avoid a fight was as commonplace in America as in England. "It was never worth it," the lugubrious gay schoolteacher in *Stranger in the Land* decides, "to outrage herd-prejudices and dare the vengeance of mob-morality."

Mattachine members on both coasts knew only too well the result of this pained complacency. They would frequently meet with something worse than apathy or fear—outright derision—in their efforts to engage new members. Even within Mattachine itself, the older members were eager to defend their low-key approach from the combative new influences reappearing on the scene as early as 1958. That year Randy Wicker, a precocious student at Washington and Lee in Virginia, spent his summer vacation in New York City and volunteered his services to the cause. On his own frolicsome initiative, he had signs printed and displayed throughout Greenwich Village to publicize a talk on "The Homosexual and the Law" to be given by lawyer Irwin Strauss—much to the dismay of Strauss, Mattachine president Arthur Maule, and other members who were used to a quiet, word-of-mouth approach to their lectures. ("We didn't know what to make of Randy Wicker," Maule remembered with affection almost forty years later. "He was, let's say, a disturbing acquisition for the movement.") Both impressively energetic and frighteningly vocal, Wicker struck a few members as just what their organization needed, but to most of the others he was a potential troublemaker.

The self-perception that homosexuals really had no business taking a public stand could apply even to situations of imminent physical danger, and the smallest gestures of activism and affirmation could land a young gay man in trouble with his own kind. In the academic year 1957–1958, playwright Doric Wilson was a freshman at the University of Washington in Seattle. He was ill at ease with most of the other gay drama majors at the school, to his mind an insufferably discreet group, but he was aware of the heavy cruising scene at Ravenna Park near the campus—and brassy enough to want to do something about the sniper who had been taking potshots after dark with his BB gun at the men in the ravine below. On the sly, Wilson used the drama department's mimeograph machine to prepare a one-page warning to the unsuspecting night-prowlers, which he handed out at the entrance to the park at sunset. The first person on his way to the cruising area to take the sheet and read it happened to be an instructor in the drama department. A few days later Wilson was called in to the office of his advisor, a man he later learned was also gay, and informed that his standing at the school was in jeopardy. In fact, it would hardly be worth his while to stay, he was told. As an "undesirable type," things could be made awkward for him. Wilson's advisor didn't need to offer a more detailed explanation or recount his conversation with the embarrassed drama instructor: the tacit understanding was that a homosexual student had conducted himself in an outrageous manner in conservative Seattle. Printing and distributing flyers—even in the interests of public safety—that named the unnameable and broadcast the existence of gay cruising spots were the actions of a rabble-rouser. Doric Wilson dropped out before the end of the next semester.

The anti-gay tenor of the late 1950s demonstrated all that was wrong with this way of thinking and gave new life, albeit slowly and in a roundabout manner, to the visionary aspirations first expressed earlier in the decade. An unequivocal rejection of *any* solidarity or activism came at a great cost. Whether or not men and women who loved, and made love to, members of their own sex were comfortable with the idea of identifying with others like them, with finding common ground and uniting in some fashion—whether or not they shared Harry Hay's faith that there was such an entity as a "gay people"—the consequences of the opposite view were everywhere to be seen. In the end, a low profile spared very few people. Western society had aggressively, even monomaniacally, set the terms, and there was no reason to assume that conditions would improve until the people who were the objects of anti-gay prejudice began to ponder more deeply the social and political context of their lives.

IV. CULTURE WAR

14

QUEER IN CAMELOT

If society can be said to be on the defensive, then it must follow that the forces of the homosexual minority are consolidating for the exploration and exploitation of that defense.

—Donald Webster Cory and John LeRoy,
The Homosexual and His Society:
A View from Within, 1963

The brisk air on Inauguration morning, a resplendent First Lady on tour, touch football on the lawn at Hickory Hill, men who wouldn't blink in a crisis, Marilyn Monroe in a tight-fitting dress rasping out a sex-kittenish "Happy Birthday, Mr. President" at Madison Square Garden: the imagery of the post-Eisenhower (and post-Mamie) age, the thousand days of New Frontier vigor and charismatic leadership, is relentlessly sensual. America was ready to pass the torch and those men who were taking their place in the corridors of power were determined to be seen as energetic, self-assured, and dynamically masculine. At the center of this earnest mythology was the president himself, whom chroniclers would wait more than twenty years after his death to describe as the humanly troubled and conflicted man that he was, a politician perhaps no better or worse than his predecessors, a victim of extraordinary physical disability (dependent on novocaine and amphetamines) whose ultimate judgments on Vietnam and many other issues we will never know. What we do know now, however, is that in contrast to the aura of youthful confidence the early 1960s acquired for a time after the fact, the real order of the day concerned just how tough the United States was going to be in the face of myriad threats, how willing to hold the line—in Berlin, in Laos, in Cuba—the nation's untested (and nervous) new leaders would be. The veneer was radically different from the 1950s, but not the substance. Brinkmanship was about balls.

In this climate, homosexuals weren't destined to fare very well, and gay men and lesbians in government service did not find the Kennedy years appreciably better than the heyday of Senators Wherry and McCarthy. The Navy was still discharging more than 1,600 enlisted men and women a year after investigating their sexual orientation, and anyone who worked for a company doing business with the government was subject to the same scrutiny. What *was* different was that homosexuals watched other groups take their place as recognized minorities while the "perverts" of old remained perverts. Civil Service Commissioner John Macy was on record as standing for equal employment opportunities for all government positions and an immediate end to discrimination based on "race, creed, color, sex, and other non-quality measures." But in 1961 Macy declined to meet with a gay delegation to discuss the commission's policy of not hiring or retaining gay employees. Homosexuality was a fair job "quality measure," in the view of Macy and everyone else who had any say in the matter. Dean Rusk, a man not known for his mirthful countenance, could scarcely keep a straight face when announcing to reporters the Mattachine Society's first picketing of the State Department a few years later, and Robert Kennedy made no distinction between J. Edgar Hoover and the First Lady's cousin by marriage, Gore Vidal. When Clyde Tolson was admitted to the hospital for surgery in the early 1960s, the attorney general asked amused aides if Hoover's boyfriend had gone in for a hysterectomy; when Vidal incurred his wrath at a White House party one evening, he was audibly denounced as that "New York fag." The president was more sophisticated than his brother and had no problem inviting Vidal or Truman Capote to the White House, but a New Frontier focus on vigor and stamina precluded any acknowledgment of that tolerance for the window dressing of literary queers.

Across the country, anti-gay ferocity seemed, if anything, stronger than ever. "For the first time in several generations," *ONE Magazine* reported in May 1960, "just about every New York City gay bar has been shut down." Even Mary's on Eighth Street, in business for fifteen years and the "symbol of gay life" in Greenwich Village, lost its liquor license. In San Francisco, a 1961 raid on the Tay-Bush Inn, the largest raid in the city's history, saw eighty-one men and fourteen women taken to jail. (A number of the better-dressed white customers were allowed to leave the bar, while the black, working-class, and more obviously gay patrons were detained.) On a wild summer night in 1960, the family estate of Jack Adair in Radnor, an exclusive suburb of Philadelphia, was raided and eighty-four people were arrested when they gathered to screen one of Kenneth Anger's underground films and to discuss reopening a Mattachine chapter. At the start of the decade, administrators at the University of Michigan in Ann Arbor were having a difficult time keeping the city's undercover police off the campus, and arrests of professors, students, and locals continued apace, as they had since the early 1950s. In Florida, the tone was especially nasty. Crowing over the 150 arrests his men had made in ninety days, the police chief of Tampa, Neil Brown, vowed in 1961 to "run every homosexual out of the city," at the same time that the Johns Committee was denouncing the state's public school system as "a veritable refuge for practicing homosexuals." As Leslie Fiedler had observed several years earlier, with the acceptability of racism and anti-Semitism on the decline, homosexuality stood to become the perfect scapegoat for all of society's ills and the last allowable prejudice.

Fiedler was on the mark. Strom Thurmond knew that his antagonism toward black Americans was a thorny issue and had to be couched in more diplomatic language than he had used in Dixiecrat days, but without a second thought he could attack Bayard Rustin, a key figure in the civil rights movement, on the floor of the Senate in 1963 for his deviant sexuality. (Rustin, one of the organizers of the March on Washington, was also criticized by Adam Clayton Powell, Jr., and Roy Wilkins, who didn't want a left-wing homosexual representing their cause. James Baldwin, to his surprise, found himself in an identical position. He expected that as the country's most famous black writer and a capable orator he would be one of the many speakers at the historic event. Attend as a celebrity guest, certainly, King and his advisors agreed, but stand at the podium?—out of the question.) "Science," as much as religion and law, still backed the old prejudices.

Throughout the early 1960s, Irving Bieber, now the undisputed authority on homosexuality, chided colleagues who wasted precious time helping their patients adjust to their sexuality when they might be helping them alter it, a task at which Dr. Charles Socarides claimed a 50 percent success rate. In 1963, the lordly Karl Menninger wrote the introduction to the American edition of the Wolfenden Report, the British government's study of homosexuality, and praised its call for decriminalization while reminding his readers that "legal" and "healthy" were not synonymous terms. "Whatever it be called by the public," he wrote on behalf of his profession, "there is no question in the minds of psychiatrists regarding the abnormality of such behavior." On the contrary, there was some question in elite intellectual circles. A few psychiatrists, most notably Judd Marmor, worried in print about the skewed patient samples the studies relied on, and a handful of brilliant sociologists—Erving Goffman in *Stigma* (1963), Howard Becker in *Outsiders* (1963), Edwin Schur in *Crimes Without Victims* (1965)—wrote about nonconformity, deviant populations, and society's power structures in the earlier, critical spirit of Mead and Benedict. But it would be some years before the impact of their thinking would be widely felt and disseminated in a conformity-minded culture.

Of more immediate relevance, pointing to larger impending changes, was an indisputable fact: America was becoming a country at ease with open expressions and discussions of sexuality. Americans readily accepted the hormonal struggles of teenagers and the reality of discontent in the bedroom, and viewed sex with less shame and, as a product-selling commercial tool, with more avaricious delight than previous generations. A trend whose origins could be traced back to World War II, or even to the 1920s, was accelerating at a brisk clip. Its momentum, dramatically chronicled by Gay Talese in *Thy Neighbor's Wife*, had been advanced for a willing public in the 1950s by men and women of diverse styles and motivations—assorted crass studio heads and brave publishers, Marilyn Monroe and Jane Russell, Elvis Presley and Marlon Brando, Hugh Hefner, Allen Ginsberg, Justices Douglas and Brennan—and brought forth results few liberals or intellectuals (except gay men such as the author of *Howl*) would have imagined. Heterosexuals were not the only ones to profit by the more eroticized tone of American life on the eve of the counterculture explosion.

A self-conscious, self-congratulatory sexual identity defines itself by comparison with, or in reaction to, other modes of sexual expression. Once upon a time, for straight men, that point of contrast was female sexuality (or alleged asexuality), submissiveness, or innocence. No one with any experience of real women in high school, college, or adult life—no one who went to the movies, glanced at popular magazines, or spent an afternoon at the beach—was ready to defend that canard any longer. On the other hand, celibacy for the single, or unglamorous monogamy for the married, was even less usable as an opposing mode for the millions of Americans who were stirred by Jack's virility and Jackie's mystique, the exploits of James Bond and Pussy Galore, the bed-hopping of John Updike's suburbanites, tabloid reports on starlets' busts, or the credo of *Playboy*. The true field for comparison—allowing for both titillation and a comfortable validation of the dominant sexuality, the "right" way to be—was the no-longer-so-twilight world of the limp-wristers, the boys who were a little light in the loafers. Confirmation that homosexuals were sadly not like normal people, nature's blessed, could be satisfied now only by an extraordinary amount of attention to the subject in mainstream venues.

Norman Mailer was the most honest writer in this area. A man's defeat of his homosexual potential, in Mailer's novels, is a stage on the road to manhood and therefore a highly personal, life-or-death matter. It is a means of measuring and evaluating one's maleness. Many other writers opted for a more disinterested guise. R. E. L. Masters's *The Homosexual Revolution* (1963) was a model of condescending liberalism full of preconceptions and misplaced goodwill. Distressed by the lack of basic civil rights accorded to homosexuals, Masters found it absurd that gay men should ever expect to be admitted to the armed forces or allowed to marry another man. (He did get one thing right: however much people said they disapproved of gay promiscuity, he noted, society would rather gay men were completely debauched than lawfully wed to one another.) Jess Stearn, a freelance journalist, enjoyed three months on the bestseller lists with *The Sixth Man* (1961), his breezy, scornful account of "the enigma of the rising homosexuality in our midst." *Newsweek,* like other magazines and dozens of daily papers around the country, matter-of-factly gave space to juicy stories it would have ignored in the past. In the fall of 1960, the magazines reported on two small scandals that made related points about the pathetic nature of homosexual lives. ("Under the willows of Frame Park" in Waukesha, Wisconsin, ten men were arrested for a nocturnal frolic, including a dean at Carroll College, a Catholic priest, a businessman, and a dentist; at Smith College in Massachusetts, the eminent literary scholar and Melville biographer Newton Arvin was arrested along with seven others for possession of gay pornography.) Abe Rosenthal of the *New York Times* was startled to discover that many gay men hung out on the street in the East Fifties in Manhattan. The article he assigned to Robert Doty, "Growth of Overt Homosexuality Provokes Wide Concern," was a milestone for the paper of record in 1963, as well as a classically smug bit of reporting about gays' "colonizing" certain neighborhoods and their inability to resist a pickup.

That sort of attention was a trial for gay men on the surface, but also a roundabout means to a larger end. The mid-1950s and the mid-1960s form two sides of a great divide in this regard; within the space of a decade, access to information about gay life was transformed, and young gay men were being told more about homosexuality than they knew to ask. The jackpot was a *Life* magazine article of June 26, 1964. The fourteen-page spread with fourteen photographs announced the official arrival of deviance on the American scene. It was a "sad and often sordid world," this "gay world," the article opined, as it proceeded to make the psychiatrists seem as smug as they could be and the police as devious as they were (the latter by way of a transcript of a potential entrapment setup that provided abundant clues about how to talk to a "trick" who might actually be a vice cop). The coverage reflected the bias of the day in that no one would guess there were also black and Hispanic homosexuals in the world, but in other respects, it was remarkably thorough. Timid gay men read about homosexuals "discarding their furtive ways," about a secret world growing "opener and bolder." Lonely gay men read that, rejected by the straight world, "homosexuals build a society of their own" that includes bars for every taste and personality, organizations that worked to end discrimination, and magazines with gay stories and articles. "The first time I ever heard of *ONE* or Mattachine was in *Life*," a Texas man in his forties at the time commented. "It never would have dawned on me that anything like that was out there." For hundreds of thousands of gay men, Henry Luce was generously, if unintentionally, instructive: yes, such things were out there; yes, such things were possible in America in the 1960s.

Perhaps the *Life* photographs did as much, or more, than the words to circumscribe gay despair: dark and uncheery as they aimed to be at first glance, the pictures implicitly validated what existed, celebrated all who had survived the nationwide "purge of the perverts," and demolished the Wing Biddlebaum scenario. There were so many homosexuals, so many habitats and styles. The men in leather standing before Chuck Arnett's mural at the Tool Box in San Francisco are an odd but sexy bunch—no one turns away from the camera—while the Monday night crowd at the Jumpin' Frog is obviously having an unkinky time of it at the bar's screening of *Some Like It Hot*. Alexander the Great, Leonardo da Vinci, and Michelangelo make a noble if dainty appearance. Hal Call, who helped with the arrangements for taking pictures in the two bars, stands at his printing press in his shirt and tie like any struggling small-circulation publisher. Don Slater of *ONE* could be an editor, a lawyer, or a banker. The one person who is photographed to look as if he needs serious professional help is Barney Anthony, homophobic proprietor of a Los Angeles bar long known for its sign FAGOTS—STAY OUT, a decrepit Archie Bunker type whose problems go beyond illiteracy. A better foil couldn't have been found to make a point about the heart of the opposition. For "Dan," in high school in 1964 in a tiny Roanoke Valley town in Virginia, as for thousands of others of his generation, coming upon the *Life* story was a seminal event: "I read it when nobody was around. It helped that my mother was the postmistress, so I got to look at all the magazines before they went out. I hung on every word of it. I thought, *I* want to go to a big city. *I* want to find out what this is all about."

Other changes followed in rapid succession in the four-year period that saw the miniskirt reinvent fashion, the crew-cut give way to Beatles bangs, and a proliferation of skin magazines in the wake of the Supreme Court's 1962 *Manual Enterprises* v. *Day* decision. (Monthly sales of physique magazines at Manual Enterprises, Herman Womack's company, jumped from 40,000 to 750,000 between 1960 and 1965.) Varieties of passion—black-white, male-male, female-female—became less alien when a major novelist pushed at old boundaries, as James Baldwin did in his best-selling *Another Country* (1962), though it took further judicial rulings for the last restraints to give way. These cases, too, established a linkage between the new heterosexual and homosexual privilege. The case that allowed adults to buy Henry Miller's *Tropic of Cancer* meant that other adults could buy John Rechy's *City of Night*, Jean Genet's *Our Lady of the Flowers*, William Burroughs's *Naked Lunch*, and Hubert Selby's *Last Exit to Brooklyn*. By the time Richard Amory published *The Song of the Loon* in 1966, a mass-market novel that was probably the most popular gay book of the decade, he had no reason to fear the censors with his descriptions of homosexual Indians and fuck buddies in the wild. The prose managed to be both dull and penis-obsessed ("Singing Heron gazed casually at Ephraim's cock, thick and muscular like an oak tree"), but High Art wasn't the point.

The relaxation of the Hollywood Code in the early 1960s mirrored the times just as vigorously, both in openness and in nervous limitations. The best film of the day, Basil Dearden's story of a blackmailed British lawyer, superbly acted by Dirk Bogarde, was released in the United States in 1961, but without Code approval; *The Victim* was too honest and too explicit. Hollywood preferred that the cause of all the hand-wringing in the plot be suggested or ill-defined to the point of obscurity, the slant that best fit the new guideline of allowing depictions of homosexuality "provided the references are treated with care, discretion, and restraint." And so it was in the 1962 films *The Children's Hour*, *Lawrence of Arabia*, and *Advise and Consent*. In *Advise and Consent*, based on Allen Drury's novel about circles of power in the nation's capital, Otto Preminger gave audiences their first glimpse of the interior of a gay bar since *Call Me Savage* thirty years earlier, though, since the all-male bar is not spoken of as gay and the reason for Don Murray's suicide is not spelled out, many gay teenagers had their first lesson in "reading between the lines." In Greenwich Village, the Off-Off-Broadway movement provided a forum for much more blatantly gay material. The Caffe Cino, a free-floating collective of gay writers and actors who found a home in Joe Cino's ramshackle Cornelia Street bar, was followed by the Judson Poets Theatre, La Mama, and the Playhouse of the Ridiculous. It was from this sexy, anarchic, creative milieu that young playwrights like Doric Wilson, Robert Patrick, Tom Eyen, and Robert Heide took their sustenance, or that a character like the aging queen of Lanford Wilson's *The Madness of Lady Bright* was born. "The old fey mare ain't what she used to," Leslie Bright announces in her demented quasi-monologue, which is no public relations one-act for the movement, but at least she spoke in her own voice, or the voice she chose.

THE DAYS OF silence and unending victimization were numbered, and the impending change had to do with more than heterosexual curiosity about, and willingness to publicize, a deviant group or with the beginnings of a gay cultural renaissance. Younger gay men and lesbians who had been born during the war and who had no experience of the polite or frightened reserve of the 1930s and 1940s were simply less patient than their elders. Spontaneous and aggressive, informed and passive, or political and highly organized, various modes of resistance to anti-gay bigotry were on the rise.

The little moments can be as telling, as resonant, as the larger examples. Gay residents of southern Florida recall an episode at Dania Beach in 1962 that dramatized two contradictory impulses: the extent of the loathing young straight men felt they could openly display toward homosexuals, and the realization on the part of some young gay men that it was up to them to do something about it. A problem that summer was that the stretch of beach where gay sunbathers congregated was under attack from a gang of redneck kids in their dune buggies who thought it was hilarious to drive at top speed across the sand, screaming at the queers, and veering as close to the men on their towels as they could without actually running them over. Not an unheard-of pastime, nor one in which the Florida police would have been especially interested. The influx of gay men to Dania Beach and nearby Fort Lauderdale was more bothersome to the authorities, who had in recent years taken to bringing television camaramen with them on bar raids to further humiliate the arrested patrons. One weekend, a few gay men, most around twenty years old, decided to fight back by burying pieces of wood with protruding nails in the sand to disable the vehicles. To their surprise, they weren't alone on the beach early the next morning. As many as a dozen gay men turned out to help, several with baseball bats. When the riders came by later in the day, their tires got punctured and the occupants jumped out ready for a brawl. When the baseball bats came out from under the beach blankets, the local toughs beat a hasty retreat on foot, and four dune buggies were left in the sand. They were retrieved by their owners during the night—every light, windshield, and hood smashed—and so ended the troubles on the beach. "They didn't call the police," Jerry Mitchell of Fort Lauderdale observed, "either because they didn't want to say a bunch of faggots had sent them running, or they didn't want to deal with us anymore and they knew we'd use the bats. But it had the same result. There's always a limit to how much you're going to take."

In a different context, the power of a quiet refusal to be unnerved by threats or accusations had an effect. The U.S. Postal Service wasn't moving into the modern age at breakneck speed, and many of its employees still acted as if Eisenhower's fulminating Postmaster General Arthur Summerfield—the "scourge of pornographers"—were still in charge and the important legal cases about mailing rights were still unheard. In his first year of law school at the University of Pittsburgh in 1963, Michael Lavery returned from his constitutional law class to discover "two men in brown shoes," as he put it, sitting in his dorm room. They wanted to chat about certain publications he had been receiving through his post office box, namely *ONE Magazine: The Homosexual Viewpoint*. Lavery's response was a simple comment to the effect that he believed a Supreme Court decision had been handed down on that subject, and on that very periodical, five years earlier. The postal inspectors mused that the dean of the law school might find his tastes in reading matter interesting. "Do whatever you have to do," Lavery answered, and nothing more came of the incident. But before they left, "the brown shoes" tried a more solicitous approach, suggesting that it was for the young man's own good that they had stopped by. Lavery shrugged. They didn't want to bother him, they said, but they did want a list of names of other gay men in the area, and no one would be the wiser if he provided it. Lavery showed them out.

Admittedly, the display of nerve by Mitchell and his cohorts on Dania Beach and Lavery in his Pittsburgh dorm room were atypical. Most gay men in 1962 or 1963 would have decamped to another sunning spot or told the postal inspectors what they wanted to know for fear of seeing a promising career lost before it began. (It is not a surprise that Lavery used his legal skills as a member of the Gay Activist Alliance in New York City several years later.) But neither are these moments as isolated as they might at first seem: anger, as in the case of the dune buggy smashers, or knowledge of the law, as in the case of Lavery and *ONE*, were informing the reactions of more gay men and lesbians to their oppression than ever before. Like everyone else, they read about the Freedom Riders testing segregation laws in southern bus facilities in 1961, they watched James Meredith demand entry into the University of Mississippi in 1962, they read about Selma and Birmingham, and they watched on television—and some participated in—the March on Washington in 1963. From the Lincoln Memorial, they heard Martin Luther King, Jr.'s call for a new America, and they listened to A. Philip Randolph characterize those who deplored militance and exalted patience as nothing more than apologists for the old order, voices of "social peace at the expense of social and racial justice." The example of black America was changing all of America.

As subsequent history was to show, a little reckless energy and indifference to authority were just what was needed; those were the qualities America in the 1960s would most admire. Certainly the value of the safe, middle-of-the-road approach was looking more doubtful by the minute. At the start of the decade, the homophile movement was in trouble. Membership had not grown at a meaningful rate—a survey suggested that only 2 percent of homosexuals even knew that any gay political groups existed in the early 1960s—and the combined national circulation of the three gay magazines (*ONE*, *The Mattachine Review*, and *The Ladder*, put out by the Daughters of Bilitis) had yet to exceed eight thousand. Internal strife was taking its toll, as lesbians such as Del Martin accused the men of relegating their sisters in struggle to peripheral roles in their writings, debates, and conferences, while some of the men lashed back by branding the Daughters of Bilitis a timid, obstructionist bunch. Dorr Legg was particularly volatile, charging that the women who questioned the stridency of ONE Institute's 1961 midwinter theme, "A Homosexual Bill of Rights," had been "brainwashed" by straight society. When the Mattachine Society in New York questioned the central office's handling of its dues, Hal Call dissolved Mattachine as a national body, letting each chapter fend for itself. By the end of 1961, the Detroit, Denver, and Boston groups had disbanded.

Many gay men had never put their hopes in the parliamentarians, in any case. The first overtly political statement of "gay pride," in fact, had its roots in the bar culture, not the lecture hall, the committee room, or Dorr Legg's library. By 1961, Jose Sarria had been entertaining the patrons of the Black Cat for more than a decade. More important, he had been watching its intrepid owner, at great expense, continue to fight off the police who wanted to close the cafe, despite multiple court rulings in California that gay bars were not in and of themselves illegal establishments, and he had been joyously hectoring and rousing his friends and admirers on the subject of their second-class citizenship. As George Mendenhall told his interviewers in the 1978 documentary *Word Is Out*, Sarria's camp operas and "God Save Us Nelly Queens" approach to gay life was, for many who heard it, the first glimmering of a new consciousness about their sexuality. It was not enough for Sarria, though, and in 1961—fifteen years before Harvey Milk—San Francisco's most popular chanteuse decided to take his message into an even more public arena than Sol Stoumen's Montgomery Street bar.

Sarria's run for the Board of Supervisors, the governing council of the city, was something new in American politics. Common wisdom said that whispers about a candidate's sexual orientation were a guarantee of defeat, as was any hint that the candidate was soft on the pervert issue. Sarria took a different approach, neither discussing nor denying his sexuality and not actually campaigning at all. His hope was that the gay vote itself would be sufficiently large and united to do the job, and he used the grapevine of the bar circuit as his most effective tool. The time seemed ripe: in 1959, mayoral candidate Russ Worden had tried to unseat incumbent George Christopher by charging that Christopher had allowed the city to become "the national headquarters of organized homosexuals," a tactic that backfired and ensured the mayor's reelection, and in 1961 the "gayola" scandal, in which local police and state Alcoholic Beverage Commission officials were tried and acquitted for extorting money from bar owners, infuriated the gay community. But, in the end, there was no "bloc" of gay voters, or no bloc that wanted homosexuals to be represented by the nightingale of Black Cat fame. Sarria polled 5,613 votes, coming in twenty-ninth out of a field of thirty-three candidates.

However discouraged Sarria was by his loss at the polls, the ripple effect of his audacity was undeniable. Gay men who had no intention of voting for a drag entertainer for city supervisor pondered this break with tradition. Younger gay men were thrilled by Sarria's outlook. "People in those days didn't believe [gays] had rights," Sarria noted, and if nothing else, his candidacy was an assertion of democracy's most fundamental right. In October 1961, Guy Strait, running his own "League for Civil Education" as an alternative to Mattachine, began distributing the *LCE News* in the bars, a free paper that publicized police abuse and called on gay men and lesbians to register to vote. William Plath and several bar owners and bartenders organized the Tavern Guild the next year to further some of the same goals. "The police did these little dirty things . . . nasty stuff," Plath recalled. "They'd park a paddy wagon outside your door on Friday evening about ten o'clock and then they'd go down to the corner for a cup of coffee. Well, you can imagine what [a paddy wagon sitting there] would do to your business." Hiring a lawyer and a bail bondsman to assist patrons who had been arrested or meeting with the police as a group did not turn things around overnight, but, in its rudimentary stages, the concept of a united front took root.

In the East, the value of anger, of bottomless indignation, was nowhere so apparent as in the towering figure of Frank Kameny. Kameny's dismissal from his job as a government astronomer in the purge of the late 1950s reduced him to poverty and made it impossible for him to find work, even with a Harvard Ph.D. and teaching experience at George Washington University. The government had created a monster of tenacity in Kameny.

Unlike most other men and women in his position, he did not go quietly. For four years, he followed the appeals process through every level of the bureaucracy and the courts, eventually petitioning the Supreme Court to hear his case, a plea denied in 1961. In Jack Nichols, a twenty-three-year-old native of Washington, D.C., Kameny found a sympathetic ear, and that summer the two men contacted Curtis Dewees of New York Mattachine for help and set about organizing a gay group in the nation's capital. "I realized," Kameny said, "that my faith in the system had been misplaced. No one was playing fair. No one was going to come to the rescue. If we were on our own, so be it."

The makeup of the Mattachine Society in Washington was as varied as it was elsewhere, but it ultimately benefited from more youthful, questioning, and risk-taking adherents. Kameny and Nichols were able to attract a core membership that saw nothing to be gained from existing in the shadow of New York Mattachine or from devoting too much time to lectures or research. (The total membership never exceeded one hundred, with only fifteen to twenty of that number doing the real work.) Lilli Vincenz, a Columbia University graduate recently discharged as a lesbian from the military; Bruce Scott, fired from the Department of Labor after seventeen years' service for loitering in Lafayette Park; Otto Ulrich, a brilliant linguist at the Library of Congress; Perrin Shaffer, a computer expert known for his financial generosity to Mattachine and his sexual humor ("A second Mae West," a friend remarked of Shaffer); Lige Clarke, a Kentucky-born Army officer in his early twenties with a Pentagon top security clearance who became Nichols's lover came forward—the kind of people who had already paid the price of intolerance or were ready to do so and, despite their professional positions, were of a decidedly unstodgy, devil-may-care temperament.

Nichols was wondrously quirky. An ardent student of Baha'i and all things Persian in his teens, he had come out to his family at an early age and, in 1952, found an unusual source of support in his junior high school principal. (Getting on in years, Miss Bertie Backus lived with another woman and introduced her eager student to Walt Whitman's poetry. From there, Nichols found his way to Edward Carpenter and Tom Paine.) Nichols's father was an FBI agent who worried in the early 1960s that his son's openness would get him into trouble with his boss, but the still-common practice of using pseudonyms in Mattachine took care of that. For all intents and purposes, Nichols was "Warren Adkins." Kameny and Nichols made a strange team, embodying the best of the next phase of the gay movement precisely because of their complementary styles; they suggested that there was room for both relentless, take-charge fervor and the quieter passion that came from a love of literature and an easygoing, confident sexuality.

From its inception, Washington Mattachine took an activist stance. It was an organization determined to be noticed, to have an ongoing public life. It was high time, Kameny urged, to drop the facade of the debate club and the think tank and get involved in "the rough and tumble." Letters were sent to members of Congress, the Cabinet, the Selective Service, the Pentagon, the president, and heads of departments known to have gone after their gay employees. The local branch of the ACLU was lobbied for its help (Kameny's style was "pure bulldog," one lawyer commented), press releases were dispatched, and complaints about police brutality were lodged with city officials until a response was given. Four hundred copies of an informative newsletter, *The Homosexual Citizen* edited by Lilli Vincenz, were sold or given away around town every month in 1966 and 1967. A topic that was especially high on Kameny's agenda, not surprisingly considering his own plight and the city he lived in, was the Civil Service Commission's anti-gay policy, and so he saw to it that Mattachine did all it could to advance any legal challenges that arose. The 1965 U.S. Court of Appeals decision in *Scott* v. *Macy*, overturning Bruce Scott's dismissal from the Labor Department on the grounds that the Civil Service Commission was too broad and too vague in its charges, was a proud moment—a slap at Commissioner John Macy, who continued to insist that homosexuals had no place in government, and a harbinger of other, deeper changes. "Don't talk about homosexuality, and everything stays the way it is," Jack Nichols summarized the Washington Mattachine philosophy. "Bring it out into the open and people begin to think, to move beyond their prejudices."

The most enduring accomplishment of Washington Mattachine, though, was in another area entirely. Kameny and Nichols were both of the opinion that the psychiatric model of homosexuality as an illness to be understood, modified, or cured (a view the press was popularizing more diligently each year) was their main obstacle. In October 1963, Nichols urged the Mattachine executive board to take a stand on the subject, and toward that end he prepared a cogent position paper that reviewed the medical literature on both sides. Not everyone thought Nichols's idea a wise one; more than a year elapsed before a consensus was reached. It seemed a too radical, even presumptuous gesture. That homosexuals debated the health of their own sexual urges as recently as the 1960s is often commented on today with incredulity—as if those benighted souls scarcely fit with the conception of the modern world, as if thousands of gay men and lesbians don't act out their self-hate in frightening ways even in the 1990s, as if society's messages about central and marginal experience aren't always powerful and insidious. But the notable fact isn't that many homosexuals felt that they were not as stable as heterosexuals, but that a few perceptive people understood that self-knowledge and self-acceptance were even more important, and ultimately more politically charged, than a simple appeal for one's rights. In an impassioned speech before the New York Mattachine Society in 1964, Kameny went so far as to maintain that the entire gay struggle in America would stand or fall on this one question. To ask for tolerance for a life defined by a handicap, to imply that homosexuals lived with a condition over which they had no control, was not the basis for a dynamic political movement, Kameny asserted. Jews and blacks saw no need to inquire into the origin of their Jewishness or their blackness, let alone to apologize for it. That was the path, the spirit, gay men and lesbians needed to adopt. As the country mourned the death of John Kennedy, adjusted to the new style of Lyndon Johnson (even more masculinity-obsessed than his predecessor), and watched with some perplexity the beginnings of the military buildup to "make a stand" in Vietnam, these were revolutionary sentiments. Most heterosexuals would have found them laughable or appalling. The stridency with which Kameny expressed them drove some veterans, including Donald Webster Cory, from the movement and invigorated others.

Kameny's aggressiveness, unfailingly useful at the podium, was not to everyone's liking, especially when it was turned on friends and allies. "Frank was not democratically inclined, to put it mildly," one Mattachine member observed. He was voted out as Mattachine president within two years of founding the group, but continued throughout the 1960s to be its most vocal board member and most visible spokesman. (Seen in one light, this is hardly a fact to be marveled at. A strong ego is a prerequisite for frontline participation in any dangerous cause. Yet the Kameny persona registered a deeper problem, too: the gay movement was—and still is—bedeviled by a lack of leaders who inspire trust and affection in the manner of Martin Luther King, Jr., or Cesar Chavez. From Harry Hay, Dorr Legg, and Hal Call to Frank Kameny and Larry Kramer, the roster of difficult personalities grows.) *The Homosexual Citizen* came to a needless end as a result of just such temper and inflexibility. For the June 1967 issue, Lilli Vincenz commissioned an entertainment piece on astrology. Kameny, as an astronomer, would have none of it and, despite Vincenz's agreement with the writer to print his work, demanded that the article be dropped. Backed into a corner, Vincenz quit. She was the one who saw to it that the newsletter came out each month, so her resignation terminated a worthy project.

Abrasive and dictatorial as Kameny could be, the real problem seems to have been that he was far ahead of many in the homophile movement and of American homosexuals in general in the years 1960 to 1965. Having nothing left to lose, which was not the case for most gay people, he was as intolerant of timidity as he was of challenges to his authority. But no one else would have taken on Representative John Dowdy of Texas in 1963, when Congress considered a bill to revoke the Mattachine Society's permit to fund-raise as a nonprofit body. Dowdy—later jailed on bribery charges—railed on about unnatural lifestyles and the decline of American values. Unflappable, in his element, Kameny defended his group to the congressional committee, saw his clarity favorably contrasted to Dowdy's bombast in the *Washington Post*, and was ultimately vindicated when the bill failed in the Senate. And there was no one else who would have continued so splendidly to tweak J. Edgar Hoover by keeping him on the Mattachine mailing list even after FBI agents insisted that this insult to the director must stop. Release your files on Mattachine and put an end to the surveillance, Kameny told them, and I will be happy to oblige. The agents gave up.

Such confidence and gusto should, it would seem, have attracted a bigger following, but it did not work out that way. Washington's large black gay community kept its distance—holding on to high-paying government jobs was not a pertinent issue for them—while the Georgetown set found the closet a comfortable space, and the bar crowd saw the Mattachine Society as too dour and political. New York activists were having the same problems in the early and mid-1960s. Though a new brand of leadership emerged when Craig Rodwell, Dick Leitsch, and Julian Hodges (a relative of Luther Hodges, JFK's Secretary of Commerce) became involved in New York Mattachine, others had long since given up hope; the indifference of gay men who "passed" (or thought they did) and the fear of rocking the boat that preoccupied old-time Mattachine members were too much for someone like Randy Wicker.

More than anyone else interested in rights for homosexuals, Wicker intuited that the new decade called for a new outlook. Not only did the militancy of the black civil rights movement offer encouragement, and not only were the early discussions about abortion-law reform and the legalization of marijuana of relevance, but the growth of the media as well was pointing to a different America in the making, one in which the only true failure was a lack of attention in the press and on radio and television. Notoriety conferred its own power and opened doors that prim respectability couldn't budge. After transferring from the staid Washington and Lee to the University of Texas in the late 1950s, Wicker became a campus radical whose taste for the limelight was not easily satisfied. Moving to

New York City in 1961 at the age of twenty-three, he was viewed by conservative gay men in New York as something of a crackpot with an ungovernable need to talk to reporters. His one concession to the older generation was in changing his name (he had been born Charles Hayden) to allay his father's anxieties about his son's pursuits.

Wicker's public relations whirlwind began in the summer of 1962 after he founded the "paper organization" known as the Homosexual League of New York, a move designed to give Wicker room to act more publicly than was possible under the auspices of Mattachine. When the radio station WBAI aired a psychiatrists' panel about homosexuality, which said all the usual things, Wicker convinced the station manager to schedule a program in which he and other gay men would "rap" for ninety minutes about gay life and present their own side of the story. After being rejected by every homosexual he knew who was over thirty, Wicker found several younger friends willing to participate, including an interracial couple, and the tape was broadcast in July. Jack O'Brian, a *New York Journal-American* commentator, used his column the next day to attack the pollution of the airwaves by a "card-carrying swish" like Wicker, a diatribe that gave the program far more attention than it would otherwise have received. (Wicker made sure that copies of the column reached every editor in the city.) RADIO: TABOO IS BROKEN, the *Times* reported a few days later, " 'Live and Let Live' on WBAI Presents Homosexuals Discussing Problems." *Variety* and *Newsweek* ran columns as well, and overnight Randy Wicker found himself in exactly the position he wanted, spokesman for the cause. Some of his views, especially his tendency to blame women for stifling men who then preferred to be homosexual, grated on other gay men ("I'm an emotional misogynist and an intellectual feminist," Wicker admits), as did his willingness to discuss what he saw as the drawbacks of gay life; for instance, the frequency of one-night stands. The Mattachine policy had been to avoid airing dirty laundry in public; the Wicker policy was bluntness in everything at all times.

Throughout the rest of 1962 and into 1963 and 1964, Wicker made himself the most accessible homosexual in New York. He arranged speaking engagements at area churches and colleges. He saw to it that a transcript of the WBAI tape appeared in print (in *The Realist* in August and September 1962) and lobbied the *Village Voice* to begin coverage of the gay rights movement and gay life in Greenwich Village. He worked with *Harper's* as it prepared its groundbreaking article, "New York's Middle-Class Homosexuals," for the March 1963 issue and escorted Dan Wakefield on a tour of gay hangouts for a highly sympathetic article in *Nugget* in June 1963 ("A knight of Manhattan proudly unfurls the wholesome new homosexual banner" ran the subtitle). Robert Doty requested his help in researching his 1963 *Times* article, but ignored most of the pro-gay literature Wicker provided him. On January 31, 1964, an East Coast "first" occurred when Wicker took part in a television panel discussion on homosexuality on the Les Crane show, an appearance that even his detractors agreed was helpful and impressive. (Two local television programs in the 1950s, one in Los Angeles and one in New York, presented gay men speaking on their own behalf, though their faces were not visible, and in 1961 Hal Call and two other men appeared in a San Francisco television documentary.) Supportive or questioning letters from gay men in out-of-the-way places around the country confirmed Wicker in his belief that visibility was all-important. In the spirit of the times, the cause had to be made to seem youth-oriented, brash, and sexy.

Gay activism took a different turn in the autumn of 1964 when Wicker suggested to Craig Rodwell, the youngest member of New York Mattachine, and Jefferson Fuck Poland of the League for Sexual Freedom, that the time might be right to try a picket line. The idea found few takers. (Poland's group, of which Wicker was a member, was not a gay organization, but advocated freedom and privacy in all areas of sexual life. Poland maintained that his name, expletive included, predated his cause.) On the weekend of September 19, 1964, Wicker, Rodwell, Poland, another man, three women, and one baby in a stroller paraded in front of the Whitehall Induction Center in lower Manhattan with signs that protested the military's policy of excluding homosexuals and, more important, of discharging them in a manner injurious to their future well-being. Remembering this mini-demonstration thirty years later, Renee Cafiero noted with amusement: "We had no spectators, actually. There was nobody there! It was a Saturday! This was before people put in all those weird hours working on a weekend." Yet even without an audience or press coverage other than in the homophile newsletters, to Cafiero (a lesbian member of Mattachine), the whole event had the satisfying feel of "testing the waters" before embarking on the real thing in 1965. Three months later, Wicker and three others caused a ruckus at the Cooper Union lecture hall at a psychoanalyst's talk, demanding—and receiving—a ten-minute opportunity for rebuttal. Between his first venture in September and his second in December, Wicker suggested a picketing of the FBI Building in Washington in response to the arrest of LBJ's aide Walter Jenkins in a local men's room. (Frank Kameny vetoed the idea, though Wicker jokingly badgered Kameny, who was not amused, that the least they could do was to put up a plaque in Jenkins's honor in a stall at the YMCA.) "With each advance," Wicker noted, "the next step was easier."

The news the following spring that Castro's government in Cuba had begun rounding up homosexuals and placing them in detention camps led the way to the biggest "next step." There was no Cuban embassy in Washington at which to stage a protest, but Jack Nichols targeted the White House as a plausible site—"Who knew they wouldn't start doing the same thing here?" Wicker maintained—while Wicker and Rodwell distributed leaflets throughout Manhattan to advertise a New York demonstration outside the United Nations. The Washington action, with ten participants (seven gay men, two lesbians, and a straight woman friend of Nichols), took place on Saturday, April 17, 1965; its New York counterpart, with twenty-odd participants (including Allen Ginsberg, Peter Orlovsky, and Prescott Townsend from Boston), on Sunday, April 18.

The issue of a gay picket line outside the White House and the UN, like the subsequent decision to stage yearly pickets on the Fourth of July at Independence Hall in Philadelphia, was the most contentious yet raised in the gay political circles. One older member of Mattachine thought the whole enterprise "unforgivable," declaring that it was going to set the movement back irreparably. Dick Leitsch, a participant, argued that a small group of demonstrators looked "kind of silly." At a time when tens of thousands of blacks were taking to the streets in a real show of muscle, the fact that only ten or twenty homosexuals could be counted on for a public protest made the cause look even more marginal than people assumed it was. But, as Leitsch freely admitted, his roots in the South were a factor here; in Louisville, the down-home social and the heatedly political overlapped ("That's the way I grew up, that's my understanding of politics—you know people and they take care of things, you don't parade around . . . I believe in backroom politics"). "My response in 1965, when I heard about it from a friend in Philadelphia," a gay man in the Midwest stated, "was that this was the last thing in the world we needed. It was the height of craziness. Now they'll really go after us."

A widespread reaction against uppity homosexuals was not the problem, though. The New York march had taken place on Easter Sunday and Wicker later bemoaned his choice of UN Plaza, which was deserted ("If only we had set up at Forty-second Street and Fifth Avenue! An Easter parade!"), while in the capital the *Washington Afro-American* was the sole paper to cover the picket. A second White House protest in May did much better, leading to wire service reports with A.P. and U.P.I. and a short article in the *New York Times*. Pickets at the State Department, the Pentagon, and the Civil Service Commission followed. "The numbers didn't matter to me," Lilli Vincenz commented. "To get a thousand people marching, we'd have to have waited another ten years. What mattered was that the word got out that some of us were ready to demand our rights." But as journalist Edward Alwood observed in *Straight News: Gays, Lesbians, and the News Media* (1996), getting the word out wasn't easy. The lack of extensive mainstream attention to homophile activities had to do with more than the small number of people willing to carry placards. Even when the count was much higher in the 1970s, newspapers continued to give heterosexual readers and advertisers what they wanted and expected—features about sickness and lifestyle, not a serious look at a burgeoning gay political consciousness. It served society's purposes in the 1960s to do its best to keep homosexuality out of the realm of the political and firmly in place as a psychological and moral dilemma. The five-part series in the *Washington Post* (January 31–February 4, 1965), the seven-part series in the *Atlanta Constitution* (January 3–8, 1966), and the six-part series in the *Denver Post* (February 13–18, 1965) all stressed the loneliness and alienation of gay life, making the by now threadbare pun on the word *gay*, even when the reporter's intentions were to avoid heartless stereotypes. A much quoted *Time* essay in 1966, on the other hand, made no effort to avoid stereotypes, bewailing the "homosexual mafia" in the arts (the famed "homintern") and the gay man's need to degrade everything that "normal men take seriously." The new hedonism toward all sex had "converted" many who would have wisely repressed their homosexuality in another age, *Time*'s editors believed, and readers were urged not to glamorize what was in fact "a pathetic little second-rate substitute for reality, a pitiable flight from life . . . a pernicious sickness."

The drive to fight both the liberal's cloying sympathy for the homosexual lot in life and the hard-core opposition was best displayed when the picketers gathered in Philadelphia every July Fourth from 1965 through 1969. The "Annual Reminder" (a reminder that all Americans did not enjoy equality before the law) brought together a slightly larger group from several cities and guaranteed a modest—and usually polite, if amazed—audience of tourists in town to see the Liberty Bell. It also brought together for one afternoon elements of the movement usually at odds with one another: those who wanted to fight their way back into a system made more humane by their teaching (such as Frank Kameny, who mandated a dress code—ties and jackets for men, skirts for women—for all protestors so that they would look presentable and "employable") and those who abhorred the establishment, exemplified by the fiery Clark Polak of Philadelphia, who in 1965 had just started publishing *Drum* to tout the joys of nudity and gay sex side by side with gay politics. Lesbian activists such as Barbara Gittings, Kay Tobin, Shirley Willer, and Ernestine Eckstein came without the backing of the Daughters of Bilitis, which disapproved of

public protest, and offered some faint hope that male and female cooperation hadn't entirely died out.

It is true that the picketing of the White House and Independence Hall
went largely unnoticed at the time, and so it could be argued that its significance is nil. This was not the birth of SDS or the first stirrings of Black
Panther rage. Yet its impact was felt in two ways. Many of the participants
were thrilled and emboldened by what they had done, dress code or not,
and went on to work for the gay movement in more radical capacities later
in the decade. More important, and somewhat ironically, meaning accrues
to the small demonstrations today with a kind of retrospective power: the
photographs of these men and women speak to millions of gay and lesbian
Americans who were raised to assume that they had no definable history
before the 1970s, that all pre-Stonewall lives were characterized by shame
and forebearance, and that the upheavals of the 1960s applied to everyone
but them. The pictures, appearing more frequently now in books, magazine
articles, and television documentaries, reach across the decades. They point
to what has been omitted from the history texts in both high schools and
colleges and in the lopsided chronicles of America still touted by both
political parties. Belatedly, they situate gay life as part of the story of the
1960s.

15

THE FRIENDS OF EMMA JONES

I'm sort of political, but not really political, if you know what I mean.

—J.D., southern drag queen

Resistance comes in many forms. In the autumn of 1965, several gay men in Pensacola gathered at the turn-of-the-century manor two of them had recently bought to hatch a plan to acquire the books, magazines, and movies they wanted but were reluctant to order on their own through the mail. Area postal authorities had a habit of opening the plain brown wrappers of deliveries for single men and, between the intelligence officers at the nearby military base and the local police, the existence of a list of the names and addresses of gay men in Pensacola was an open secret.

What these friends were seeking to buy ran the gamut from John Rechy's *City of Night* and assorted physique magazines to the grainy stag films (mostly straight) that were being produced in larger numbers each year in the mid-1960s. The idea they came up with was to have a woman they knew open a post office box under a phony name, pool their money for their purchases, and meet once a month in their hosts' ample living room to screen the films and circulate the reading matter. A closed circle; a safe enterprise. And so "Emma Jones" was born, with an elementary last name, a first name everyone found suitably unattractive, and a willing and eager female to collect the the goods on a regular basis—a woman of robust urges who also wanted to be on hand for the screenings, gay or straight, with the boys. The scheme worked flawlessly. Not an eyebrow was raised at the post office as the packages poured in over the next few years.

But the collective Emma Jones was a restless spirit. By 1966 the four men at the center of social life in conservative Pensacola were looking for a way to widen their circle of acquaintances and stimulate more socializing. ("In those days," one of Emma's founders recently remarked, "it was an area of *extreme* closet cases, young men living with their families, nervous, secretive men—a place of *no* outward freedom at all.") They decided that Emma would host a beach party on the weekend of the Fourth of July and sent out twenty-five invitations in her name. Fifty people showed up. The next summer two hundred men and a fair number of women came to roast hot dogs, stuff themselves with shrimp and potato salad, and frolic on a section of the famous Gulf Coast beach of snow-white sand and pure blue water, far from the family section and the gaze of the police. By 1968, with gay men from Mobile, Birmingham, and Tallahassee indicating that they were planning to join in the fun, Emma was pleased to think that a need for community was being met far beyond her original impulse and, at her own expense, saw to it that the supplies were ready and the event properly coordinated. More than four hundred people were on hand for the third celebration.

The Pensacola police had taken notice by this point, naturally, and accepted the group's assurances that they would keep to themselves, out of sight, and clean up when the party was over. But the containment of an event that was rapidly acquiring a life of its own in the South, discussed months in advance by men in New Orleans, Atlanta, and Tampa, was not a casual affair. Eventually its organizers took the next step and approached the management of the local hotel where many of the visitors had been spending freely, and arranged to use its facilities for a new aspect of the weekend's entertainment. With word out that the ever-inventive Emma was hosting a drag revue as part of the festivities, attendance skyrocketed the next summer. Queens descended en masse from every part of the country, and local merchants and restaurateurs, not to mention the hotel staff, saw a dramatic increase in their holiday earnings. The family crowd tended to drink less, eat less, tip less, and carry away fewer expensive souvenir purchases than the gay crowd.

An extensive mailing list had been compiled by this time and printed invitations announced each year's theme for the shows. "Duck Lake," a spoof of *Swan Lake* with hunters in search of their quarry *en pointe*, or a red-white-and-blue parody of the Broadway musical *1776* gave the drag queens and the costume and set designers in the group ample room to camp and create. Bikini-clad studs competed in a Mr. Gay U.S.A. contest. There was even a schedule by this point: "We were on the beach from four till seven, a mass of gay humanity," one man recalled. "Then from seven to nine, you and your boyfriend went back to your room, or you and your boyfriend and whoever went back to your room, and you did whatever, and you were ready at nine." From nine until the early hours of the morning, the Fiesta Room of the old San Carlos Hotel was the site of a kind of pageantry that Pensacola had never witnessed. An equally noteworthy feature of the weekend, given that white gay men have rarely been any more sensitive to race than their heterosexual counterparts, was its interracial quality (though this has generally been true of most drag circles since early in the century). "But in the South twenty-five years ago, it did mean something," an African-American friend of Emma's noted. "Black, white, Hispanic, we were there—in drag or not, whatever your preference—having a great time."

With over two thousand men descending on Pensacola every Fourth of July weekend in the early 1970s, Emma was in effect sponsoring the largest gay gathering held in the South to date, and—with the exception of the few cities that were holding gay pride marches by that point—the largest gay gatherings in America since the days of the great drag balls. By the time the event radically changed course in 1974, when the Mafia wanted a piece of the action and local politicians stepped in, innumerable friendships had been made, an example of gay economic clout had been established, and an exuberant gay presence had asserted itself on the Florida Panhandle that, whatever the setbacks ahead, would never disappear entirely.

The "gaying" of Mardi Gras is another example of the same phenomenon, though it cannot be called an interracial one. The theatricality of the experience—its history of extravagant costume displays, the theme parties and parades, the artifice and the masks—had always had a special meaning for gay southerners, but before the late 1950s any specifically gay dimension to it was obscured and seldom discussed. The first gay carnival clubs, or krewes, were the Krewe of Yuga and the Krewe of Petronius, founded in 1958 and 1960, respectively. Petronius fared better than Yuga and lived on to become one of the seven gay krewes still holding formal balls or pre-Lenten galas of some sort into the early 1990s. The pioneering Yuga met with an abrupt demise when its organizers took their drag balls out of one member's house in New Orleans where they had previously gathered and rented a space in neighboring Jefferson Parish.

The tale of the raided Yuga ball of 1962 is almost folkloric in older Louisiana gay circles. Evidently the police had been tipped off that a queer group from the Big Easy was gathering within their jurisdiction, and they showed up early, without sirens, while the first guests in costume—many in drag—were arriving and the band was setting up. Some members and guests had time to drive off at breakneck speed as soon as they pulled into the parking lot and saw the men in uniform and the dogs. "They knew it wasn't the caterers," one participant commented. Dozens of their friends, however, were caught in the building, running in high heels down side streets, seeking refuge in the Dumpster behind Schwegmann's. Locals credit Tommy Hopkins and Miss Dixie and Miss Irma, the famed Fasnacht sisters, with securing the release of the arrested men. Hopkins was the owner of Cafe Lafitte's in Exile, the closest thing to an openly gay bar in the city at the time; the Fasnachts had opened Dixie's Bar of Music, a legendary Bourbon Street nightspot with a varied clientele (favored drink: the soixante-neuf), in 1939. They emptied their cash registers and sent an emissary to Jefferson Parish. What he encountered, Karl Ezkovich reported, was "sickening." The police had called their wives and girlfriends to come down "to see the fruits" and bring their cameras. A laughing crowd circled around the unloading paddy wagons and filled the courtyard of the jail where the Yuga men were assembled in various states of ostentatious dress and undress. 96 ARE BOOKED IN JEFF RAID, the *Times-Picayune* headline read the next day. Some of the men lost their jobs. Others were disowned by mortified families.

The lesson of the Yuga raid was not that gay men were better off trying to blend in with their straight neighbors—though the still extant Steamboat Club, founded in 1958, is about as discreet as a gay men's social group could be—but that they had to regulate their public profile "outside the family" (and stay out of redneck Jefferson Parish), and that is just what the gay men of the area learned to do. Journalist and local historian Roberts Batson wrote that the end of Yuga actually marked "the beginning of gay carnival organizations in New Orleans ... a second, and parallel, progress" toward gay liberation. The Krewe of Petronius hosted its first balls in the early 1960s, with Amon Ra following in 1966, Ganymede in 1967, and Armeinius in 1969. There was an element of parody in these events as the revelers made fun of the seriousness of Mardi Gras dress-up by straight citizens, who otherwise scorn gay fantasy dress-up and enact laws about cross-dressing to keep homosexuals in line, along with an equal measure of campy delight and exclusivity, which is still the case. Membership in the krewes is limited, tickets to the balls are hard to come by, and no one pretends that gay Mardi Gras reaches out across social, economic, or racial barriers.

A more universal concern throughout the 1960s was finding a safe haven for dancing. A place to have a drink, have sex, make friends, or find a mate wasn't impossible to locate or to create. What was more difficult was the establishment of a setting in which another level of intimacy, of assertiveness and physical expression, could be achieved—a level more threatening to the established gender order in that it wasn't part of the known territory for homosexuals, the brutely sexual or the quietly domestic. Pickups and so-called spouses; most people knew about that. Dates and boyfriends were another matter, another form of attack on the restrictive stigma and the labels. In the 1930s, the obstacle for homosexuals had been in carving out any gay space in an increasingly hostile public sphere. In the 1940s and 1950s, the battle concerned keeping the police out of gay bars. By the 1960s, gay men and lesbians were chafing at the strict rules enforced within the bar (even when the police weren't around) by owners nervous about their licenses. *If* a woman was on the floor to make it seem as if the men nearby were dancing with her; *if* the men were in a line and never facing one another; *if* the monitor on the ladder with the flashlight was satisfied that no one was too close; *if* the red light behind the bar wasn't flashing to indicate the sudden approach of the police—then what ensued might be called "dancing together." But many gay men and lesbians were fed up with the narrow terms of their interaction in what they had come to feel should be their own space. Not that outright partner-to-partner dancing wasn't taking place in some cities, usually smaller ones with less well-staffed or less intrusive police departments. Countless bars had small back rooms for that purpose. Rolland's Tavern, the first gay-owned gay bar in Maine, opened in 1967 and Portland residents recall dancing there without much trouble. Yet Rolland's made use of the flashing red light, suggesting that a police visit was a possibility, and to be on the safe side a short ride across the state line to New Hampshire was advisable. At the gay bar in Portsmouth, men always seemed to be dancing together without fuss. In cities like New York, San Francisco, and Los Angeles, that freedom was harder to come by.

If bars were only intermittently secure sites for dancing, as their existence was usually known to the police, a better alternative was a clandestine, moveable setting. One group known to have done this with effectiveness on a large scale, at least as early as the mid-1960s, was the Corduroy Club in New York. Renting an entire floor of a building in the Garment District for a Friday or a Saturday night and relying on the grapevine to get the word out, club members were successful in bringing together men and women who wanted to dance in a gay-defined, gay-controlled atmosphere. A jukebox carted in for the occasion provided the music and a soda bar was available with a B.Y.O.B. liquor policy. The other notable feature of the club's dances was that blacks and whites danced together. In the bars, that was a much less common occurrence. By the late 1960s, the Corduroy Club was sponsoring day cruises on the Hudson River and twenty years later was still the largest gay organization in New York City.

The nature and the evolution of the Corduroy Club raises other issues beyond the generalized urge to form social ties. In *Heartlands: A Gay Man's Odyssey Across America* (1992), Darryl Yates Rist reported on one member's understanding of the group's origins as a white club that admitted black men, but eventually became "too black" for almost all the whites, who then dropped out. As an all-black organization, it became increasingly (and understandably) suspicious of any white participation, which explains the fact that by the 1980s the existence of a 2,000-member gay social club based in Harlem was unknown to most white gay men in New York City. (Northern white condescension to southern racists in the 1960s—as if northerners were without prejudice themselves—was never any less incongruous among homosexuals than among heterosexuals: the distance is slight between the all-white krewes of New Orleans and the "white flight" from the Corduroy Club, if that account of its development is true.)

The Corduroy Club's longevity also attests to the skill with which it catered to its members' needs and desire for discretion and its leaders' ability to work together and to ensure continuity with the next generation. In that sense, once the white membership dwindled, the club became part of a dynamic tradition in the black gay world. After World War II, many such clubs—with regular picnics or annual banquets or balls—were started in cities in every part of the country, almost all of them unnoticed by white homosexuals, by the police who always paid less attention to what was happening in black neighborhoods, and by most heterosexuals in the black communities as well. For some members, these clubs were their primary means of affirming their bonds with other gay people. Gay politics, the province of white homosexuals, was not yet a realistic or even an interesting option. For black Americans, changing the laws about homosexuality and developing a more tolerant climate were desirable but necessarily less crucial goals. Segregation and racial discrimination were more pressing concerns, and if any joining-the-ranks was to be done, the black civil rights movement would have been the natural cause.

THE LINK BETWEEN the social and the political is never a tight one for any group of people. Partying does not always lead to thoughts about fellowship or an impulse to make a better world; it sometimes just leads to more partying. Yet many gay men in the mid- and late 1960s were reevaluating the strategy of the homophile movement in the light of its unwillingness to establish at least some connection between the pleasures of homosexual life and the need for action. They saw the limitation of Mattachine as, in part, a failure to accept that gay men and lesbians, in terms of pickets and conferences, were no more political than anyone else. A small following in the 1950s and early 1960s could fairly have been credited to a bold idea ahead of its time. A small following in the late 1960s meant that the movement had failed to ignite.

Good work was still being done, and when members of Philadelphia's Janus Society held a sit-in in 1965 at a local restaurant to protest the owner's refusal to serve obviously gay patrons (the protestors were hauled off to jail for their troubles), they were acting in the useful context of modern civil disobedience. When Dick Leitsch, Craig Rodwell, and John Timmons staged their "sip-in" at a Manhattan bar in 1966 to initiate a legal challenge to New York State's law against serving "known homosexuals" in a bar, they were addressing an important issue. Leitsch's fury at the way Suffolk County police would sweep down on Fire Island for mass arrests of Cherry Grove vacationers led to energetic, and ultimately successful, efforts by Mattachine to call a halt to the raids. Colleges and television talk shows were beginning to ask for lecturers or spokespersons, which movement sources could provide. Jack Nichols, for instance, did his best on Mike Wallace's 1967 documentary *The Homosexuals* to counteract the effect of other guests speaking from the shadows and from behind potted palms. (Nichols was fired from his job as a hotel sales manager the next day. Not for nothing did the CBS producers offer face-obscuring palms.) In Chicago, Bob Basker, William B. Kelley, and the others who got Mattachine Midwest off the ground in 1965 were surprised by the range of people who turned out for their first meeting—"a hundred or so people from different backgrounds, in all kinds of jobs," Kelley remembered—and the enthusiasm they showed. The Dorian Society of Seattle, the Promethean Society of Houston, and the Phoenix Society of Kansas City all helped victims of harassment and discrimination in their region, either by means of personal contacts with politicians or through the ACLU, which was finally awakening to its responsibilities in this area. But too much of the movement was bogged down by displays of both ego and timidity, procedural fights of no consequence to anyone but the combatants, and futile efforts to form a national coalition.

A devastating example of this failure was the appearance of homophile activist Richard Inman on Florida television in 1966. Inman, a voice in the wilderness in Miami (where he ran an essentially one-man Mattachine), was the lone spokesman for gays in a WTJV documentary intended to warn Floridians about the dangers of perversion in this time of moral laxity. His was a performance that suggested gay men and lesbians would be better served by silence. Uncomfortable on camera and looking as if he had suddenly realized that acknowledging his sexuality was tantamount to admitting a crime for which he might be arrested, Inman squirmed before his interviewer's questions, ending with the claim that he had given up homosexuality four years earlier—"It's not my cup of tea"—though he believed that homosexuals deserved fair treatment. He giggled at the suggestion of gay marriage or gay adoption. "You weren't exactly inspired to run out and join his organization," a Fort Lauderdale gay man, then in his twenties, noted. "Actually, he scared me more than the cop they had telling the eighth-graders that any one of them could become a deviant if they weren't careful."

In presenting a more confident image and in seeking to merge sociability and advocacy, California was far in the lead of the East Coast by 1966. The great value of the Society for Individual Rights, an offshoot of the Tavern Guild known by its acronym SIR, was in its services to people who would never have joined a march but wanted to connect with other gay men in nonsexual ways. The premise of SIR was that a solid community had to take shape first; only then could a movement evolve that would advance the rights of that community. Or, in a less tidy, sequential manner, community-building couldn't be ignored while the political strategizing was under way. The group's constitution, drawn up in bar owner William Plath's San Francisco living room in the summer of 1964, stressed a mission that was as all-inclusive as possible. Bringing about "changes in unjust laws concerning private relationships among consenting adults" was an important endeavor, but so was "the giving of real and substantial aid to members in difficulties; the promoting of better physical, mental, and emotional health; the creating of a sense of community; and the establishment of an attractive social atmosphere and constructive outlets for members and friends."

Plath, Bill Beardemphl, Marc Forrester, Bob Ross, Dorr Jones, Bill and Nancy May (Bill was gay, but his wife was not), and the several other charter members wanted a more democratic, membership-driven body than Mattachine had been. Instead of limiting themselves to lectures and symposia, they brought people together in a variety of less overtly educational settings—for picnics, bridge parties, art and tennis lessons, classes in meditation, hikes in the countryside, ballet and theater outings, bus trips, and, most popular of all, a bowling league, which eventually took over the better part of one bowling alley and, like SIR's fund-raising thrift shop, long outlasted SIR itself. *Vector,* the organization's newsletter-turned-magazine, available on San Francisco's newsstands, included social as well as political news. *The Mattachine Review* had all but pretended that gay bars and drag clubs didn't exist; *Vector* took their ads, reviewed them, and celebrated the culture that had produced Jose Sarria and "God Save Us Nelly Queens." By 1967, editor Bill May wrote a regular bar guide under the nom de plume Tequila Mockingbird, Bill Beardemphl offered cooking tips in his "March of Thyme," and "Madame Soto-Voce" was dispensing wisdom in her offbeat advice column. At its peak, SIR numbered almost one thousand members.

SIR's more earnest activities took into account the darker side of gay life in San Francisco—the rise in sexually transmitted diseases, the lack of gay political clout, and everyone's vulnerability before a Gestapo-like police force. (It wasn't unknown for men leaving the bowling alley to be picked up by the police, taken to the station house, beaten senseless, and thrown out into the street without any mention of charges against them.) Working with the city's health department, SIR launched a VD awareness and testing campaign that said, in effect, "We are capable of looking out for our own." Candidates Night, at which office-seekers were asked to present themselves to SIR's membership much as they would to any other ethnic or neighborhood club, was similarly adventurous. At first, responses were few and far between—political aspirants in 1964 did not look on the homosexual vote as worth courting—but by 1966 candidates began to show up for the question-and-answer sessions. Within another year, some were advertising in *Vector.* Admittedly, the receptive parties were the underdogs and the unknowns, never the incumbents, but the groundwork for a heterosexual view of homosexuals—and a homosexual view of homosexuals—as a discrete, informed component of the urban scene was being established, and that was exactly the intention of SIR's leadership. The opening of the nation's first gay community center in April 1966, on one floor of an old union building on Sixth Street between Mission and Market, advanced that goal even more emphatically. In a day and age when "gay space" meant a bar or a bathhouse, a center that could accommodate up to five hundred people for meetings and social functions, counseling and referral programs, art exhibitions and weekend brunches, was something new and, to some older gay men, unnerving.

The thrust in San Francisco was against the root problems still disabling gay men: estrangement from the wider social bonds they wanted and self-laceration. It was the right time to be attacking them head-on. The view of male homosexuality as a sort of ersatz womanhood was on the wane, as was the notion of trade as the best—most masculine and satisfying—sex partner. Those were "auntie" ideas, and the much-touted generation gap was beginning to manifest itself in homosexual circles, too. The change could be detected even in some of the pulps written that year. In *Born to Be Gay,* an especially lurid example of the genre, the high school–age queer is forcibly taken out to the woods by some eighteen-year-old thugs who can't find an available girl. An ancient formula, a quick reader arousal. But the reader isn't the only one shamefacedly turned on. The gay character has to deal with the stimulation he feels as he is being brutalized—the inevitable connection of hot sex and degradation, a psychological pattern familiar to many gay men trained to equate eros and power. Yet the story has a twist it wouldn't have had in a pulp of the 1950s or in a novel like *Stranger in the Land* in the 1940s. Terry Cabot actually wants a *gay* boyfriend, not a trade stud in denim. He wants to find what the world, and the trashy paperbacks, tell him can't be had: gay love, gay friendship, affectionate sex, a view of himself as whole and worthy.

Lofty goals—and skeptics wondered what any of this had to do with a building in the Tenderloin in San Francisco. But the hope of the men and women who founded SIR and its community center was that they were going to offer new avenues by which gay people might meet and a new context for evaluating what it meant to say that one was gay. Their dances were by far the best proof that they were on the right path. They were "tremendously successful" affairs, Nancy May recalled. Lines formed early and guests stayed late. The dances were popular for a good reason; an openly gay, publicly held dance was a new entity in 1966. By the end of the decade, SIR's leadership was disappointed that more gay men and lesbians hadn't become involved in its political actions. As soon as the gay bars were able to allow dancing, the crowds went there and forgot about SIR and its underlying purpose. But that self-evaluation is too harsh. The task of enabling gay men and lesbians to feel more at ease with themselves— ultimately, a political objective—was set in motion by the dances and other activities sponsored by the community center. The concrete benefits of that change were not immediately apparent, but they were nonetheless real.

As others saw it, social networks and male conviviality, dances and picnics, weren't the only things that had been lost sight of, or perceived as dangerous territory in homophile circles and gay periodicals. Clark Polak, founder of the Janus Society in Philadelphia, was adamant that sex itself had been avoided for far too long by those who wanted to "raise consciousness," and that reticence had created another large gap between audience and activist. In 1964, he began publishing a low-budget periodical to make some money and to rectify that omission. Polak called his monthly magazine *Drum*, alluding to the famous Thoreau line about marching to the beat of a different drummer, and within a few issues was interspersing its news reports with articles like "The Beginner's Guide to Cruising" and photos of young men in tight bathing suits and, a few months later, young men without their tight bathing suits. *Drum*'s philosophy was plain enough: it was time to raise a little hell. Polak went after a younger, more hip crowd and scorned the "Aunt Marys who have exchanged whatever vigorous defense of homosexual rights there may be for a hyper-conformist-we-must-impress-the-straights-that-we-are-as-butch-as-they-are stance." (Not surprisingly, Polak was one of the loudest critics of the dress code enforced by the protestors at the Annual Reminder, though he never missed a picket.) His readers were amused by the first gay comic strip (*Harry Chess: The Man from A.U.N.T.I.E.*), his scathing editorial tone, and the pages of trivia quizzes ("Q: What TV actor can be counted on to strip to the waist every week? A: Robert Conrad in *The Wild Wild West*.").

In arguing that the struggle for gay rights and the development of gay solidarity must come out of an affirmation of the reasons men wanted to be gay in the first place—that they loved the male body, that they wanted to have *fun* with other guys—Polak touched a nerve. The national circulation of *Drum* reached ten thousand by 1966, quickly surpassing the total of all other homosexual publications combined. Those ten thousand copies were passed from friend to friend in a way that *Mattachine Review* or *ONE* were not. Like Hugh Hefner's monthly bible for straight swingers, *Drum* championed the joys of ogling firm young flesh, scoring in a bar, "doing it" till you dropped, and (in later issues) relishing a marijuana high or the more ecstatic experiences offered by stronger hallucinogens. Judicial rulings, employment discrimination, Richard Burton and Rex Harrison flitting about in *Staircase*, Francis Bacon's paintings, and getting crabs were all relevant topics. In 1965 Polak founded the Trojan Book Service, a mail-order house for the sale of erotic photographs and gay novels. The post office and the police were after Polak from the start—and did succeed in forcing him out of business and out of Philadelphia in 1969—but not before important inroads had been made against censorship of gay reading matter.

Clark Polak was an irritant to most of his fellow members of the homophile movement and he could be fiercely undiplomatic, but he raised a key issue at an early date. Behind all of his efforts, the question is asked, To what extent will gay men go to achieve their place at the table, while avoiding an indelicate focus on what they do in private when they are not at the table? As Polak knew, it wasn't only men turning from marriage and living with other men that stirred opposition. The thought of men kissing, touching, masturbating, sucking, and fucking each other, and (worse) proudly admitting it, was what drove people crazy. The Frank Kameny school of thought—an approach both civilized and plausible—was tactically to circumscribe the debate at the level of civil rights, equity, privacy, and tolerance for difference. The Clark Polak stance suggested that the world might as well know what it was being asked, even (or especially) in its grubbiest form, to rethink and accept. Discretion, for Polak, was a trap in and of itself. This debate would resurface on a more public level in America a dozen years later, when a Baptist singer–turned–Florida orange-juice promoter went into high gear.

Craig Rodwell's Oscar Wilde Memorial Bookshop in Greenwich Village, which opened Thanksgiving weekend in 1967, was another aspect of the same effort to bridge the gap between those who saw their sexuality as an aspect of identity politics and those who believed it had no real meaning outside the bedroom or the bathhouse. For Rodwell, community and liberation were natural by-products of a sense of cultural heritage and intellectual exploration. Many homosexuals were unaware that same-sex desire had ever been a theme for serious gay and lesbian poets, playwrights, novelists, and essayists. If they took their instruction from schools and the media, they concluded that their experience had never been the stuff of literature. They might know about the pulp novels and skin magazines; they didn't always know about James Barr or Fritz Peters, or even Gide, Firbank, Vidal, and Baldwin. The Oscar Wilde, the first store of its kind, was explicitly intended (as Martin Duberman wrote in *Stonewall*) to be a vehicle for changing that perception and "for promoting a more positive view of homosexuality." Rodwell declined to sell pornography, which he found demeaning and exploitative, and by the standards of a Clark Polak was something of a prude. (Plenty of early customers let him know that that was their opinion.) But in filling his shelves with what the twenty-six-year-old owner judged to be the better books (a stock that was at first 70 percent gay male to 30 percent lesbian—another bone of contention with customers), Rodwell was hoping to make a didactic as well as a commercial point. It was a gamble to be the proprietor of the "Bookshop of the Homophile Movement," as one sign in his window read, and to keep a business going with another sign announcing to passersby, "Gay Is Good." Rodwell had invested his life savings of $1,000 in this project. The job required seventy-hour weeks and a high tolerance for abuse. Many gay New Yorkers were skeptical about the wisdom of a "separatist" store and its chances for success. Dealing with belligerent phone calls, swastikas painted on his doorway, and a landlord who was not happy when he discovered the nature of the business he was renting to, Rodwell survived the first rough years and helped to create what is today a large and highly literate market.

THE OSCAR WILDE Memorial Bookshop celebrated its thirtieth year in business in 1997. At the same time, A Different Light bookstore operates a three-city chain and the Gayellow Pages lists more than forty nonerotic gay and lesbian bookstores nationwide. Yet, despite the myth of gay affluence and education promoted for various reasons in the 1970s, there has never been any reason to believe that gay men are, in the main, more apt to buy and read books than straight men. In a similar vein of assuming differences where they don't verifiably exist, gay men were long taken to be less religious than their heterosexual counterparts. Most church teachings are not sympathetic to homosexual sex or love; therefore, most gay men do not hold or practice a religious faith. The shakiness of that logic troubled some gay men in the 1960s. It didn't correspond to their own experience and it fit too neatly with society's wishful stereotype of homosexuals as odd and un-American in another way, their godlessness. It certainly bore no relation to the situation of black gay men, thousands of whom continued in big cities and small towns to be active, if discreet, members of their church congregations, choirs, and boards.

Concern about developing ties between organized religion and homosexual men was evident in the late 1950s and early 1960s in Chuck Rowland's Los Angeles Church of ONE Brotherhood (doomed to fail in that Rowland wanted to address the need for gay spirituality but was not a cleric or even a believer) and in the readiness of the Quakers to open their meetinghouse to the Mattachine Society of San Francisco when a place was needed for its gatherings. *Christ and the Homosexual* (1961) by Robert Wood, an oblique plea for tolerance by a Catholic priest, had a wide gay readership, while the publication of *Toward a Quaker View of Sex* two years later was hailed as the first significant breakthrough in establishing a dialogue. The Quaker idea that the spirit motivating any sexual act—humane or self-destructive, loving or exploitative—was of greater moral consequence than the mechanics of the act itself or the gender of the partners was a radical one even to some Quakers, who feared that their document might be interpreted as an endorsement of promiscuity, but the Society of Friends (never vulnerable to the charges of 1960s hedonism decried in the popular and religious press) had introduced a note of hope and expanded the debate as never before.

Homosexuals in the movement who were not traditionally religious themselves understood the usefulness of seeking allies in the church. Many Mattachine boards between 1957 and 1964 had made contact with liberal clergymen in their states, inviting them to speak or to bring their colleagues to panel discussions with the membership. Cecil Williams, the black minister of the Glide Memorial Church in San Francisco's Tenderloin, and Ted McIlvenna, a white minister and social worker, were especially interested in learning more and opened their doors to various groups. Both were key figures in setting up the Council on Religion and the Homosexual at the end of 1964. A "new rapport" was in the making, Del Martin wrote in *The Ladder* that year, and the rapid growth of the Council in California and elsewhere verified the optimism. "By 1964 the ministers' consciences had become aroused," Evander Smith, a gay attorney in San Francisco at the time and an early Council participant, agreed. That arousal had a practical purpose for an outcast group with very few bridges to the mainstream and a long-range larger dimension for those gay men and lesbians who felt unwillingly alienated from God and communal worship.

Except for a short period during the black civil rights movement, clerical activism was never a widespread phenomenon, and the disdain for clergymen who spoke about, or worked toward, fellowship with homosexuals wasn't restricted to other clergymen or uncharitable parishioners. Law enforcement officials tended to be astonished, and then outraged, at the betrayal of social conventions from an unexpected quarter. The most egregious example of this response aimed at putting the ministers in their place and restoring the gulf between the deviants and respectable society took place in San Francisco on New Year's Day 1965. A costume ball fund-raiser for the Council on Religion and the Homosexual had been announced and the necessary permits obtained, but no effort was made to secure police permission concerning the attire of the paying guests. (Police departments in many cities granted gay men permission to appear in drag in public once a year, usually on Halloween.) The police let it be known that the queers and "queer-lovers" had best drop the whole idea. The ministers met with the police, to no avail. ("There was one cop at the meeting who said he couldn't rest until he wiped out all queers," Evander Smith noted. "He was a good Catholic.") The benefit proceeded as planned, and the inevitable confrontation took place. As the five hundred guests arrived at California Hall on Polk Street, some in tuxedos and some in drag, they were greeted by lines of paddy wagons and a massive police presence photographing them as they entered and attempting to badger their way inside. A ticket taker and three gay lawyers who intervened were illegally arrested, including Smith and Herb Donaldson, who later became a San Francisco municipal judge. All charges were quickly dropped, though Evander Smith was fired by his boss all the same.

The 1965 New Year's ball and police action drew the lines of the conflict with great precision. Several important beliefs were under attack that night, by the gay participants and the ministers and by the police. The Council was disputing the right of the police to determine the limits of social and moral acceptability in America. They were also challenging the long-standing notion that cultural norms and spiritual truths were necessarily the same. The police, for their part, were determined not to yield an inch of their authority—arresting lawyers for an unpopular cause, the ACLU charged, was a dangerous precedent—and to make their own statement about clerical involvement in political issues. Psychiatrists, sociologists, and legislators might change their minds over time about "perversion," but there was something uniquely shocking about ministers doing it. Homosexuals incorporating their societies, circulating their magazines, dancing together, refusing to be ashamed of their sex lives—that was bad enough. A *spiritualized* homosexual, a gay man or lesbian convinced that he or she enjoyed God's blessings as fully as anyone else, was a new kind of threat. "I think," said one man who attended the ball, "that if it had been anyone other than a bunch of ministers backing us up, [the police] wouldn't have gone so crazy. Somehow that drove them wild."

Throughout the spring of 1965, the San Francisco Police Department continued its provocative stance: raiding a SIR fund-raiser, harassing bar owners and patrons, stopping gay men on the street, beating them at whim. The Council on Religion and the Homosexual fired back with "A Brief on Injustices," a report intended "to expose a pattern of social, legal, and economic oppression of a minority group." In America, the ministers bluntly wrote, "there is very little justice for the homosexual." Later that year when several gay groups came together to form Citizens Alert, a hotline offering advice, legal aid, and emotional support for victims of police brutality, it was with the active support of the Council. This mattered; it was far more than token encouragement. Gay men and lesbians who had been made to feel unwelcome by their priests, ministers, and rabbis had reason in the mid-1960s to conclude that all spiritual leaders were not equally bigoted.

Yet the leap had to be made, eventually, from clerical alliances to gay self-direction, from relying on the goodwill of a small minority of clergymen to carving out a secure niche for gay worshipers in the edifice of modern American religion. At the time Troy Perry, a twenty-eight-year-old gay man and former Pentecostal minister, founded the Metropolitan Community Church in 1968, he assumed that a need for a "gay church" would be obviated within a few years as the larger churches opened their doors and rethought their exclusion and denigration of homosexuals. That hasn't universally been the case. Perry had ample experience of the problem, having been dismissed from two different fundamentalist churches after admitting his homosexuality. A tall, well-built bear of a man, Troy Perry had been brought up as a snake-handling Pentecostal in Florida and Georgia and was preaching by the age of fifteen. Dropping out of high school in eleventh grade, he traveled throughout the South in the late 1950s as a paid evangelist and, at eighteen, married the daughter of another preacher. (Speaking to his future father-in-law about his sexual ambivalence, he was cut short and told that marriage to a good woman would end all such speculation.) Perry served as the pastor of a small Church of God in Joliet, Illinois, until he was denounced by another gay Pentecostalist who was jealous of a one-night tryst Perry had confessed to him. A few years later, as a minister in the Church of God Prophecy in California, now the father of two sons, he broached the subject with an overseer of the church. He was troubled by what he had read in a book he had come across, Donald Webster Cory's *The Homosexual in America*, and by his own marital discord. That moment of honesty ended his affiliation with the Pentecostalists as well as his marriage.

A tour of duty with the U.S. Army in Germany in the mid-1960s, where Perry befriended a black soldier who was openly gay, was followed by a full coming out and a move back to California. Perry's continuing interest in questions of faith seemed to some people at odds with the new life he was cultivating in Los Angeles. "You are the only gay person I know who talks about religion," his roommate at the time assured him. Perry was not convinced. In the aftermath of a suicide attempt and after observing the agony of a friend who had been arrested in a bar raid, he felt the call to bring together the two parts of his life that meant the most to him, his belief in a God who was better represented by the Sermon on the Mount than by Leviticus and his own identification as a gay man. To his roommate's dismay, he placed an ad in a new gay newspaper, *The Advocate*, which announced a gathering of Christian homosexuals and provided his address.

The first service of what became the Metropolitan Community Church, held on October 6, 1968, in Perry's living room, was not without its awkward moments. Nine people Perry knew attended, including a few who came to chuckle; three men who had seen the ad showed up. Departing from the Pentecostal tradition, Perry wore black robes for the first time in the hope that a more ecumenical appearance (and a less histrionic demeanor) would attract a larger, more diverse following. Perry preached, sang, and offered communion. Enough guests wanted to repeat the experience, and spread the word among their friends, to justify renting a women's club several weeks later and then an auditorium. The first service outside Los Angeles was in the back room of a gay bar in Orange County near Disneyland. An interview in *The Advocate* led to an "unbelievable jump" in attendance and, by the end of 1969, the Metropolitan Community Church owned its own property in Los Angeles with a thousand weekly worshipers, male and female. (Today branches of the Metropolitan Community Church are active in forty-eight states with approximately 48,000 regular members.)

A good deal needed to be sorted out in the months after the first few services, as a board was elected and contacts were made in other cities. "Growth was rapid," Perry noted in his autobiography, "but not always easy." Some of the original board members were uncomfortable with the idea of a high-profile, aggressively gay, activist church. A feeling of peace and security for the emotionally wounded was important, Perry agreed, but he was adamant that the new church "would not be another closet." On that point, he was unrelenting and ultimately persuasive. The gospel he preached was three-pronged: salvation through Jesus, community for those in need, and vigorous Christian social action. "If you're fired from a job because you're gay," he maintained, "you've got to fight, you've got to sue, you've got to do something. That's an injustice and it's our duty to stand up to injustice against ourselves and others. Wherever and whenever." In March 1969, Perry led 120 marchers to a rally at the Dover Hotel, site of a grisly murder of a gay man by three LAPD officers, and the next year he camped out and fasted on the steps of the Los Angeles Federal Building for eleven days to protest the city council's refusal to discuss gay rights. Clerical activism took a new turn.

In its earliest days, some people wondered—and it was a fair question—whether MCC, as it was soon known, was flourishing because it truly spoke to unanswered needs or because the founder was so determined, handsome, and charismatic. The question was answered as MCC branched out over its first two years into previously unattempted types of social work (a youth group for gay teenagers, a class in sign language for deaf homosexuals) as well as traditional but still undermanned endeavors (a suicide hotline, a medical and legal referral service), and opened new churches in other cities. Men who avoided gay bars and cruisy beaches, and those who were most at home there; older men who would never have joined a picket or signed a petition for a gay cause; younger men who were ready to take on the world—everyone was made to feel welcome. Lest there be any confusion on the point, Perry liked to make clear that the church was not more gay than it was Christian (10 percent of the membership was usually heterosexual), that a doctrine based on an acceptance of Christ and the New Testament was essential. Styles from city to city might vary as the congregations did, from the more formal tone of some to the casualness of MCC in San Francisco, which advertised with the slogan "Take a Trick to Church." The common ground was a less rigid understanding of Christianity, an emphasis on love, and a social philosophy captured in the line from Dag Hammarskjold displayed in Perry's office: "Never for the sake of peace and quiet deny your own experience or convictions."

Troy Perry's vision had all the fervency and even theatricality of the Pentecostal ministry he had been bred to, and in some ways it was a larger perspective than that of the gay activists who preceded him. Like Hay, Kameny, Gittings, Wicker, Polak, Rodwell, and so many others, he was calling on gay men and lesbians to be political beings, to demand their rights. But he was also urging them not to cut themselves off from a rich spiritual life because centuries of biblical interpretation by fallible, often hard-hearted men had turned organized religion against them.

Moreover, Perry articulated both of these goals in the context of self-understanding and self-acceptance, including a healthy attitude toward romance, sensuality, and sexual appetite. His own persona had nothing to do with old-fashioned ministerial worries about being seen in a gay bar, dating good-looking men, or dancing in a club. ("A man to give the phrase 'sex-positive' new meaning," one friend remarked.) Nor was he loath to talk about his own missteps, times of doubt, and suicidal despair before "the small, still voice" of the divine spoke to him. The Metropolitan Community Church wanted to bring its parishioners closer to God; its founder wanted to see them more thoughtful about, and sensitive to, the range of their needs as well. But before any of this was possible, gay men and lesbians had to confront their own demons, which meant identifying themselves as different, reflecting on the pain and ostracism they had known, acknowledging and temporarily embracing the separateness society had created and enforced, and finding joy in the company of other homosexuals: "We who were not a people, God has made a people."

A frolic with Emma Jones in Pensacola, a Corduroy Club dance in New York, a night out with the SIR bowling league, or a prayer meeting at the Metropolitan Community Church were, in this sense, aspects of the same gradual but important shift in gay life in America in the 1960s. They all whittled away at the archetype of the lonely, depressed, unlovable homosexual. They rejected the view of homosexuality as a handicap or an incidental fact in one's life. They presupposed that some level of community, ongoing or intermittent in the lives of its participants, was needed. A drop-in center, a bookstore openly displaying dozens of novels about same-sex relationships, a church where one would hear sermons about Christ's love and nothing about the fictitious damnation awaiting homosexuals: these were developments hard to imagine a decade earlier. They were made possible by farseeing individuals, but they were also evidence of changing times, and they signaled even more creative tumult to come.

16

THE BOYS IN THE BAND

Now they call it a gay play. Once upon a time it was just a play.

—Mart Crowley, 1990

Critics and commentators interested in the American theater felt they had a great deal to worry about by the mid-1960s. They pondered declining audiences and rising production costs, the imminent death of Broadway and the national indifference to repertory. They watched good actors decamp for Hollywood in ever larger numbers and young writers, who would once have been playwrights, devote themselves to the perfect screenplay. They worried, with good reason, that there weren't any more Eugene O'Neills on the horizon and that Arthur Miller and Tennessee Williams, pillars of the 1950s, had long since done their best work. They also felt a mounting unease about that once unmentionable subject, now very mentionable indeed.

Amazement that homosexuals figure prominently in the theater is akin to surprise that Jews play a large part in the performing arts scene. (As one prominent elderly actress exclaimed on hearing that Yale was about to open a repertory playhouse in 1968: ridiculous, you can't have professional theater without Jews and homosexuals! Her concern, that New Haven lacked sufficient numbers of either group, proved unfounded.) But to journalists in post-Kinsey, pre-Stonewall days the issue of "the gay strangle-hold on American theater" was something of an idée fixe. At its lowest level, it was a feature in *Tip-Off*, a forerunner of the *National Enquirer*, that sought to alert its dime-store readership in 1956 to the crisis in the entertainment industry with "Why They Call Broadway the 'GAY' White Way." At an only slightly higher level than this "exposé" of gay casting-couch lore was Howard Taubman's 1961 analysis in the *New York Times* of "the infiltration of homosexual attitudes" that was corrupting American drama as gay attitudes found their way into heterosexual situations. Yet Taubman's concern about the "rot" at the core of any play written by a gay man who took a dim view of marriage or modern family life carried a liberal veneer that the tabloids never bothered with: he wasn't attacking homosexuals per se, he wanted his readers to know, but the insidious, covert nature of gay writing that was trying to "pass." Homosexuality was not a forbidden topic in 1961, Taubman insisted without irony, and the authors of *A Streetcar Named Desire* and *Picnic* and *American Dream* were advised to treat gay themes more forthrightly, leaving the depictions of women and heterosexual life to—well, to someone not gay. Edward Albee seems to have roused the ire of the critics more than most when *Who's Afraid of Virginia Woolf?* was unceremoniously decoded as a play about an alcoholic gay couple, and *Tiny Alice* was unmasked as a castration drama complete with Woman as Destroyer. It was time for a return to "a masculine theater," Elizabeth Hardwick urged, and in the view of Philip Roth (of all people) an end to mean-spirited portrayals of castrating bitches.

By 1966, when Stanley Kauffmann wrote his more famous essay on the subject during his brief stint as the *Times* drama critic that year, the best that could be said about the level of the debate was that outright disdain for a gay presence in American cultural life was no longer acceptable in sophisticated circles. The topic had truly become a subject for debate rather than a series of pronouncements from on high.

Kauffmann's thesis wasn't so very different from his predecessor's at the paper of record. "Homosexuality and Its Disguises" agreed that there was substance to the charge that contemporary American drama presented a distorted picture of women, families, heterosexual love, and society in general, and that much of this distortion could be charged to three of the most prominent playwrights of the day (unnamed in the article, as always). These three men—Williams, Inge, and Albee, presumably—just hadn't gotten it right. Fading southern belles lost in a haze of liquor and anonymous sex, the glorification of the stud, incestuous families and suburban lust, role-playing and dissipation and bitter, brittle humor: this was gay life or gay fantasy, but not American life as Kauffmann and his colleagues knew it. The one twist Kauffmann provided to the discussion was his readiness to fault heterosexual society for the gay writer's need to forgo his own story while he pretended to tell America's. "In society, the homosexual's life must be discreetly concealed," he wrote. "As a material for drama, that life must be even more intensely concealed." Heterosexual repressiveness and hypocrisy: therein lay the problem. We have no one to blame but ourselves, Kauffmann suggested, if homosexuals couldn't be honest in their writing about their own world and of necessity continued to get "our" life wrong. We have no Jean Genets in America because we had no one who felt comfortable enough, strong enough, about his homosexuality to create an art without subterfuge.

By the summer of 1967 a young writer was at work on a play of remarkable bluntness on the subject of homosexuality. Not that *The Boys in the Band* was a theater event utterly without precedent. Since the days of the Caffe Cino and Lanford Wilson's Lady Bright, gay characters had found their way to Broadway and the larger Off-Broadway houses in many plays: Lorraine Hansberry's *The Sign in Sidney Brustein's Window*, Edward Albee's adaptation of James Purdy's novel *Malcolm*, Joe Orton's farces, and, most sensationally, in Frank Marcus's *The Killing of Sister George* and John Herbert's *Fortune and Men's Eyes*. But the social acceptance of the incidental gay character or the horror of prison rape was far removed from what the thirty-one-year-old Mart Crowley was attempting in his story of several contemporary gay men and the campy, ludicrous, oddly fraternal nature of their lives.

Born in 1936 in Vicksburg, Mississippi, to an Irish-Catholic family, Crowley had been existing on the fringe of the film world for some time when he began his most famous play. With a pile of rejected screenplays and unfinished work on his desk, he felt a mounting anxiety about the future. Natalie Wood had given him the money to go into therapy, but that experience hadn't done much to dispel the consuming "personal rage" that was getting the better of him. The play he started while staying in a friend's Beverly Hills mansion and then finished five weeks later on Fire Island was a kind of therapy in itself.

Originally entitled *The Gay Bar*, the two-act drama was at first set in a Manhattan bar—with the cowboy-hustler, who appears near the end of Act I in the final version, already onstage. The next draft switched the setting to a living room, brought the hustler in later, and was called *The Birthday Party*, until Harold Pinter's tour de force came along and eliminated that title in favor of *The Boys in the Band*. Though the script was too long and needed judicious cutting before production, the essence of the characters and their relationships had been set from the start. These were people Crowley knew. Doug, a friend from Laguna Beach who came into Los Angeles each week to see his psychiatrist, became the sweet, neurotic Donald who braves the Long Island Expressway every Saturday to throw himself on his New York analyst's couch; Eddie, effeminate and witty, evolved into the outrageous, mincing Emory; Bernard was based on a handsome, reserved black man Crowley used to talk to in a bar he frequented.

Deciding to hold nothing back and to re-create the tenor of gay life as he knew it, Crowley placed himself in the most unsparing light of all. Mart became the bitchy Michael, a manic shopper, guilt-ridden Catholic, both confidant and tyrant to the people who know him best. The party Michael throws for Harold, an even more grandiloquently tortured queen, is the excuse to bring together several men who don't so much represent a cross-section of gay life in New York as a plausibly diverse circle of friends and acquaintances. Emory is the decorator-sissy who refers to everyone by feminine names; Bernard, a librarian, is the most stable of the group in many ways; Hank and Larry are a likable couple struggling with Larry's desire to play the field and Hank's interest in monogamy. Complications, alternately (or simultaneously) funny and serious, follow upon the arrival of Emory's "present" to Harold, a hustler he's picked up in Times Square, and an unexpected visit from Alan, a married college friend of Michael's who may or may not have had some homosexual experience in his younger days and who loathes Emory on sight. Worlds Michael has long tried to keep separate collide at a dizzying pace. Magnificent innuendos and insults are bandied about, Alan attacks Emory, and Harold belatedly arrives in the midst of the chaos. The midnight cowboy launches into "Happy Birthday" and the first act of *The Boys in the Band* closes in the grand tradition of classic stage farce.

A more contrived, less freewheeling second act takes its structure from a party game that Michael, getting drunker and nastier by the minute, forces upon his guests. Everyone will place a phone call to the one person he loves, or has loved, the most, winning points for dialing, for connecting, for finally pouring out his heart's truth. The purpose of the game is humiliation. By the end of the evening, Michael succeeds in embarrassing most of the participants, though Harold holds his own against Michael's spite; Hank and Larry have affirmed their love; and Emory and Alan have made up. Michael's unappeasable self-hate, however, dominates the closing minutes of the act, and the most frequently quoted snippet of dialogue from the play (not surprisingly) is his lament, "You show me a happy homosexual and I'll show you a gay corpse."

The first person to read *The Boys in the Band*, director Robert Moore, knew that his friend had written something quite extraordinary. He also suspected it would be a hard sell. Indeed, the agent Crowley sent the manuscript to was appalled at the idea of representing so offensive a piece of work. Heterosexuals who had seen *Staircase* or *The Sergeant* had watched homosexuals camping it up at home and blowing their brains out, so that wasn't the problem—postwar America had always made room for plays and movies that fostered a sense of audience superiority toward the sadsack deviant. Rather, what was unnerving in Crowley's play was his indifference to any of the usual limits. Just how much did heterosexuals want to know about the private lives of gay men, and just how much did gay men want revealed and examined on stage? Crowley wrote as if he couldn't care less. Joking references to poppers, VD, vice arrests, and the baths (where Emory spends his vacations in San Francisco) crossed the line. But the playwright had made it clear from Michael's first words (moved back a few pages in revision) that he wasn't going to pull his punches. "One thing you can say for masturbation," Michael remarks as he studies himself in the mirror, "you certainly don't have to look your best." Nor, when Harold stares at Emory's purple lips, recently bloodied by Alan, and asks if he's been rimming a snowman, is Crowley giving any quarter to the *Plaza Suite* or *Man of La Mancha* crowd.

Yet the skeptics underestimated, or misread, an artistic climate that was rapidly becoming both more tolerant and more sensation-seeking, embracing *Hair* as fervently as *Hello, Dolly*. Producer Richard Barr arranged for a well-received showcase production in the Village before transferring the play to Theatre Four, an Off-Broadway house. A superb cast was assembled. Word of mouth in New York promised an exciting event, and from the night of its official opening on Easter Sunday 1968, the play was a huge success.

THE LAUGHTER AND applause, interestingly, weren't only from gay audiences. *The Boys in the Band* was equally popular with straight reviewers and theatergoers, a development that would have been hard to imagine even two or three years earlier. Clive Barnes in the *Times* wondered if the humor had to be quite so lacerating and if gay life was quite as painful as Michael suggested, but praised the play's humor and frankness. The staid *Saturday Review* and the usually homophobic *Time* found good things to say. *Time* recognized the play as "funny, sad, and honest," although the reviewer was a little too pleased that his worst preconceptions of gay life were being verified and confused the characters Harold and Hank. Like many straight theatergoers, Frank Rich (then in college) assumed he was getting "the definitive insider's tour" of the gay world and reveled in the atmosphere at Theatre Four, "itself reeking of the secret and the contraband." A Presbyterian church in Brooklyn invited the cast to meet its congregation after services to discuss the play. As *The Boys in the Band* made the rounds of regional theaters and college playhouses over the next three years, local papers tended to be similarly determined to avoid an overly philistine slant. The *Chicago Tribune* hailed Crowley's integrity and the *Washington Post* thought that he might prompt understanding of a problem that had finally "caught the spotlight after years of darkness." The *Hartford Courant* decided that a night with the boys was harmless fun, "a bit of curiosa akin to the study of exotic tribal customs and rituals." Even Caesar's Palace in Las Vegas booked the show. Only in Atlanta did problems arise, where the production was canceled when county commissioners threatened to withhold their annual grant from the theater if the production went on—an arts-agenda tactic Cobb County was still fine-tuning in the 1990s.

Gay reactions were another, messier story. Many of the gay men who packed the theater on West Fifty-fifth Street were delighted by Crowley's nerve and crackerjack dialogue, just as many homosexuals outside New York City were pleased that a gay play was finally being staged in their area. "This was a significant breakthrough by any standard," an associate of Barr's commented. Others appreciated the craft involved, especially the bravura performances of Kenneth Nelson, Leonard Frey, Frederick Coombs, and Cliff Gorman, but not the self-pity of the principal characters. "I laughed from start to finish," one playwright admitted, "and I just hated Crowley for what he was doing." The earthy, sexual conversation was a sticking-point for some. "We'll all pay for this," an opening-night patron told David Rothenberg, the play's publicist. Often the divisions were along generational lines, with gays in their twenties disliking the faggy self-deprecation and men Crowley's age and older insisting that he had gotten their story "just right." Dick Leitsch wrote one of the few vigorously sympathetic gay reviews of the play, defending the author's version of the truth and his right to tell it. He titled his piece "Mart Crowley: Harriet Beecher Stowe in Drag."

The real enemies of the play—and they did in fact see themselves as enemies, not merely critics—hated almost everything about it, and grew in number and vociferousness for the four or five years the play continued to be a hot property. Writing in the *Times* about the release of the original-cast album in 1969, Donn Teal called *The Boys in the Band* "a satanic gem" that offered a "distorted picture of a subculture" and a "debasing dramatic debut in heterosexual society." Modern homosexuals, he argued, were by no means as unhappy as the limited specimens that Crowley was feeding to straight audiences. Others were much more strident than Teal, insisting that Crowley was actually doing great harm to the cause of gay rights and that Richard Barr had no business promoting what was essentially an anti-gay diatribe in the guise of slick entertainment. The Kalos Society picketed the Hartford Stage Company production in May 1971, handing out leaflets decrying stereotypes, and when William Friedkin's film version was released that same year, activist Morris Kight led a demonstration at the opening in Los Angeles. One sign captured the essence of all the grievances: "*The Boys in the Band*: Best Gay Movie of 1947."

Crowley was stung by the attacks. His belief that, as an artist, he should be able to dramatize any aspect of life he chose (and the psychological morass Michael, Donald, Harold, and their friends typified was authentic to his experience) had run up against an always impenetrable wall—the loud, urgent political needs of the moment. Especially in the wake of Stonewall a year after the play's opening, Crowley became a symbol for what the next generation of gay men wanted to bury and forget. "Gay Power!" and overdrawn charge accounts at Bloomingdale's, taking to the streets and knowing the difference between cashmere and vicuna, coming out and passing: the gap seemed to preclude any point of mutual understanding. The activists Crowley had ignored weren't uniformly opposed to an effeminate manner, but they certainly despised (or professed to despise) the tendency of people such as Michael and Donald to see their homosexuality as a cross to bear, an attitude reinforced by religion and therapy. They hated Emory's maudlin streak ("Oh, Mary, it takes a fairy to make something pretty") and the whole obsession with Bette Davis and Judy Garland. The bravery that the author of *The Boys in the Band* was exhibiting when he sat down to write his play in 1967 was little appreciated in some quarters by 1969. Gay America was changing faster than anyone could have predicted.

The most striking encapsulation of the change in outlook was journalist Tom Burke's article for the December 1969 *Esquire*. The author of "The New Homosexuality" was as sure of himself as Crowley was self-doubting. "Pity," Burke began, "just when Middle America discovered the homosexual, he died." The old-time queen was an unmourned victim of natural law: "He has expired with a whimper, to make way for the new homosexual of the Seventies, an unfettered, guiltless male child of the new morality in a Zapata moustache and an outlaw hat, who couldn't care less for Establishment approval, would as soon sleep with boys as girls, and thinks that 'Over the Rainbow' is a place to fly to on 200 micrograms of lysergic acid diethylamide." Burke's piece was vintage late-1960s *Esquire*, and his animus wasn't directed only at Crowley and the boys. He spoke for those who hated the whitebread world of the aging nellies, the urge to polite assimilation, and Mattachine reform strategies. Dick Leitsch was the journalist's straw man set up as a contrast to Jim Fouratt of the newly formed Gay Liberation Front, a street fighter par excellence. Burke effectively captured something of the impatience younger gays felt with the "dress right, act right" approach of the previous generation, though his own stereotypes are as shallow as the ones he attacks. Burke's interviewees, the "groovy" guys who "ball chicks" on occasion and prefer pot to dry martinis, had no reason to condescend to anyone, least of all to men who had survived the homophobic 1950s.

Inevitably, many aspects of Crowley's play were obscured by the heated response it evoked. For all the gloom that underlies Harold's ill-fated birthday party, no one—including Michael—is really any more lost or self-absorbed than countless other malcontents of American realist drama. But the temper of the times demanded that Crowley's characters be taken as representatives of their kind rather than quirky, suffering individuals; straight audiences were still too eager to see the homosexual as a grotesque in a category of his own, and gays wanted role models. Biff Loman or Jamie Tyrone are misbegotten, but Michael and Harold are pathetic. In this light, Michael's personal hell becomes an authorial statement about an entire group's identity, something Crowley insisted was never his intention. Also minimized by many irate observers were the bonds that still exist among the characters after all the bloodletting. Their bitchy ways aside, Bernard and Emory have always looked out for each other, Donald and Harold will continue to stand by Michael in his craziness, and Hank and Larry—like any male-female couple out of Cheever or Updike—will go on stumbling their way toward a workable union, despite Larry's dalliances and Hank's jealousy.

Mart Crowley's real accomplishment, the fashioning of a truly funny comedy out of his grim material, was acknowledged by almost everyone, but even this dimension of the play was relegated to a secondary status by his critics, as if wit and rhetorical skill were incidental qualities. But Harold isn't a run-of-the-mill mess. He is a camp diva on the theme of his life, his mother, his rabbi, his bad pores, and his hang-ups. Emory may be a "butterfly in heat," as Alan charges, but he artfully defends himself with the quick comeback. (He is also astute enough to remind his Catholic host that the need to seek absolution "depends on what you think sin is." In his heart, Emory understands better than anyone that society is in the wrong, not him.) Michael means to hurt, but his targets know how to take him. For certain gay men, Crowley's particularly, language is a kind of brawn. The *way* they speak belies a spirited affection for one another, just as it manifests a subtle power and a healthy theatricality, a love of gesture, competition, and tireless verbal energy. It also hints at, or aims to communicate, what is always hardest to express to friends—sorrow and concern.

Five years after its premiere in New York City, on the eve of its eclipse, the play was still attracting attention in unlikely quarters. A Westchester County amateur theater company in Yorktown Heights, revived the drama—in spite of some town protests at the "morally decadent" nature of the work—with a pointedly heterosexual "family man" cast, including two lawyers, two IBM executives, and a teacher. (The Off-Broadway cast had been largely gay.) The director noted that the production was the most successful venture in the company's eleven-year history, though he admitted that not all of the actors' relatives had been happy about or willing to attend the play. The actors themselves were fulsomely self-congratulatory on the insight Crowley's writing and their own acting shed on an aspect of experience most suburbanites wanted to ignore. References to wives and children in the program notes were abundant, lest any misconceptions occur.

It can't be said that *The Boys in the Band* presaged a renaissance in gay writing for the American theater, not in the immediate future at any rate. *Norman, Is That You?* had "dinner theater" written all over it when it opened in New York for a short run in 1970, and even as late as 1974, when Broadway wanted to be meaningful and serious about the issue, the result was a solemn play like *Find Your Way Home* in which Lee Richardson must spend two hours finding the courage to leave Jane Alexander for Michael Moriarty. The more important developments over the next few years took place Off-Broadway and in small community-based theaters across the country, where writers focused on the varieties of gay experience—often with the characters' homosexuality treated as a given, not a choice to be debated or a revelation for the character's parents. Sometimes the results were controversial in their use of the old stereotypes for the purposes of transgressive humor, as was the case with Al Carmines's popular musical *The Faggot* (seen by novelist Michael Grumley as a liberated "reshuffling of the cliché cards" and by historian Martin Duberman as a Stepin Fetchit revue); others, like Jonathan Ned Katz's docudrama *Coming Out!*, were explicitly political and inspirational.

One thing that changed for good after Mart Crowley's experience was the feeling toward gay writers who weren't inclined to be open, or open enough to satisfy the modern public, concerning their own sexual identity. The grumblings about Tennessee Williams and Edward Albee were renewed, despite the fact that neither had ever hidden his sexual orientation, and Williams even became the subject of a play based on his alleged timidity and ambivalence. *Nightride*, the story of a famous playwright in decline who is challenged by a publicly gay rock star about his closeted way of life, ran for a short time Off-Broadway in the fall of 1971 and might have faded from the scene without comment had not the author of the play used a pseudonym. "Lee Barton" then found himself in the strange position of having to account for his anonymity in the pages of the *New York Times* after theater historian Eric Bentley and others accused him of hypocrisy and unfairness to Williams. "Barton" hotly asserted that someone in his position, with a day job in business, would be fired and impoverished if he came out, in contrast to the authors of *Cat on a Hot Tin Roof* and *Tiny Alice* who had less to lose and should therefore lead the way. "Only the rich, the self-employed, or the social outcast has nothing to fear from being labeled a homosexual," he told his critics. "Freedom, even in 1972, is something one must be able to afford."

In the same month Williams was being taken to task by Barton, he was proving the charge unfounded, or outdated. *Small Craft Warnings*, a full-length version of a play he had been laboring over for five years, was finally being readied for production in the winter of 1971–1972, and in it Williams created his most explicitly homosexual characters. The results were forbidding. Middle-aged Quentin, his face looking as if he had been "burned thin by a fever," is happiest paying for his pleasures and loses interest when the boy he picks up responds with affection and enthusiasm. Bobby wants love, not the older man's money and cynicism. When a fellow barfly tells Quentin that she knows the gay scene he is a part of and "how full of sickness and sadness it is" because her late brother was gay (like Blanche's poet, another boy too delicate to live), Williams seems to be speaking in his own voice, having reached an end-point of sexual and spiritual weariness. Quentin's belief that there is "a coarseness, a deadening coarseness," at the heart of gay life is only a more exhausted rendering of Michael's dirge at the end of *The Boys in the Band*. Yet in Bobby, this unformed teenager wandering the country in his sweatshirt and denim, Williams also strains to acknowledge an outlook different from his own, embodied in a teenager who doesn't use the term *gay*, who is neither Tom Burke's "New Homosexual" nor an old-time queen in the making.

What was difficult for any writer for the stage to achieve at the time (and impossible for screenwriters) was exactly what gay audiences craved: "a gentle, romantic, and loving encounter between two men," as playwright Martin Sherman termed his own excellent venture in that area. Short and charming, *Passing By* is a story in which two young men pick

GENDER-ROLE VARIANCE: TURN-OF-THE-CENTURY AMERICA

Postcard circa 1905

COLLECTION OF WILLIAM WALKER

Julian Eltinge, a popular
female impersonator, in 1920

PHOTOFEST

Picking up sailors in
Charles Demuth's watercolor
"On *That* Street," 1932
CHICAGO ART INSTITUTE

Best known for his elegant still lifes and industrial landscapes, Demuth
depicted gay life between the wars in his drawings of men cavorting
on the beach, bathhouse encounters, and morning-after scenes (*Eight
O'Clock, Morning #2,* 1917). WADSWORTH ATHENEUM

Gender-role pressures: in the 1953 movie *Tea and Sympathy*, a "sensitive" boy is counseled to walk like a "regular guy."
CORBIS-BETTMANN

A drag party in San Francisco in 1959
PHOTOFEST

one

THE HOMOSEXUAL VIEWPOINT

JANUARY 1960
FIFTY CENTS

"I Just Had to Write"

More important than their circulation figures would suggest, "homophile" magazines kept readers informed about police harassment and early activism in the 1950s and 1960s.

The mass-market paperback boom led to the publication of hundreds of cheap novels about gay life, part exposé and part pornography.

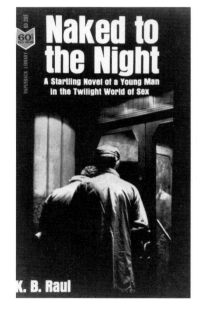

Naked to the Night

A Startling Novel of a Young Man in the Twilight World of Sex

K. B. Raul

The window was thrown back. There was a second's silence, then a terrible muffled thud . . .

The homosexual's lot: morning-after guilt and suicide (an illustration from the 1957 paperback edition of Andre Tellier's *Twilight Men*)

1960s ACTIVISM

Jack Nichols, Frank Kameny, and Lilli Vincenz head a gay-rights picket line outside the White House in the spring of 1965. CORBIS-BETTMANN

Demonstrators outside the U.N. on Easter Sunday, 1965, protest Castro's internment of Cuban homosexuals (Dick Leitsch in front, Craig Rodwell behind). RANDY WICKER

Randy Wicker's media blitz in the mid-1960s brought attention to the discrimination and stereotypes gay men had to live with. RANDY WICKER

The 1962 movie *Advise and Consent* brought the interior of a gay bar to the screen for the first time since *Call Her Savage* thirty years earlier

Mart Crowley's play *The Boys in the Band* provoked sharp reactions to its comic and bitter view of gay life.
PHOTOFEST

July 4, 1970: The Emma Jones Society of Pensacola invited its friends to a beach party and drag revue.

Gay liberation
rally in Albany, 1971
RICHARD WANDEL/CORBIS-BETTMANN

Television broached the subject
of gay relationships and family
ties with *That Certain Summer*
(1972), starring Hal Holbrook
and Martin Sheen. PHOTOFEST

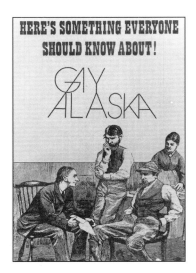

By the end of the 1970s,
gay periodicals were
published in almost every
state, introducing new
ideas about gay identity
and community.

Changes in the style, safety, and social acceptance of the baths in the 1970s transformed the experience.

Reverend Troy Perry of the Metropolitan Community Church performs a wedding in Los Angeles in 1972. UPI/CORBIS-BETTMANN

The gay influx to San Francisco in the 1970s created a "gay mecca" in the Castro neighborhood that illuminated the benefits and drawbacks of separatism.
CRAWFORD BARTON/
GAY AND LESBIAN
HISTORICAL SOCIETY OF
NORTHERN CALIFORNIA

Harvey Milk's election to the San Francisco Board of Supervisors in 1977 gave him a forum in which to champion the cause of tolerance and diversity.
UPI/CORBIS-BETTMANN

The lenient sentence given to Harvey Milk's murderer prompted the "White Night Riots" of May 21, 1978, the most violent display of gay anger ever seen.
CRAWFORD BARTON/
GAY AND LESBIAN
HISTORICAL SOCIETY OF
NORTHERN CALIFORNIA

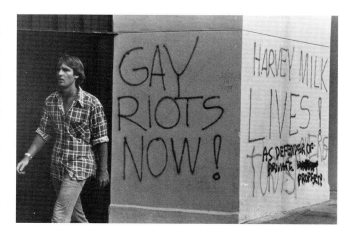

The flamboyant author of *The Naked Civil Servant* (center), seen in a gay pride parade in 1982, Quentin Crisp often found himself at odds with the new gay activism and ideology.
RICHARD WANDEL/ CORBIS-BETTMANN

The idea of gay activist Cleve Jones, the NAMES Project AIDS Memorial Quilt was displayed in numerous cities between 1987 and the mid-1990s.
CORBIS-BETTMANN

Marlon Riggs's controversial film *Tongues Untied* examined social and sexual issues particular to African-American gay men.
RON SIMMONS/FRAMELINE

In *Clean*, Edwin Sánchez wrote about a Puerto Rican teenager who accepts his homosexuality without guilt and a gay black drag queen who (to his own surprise) falls in love with the young man's mother.
GERRY GOODSTEIN

Bridging and clashing cultures: B. D. Wong (front) and David Drake as ex-lovers in a scene from Chay Yew's play *A Language of Their Own*.
MICHAL DANIEL

FIGHTING BACK

George Stewart, a member of the group OUT, participates in a demonstration outside the White House in 1991.

REUTERS/CORBIS-BETTMANN

An ACT-UP group stages a "die-in" in Kennebunkport, Maine, during the town's Memorial Day Parade in 1992.

REUTERS/CORBIS-BETTMANN

each other up at the movies and see the ups-and-downs of their relationship, including the hepatitis one has given the other, as the real issue—not their gayness. Sherman's characters live a life as distant from the anguished confessional spirit of *Small Craft Warnings* as they do from the horrors of *Bent*, Sherman's later drama about gays in the concentration camps. But the weak production his boy-meets-boy story received in New York emphasized the disparity between artistic and political goals on the one hand and overriding commercial realities on the other. American actors, gay or straight, didn't want to play happy, well-adjusted homosexuals. "They were quite willing to limp their wrists onstage, indeed even to cut them— that constituted 'character' playing," Sherman noted. "Anything free and natural was thought to be a threat to future employment." Before Cliff Gorman's spectacular success as Crowley's "butterfly in heat," agents had sternly wanted their clients away from femme roles. Post-Gorman, those were the best, and often the only, gay parts agents would consider. This was, and still is, a serious problem in a field where making a living is a depressing struggle. The story made the rounds in the 1970s that the president of a famous coffee company instructed his ad people that no one who had performed in *The Boys in the Band* was ever to appear in a commercial for his product, including the heterosexual Gorman and Laurence Luckinbill.

A related dilemma confronted playwright-director Doric Wilson in 1974 when he formed TOSOS, or The Other Side of Silence, as a nonprofit workshop for gays and lesbians working in the performing and the visual arts. TOSOS presented plays by Terrence McNally, Robert Patrick, and other veterans of the Caffe Cino and popular revivals of Noel Coward and Joe Orton. Unsettled by the joylessness of *The Boys in the Band* and stirred by his own involvement with gay politics, Wilson hoped that in a supportive atmosphere talented artists would create a new aesthetic, sidestep the confines of the marketplace, address the realities of gay life without alluding to heterosexual preconceptions. "But the scripts weren't there in the end," Wilson remembered of his three-year project. Like the actors Sherman referred to, gay writers were also mindful of the doors they were closing in too strong an affiliation with an all-gay enterprise.

Martin Sherman's and Doric Wilson's observations, as much as Tennessee Williams's sentimentality about gay life and Lee Barton's confused indignation, only underscore the unique achievement of *The Boys in the Band* in 1968. In an art form governed by conservative business interests and unpredictable audiences, Mart Crowley could be said to have done what only a few writers had managed since the war. He wrote a play that in its time mattered passionately to large numbers of people (detractors and admirers), a ribald entertainment with social and even political resonance. That Crowley saw himself—and still does—as apolitical is beside the point. To the young men far from Manhattan and San Francisco who saw or read *The Boys in the Band*, he served a vital purpose of opening a window on lives that the American theater had ruthlessly ignored, subjecting the experience of those lives to an invisibility that was more damaging than the worse anxieties of Crowley's characters. To the young radicals of Stonewall, he was a lightning rod for their discontents and the collective need to eliminate or refashion a suffocating stereotype. Most important, to the Emorys of America, not yet ready to give way to the New Homosexual, he was a fair chronicler and a clever ally.

17

1968–1969: MAELSTROM

Homosexuals can effectively demand respect from others only if we first respect ourselves—as homosexuals. That requires that we admit to ourselves that we are homosexual; that we affirm it, understand it, realize it in all its implications. I am a homosexual. Say it! aloud; "I am a homosexual." Shout it, whisper it. Laugh it, cry it. State it, proclaim it, confess it in sobs, but *say* it. . . . Not "Leonardo da Vinci was homosexual," but "I am homosexual."

—Craig Schoonmaker, founder
of Homosexuals Intransigent

LOS ANGELES: AUGUST 1968

The Patch, a dance bar near Long Beach just south of Los Angeles, had been having trouble all summer with local hoods who gathered in groups to slash tires and harass gay men in the parking lot of the popular Wilmington nightspot. On the evening of Saturday, August 17, the LAPD took its turn at harassment. When Lee Glaze, the manager of the bar, noticed two vice squad regulars at the bar eyeing his customers, "the blond darling" did just what he had on other occasions—took to the stage to issue a warning to potential victims in the form of a comic monologue that pinpointed the cops, "a pair even more homely than they usually send our way." Everyone laughed, including the two policemen, though there was a significant risk involved: a bar employee could be arrested for breaking the cover of a policeman.

At midnight, with over 250 people at the bar or on the dance floor, the plainclothes team was joined by several uniformed police who fanned out to check IDs and, at random, place two men under arrest. One of them, a married twenty-two-year-old Hispanic man, had been dancing with Reverend Troy Perry and was handcuffed and charged with "lewd and lascivious behavior." Again, Glaze went to the stage and this time spoke more in anger than humor, asking how long they were going to put up with this craziness. "Two people who are totally innocent have just been arrested," he told the crowd. "The cops are trying to put us out of business by keeping us frightened. It's time we did something. Is anybody with me on this? We have rights, and one of them is to be left alone in our own bars." The crowd erupted in applause and, as one news account read, "the scene very nearly took on the aspects of a political rally." Glaze announced that the Patch would post bail for the two men and provide a lawyer. He then left for the police station to find out when the men would be released. Upon his return, he asked everyone who was willing to join him back at the station to greet them. But they would need to make one quick stop en route.

In a summer of rebellious gesture and political spectacle—African-American athletes receiving their Olympic medals in black gloves, raising their fists in Mexico City as "The Star-Spangled Banner" played; a sheep done up in ribbons and bows and a public burning of bras and girdles at the Miss America pageant in Atlantic City; the theatrics of Abbie Hoffman, Jerry Rubin, and Myra Breckenridge—Glaze was a man in his element. The stop he had in mind was to empty out a nearby flower shop owned by a gay man. "We made up some hasty-ass bouquets," Glaze said, and arrived at the sergeant's desk—two dozen gay men, arms loaded with mums, daisies, carnations, roses, gladioli—"and said, 'We are here to wait for our imprisoned sisters!' " And wait they did. The police took their time about processing the offenders, who weren't released until five A.M., at which time they were loudly cheered and presented with the flowers.

All did not end happily, however. "We won the battle," Glaze noted—intimidation within the bar ended—"but we lost the war." The police "made it sheer hell" for customers leaving the Patch, stopping their cars, writing down license numbers, and in many ways behaving more threateningly than the tire slashers. A short time later, the club relocated and became Patch II. Troy Perry, for one, was not inclined to minimize the episode, though, as an event isolated from a wider questioning about self-worth and fundamental rights. "Showing up as a group at the police station to say, 'We'll wait for our friends you have illegally brought here' was a response the L.A. police weren't used to. They looked startled. Before, people would take off and be glad it wasn't them. This was a response *we* weren't used to, and that was Lee's doing." A month later, Perry placed his ad for the Sunday service that evolved into the Metropolitan Community Church.

Another change indicative of the time had to do with the way news of this kind was communicated. In years past, neither Lee Glaze's botanical protest nor Troy Perry's wish to meet other gay Christians for prayer would have spread much beyond their own circle of friends and acquaintances. The mainstream press restricted its coverage to pedophiles, psychiatric reports, and formal bar raids and never ran ads with a gay content. The founding in September 1967 of *The Advocate*, at the time a monthly known as the *Los Angeles Advocate*, meant that gay readers finally had a newspaper of their own. Perry found a meaningful point of contact, and Glaze's display of nerve had an audience of several thousand men who never set foot in his bar. The two-page article in the September *Advocate*, headlined "PATCH" RAIDS POLICE STATION, speculated that "if the reaction of [Lee Glaze's customers] is any indication, a new era of determined resistance may be dawning for L.A.'s gay community." Its editorial was entitled "Courage Catches On." The photo of beaming faces and waving gladioli was captioned "Flower Power."

CHICAGO: AUGUST 1968

Several days before the Democratic National Convention opened in Mayor Daley's hometown to nominate Hubert Humphrey and to witness a police rampage in the streets, a smaller convention met in Chicago for a similar purpose: to declare a unity that didn't exist and to put a positive face on a future that the delegates could not predict, control, or even significantly influence. The 1968 meeting of NACHO—the North American Conference of Homophile Organizations—marked the fifth time gay rights groups from around the country had gathered at one site to plot their course, and the parliamentary wrangling and behind-the-scenes name-calling had only worsened with each year. "The greatest issue at the Chicago conference," Stephen Donaldson wrote in *The Advocate* in October, "one that took up a day and a half of floor time and two days of committee time, was the set of by-laws recommended by a divided Unity Committee. These were tabled and taken from the table more often than Mother's coffee cups."

Donaldson's account in *The Advocate* had a satiric edge, though the comedy arose simply from the writer's deadpan chronicle of endless roll calls, procedural fights, speeches, motions, committee reports, and haggling over minutiae. Just to be admitted to voting status, a local or regional group had to be painstakingly vetted by Foster Gunnison's Credentials Committee, a process that many found high-handed. (Gunnison's minutes of his committee's deliberations—sixty typed pages, single-spaced—were legendary documents, impressive to those who wanted to keep radical or "fringe" groups out of NACHO and galling to those who favored more openness. The irony was that some organizations given official status represented no one beyond their founders. The Circle of Loving Companions in Los Angeles consisted primarily of Harry Hay, now intermittently back in the movement, and his lover, while Foster Gunnison *was* the Institute for Social Ethics of Hartford, Connecticut.) Disagreements about the direction of the movement, which the very existence of a credentials committee spoke to—militants vs. ameliorists, activists vs. educationists, hippies vs. ties-and-jackets, men vs. women—were getting nasty, and longtime allies found themselves not speaking to one another.

Looked at from one angle, NACHO in 1968 could claim to have accomplished a good deal, shaking off the dust of 1950s homophile reserve. A Homosexual Bill of Rights had been adopted, and its tone was clear and forceful. Five basic demands were articulated—the legalization of private consensual sex acts among adults, an end to police solicitation, equal opportunity in employment, unrestricted service in the armed forces, and (in matters of citizenship) security clearances and the granting of visas—and ten "areas for immediate reform" were listed. The slogan "Gay Is Good," promoted by Barbara Gittings and Frank Kameny, was accepted as the movement's motto, a cheery allusion to the successful public relations of "Black Is Beautiful." Yet few of the 135 delegates left Chicago satisfied. The Daughters of Bilitis resented the push for a unified national organization and a powerful board, and let it be known that it would not be part of any NACHO proceedings in the future. SIR delegates, representing the largest gay group in the country, bitterly complained that no one in NACHO wanted to discuss direct action. Everyone worried that New York Mattachine, the nation's second largest group, had boycotted the convention altogether. Not only was a single charismatic leader not emerging from these sessions, but the danger of splintering and stagnation grew as membership in the various organizations slowly increased. "After a while, it was like the one-minute egg and the two-minute egg factions in *Gulliver's Travels*," a delegate recalled. The fervor with which beliefs were held overshadowed the issues themselves.

"Gay Is Good" signaled a determined step away from timidity and self-hate, but the tenor of social protest outside NACHO was taking a different form. Stephen Donaldson, a protégé of Frank Kameny and the founder a year earlier of the Student Homophile League at Columbia University (the first gay group on a college campus), was one of many participants acutely aware of the gap. He had been at Morningside Heights for the takeover of the campus that spring. "I relished the internal politics" of NACHO, Donaldson admitted. "It appealed to me, the machinations—and I liked being the young radical from New York. But of course it wasn't Columbia. Students were closing down a major institution. Blacks and women were becoming really loud, disruptive . . . radicalized. That wasn't happening in gay politics, not like that, not yet." The conditions to encourage that loudness, disruptiveness, and radicalism were, however, falling into place.

FORT BELVOIR, VIRGINIA: NOVEMBER 1968

Throughout the 1950s and 1960s, the Defense Department had spent vast sums of money to ferret out and discharge gay men and lesbians in the military. This policy overlooked the three extensive reviews conducted by the Navy (in 1948, 1952, and 1957) that found no evidence that homosexuals were unfit to serve. But Vietnam, changing everything else about America, was changing that, too.

The Tet Offensive in January had brought Viet Cong soldiers to the front yard of the American Embassy in Saigon and shattered confidence in the war effort among everyone but die-hard hawks. Walter Cronkite confessed his uncertainties to millions of viewers on the *CBS Evening News*, while the *New York Times* suggested that, after years of government statements about a weakened enemy, "the American people have been pushed to the limits of gullibility." Yet even as support for the war eroded overnight in Congress and in the heartland of America, General Westmoreland was telling President Johnson that he would need another 200,000 troops to bring into focus that much-discussed "light at the end of the tunnel." Homosexuals, it turned out, were not such a threat to morale and combat readiness. "The exigencies of wartime," as Randy Shilts wrote in *Conduct Unbecoming*, "overrode the military's usual antipathy for those with nonconforming sexual orientations." The 1,600 enlisted men and women regularly discharged by the Navy each year had dropped to half that number in 1968, to 643 the next year, and to 461 in 1969. Not since the Korean War had the government been willing to turn so blind an eye to what, under other circumstances, was anathema. Gay soldiers returning from Southeast Asia told friends of a hectic gay subculture in Saigon and other cities—a nightworld of bars, clubs, and illicit relationships flourishing right under the noses of the brass, who were oblivious or uninterested.

Perry Watkins's friends in Tacoma were surprised by his induction into the Army in May, four months after Tet. Even at Lincoln High School, Watkins had been out. He had to listen to the usual comments, more from other black students than his white classmates, but in general had been left to go his own way. When he received his draft notice, it never occurred to him to lie. The two psychiatrists he spoke to didn't seem concerned. Questioned about his sexuality that fall by the commandant at Fort Hamilton in Brooklyn, Watkins acknowledged yet again that he was gay and had had sex with other young men. The result of that interview was Watkins's transfer to Virginia; denied permission to be a chaplain's assistant, the job he wanted, he was told he would be given work as a clerk-typist. "I'm too queer to be a chaplain's assistant, but I'm not too queer to be in the Army," Watkins marveled. Though his case was destined to become a famous one in the tangled history of gay servicemen and the U.S. military (earning him the label of "the Rosa Parks of gay soldiers"), Watkins had no strong feelings yet about wanting a discharge. It was galling, though, to learn that the white gay men he met had no trouble getting out of the military once they admitted their homosexuality. Black gay servicemen were given the runaround.

At his new post, Fort Belvoir, an anomalous situation quickly became a nightmare. On a Sunday afternoon in November, five soldiers approached Watkins in the empty barracks, told him they had heard he was a faggot, and demanded oral sex. When he refused, they became belligerent. He successfully fought them off with a ferocity that surprised them and himself. Then, in a rage, Watkins went to see his new commanding officer. Now he wanted out. "You put me in here knowing I'm gay," he told him, "and it's your job to protect me." The Army Criminal Investigation Division did in fact begin to take him seriously at that point and began an investigation—not of the men who had tried to rape him, but of Watkins himself. They concluded there was insufficient evidence to accept Private Watkins's characterization of himself as homosexual and so he would remain in the military, where he was needed in this year of crisis. Too many young men were declaring themselves homosexual to avoid serving their country in Pleiku and Danang. Watkins let it be known in the barracks that if anyone attempted to molest him again, he wouldn't fight them off. He would kill them in the middle of the night when they were asleep.

NEW ORLEANS: MARCH 1969

The assassination of John F. Kennedy in 1963 marked the end of one form of American innocence—murdered presidents were taken to be a reality abroad, in the distant "Third World," but not in the United States. Modern political violence was brought home even more emphatically in 1968 with the shooting of Martin Luther King, Jr., and Robert Kennedy. Yet the deaths of King and the younger Kennedy possessed a clarity that the Dallas tragedy did not. Skepticism about the Warren Commission Report lingered, grew, and took on a life of its own. Pat answers and unexamined leads that were accepted by a trusting nation in 1964 became further proof that governments told lies and manipulated their citizens. A Harris poll in 1969 indicated that a majority of Americans did not believe the full story of the assassination had been told. That number included elected officials. In 1967, New Orleans District Attorney James Garrison, a master manipulator himself, found in gay businessman Clay Shaw a vehicle for three distinct ends: a high-profile critique of the Warren Report's lone assassin premise, a national forum for his own political ambitions, and—of least consequence to many of the people involved—another means of keeping the New Orleans gay community in line. The Shaw case came to trial early in 1969.

From the beginning of his tenure as district attorney, Jim Garrison had made several things clear. He was a man with no tolerance for the increasingly public nature of gay bars and gay street life (homosexuals openly congregating were in the same category as the Bourbon Street strippers and prostitutes he went after), he was not a person to cross, and he rarely backed down or acknowledged an error. By 1966 the future Frank Capra–style hero of Oliver Stone's film *JFK* was sifting through the glaring inconsistencies of the Warren Report and following up the oddest of leads. When he came upon David Ferrie, a gay drifter alleged to have known Lee Harvey Oswald (Ferrie was also a pedophile, part-time pornographer, and self-professed bishop of "the Old Catholic Church of North America"), he was convinced he was on to something. A person variously named "Clem Bertrand" and "Clay Bertrand" was mentioned, by an informant of even more doubtful veracity than Ferrie, as having known both Oswald and Ferrie. Ferrie died of a heart attack while Garrison's investigation was in its early stages, but the death of his original untapped source was not an obstacle. Garrison soon announced he had found the mysterious Clem or Clay Bertrand who had conspired to kill the president with the late David Ferrie, and that his real name was Clay Shaw.

The announcement left most residents and civic leaders stunned. A man like Clay Shaw—a Kennedy Democrat, no less—seemed an unlikely conspirator. Whatever his private life, about which he was always discreet, Shaw was a respected figure in the community, a decorated veteran of World War II and a patron of the arts, an exemplar of the New South. He was a courtly, affable, modest man who had been a guiding force behind the preservation movement in the French Quarter and the development of the International Trade Mart, both of which had had a favorable impact on local revenues. When he retired in 1965 in order to write and travel, the city awarded him the International Order of Merit, its highest honor. But, as local reporters Rosemary James and Jack Wardlaw astutely noted in their 1967 review of the case, *Plot or Politics?*, the brashness of Garrison's manner had the power to take root in the collective unconscious of the city. "A man like Clay Shaw"—what did that mean, when you came down to it? Jim Garrison was a known entity in the land of Huey Long—straight, married, ambitious, arrogant, anti–Washington establishment. Did a normal citizen, a family man, reading of Garrison's extravagant charges know what the world of any homosexual entailed, the secrets and associations it might encompass? The judge who was to preside at the trial touched on this line of thought when he remarked to an out-of-town writer, "Queers know queers. . . . They've got a clique better than the CIA." In Clay Shaw, then, Garrison had a perfect straw figure: wealthy and smart enough to be a major player in a complicated plot (unlike the "little man," the tawdry David Ferrie), but not above suspicion as a fifty-two-year-old bachelor who lived in a tastefully furnished carriage house and aspired to be a playwright. Though the ACLU of Louisiana and newspapers across the country attacked the investigation as a travesty of justice, Garrison was betting that no one in Baton Rouge or Washington would stop him. That would mean speaking up on behalf of "a man whose private life made him vulnerable," as *The New Republic* delicately put it. *Look* magazine was equally genteel about the object of Jim Garrison's fishing expedition. Clay Shaw was "a prominent man with a weakness."

The case was heard by Edward Haggerty, a judge with a reputation "for liking his spirits not infrequently spaced" (this was a trial to set new records for reportorial euphemism), who was arrested later that year in a raid on a motel room stag party. Two obvious homosexuals were excused in the voir dire amid grins and chuckles, and the jury was lectured about wearing ties and looking neat, as Judge Haggerty "didn't want 'em lookin' like the Scopes trial." Yet the parade to the witness stand of eccentrics, chatterboxes, busybodies, publicity seekers, perjurors, and near-psychotics in February 1969 went far beyond anything seen in the Scopes trial. Garrison's case, it turned out, was built on the testimony of scandalously unreliable sources: a jailed narcotics addict angling for a parole deal, a man who regularly fingerprinted his daughter to be sure she had not been replaced by a double, a postman indebted to Garrison who was able to swear he had delivered mail in the French Quarter to "Clem Bertrand" (and to any other name any lawyer threw at him), an attorney who admitted on the stand that he was making up his version of events as he went along, a policeman whom the judge himself called a liar from the bench, and an elderly handwriting expert who studied evidence with her binoculars. Garrison's chief witness, Perry Russo, was so inconsistent as to be useless. Garrison's closing remarks dealt with fighting for truth, the Zapruder film, and the sinister nature of big government, with only a single passing reference to the defendant—and no mention of why the defendant would have wanted to kill Kennedy. Pershing Gervais, a former investigator with Garrison's office, acknowledged to a reporter, "All of that bullshit doesn't mean a thing. Who's right or who's wrong—this is New Orleans!"

Feeling against the Warren Commission and the undercurrent of suspicion about homosexuals in general was strong enough to suggest that Shaw might still be found guilty, but the jury returned from its speedy deliberations on March 1 with an acquittal. Judge Haggerty was heard to comment that he had won a nickel on a bet that the jury would be back in court in sixty minutes flat. The *States-Item* demanded Garrison's resignation. The president of the American Bar Association said that he hoped the Louisiana Bar Association would take action against the district attorney for the "charade" he had perpetrated in a court of law. *Look* entitled its August article "The Persecution of Clay Shaw." But Garrison did not resign and was not censured. He was reelected in November, though that election proved to be his last. In February 1970 Jack Anderson reported in his nationally syndicated column a thirteen-year-old boy's accusation that Jim Garrison had fondled the boy's genitals at the New Orleans Athletic Club.

Clay Shaw returned to his French Quarter home after his acquittal a relieved, if shaken, man. He declined to issue any vindictive statements against his accuser. Two days later, on March 3, 1969, Garrison arrested him again, this time on a trumped-up charge of perjury. Almost a year would pass before Shaw could get a federal court order ending Garrison's tenacious harassment. One of the most prominent gay men of the South was by then exhausted and financially ruined. As a gay resident of Louisiana at the time remarked, "We got the point."

LOS ANGELES: MARCH 1969

The Dover was a hotel for indigents, transients, and men who signed the guest book with an alias if they were there with a trick. At one in the morning on March 9, Howard Efland, a slightly built nurse who had registered under the name "J. McCann," was dragged handcuffed and screaming from his second-floor room. Other residents of the hotel came out into the halls to see two vice officers holding Efland down while a third kicked and beat him and then jumped with his full weight on his stomach. One of them shouted at the witnesses, "Get the fuck away! It's none of your business!" A hotel clerk called the police, who arrived as Efland was being thrown, still alive at the time, into an unmarked car. The exact hour, or even the date of his death, was never made clear.

Gay men of the Los Angeles area turned out in large numbers at the inquest, only to learn that Efland's embarrassed family had not retained a lawyer to represent them and that the district attorney's office was uninterested in the testimony of the witnesses. The police version of events—that the vice officers had seen Efland fondling another man in his room and that Efland had groped one of the officers when he entered—was taken as unquestioned fact. The coroner's jury ruled Efland's demise an "excusable homicide" as a result of injuries sustained while resisting arrest. "The family of the deceased will not press charges against the police," a reporter for *The Advocate* wrote, "and no civil rights organizations have expressed an interest in the matter." But *The Advocate* itself had something to say. An editorial advised homosexuals to attend inquests in the future, to see what the LAPD got away with. "Frequent attendance at such whitewash parties might even make the homosexual community less passive in the face of the shit the cops dish out in the name of law and order." In the spring of 1969, in a groundswell of liberalism, courts, legislatures, and civil service commissions in several states began reevaluating archaic laws governing the existence of gay bars, loitering statutes, and restrictions on the states' employment of known homosexuals. Police departments were having none of it.

The following March, in full vestments, Reverend Troy Perry led 120 gay men and lesbians to the Dover Hotel to commemorate the first anniversary of Howard Efland's murder. Their message: We will take notice. We will remember.

SAN FRANCISCO: APRIL 1969

One of the many journalists who witnessed the assault of Mayor Richard Daley's police force on the Grant Park protestors in Chicago at the Democratic National Convention and came away sickened by the violence was a California reporter named Leo Laurence. Laurence's transformation from a political moderate into a countercultural radical was more far-reaching than that of his peers, however. He became a biting critic of mainstream politics and bourgeois America, gay or straight. Several months later, in the spring of 1969, the thirty-six-year-old writer with the Honest Abe beard was elected to the nonpaying but still influential editorship of *Vector*, the monthly journal started by the Society for Individual Rights. It was not a marriage made in heaven. SIR's declining membership was middle-class and unflamboyant; Laurence's was the spirit of Haight-Ashbury and Woodstock. In his brief time as editor of *Vector*, he managed to alienate a sizable number of the magazine's traditional readers and many of its allies. In his columns, he lashed out at the Tavern Guild, calling it a racist alliance of white bar owners. He favored a Clark Polak approach to the visuals in the magazine. He attacked the failure of more established gay leaders to align themselves with the cause of countercultural revolution. He had a take-no-prisoners attitude toward men who, in the interest of keeping their employers and parents happy, declined to use their real names and pictures in the gay press.

Laurence and his lover, Gale Whittington, a twenty-one-year-old accounting clerk with the States Steamship Company, had no qualms about putting into full practice what they preached. To that end, Whittington posed for the April cover of *Vector* in torn shorts with a come-hither look and a bed in the background, and the two men posed for the *Berkeley Barb*, an alternative newspaper, effectively announcing their status as a couple. Whittington, with a hairless high school boy's chest, posed shirtless. Laurence, looking like a gay Abraham Lincoln, stood snugly behind him with a wide grin, a rapt gaze, and his arms around his boyfriend's waist. It was a puppy-love image—a little daffy, more tender than hardcore sexual—seen countless times each week by Americans flipping through magazines, glancing at advertisements, or watching a movie, but in this case both figures were male and that made all the difference. The San Francisco–based freighter line that employed Whittington saw the photo and promptly fired him. The two men then organized what they called the Committee for Homosexual Freedom, a group of several good friends who agreed to participate in a daily noontime picketing of the steamship downtown offices. For several days, they carried signs reading "States Line Hates Homos," "Freedom for Homos Now," and "Let Gays Live." The company refused comment and refused to reinstate Whittington. Laurence lost his day job as a reporter for KGO Radio a short time later.

The directors of SIR were also at the end of their patience. They were dismayed by Laurence's arrogance and what they saw as his exhibitionism. Though *Vector* had evolved into an independent publication far beyond its origins as SIR's newsletter, the funding still came from SIR, and their renegade editor was given the boot that spring. "The SIR leadership and the Tavern Guild couldn't take the heat," Laurence told *The Advocate*, "so they decided to hang me." The leadership of the gay movement was nothing but "a bunch of middle-class, uptight, bitchy old queens," he went on to say, and he, for one, welcomed their passing. They would be supplanted by tougher men who used their own names, proclaimed their affections to the world, and didn't ask for their rights but demanded them. Laurence left the editorial limelight, though, on an interesting note of prophecy. His last column for *Vector* in April—two months before Stonewall—stated that "the only people with that kind of courage [to say 'I'm gay and I'm proud!'] are the new breed of young kids. The old-timers are scared that these kids will come in and really create a gay revolution."

COLUMBUS, OHIO: MAY 1969

The trial of nineteen-year-old James Allen Stitt was quick, like the death of Emil Zbinden the previous fall, and not at all in the Clay Shaw league for high courtroom drama. In the end, despite the fact that the story made the front page in many Ohio newspapers, there was nothing much to say about it on the editorial page. A gay man was shot dead. His murderer was given a fresh start.

In September 1968, forty-eight-year-old Emil Zbinden approached Stitt to go fishing with him. Stitt agreed, taking with him a .32-caliber revolver. As he later told police, he was aware from a previous meeting that Zbinden was a homosexual. Stitt's brother suggested that he keep the date and take the queer for whatever he could. Zbinden's body, stripped of identification, was found on the bank of a creek outside town near Route 23. Stitt was located the next month in Daytona Beach, Florida, where he was hiding out with Zbinden's car. The district attorney felt he had a good case: a motive, a weapon, a confession of premeditation and of the shooting itself. The defense attorney described the older man's "immoral advances" to the unwilling younger man. The case went to the jury on May 29, 1969. The next day Stitt was free.

NEW YORK CITY: JUNE 1969

Like most gay bars in major cities in the 1960s, the Stonewall Inn at 53 Christopher Street just east of Seventh Avenue in Manhattan was raided with some regularity. The more-or-less monthly event was usually announced to the bar's Mafia management in advance. It consisted of a check for IDs; the removal or arrest of any patrons who were without an ID, not wearing three items of clothing "appropriate to their gender," or were obviously underage; and some predictable scattering of police insults among the clientele and staff. Everyone would be hustled out into the street and the bar shut down. As this display of authority often occurred early in the evening (that is, if the owners' payoffs to the local precinct captain and desk sergeants had been punctual), the bar could be back in operation for its peak business hours after midnight.

What went wrong during the night of June 27–28 has never been fully determined. The notoriously corrupt Sixth Precinct had been receiving its $2,000 a week without any problem for the three years the bar had been a gay hangout in Greenwich Village, but Mario, Zucchi, and Fat Tony Luccia—the three mobsters who owned the bar, the last of whom was gay himself and reportedly killed later by the mob—apparently hadn't been told of the planned police action. Speculation about this break with tradition takes four discrete paths: the new captain at the Sixth didn't think much of the arrangement; a payment had been missed; the Stonewall's profits, higher of late, warranted a larger payoff and a show of muscle was part of the negotiation; or the Sixth Precinct hadn't scheduled the raid but had been ordered to at the last minute by the Bureau of Alcohol, Tobacco, and Firearms, which was investigating the Stonewall's bootleg supply of beverages.

The Stonewall was an unlikely setting for a climactic moment in modern gay history. Generally described by those who frequented it as a dive where the drinks were watered and the lack of running water to clean the glasses created a serious health hazard, it nonetheless attracted a diverse crowd. The Village had its specialty bars—Keller's for leathermen, the Washington Square for transvestites, Julius's for men over thirty-five, the Ninth Circle for hustler pickups—but at the Stonewall, the "fluffy sweater types . . . the giggle girls" (as Dick Leitsch termed them) mixed with the "chino-and-penny-loafer crowd" (in Martin Duberman's phrase), a handful of young men in "scare drag" (almost never in full drag), and occasionally a few hippies and lesbians. The interior was painted charcoal black, though the dimly lighted space could suddenly be "lit up like Luna Park" when the police sauntered in. A doorman exercised right of refusal, and signing your name, or some name, in a book by the door was required to preserve the fiction that the Stonewall was a private "bottle club." For three dollars on weekends, a patron got two tickets for two drinks. From time to time, an underdressed go-go boy would dance in a cage atop the bar.

The trouble began shortly after one A.M. on June 28. The timing itself suggested problems, coming as late as it did, and when several detectives (two of whom were women) arrived, there was a feeling in the bar that something was amiss. Zucchi and Mario were out the back door in an instant, the bartenders gathered the cash from the cigar boxes and left their posts to blend in with the crowd, and everyone else prepared to run the ID gauntlet at the front door. "As some of the gays came out of the bar, they would take a bow and their friends would cheer," Morty Manford recalled.

A crowd had gathered rather quickly, applauding and heckling. Lucian Truscott IV, a *Village Voice* reporter on the scene, thought that the spectators assembling along Christopher Street and in Sheridan Square Park easily numbered four hundred—a festive but skittish group. (The emotional dimension of what has been called "the Judy Factor" should be noted here: some of the men in the crowd that night had been part of the throng lining Madison Avenue earlier in the week to pay their last respects to the great gay icon Judy Garland—but as Bob Kohler, a longtime Village resident and astute observer, commented, it would be foolish to make too much of this coincidence. The street kids he knew, who made up the better part of the mob on Christopher Street, were not the type to moon over Judy Garland records or attend her concerts at Carnegie Hall. They were more preoccupied with where they were going to sleep and where their next meal would come from.)

The exact spark that ignited the riot has been lost over the years in a welter of contradictory eyewitness accounts. Some people insist that a cross-dressing lesbian struck in the head by a policeman provoked those who saw the attack to turn on the police. Others contend that an occupant of the paddy wagon who managed to jump out and was immediately caught again inspired a reaction. Craig Rodwell, whose bookstore was just down the street, spoke to Martin Duberman about the simultaneous incidents that people were observing, which resulted in "a flash of group—of mass—anger." Suddenly pennies were being thrown at the cops. "You already got the payoff, but here's some more," drag queen Sylvia Rivera started yelling. Beer cans, rocks, and bottles followed the coins. To the loud cry of "Fuck the pigs!" and "Motherfuckers!" the paddy wagon sped away, while the remaining detectives, surprised at the unruliness of people they usually controlled without any problem, took refuge back in the Stonewall. Several men on the street uprooted a broken parking meter and began smashing at the thick wood door of the bar. The detectives responded by opening the door and turning on the crowd a fire hose taken from the back of the bar, but the thin stream of water was more comical than injurious. Its only effect was to impress everyone on both sides of the street with the vulnerability of the police. The parking meter was sent crashing through the front window in the next minute, and the men and women inside drew their pistols. A spray of lighter fluid came through the broken window, then several lighted matches, starting a small, quickly extinguished blaze. The first attacker to get past the door, Inspector Seymour Pine admitted later, would have been shot dead. A 10–41 emergency call for help was made.

The arrival of a phalanx of the Tactical Patrol Force, the helmeted and fully armed riot-control squad of the NYPD, raised tensions still higher but did nothing to diminish the size or fury of the mob. Given the winding, nongrid pattern of Greenwich Village streets, any group of hecklers or bottle tossers forced to move had only to dart around the block and reassemble to the side or rear of the TPF. On and on it went: the taunting on both sides grew more belligerent, trash cans were set ablaze, traffic came to a standstill, police cars were pelted with rubbish, and when a pair of cops chased their quarry down a smaller side street and discovered themselves suddenly outnumbered, it was their turn to retreat, panicked by the shouts of "Catch them! Rip their fucking clothes off! Fuck them!"

"The cops got what they gave," Stormé DeLarverie pronounced later. A Rockettes-style chorus line added a camp note as the assembled queens belted out a more audacious version of "Gay Is Good":

> *We are the Stonewall girls*
> *We wear our hair in curls*
> *We wear no underwear*
> *We show our pubic hair . . .*
> *We wear our dungarees*
> *Above our nelly knees!*

The chaos didn't end until almost four in the morning, by which time one policeman had suffered a broken wrist, four others claimed injuries from kicks and bites, thirteen people from the bar were in jail, and an unknown number of men and women had been beaten bloody with nightsticks. A young man reportedly lost two fingers when a car door was slammed on his hand.

Splendid, frightening, distressing, and carnival-like as the confrontation had been, the true meaning of the Stonewall riot took shape after daylight on Saturday as the participants gathered to survey the ruin of the bar, which had been vandalized front to back by the enraged police when they took cover there, and to talk about the impact of the riot on their state of mind. As a one-time incident, it would soon be forgotten, but there was an urgent feeling that the momentum of resistance should not be lost. It had been reflected the night before in the shouts of Jerry Hoose, a nineteen-year-old from Brooklyn, who kept screaming, "To City Hall! Let's march on City Hall!"—an idea, he later observed, that wouldn't have accomplished much at three in the morning—and in the anger Sylvia Rivera couldn't contain that compelled her to wander the streets long after everyone else went home to bed, setting trash cans on fire and cursing the police. It had been an element of the high-kicking chorus line Vito Russo and his friends staged—the ultimate fuck-you to the big brave men with the shields and the billyclubs—and in Jim Fouratt's unsuccessful efforts to rouse his straight radical friends to join him in the square in standing up to the authorities. "We had been treated so badly for so long by the cops in the Village," Hoose remembered. "You'd be standing on Greenwich Avenue talking with your friends and they'd come along, 'Let's get moving, girls.' You weren't a person to them, you weren't a citizen like anybody else. They felt they could talk to you any way they damned pleased. After the riot, we were overcome with this sense of, '*Enough*, damn it. It's got to stop now.' " Once seriously challenged, authority is hardly ever regarded in the same light: "I remember thinking, when it was over," Dario Modan told an interviewer in 1994, "that I'd never have to be afraid again."

So the crowds were back on Saturday night, milling about, as was the Tactical Patrol Force, stationed across the street from the Stonewall and obviously spoiling for a fight. But the civilians—gay and straight, the curious and the rowdy—were far more numerous than the night before, and they had no intention of going home when they were told. A nightstick was poked into someone's ribs, a bottle was thrown, Marsha P. Johnson (a black drag queen and friend of Sylvia Rivera's) smashed the windshield of a police car by throwing a package down from her perch on a lamppost, and the violence of the previous day was set in motion again. This time, according to some accounts, the TPF acted even more randomly and aggressively, clubbing anyone in reach. On Sunday, the Stonewall Inn reopened for business, despite the fact that the police had broken every mirror, ripped out every phone, and plugged up every toilet in the place thirty-six hours earlier, and on Monday and Tuesday nights, the rain prevented anything more than sporadic demonstrations of gay rage and police indignation. Wednesday, July 2, however, provided a third and final opportunity for a clash, and more insults were exchanged between police and homosexuals, more trash cans set ablaze and rocks thrown, more men beaten and taken off to jail. "There was no way," commented Doric Wilson, who had been on the spot all five nights, "that this could simply come to an end. There was too much energy and anger involved. Too many people were fired up."

The mythology of the riot assumed a formidable character by the time of its tenth, twentieth, and twenty-fifth anniversaries—as Eric Marcus has suggested, can Andrew Lloyd-Webber's *Stonewall: The Musical* be far behind?—and, in its crudest form, implies that gay life in America was immediately and dramatically transformed one summer night. In reality, most gay men and lesbians in the United States did not hear anything about Stonewall until years later, if only because the media outside New York City did not cover the riot. For wealthy or middle-class gay men, the antic life of Greenwich Village queens was never a topic of interest, anyway, and their street activism didn't register as important in 1969—"Not so much as a blip on the screen," Marvin Liebman commented. Nor did a word about the riot reach Paul Monette that summer, teaching at a Connecticut prep school only seventy miles away. As was the case with many otherwise thoughtful people, the connection for Monette between his antiwar work and homosexual rights was nil: "My leftist politics stopped at the closet door." Others who later assumed important positions in the modern gay rights movement learned of the riot only after joining the various political groups that rose from the event. In *Farm Boys* (1996), Will Fellows's oral history of gay men from the rural Midwest, the word *Stonewall* never appears in a single interview. Indeed, in the 1990s, it is possible to meet gay men in many parts of the country who identify as gay and have always been in the life, but who have only the sketchiest associations with an incident they perceive as a much-hyped, slightly confusing Manhattan story.

In New York City, though, "the hairpin drop heard round the world," as Dick Leitsch called the riot in his July column in the Mattachine Society newsletter, did excite mention, by degrees. The *New York Times*, always uncomfortable with gay news, waited until Sunday to place a six-paragraph article on page 33, which emphasized the threat to law and order ("Four Policemen Hurt in Village Raid . . ."). Truscott's flamboyant *Village Voice* account appeared on July 2. A full week after the riot, the *Daily News* followed up its original article with a more sarcastic piece entitled "Homo Nest Raided, Queen Bees Stinging Mad" and, on July 8, the *Post* carried its own patronizing version of events, which at least made an effort to establish some context for its readers. "People are beginning to realize," the Stonewall's doorman was quoted by the *Post* reporter, "that no matter how 'nelly' or how 'fem' a homosexual is, you can only push them so far." Later in July, Jack Nichols and Lige Clarke referred excitedly to "the revolution in Sheridan Square" in their column on homosexual news in Al Goldstein's sex tabloid *Screw*. They expressed the hope, similar to Doric Wilson's, that June 28 was merely the start of something momentous and quoted Allen Ginsberg's remark, upon the reopening of the bar, about the beauty of the young men at the Stonewall Inn: "They've lost that wounded look that fags all had ten years ago."

The start of something momentous, but it was also the end of several groups and rituals—several ideas about gay rights—whose time had passed: the mood at the Annual Reminder in Philadelphia on the Fourth of July was the first sign of the change. A precise, orderly demonstration in front of a national landmark struck many angry gay men and lesbians as too decorous and mild-mannered an endeavor. The New Yorkers were especially annoyed by the still-honored dress code rules, and when two women broke out of the single-file line to march together holding hands, Frank Kameny's demand that they walk separately was met with quiet rage. Several participants assumed, rightly as it turned out, that this would be the last of the civil rights–era Independence Hall gatherings. Back in New York, in San Francisco and in Los Angeles, a more aggressive group of younger gay men and lesbians, who had never heard of NACHO and were largely indifferent to SIR or Mattachine, were meeting to figure out how to make use of the "fire in the streets" that the homeless kids, the drag queens, the "giggle girls," and the all-round pissed-off queers and dykes had set in motion.

V. GAY AWAKENINGS

18

THE NEW ACTIVISM

If the best the liberal establishment wants to offer us is its traditional defense—leave them alone, they're sick, not criminal—we will show them that no dream for a new America can exclude us.

> —Marty Robinson, "Homosexuals and Society:
> The 'Cure' Is Rebellion," *Village Voice*,
> 29 April 1971

For all their straightforward drama, the new ideas about what it meant to be gay in America that were developed and articulated by the men and women of "gay liberation" represented a juggling act. *Gay* definitively replaced the more clinical *homosexual*, *pride* was the watchword of the day, and *coming out*—to the world as well as to yourself and your gay friends—became the cornerstone of the liberation process. Yet even as the wonders of embracing a contentious label were broadcast far and wide, acknowledgment had to be made that any labeling, even self-labeling, was problematic. "Saying 'I am proud to be a homosexual,' " complained gay activist Thane Hampten, was in the same league as saying "I am proud to drink water" or "I urinate, therefore I am." Many of his militant brethren in groups such as the Gay Liberation Front also doubted the wisdom of perpetuating a category that implied a separateness from the rest of humanity. Mattachine founder Harry Hay talked now, with great passion, about "a gay people" and a special brotherhood that avoided imitating the "heteros." But others argued that a higher goal was to render all such designations meaningless. A vocal gay identity in 1970 was more in the nature of an expediency, according to this line of thought, which would lead to an era in which everyone would realize his potential to love and lust in myriad ways. The disappearance of "the homosexual," as Dennis Altman wrote in *Homosexual: Oppression and Liberation* (1971), was the promised end, bringing with it the demise of heterosexual absolutism as well.

At the same time, the label itself was being energetically recast. To be gay and out after Stonewall meant establishing a distance from the earlier stereotypes of meekness and frailty, of pansies who wouldn't hit back. Some liberationists looked to Che, the Young Lords, and the Black Panthers for inspiration. Yet two paradoxes came into play here. One was that a self-congratulatory toughness was perceived by many militants, not only the women, in a skeptical light. Swaggering gay men mimicked the oppressor; there was a fine line between the gutsiness of the street fighter in work boots and the bluster of a John Wayne. The other paradox concerned the place of the drag queen in this new phase of the movement. A rejection of hypermasculinity, as it turned out, did not mean a wholehearted welcome for men in heels and mascara. "We were tolerated at best," Sylvia Rivera insisted. "We made everybody uncomfortable, gay or straight, radical or conservative. That didn't change overnight with Stonewall." Indeed, some gay theorists were ready to predict the demise of the drag queen, too, as role-playing was consigned to the dustbin of gender history.

Likewise, attitudes toward sex became more complicated than the rhetoric implied. No more furtiveness, no more sex-negative judgments: everyone in the new generation of activists could agree on that. At its most extreme (or honest), the belief in polymorphous ecstasy could take the form of Charles Shivley's writing in the Boston paper *Fag Rag*, founded in 1971. His series, "Cocksucking as an Act of Revolution," took aim at gay men as well as straight, at those who were squeamish about group sex, paid homage only to the young and pretty, and secretly upheld the prejudice that to be sucked was manly while to suck was degraded. But guilts bred in childhood and adolescence were not to be dismissed at will, nor was there any agreement about the appropriate sites for all of this revolutionary, nondiscriminatory cocksucking. One side of the debate, circa 1969–1973, asked if it were giving in to the system—an objectifying, commercially based, affection-destroying system—to pick up tricks in a bar, cruise the parks like hunters, patronize the baths, hang out at truck stops or tearooms. The other side of the argument pointed to gay male sexual freedoms (wherever they were exercised) as part of the critique of marriage, monogamy, the double standard, hypocrisy, and sexual possessiveness that gay liberation was uniquely qualified to lead, now that feminism and the counterculture had paved the way. From this perspective, civil rights had always been a limited goal. A true liberation movement aimed to remake, not reform, society.

Finally, to achieve the kind of progress gay liberation had in mind, or even to keep the debate going, it was necessary to do more than create a stir in the present and envision a far different future. It was also necessary to rewrite the past. As the story went now, men and women of the pre-Stonewall years were full-time denizens of "the closet" (a metaphor whose day had arrived with a vengeance), sad souls defined by their isolation, misery, and bitchy defensiveness. Earlier groups and political strategies didn't fare much better. SIR now stood for the "Society of Idle Rap," the *San Francisco Free Press* told its readers in an article about a disruption of a SIR meeting by Leo Laurence's Council for Homosexual Freedom. A photo of a young gay activist burning his SIR membership card accompanied the article, with a caption that quoted a line from the recent movie *Putney Swope*: "Rocking the boat is a drag. You gotta sink the boat." The Mattachine Society, the Young Turks maintained, probably did more harm than good. Fortyish homophiles were "part of the problem, not the solution." When his name came up at all, Donald Webster Cory, once the most revered figure in gay political circles, was derided as a self-abasing "closet case." *ONE* and *The Mattachine Review* might as well have been the names of medieval manuscripts. For the moment, the past would offer no guide to the future.

THE PEOPLE WHO gathered in July 1969 at New York City's Alternate U, a radical educational center in Greenwich Village, to form the Gay Liberation Front were determined to distance themselves from their well-bred predecessors with all possible vigor. The name itself, alluding to the Viet Cong's National Liberation Front, was meant to be confrontational, but it also reflected the left-of-liberal bent of the individuals who made up the coalition. Some, like Michael Brown and Marty Robinson, came from the newly formed Action Committee of the Mattachine Society, the latter organization's means of accommodating radicalized young gays who didn't want to hear any more about backroom politics and quiet political influence. Others—radical feminists Lois Hart and Martha Shelley or men like Jim Fouratt, John O'Brien, and Ron Ballard—were veterans of the New Left who saw a need for an alliance of the homosexual cause and the black and workers' movements. Still others, like Bob Kohler and Jerry Hoose, were less doctrinaire but had observed too much in the Village (not only on the night of June 28) to let pass an opportunity to do something about the injustices that outraged them. The mix was more heterogeneous than it initially seemed, but it worked for a time. In *The Politics of Homosexuality* (1980), Toby Marotta summarized the spirit of the first weeks of GLF, as it was called: "Radicals and revolutionaries shared the conviction that since every dimension of the existing system was bankrupt, a total transformation of society was desirable, and that to effect such change, it was necessary to unite all oppressed minorities into a broad-based movement." Those who had assumed they were involving themselves in an exclusively gay cause were quickly disabused of that notion. The implications of that approach would become apparent later in the year.

At first, it was all wonder and rage, a creative chaos that unnerved everyone but the most stridently political of the couple dozen people who showed up for the meetings. "Wild meetings, screeching meetings, arguing meetings," in the memory of one participant. "I began to doubt if we'd ever get anything done." Gradually, a shape and a purpose emerged. Though it saw itself not as a civil rights or protest organization but as a loose association of men and women at odds with racism, sexism, militarism, and the consumer culture as well as homophobia, GLF was capable of concrete, practical "actions" when they were called for. A number of those actions had to do with simply getting the word and the idea of "gay" before the public, doing everything possible to end invisibility once and for all. Advertisements in the *Village Voice* for a GLF newsletter and later for a dance were censored after they were paid for. The phrase "Gay Power to Gay People" was judged obscene and therefore inappropriate for a liberal Greenwich Village weekly. A noisy picket line and several thousand leaflets charging the *Voice* with discrimination brought the paper's publisher to a new view of the matter. Dogging the steps of the mayoral candidates, who never imagined having to air an opinion on the subject, proved useful in the same way throughout the fall 1969 campaign. "This is 1776—the homosexual revolution has begun!" Marty Robinson cried out at a League of Women Voters forum as GLF queries were brushed aside and the police led the disrupters away. "The main idea, the first idea, was 'no more ignoring us,' " Jerry Hoose commented. "We were saying, or yelling, 'We're here and you're going to pay attention.' " To the militants, middle-class decorum was a proven dead-end in politics, at least for homosexuals. The only way to be heard, short of violence, was by means of raised voices, undaunted rudeness, guts in the face of intimidation by police and politicians.

The GLF newsletter became a perfect encapsulation of those loud, rude, gutsy qualities. It went after the Mafia and the police for their stranglehold on the bars (a subject no one had ever touched on in print), trashed other gay periodicals that were insufficiently critical of the establishment, provided reports on life in Cuba, analyzed the tyranny of sex roles and the joys of consciousness-raising, and publicized the need for a gay community center. *Come Out!* was also vintage GLF in its antimanagement style. "Editorship," or even a staff with regular duties, was old-fashioned and authoritarian; instead, lots were drawn each month, and those who had volunteered to see that the 6,000 copies of the publication were laid out, printed, distributed in New York, and mailed across the country took on different tasks with each issue. Spreading the word to gay radicals in other cities who might be interested in forming their own versions of GLF was not the least part of the value of *Come Out!*. Within a year of the founding of GLF in New York, Gay Liberation Fronts were meeting in Atlanta, Boston, Chicago, Iowa City, Los Angeles, Milwaukee, Portland, San Francisco, Seattle, Washington, D.C., and more than fifty other cities. Many of these groups were based on college campuses, created by gay students tired of marching for every cause but their own. Others were the work of a tiny handful of individuals determined not to miss out on what promised to be a major social upheaval, even if the gay population of their respective cities was ambivalent about greater visibility.

The rapid proliferation of these groups, all of which were separate bodies answerable only to themselves, surprised everyone. By 1972, conservative estimates placed the number at five hundred. "We felt that we were an idea whose time had come," Los Angeles GLF leader Morris Kight affirmed, "but the thrill it generated surpassed most people's expectations. That's because it wasn't 'homophile education.' It was street theater and a call to change the world. It was an invigorating moment to be gay." In Los Angeles in 1970, GLF members broke up a conference of mental health professionals at the Biltmore Hotel and stopped the showing of a film on aversion therapy. "You people," Don Kilhefner told the psychiatrists, "have been conducting a monologue for over half a century and we would like to start a dialogue." Several months later, the same group invaded the West Hollywood office of primal scream therapist Arthur Janov to hold their own "scream-in" protesting his anti-gay writings. GLF in the nation's capital joined the 1970 Moratorium Against the War in Vietnam march with their own version of the chant "Make Love, Not War" ("Suck Cock, Beat the Draft") and held a "nude-in" at the reflecting pool in front of the Lincoln Memorial. Less carefree was the earlier protest in San Francisco, a joint GLF and SIR action, known as "Bloody Friday of the Purple Hand." Sixty picketers, gathered outside the *San Francisco Examiner* building to stage a peaceful protest against the epithets used by the paper in its coverage of gay life, were doused with purple printer's ink dumped from a third-floor window by someone on the paper's staff. They pressed their ink-stained hands on the building's white facade. The police arrived, not to investigate who had dumped the ink, but to take the gay men and lesbians to jail, clubbing a number of them to the ground in the process.

Though the Gay Liberation Front ideology and manner appealed primarily to iconoclastic youth, some older gay men were thrilled by the renaissance they were witnessing. Morris Kight, a veteran anti–Vietnam War activist, was fifty. Jim Kepner, in his late forties, was ready to take part, leaving Dorr Legg and the *ONE* crowd behind to steam about the rabbler-rousers. Harry Hay had been living in hope of just this development and rejoiced in the downfall of those who had opposed his vision of community in the 1950s. "The counterculture had cast its spell on him," his friend Will Roscoe wrote. Young GLF members who attended the last homophile conferences of 1969–1970 were only too ready to outdo Hay in showering abuse on those they characterized as sellouts, but in the rush of events, even sympathizers from the older generation were given a hard time. Activists such as Frank Kameny and Barbara Gittings showed up at GLF meetings in New York only to be challenged for their credentials by people who weren't in high school when Kameny was testifying before Congress and Gittings was editing *The Ladder*. The middle-aged Foster Gunnison, a movement fixture, looked like an FBI plant to those who eyed his crew cut and bow tie with disdain. "You have to understand," Kiyoshi Kuromiya of the Philadelphia GLF pointed out, "that the white middle-class outlook of the earlier groups, which thought that everything in America would be just fine if people only treated homosexuals better, wasn't what we were all about. On the contrary, we thought, 'Screw that attitude.' We wanted to stand with the poor, with women, with people of color, with the antiwar people, to bring the whole corrupt thing down. GLF had no use for people who weren't with us in thinking that big and making those connections."

Serious divisions were not long in making themselves felt, first in New York and then elsewhere. The Gay Liberation Front—by its nature a magnet for extreme opinions and histrionic personalities—was an ideal vehicle for exposing and amplifying rifts that had always existed in more diluted forms. For years, most of the literature about homosexuality had stuck to the same script: it was a predominantly white male phenomenon, and those white males were arty and middle-class, apolitical and easily cowed. The consciousness-raising dimension of GLF demanded that all such myths be confronted, but some were more easily dealt with than others.

Gender was the first tear in the delicate fabric of GLF unity, especially in New York. As lesbians worked to open the women's liberation movement to their concerns, women's liberation had in turn led many lesbians to question their priorities and to ask whether their true oppressor was straight society (which included other women) or male society (which included their black and white brothers in gay liberation). The lesbian critique of gay men was cutting and not without validity: you want us to be your coffee-servers and back-patters and earth mothers, not your empowered equals, Del Martin told male activists in a famous 1970 speech announcing her departure from homophile ranks. In GLF, the same complaints were heard. Men were better trained to shout down opposing views during debates, to throw their weight around. In a group that espoused "structureless structure" and resisted formal voting as a bourgeois contrivance, this meant that some revolutionaries were more equal than others. The crowds, dark lighting, loud music, and sexualized atmosphere of GLF's fund-raising dances were also denounced as a "male thing" that unfairly kept many women away. ("Gay men are obsessed with sex. Lesbians are obsessed with love," one exasperated lesbian writer summarized the difference in *Come Out!*.) Language revealed the disparity as well; men were "men," but women were, as always, "the girls." In the final analysis, there was as much implicit male chauvinism among gay men, they believed, as among straight men.

Some of the GLF men agreed with that assessment and argued that the necessary corrective was to defer more automatically to the women's judgments and to play down the pride they felt as macho fighters for the cause. The self-proclaimed "faggot effeminists" of GLF went further, urging men to cultivate their feminine side. Centered on the male bonding ideal, male homosexuality was, after all, misogynistic and "counterrevolutionary" by definition. Not everyone bought this idea, but even those men who saw the point of the feminist concerns balked at the women's unilateral appropriation of dance funds that had been earmarked for the community center. Tensions heightened. Eventually, many women departed GLF on angry terms to become part of Radicalesbians. The "woman-identified woman" needed her own space, her own leadership, her own style of bonding.

The Gay Liberation Front relationship to black radicalism was no less fraught with complications. Everyone agreed that a problem with the earlier gay movement had been its lily-white character. Now, finally, black gay men were stepping forward. But for white gays, there was a big difference between honoring Dr. King and reading James Baldwin and aligning themselves uncritically with the new cutting edge of black politics and culture. LeRoi Jones still prattled on about gay love as a white man's illness (a position he would later amend), Eldridge Cleaver compared homosexuality to baby rape in *Soul on Ice*, and the Black Panthers behaved none too hospitably to the "sex freaks" who wanted to fight with them against a racist power structure. The GLF presence at the Revolutionary People's Constitutional Convention in Philadelphia in September 1970 was greeted with snickers, and most of the lesbians walked out after the Black Panthers made it clear that they did not regard the gay or feminist causes as equivalent to theirs. Yet those who dreamed of a wider solidarity, a change of consciousness as well as economics, were quick to point out that there was no reason to expect that America's revolutionaries—black or white straight men—would be any less homophobic than anyone else, but there *was* reason to think they were more educable. Each time gays marched in an antiwar demonstration as a gay group or spoke up for the Panthers, they showed their sincerity, their courage, and their compassion for other victims of oppression. That was important, and sometimes brought results. Huey Newton's statement in the August 1970 issue of *Black Panther* that blacks needed to overcome their insecurities about homosexuality "to unite with [gay militants] in a revolutionary fashion" as "friends and potential allies" (a letter that led to the inclusion of New York's GLF in the Philadelphia conference) was taken by left-wing gays as a sign of a budding mutual empathy. A mere grasping at straws, other gay activists felt. In the modern hierarchy of causes, they concluded, homosexuality would never hold its own with the masculinity-obsessed black militants.

An unpleasant truth needed to be faced. The woman-gay, black-gay dichotomies were, for the moment, irreconcilable. First and foremost, the understanding the women and the men had of each other was too rudimentary. It amazed some of the men that they were viewed as an obstacle to lesbian empowerment. Second, white homosexuals (male or female) were not about to align themselves with straight groups or individuals who treated them with hostility or condescension. That approach replicated early Mattachine ties to the psychiatrists. "Were we trying to buy their respect?" Martha Shelley asked after New York's GLF voted to give money to the Panthers for their bail fund. At the same time, white gay men would not, or could not, see that few lesbians and even fewer blacks were prepared to rally around the gay banner alone. Their war had multiple fronts. For them, the overlap of gender and sexual orientation, or race and sexual orientation, was crucial, and if their white peers would not accept the ramifications of that fact, they were chauvinists or racists. The ensuing arguments were fierce, and in many cities the Gay Liberation Front splintered within months of its founding on the basis of these antithetical philosophies (fighting the people's war vs. fighting for gay rights) as well as contradictory organizational concepts (consensus vs. parliamentary procedure). The modern gay movement, then, was born in a spirit of euphoria and unity that was short-lived. Gay politics existed in a competitive context with all other forms of politics and thrived and suffered accordingly.

The fragmentation of the Gay Liberation Front in New York wasn't mourned by all who had endured its acrimonious meetings. As early as November 1969, a dozen of the discontented got together to form a breakaway group that would steer a different course, abandoning both GLF's inflated oratory and its ties to nonhomosexual left-wing causes. Their aim was a tight one-issue focus. The constitution of the Gay Activists Alliance was aggressive in its preamble about the rights "liberated homosexual activists" were demanding, while its articles and bylaws evoked mainstream precision and efficiency. The document struck a few of the individuals who read it that winter as a step back to the worst days of Mattachine and NACHO (it was "an elitist fuckup" in the words of one dissenter), but its rules about membership eligibility, quorums, dues, committees, election procedures, officers, and expulsion of members were just what was needed to avoid the paralysis that was overtaking GLF, in the view of founders such as Jim Owles and Marty Robinson. Tom Doerr's suggestion of the Greek letter lambda as the organization's logo struck an appealing note. The traditional symbol for wavelength in quantum physics brought to mind dynamism, motion, constant change. An early statement, "What Is GAA?," emphasized the group's commitment to a militant but nonviolent homosexual civil rights struggle and a membership open to all who shared this approach and objective. "Well-mannered conformist shit," in the words of GLF stalwart Bob Kohler; "An exciting place for a range of us who weren't out-and-out revolutionaries," in the view of Kay Tobin, one of the few women present at the birth of GAA.

Later characterizations of the Gay Activists Alliance (such as Arthur Dong's 1995 film *Outrage '69*) have made it seem as if it were a monolithic entity whose skepticism about the Panthers necessarily implied a deep-seated racism, but in fact its original members gravitated to the new group for various reasons. Some had been comfortable with the Black Panthers connection, but broke with GLF specifically over the gender divisions. "I wasn't offended by the GLF contributions to the Panthers any more than I was by Leonard Bernstein's party for them," Michael Lavery observed. Rather, he felt that "the GLF women were trying to blackmail the men over the nature of the dances"—and that was sufficient cause to walk. "It was the politics of the time. It couldn't be avoided." In fact, Lavery became uneasy about the "purity" of the GAA focus on gay civil rights. Others were ready to abandon GLF precisely because of the diffuse nature of its revolutionary agenda, while a few members just felt that the "consciousness-raising had gotten a little too weird." ("You opened your mouth, you offended somebody. It wasn't worth opening your mouth after a while.") In the emphatic recollection of Phil Raia, who joined GAA in 1970 but left by the end of the year, its initial spirit was not as bound to a *Roberts Rules of Order* mode at the start as its detractors would have it. "That unfortunate tone came a little later," Raia said. "The atmosphere at the beginning was idealistic and energetic or I wouldn't have joined. People were ready to fight."

Those fights took a distinct form. In contrast to the gay Marxists who wanted to bring Wall Street to its knees or take up arms in the name of that amorphous cause, The Revolution, GAA was bound to seem conventional. Yet in contrast to the homophile movement or to middle-class America, it was plenty brash and threatening. Its thrust was legislative reform—repeal of the sodomy statutes, passage of laws guaranteeing equal employment and housing opportunities—but its tactics were closer to those of GLF than those of the White House picketers or the Annual Reminder crowd. "Zapping" public officials, which involved challenging those individuals to address their gay constituents, was especially popular and effective. Mayor Lindsay was hounded from one cultural event and podium to another in Manhattan; the threat of a disruption persuaded Dick Cavett to allow GAA spokespersons onto his show after comedian Mort Sahl made anti-gay remarks as a Cavett guest; a sit-in at the Republican Party headquarters led to the arrest and trial of "the Rockefeller Five." Twenty-four-year-old Jim Owles, GAA's first president, talked of cultivating gay anger, of finding the usable middle ground between polite remonstrance and destructive rage, while vice president Marty Robinson, a carpenter from Brooklyn in his late twenties, epitomized for many members the best of the emerging style—outspoken, off-the-wall, caring, proud of his working-class job, sexually uninhibited, equally insistent about legal reforms and the right to walk the street hand-in-hand with his lover.

A sense of the theatrical enlivened GAA. Long gone was the solemn tone of late Mattachine. When the Taxi Commission announced that it would not issue hack licenses to gay drivers without a psychiatrist's letter testifying to their mental health, the group invaded the commissioner's office in white coats carrying a couch for the commissioner's own analysis. When a large apartment complex let it be known that gay renters were not welcome, tents were pitched and the demonstrators dragged off the grass by police, taking as much of the lawn with them as they could. While inherently confrontational, a zap also had the potential to be a warmly offbeat, sociable experience. Protesting anti-gay remarks by the head of New York City's marriage bureau, a large GAA contingent occupied the office in 1971 to make a statement about society's refusal to legitimize gay relationships and to hold a party of their own (they brought a wedding cake and a guitar along with the usual leaflets). The office manager, barely able to contain his rage at the invasion of a bureaucratic inner sanctum, exchanged heated remarks with the ever-indignant Arthur Evans, GAA's resident intellectual, but on the whole the tone of the action was eminently civilized, even light-hearted. Randy Wicker's videotape of the hour-long zap captures the amiable curiosity of most of the staff—they were, or course, being plied with free coffee and pastries and an unusual break from their routine—and the reasonableness of both the GAA membership and the police. The right of gay men and lesbians to marry was not a movement priority in the 1970s (it certainly didn't mean a thing to anyone in GAA), but in the larger sense, the target of the zap was appropriate. Those in leadership positions had to be educated about the name-calling and statements of private prejudice that were no longer going to be tolerated by the taxpayers they singled out for insult.

Despite the inevitable strife of its internal politics, the camaraderie the Gay Activists Alliance inspired was another, not insignificant feature of the group. The rental of a large space in SoHo accomplished what GLF had only talked about, giving New York City its first gay community center. The Firehouse at 99 Wooster Street soon became a vortex of activism—political activism as strategies were debated and zaps and media appearances planned; social activism by way of weekend dances, attended by well over a thousand men and women happy to find an alternative to the bars; cultural activism in readings and screenings of gay films organized by Vito Russo. "If you had any problems accepting yourself," commented Fred Goldhaber, a GAA member who was first taken to the Firehouse by friends in 1971, "an evening there was tremendously uplifting." But from the perspective of another time, that camaraderie and cultural exchange were suspect as an overwhelmingly middle-class white male experience. Nor was any member of the group going to deny that the Gay Activists Alliance appealed to women and people of color even less than the Gay Liberation Front had. The Owles-Robinson take on this complaint took three distinct forms. The first, that nothing about GAA's stated purpose excluded any gay man or lesbian who shared its philosophy, was disingenuous in that its gay focus ignored feminism and race except in a token way, and lesbians and black gay men were not about to do that. The second, that white middle-class gay men had their own legitimate needs to address and the right to do so, was perfectly true. The third was more an unproven hope, a progressivist vision of change, which implied that any gains GAA achieved would indirectly benefit everyone. Certainly in its prime, from 1970 to 1972, GAA generated media attention and, even outside New York City, goodwill as no other group had. A few of its members traveled to other states to help with local organizing, staying with anyone they met in the gay bars who expressed the least interest in activism. "It wouldn't matter to us how small the interest was. We wanted to see what could be done," Rich Wandel recalled of a 1971 trip to Iowa, Wisconsin, Illinois, Indiana, and Ohio. Their example and their presence meant a great deal to fledgling groups.

Not surprisingly, the multicultural and gender issues, which had also bedeviled GLF, were a part of the gradual undoing of GAA. The sensitivity of the men toward the women, or rather the lack of it, was an ongoing problem. An even more inflammatory subject was how drag queens were unwelcome in the ranks. Jim Owles's decision not to allow Natasha, a black transvestite, to perform an outré (and underdressed) skit at a GAA dance, despite the Pleasure and Fund-raising Committee's imprimatur, stirred considerable debate. The "Natasha incident" riled those members who felt smothered by what they saw as GAA's autocratic, anti-camp, image-conscious leaders ("the middle-class white boys") and its emphasis on the electoral process over consciousness-raising and gay culture. Ironically, within two years, many more members were ready to leave for the opposite reason, complaining that GAA was filled with "too many zanies, too much wild talk."

But other factors—time and energy, particularly—were relevant. The faith manifested by Owles, Robinson, and their friends in charge within the system did not produce expeditious results. Often, the pace of change-within-the-system was downright glacial. (A classic example: the gay rights bill first introduced to the New York City Council by way of GAA's lobbying efforts in 1971 was not passed until 1985.) The practical value of legal reform was also fairly called into question. Illinois decriminalized sodomy in 1961; Connecticut, in 1971. But discrimination in both states was rampant. Some gay men argued that in Chicago police brutality against homosexuals actually increased in the 1960s. Would new laws on the books and deference from zap-conscious mayors and city councils mean much if society remained sexually, racially, and economically divided, imbued with an Old Testament ethos, and wary of nonconformists? Finally, the burn-out factor was perhaps the hardest to own up to. Energy expended on intra-organizational battles depleted participants as surely as the demands of street actions and lobbying. By 1973, GAA's leadership had passed from Owles to other hands—the less contentious Wandel, the charismatic Morty Manford—but a fractious, declining membership and a suspicious blaze that destroyed the Firehouse spelled doom.

Outside New York, San Francisco, and Los Angeles, assertions of gay pride and outrage took the same toll and were sometimes made at a cost even beyond what was exacted in larger cities. As David Williams noted about the course of homosexual politics in Kentucky, "The emergence of gay liberation groups in Louisville and Lexington in the early 1970s inaugurated a brief era of brutal repression by law enforcement officials and politicians, who succeeded in curtailing any further effective gay/lesbian political activity in Kentucky until 1984." The youth, indignation, and general antiestablishment style of the activists made an inspiring combination, though, and (as always) it helped that they had less to lose than their homophile predecessors with nine-to-five jobs.

In Louisville, for instance, a small Gay Liberation Front formed in the summer of 1970 to protest the policy of a local bar that excluded drag queens. In the fall they initiated a gay studies course as part of an alternative curriculum at the University of Kentucky, precipitating a battle with state legislators and campus administrators, and later joined several hundred other demonstrators who turned out to heckle Vice President Spiro Agnew when he came to town. At the Agnew demonstration, gay protestors refused to downplay their sexual identity in the fashion of pre-1969 countercultural days; their banner read "Freaking Fag Revolutionaries Against Agnew," an allusion to the famous remark by the prosecutor of the Chicago 7 that America's children were being lost "to the freaking fag revolution." That autumn, Denver's GLF prepared guerilla theater programs for use on Colorado's college campuses, Hartford's Kalos Society held a "confrontation picnic" to challenge restrictions in Connecticut on the gay right to assembly, and Cornell University's GLF liberated an Ithaca bar that had refused to serve gay patrons, an event reported in *The Advocate*. In January 1971, the New Orleans Gay Liberation Front staged a noon march on City Hall—an unheard-of development in that city—and elsewhere throughout the South, Midwest, and far West, local versions of GLF or GAA made their presence felt.

Again, any image of unity and coordinated effort misses a vital point. Even among the campus groups, no single dominant idea emerged of how best to proceed toward the goal of changing the conditions of life for gay men and lesbians in America. In fact, gay antagonists tended to be as intractable toward one another as they were toward straight adversaries. Only rarely over the next two decades were those differences even temporarily resolved.

SOME OF THE same conflicting values were vividly apparent in the flood of prose—papers and mimeographed sheets, books and broadsides—that was another aspect of gay liberation in the early 1970s. A key aspect, in fact: tens of thousands of gay men and lesbians who weren't in a position to join a group were made aware of the movement by what they read.

The new periodicals were often written and published by the more militant activists and reflected their impatience with liberalism and amelioration. Chicago's *Killer Dyke* was unequivocal in its support of armed action to end discrimination immediately, as was New York's *Gay Flames*, which looked to the Panthers as a model more than an ally. ("We are faggots and we are flaming with rage," the first issue declared.) Charles Thorp, founder in 1970 of the *San Francisco Gay Free Press*, knew about violence first-hand, having been slashed in the face and hit with a baseball bat while passing out gay leaflets on the street. "Violent gay revolution" was the only answer, he told his readers. New York GLF member John O'Brien, a hard-core Marxist and a participant in the Stonewall riots, was probably among the most vocal radicals on that subject. His mimeographed paper, *Gay Times*, made use of a logo (a hand grasping a rifle) and a motto ("To Love We Must Fight") that were unambiguous, and O'Brien himself claimed responsibility, long after the fact, for burning a Greenwich Village record store to the ground in retaliation for the anti-gay practices of the owner, who subsequently died of a heart attack. "I'm very proud of that," O'Brien told interviewer Rodger Streitmatter in 1993. "Some people deserve to die." (The FBI was certain that O'Brien was a heterosexual who had latched on to the gay movement for his own subversive left-wing purposes. He was, in their view, too tough, abrasive, and threatening to be a gay man.) Boston's *Fag Rag* attacked assimilationist goals in no uncertain terms—"We do not want a slice of the pie; the pie is rotten"—and Detroit's *Gay Liberator* joined the chorus celebrating disruption and anarchy.

Emerging as "papers of record" in this period were two less aggressive publications, one from each coast. Both spoke to readers who were more interested in significant change than revolutionary upheaval. *The Los Angeles Advocate*, later simply *The Advocate*, had been founded by Dick Michaels to report on news ignored by other papers (bar raids, protests, gay conferences, and movies), and by 1970 reached beyond California to more than 20,000 subscribers in Chicago, New York, Boston, and Miami. Michaels was keenly alert to the need for a fact-oriented national periodical to give homosexuals a sense that their concerns were widely shared. His editorial slant was galling to those who viewed "Amerika" as a gay-genocidal police state on the verge of a long overdue collapse. Michaels and his writers proceeded on the assumption that most gays had no special fondness for the SDS or antipathy to capitalism. They wanted humane leadership of existing institutions rather than an end to those institutions.

Gay, out of New York, shared Dick Michaels's opposition to violence and angry rhetoric, but was more frolicsome in every other respect. When a Greenwich Village bookshop was raided by police and its gay pornography seized, editors Jack Nichols and Lige Clarke ran a news item with a five-by-twelve-inch nude photo of the store's young, prodigiously endowed cashier. Coverage of new bathhouses necessarily included photos of patrons in towels, and gay pride and gay history meant lively interviews with Paul Goodman, Allen Ginsberg, Troy Perry, and elderly activists like Prescott Townsend, the guru of Beacon Hill. Financed by Al Goldstein, *Gay* resembled nothing that had ever been published in America. It exhibited all the irreverence of its heterosexual sponsor, the demonic founder of *Screw*, but it also aimed at times to transcend, or subtly subvert, its own roustabout flavor. Nichols and Clarke's agenda raised their weekly to another level.

Jack Nichols and Lige Clarke had been leaders in the Washington Mattachine Society and were a much admired couple who participated in all the early pickets and conventions. After they relocated to New York, Al Goldstein offered them a column in his new—decidedly straight, decidedly tawdry, and very successful—tabloid. He gave them carte blanche over content and even accepted his columnists' veto of the *Screw*-style title he wanted, "The Cornholing Corner." They opted for the more sedate title of the old Washington Mattachine newsletter, "The Homosexual Citizen." In return, though, the publisher reserved the right to decide on the articles' headings, captions, and photos. Clarke's piece on the Oscar Wilde Memorial Bookshop became "Stalls of Balls" and Nichols's article on anti-gay psychiatrists went to press under a classic Goldstein title, "Does Dr. Albert Ellis Suck?" Similarly, when Goldstein agreed in 1969 to underwrite the expense of a separate gay tabloid, he had in mind a homosexual version of *Screw* but ended up with, and supported, something else entirely. *Gay* provided its 25,000 readers with creditable journalism, opinionated commentary (debates about drag queens, S&M, and duty-bound monogamy), intelligent book and theater reviews, erotic ads, a politically moderate tone (strictly GAA), and innumerable sexy photos.

The explicit photographs, of models and of its own undressed columnists, and the coverage of the bathhouse scene annoyed people from two opposing directions. To more prim-and-proper tastes, *Gay* made homosexual life look debauched. To the GLF Marxists, it was a pornographic tool of a capitalist oligarchy (Who owned the bars? Who owned the baths? Not the people!) and promoted self-indulgence over politics. What critics saw as a lack of seriousness, Nichols and Clarke understood as a different, less constrained outlook. This was part of a "vision of liberation," as novelist Michael Rumaker wrote, encompassing more than gay rights: "The larger vision was the death of flesh hatred and shame."

For most of the 1950s and 1960s, America warmed to the message of Hugh Hefner (whether or not the man of the house was ready to buy the magazine itself) and the teasing of big-bosomed starlets and, more recently, the libidinous freedom of the shaggy-haired kids in jeans. But the ease with which the country discussed and displayed the varieties of heterosexual sex had nothing to do with gay men and lesbians. The strictures of psuedo-scientist Dr. David Reuben—"penis plus vagina equals sex," anything else is repulsive and unnatural—was still the final word on the subject. (Reuben's amazing book, *Everything You Always Wanted to Know About Sex, But Were Afraid to Ask*, informed eight million credulous buyers in 1969 that male homosexuals were a particularly grim lot, unsuited for long-term relationships and given to inserting lightbulbs in their rectums and masturbating into carved-out cantaloupes, when papayas weren't available.) For the generation of gays coming of age in 1970, then, ending police brutality and job discrimination were important tasks, but the cause had to have a more psychological and social dimension. It had to be about the rightness of one man taking another man's penis in his hand or mouth and an *insistence* on the equality of those acts with any other between consenting adults. A focus in public discourse, linked to political action, on the body and unfettered sexual pleasure did not outlast the 1970s, especially in the aftermath of the Anita Bryant campaign of 1977–1978 when gay rights appeared to be a more suitably referendum-oriented goal. Yet in the early 1970s an erotic emphasis became part and parcel of the whole endeavor. "We wanted gays to rejoice over what they did in bed, or wherever they did it with another caring partner," Jack Nichols observed, "as much as we wanted them to fight for their legal rights. The two couldn't be separated. The two shouldn't be separated."

Just as *Gay* wasn't only about sex or only about politics, some of the most popular books of the day explored that overlap. Angelo D'Arcangelo's *The Homosexual Handbook* had been steadily finding readers since Maurice Girodias's avant-garde Olympia Press brought it out in 1968 and, by 1970, had reportedly sold over 250,000 copies. (Another sign of the times: in June 1969, two weeks before Stonewall, Olympia hosted a party for the book's second printing at the Luxor Bathhouse in New York.) D'Arcangelo's book was chatty and amusing, with chapters on cruising techniques, bars, gay theater, and a list at the end of famous homosexuals, living and dead. Some of the inclusions were doubtful (Paul McCartney was wishful thinking, D'Arcangelo admitted in the text) and others, from assorted popes to Somerset Maugham, were old hat. But mention of J. Edgar Hoover as the *"eminence froide* of our secret society" caused a publisher's nightmare when the FBI threatened reprisals if the unsold copies of the first edition were not recalled and the director's name deleted from future printings. John Paul Hudson's *The Gay Insider* (1972) went several steps beyond D'Arcangelo's work in both chattiness and scope. A travel guide for all fifty states that evaluated the opportunities for both connecting to the movement and getting laid, Hudson's hefty book was considered indispensable in its day. Hudson the horny Baedecker, Hudson the GAA activist, Hudson as a model of the New Homosexual were hard to separate. Similarly, Arthur Bell's *Dancing the Gay Lib Blues* (1971) was as much about his tempestuous relationship with his lover, GAA leader Arthur Evans, as his impressions of the movement. The feminist principle, "the personal is political," was by now an adage.

In this climate even an older generation of gay men could be stirred to greater boldness. Journalist and Truman biographer Merle Miller caused a sensation when he published a memoir-essay, "On Being Different: What It Means to Be a Homosexual," in the *New York Times Magazine* in January 1971, the most public coming out in American history. Miller described his childhood as a "four-eyes" sissy in Marshalltown, Iowa, his escape into the Army during World War II where he learned to lower his voice and make comments about queers, and three decades given over to "passing" and internalizing the judgments of a culture that taught him he was malformed by nature. He wrote about his sexual history with men and his failed marriage. He discussed the outlook of gay men twenty years his junior (quoting Jim Owles and Marty Robinson, who had invited him to GAA meetings), his admiration for their bravery, and the emotional distance between his generation and theirs that would always exist. Miller's work was published by Random House a few months later and, as a short and widely read book, prompted even more discussion than it had as a *Times* article. Many gay men were unhappy with Miller's admission that his life as a gay man involved enormous sadness or his wish, all things considered, that he had been born straight. In the pages of *Gay*, Dick Leitsch, who had been living the motto "Gay Pride" since his teenage years in Louisville in the 1950s, acidly named Miller a candidate for the Irving Bieber Award for 1971. "I never had any tolerance for that oh-poor-me way of thinking," he later remarked. That the book would be criticized from both sides (as indiscreet by his straight friends, as politically timid by the liberationists) didn't surprise Miller, who understood and even relished the contradictory time he was living in. He had his eye on a different audience, the young Merle Millers still trapped in Marshalltowns everywhere wondering about their choices and the viability of the closet.

Aspects of society's growing fascination with gay life, its sexiness as much as its sorrow, inevitably brought a number of quaint stereotypes to the forefront. Gordon Merrick's romantic novel *The Lord Won't Mind* was an unexpected bestseller in 1970, despite its edge of racism and the breathtaking shallowness of its handsome, masculine, genitally obsessed characters. As one straight "liberal" reviewer commented, at least America was learning something about what mattered to homosexuals, and indeed an interest in penis size is an embarrassing given in Merrick's world. A perky member is often referred to abstractly as "the sex," as in "the sex drove deep within him," and terms of endearment are apt to sound like the corniest phallus worship ("I belong to you, big boy," a satisfied Peter tells the lusty Tim). What straight society was really learning was that Jacqueline Susann had her gay male counterparts and that homosexual mass-marketing reading tastes were no more elevated than heterosexual mass-market reading tastes. But for the teenager who never imagined that a paperback with descriptions of men in bed together could be on sale at the local drugstore, *The Lord Won't Mind* served a purpose. Twenty-two years after Gore Vidal had been told that he was committing professional suicide with *The City and the Pillar*, New York publishers were talking about a "breakthrough" love story. To the money men following the latest trends, the voices of gay liberation announced something more than radical social change and a new kind of talk-show guest. They announced buyers to be heeded, markets to be tapped. The commercializing of gay life began at the very moment the new activist spirit peaked, with consequences that would be every bit as profound.

19

CREATING A SCENE

Yet if heterosexual life has come to seem impossibly difficult, homosexual life still seems more nearly impossible. For to be a homosexual is to be a hostage to a passion that automatically brings terrible pressures to bear on any man who lives with it; and the pressures, which only a few rare homosexuals are able to rise above with any success, can distort a man, can twist him, and always leave him defined by his sexual condition. The same, I think, cannot be said about heterosexuals. With the possible exception of prostitutes and heterosexuals driven by abnormal appetites, the general run of heterosexuals are not defined by their sexuality at all. . . . If I had the power to do so, I would wish homosexuality off the face of this earth. . . . Cursed without clear reason, afflicted without apparent cure, they are an affront to our rationality, living evidence of our despair of ever finding a sensible, an explicable design to the world.

—Joseph Epstein, "Homo/Hetero:
The Struggle for Sexual Identity,"
Harper's, September 1970

Ultimately, the Gay Liberation Front, windy rhetoric and millenarian fantasies aside, was right. The obstacles for a gay political movement with minimal ties to feminism and none at all to the cause of racial equality proved formidable. More important, the core GLF principle, which carried over into the framework of GAA and similar groups—namely, that silence is the real enemy; coming out, the path to full humanity—transformed American society. The love that dare not speak its name had become, in a popular line of the day, the neurosis that didn't know when to shut up. But that very act of refusing to shut up changed the way in which homosexuality was discussed and attacked, which in turn changed the way in which gay men and lesbians chose to take on their opponents. Though the crudest form of denunciation (the homosexual as demon and child molester) was in full force again at the end of the decade, many mainstream commentators in the 1970s sought to distance themselves from the ugliness of Johns Committee witch-hunts and police-state terror. They wrote with sympathy about the "handicap" of being gay or spoke in favor of tacitly agreed-upon private rights. Full acceptance was another story.

Not surprisingly, then, reassuring straight society that homosexuality posed no threat to the order of things became the preferred response for some gay men. GLF stridency and, eventually, GAA zaps were seen as a relic of 1960s utopianism. To others, the better strategy was to open an aggressive educational attack on more fronts than the early activists had thought possible, laboring to institute a discreet gay presence in America's libraries and classrooms, law offices and television studios, stores and theaters, churches and corridors of power, both civilian and military.

The hardest lesson for gay men and lesbians to learn at this point (one still not fully absorbed in the 1990s) was not to expect help from that part of the establishment that was, or saw itself as, liberal or sophisticated on other issues. State senators in many parts of the country were willing to debate the repeal of sodomy laws, which after all governed male-female sexual congress as well, but the political risk of declaring the bedroom off limits to the state was never high. As Ken Ross wrote in the *Nation* in 1977, "The passage of consenting-adults legislation was doing well precisely because it had no effect on public life." It was the demand to acknowledge the truth of gay relationships and affections *in public* that set people on edge, inspiring what Paul Robinson called "the horror of visibility." Let them do what they will behind closed doors, so long as it isn't rubbed in our faces. In this area, the liberal media was as clear about the limits of tolerance as any other institution. The *New York Times* published Merle Miller's startling essay in the *Magazine* section in 1971, but Abe Rosenthal's editorial ban on the use of the word *gay* remained in effect until 1987. The atmosphere at the paper was known to be far from sympathetic to gay journalists or gay concerns in the 1970s and early 1980s. The *Miami Herald* adopted its own antidiscrimination employment clause as early as 1973, which, as Ransdell Pierson noted in the *Columbia Journalism Review*, "did little to change an oppressive atmosphere [beyond putting] a stop to the routine faggot jokes at news conferences" and meant nothing at the time of the Dade County referendum in 1977 when the *Herald* came out against the "new deviate freedom." The *Los Angeles Times* was the object of demonstrations and sit-ins in 1973 and 1974 to protest its refusal to cover newsworthy stories about gay events. As late as 1979, Jimmy Breslin felt comfortable mourning the changes at the *Village Voice* that had made a once-great publication into a "fag paper," while noted columnist Murray Kempton extolled the dignity of the closet. At the networks, coverage of gay life inched its way onto the screen, but only rarely with a positive angle on the coming out phenomenon.

The true masterpiece of clarity on this theme appeared at the start of the decade as an essay in *Harper's* magazine, accompanied by a cover picture of a man's bulging biceps and inflated torso stuck into a red dress, and by two pansyesque photos in the text. "Homo/Hetero: The Struggle for Sexual Identity" by Joseph Epstein, a literary critic and contributor to some of the leading scholarly journals in the country, was part autobiography, part analysis of the late 1960s, part sleight-of-hand diatribe. Careful to establish his credentials as a worldly man (having talked and socialized with many of "them") and to cite his own culture-bound habits (including the use, "without hesitation," of all the epithets), Epstein gave the appearance of offering long and sober reflections on the topic, but in the end boiled the matter down to a simple core: he could not abide the idea of two men making love to each other, and consequently was convinced that homosexuals were a people made ludicrous by nature, whose unhappy existence he would gladly wish "off the face of this earth." There was much that his sons could do that would dismay and embarrass him, Epstein wrote, but nothing that would sadden him as much as the knowledge that they were so cursed. The GAA occupation of *Harper's* New York offices the next month, in October 1970, suggested that the time of homosexual passivity toward anti-gay prose, particularly genocidal fantasies in the guise of a professor's musings, was over. At the very least, editors could expect to be confronted by furious readers.

Harper's editor Midge Decter was right in maintaining that Epstein's essay dealt with a subject that cried out for honest debate. More than that, Epstein had been admirably, brutally, direct in his refusal to pretend that in their hearts well-educated people felt differently from redneck gay-bashers; they just used words better. But, as Arthur Evans argued on Dick Cavett's show that fall, it wasn't likely that a magazine such as *Harper's* would have given space to even the most articulate essayist who concluded that the world would be better off if there were no Jews or blacks because their lot in life had been painful and the writer found them unpleasant. (The ex-liberal, soon to be neo-conservative movement, of which Epstein and Decter were a part, would never advance much beyond this point. By 1977 Decter's husband, *Commentary* editor Norman Podhoretz, was attributing the appeasement of the Nazis and the decline of anti-Communist fervor to gays, and in 1980 Decter wrote about the gay men of her limited acquaintance as misogynists and debauchees to a man. Ultimately, for Podhoretz and Decter, homosexuality represented an unpardonable "flight from fatherhood" and a worrisome model for the young ones. That little Johnny might grow up and elect not to marry and sire children, and yet still be a responsible citizen and anti-Communist, was a hard idea for some nervous parents to grasp.) Yet an air of civilized concern went a long way toward keeping alive the acceptability of hating fags. As the dean of students at Fordham University told a campus group in 1973 in rejecting their petition for a gay lounge, "This is still an issue on which reasonable men disagree."

In popular culture, that image of reasonableness and sagacity was embodied in the middle-aged family doctor played by Robert Young on *Marcus Welby, M.D.*, one of the best-loved characters in the history of television. Welby was an object of "national adoration" in the early 1970s, one media critic wrote, appreciated as much for his bedside manner as his medical knowledge. When gay insiders at ABC slipped an advance copy of the script for "The Other Martin Loring" to New York's GAA media committee, the response was swift. "It was incredible," Ronald Gold recalled. "Here you had the 'voice of reason' for all of America telling a patient who came to him with this 'problem' that the best thing he could do was to suppress it because it was a shallow and disgusting thing." GAA protests effected only a few minor changes in the script, and in January 1973 millions of viewers heard Dr. Welby play Joseph Epstein for the masses: Martin Loring's urges were not legitimate desires. They were insurmountable obstacles to happiness and self-respect. The following year, Gold and his associates (having split from GAA and working under the aegis of a new organization, the National Gay Task Force) were more effective in showing ABC that it could make life difficult for the corporation if it chose to air "The Outrage," an even more troubling *Welby* episode about a homosexual high school teacher who rapes a male student. The clamor resulted in lost advertising revenues from sponsors, who shied away from any controversial programming, and in affiliate cancellations. The gay media team persuaded the National Organization for Women and the National Educational Association to support them with their own statements, deriding the script as "misconceived" and prejudicial.

The two *Welby* programs were not the first time the subject was raised in prime time, but they were the most offensive to appear in a serious dramatic context. (In 1970 *Rowan and Martin's Laugh-In* took stock of gay liberation at the rate of a joke per week.) The activists who took on ABC were conscious of the stakes in letting the network go unchallenged. It wasn't far-fetched to see "The Other Martin Loring" as ABC's temporizing response to its own broadcast two months earlier of *That Certain Summer* with Hal Holbrook and Martin Sheen, a made-for-TV movie that avoided the mental illness assumptions and was regarded as the breakthrough TV program on the issue of male-male relationships. "The Outrage," with its implicit equation of homosexuality with pedophilia, represented several steps backward. From 1972 to 1974, a careful line was being drawn to delineate, as one minister phrased it, "the difference between liberalism and license, between compassion and complete moral surrender." To endorse homosexuality without caveats was, evidently, to approve of a sweeping amorality.

THE DRIVE TO influence television's portrayal of gay life, and the excited realization that to an extent such a thing was actually possible, provided important fuel in the struggle to change America's overall view of gay men and lesbians. With each battle, gay activists became more adept at figuring out how to work the system. Between the East Coast's National Gay Task Force and the West Coast's Gay Media Task Force, "gay activists had become so institutionalized in network television," by the mid-1970s, according to one academic study of the industry, "that they rarely needed to use protests." Instead, they were consulted on scripts and asked to meet with writers and directors. "Lisping gays and homosexual murders and child molesters [were] all but gone" from the TV screen, a writer for *LA Weekly* concluded in 1982, and the credit went to the advocacy groups who hit their stride in 1973. Their labor, Ronald Gold observed, "had an impact that went beyond media. We were an example of how *capable* gay activism was becoming."

It was a varied capability, evident in several different dimensions of public and professional life. Some of it was the work of those 1960s activists who had never really bowed out. In Washington, Frank Kameny, who ran as an openly gay candidate for the District's seat in Congress in 1971 and helped form the Gay Activists Alliance there, pressed his fight against the Civil Service Commission's policies that had cost him his government job in the 1950s and, after assisting in numerous court battles, saw those policies reversed in 1975. Henceforth, homosexuality in itself would not be a sufficient reason to exclude an applicant or dismiss an employee from most federal jobs. Working through the American Library Association, Barbara

Gittings focused her energies on educating librarians about the dearth of serious gay literature in public collections. Michael McConnell (who had appeared with his lover Jack Baker in "The American Family" issue of *Look* magazine in 1971) protested the loss of his job at the University of Minnesota through years of highly public litigation even as he and Baker kept alive the heated issue of same-sex marriage in their state. Other movers and shakers were considerably younger. Mark Segal of Philadelphia, scarcely out of his teens in the early 1970s, was a one-man juggernaut against talk-show smirks and nightly news myopia. Johnny Carson, Mike Douglas, the *Today* show, and Walter Cronkite were all interrupted on the air by the same long-haired young man in a suit handcuffed to a camera or plopping himself down on the broadcaster's desk. Dubbed "Supergay" by one midwestern newspaper, Segal seems to have made an impression on Cronkite, who spoke with him after his 1974 trespassing trial. CBS coverage of gay news did, in fact, increase during the next year.

The lack of a centralized gay leadership or organization worried some observers, who looked to the black civil rights movement and saw (or, more accurately, thought they saw) a cohesive structure and a unified philosophy for achieving racial equality. The National Gay Task Force in New York was one answer to this perceived need. Born out of frustration with GAA's wayward energies, the NGTF aspired to be that directive overarching body, but even the commanding personalities of its first leaders, Bruce Voeller and Jean O'Leary, couldn't buck the tide, which was emphatically local or regional or issue-specific, dynamic but haphazard. Student groups, holding dances and rap sessions, came and went on this campus and that; on shoestring budgets, dedicated individuals in Los Angeles and Minneapolis kept the doors open at busy gay community centers. Liberal ministers raised the subject with their bishops and parishioners and with the press, and the Metropolitan Community Church network grew. Gay lawyers lobbied the American Bar Association for support and, in New York City, formed the Lambda Legal Defense Fund to prosecute gay-related cases. (Harris Kimball, whose disbarment in Florida in 1957 was discussed in chapter 13, began a challenge in 1971 to the exclusion of open homosexuals from the New York State Bar. A landmark 1973 decision, *Matter of Kimball*, determined that professional licenses could not be denied solely because of the applicant's sexual orientation.) High school teachers like Joseph Acanfora, who appeared on *Sixty Minutes* to tell his side of the story of his firing, no longer went meekly from their classrooms when confronted by principals and school boards. Gay university academics met for the first time in 1973 as part of the newly formed Gay Academic Union.

In some areas, such as elementary and high school education, the outlook was grimmer than in others, and some groups (the Gay Academic Union and the National Gay Task Force) were more immediately rent by internal strife as lesbian-feminist priorities clashed with traditional male perspectives. Yet the good of these disparate endeavors was that they reiterated the message again and again: We will not be quiet any longer, we are too numerous and too entwined in the very fabric of America to retreat into the closet ever again. "I left the first meeting of the Gay Academic Union" in New York in November 1973, John C. Graves, a philosophy instructor at MIT, recalled, "and I went back to Boston and came out in class the next week by talking to my students about this conference I had gone to, the way professors always talked about conferences. They sat absolutely rapt." Graves then taught the first gay studies course at MIT and started a New England chapter of the Gay Academic Union. "That's how it was done. Individuals inspiring other individuals. There was a great optimism in this period."

Even something as closed off to homosexuals as electoral politics began to seem, by degrees, more open. In 1970, the Gay Liberation Front of Los Angeles created a ruckus when Don Jackson and other activists announced their intention to legally "colonize" tiny Alpine County near Lake Tahoe. The thought that gay people might move to the area en masse, register to vote, and elect an all-gay county government sent shock waves throughout California; only later did it become clear that the plan was, in part, a media-savvy hoax. But by 1972, more authentic gay inroads had been made within the system. Jim Foster of SIR was invited to give a nationally televised address to the Democratic National Convention that nominated George McGovern and spoke on behalf of a gay rights plank (to the horror of many delegates), and within two years the first openly gay politician won elective office when Elaine Noble took her seat in the Massachusetts state legislature. Inspired by Noble's example, Minnesota state senator Allan Spear came out not long after on the front page of the *Minneapolis Star*. In the eyes of revolutionary activists, a dubious sort of progress and just so much tokenism, but the same developments were again taken as encouraging harbingers of change by the rest of America's gay population.

An uncontestably positive step was made in December 1973 when the board of trustees of the American Psychiatric Association voted to delete homosexuality from the official *Diagnostic and Statistical Manual* list of mental disorders. This, too, was not simply a matter of a group of doctors suddenly reevaluating their perceptions of gay life. Gays themselves played an active and carefully plotted role in the complex process that led to the psychiatrists' vote. Perhaps no other venture showed the tactical skills of the Gay National Task Force and its predecessors to better advantage. A louder watchdog presence at psychiatric conferences, behind-the-scenes lobbying, alliances with friendly and influential members of the APA, contact with regional psychiatric societies, the presentation of alternative papers, and a parade of "healthy homosexuals" who had never needed the services of the mental health profession were "the politics of diagnostic change," as Ronald Bayer termed it. The action called for varying strategies, and the activists were scrupulously attentive to all of them. "Knowing when to scream and shout and when not to," Ronald Gold commented, "it's an art. It's the art of politics." Hard-liners led by Irving Bieber and Charles Socarides complained that the APA's board had been intimidated by a pressure group with an increasingly threatening posture, but the membership backed the board's decision by a sizable majority in the balloting the next spring. "Sick No More," *The Advocate* trumpeted.

Yet if homosexuals were no longer officially sick, they were no less hated by violent predators and by police and city officials unhappy with the prospect of queer civil rights. A particularly traumatic year, 1973, created a backlash. The Metropolitan Community Church building and two gay bars in San Francisco were destroyed by arsonists, as was the Gay Services Center in Buffalo and a gay lounge in Springfield, Massachusetts. The MCC building in Los Angeles ("the mother church") was firebombed twice within six months. In San Antonio, Gene Elder and Hap Veltman opened The Country, the biggest gay bar and disco in that part of Texas, triggering a harassment campaign by local and military police intent on driving patrons, both civilians and soldiers, away. Most tragically, thirty-two men were killed in an arson blaze at the Upstairs Lounge, a popular New Orleans bar, after which some of the city's churches closed their doors to funerals or memorials for the victims.

But Stonewall was a living legacy now, and the news blackout about gay resistance and collective action long since over. The owners of The Country took the San Antonio police to court. Troy Perry and other gay activists went to New Orleans to conduct services for the dead and offer various kinds of aid. Within weeks, a gay switchboard opened there. The burned-out churches in California were rebuilt. "We did not see 1973 as a time to take a lower profile," Perry said. "On the contrary."

THERE WERE CRITICS. A raised profile invited trouble was one argument, made both by heterosexuals who wanted to know why discretion was suddenly being thrown to the winds and by an older generation of homosexuals who looked on the 1970s as a repudiation of an entire way of life. An element of understandable defensiveness crept into these exchanges between the generations. "Why make such a fuss? I don't want to be defined by what I do in bed" was a complaint that conveniently ignored the fact that those distinctions had been a part of American life for a very long time, to the detriment of all concerned. "A fag is a homosexual gentleman who has just left the room," Merle Miller noted in his *Times* essay, a truth Joseph Epstein readily confirmed in *Harper's*. If we are going to be so named and categorized by heterosexuals, the gay activists answered, in effect, then it is necessary to participate in—or control, to whatever extent possible—the process of defining. And that was a vocal, not a discreet, task.

A less easily answerable challenge from older gay men concerned sex practices themselves. "Gay liberation killed sex with straight men," as one elderly gay man summarized the change (not without annoyance) in a 1994 interview. Before the 1970s, the lines could, on occasion, be pleasantly blurred. For reasons of financial need, curiosity, convenience, or lust, a young man who dated women and planned to marry might bed down, or go into a park or a movie theater, with a man who self-identified as homosexual. But in an era when "gay" and "straight" assumed monolithic and antagonistic proportions (not unlike "Communist" and "anti-Communist" in the 1950s), the straight guy who wanted from time to time to get off with—or on, or in—a queer risked being branded something worse than trade or just plain horny. "Every schoolboy knows what a 'pansy' is," LaForrest Potter had written in 1933, and he might have added every schoolboy knew that he wasn't one because he didn't lisp and mince. Forty years later, every schoolboy knew what gay was and knew what he had to do to avoid the label. In the 1970s, letting a queer do him, even for money or laughs, could tarnish the reputation of both participants. Another goal of gay liberation, then, was to remake homosexual desire *for homosexuals* as a satisfaction in itself, to whittle away at the longtime need to evaluate sex with straight men as a more potent thrill.

At the same time, gay male life was changing in other ways, particularly in its own understanding of sexual object-choice vs. gender-role identification. In 1970, it was still possible to come out in a circle of friends who encouraged the use of a feminine nickname, taught you all the fey mannerisms, applauded bitchy wit, and included in their ranks at least one classic camp queen. By 1975, that milieu was much less common and began to seem more specialized, even quaintly historical. A gay man now was apt to describe himself, a bit defensively, as a *man* who wanted men. Camp and androgynous play didn't disappear, far from it. They were welcomed into one aspect of society at large, reborn as performance and ritual and tamed as entertainment for any suburbanite. Approximating styles that had been a feature of gay parties and drag balls for decades, stage artists as varied as the Divine Miss M, David Bowie, Alice Cooper, and Mick Jagger captivated large audiences. The personae and the popularity of rock stars like Jagger weren't emblematic of a new gender-role flexibility but, like the pansy craze of the late 1920s or the Michael Jackson craze of the 1990s, played an ironic role in transmuting a still-powerful threat. The same teenagers who beat the life out of a male classmate for wearing makeup in the cafeteria also attended rock concerts in which a studied masculine/feminine confusion was a key part of the act; Tiny Tim sat down to chat with Johnny Carson and Ed McMahon in the studio, not in their off-camera lives. Day-to-day reality became, if anything, less hospitable to the truly feminine male or real-life camp queen.

For those gay men who had found hyperfemininity an affectation and a trap, the newly acquired masculine style of the mid- to late 1970s—moustaches, pectorals, and jeans replacing the limp wrists, vicuna sweaters, and giddy humor of *The Boys in the Band*—was in itself a form of liberation. Yet there was a dark side to the glorification of gay masculinity. Freedom from clichés about queer boys who wouldn't fight back was invigorating, and there was no reason to fault gay male adoption of butchness as more superficial than it was among straight men. But the cultivation of a stance that was once used to marginalize and degrade gay men necessarily had different implications for them. Seymour Kleinberg pondered the trend in one of the most thoughtful essays of the decade, "Where Have All the Sissies Gone?," published in *Christopher Street*. "Young gay men," he wrote in 1978, "seem to have abjured effeminacy with universal success. Muscular bodies laboriously cultivated all year-round are standard; youthful athletic agility is everyone's style. The volleyball game on the beach is no longer a camp classic; now it takes itself as seriously as the San Francisco gay softball team. Hardness is in."

Kleinberg doubted that these men were any happier than those of his generation who came out in the 1950s, but more to the point, he wondered if the new look of homosexual life might be subtly aggravating old problems, binding gay men to a primitive, conservative notion of virility and worth: "The homosexuals who adopt images of masculinity, conveying their desire for power and their belief in its beauty, are in fact eroticizing the very values of straight society that have tyrannized their own lives. It is the tension between this style and the content of their lives that demands the oblivion of drugs and sexual libertinism. In the past, the duplicity of closeted lives found relief in effeminate camping; now the suppression or denial of the moral issue in their choice is far more damaging. The perversity of imitating their oppressors guarantees that such blindness will work itself out as self-contempt." Or, if not always in self-contempt, then in contempt for those who obstinately remained different, who clung to the defiant ambiguity of what soon came to be known as "gender fuck."

Drag queens never had any doubts about what this development meant for them. If the status of cross-dressers (the *"sans culottes* of gay liberation," as Kleinberg wrote) had been an unresolved issue in 1970 when GLF and GAA groups were first flexing their muscle, there wasn't much room for debate a few years later. Lesbians attacked the practice as a blatant insult to their biological womanhood, "manly" gay men denounced it as a sexual turnoff and an affront to the streamlined modern concept of gay, and gay politicos feared that the civil rights agenda for "normal" homosexuals was going to be sidetracked by attention to something that "confused the issue." The best way to placate the Marcus Welbys of the world, or one's own family or colleagues, was to demonstrate that gay men weren't weird or nellie and, furthermore, rejected offensive nellie behavior themselves. That approach begged a larger question, however, a question that seems to plague many radicals movements at one time or another: specifically, was the battle going to be won only by changing the terms of the conflict, refining away the abrasiveness of the initial threat to the status quo? In the case of sexual deviance, that meant narrowing homosexuality (or, more properly, gayness) to a set of physical acts, working against the view of gay liberation as a springboard for a larger investigation of conformity, role-playing, intolerance, and patriarchy in American life. It meant keeping drag queens off the podium at marches and wording civil rights legislation in such a way as to minimize its relevance to anything other than privacy in the bedroom.

In the midst of all this celebrating of gay sexuality for the firm-of-muscle and against a background of much irrelevant talk about numbers and statistics (with "10 percent" assuming a hallowed, artificial power), some gay men tried to steer the discussion on a different course. Worrying about the approval of middle-class America was not only futile, they argued, it will sidetrack us from the more important business of deciding what *we* think about ourselves. Defense of something now termed a "lifestyle" sapped energies put to better use elsewhere. "Who are we? Where do we come from? What are we for?"—these were the questions Harry Hay and the original Mattachine members had posed as essential to gay fulfillment. By the mid-1970s, those queries were in danger of being dismissed as silly.

A less tortured view of homosexual sex was all well and good, the skeptics noted, but it could hardly be the basis for a real community. Likewise, an exclusively political outlook had its limitations in terms of psychological or spiritual transformation and was apt to devolve in the end to a co-optation by those who simply wanted our votes. As Don Kilhefner noted, "a gay 'bagman' for the Democratic or Republican Party is indistinguishable from his non-gay counterpart." It was in the domain of consciousness itself that some gay men wanted to see more striving, and their critique of gay life was not unconnected to the precipitous gay male retreat from androgyny and femininity. Various San Francisco–based theatrical groups such as the Cockettes, the Angels of Light, the Sisters of Perpetual Indulgence, and a few performance artists of great ingenuity kept alive the "tradition of radical drag," as Mark Thompson called it in his essay "Children of Paradise: A Brief History of Queens." Their objectives were not always the same. When Logan Carter performed in "Gender," lip-synching "What Makes a Man a Man," he transformed himself onstage from a credible femme fatale to a trim young stud in sneakers and jeans—the emerging "gay clone"—demolishing along the way the plausibility of a gender-style essence. On the other hand, members of the theater troupes as well as the Imperial Courts of drag queens in numerous cities wore veils, tiaras, and dresses to downplay the real-man-in-pants ethic and to reclaim a sissy identification that most gay men were fleeing from. They were in full agreement with Kleinberg's thesis: rejecting any traces of delicacy or whimsy and assuming the guise of those who had always made life miserable for gay men (the rugged men of the world, the only world that counted) was a tragic error, a capitulation rather than an advance.

This line of thought and expression went beyond gender politics. For those who organized the far-flung branches of the Radical Faeries in the 1970s (a phenomenon of the western and southern states), the purpose was loftier and more unconventional. It spoke to a wish to go beyond science and psychology (with its focus on aberration and adjustment), beyond the usual notions of social acceptance and liberal philosophy (we are all the same at heart and so should tolerate one another). It entered into the realms of neo-paganism, historical and anthropological exploration, and "gay soul" or "gay spirit." In *Witchcraft and the Gay Counterculture: A Radical View of Western Civilization and Some of the People It Has Tried to Destroy* (1978), Arthur Evans posited a link between modern gays and the nature-worshiping, goddess-led tribes of Celtic, Roman, and early Christian times who, later outlawed and known in folklore as "fairies," reemerged in the Middle Ages to be labeled—and destroyed—as heretics and witches. In his influential essay "Visionary Love" (1976), published as part of a longer book in 1980, Jungian psychologist Mitch Walker endeavored to create a gay mythology of identity formation in contrast to the "false-self system" of presumptive heterosexuality. Inspired by his study of tribal shamans and particularly the Native American "Two Spirit" tradition of the *berdache*, Harry Hay began to write and lecture about gay consciousness as something that was innately different from "hetero consciousness." The former arose from what he called an egalitarian "subject-subject" view of the world; the latter, a "subject-object" view marked by competition, alienation, and the ego-driven need to fight and subjugate. Those men who—like Evans, Walker, and Hay—were ready to take the word *fairy* back from those who had degraded it as an epithet, and to stop running from the little boy within who had learned to hide his gentleness from the disapproving eyes of parents and schoolyard bullies, came together in outdoor ritual gatherings, or Faerie Circles, to nourish a noncompetitive "gay soul" of fraternity and openness.

Described by Stuart Timmons, Hay's biographer, as "a mixture of a political alternative, a counterculture, and a spirituality movement . . . a networking of gentle men devoted to the principles of ecology, spirituality, and, in New Age terms, 'gay centeredness,' " the Radical Faeries met for their first large convocation in Arizona in 1979. Hay himself was leery of the term *movement*, preferring to think of the Radical Faeries as part of a process or way of life, one that went against the grain of the more visible aspects of modern urban gayness as fiercely as it went against the grain of bourgeois heterosexual America. The main point was that its participants believed they had answered the original Mattachine questions: despite millennia of persecution, gay men (as distinct from those who merely performed homosexual acts) had survived for a reason. They served an evolutionary purpose. Though most gay men might end their days as docile citizens and eager conformists, identical to their straight neighbors save for their sexual tastes, *they did not start out that way.* The Radical Faerie philosophy called on them to remember the intense social conditioning that molded them and to become, once again, what they were as children, a force the world desperately needed—neither inferior men nor imitation women, but a playful, imaginative, heretical tribe who by their nature loved camaraderie and disliked aggression, swagger, and ruthless competition.

It wasn't likely that vast numbers of men in late twentieth-century America were going to gravitate to a revised version of the nineteenth-century concept of the "third sex," any more than they would stand naked and mud-covered in the Arizona sun or exult in the hated "fairy" label, whatever its mythopoetic roots. (And it probably wasn't until later in the 1980s when Mark Thompson's fine anthology *Gay Spirit* was published that many eastern or midwestern gays even heard of this new intellectual, or spiritual, current.) Furthermore, rancor among strong-minded men was more easily banished in theory than in reality—Hay, for one, was a model autocrat, in his detractors' eyes—and the rural land trust they hoped to create never got off the ground. Yet the Faeries rightly believed that theirs was a much-needed questioning of self and society. The energies of Western culture were devoted to elevating science and denigrating myth and mysticism, to grinding all experience through one standardizing lens, to ever more fevered worship of Normality. The Faeries wanted their peers to speculate about gayness not as something that just happened (fortunate or otherwise), but as something nature *intended*, and to awaken in gay men a feeling that they had to think more grandly about identity, or to dig deeper, than they had before.

ANOTHER AWAKENING OF comparable magnitude was in its nascent stage in the 1970s. Gay men of Latino, African, Asian, or Native American descent were, at different moments and in different places, beginning to clarify what gay liberation meant to them and the ways in which it was not an endeavor—particularly as a mainstream political cause—that could speak to all, or even many, of their needs. They were outnumbered by white men who more easily and quickly took charge in organizational hierarchies, and even at their most well intentioned, the bonds between gay men of different colors were tainted by a cultural heritage of inequality or outright belligerence. Black men, who were asked to show double or triple IDs at gay bars, while white patrons might not be carded at all, had good reason to bristle at the inflated claims of progress made in the decade after Stonewall. Asian-American gay men who learned that they were regarded as a specialty taste among white gay men—an object of interest to the "rice queen," much as the black man was to the "dinge queen"—understood that most American homosexuals were no less racist or imbued with colonialist fantasies than heterosexuals. As Gil Mangaoang wrote in a 1996 essay about his political, racial, and sexual identity, it was difficult enough twenty years ago to develop a strong sense of self as a Filipino-American and a left-wing activist in a country with scant use for either, but it was a much harder feat "to tap into the exhilarating feeling of being openly gay and to become an integral part of that '70s generation of gay activists." The earlier GLF concern that *gay* could never embody a sufficiently universal experience, or one set of aspirations, or even one way of speaking, if it failed to take into account race and class did not die with the Gay Liberation Front.

Separatism has always been a highly charged word in a society that has so much invested in the image of the melting pot. But as the lesbians who moved out from under the male banner of "gay" knew, a pretense of unity mainly benefits the numerical majority. Lesbians came into their own as a political and cultural force only with, or after, their break with the men. At some point, separatism—as a permanent state or a transitional stage—is both natural and productive. Such divisions have the potential to be enormously creative. The first steps in that direction for men and women of color were necessarily small scale, but the groundwork for a new kind of 1980s activism was laid. In Los Angeles in 1970, Unidos came together as the first Chicano/Chicana gay organization, and in San Francisco in 1975, Randy Burns, a Northern Paiute, and Barbara Cameron, a Lakota Sioux, founded Gay American Indians, which began as a small social club and numbered six hundred members as a national body ten years later. Though it was important, Burns agreed, "to break down the image of the Indian as a macho militant," mutual support was a more pressing goal. "Gay American Indians is first and foremost a group for *each other*," Cameron added in a 1976 interview. Elsewhere, local or college groups, such as the Philadelphia Black Gays or the Gay Studies Circle at the University of Puerto Rico or San Francisco's Asian-American Alliance, were based on the same premise. At the time of the first National Lesbian and Gay March on Washington in October 1979, a Third World Lesbian Gay Conference held at Howard University included a second march of its own. "The early morning march through the Black neighborhood and through Chinatown was the first time Black and Asian lesbians and gay men had paraded through their own neighborhoods," according to activist Daniel Tsang. The symbolism of that event was vital. Hurdles cleared with the Civil Service Commission, the television networks, or the American Psychiatric Association were victories that naturally spoke more to whites than to people of color, a fact that is not a criticism of those accomplishments but a statement about racial imbalances in employment, the media, and the mental health profession.

Even as seemingly straightforward a topic as the place of gays in the military went beyond homosexuality itself, raising the more complicated issues of race and gender-role definitions. Though Pentagon officials had no reason to be surprised, middle America was shaken to read in the waning days of the Vietnam fiasco about the extent of sexual deviance in the armed forces and the brazenness of the accused who decided to fight back. In 1972, Petty Officer Third Class Bob Martin (a.k.a. Stephen Donaldson) became the first sailor to refuse to go quietly when confronted with confessions from his sexual partners. As the founder in 1967 of the first college gay group, at Columbia University, and as a longtime member of Mattachine, the twenty-six-year-old Martin had plenty of experience standing up to intimidating authorities. He eventually won a general discharge. At the same time, eighteen-year-old Jeffrey Dunbar went public with his case, enlisting the support of Frank Kameny, the *Washington Post*, and the Washington Gay Activists Alliance. (The GAA picket at Quantico brought an unnerving sight to the Marines at the base where Dunbar was stationed: protestors carried signs reading THE MARINE CORPS BUILDS CLOSET CASES: ASK A MARINE and YOUR DRILL SERGEANT COULD BE GAY.) The case of Ensign Vernon Berg received even more press, as he was the son of a Navy commander and chaplain who stood by him at his trial.

None of the cases prior to Vernon Berg's elicited much interest or support from the gay movement. The much-favored term *diversity* was not meant to include men or women in uniform who believed in military service and honored the flag. As an Annapolis graduate who had served as an assistant chief of staff to a NATO vice admiral, Berg seemed to Bruce Voeller of the National Gay Task Force and the lawyers of the Lambda Legal Defense Fund to be a good candidate for a test case, and his litigation did in fact end with an upgraded discharge and a cash settlement. Air Force Sergeant Leonard Matlovich's qualifications for that role were even more impressive. Winner of a Bronze Star and a Purple Heart from his three tours of duty in Vietnam, Matlovich was a white, middle-class patriot of the first order, a gay man who had come out for the sake of honesty and who dreamed of monogamy and a quiet suburban life with a male partner. Throughout 1975 and 1976, gay groups around the country made use of him, to the point of exploitation, to raise funds and enhance the profile of the movement. Even *Time* magazine agreed with the assessment of Matlovich as the ideal poster boy. In September 1975, he appeared on the cover in uniform, with a blunt caption in large letters: "I Am a Homosexual: The Gay Drive for Acceptance."

In contrast to the Matlovich case, which was later the subject of a TV movie, the experience of Perry Watkins never held the attention of the media, the gay movement, or gay men in general. Yet his story was at least as fascinating, and Watkins no less bold and no less committed to the service than Berg and Matlovich. But one key difference existed. Watkins was, in his words, "a little black nelly queen." In 1967, at the age of nineteen, he had been drafted and accepted into the Army despite checking the "Yes" box on the medical history form at his induction that asked about homosexual tendencies. He remained in the service for the next several years and was highly regarded for both his crackerjack clerical skills and his flamboyant performances as "Simone Monet," who could do Diana Ross or Eartha Kitt like nobody's business. In lavish gowns and heels and with a trademark seven-foot boa, "Simone" was a hit with the Army's recreational program in West Germany; the *Army Times* even ran an identifying photo of the African-American female impersonator in sequined glory next to a photo of

Staff Sergeant Watkins in uniform. Beginning in 1975, the Army decided that their approval of Watkins's drag act and the high marks he had always received on his job evaluations were no longer relevant, especially in light of his refusal to deny his homosexuality and the Pentagon's smaller manpower needs. They suddenly wanted him out. Watkins then endured a back-and-forth journey through the legal system that lasted from the mid-1970s into the 1980s, a battle he refused to walk away from. In 1990, the U.S. Supreme Court, by declining to hear the government's appeal, backed up an Appeals Court decision ordering Watkins's reinstatement. But, given his color and effeminacy, he was made to feel on more than a few occasions that he was not a desirable spokesman for the cause. During the Sam Nunn hearings on the proposed Clinton executive order in 1993, as Margarethe Cammermeyer and others made the trip to Capitol Hill, his phone was conspicuously silent.

The National Gay Task Force and the Radical Faeries, Bruce Voeller and Ronald Gold, Harry Hay and Randy Burns, Leonard Matlovich and Perry Watkins—the achievements of many groups and individuals of different, even antagonistic styles merit remembering. But there is no doubt that the white, straight-acting homosexual was perceived to be the safer bet in publicizing the fight to open doors and secure rights for gay men and lesbians. The unresolved question was whether that belief—that tactic—would yield sufficient gains to justify its failure of nerve and spirit.

20

THE PLEASURE PRINCIPLE

It was like discovering candy as a kid—better. It wasn't just the physical sensations. It was the idea that no one from any of the other areas of my life knew where I was at the moment. I felt *comfortable* there, and that was a great surprise to me.

—Sam Garrison, staff lawyer for
Vice President Agnew, describing his first
visits to the baths in Washington, D.C.,
in the early 1970s

With gay politics and culture regularly in the news and the campaign for legal reform gaining momentum, it was easy to forget that life for most gay men in the early 1970s was still a matter of keeping a big secret and making compromises. The American Psychiatric Association's about-face did not transform the analyst's couch into a welcoming space overnight. Many gay men and lesbians continued to fear for their jobs. Family disapproval remained an emotional stumbling block of staggering proportions. The more universal difference from pre-Stonewall days involved a gradual decline in police harassment of gay activities conducted in private and a corresponding increase in the opportunities for uninhibited sex.

Bathhouses were the most obvious gauge of the new atmosphere. Men who would never have imagined setting foot in a gay bathhouse in the 1960s, or who would have had to travel a great distance to do so, became

"Buddy Night" regulars a few years later. The aura and the physical circumstances of the experience were different, its outlaw status revised, and
the number of such places had grown dramatically. "Skipper's Newsletter,"
published out of Danville, Kentucky, listed 102 bathhouses in the continental United States and Puerto Rico as of the fall of 1972. (In 1976, Randy
Shilts put the number at 150 and, by the early 1980s, Allan Bérubé estimated in his essay "The History of Gay Bathhouses," that the number had
reached 200.) No longer a phenomenon exclusive to major metropolises,
bathhouses of one kind or another could be found in the 1970s in
Akron, Billings, Camden, Duluth, East Hartford, Galveston, Louisville,
Portsmouth, Savannah, Tampa, Toledo, and Kenosha, Wisconsin.

None of this is to suggest that bathhouses did not figure prominently
in the lives of gay men throughout the century. Charles Demuth's World
War I–era watercolors depict an erotically charged space of towel-clad men
wandering bathhouse corridors, and George Chauncey's *Gay New York*
documents pre-1930s raids on various Manhattan bathhouses, including
the Lafayette, which Demuth frequented. A 1903 raid on a sauna in the
basement of the Ariston Hotel at Broadway and Fifty-fifth Street led to a
twenty-year prison term for one patron, while other defendants caught in
the act received sentences of several years in the penitentiary. Yet, despite
the risks, the baths were, as Chauncey wrote, "the safest, most enduring,
and one of the most affirmative of the settings in which gay men gathered
in the first half of the twentieth century." New York's Everard was sufficiently famous in gay circles by the late 1920s to be a topic of discussion
among European men. London offered "*nothing* compared to it," a
Parisian friend told British actor Emlyn Williams, who was advised to pay a
visit. The Palace Baths near the Palace Hotel in San Francisco also attracted
"our kind, in significant numbers," a visitor from Germany was instructed
in the same period.

The appropriation of public baths, or more commonly private Russian
or Turkish baths, into gay spaces—at certain times of the day or in certain
parts of the bathhouse or, eventually, in toto—was an old practice by the
time of Pearl Harbor. Thousands of young servicemen eager to experiment
but who knew of the MP raids on off-limits bars learned that a bathhouse
was the better place to try their luck. Besides being a less public site, the
owners often developed a more secure relationship with the police than bar
owners, and in the event of trouble, a visitor could always claim he didn't
know what kind of bathhouse it was, a less credible excuse in a bar. The
social dynamic allowed for more freedom as well: exchanging names and
making dates to meet again was possible, but complete anonymity was
easily maintained in a steam room or on a mattress beneath a forty-watt

bulb. In the early 1940s the bathhouse scene thrived as never before. "It was so easy to tell when they were in the service, even though they checked their uniforms before they got there," recalled a civilian gay man of his numerous wartime encounters in Chicago's four bathhouses. "I had sex with hundreds, thousands, of guys in those years who would never have looked at me on the street or in a bar." (Illegal "locker clubs" in many cities enabled soldiers to check their uniforms and rent civvies for street wear.) In an interview in the 1990s, one World War II marine spoke of running into two other men from his company on furlough at the Liberty Baths in Pittsburgh, not one of them knowing beforehand that the others were so inclined, while the activity among soldiers at the Bellevue Baths in Philadelphia, Henry Gerber told a friend, was nothing short of "bacchanalian." Any city with a Navy shipyard or an Army base nearby was fertile territory.

Though they remained for the most part physically unpleasant—or at least inelegant—places, located in dangerous neighborhoods and staffed by rude (often straight) attendants, bathhouses found a stable, relatively uncomplicated niche in gay life in the postwar years. Race remained a great divider (the Mount Morris Baths in Harlem catered to black men who were often denied admission to bathhouses in midtown Manhattan), but the issues and pressures of the bar world were often kept at bay, or altered. Cruising is different in a towel, which negates worry about a proper outfit, lengthy barstool conversation, vice squad entrapment, or unpleasant surprises when the clothes come off. Plenty of gay men regarded a trip to the baths as beneath them and marveled at friends who were tacky enough to go, but in a hostile society many others felt more relaxed there than in any other exclusively gay setting. The feeling of security wasn't always illusory. Even when raids and closings of gay bars swept "clean" an entire city, it was often the case that the bathhouses—less visible and therefore less noted by newsmen and politicians—were left untouched. By the late 1960s, some sociologists and psychiatrists, influenced by the new mores like everyone else, found it hard to register much indignation on the subject. "If one were called upon to justify the existence of the homosexual baths," Martin Hoffman wrote in *The Gay World* in 1968, "this would not be too difficult a task, since they are basically only known to those who are already homosexually oriented, and provide no nuisance to the public. If anything, they keep homosexuals out of those public places where they most frequently run into trouble with the police. The almost exclusive focus there on genital activity in preference to any other kind of relationship that might take place between two persons is, of course, not one which can evoke much enthusiasm from anyone who feels that sexual activity should be integrated into a meaningful human relationship. Nevertheless, it is difficult to see how the baths do any harm, since their clientele have already reached the stage which perhaps could be best described as a concentration upon sexual activity for its own sake."

One of the most significant developments in the contemporary history of the baths involved gay ownership and the founding of one particular bathhouse chain. In 1965, Jack Campbell and two partners opened their own bathhouse in Cleveland. "There had been a bathhouse in the downtown area that was straight during the day and gay at night," he remembered. When it was torn down, the owner decided he didn't want anything more to do with a gay clientele and moved his business out to Shaker Heights. Campbell took advantage of the situation, bought an old sauna that was for sale in the Finnish section of the city, and fixed it up. "I had been to San Francisco and so I knew that bathhouses didn't have to be so dumpy, like the ones in New York and Chicago. I specifically wanted a better, cleaner atmosphere." His Finnish clientele quickly figured out what was going on—Cleveland's gay men were being welcomed, not discouraged, at "The Club"—and departed altogether. Business soared. The next year, Campbell and his associates opened a second bathhouse, the Sixth City Sauna, followed in 1967 by another using the name The Club, in Toledo. As the Club chain expanded, the investors at first went only into smaller towns close to larger cities (Hammond, Indiana, rather than nearby Chicago itself) or to outlying areas near highways offering convenient access. "It was all thought out very carefully," Campbell explained. "We didn't want to go into residential or upscale neighborhoods. We looked for areas with business or industry during the day and not much going on at night, which guaranteed privacy, and we looked to take in a partner from the new city, someone to keep an eye on the till." The response in each community among gay men exceeded Campbell's expectations. "For men who were married or didn't have a place to take somebody, we were a godsend. And there wasn't any nonsense about straight managers or attendants looking down on the men who went there." By 1971 the Club chain included fourteen bathhouses from Atlanta and New Orleans to St. Louis, Buffalo, and Newark, offering student discounts and special rates for men who arrived in pairs on Buddy Night.

From furtiveness and squalor to middle-class tidiness to bathhouse chic—the changes in quality and perception followed quickly. Paving the way toward the latter plateau was Stewart Ostrow's famed Continental Baths in New York City. Opened in 1968 in the basement of a landmark hotel, the Ansonia, the Continental adopted the Jack Campbell approach of pleasant, gay-friendly surroundings and included a pool and dance floor.

An added attraction was the entertainment. Melba Moore, Cab Calloway, Tiny Tim, Dick Gregory, and, most spectacularly, Bette Midler performed in the discotheque area to crowds of cheering men in various states of undress or stark naked in the pool. "My career took off when I sang at the Continental Baths in New York," Midler commented in 1972. "Those tubs became the showplace of the nation. I made 'em respectable." A year later, soprano Eleanor Steber sang for the same unusual audience for what was called a "black towel" concert. When the *Pat Collins Show* on WCBS broadcast in February 1974 from "the Grossinger's of the gay set," as Collins called it, over 100,000 unfazed New Yorkers watched the program, with the network reporting only a single irate caller. The unspeakable had become the fashionably interesting to gays and straights, at least in New York. Terrence McNally's 1973 play *The Tubs* (rewritten for Broadway and Hollywood two years later as *The Ritz*) was set in a bathhouse, as was A. J. Kronengold's *Tubstrip*.

The legitimization of the bathhouse experience had a profound impact on gay male life. Gay sex was now, for the first time, protectively zoned. Police harassment didn't end all at once, but a more liberal judiciary was clear in its dealings with those police officers who were slow to get the message. A raid at the Club Baths in Miami in 1975, for example, was disturbing, but all sixty-four cases were immediately thrown out of court by the judge. By the end of the decade, a bathhouse was one of the most secure of gay sites, and hundreds of thousands of gay men recognized them as a choice for an evening's pleasure equivalent to a bar or disco. "There was so much business to go around," according to Chuck Renslow, who owned Man's Country in Chicago, "that competition was not a problem." Large cities could easily support two or three bathhouses, each of which had three or four thousand customers a week renting a room or a locker for the night. The scant documentation that exists offers a plausible picture: 54 percent of the male respondents to Karla Jay and Allen Young's *The Gay Report* (1979) visited the baths more than once in their lives, and 20 percent of the 5,000 men surveyed described their visits as "somewhat" or "very" frequent; 47 percent regarded a bathhouse as a "somewhat" or "very" desirable site for sex.

The popularity of the baths wasn't greeted with unanimous approval among gay men. To former GLF types, the situation spelled trouble on many counts. What gay men did at the baths was no different, they argued, from what straight men did to women in society at large. Using individuals as sex objects, so many notches in the belt, was not a gay liberation goal. Equally distressing was the way in which sexual indulgence tended to supplant activism as a means of identification with homosexuality, which in turn reinforced the worst kind of barriers. Only the naive thought it was coincidental that most bathhouses were populated by men of the same skin color and social affect. Diversity, like political commitment and consciousness-raising, never made it past the front door. The other oft-heard criticism was medical. The baths made sex too easy, and gay men were consequently having more of it with more partners, and so became infected with venereal diseases and virulent strains of hepatitis at an alarming rate. The baths encouraged the use of stimulants such as Quaaludes and poppers, which were likewise dangerous. Gay men didn't altogether ignore the sex-hazard theme—articles about sexually transmitted diseases appeared in the gay press, free VD tests were provided at some bathhouses, clinics staffed by gay doctors for gay patients made treatment easier and less embarrassing—but the warnings of a Pandora's box scenario did little to stem the excitement the baths inspired.

The post-AIDS take on the baths has been so negative, and the characterization of sexually active gay men of the 1970s so dismissive, that it is worth reflecting on the multiple positive meanings the baths offered for a generation that was more politically optimistic than psychologically at ease with being gay. Bars, cruising spots, dances, books, movies (X-rated or otherwise), rap sessions, drop-in centers, campus organizations, and gay pride demonstrations taught young gay men many things, some (such as the lessons of the tearooms and pornographic movies) more troublesome and complex than others. None, however, could teach young men how to feel the *joy* in making love that Western culture affirmed in dozens of ways for heterosexual couples, from the onset of adolescence. In its bathhouse dimension, "the Stonewall experiment," to use poet Ian Young's apt phrase, took that as its mission and amply succeeded. It was not that the baths ruled out wider human connections, as some critics maintained. It was often easier to meet people in a less pretentious atmosphere, and many friendships and lifetime-partner relationships were forged there, especially in those bathhouses that had space for eating and socializing. The television rooms, vending machines, Jacuzzis, shag carpeting, and wood paneling of the Club chain made a statement that set it apart from the grubby-barracks quality of those places that discouraged casual conversations or postcoital hanging out. (The fact that the older, dumpier establishments continued to thrive, even as the new bathhouses emphasized cleanliness and civilized decor, suggests that a significant number of gay men didn't want their sex venues tidied up. The back alley did not lose its aphrodisiacal allure, ten thousand "Gay Is Good" banners to the contrary.) The codes evolved at the baths over the years also lessened traditional sexual tensions. Rejection at the open door of a room was routinely and delicately handled in the set phrase "Just resting," and the position of the room's occupant—on his back or on his stomach—made for a useful, immediate clarity about sexual tastes and compatibility. In a subculture with only a catch-as-catch-can tradition of dating and "parking," the baths allowed for sex play as much as anything more hard-core, for controlled situations and levels of intimacy.

The barriers that did exist were by no means as apparent as those that seemed to be stripped away: shorn of clothes, rich and poor look pretty much alike. The dark of an orgy room gave old and young, handsome and unsightly, a more level, less brutally competitive playing field. Married men, who were more accustomed to a quickie in a car or a rest room, could relax without worrying about a surprise police presence. (Priests or young men still living with their parents or with straight roommates enjoyed the same advantage in this regard.) Lovers who would have recoiled at an affair as a relationship-threatening breach of trust might accompany each other for a night of anonymous sex that didn't carry over into their lives at home. Communal showering replayed the high school gym class experience with a delightful twist. Staring appreciatively at other nude male bodies was finally the norm, not the mark of the misfit queer. Describing his first visit to New York's St. Marks Baths in 1963, science-fiction writer Samuel Delany wrote of the "heart-thudding astonishment, very close to fear" he felt on that occasion, a fear born of the contradiction between public perception (homosexuals as a small, isolated group) and unexpected reality. "The first direct sense of political power," Delany concluded, "comes from the apprehension of massed bodies."

Yet the nature of the baths wasn't static, and it isn't anything that is plausibly cast in too Pollyanna-ish a light twenty years later. Sexual energy resists channeling into neat paths, and in a nation of Disney theme parks, imagination and money are often put to service in the strangest causes. Within a few years, the simplicity of Jack Campbell's 1965 concept underwent some lurid adaptations. From the infamous truck—a life-size, fully assembled replica—on the ninth floor of Man's Country in Manhattan, in the back of which patrons could act out trucker fantasies in near-total darkness, to San Francisco's cavernous Bulldog Baths, reputedly the largest in the country (and the sponsor of the Biggest Cock in San Francisco Contest), gay men in the late 1970s created boundless opportunities to test the limits of their libido in progressively more outlandish settings. Having sex with someone you'd never see again, with a man whose name you didn't know, with the embodiment of your most powerful fantasies, with a group of strangers, in the privacy of your own jailhouse cell or faux-flophouse room, or in front of spectators: this was a way of life, anathema to most of America, that gay men chose to explore in a fairly unapologetic way in the decade after Stonewall. That exploration was plausible in the context of the most erotically hyped decade homosexuals or heterosexuals had ever known in the United States, and beneficial—psychologically rein-forcing—to men brought up as the American family's dirty little secret. As is true of all explorations (whatever the intentions of its individual partici-pants), it couldn't last indefinitely in the same form. Time quickly altered both the content and the meaning.

IRONICALLY, THE MOST succinct and cogent case for the world of the bath-house came not from a gay man, but from a lesbian. In 1975, novelist Rita Mae Brown dressed in male drag and paid a visit to a gay bathhouse in New York City with her friend Arthur Bell. Recounting her experiences in the essay "Queen for a Day: A Stranger in Paradise," Brown was anything but horror-struck by the towel-clad men socializing and the naked coupling she observed. In fact, she saw it as an option lesbians should have for them-selves. The desire for the purest physical gratification wasn't a character flaw, Brown noted, and the bathhouse she visited seemed more than any-thing to be a place of "relief, refuge, release," and a situation that offered choices. Short-term sex didn't preclude long-term relationships. An evening at the baths didn't make you a terrible person, a lost soul, or a basket case.

But what about many evenings at the baths? Or years of weekly out-ings? What about the baths as a primary form of sexual expression, so that two men at home alone in bed could begin to seem quaint, or sex without poppers and an audience nice but unarousing? The trap inherent in the use of sex as a regular, or ritualized, means of self-validation is that the glands end by demanding parity with the intellect. Choice is eventually relin-quished to need, to hunger and habit. If there was always a danger in mak-ing gayness a central element of identity—it lacked a widely known history and common culture, it meant too many different things to different people—that danger was compounded by making arousal itself the very core of that part of identity. The stimulation doesn't end when those goals ancillary to orgasm are achieved; a young man who has long since decided he likes being gay and is comfortable with gay sex and socializing might then integrate an occasional trip to the baths into the fullness of his life. But he might—and many did—find himself caught, the lightheartedness gone out of the venture as the addictive and enervating quality of the bathhouse experience took its toll. The voluminous sexual diaries of Ron Hardcastle, discussed in Douglas Sadownick's *Sex Between Men* (1996), make the point in fascinating detail. "Sex gave Hardcastle's life meaning at a time when he was struggling to find firm ground to stand on as a gay man," Sadownick wrote, but the casualness and vast number of encounters both expanded and radically constricted his world.

Then, too, the baths were only one aspect of the new model of liberation. What had originally been advanced as an implicit critique of heterosexual values—asking perfectly reasonable questions on the order of: Was monogamy essential to love and lifelong commitment? Whose interests were served by accepting society's definitions of fidelity and promiscuity? Could sex be divested of its aura of dominance and submission?—became, for some men, a search for the arousal and gratification that older, tamer acts and settings could no longer provide. Anecdotal evidence suggests that the advent of fisting, or fist-fucking, dates from 1969 to 1970. Sadomasochism and leather fetishism seemed to find a larger, more responsive audience over the next few years. The decaying piers next to the Westside Highway in Manhattan became a favored cruising spot. Porno shops even in small cities and outlying areas opened backroom spaces for quick sexual contacts in kinky settings. By the middle of the decade, backroom bars and clubs in several cities attracted thousands of urban men who led middle-class lives by day but conducted the sexual hunt between midnight and dawn in warehouse and meat-packing district bars where the dress code kept the fairies out, and where, in darkened rooms behind the bar or in the basement, anything was possible against the wall, on the urine-encrusted concrete floor, or in the bathtub provided by the management. "The Anvil on a Saturday night is more popular than the Concord on a holiday weekend," Arthur Bell quipped in the *Village Voice* in 1977, and he might have added that New York's Anvil was no less respectable, no more otherworldly, to a certain strata of gay urban culture than the Catskills resort was to its middle-class Jewish patrons.

"Promiscuity knits together the social fabric of the gay community," the Canadian gay magazine *The Body Politic* suggested at the time. But it was remarkable how many different styles and levels of promiscuity there turned out to be. And how different this new model of liberation was from the more transforming program of GLF and GAA, which had envisioned, in their different ways, sexual celebration as linked to empathy, outreach, activism, and social change. And how charming and antiquated it rendered those earlier Edward Carpenter ideals of soul-bonding, evoked in *Maurice* (1971), E. M. Forster's tale of love in the greenwood—and his posthumous gift to the gay men of the 1970s. Some of the more thoughtful devotees of backroom bars argued that there was no reason to evaluate their choice in a different light from, say, the baths with their beds and private areas. The principle was the same: "To help a stranger to orgasm is a very loving thing to do," Arnie Kantrowitz wrote in one of his *Advocate* essays in 1978. "Promiscuity parlors need not threaten other kinds of relating, but may be a pleasure and a learning experience in their own right." He spoke up for honest acknowledgment of "the back rooms as a valid form of sexuality" about which those who frequented them "should feel no need to lie." To Arthur Bell, on the other hand, the dimly lit nightspots with their prison chamber affect and assembly-line style of sex resembled "combat zones" for "peak thrills" that hinted at a collective death wish more than any kind of affirmation. "When homosexuality came out of the closet," he lamented in his *Village Voice* column in 1977, "romance went in and bolted the door." A potential feast had become, in the space of just a few years, an orgy of "TV dinners for young men in a hurry."

The films and magazines devoted to gay sex were even more vitally concerned with the equation of gay liberation with unrestrained libido because they reached people who hadn't heard of the Anvil or the Mineshaft, or who were far from the fisting emporia of San Francisco or the truck at Man's Country. In 1968, a festival of Pat Rocco's soft-core films in California was a momentous event. The kind of movies nervously screened at home with the shades drawn only a few years before (nude men gamboling in the wild; no dialogue, no sex) were now shown in public cinemas. "The moon landing wasn't such a big deal in Los Angeles," joked one gay man, who had in fact been arrested in the 1950s for possession of "obscene" films. The cultural ascendancy of Kenneth Anger and Andy Warhol made a difference, not least in bringing the sublime Joe D'Allesandro to the screen, and Wakefield Poole's discovery of blond, lithe Casey Donovan led to the hard-core breakthrough of *Boys in the Sand* (1971), establishing Donovan as the first gay porn superstar and earning Poole a good profit and a *Variety* review. The slow-paced, romantic quality of the sex in *Boys in the Sand* was not destined to carry the day, however. For hip modern audiences, simple erotica was only slightly preferable to Rocco's fraternal nuzzling and smooching. Men wanted a rougher edge, whether it was in Fred Halsted's sadomasochistic *L.A. Plays Itself* and *Sextool* or in the hundreds of slam-bam garage mechanic/football coach/ cowhand/construction worker/cop stories that directors churned out as the market grew by leaps and bounds.

In 1976, studios like Colt and Falcon were making forty such films a year, and the bigger mail-order companies purportedly had customer lists of 40,000 names, with most of their sales coming from states like Arkansas, Oklahoma, and Iowa. In large cities where censorship efforts had ground to a halt entirely, some movie houses became sex sites themselves. The fantasy potential of these settings equaled that of the wildest bathhouses and made heterosexual swinging look timid. Straight guys took their girlfriends to see *Deep Throat* or *The Devil in Miss Jones* but, unlike gay men, weren't stripping in the aisles or turning the mezzanine into an arena for groping and sucking.

Sex appeal on the page aimed for a more mainstream approach, and credit for that (such as it is) goes to the likes of Burt Reynolds and George Maharis. *Playgirl* had made male nudity viable, one publisher commented in mid-decade about the magazine that had talked the two Hollywood stars into undressing, and it didn't surprise anyone in the industry that 39 percent of *Playgirl*'s readers were reportedly male. Hard-core gay pornography in books and magazines was a thriving under-the-counter business in the 1960s, but the glossy, well-photographed approach was something different, something many gay men craved. Newsstand vendors saw the point. If stocking a magazine with photos of nude men, ostensibly for liberated women, was both allowable and desirable, then there was no reason to be squeamish about the shapely pectorals of "Bruno" or Al Parker's formidable crotch. *Blueboy* was available on newsstands in 1975, after publishing its fifth issue, claiming a 26,000 subscription base and a 160,000 print run a year later, though most industry professionals considered that figure wildly inflated. *Mandate* claimed 10,000 readers for its first issue, 59,000 for the sixteenth issue in 1976, and over 100,000 by 1980.

Skepticism about these magazines and their offspring and competitors—*Honcho, Drummer, In Touch, Torso, Stallion*—was heard almost from the start. The young white models promoted a standardized image of desirability that publishers insisted was exactly what their readers wanted and that critics called narrow, racist, commercial, and dehumanizing. For young men in the hinterlands, a first sight of Jack Wrangler, pioneer of the Marlboro Man look, or the towering Michael Christopher was likely to clarify the direction of their interests, and that wasn't a bad thing. Puerto Rican was considered hot, and a token black model would turn up from time to time. But the segregation of black models to special interest magazines like *Mandingo*, which didn't always trouble with model bios or other individuating textual notes, confirmed their otherness to white readers and, to black readers, proved the sorry level of white indifference. In that sense, gay erotica was even more restrictive than its straight counterpart. Sexy Asian or Asian-American women were often part of the heterosexual fantasy package. Asian-American gay men were nonexistent, figments of demographic imagination whose absence from the photo spreads perpetuated a stereotype about musculature and penis size.

Fans of the periodicals, and those who worked for them, were quick to point out that there was more to what they were offering than an easy one-skin-color-for-all orgasm. *Blueboy* had its Truman Capote profiles and its Montgomery Clift eulogies. *Mandate* was tellingly subtitled "The International Magazine of Entertainment and Eros," an overlap that included enthusiastic coverage of the dance and theater scene and, amid the masturbatory photos, interviews with gay-friendly personages such as Sandy Duncan and Liz Taylor. Book reviews of gay novels routinely ignored by the establishment press were important to writers marginalized by homophobic editors. Yet one feature of the magazine, as omnipresent as the boy-next-door penises and the valentines to the stars, drew fire and was a little harder to explain away: the push to sell amyl nitrate and, when that was banned, butyl nitrate inhalants, commonly known as poppers.

Demonstrating the vintage 1970s flavor of "entertainment and eros," the popper ads in the skin magazines were their largest and most dynamic advertisements. Available at head shops and X-rated stores and even at some corner delis, Bolt, Rush, Hardware, Quick Silver, Bullet, Natural Brute, and Locker Room got around most legal entanglements because doctors were still divided about their long-term effects and because the ad copy contained phrases such as "liquid incense" or "room odorizer" (in the case of Locker Room, a nice comic touch). Here and there alarms sounded on the health threat these substances posed, and by implication the culpability of the magazines in their promotion of them. Writers in the 1990s have been scathing about this aspect of 1970s sexuality, but hindsight always clarifies what was less certain at the time. A balanced article in *Christopher Street* in 1979, David Reed's "The Multi-Million-Dollar Mystery High," was both investigative and critical as well as honest about the gray areas. Too little was known about these aphrodisiacs to say with certainty that they were harmful, Reed noted, though many people had their suspicions. In any event, a climate of ever-freer drug use among Americans under forty did not encourage scrutiny of something that promised more intense sexual thrills and better ejaculations. One researcher was of the opinion that the FDA had never given the use of nitrate inhalants more study because the government assumed (inaccurately, as it turned out) that popper use was exclusively a gay issue.

Yet straight America was not entirely indifferent to gay visibility, demographics, and sexual practices by the late 1970s. Heterosexual businessmen became partners in bathhouse ownership, an especially appealing prospect when they discovered that their gay partners were not fanatical about upkeep and repairs once they had cornered the market in their area. The founder and owner of Modernismo Publications Ltd., the company that produced *Mandate*, *Honcho*, and *Playguy*, was straight. George Mavety, "a man of Falstaffian proportions" (as George DeStefano, one of his writers, described him), was an energetic businessman who believed that his success with straight skin magazines could be carried over into the new field. Capitalizing on the expertise of John Devere, the gay editor of the homoerotic arts magazine *After Dark* (whose publishers spent most of the mid-1970s denying it was a gay magazine), Mavety did just what he set out to do and eventually created a near monopoly. He liked to call his work, which he claimed was never as profitable as outsiders assumed it was, a labor of love and free-speech principle—a statement *Modernismo* magazine writer John Preston labeled "some of the biggest bullshit I've ever heard." Donald Embinder, publisher of *Blueboy*, was less given to talk about serving the cause of the First Amendment and gay pride. In 1976 he ran a full-page ad in *Advertising Age* bluntly urging the business world to wake up: "Now you can reach America's most affluent minority . . . the Male Homosexual." His target group (the fashion, liquor, and hi-fi industry) acted skittish about displaying their wares in a bathhouse-poppers-Key West vacation context, but an opening wedge had been made. They held back not because they were morally offended by gay men, but because they feared alienating more conservative customers and clients.

EMBINDER'S DRIVE TO solicit mainstream advertisers, like the bombardment of popper ads or even Mavety's heterosexuality, stripped away a good deal of pretense. The momentum of change was tied, in the end, to economic factors. Huge amounts of money were to be made from open gay male sexuality and the drive to reap those profits was not to be stemmed. Homosexual-as-consumer was an easy market to develop and to tout. This designation, in turn, readily spilled over into nonsexual areas of indulgence. "We're everywhere, and we're the most affluent of any minority," the publisher of *The Advocate* proudly declared in 1979, echoing *Blueboy*'s claim of a few years earlier. By then, business analysts agreed and pointed to the surveys in the gay magazines: gays control 19 percent of spendable income in the United States; 70 percent are college graduates and 97 percent are employed; gay household income is 50 percent above the national average. Who commissioned these surveys, how and where uninhibited respondents were located, who had agreed to answer the survey and who had not were questions seldom a part of the discussion. Many gay men were only too willing to accept the premise and the image. It was satisfying to be considered part of a group smart enough to earn more, and enjoy itself more, than other Americans with their bigotry and their limited budgets. Living well is the best revenge, after all.

There was a hitch, though, or more than one. In reality, gay men weren't at all different from their countrymen in terms of income. As anyone could attest who spent time outside the gay-gentrified neighborhoods or the coastal beach houses, homosexuals in blue-collar jobs punched time clocks and struggled to pay their overdue bills like everyone else. There was no evidence to prove that black or Hispanic gay men were especially affluent, no reason to think that anyone could state with accuracy how many gay men had gone to college or stayed off the unemployment rolls, no grounds for assuming that a higher percentage of gays than straights owned expensive cars and lived in luxury. Certain urban, white, professional gay men were more prosperous than the average worker and, naturally, were in the best position to be visibly gay (after work hours) and flaunt their wealth. Unfortunately, as soon as enough gay men bought into the perception that the privileged few verifiably represented the majority, countless numbers of their brothers were excluded from the common understanding of what it was to be gay, becoming anomalies within the group, not-their-brethren. The last hope for the moment of investing the terms *gay community* and *gay identity* with a broad, durable meaning were squandered in a display of groundless self-congratulation, the white-collar myth replacing the hairdresser cliché.

The other alleged advantage of characterizing gay men as America's richest minority involved a Faustian bargain that never saw the Devil's part of the debt come due. By this line of thought, gays would be taken seriously by politicians and corporate giants, by realtors and advertisers and bankers—by the people who matter—if they were acknowledged to have economic muscle. Campaign coffers, charities, real estate values, and tax bases would rise and fall by their sense of who was being fair to them. Millionaire David Goodstein, the new owner of *The Advocate*, was only one of many entrepreneurs taken with this notion. Yet, from the ambivalence of Jimmy Carter and Walter Mondale to Bill Clinton's skillful manipulation of the gay leadership in the 1990s, that quid pro quo never quite bore fruit for homosexuals. It did bear fruit for the anti-gay right wing when it began to question the gay comparison of the homosexual movement to the civil rights struggle of racial minorities.

Any reasonable American agreed that blacks and Hispanics were not getting their share of the pie in housing, employment, or education, but many wondered, or were taught to wonder, why gay men needed "special" legal protections if they made so much money and were able to devote their leisure time to the unrestricted pursuit of pleasure. Hedonists with fat bank accounts don't elicit sympathy, or even interest. In the long run, backroom bars and out-of-sight bathhouses probably didn't rankle heterosexuals as much as the thought of country homes, swimming pools, and "discretionary income" among people who griped about all they were up against.

The "freedom from financial care" that journalist Midge Decter saw, or thought she saw, in her gay Fire Island neighbors was not unconnected in her mind to a dangerous freedom from maturity and social responsibility. The idea of homosexuals as objects of discrimination in housing and employment "took a little getting used to," she coyly wrote in 1980. Decter's "boys on the beach" didn't have it so bad after all. As the crusades of Anita Bryant and Ronald Reagan proved, the artifice of public relations had gone terribly awry. The price to be paid for that development was not small.

VI. SHADOWS

21

DADE COUNTY AND BEYOND

Anita Bryant stumbled upon the issue that a lot of people don't like fags. . . . This was going to be a Hot Button she could press. I think it began accidentally, although there is in this country a great market for washed-up show business types who discover Jesus. And she got onto that circuit. And it did well for her—that and the oranges.

—Gore Vidal

Complacency was perhaps inevitable. With Vietnam at long last out of the news and Nixon in exile, the bicentennial year had a resoundingly liberal aura. The rhetoric at the podium was about the Constitution, freedom, tolerance, and the individual, and if a gay man was to judge by the media, the day of the witch-hunt had been replaced by an era of enlightenment—both heartfelt and terribly chic. Shortly before Christmas, thirty million Americans watched *Family* to see Sada Thompson's son sensitized by his best friend's coming out. Editors at *People* magazine let it be known that they were looking for a gay cover couple (Christopher Isherwood and Don Bachardy were wary and declined). Publishers and journalists cheered a tide of self-revelation. It was a season of comings out: *The Dave Kopay Story* made the bestseller lists and infuriated sports fans with its juicy account of the author's life as a gay pro football star; Reverend Malcolm Boyd, famed author of *Are You Running With Me, Jesus?* stunned his readers when he announced that he was gay; and Marlon Brando, the Stanley Kowalski of his age, told a French interviewer that he had had sexual experiences with other men "and I am not ashamed." Indeed, disavowal of shame was reaching new proportions.

In the political realm, there was cause for guarded optimism as well. Thirty-six cities had passed laws banning discrimination against homosexuals and sixteen states had legalized sodomy between consenting adults since the start of the decade. These legislative decisions promised to alter the terms of gay life for millions of Americans and, not implausibly, gay strategists considered it only a matter of a few years before a national gay rights bill was voted on in Congress. The mood, almost euphoric, was felt even in what some viewed as the last bastion of homophobia, the U.S. military. Discharges on the grounds of sexual orientation were at an all-time low in the mid-1970s, and the Coalition for Gay Service People took shape at Vandenburg Air Force Base in California in the spring of 1976. Airman Adam Gettinger-Brizuela had been amazed to discover such a large, self-affirming gay presence in the military, and founded "the Family," as the group was called by its members. Viewed as a sustaining and safe social tie, it ultimately proved to be a dragnet trap.

Hard-core activism may have had a potentially dreary quality about it as disco fever raged, but more to the point, gay men and lesbians wondered what was left to do. In the summer of 1976, the cover article of *Vector* asked the question that was on many people's minds: IS GAY LIB DEAD? Most interviewees did not think that the answer was an automatic yes. Look back fifteen years and review the hard-won progress, ex-SIR president Bill Beardemphl charged, and then decide if the movement is moribund. It was in the spirit of agreeing that there was more to be done, and that it was doable, that the Dade County Coalition for the Humanistic Rights of Gays was formed in July 1976. Its purpose was not unlike that of SIR in its early days—to create a higher political profile for gay men and lesbians—and its primary task that summer was questioning candidates for office in south Florida about antihomosexual discrimination, sexual privacy rights, and the embattled E.R.A. before offering an endorsement. The coalition's members included Jack Campbell of the lucrative Club baths chain; Bob Kunst, co-founder of the Transperience Center, a human potential movement project; Alan Rockaway, a psychologist and Kunst's Transperience partner; and Bob Basker, a businessman with ties to leftist politics and the civil rights movement dating back to the 1950s and gay organizing in Chicago in the 1960s. Forty-nine endorsements resulted from their meetings, and forty-five of those candidates were elected in November.

One of the winners to a position on the important Dade County Commission was Ruth Shack. Shack's husband had worked as a booking agent for a former Miss Oklahoma and runner-up for the Miss America title in 1959, the singer Anita Bryant, who had also authored several books of religious inspiration and was now living on Biscayne Bay with her husband and four children. That tie notwithstanding, Shack was a liberal Democrat and, when Bob Kunst decided that it was time to "call in the chips, so to speak" and approach one of the coalition-backed candidates to discuss a gay rights ordinance, Shack was the logical choice. She was in full agreement about the need for the legislation and later in the year introduced a bill to the Dade County Commission that banned discrimination in housing, public accommodation, and employment based on "affectional or sexual preference." The commission's first reading of the proposal was favorable, with all members in agreement. A public hearing was scheduled for January 1977. Traditionally seen as the most conservative region of the country, the South now appeared to be part of the nationwide trend toward greater tolerance.

The assumption was premature. Opposition to the ordinance—horror at the very thought of it—grew throughout the fall. Baptist ministers, Orthodox rabbis, and Catholic priests were particularly incensed at the prospect of being told that they could not fire a teacher in a parochial school because of his or her sexual orientation. No one in the coalition seemed to take the groundswell of dismay very seriously, least of all when they heard that Bob Brake, a former Coral Gables county commissioner, and William Chapman, the pastor of a local Baptist church, had approached Anita Bryant about taking a role in their campaign to convince the lawmakers not to pass the ordinance or, if need be, to work for its repeal. Bryant was known to be furious with her ex-agent and his wife for their part in "promoting deviant sexuality," but it was hard for gay Floridians to imagine that they had much to worry about from a woman who read the Bible with the literalness of William Jennings Bryan and whose career niche involved a strong rendition of "The Battle Hymn of the Republic" and orange juice ads for the Florida Citrus Growers Commission. (That career niche reportedly netted her $600,000 a year.) On the day before Jimmy Carter's inauguration, a small item appeared on page 14 of the *New York Times*, "Bias Against Homosexuals Is Outlawed in Miami." By a vote of 5-to-3, the ordinance had been passed and would go into effect in ten days. "We're not going to take this sitting down," Bryant told a reporter.

Bryant's coaches paid careful attention to the right tactical language for the coming fight: the new law, she insisted, "discriminates against my children's rights to grow up in a healthy, decent atmosphere." "Preferential legislation" for a degraded "lifestyle" was an evil God called her to resist.

(Bryant and her handlers were never anything but sharp in their sense of the political power of words. Coming to the defense of nativist sentiment in *The Anita Bryant Story*, for instance, she emphatically noted that the anti-Asian immigration law of the 1920s was "an entry quota," not an "act of exclusion.") " 'Gay rights' was in trouble," one activist decided, "the day 'special rights' was born."

Within several weeks, Brake, Chapman, Bryant, and their allies founded Save Our Children, Inc., and collected six times the needed 10,000 signatures to put the matter before the voters of Dade County. Though lawyers for Save Our Children questioned the ordinance's constitutionality, and all concerned wanted to avoid the expense of a referendum, the judicial word on the subject was that nothing in the law prohibited the enactment of such an ordinance. The state's sodomy statute might have been at odds with granting protection to individuals based on "sexual preference," but not on the grounds of "affectional preference." The commission announced in March that it would not repeal the ordinance on its own and that a referendum would be scheduled. Both sides prepared for a nasty, draining battle. Jack Campbell was shocked. "I never thought that our rights—anybody's rights—once they were the law, would later be something people could vote on," he told a reporter. Imagine, Leonard Matlovich added, if the citizens of Selma had been allowed in 1965 to vote on the Civil Rights Act.

The campaign for repeal was well positioned from the start, not least because the wording that would appear on the ballot would be in the affirmative (Bryant's side would be asked to vote *for* repeal, *for* decency, not *against* something), and because its spokesperson was a good-looking wife and mother with fantastic stage presence. She claimed to have entered the fray reluctantly, but the energy Bryant showed for the task bespoke great enthusiasm, and no performer, especially one whose Hollywood ambitions had been thwarted, could have resisted the media attention she was to enjoy in 1977 and 1978. Beyond energy and enthusiasm, Bryant's savvy approach to her theme, designed to appeal to diverse audiences, raised some arguments that were almost impossible to respond to quickly and meaningfully.

The focus of the anti-gay position was expressed in the name of the new organization, Save Our Children. The homosexual-as-pedophile was one myth gay people could respond to, pointing to the government's statistics about the heterosexuality of the vast majority of child molesters. Few people who believed the stereotype in the first place, however, paid attention to the numbers. THERE IS NO "HUMAN RIGHT" TO CORRUPT OUR CHILDREN was the heading of a prorepeal *Miami Herald* ad that spring. It featured clips from news stories from around the country about scoutmasters abusing their troops and kiddie porn. (The same newspaper censored some of the antirepeal ads as "inappropriate to a family paper.") Yet most educated Americans knew that the school system—public, private, and parochial—included gay teachers, excellent teachers, who never laid a hand on their students. They worried instead about teachers as role models who might become less closeted about their private lives, referring to their life-long partners with the same nonchalance another teacher might refer to a husband or wife, acting as quietly or implicitly proud of their homosexuality as another teacher would about his or her race or religion. Observing a bright or popular teacher known to be homosexual, students might conclude that being gay wasn't a personal hell or a mark of depravity. This was the less overt and more potent aspect of the gays-in-the-classroom side of the campaign, and harder for gays to answer in a manner that would win them votes—largely because it was true. Gay teachers in the classroom who never once mentioned homosexuality could, simply by their presence and example, change the status quo. Neither recruiters nor seducers, they would by their nature usher in a new understanding.

Other angles on the subject hammered home by Bryant in her talks to parent and church groups, reporters and fans, were even less amenable to concise or cogent refutation. As always, allusions to God and the Old Testament tended to stop all discussion in its tracks. A selective reading of Leviticus, approving of its condemnation of homosexuality while ignoring its strictures about clothing, food, and dress, had long since become a staple of mainstream Christianity. Linked to this argument was the more generalized rhetoric about America's "moral decline," an outlook that stirred both religious and nonreligious older voters. Ten years of increasing drug use, sexual openness, and declining patriotism had given a rosy glow to precounterculture days; the 1950s brought to mind respect for authority, tight family bonds, regular church attendance, and the innocence of *Grease* and *Happy Days*, not Korea, the threat of nuclear war, segregation, urban decay, and limited career possibilities for women. Pegged as a central factor in the country's overall slide from the heights of a postwar unity and moral clarity to the chaos of the present, homosexuals were left to shadowbox in a sociological match that defied rational exchange. A calm, confident past that never existed invariably beats a complex, untidy present. Similarly, Bryant's emphasis on the citizen's "right to choose" and wish to keep "our basic freedoms" in the face of an "ultra-liberal," overbearing government—appeals that would sweep Ronald Reagan into the presidency in four years—were difficult to confront. Reasonable individuals agreed that hotel owners did not have the right to refuse a black man a room because he was black, or that parents did not have the right to demand that their children be taught by a white teacher; those "rights," firmly held in the 1930s, had been curtailed by the government. In 1977, though, it was possible to use the word *rights* with an Orwellian edge. TELL US ABOUT HUMAN RIGHTS? a Save Our Children newspaper ad asked. "What Right Is There To Corrupt Our Children? Vote *For* Human Rights. Vote *For* Religious Freedom."

Finally, and most effectively, Bryant opted—never too frequently and often with just the right blend of shocked directness and calculated sorrow—to evoke the worrisome image of gay male sex itself. In this, the spokesperson for morality and religious freedom was playing her best card, showing that she was a woman of her time (no point in being reticent) and, in effect, daring gay men to respond with equal candor. There was a personal dimension as well to her sexual bluntness. The news provided by a gay acquaintance that homosexual men sometimes swallowed their partner's semen elicited in Bryant a reaction unequaled since the days of Edmund Bergler. She suspected that others did, or could be made to, share that horror. "The male homosexual eats another man's sperm," Anita Bryant wanted America to know. "Sperm is the most concentrated form of blood. The homosexual is eating life." The vampires had to be stopped. Once again, lesbians got lost in the shuffle.

THE DADE COUNTY campaign is best remembered as a contest between two diametrically opposed viewpoints, the fundamentalist and the homosexual, that managed to bring middle-class America (which was neither one nor the other) into the debate. The result was an overwhelming defeat for the advocates of gay rights. The split within the gay world, though, was more than half the story. It is also the half that still has meaning, that presents unresolved questions two decades later, when Bryant herself is a divorced woman out of the limelight, "more inclined," as she told a writer for *The Ladies' Home Journal* in 1980, "to say live and let live."

When it became clear in the spring of 1977 that a referendum on the new ordinance would take place, the Dade County Coalition for the Humanistic Rights of Gays offered to raise some of the $300,000 that the election would cost the county. That offer was withdrawn in late April when two chilling facts emerged. One was that, far from ensuring the legal protection of homosexuals, the election might well go the other way. That was not something Jack Campbell's group had anticipated in January. The second was that wealthy gay men in Florida had no intention of contributing substantial sums to the cause. Many of them, Bob Basker remembered, felt that "we had been too pushy to begin with. Why bring up the subject at all? It was unseemly." They didn't want to be associated by name with the project nor did they want to see other gay men in a shouting match with a popular Baptist entertainer. Ignore the ads, the rhetoric, and the "Christians for Decency" rallies, they told the activists, and go back to leading a dignified private life. In Campbell's recollection, more money ultimately came in from the San Francisco Bay Area than from all of Florida.

. The campaign expertise also had to come from out of state. Jim Foster of San Francisco and Ethan Geto, an aide to New York politician Robert Abrams, were brought to Miami to take charge. Leonard Matlovich was on hand in his role as gay celebrity, and assorted liberal political figures, such as California Assemblyman Willie Brown and San Francisco Sheriff Richard Hongisto, came to speak or lend moral support. Norman Lear prepared a commercial starring Ed Asner. The obstacles the gay activists faced were clarified by a random-sample poll commissioned by Ethan Geto immediately upon his arrival, seven weeks before the election, which indicated considerable unease among voters about discrimination in general, but also a deep-seated antipathy toward homosexuals and, even more, toward homosexual acts. "I interpreted the poll to mean," Geto told *Christopher Street* a few months later, "that, although we were up against a lot in Dade County, if we played on the sentiments of human rights and a basic right to work, etc., maybe we could get a majority vote." There didn't appear to be a more pragmatic alternative, he was convinced, and so the Dade County Coalition for the Humanistic Rights of Gays became the Dade County Coalition for Human Rights. Unfortunately, the poll revealed that the voters most likely to turn out were those sympathetic to Save Our Children and, worst of all, that a significant number of political moderates wondered how much discrimination gay men and lesbians actually faced in their day-to-day life. The price of homosexual silence over the years, of "getting by" and not complaining, was that most Americans had no clear conception of the pain that the ostracism and the epithets, the police brutality and employer prejudice, could and did inflict.

Decisions had to be made quickly, some of which were practical (choosing between television and print advertising, given the funds and when they became available) and some of which were ideological. Hindsight suggested to one coalition member that a disastrous mistake was made in assuming that the Cuban-American community would not turn out en masse to vote on this issue, and to another gay leader (speaking in the 1990s), a major error was the failure to court the African-American vote more aggressively. The favorite charge of the repeal forces was the "recruitment" allegation. Bryant repeated her best line, "Homosexuals cannot reproduce so they must recruit," with a freshness and conviction any politician on the stump

would envy. The coalition responded in a straightforward fashion by bringing in psychological experts to talk about the nature of sexual orientation,
assumed by one and all on the gay side of the debate (or so it appeared at
the time) to be "fixed" at preschool age, hence not susceptible to the influence of "recruiters" of straight teenagers. How to deal with eager volunteers from other parts of the country who wanted to come to south Florida
as a new wave of "freedom riders" wasn't a complicated decision to make,
either; Geto, Foster, and Matlovich were already being tarred by the right
wing as carpetbaggers, and uninvited outsiders were discouraged. The
orange juice boycott was the tougher call. It was catching on in many states
as a way to send a message to Bryant's corporate sponsors, but the coalition was leary of giving its support. (The argument against the boycott was
that it would end up hurting the migrant workers who picked the oranges
more than Bryant and her backers. Others thought the coalition's stand
implied a mealy-mouthed fear of riling Floridians proud of their state's
main product.) Above all else, those directing the coalition wanted to avoid
a sensational, radical, or sex-oriented campaign.

No one was more heatedly opposed to all of these strategies than Bob
Kunst, the coalition board member who first lobbied Ruth Shack about the
ordinance. Fired in 1975 from his job as an advertising promotion director
for the Miami Toros soccer team after a brochure for a gay organization
was found in his desk and later reduced to living on food stamps, he knew
all about job discrimination against homosexuals. But Kunst doubted the
wisdom of—and wasn't temperamentally suited for—the moderate, conventional approach he saw taking shape. As he saw it, the issue went
beyond fairness to employees or minding one's own business, and was not
unrelated to the growing opposition to E.R.A., reactions against feminism,
marital discontent and divorce, sexual dysfunction, and a host of other
modern-day topics. Kunst's view, shared by Alan Rockaway but rejected by
Campbell, Basker, Geto, Foster, and almost everyone else in a decision-
making capacity, was that the original passage and the current uproar
over the ordinance had to be fought as more than a civil rights issue pure
and simple; it was a rare opportunity to discuss attitudes toward physical
intimacy—oral sex, anal sex, nonmonogamous unions, bisexuality, exploration vs. repressiveness, the right to be sexually out of the mainstream—in
a way that Americans had never done before. It was the moment to transcend liberal pieties. "I wasn't talking about human rights," Kunst said. "I
wanted to talk about what people really voted on, which was their emotional and sexual hang-ups or insecurities. I wanted to open up the entire
sexual debate. . . . *Why* do people feel the way they do about certain acts
and experiences? Where does the fear come from? What does it mean?"

To those Florida gays who were sorry the ordinance had ever been brought before the commission, Kunst was a wacked-out idealist and an egomaniac who was only going to make things worse with his sex talk and Transperience human potential philosophy. To the membership of the coalition, he was jeopardizing the outcome of the election, especially when he and Rockaway began to compete for funds with their own organization, the Miami Victory Campaign. Even his enemies had to concede, though, that Kunst did something in the closing weeks of the campaign that no one else in the field had been willing or able to do. He gave a face to the cause and broadcast a dynamic persona to complement Anita Bryant's. He also got enormous mileage out of his twenty volunteers and the $20,000 he was able to raise. Handsome, blunt, charismatic, at ease (or rather, in his glory) in the spotlight, Kunst at thirty-five was, like Bryant, a lightning rod, a seductive orator, any reporter's favorite copy, and a sexual theorist of unprecedented directness. He had no more qualms about discussing his multiple erotic experiences than he did about supporting the orange juice boycott. When Governor Reuben Askew announced at a press conference that he didn't want a homosexual on his staff or in his children's classroom, Ethan Geto prepared a statement about arbitrary judgments and the toll of bigotry. Kunst made headlines by questioning the governor's sexual insecurities.

(It isn't difficult to see why Bob Kunst ruffled feathers in 1977, but long after the referendum, enmity against him persisted that is quite remarkable in its depth and longevity. In *States of Desire: Travels in Gay America*, published in 1980, Edmund White reported that any gay anger he detected in Florida was actually directed more toward Kunst than Bryant. In St. Paul, a lesbian activist told him that she knew of many Minnesotans who had been against the repeal of St. Paul's gay rights ordinance until they saw Kunst on television there and decided to vote the other way. Fifteen years later, numerous residents of Dade County were still willing to place the blame for their defeat in 1977 squarely on Kunst's ample shoulders.)

Today it is possible to wonder how much of the vote had to do with the Bible or attitudes toward sexual acts or sexual privacy, and how much had to do with something quite different. "The Battle for Gay Rights" was *Newsweek*'s cover story the week of the referendum and it evoked a subtext, a psychological terrain, of some importance. Despite the straining to appear evenhanded, which has always characterized the major news weeklies, the *Newsweek* article conveyed the extremist tenor of Bryant herself and her crusade. In a period that thought Jimmy Carter too sermonizing, she was not the American Everywoman. But this in itself meant little. Alone in the voting booth, people will align themselves to all manner of styles and opinions they won't defend in conversation, and *Newsweek* agreed that the referendum was too close to call. Of more subtle importance was the article's "balanced" depiction of gay life. The veneer of the time-honored litany was preserved: homosexuals were doctors, lawyers, and teachers, indistinguishable from other professionals; they were artists and decorators; they were the rougher types who hung out in bars called the Ramrod. But it was an oddly narrow sense of diversity for 1977—no mention of women, of blacks or Hispanics, and no hint of blue-collar gays, of office workers and bank tellers and dishwashers—while the most evocative prose, not surprisingly, focused on the doctors and lawyers right out of *The Green Bay Tree*: "By night [in Miami], gay professional men gather over Chateauneuf-du-Pape and racks of lamb in the quiet of the Candlelight Club."

The problem, then, wasn't that Americans believed all homosexuals were "human garbage," as *Newsweek* quoted Bryant in one of her less contained moments. It was that they were perceived as far more affluent than the norm, privileged in one way if not another, and therefore were displaying colossal nerve in asking for legal protections when they were already doing quite well—better, the stereotype went, than the average struggling American worker and his family. From the time of Martin Van Buren, a more convenient target has been hard to find than the well-fed man who knows his Chateauneuf-du-Pape. And look at what they spent their money on. *Newsweek*'s descriptions of Jack Campbell's house and pool, his young lover and his pool boy, were bound to the same generalizations about decadent gay wealth. Bryant's much grander mansion came from money made singing old favorites and from the wholesome goodness of orange juice. Campbell's luxury came from men doing the wild thing in bathhouses. As if to underscore the sexual obsessiveness, or at least the sadness, at the center of the gay experience, a photo of the rescued patrons of the Everard Baths fire in May accompanied the article. A near-naked, towel-clad young man stands on the sidewalk. A dazed black man lies at his feet.

At its root, the Dade County fight posed a dilemma tersely summarized by the magazine's writers: "how to protect the civil rights of homosexuals without suggesting approval of a practice that most Americans still consider deviant?" Reasonable parents, *Newsweek* agreed, could "logically" want to draw the line at having homosexuals work in day-care centers. The question was probably meant to be an honest one, but the residents of south Florida understood its essential disingenuousness. The two goals *are* incompatible. Full civil rights—including the right of anyone to work at a day-care center who is capable of doing the job—can only be granted to those whom society deems acceptable. "Drawing the line" at certain jobs necessarily means withholding those civil rights. The people of Dade

County had no trouble making up their minds. The men with pool boys, the men in bath towels, had to be kept in their place. They had enough "rights" already.

Until the first returns started to come in on the night of June 7, both sides anticipated a close election. That turned out to be far from the case. The number supporting repeal was a little over 200,000; against repeal, barely 90,000—better than a 2-to-1 defeat. Bryant crowed that "the normal majority had spoken" and that "the laws of God" had been vindicated. Gay men and lesbians in every state were shocked and outraged. Kunst, Campbell, and other principals labored to put a positive spin on the referendum, noting the infusion of energy the movement had received in 1977. Only Ruth Shack admitted to the surprise and devastation she felt by the margin of the loss. "They came out of the woodwork," she lamented, referring to the vast numbers who voted to save America's youth from predators. Surveys suggested that even older Jewish liberals in Miami Beach, the non-gay bloc the coalition forces had counted on, voted with the Baptists, the African-Americans, the Cuban-Americans, and the non-Cuban Catholics to keep homosexuals in their own neighborhoods and out of the schools.

But liberals were never to be relied on in a crunch, Bob Kunst had maintained all along, and in any case, as he saw it, the issue wasn't liberal vs. conservative or even gay vs. straight. "The issue was, how uptight are you about human sexual expression?" "Antisex gay people," in this light, were as much a part of the problem as antisex fundamentalists. The June 7 vote was just an opening volley, Kunst believed. By the end of the year, with only a $5,000 budget this time, the Miami Victory Campaign was at work on Round II of the referendum fight. Everyone associated with the coalition was appalled that Kunst would want to put the county through the trauma of another battle, which was sure to end in a second humiliating defeat at the polls. "I was being as pesky as I could possibly be," Kunst admitted. But there was method to the madness. Let Campbell go back to his business, let Foster go back to San Francisco and Geto to New York. In the Kunst scheme of things, retreat was the worst possible strategy. Rather, show them that "we" are as tireless, convinced of our ultimate victory, and sure of ourselves as they seem to be. But who was this "we"? Kunst found himself preoccupied with the question in the weeks after the June election, brooding about the self-image the gay men and women of Florida had created for themselves. Why were they so reluctant to be aggressive, so ready to look like the pansies society told them they were, so lacking any common identity "but their own sense of oppression"? The best response to gay timidity and straight disdain, he decided, was a campaign that was more direct and focused than it had been the first time. The red-white-and-blue bumper stickers said it all: BETTER BLATANT THAN LATENT acknowledged the homosexual angle, but ORAL IS MORAL applied to any man or woman, straight or gay, who wanted the church and the state out of the bedroom. "My position has always been that there are more cocksuckers than Fundamentalists [in the general population]," Kunst remarked in a 1995 interview.

The vote on reviving the ordinance, which took place in the fall of 1978, was the defeat everyone predicted. Yet, as Kunst pointed out, something had to be made of the fact that the 31 percent of 1977 had escalated to 41 percent a year and five months later. Fifty thousand more people had decided to cast a ballot for gay rights (or the right to sexual privacy) the second time around.

SAVE OUR CHILDREN, Inc., had won decisively in Florida, but there was some pleasure to be had in the months ahead in dogging Anita Bryant's footsteps as she took her campaign on the road and continued her singing engagements. Those protests were important opportunities for gay men and lesbians to express their anger—and to evaluate the fragmented, ambivalent nature of the gay "community" as it debated the level of visibility, confrontation, and tactical rudeness people were comfortable with.

Bryant's first singing appearance after the referendum, for example, was in New Orleans. National gay leaders and local activists like Bill Rushton and Alan Robinson hoped to mark the event with a significant demonstration. Bryant had worked to undo a law protecting homosexuals in the workplace; homosexuals would respond in kind. But New Orleans wasn't a city used to political demonstrations, and many gay southerners were divided over how viciously to go after Bryant. The initial plan to pressure the New Orleans Summer Pops Orchestra to rescind its contract with Bryant fizzled and was characterized by the *Times-Picayune* as an assault on the entertainer's civil rights (an angle on the situation that always seemed to work in Bryant's favor). Organizing a major street action was almost as difficult an option. The newly formed Gertrude Stein Society was more a cultural than an activist body, but even it was deemed too radical—too visibly gay—to be the proper catalyst. A spin-off group, known by the acronymn H.E.R.E., was then set up to make the arrangements, rouse the faithful, make converts, and keep the press informed. H.E.R.E. was not a Bob Kunst BETTER BLATANT THAN LATENT/ORAL IS MORAL operation; the letters stood for Human Equal Rights for Everyone and avoided the terms *gay* and *lesbian* entirely. A fund-raising cocktail party, "Anything But Orange Juice," enlisted the support of a few of the city's progressives, including the next mayor, Judge Ernest Morial. Mainstream activists Frank Kameny, Barbara Gittings, Bruce Voeller, Leonard Matlovich, and Troy Perry were flown in to address the demonstrators. Old-time queens, accustomed to a more private approach to their sexuality, kept their distance.

The positive aspects of the June 17 rally were visceral and inspirational. "It was a whole new world for New Orleans," journalist Roberts Batson wrote twenty years later, "a weekend . . . filled with a tremendous emotional charge." The 4,000 or more people who gathered in Jackson Square to hear the speeches and then march to the auditorium where Bryant was performing constituted "the largest civil rights demonstration of any kind in the history of New Orleans." Conventional wisdom said that Big Easy locals would never get off their bar stools for a political cause, but the "orange juice woman" provided a useful focus to challenge that belief. Translating the energy of June 1977 into an ongoing force for social change in the region was another matter, however. The Gay Pride Festival organized the following year stirred little interest, the 1978 rally in Jackson Square was sparsely attended, and H.E.R.E. soon fell apart. This was disappointing to gay observers in California and the Northeast, who were then—and still are—reluctant to accept that strategies viable in one part of the country were not necessarily relevant elsewhere. "A 'Yankee town' get-out-and-cause-a-fuss style wasn't going to go here, no matter what the big guns thought," one Louisianan commented. Progress took other, less explicitly political forms: *Impact*, the city's first continuing gay newspaper, was in business by the end of 1977; the number of gay carnival clubs grew (as the gay presence at Mardi Gras became more visible in general); and the Metropolitan Community Church, Integrity, Dignity, and other religious groups found their membership increasing. According to one poll from the mid-1970s, New Orleans was not atypical in this respect. Throughout the United States, gay student and religious groups for some time attracted a more avid following than gay political groups.

The notable development over the next eighteen months was that cities not known for gay public protests were the site of some healthy uproar. In Norfolk, Virginia, three hundred people staged a clamorous walkout at Bryant's appearance in a local hall. After a rally at Dupont Circle in January 1978, 2,000 marchers encircled the Washington Hilton where she was speaking at a National Religious Broadcasters convention. ("I hear that Christians everywhere are drinking orange juice like holy water," she told her audience. The Florida Citrus Growers Commission was less optimistic.) The next month, over a thousand protesters demonstrated as she arrived in Tucson, Arizona. But gay leaders were apt to read larger meanings into these turnouts. Mobilization against Anita Bryant was satisfying on a gut level for its participants, as well as for those gay men and lesbians who wouldn't or couldn't participate but heard about it on Walter Cronkite. At least some gays somewhere were doing something, whether it was a candle-light vigil or Tom Higgins's banana cream pie in Bryant's face at a Des Moines news conference. Yet in terms of influencing the citizenry at large to rethink the old arguments about homosexuality, the effect was negligible, and the news quickly got worse.

In April 1978, the gay rights law in St. Paul was struck down by a vote of 54,000 to 31,000. Two weeks later, one of the largest voter turnouts in Wichita's history helped repeal that city's nondiscrimination ordinance by a staggering 5-to-1 ratio. Eugene, Oregon, followed suit by a 2-to-1 ratio. New York City's gay rights bill went down to defeat for the seventh con-secutive year; anti-gay purges in the military (always a barometer of the national mood) were resumed; and California state senator John Briggs announced that he had gathered the 500,000 signatures needed to bring his initiative against gay teachers in public schools to a vote in November. In the summer of 1978, Hartford, Connecticut's town council passed a gay rights bill, only to have it vetoed by Mayor George Athanson, who had "some serious questions on whether it affects teachers" (meaning, presum-ably, that the bill's weakness was that teachers would no longer be fired if openly gay). The citizens of Hartford, in the main, agreed with Athanson. More duplicitously, New York's Governor Hugh Carey reaffirmed his opposition to an executive order banning discrimination against homo-sexuals in state government hiring "because no such discrimination exists." In the cleverest move of all, religious leaders of the local antihomosexual organization in Wichita intimated that the three commissioners who had guided the city's gay bill to passage had shown themselves woefully out of touch with their constituents, and should apologize or face a recall. From the Carter White House to city halls across small-town America, the mes-sage was heard. A clear-cut identification with gay rights was political sui-cide. In October 1977, the mayor of Amsterdam showed up at a revue where popular Dutch entertainers satirized Bryant. Its purpose was to raise $40,000 to place an ad in *Time* magazine attacking Save Our Children, Inc. But that was the Netherlands; no American mayor would have dared give his blessing to parodies or to the strong tone of the ad. An electable official was one who tepidly supported privacy or equality under the law, not one who called Bryant a zealot and approved of men sleeping with men.

Outlandish statements about homosexuals by elected officials became increasingly common in 1978. State Senator John Briggs of Fullerton, Cali-fornia, had gone to Miami the day before the referendum, celebrated the victory of Save Our Children with Bryant, and taken note of the housewives and grandmothers who turned out by the hundreds to distribute leaflets and lick envelopes. These were people receptive to talk about a "homosexual takeover" of America (Briggs was especially pleased with his joke about granting San Francisco "captured nation status"). They, or the counterparts on the West Coast, were also a potential army of volunteers to aid a folksy conservative of no special talents with his gubernatorial aspirations. (In his biography of Harvey Milk, Randy Shilts assessed Briggs's political ambition and search for the right hot issue as considerably more important to the man than any actual dislike of homosexuals he may have felt.) Briggs wisely restricted the scope of his own initiative in California, leaving the matter of housing and public accommodation aside. What stirred people to action was homosexual proximity to children and teenagers. Proposition 6, calling for the dismissal of gay teachers presently employed by the state, was worrisome not only in light of Bryant's successful scare tactics regarding "recruitment" and molestation. The Supreme Court had recently refused to hear the much-publicized case of James Gaylord, a Tacoma high school teacher fired for acknowledging his sexual orientation to his principal. Gaylord had a thirteen-year record as an outstanding educator and the subject of homosexuality had never been raised in his classroom. Should Proposition 6 become law, there was no reason to assume it would be struck down by the courts. *McCall's* magazine speculated that most Americans would accept a gay teacher in their child's classroom who was good at his job and kept his private life private, but its own nationwide survey of 1,400 principals was more ominous. Forty-two percent said they would dismiss such a teacher automatically.

The California legislature was unreceptive to Briggs's proposal, and at first it seemed as if getting the requisite number of signatures to place the issue on the ballot would be hard to amass. The deadline for the 1977 fall elections came and went. But in the new year, all that changed. Audiences were mesmerized by Briggs's spur-of-the-moment statistics (20 percent of Los Angeles's teachers are gay; 30 percent of San Francisco's) and his characterization of the debauchery that would become part of mainstream American life if the deviants were not stopped at the source of their growth, the schools. The hyperbole and untruths directed against them galvanized gays throughout the state. A record 250,000 marchers turned out for the Gay Pride Parade in San Francisco in June 1978. Harvey Milk, San Francisco's newly elected city supervisor and rapidly becoming the most prominent gay politician in the country, toured the state, debating Briggs with his usual flair.

The California contest had dimensions peculiar to itself, however, that in the end substantially enlarged the opposition to Briggs. The diversity of the state's vast population meant that those deciding the issue would be a much less homogeneous group than was the case in Miami, Wichita, St. Paul, or Eugene. Furthermore, Briggs undermined his own appeal to the middle ground by sponsoring Proposition 7, a capital punishment bill, on the same ballot and by implying that even a teacher's presence in a gay bar—anywhere, anytime—would be enough to justify a dismissal. As a result, liberals could either support gay rights or simply distance themselves from the capital punishment tie-in; moderates could take issue with the breadth of Briggs's definition of "openly gay"; and conservatives could worry about the implied extension of state control over private life. So Paul Newman and Joanne Woodward made their own fund-raising appeal, Governor Jerry Brown eventually took a stand, President Carter was persuaded to say a few words about voting "no," and both ex-Governor Ronald Reagan and former President Gerald Ford came out against Proposition 6 (though neither Reagan, Ford, nor Carter wanted to be thought too sympathetic to the individuals who would actually suffer under the proposed law, should it go into effect). Despite the frightening September poll that promised an easy 60 percent win for Briggs, on November 8 Proposition 6 was beaten by that same wide margin. Harvey Milk speculated that a closer call—followed perhaps by some angry gay demonstrations—would have been better for the consciousness-raising goals of the movement, but most gay men and lesbians were simply relieved.

A second victory was celebrated the same night, in Seattle, though the national press gave it considerably less attention than the California vote or, the year before, the Dade County vote. Initiative 13, another attempt at a repeal of an ordinance already in place, was pushed through in Washington State's principal city by two policemen as part of the anti-gay tide that gained momentum after the elections in St. Paul, Wichita, and Eugene. "But Wichita was one thing. How they got it through there in the first place is the mystery," a Northwest resident remarked. "A rejection of a gay rights law in a city like Seattle that was assumed to be more progressive would have been a catastrophe." Local gay leaders did not wait long to act, though.

Charles Brydon, one of the gay businessmen who formed the Dorian Group, which met for monthly luncheons with city officials and prided itself on its access to the corridors of power in Seattle, went to St. Paul to assess the situation (both cities had large Scandinavian populations, among other similarities) and commissioned an early poll at home. The results were not very different from the poll Ethan Geto consulted in Miami: a "right to privacy" campaign had a fighting chance. Any thrust implying legitimization of homosexuality was much riskier. A greater liberal base and a smaller fundamentalist one also helped the antirepeal side. And Citizens to Retain Fair Employment, as the gay group named itself, was not alone. Three other local organizations played a part, including Seattle Citizens Against Thirteen (SCAT), which—in the feisty spirit of the Miami Victory Campaign—disdained the Brydon camp as a tie-and-jacket crowd too establishment oriented to stand by the banner of gay liberation. (The Dorian Group, and Brydon in particular, incensed many younger gay men and lesbians by refusing to endorse a gay pride march in the city while the campaign was under way.) A fair amount of energy was spent "preventing war between the organizations," Brydon conceded, but in the end the issue was defined largely as a universal civil liberties question. "And those were the only terms on which we could be reasonably sure of keeping the law in place," he added. "We had to make people feel as if everyone could be affected by this type of legislation." One campaign poster showed a huge keyhole with an eye peering through it; television ads depicted ordinary people living inside a fishbowl. Initiative 13 was defeated by a 2-to-1 majority.

The events of 1977 and 1978 clarified what heterosexual America thought about gay men and lesbians. The change from even the late 1960s was considerable. Fewer people wanted homosexuals driven from their midst, imprisoned, beaten by the police, or handed over to psychiatrists to be forcibly "cured." The sodomy laws continued to be repealed by legislatures in state after state. But heterosexual Americans were not prepared to embrace the degree of openness and equality gay liberation called for. When the emphasis was on privacy rather than lovemaking, tolerance was possible; full acceptance was not. If anything, most Americans probably shared the feeling of the Georgia housewife who wrote an article for the *Atlanta Constitution* in 1977 entitled "Enough! Enough! TV Is Killing Us with Gays" who said, "I don't hate homosexuals, or think their sex life is my business," but talk shows and sitcoms featuring gay men had exhausted her patience and interest. "Now when I see one coming, off goes the set." Benign neglect had its appeal on subjects other than race.

Millions of gay men and lesbians could live with that level of attention. Their jobs and their income, their polite relations with family and colleagues, insulated them from the harshness of their second-class status. The claim of gay leaders from the early 1970s that such equivocation was a grave error had been largely unheeded, and in that sense Anita Bryant, John Briggs, and others offered some timely provocation, forcing more gay men and lesbians to think about how they chose to view themselves and their place in America. Many wanted a roomier closet and less challenging rhetoric from the likes of Harvey Milk and Bob Kunst. But events were moving at a pace that would soon transform the leisurely, haphazard process of deciding how much one wanted to be identified as "gay" into a luxury most homosexuals could not afford. By the early 1980s, shame masked as discretion was to have deadly consequences. Milk's fantasy of a large-scale coming out and Kunst's insistence on a public discussion of variant sexual practices would come to pass, but not for the reasons they imagined or desired.

22

CALIFORNIA FERVOR

Like would-be stars flocking to Hollywood, gay men migrate to the golden gates of Castro Street, where even the clothing store mannequins have washboard stomaches; a liberated zone that calls, "Give me your weak, your huddled, your oppressed—and your horny, looking for a little action."

—Randy Shilts,
"Castro Street: Mecca or Ghetto?"
The Advocate, 1977

A rift between the East and West Coast had long been a feature of the gay movement, a tension that the glamorous notoriety attached to Stonewall did nothing to assuage. And it was with some justification in the 1970s that Californians working to advance gay rights complained that New Yorkers often acted as if they had gotten the ball rolling all on their own.

In fact, gay New York had originated nothing comparable to Harry Hay's Mattachine Society or Dorr Legg's ONE Institute or Troy Perry's Metropolitan Community Church, all products of southern California in the 1950s and 1960s. It was the upfront patrons of San Francisco's bars who had been photographed in the famous *Life* magazine article in 1964, and it was also that city's social and political groups, especially in its heyday the Society for Individual Rights, that established a more militant tone than anything seen on the island of Manhattan before the Gay Liberation Front in 1969. Brazen demonstrations such as those protesting police raids at Compton's Cafeteria in San Francisco in 1966 and the Black Cat Cafe in Los Angeles in 1967 were events of more than local importance, and Carl Wittman's "Homosexual Manifesto," a call-to-arms document quoted more than any other in liberationist circles, was a Bay Area creation in the spring of 1969. The Gay Community Center established by Morris Kight, Don Kilhefner, and others in Los Angeles in 1972 served as a model for the rest of the nation long before most other major cities opened such facilities, and no state boasted as many gay magazines and newspapers as California in the 1970s.

In time, all of this energy and activism—this excitement and euphoria—came to be embodied in the words *the Castro*. This activism's roots—not merely in this one neighborhood, but in all of San Francisco—are currently being examined in depth by several historians, but the advantages of life in a midsized seaport city with a history of intermittent tolerance for untraditional ways and an influx of gay men and lesbians during World War II (many of whom stayed on after they left the service) are significant factors. As John D'Emilio noted in his essay, "Gay Politics, Gay Community: San Francisco's Experience," postwar census figures "hint at the degree to which San Francisco, even before the 1970s, was attracting a gay populace. From 1950 to 1960 the number of single-person households doubled and accounted for 38 percent of the city's residence units." Word of mouth played no small part of the process. "The mistake of my life was in returning to Connecticut," commented one man interviewed for this book, who moved back to the Bay Area in 1953 (after leaving the Navy in 1946), at the urging of his gay friends there. "That was seven wasted years before I got back to where I could function like a gay man again." The visibility of the North Beach beat culture in the late 1950s, dominated by openly homosexual men such as Allen Ginsberg and Robert Duncan, heralded another set of possibilities, as did the nerve of Jose Sarria as an office seeker in 1961 or the mid-1960s fraternity of Tavern Guild picnics, leather bars, motorcycle clubs, and an active gay house-party circuit, particularly among black gay men and lesbians.

Freewheeling electoral politics and uncloseted social bonds played a large part in shaping the gay scene over the next twenty years. Yet San Francisco also offered at the end of the 1960s something few cities could: an opportunity to build a gay neighborhood from scratch, a development that played to the needs—only occasionally overlapping—of both affluent and working-class gays. Waves of young gay men had arrived in Haight-Ashbury circa 1967–1970, some of whom knew they were gay at the time and were eager to make a new life away from their hometowns and some of whom discovered their different interests only after settling in. But the transformation of the Haight into a zone of antibourgeois values and free love foundered by the end of the decade in the face of the more desperate realities of heroin and poverty, so nearby Eureka Valley, an area that includes the blocks known today as the Castro, became a sensible alternative for the long run. Apartments were cheap but habitable, and the rows of shabby-genteel Victorian houses, once home to the extended families of the Irish who relocated to the suburbs in the 1950s and 1960s, were there to be picked up for a song by anyone with the capital to invest. The resulting gay migration assumed many styles. Classic gentrifiers arrived with the idea of taking up residence and earning a livelihood in a more hospitable milieu than they had known. Others thought of the area as a place in which to continue what the Haight in its most serious questioning form had started, but under manageable, even middle-class circumstances. Still others, such as Harvey Milk—leaving behind a job as a financial analyst in New York to open a camera shop in the Castro—had a mind to do a bit of both.

Gay gentrification was not unique to San Francisco in the 1970s. A number of cities could point to neighborhoods where gay men had settled and quietly upgraded the properties. Nor was the phenomenon new to that decade; a 1968 forum in *Vector* remarked on the "queenizing" of apartment buildings in various parts of San Francisco in the 1940s. What was different about the development of Eureka Valley was its speed, its blatancy as a gay enterprise, and its comprehensiveness. In his 1969 "A Homosexual Manifesto," Carl Wittman referred to San Francisco as "a refugee camp for homosexuals." Only a few years later, a single neighborhood of that metropolis was viewed, as Frances Fitzgerald wrote with only slight exaggeration in *Cities on a Hill*, as "a world apart from the rest of the city . . . [a place where] gay men could spend days, or an entire week, going to their offices, to the cleaner, the bank, and the health club, dining in restaurants, attending political meetings, and going to church without coming into contact with anyone who was not gay." Not even Greenwich Village could make that claim—if, in fact, this was a claim to be proud of, a point still in dispute among gay men twenty years later. But what no one disputes was the potential impact of these numbers, their power to bedazzle the uninitiated. "I had no idea there were so many faggots in the world," Armistead Maupin's wide-eyed hero exclaims about his own delighted first impressions in *Tales of the City* (1978). Citywide estimates in 1977 put that figure at approximately 125,000 to 150,000 out of 750,000, or almost one-fifth of the total population.

The Castro as an actuality and as a symbolic center was a test of anyone's idealism from its inception. The ugly side of gentrification was never far from the surface. Poor families were displaced rapidly and heartlessly. Gay landlords could be as mercenary toward their tenants (gay or straight) as their heterosexual counterparts, and hopes for an economically and racially diverse neighborhood were short-lived. The gay bars that opened were often unwelcoming to men of color. "It wasn't necessarily our mecca, too," Thom Bean remembered, and in his essay "Racism from a Black Perspective," he quoted a friend: "I've lived in New York, Chicago, and Los Angeles, and San Francisco is the only place I've ever had to file a housing discrimination suit. It was against a prominent gay businessman who rents only to gay male WASPs in their twenties and thirties." The disproportionate number of men also ensured that the homosexual gender gap would continue or worsen, and many lesbians in the 1990s have few positive memories of time spent (in the angry words of one woman) "among the boys-only crowd." Yet many gay men felt the need for a territory that would be as male as possible, confirming what lesbian-feminists had long argued—that gay men had more in common with straight men than with homosexual women—and were glad to see talk of solidarity go by the wayside. The result, in a city less career obsessed and (at the time) less expensive than New York, with a gay population more centralized than in Chicago or Los Angeles and more politicized than in Houston or Dallas, was a unique opportunity to see what kind of life gay white men could make for and by themselves.

Critical mass was certainly in place by 1975. Such a concentration of men in so small an area guaranteed a high-profile sexual intensity, rich costume drama, and a consolidation of economic power that was exciting to residents and appealing to gay men elsewhere, who now had a model for well-advertised trend setting and a site for pilgrimage. The reborn Castro also served to reiterate the obsolesence of the older stereotypes. "If one imagines a world of hairdressers and interior decorators, painted flower window boxes and poodles, one imagines wrong," novelist and longtime San Franciscan Herbert Gold noted in 1977. Instead, what one saw was alternately more eclectic—as befit a city that was soon home to both Reverend Ray Broshears's armed Lavender Panthers (scourge of teenage gay-bashers) and the habit-wearing Sisters of Perpetual Indulgence—and more uniform. The uniformity involved the macho apparel and affect that young and middle-aged gay men were adopting, the de rigueur jeans or army fatigues, leather jacket, moustache, muscular build, and handkerchief codes that assigned pastels, limp wrists, and aunties to the netherworld. To the surprise of the older generation, the "clone" style took hold as tenaciously as had the earlier conformity about the use of feminine nicknames and carefully limited butch/femme sex roles.

This hypermasculinization of male homosexuality was tied to another development that widened the gulf between the generations. Prejudices about specific activities in bed collapsed as hard-muscled young men made it clear they wanted to be the passive as well as the active partners in anal sex and stigmas about penetration by a man as a feminine desire became untenable. (In *A Homosexual Manifesto*, Carl Wittman cited the line "I like to fuck, but don't want to be fucked" as an example of "role-playing at its worst," an anti-gay mimicry of heterosexual maleness.) Nor was there reason any longer to glorify trade, masculine straight men willing to follow the top-bottom patterns in oral and anal sex that provided the thrill of the dominance-submission game. All around, gay men looked like the embodiment of fantasies that in adolescence had been associated exclusively with heterosexuals. On Castro Street, the man of your dreams was just as apt to be queer, out, and ready to assume any or all positions in bed.

The New York City–Fire Island circuit got its share of journalistic and literary attention at the same time, and the hot clone look was ubiquitous by mid-decade, but San Franciscans were seen as the embodiment (if not the actual, or lone, originators) of the new style and freedom—"advanced homosexuals," as a character observes in Andrew Holleran's *The Beauty of Men* (1996). It was a mythology that filled a need; there had to be advanced homosexuals *somewhere*. A self-defined group requires a cutting edge, actual or invented, a group of people who live just a bit ahead of the rest of us. Men dancing the night away, pressed against one another in shirtless, sweaty, randy crowds; men wandering the maze of the Barracks, meeting for fisting parties at the Catacombs; men holding hands on the street (not a common sight in New York), doing without women or heterosexuals—this added up to a vivid terrain experienced by many as a final triumph of brotherhood and pleasure over recrimination and loneliness.

America's new gay male image had its own critics, who tended to be based in the East. The narrowness of a life lived exclusively in the subculture was most deftly evoked in Andrew Holleran's *Dancer from the Dance* (1978), the strongest novel by a gay writer of the post-Stonewall era and one of the few gay books that continues in each decade to find a new audience. Holleran's narrator knows that the world of single-minded eroticism, of nights spent in search of the perfect *discaire*, the right club, or a new Puerto Rican trick is suffocating, addictive, absurd, racist—and scarcely plausible as a way of life. A landscape requiring constant imaginative labor to keep it in focus, Holleran's Manhattan isn't any more realistic than

Dickens's London or Balzac's Paris, with their youthful innocents, diabolical climbers, and Machiavellian tempters. The novel's lost Ivy League beauty, Malone, and his friend Sutherland, the camp queen who always schedules a stop at the Times Square men's room before bridge with Helen Auchincloss, are part of "a strange democracy whose only ticket of admission was physical beauty" and where a small penis ("the leprosy of homosexuals") is a curse. To be sure, this was not life as most gay men of any class, color, or region knew it, not exactly, but neither was it a mindset that was entirely alien to most gay men, either. By avoiding obvious satire and explicit judgments, relying instead on a prose style that subjects the reader to the same daze, the same ache his character has known since entering into a life without family obligations or erotic limits, Holleran offered a lasting—if affectionate—critique of the values gay men were examining. In *Tales of the City*, Armistead Maupin's valentine to San Francisco, the homosexuals aren't that different from the heterosexuals (everyone wants a lover, everyone has a healthy libido). In Larry Kramer's novel *Faggots* (1978), gay life is the last circle of hell the Krafft-Ebing–era psychologists warned about, a comic descent into erotomania that precludes love or self-respect. From Holleran's perspective, Maupin misses the darkness, the compulsion; Kramer misses the élan and the yearning.

IF THERE WERE psychological and emotional risks in unbounded sexual freedom, in separatism, and in a flourishing entertainment culture of discos and drugs, not too many men wanted to ponder their implications in the mid- to late 1970s, and Kramer deserves credit for ruffling feathers with his controversial story of Fred Lemish, love-starved but "cock-drunk" (in Christopher Bram's phrase), a brittle satire that many gay readers dismissed as hyperbolic and self-hating. But another, more political critique asked a different set of questions, at least as timely. Others wondered if gay men were becoming less politicized as they expanded and codified their social world. Had the gay movement lost steam because of its success in increasing gay space, visibility, comfort, and some economic security? The career of Harvey Milk, a distinctly California phenomenon, was intimately linked to these concerns.

An unlikely gay politico, and an even more unlikely gay hero, Milk came from a middle-class Long Island Jewish background. At Bay Shore High School and later at the New York State College for Teachers in Albany (class of 1951), he was a middling student with no special talents or intellectual gifts, an unexceptional athlete, gregarious, at moments oddly reserved, but not someone readily pegged as a queer. Milk knew his own nature, though—well enough to be looking for sex partners on teenage excursions to New York City during the war. Having been picked up at least twice by the police, he also knew the advantage of "passing" and secrecy. After a brief stint in the Navy in the mid-1950s, which included a busy exploration of the homosexual opportunities in San Diego, he moved to New York to fashion the sort of life tens of thousands of college-educated gay men of his generation did. That meant a job in business, a well-decorated apartment, a series of lovers, a willingness to accept the situation in which he found himself and which required living with what Mattachine writers of the time called "the mask." Occasionally, a volcanic temper behind the mask revealed itself, as when Milk lunged at a diner in a Manhattan restaurant in the late 1950s who muttered "faggots" when he and his lover walked by. The subject of the Holocaust and the complicity of German civilians often elicited a similar unpredictable rage from Milk.

In his choice of lovers, Milk gave further hints of the other dimensions of a temperament at war with its own conventionality. The staunch Republican who supported Barry Goldwater in 1964 tended to fall for more outré partners, among them Craig Rodwell, future Mattachine activist and founder of the Oscar Wilde Memorial Bookshop. So it isn't entirely surprising that Milk, who was never excited by the nine-to-five routine of the financial analyst or tempted by the lure of big money, drifted into a Bohemian circle of friends around *Hair* director Tom O'Horgan, joined in the late-1960s taste for beads and jeans, and eventually relocated with a boyfriend to "Baghdad on the Bay." San Francisco allowed for a reinvention of identity and a more relaxed gay life: the plate-glass windows at the Elephant Walk on Castro and Eighteenth Street were alien to New York, where gay bars remained dimly lit and protected from the gaze of passersby. Opening a camera shop in the heart of the emerging gay neighborhood was, for Harvey Milk, less a career choice than grudging admission that one had to do something to make a living.

The real "something" that came to interest Milk not long after his move was electoral politics. His professed reasons for attempting in 1973 an act as brash as running for the Board of Supervisors, the city's governing body, were his pique at being forced to make a deposit against future sales tax payments before he could open his business, concern about inadequate funding for local schools, and indignation over the Watergate hearings, but those statements (like many that originated with Milk himself) should be taken skeptically. He had a restless, theatrical side and an impatience with concepts of private life that sustained other men—the cozily domestic or the exclusively social and sexual was not for him. On the verge of middle age, he was too old to be a foot soldier in any cause but his own. In any case, Milk's decision—regarded as slightly batty even by his closest friends—

was not made in a vacuum. The political scene he wanted to enter in the waning days of the conservative Alioto administration was a volatile one, and already established gay organizations and their power brokers promised to be the means to significant change for homosexuals—if that constituency bided its time and made the right alliances. To people such as the wealthy *Advocate* publisher David Goodstein or SIR leaders such as Rick Stokes and Jim Foster (whose contacts with the McGovern campaign allowed him the chance to deliver a moving televised speech on gay rights at the Democratic Convention in 1972), the man with the ponytail and the big mouth was only going to be an obstacle to their incremental strategies for repealing the state's sodomy law, ending police brutality, cementing ties with Democratic liberals, and—some day, probably in the 1980s—electing a gay supervisor.

On the latter point, Milk was belligerently clear. He was against caution and timetables. Attuned to homosexuals' expanding minority consciousness without having participated in New York's GAA or GLF activities himself, he wanted gays to represent their own interests in the circles of power. To Jose Sarria, a forefather in the struggle, and other drag queens, that line of thought alone was worth an endorsement, but the Alice B. Toklas Democratic Club (a political offshoot of SIR) was furious at his effrontery in suggesting in *The Bay Area Reporter* that Toklas Club gays were Uncle Toms "satisfied with crumbs." At candidates' forums, Milk presented himself, often with considerable eloquence, as a vigorous alternative for all citizens. He spoke out against the transformation of San Francisco into a tourist and corporate center, high assessments on small-home owners, neglect of the public bus system, the razing of whole neighborhoods, the loss of a city's soul to its business interests. In a citywide contest, Milk came in tenth out of thirty-two candidates for the five spaces that were open on the board. For a campaign run on a shoestring budget of $4,500, those numbers were a respectable tally. As Randy Shilts wrote in his biography of Milk, *The Mayor of Castro Street*, "The political analysts had been looking toward the Milk campaign as a clinical study of whether a gay vote actually did exist. [Harvey Milk's] 17,000 votes showed that it clearly did."

The election also clarified Milk's relish for campaigning and his ability to maneuver between the traditional poles of political life: brazen self-promotion and idealistic pronouncements. His tall tale about having been discharged from the Navy in the 1950s in an anti-gay purge won points with gay audiences and his temper tantrums when anything went wrong at his headquarters got the job done, but at the same time Milk could be genuinely inspirational in ways that few politicians were. Indeed, his combination of cranky, high-minded, driven, and pleasantly zany qualities was what appealed to many acquaintances. The man who later donned a clown costume—suit, hat, nose, and makeup—to greet cable car riders was the same street-smart coalition builder who helped the Teamsters bring their Coors boycott to the attention of gay bar owners. He was the same strategist who put together the Castro Village Association for those gay merchants who were frozen out of the Eureka Valley Merchants Association, organized the first Castro Street Fair in 1974, and offered his store as a collection point for defense funds for the Castro 14, a group of gay men fighting their treatment by the SFPD. He was the same bold editorialist who referred in print to one of the gay-bashing policemen in that episode as "Officer Chickenshit" and who openly charged the leaders of the local Teamsters union with taking bribes to back out of the Coors fight in 1975. He was the same shrewd tactician (whose neglected camera store never seemed to make a profit, whose romantic life was always a shambles) who secured the endorsement of the firefighters' and the construction workers' unions with his prolabor stand. In his 1975 run for the Board of Supervisors, he more than tripled his earlier total, winning over 50,000 votes. The six incumbents up for reelection carried the day, but Milk, in seventh place, came closer to his goal.

Milk's reward for supporting George Moscone, the liberal Democrat who squeaked into office as San Francisco's mayor in 1975, was a spot on the city's Board of Permit Appeals. As part of an important commission, the job was looked upon as a political plum, but Milk didn't last long in the post. His decision to run for a vacant seat in the Assembly only five weeks into his appointment alienated Moscone, who fired him, and made enemies of almost the entire Democratic machine. He lost the primary and had to live with renewed accusations that he was more an opportunist desperate to hold office than a roll-up-his-sleeves man on the job. "And," noted a sometime campaign worker, "that was true. [That fact] just doesn't happen to mean all that much. Permit appeals weren't Harvey's idea of his destiny."

Two developments of equal consequence allowed Milk to move into the larger arena he needed. One was a change in election procedures. The shift from citywide to district elections for supervisors meant that an openly gay man running from District 5—Eureka Valley, Noe Valley, the Haight— could now play to his strengths. He didn't need to worry about carrying those parts of town that would never vote for a queer. The other was the Dade County steamroller and John Briggs's initiative, highlighting the urgency of a gay rights debate and the limits of straight support. Gay men and lesbians were talking about their dubious legal status as never before. The gay-bashing murder of Robert Hillsborough, a thirty-one-year-old man on a date with his boyfriend, only days before the Gay Freedom Day

Parade in June, prompted the largest showing ever for that event anywhere in America—a quarter of a million participants, by most estimates. This was a climate in which Milk could unfairly characterize Rick Stokes, his principal opponent, as a gay sellout and rightly characterize himself as the voice of change. In November 1977, on his third attempt, he was elected to the Board of Supervisors.

AN ESSENTIAL INGREDIENT in Milk's rise, as it is for all politicians perceived as leaders rather than mere officeholders, was the element over which individuals have the least control: timing. Between 1972 and 1977, the temper of gay male life changed more than the older activists realized, not merely on the coasts but everywhere in the country. A less stodgy, more hip, more aggressive style was vital; looking as if you knew your way around the dealmakers' back rooms and the black-tie fund-raising circuit was not. Modulated anger was crucial. In the minds of younger gay men (those who were likely to be the objects of victimization and, as baby boomers, the largest voting bloc), Harvey Milk was the public figure who seemed most indignant about the arrogance of the Officer Chickenshits who preyed on them, the city officials who didn't stop the abuse of power, and the Anita Bryants who implicitly encouraged it. Best of all, he didn't care if the tone of that indignation sometimes offended heterosexuals.

Yet Milk's rhetoric never reached the point of irrational or destructive anger, off-putting to middle-class gay men. The fantasy of a gay riot was not without appeal, but was nothing to be advocated from the podium or in print. As a former Republican and owner of a small business, Milk believed in the methods of the system. He was as impatient with Marxist gay radicals as they were with him. Yet he had the wit to articulate the difference between shaking up the system and simply buying into it. He got rid of the ponytail, but still talked like an outsider and an eccentric. At the same time, he managed this juggling act while adopting a warm approach to the heightened sexuality of the day, its hedonism and flagrant rejection of assimilationist values. Part of this refusal to criticize was a reflection of Milk's own roots in the counterculture and in his own active libido. Even when he was in a suit, Harvey Milk looked like the type who was just as comfortable in jeans or a bathhouse towel. (How buttoned-down is a man going to seem who was thrilled to be photographed on the street in a clown suit?) An effort to channel gay energies into political action made more sense than pious judgments about what went on in the bushes at Buena Vista Park or at the Sutro Baths. The avid pursuit of pleasure and productive social change were not mutually exclusive, Milk believed, nor were the style and needs of the mid-1970s necessarily going to be the style and needs of the 1980s or the 1990s. He was more concerned about the dehumanizing effects of technology, inflated rents, corporate competition, skyscraper-based urban renewal.

Once established in City Hall, which he grandiloquently referred to as "my stage," Milk set out to be the kind of elected official he always said he would be—mindful of his promises, alert to moments of symbolic importance, and attentive to the smaller quality-of-life issues. He billed himself as the city's "number one queen," but his time was devoted to tax rates and pooper-scooper laws, stop signs and potholes, as well as the city's gay rights ordinance, whose passage he oversaw, and the coalitions he hoped to build, especially between San Francisco's Chinese-American and gay population. He took more joy, it seemed to some observers, in needling lukewarm allies like George Moscone and Dianne Feinstein than in squaring off against the Board's lone conservative, ex-cop Dan White. White was dumb but "educable," Milk insisted. The turmoil of Milk's home life, which culminated in the suicide of his lover that fall, was offset by productive twelve-hour work days. This, Milk told friends, was the work he was born to do—and would do even better when he was mayor.

Like politicians as different as the Kennedys and Ronald Reagan, Harvey Milk was smart enough to know that no matter how consuming the labor or details of his job might be, a leader exists to provide energy and hope to those who share his philosophy and needs to be identified with an overarching theme. Hope for a better future, hope for gay teenagers grappling with questions of identity and bigotry, became almost a litany in Milk's speeches and functioned as a corollary to his larger message about coming out. Though he was able to express his view without making audiences feel guilt-ridden or hectored (no small feat), its thrust was, if not accusatory, then demanding: gay liberation and the noisy activism of a minority notwithstanding, gays had not been honest enough or brave enough. Their tendency to hide—their ability to make a life that skirted the issue—was the problem in 1978 as it had been in 1958 or 1938. "We will not win our rights by staying quietly in our closets," Milk told the ecstatic crowds in front of City Hall on Gay Pride Day in June 1978. Coming out was essential to "fight the lies, the myths, the distortions," to battle those who played "fast and loose with the true meaning of the Bible" and perpetuated the shallowest stereotypes. Waiting for help from Jimmy Carter or anyone who talked glibly about human rights was folly. The "conspiracy of silence" should be ended by gay men and lesbians themselves, who still refrained from talking about love and sex with their families, neighbors, and colleagues out of a misplaced sense of discretion that was their adversaries' best weapon.

When push came to shove, Milk was not averse to forcible outings to counter those adversaries. As a onetime boyfriend of the man who thwarted Sara Jane Moore's assassination attempt on Gerald Ford in 1975, he knew about Bill Sipple's homosexuality and had shared that privileged information with the press for the sake of advancing a positive role model, a specifically gay hero—much to Sipple's horror. Linking the gay cause to the plight of other minorities and to a failure of heart and will—"No more racism, no more sexism, no more ageism, no more hatred!"—Milk called for a gay and lesbian demonstration in Washington the following summer to tell the nation "what America really stands for." Shame, timidity, and a desire for privacy inevitably aided our oppressors, he asserted, no matter how understandable their origins in personal suffering.

Milk had every reason to anticipate a brilliant second year in office. His travels throughout the state to challenge Briggs and Proposition 6 increased his visibility and promised him a significant place in the national gay movement. But he did not live to see the 100,000 participants gather for the National March on Washington for Lesbian and Gay Rights in the summer of 1979. His violent death came from a source closer to him than the dozens of anonymous death threats he received by mail every week. On November 27, 1978, three weeks after the defeat of the Briggs initiative, Dan White, his pockets packed with extra bullets, unloaded his revolver into Mayor Moscone and Harvey Milk. Worn down by personal problems and furious at Moscone for not reappointing him to the Board after his precipitous resignation the week before (a decision Milk had leaned on the mayor to make), White cracked under the strain and, alone with them in their City Hall offices, murdered the two men who embodied what he most feared about the cultural changes of the 1970s in San Francisco.

The news shocked the city and devastated residents of the Castro, but also caused gay men elsewhere to reflect on Milk's stirring words and example. "I had very little idea of what he was doing, what he was trying to do," commented a gay man from Arizona interviewed for this book, "until the coverage when he died." Half a continent away, in Chicago, writer Darrell Yates Rist felt the impact as a visionary experience: "The gunshots that killed Harvey Milk that day gave shape to San Francisco in our minds, not so much as a place by the bay, but as the idea of freedom. It became the place of martyrs—the Promised Land we longed to create wherever we lived." Larry Kramer had "only vaguely heard about" Milk before the assassination, but visiting from New York that week promoting *Faggots*, he felt "shivers of pride" at the form the city's grief took, its scope and beauty. Tens of thousands of tearful marchers walked from the corner of Castro and Market Streets to Civic Plaza after dark, holding candles aloft.

"It was one of the most eloquent expressions of a community's response to violence that I've ever seen," remembered activist Sally Gearhart, who had joined Milk in debating Briggs and rallying the troops. "I think we as lesbians and gay men, and all the straight people who were marching with us that night, and there were thousands . . . we sent a message to the nation that night."

A different message was sent six months later. The trial of Dan White in May 1979 did not provide closure. After eleven days of testimony and lawyers' arguments (marked by a suspiciously weak prosecution) and six days of jury deliberation, the former supervisor was found guilty on the lesser charge of voluntary manslaughter. In the voir dire, his attorneys had managed to exclude any gay men or lesbians from the jury and, during the trial, capitalized on White's Catholic, wholesome family-values background and the stress he had been under after leaving his position at City Hall. The so-called Twinkie defense emphasized White's consumption of vast quantities of sugar and junk food in the days leading up to the murder. "Good people—fine people with fine backgrounds—simply don't kill people in cold blood," the defense lawyer contended. Dan White "was honest and fair—perhaps too fair for politics in San Francisco." The largely working-class, Catholic jury agreed. The woman whom Bill Sipple had prevented from shooting President Ford in San Francisco four years earlier was serving a life sentence; Dan White, having actually murdered the mayor and the city's most prominent homosexual leader, received a prison term that made him eligible for parole in five and a half years.

The night of the verdict, gay men and women took to the streets, indignantly sharing the sentiments of activist Cleve Jones about the jury's attitude: "in America, it's all right to kill faggots." Chanting "Avenge Harvey Milk" and "Dan White, Dan White, hit man for the New Right," five thousand demonstrators converged on City Hall. Outside the building, marchers who urged nonviolence were outnumbered and outshouted by an enraged mob. They smashed windows, hurled rocks and bottles, and set rows of police cars ablaze. The White Night Riots, as the evening of May 21, 1979, came to be called, dwarfed Stonewall and all previous displays of gay rage in size, intensity, and media coverage. The feeling even among those previously committed to nonviolence was that "*things* had to be destroyed," in the words of Allan Bérubé. No better symbol than a burning police car could be found—the SFPD had been too nakedly sympathetic to Dan White and almost gleeful over the demise of Moscone and Milk. But the police were quick to take their revenge for the arson and taunts of the crowd. After midnight, they invaded the Castro in riot gear, stormed the Elephant Walk, dragged its occupants into the street, and (having removed their badges and other ID) clubbed dozens of men—bar patrons, passersby, journalists—to the ground over the next hour.

Like Milk himself, the aftermath of his death was not all of a piece. Movingly eulogized at the time, the subject of a biography in 1982, a film in 1984, and an opera in 1994, he became the kind of role model he believed gay people needed. His influence was sufficient to guarantee that the new mayor, Dianne Feinstein, would appoint a gay man to take his place, and a Milk protégé, Harry Britt, assumed the position. But the momentum stopped there, for the time being. No leader of equivalent strength or personality emerged. In its December 1978 report on the slayings, which had happened only days after the Jonestown mass suicides in Guyana (taking the lives of many former San Francisco residents), *Newsweek* editorialized that the problems in the city perhaps stemmed from its very tolerance, its openness to all manner of deviance—which was a slap at "gay demands" and "gay excesses" rather than Dan White's socially sanctioned homophobia. The magazine's editors evidently weren't the only ones who thought that way. Street violence against gays continued to rise and police harassment continued unabated. In 1980, San Francisco voters repealed their new district voting system, curbing the likelihood that a man whose primary strength lay in a gay neighborhood would again be elected to the Board of Supervisors, and CBS offered its reading of the situation in a prime time documentary suggesting that the gay population of San Francisco had far too much power and far too little respect for decent values.

23

HISTORY MAKING

The only way we'll have real pride is when we demand recognition of a
culture that isn't just sexual. It's all there—all through history we've
been there; but we have to claim it, and identify who was in it, and
articulate what's in our minds and hearts and all our creative contributions to this earth.

—Larry Kramer, *The Normal Heart*

In the end, the tumult of the late 1970s tended to conceal as much as it
revealed. Large parades each June commemorating Stonewall became a significant urban phenomenon in the wake of Bryant, Briggs, and the murder
of Harvey Milk, and gay visibility acquired a sexy Hollywood cachet. Jane
Alexander and Gena Rowlands made respectable lesbians in the TV movie
A Question of Love in 1978, but four years later in *Making Love*, Harry
Hamlin and Michael Ontkean thrilled gay moviegoers more for the ripple
of shock their smack on the lips occasioned in mixed audiences than for
the heat of the image itself. Important alliances continued to be made with
labor and religious leaders, and the communications network within the
gay world expanded by leaps and bounds. In his landmark study of the gay
press, Rodger Streitmatter analyzed this period as the time of the "national-
izing" of gay news as local papers began to cover stories from other
regions, thus providing their readers with a sense of shared obstacles and

accomplishments. But the *symbols* of progress were the heady stuff, and those symbols became more potent and creative all the time. Gilbert Baker's rainbow flag was popular from the moment of its first appearance at a 1978 Pride March in San Francisco, and the sight of gay and lesbian activists around a conference table at the Carter White House presented public relations material of a high order.

The March 1977 West Wing meeting of fourteen movement leaders with Carter aide Midge Costanza, arranged by the National Gay and Lesbian Task Force, is nothing to disparage in the context of a system that values access to power, but the questions asked at the time had to do with how real that access was, and to what that access might plausibly lead. (The fact that Costanza was a lesbian, though not out at the time, and did not last long at the White House contributes to a retrospective air of unreality about the event and makes for a different, less elevating kind of symbolism: gays talking to gays in the Roosevelt Room, while the real policymakers are out of town.) The truth was that Jimmy Carter had shown less interest in gay rights than his Democratic rivals in 1976. Birch Bayh and Morris Udall attended fund-raising brunches in gay bars; Carter paid lip service to support for a federal civil rights bill, but withdrew his backing for an antidiscrimination plank in the party's platform once it became clear that he had the nomination sewn up. He never intended to meet personally with the gay leadership at any time or, more important, to work to change archaic policies. Only with great reluctance did the president speak out against Bryant and Briggs, and vicious new Pentagon purges were in full swing by the middle of his term. "The Carter years," Randy Shilts wrote in *Conduct Unbecoming*, "would prove to be even worse ones [than the Ford years] for homosexuals in the armed forces." The White House conference, then, was both reassuring and highly misleading. Yet for people committed to traditional politics, symbols are all but irresistible: at the Democratic National Convention in 1980, the Gay and Lesbian Caucus was allowed to place the name of Mel Boozer, an African-American gay activist, in nomination for the vice presidency and he was given a few minutes at the podium, which he used to great oratorical effect. This was arranged, however, with the understanding that his nomination would then be immediately withdrawn.

After enough symbolic moments, who could tell the pleasing image from the bruter fact? In the same way, the nature of the opposition was sufficiently histrionic to mislead those who saw the trajectory of American life as one of steady progress toward a less divisive society. Donald Wildmon, founder of the National Federation for Decency and the Coalition for Better Television, was every bit the Mississippi redneck, a man to make Bryant look sophisticated. It wasn't likely that he was going to cow the networks into submission. Jerry Falwell was an equally absurd figure when he announced the organization of the Moral Majority in 1979, whose mission would be to reclaim "the Christian foundation" of God's country, now lost to feminists, liberals, Communists, and homosexuals. After Anita Bryant's reappraisal of her anti-gay campaign in a famous 1980 interview, at which time she turned on fundamentalists who were "too legalistic and letter-bound about the Bible" and conceded that she had been needlessly belliger-ent, it seemed as if the reactionary stance toward homosexuality was destined to fade away. What was less apparent at the time was the way in which the New Right was more subtle and clever than it seemed, especially in the development of huge war chests and extensive mailing lists that could be used for the election of those candidates who shared many of Wildmon's and Falwell's views but who appealed to voters not willing to put an evan-gelist in office. On gay issues, whether it was legislated "approval" of a deviant lifestyle or the soon to be life-or-death topic of public health priori-ties, the distance between Jerry Falwell and Ronald Reagan was slight. Fal-well's grasp of the national mood, and his sense of how to achieve many of the goals of the Moral Majority, was superior to that of any strategist from the other end of the spectrum.

A decade later, the computer revolution would provide a new twist to an old adjective that evoked the spirit of the gay dilemma circa 1980 and into the 1990s. On the screen, high-tech virtual reality simulates experi-ence, making the artificial appear real, and for a number of cyberspace junkies the difference between the two, for all intents and purposes, can be negligible. In *Virtual Equality* (1994), Urvashi Vaid made the case that gays in America were becoming products of the same confusion in perception. "Virtual nondiscrimination" ensures that no one will be penalized in the workplace so long as he or she pretends to be straight or asexual; "virtual respect" allows everyone to remain on good terms with family members so long as homosexuals pretend their dates or spouses are simply friends or roommates. Blatant inequality, like obvious hatred, inspires one set of responses. Its clarity is bracing, even useful. Yet in a climate of virtual equality, the danger is no less menacing. The world simply appears more benign than it really is.

A telling example of the mainstream's still vigorous need to demonize the homosexual was the television networks' idea of a serious documentary on the subject. Twelve years after Mike Wallace's discouraging program for CBS, *ABC News Close-Up* aired its own hour-long study in 1979, which went on without a single sponsor and dealt more with gay suicides and numbers of sex partners than anything else. *CBS Reports*'s more controver-sial broadcast in April 1980, "Gay Power, Gay Politics," was purportedly a look at gay influence in San Francisco, but lacked even the most rudimentary conceptions of objectivity. To her credit, Dianne Feinstein asked her interviewers to leave her office as soon as the first question was out of producer George Crile's mouth ("How does it feel to be mayor of Sodom and Gomorrah?"). Others in San Francisco felt badly used by the journalists they agreed to help when they watched a program that emphasized S&M brutality as a widespread and uniquely gay practice (though filming its S&M scene in a heterosexual club), unrestrained public sex, and a political movement intent on humiliating the mayor and violating all community standards. Five months after the broadcast, the National News Council rapped CBS for airing a documentary flawed by questionable editing practices and the use of stereotypes. Three African-American members of the council's review panel compared the network's coverage of homosexuals to its lopsided and prejudicial coverage of blacks twenty years earlier. The "liberal media" was—is—a perennial right-wing bogeyman, but its biases were nothing gay men and lesbians could appreciate.

THE ELECTION OF Ronald Reagan, swept into office in 1980 on an anti-ERA, family values platform, validated a yearning in America, a wish to return to a more ordered world where deviance and disruption were supposedly nonexistent or invisible. For the next several years, any expectation that society would change more than it had on sexual-political issues was unrealistic. Instead, more than ever before, it was incumbent upon gay men and lesbians to challenge this limited view of history and culture, speaking to each other if not to the rest of the country. In the period since Stonewall, a number of talented researchers and writers had been doing just that, and as a consequence the late 1970s and early 1980s witnessed a development at least as significant as the founding of a gay political movement—the excavation and examination of a rich history most people presumed was not there to be found, and the flowering of a self-identified gay culture.

In this endeavor, the labors of Jonathan Ned Katz were paramount. His book *Gay American History* was published in 1976 and his *Gay/Lesbian Almanac* seven years later. Both were bountiful documentary collections, the result of the author's interviews and wide-ranging survey of court records, government files, medical journals, diaries, newspapers, biographies, and novels from colonial to modern times. The staggering amount of information Katz uncovered about homosexual sex, homosexual love, and gender-role differences—which he divided into the categories Trouble; Treatment; Passing Women, referring to the many nineteenth-century women who wore male attire and successfully made a life for themselves as men; Native Americans/Gay Americans; and Resistance—proved, definitively, that the raw material was there, that homosexuality (like race and gender) had a history that could be studied. Contrary to the judgment of the many publishers who rejected the first manuscript, there were plenty of readers who wanted to know more about the origins of aversion therapy or the Radclyffe Hall controversy or the early anthropologists' reports on cross-dressing Indians; *Gay American History* eventually sold 40,000 copies. The book was dedicated to "My people, in love, in struggle" and to "two pioneers," Jeanette Foster, who had written an early study of lesbianism in literature in the 1950s, and Harry Hay.

Several interesting books followed in quick succession: Christopher Isherwood's memoir of Berlin between the wars, *Christopher and His Kind* (1976); A. L. Rowse's *Homosexuals in History* (1977); and, especially important in the academic world, Jeffrey Weeks's *Coming Out: Homosexual Politics in Britain from the Nineteenth Century to the Present* (1977). In 1980, Yale professor John Boswell stunned the serious reading public with the erudition of *Christianity, Social Tolerance, and Homosexuality: Gay People in Western Europe from the Beginning of the Christian Era to the Fourteenth Century* (1980). Boswell's thesis—that Roman Catholic opposition to homosexuality was not an original or inherent element of the Church's teaching, but was actually a medieval development—earned him enemies among both religious traditionalists, who branded this view of Catholic history as heretical, and gay radicals, who called it wishful thinking. (Boswell's coyness about discussing his own homosexuality, on the grounds that he wanted his text read for its own merits rather than as an example of special pleading, illustrates the bind that even tenured academics found themselves in in 1980. Gay radicals accused him of special pleading from the other angle—wanting as a Catholic gay man to justify his own ties to a Church that called him a sinner.) More recent but still largely unknown history was brought to life in Toby Marotta's *The Politics of Homosexuality* (1981) and John D'Emilio's *Sexual Politics, Sexual Communities* (1983) that chronicled, from different perspectives, the rise of the gay movement in the United States from the 1940s to the 1970s. Other scholars, both university-based and independent, vigorously pursued their own areas of interest: Eric Garber and the Harlem Renaissance; Gregory Sprague and gay life in Chicago; Allan Bérubé and the gay experience during World War II; Richard Plant and homosexuality in Nazi Germany. Community-based history projects got under way in several cities by the end of the decade gathering oral histories from older homosexuals and soliciting relevant papers and photographic collections. The vast private libraries amassed over the years by Jim Kepner, Dorr Legg, and Don Slater suddenly became indispensable resources for a younger generation of writers.

The popularizing of information and ideas about a shared past was furthered in these years as room was made in the gay press for articles by historians scouring out-of-the-way archives and for random reminiscences by longtime participants in gay life, such as diarist Donald Vining and poet Havilland Ferris. It was also advanced by writers, particularly dramatists, who were enlivened by a new sense of audience and the prospect of new venues for their work. Theater Closet in Baltimore, the Triangle in Boston, Speak Its Name in Chicago, Celebration Theatre in Los Angeles, Out-and-About in Minneapolis, the Glines in New York, Janus Productions in Phoenix, Carpenter's Children in San Diego, and Theatre Rhinoceros in San Francisco all began their catch-as-catch-can existence in this era. The gay theater network was crucial for playwrights whose subject matter kept them from the larger audience that a writer treating a supposedly more universal theme could aim for. The notable exception of the 1979–1980 Broadway season, Martin Sherman's drama about homosexuals in concentration camps, owed its unusual status in large part to the presence of Richard Gere in the lead. Many of Sherman's concerns in *Bent* were relevant to the lives of contemporary gay men—self-acceptance, family rejection, the danger of an apolitical hedonism, generational differences about openness and secrecy, and the place of the homosexual in the pecking order of outcasts—but his story's signal contribution was in placing genocide against gays in the context of twentieth-century history. *Bent* was a flat-out rebuke to those who did not want homosexuals to share in the memorializing accorded Jewish, Catholic, Slavic, or gypsy victims of Nazi tyranny. It was a rebuke to those who insisted that being gay never entailed the same suffering other groups had endured. (Not surprisingly, the pink triangle worn by gay prisoners in the camps quickly became the new symbol of gay resistance.) With *Bent*, Martin Sherman also brought a new explicitness to theater about gay men, whether it was in the onstage nudity of the storm trooper Gere brings home for the night, the details of gay lovemaking, or the acknowledgment of the problematic truth that it is easier for a gay man to hide his homosexuality than it is for a Jew or a black to hide his ancestry or race. On that point, Sherman's protagonist wavers until the final hour between self-preservation and an identification, both psychologically and spiritually necessary, with "his people."

Like *Bent*, the best of the imaginative historical re-creations of the time weren't intended to generate plaster saints. In William Hoffman and Anthony Holland's *Cornbury: The Queen's Governor* (1976), New York's transvestite, and probably homosexual, first governor is a cad as well as a free spirit. In *Lord Alfred's Lover* (1978), Eric Bentley's Oscar Wilde has no interest in martyrdom or the Uranian cause and—before the nightmare of Reading Gaol—little understanding of his society's calculated support for "the double life," insofar as it remains double and never admittedly homosexual. The thinly fictionalized Guy Burgess in Julian Mitchell's *Another Country* (1981) is a victim of an oppressive boarding school system that tolerates a certain amount of adolescent messing about, but the future spy for the Soviets is too complicated to be read exclusively as an innocent victim of British homophobia. Edward Carpenter in Noel Greig's *The Dear Love of Comrades* (1979) can be a difficult and egotistical man. The author of *Love's Coming of Age* finds integrating his concept of nonbinding relationships into his day-to-day life easier said than done. Yet he remains an eminent Victorian with a more daring vision than most and declines to please his allies by putting his Socialism before his faith in "homogenic love." The heroes we need, in Greig's view (as in Bentley's or in Sherman's), are individualists who grope their way toward a deeper knowledge of social and political forces, not scapegoats or happy libertines.

The tradition of representing homosexuality as a frequently British, and largely educated or upper-class, experience—the *Brideshead Revisited* syndrome—was revitalized in the 1970s and early 1980s for many good reasons. Less was known at the time about gay life elsewhere, and the always classy, always marketable circle of Oxbridge, Bloomsbury, and Auden-Isherwood-Spender invested the subject, made tawdry by the mass media, with a safer, tweedier image. Yet when a flesh-and-blood child of the Edwardian Age arrived in the United States—first by way of a BBC film of his memoirs, then by means of his book, and finally with the appearance of the "naked civil servant" himself, eager to settle in the New World and share his musings from the podium—a new take on the subject was provided. Quentin Crisp was a shock to the system, to everybody's system. He had been parading around London for six decades as "a self-evident ho-mo-sexual" and, before the BBC elevated his autobiography to a cult classic with John Hurt in the title role, he had known his share of anti-gay violence ("though all that is past now . . . I've been *interviewed*. The same people who used to kick me in the shins at the bus stop now come up and said 'Oh, love, I saw you on the telly!' "). His one-man show, *An Evening with Quentin Crisp*, was a bit of time-travel itself; the didacticism and extemporaneous wit dispensed from the stage at his talks had more to do with potted palms and Oscar Wilde than street theater and GLF sloganeering.

Crisp's popularity with gay audiences says a great deal about the ebullience with which the late-1970s examination of the past and the discussion of gay identity were being conducted. The conservatism of his message ("Don't tell your parents . . . don't be silly, they don't want to know") should have left Crisp facing empty theaters in the era of gay pride, but his persona, alternately fey and regal, was as seductive as the story of his life. He didn't apologize to anyone in 1929 for going about London in painted nails and henna-dyed hair, and he wasn't going to do so in 1979, but neither was he here to praise the modern ideology that saw his as a sad, unliberated generation. We are oppressed by heterosexual men, and one way we have made the pain bearable throughout the ages is to worship their muscular power, to make our abasement sexual, he said. For Crisp, it was silly to act as if the world were otherwise. A line such as "I regard all heterosexuals, however low, as superior to any homosexual, however noble" struck some listeners as an infamous comment to make ten years after Stonewall, but to others, Crisp's lectures and subsequent writings were something more than a bathetic commentary on self-hate by a survivor. They were a fair, if oblique, rap at masculinized clones and assimilationists: pretend that you are their equals if you want to, darlings, by pumping up and wearing denim and ignoring what they say behind our backs. The truth of our situation lies elsewhere. Irony, wit, camp, chic, a thick hide, and ostentatious honesty will better serve us than bravado and banners. (The pleasure of being lionized in one's golden years by pumped-up young gay men in denim was nothing to be shunned, however. In the 1980s and 1990s, even as he approaches the age of ninety, Crisp is a staple figure at gay pride events.)

Quentin Crisp was also a wonderful reminder to an unhistorically minded generation that the past is, to use L. P. Hartley's metaphor, a foreign country. Yet an appetite for information about sexual nonconformity in the past had been stirred, and when that curiosity was fed, as it was by Crisp, or in the film *Word Is Out*, first shown on PBS in 1978, the impact was incalculable. A product of five years' worth of interviewing by Peter Adair and the Mariposa Film Group, *Word Is Out: Stories of Some of Our Lives* is an unnarrated collection of faces, reveries, and vignettes. As a panorama of contemporary life, it aimed for the greatest possible breadth. A black athlete-scholar reflected on the multiple identities he had to juggle at home and school. Two divorced women in the suburbs discussed their lesbian union and their bonds with their respective children. An affluent businessman, a "gender-fuck" queen, rural couples, and urban activists invited the camera crew into their homes. The interviewees, articulate or taciturn, collectively suggested a mosaic that no one before Adair and the Mariposa Film Group had quite managed to evoke. Another key dimension of *Word Is Out* was in its window onto preliberation days. Watching PBS, thousands of gay viewers heard for the first time about the Black Cat Cafe and the Nightingale of Montgomery Street (the description of Jose Sarria leading patrons in a round of "God Save Us Nelly Queens" is a not-a-dry-eye-in-the-house moment); first heard of Harry Hay; or first learned, through the riveting testimony of Pat Bond and other women, about wartime camaraderie and the WAC purges after the war.

The great irony of the moment was that just as a body of work about a past "hidden from history" (in Martin Duberman's phrase) was attracting a general, unspecialized, enthusiastic audience, a new current of scholarship was calling into question the premise of some of that research. Katz's *Gay American History*, Rowse's *Homosexuals in History*, and Boswell's *Christianity, Social Tolerance, and Homosexuality* were predicated to varying degrees on the assumption of a continuity of experience between modern homosexuals and people who felt and loved in the same manner fifty, a hundred, or, in Boswell's case, a thousand years ago. Boswell explicitly used the term *gay people* in his discussion of those who had romantic and erotic attachments to members of their own sex in the Middle Ages and believed that the term was valid even when applied to ancient people who had no equivalent noun in their vocabulary. This was a position he held to the end of his life, in 1994, the year his book *Same-Sex Unions in Premodern Europe* was published, which documents same-sex commitment ceremonies as a little-known part of Western culture over several centuries. Yet other scholarship, precipitated by Jeffrey Weeks's *Coming Out* and the surging interest in Michel Foucault, rapidly took sexual history in a different direction. Weeks's view, amplified by Katz in his second anthology in 1983, was that gays falsely read their own post–Industrial Age urban expectations into the past when they imagined that men who had sex with other men in bygone days conceptualized themselves as a different category of people. In considering a time when an identity as "a homosexual" or "a gay person" was literally inexpressible, when the issue was an illegal act (sodomy), or the degree of a man's masculinity and not a way of life or a way of being, and when sodomist practices themselves were looked upon as sins that any man of weak character might commit, it makes little sense to refer to "gay men of the Middle Ages"—or even Lord Cornbury or Walt Whitman—as ancestors of the modern homosexual. From this perspective, "gay" was a recent idea lacking a fixed or universal meaning.

By the mid-1980s, the intellectual differences between the two schools of thought—known as "essentialism," which saw homosexual identity as a constant throughout history, and "social constructionism," which disputed the idea of any such transhistorical category as "gay"—formed more of a chasm than a difference of opinion in academia, with the social constructionists carrying the day and statements about the homosexual as an invention of the late nineteenth century repeated ad infinitum. Most gay men and lesbians not a part of the academic world who paid any attention to this topic probably saw the truth as occupying a gray middle ground. Questions nagged: Is every same-sex coupling in Aristotle, Plato, Plutarch, or the *Satyricon* a pederastic bond of limited duration and circumscribed emotions (the usual model in the literature about Greco-Roman homosexuality)? Did all of the thousands of Renaissance Florentines brought before the Office of the Night go on to marry and forget the pleasures of homosexual intimacy in their youth? Was it impossible that some of those who frequented London's molly houses in 1700 saw themselves as different from other men in profound, discrete, even self-categorizing ways that preceded the adoption of the term we now use and had to do with more than wearing women's clothes? Did the word *sodomite* ever mean something, at least to some of those it was applied to, that was akin to "homosexual," a label that can speak to a forbidden romantic love of men as much as a taste for buggery? Social networks that might have been too small, rudimentary, and secretive to leave a record for posterity were nonetheless declared nonexistent before the nineteenth century, with the same absoluteness that same-sex eroticism had been dismissed by earlier historians and teachers. In some quarters, as philosophy professor Richard D. Mohr pointed out, *gay* was now defined with a calculated specificity that necessarily precluded any ties to the ancient world or the Renaissance.

Yet if social constructionism in its more extreme forms had a dogmatic cast and appeared to threaten gay political solidarity (if "we" have no shared past and are a recent and possible transitory ideological creation, then "we" have no certainty of a meaningful future as a group), it did inaugurate a more rigorous, less homogenizing approach to historical inquiry. The followers of Weeks and Foucault properly reminded modern gays that homosexual activity and homosexual identity are not synonymous, just as untraditional gender roles in other cultures (for example, the Native American *berdache*) should not be taken as examples of homosexuality, pure and simple. The constructionists introduced a complexity to the subject that few people were ready for, especially when it was in the interest of modern gays to disparage the bisexual movement as a cop-out and to define any male heterosexual who harbored feelings for men as a closet case.

THE SCHOLARLY DEBATE over whether gay people could be said to have existed throughout history had ramifications for the here and now. First, there was the matter of all those lists, the Alexander the Great to Hans

Christian Andersen catalog of forebears. Modern gays were being asked to consider whether the urge to locate gay individuals in history was really a purposeful endeavor or an act that simplified the past for the sake of the political agenda of the present. Then, too, if homosexuality was not only a capacity shared by all people (unlike race or religious heritage) but part of a *role* whose characteristics were variable, the comparisons to other, protected minorities began to lose some of their credibility.

One response to this morass (not the least common) was to ignore the whole matter, chalking it up to abstruse academics. Another was to reflect on the ways in which a group need not have been unchangeably present throughout the ages to be accepted as a viable category today. (In terms of empowerment and victimization, outsider status and self-definition, a Jewish identity, for instance, has not meant exactly the same thing in every society over the last several thousand years. Similarly, Alan Dershowitz's 1997 *The Vanishing American Jew* asked what it will mean, if anything, to say "I am a Jew" in a time of declining anti-Semitism.) Yet another approach was to make more precise distinctions between those gay people who readily identified as gay and those who were not comfortable with the label/role because it did not correspond to the reality of their lives. They had less need of a gay identity connected to a gay history or a gay culture because they lived in a way that was not largely or exclusively homosocial or even homosexual. The most existential stance, perhaps, was to act as if historical certainty and philosophical clarity were relevant, but not all-important. If *gay people*, as modern Western societies know the term, didn't always exist, and even if they won't exist in some far-off future when homophobia has ended or sexual object-choice ceases to be a defining characteristic, gay people *do* exist now. The term means something to gay-bashers, to politicians and sociologists, to the tens of thousands of individuals who apply it to themselves and their lovers and friends. Their experience, in this country and in this century, has assumed certain contours, albeit never uniform ones that could pertain to all people who practice homosexual sex. But to be a gay man in the United States circa 1980 denoted something more than a psychosexual condition or a lifestyle choice, and numerous individuals and groups struggled to articulate that state of mind.

This cultural and psychological tie was charted, examined, expanded, celebrated, and critiqued with amazing fullness in a remarkably short period of time. The anthologies of GLF veterans Karla Jay and Allen Young addressed themselves to that end, for example, as did their own probing journalism; *After You're Out* (1975) included essays by gay writers on rural versus urban lifestyles, lesbian–gay male relations, and gay white racism, and selections in *Lavender Culture* (1978) covered the glamorizing of the baths and the changing bar scene to the gay impact on the visual arts, theater, dance, poetry, and rock music. *The Gay Report* (1979), modeled on *The Hite Report* and other sexual survey books of the period, was an 800-page tabulation analysis of the 5,000 questionnaires Jay and Young distributed nationwide, asking about sexual histories, techniques, and fantasies as well as respondents' stories of discrimination and attitudes toward gay liberation. Aside from its implicit point of announcing that gays were now to be studied on a large scale, like any other group in survey-crazed America, *The Gay Report* argued the need for homosexuals to continue establishing their own perspective on their lives, especially considering that the heterosexual "experts" had yet to surrender the field. (Masters and Johnson's abysmal *Homosexuality in Perspective* was also published in 1979, based on a study originating in the mid-1960s of a scant 176 gay men.)

Though the bulk of *The Gay Report* dealt with sexual topics, its concluding chapters on lifestyle offered some important refutations of two key, but divergent, myths about gay men—their leftist politics and their above-average incomes. Twenty-three percent of the respondents described themselves as moderate or conservative in their political leanings (with 11 percent registered as Republicans). Sixty percent reported a yearly income of $15,000 or below; 36 percent reported an income of $10,000 or below. Self-acceptance, not surprisingly, was high. Only 6 percent of the gay men answered affirmatively to the question, "If you could take a pill to make you straight, would you do it?" (None of the lesbians answered yes.) Sixty-five percent expressed the belief that their gayness was more than a matter of sexual orientation, with over 70 percent describing the concepts of gay community and gay culture as "important" or "somewhat important" to them. Wrote one respondent: "It's an attitude—one of the benefits of seeing America from the outside." "While I am doubtful about the idea of a workable gay community," wrote another, "since too many people with too little in common are included, I strongly support the concept of a gay culture . . . a heritage of idealistic, somewhat alienated, romantic creativity." There are such things, a third man argued, "as unmistakably gay contributions" to society.

A more impressionistic tour of the same milieu was novelist Edmund White's *States of Desire: Travels in Gay America* (1980). From Seattle and Salt Lake City to Houston and New Orleans, through Cincinnati, Minneapolis, and Boston, White wandered in search of the tone and texture of postliberation gay life. His well-received travelogue was also heavily, even primarily sexual, enough to leave some readers wondering if gay male interests ever went much deeper. John Boswell complained about what he perceived to be an unresolved problem in White's book: in describing so much casual sex and so many open-ended relationships, was White merely chronicling what existed or positing this freedom as a moral good? But it is hard to believe that Boswell didn't know the answer. Indeed, in other forums, White was very clear: though the dangers of elevating sex to the level of a transcendent value were real, gay men were also advised to accept their bouts with clap and herpes as badges of courage in a war against Puritanism. Nothing appeared to interest White less in *States of Desire* than the attempt of someone like Boswell to reconcile his homosexuality with traditional Catholic ethics. Gayness was about seeing what kind of bonds could be made when monogamy was not the most important feature of a love relationship, when walking the tightrope between anti-Puritanism and the "cooperative delusion" (White's phrase) of sex as ecstatic performance had become a way of life.

Yet the time and energies of gay men were also occupied by a wide range of other issues, originating in sexual quandaries or not, particular to homosexuals or not. The novels, poetry, theater, independent films, anthologies of stories and essays, and the gay-press journalism of the late 1970s and early 1980s were thematically broader than most critics have acknowledged. Fear of commitment and the need to redefine commitment when sexual fidelity is no longer, or not always, paramount; the tyranny of body image; the gap between political idealism and real-life compromise; mentoring and adoption; the ongoing lure of the closet; the yearning for an identifiable gay past; the pleasures and drawbacks of a gay ghetto; the difficulties facing gay men who have left wives and children to make a new life with a male lover—perspectives on these topics varied from the sentimental and the hortatory to the challenging and ambiguous. The antiseptic *Making Love* and the proctological *Taxi Zum Klo*, the aesthetic labyrinth of *Dancer from the Dance* and the bitterness of *Faggots*, covered a vast stylistic territory. And no less important than this productiveness was the creation of outlets and support systems for those who wanted to see the public discourse about homosexuality taken from the politicians and the sociologists. For every crossover success story like *Tales of the City* or Harvey Fierstein's *Torch Song Trilogy*, dozens of other projects and careers threatened to languish. In response, writers established their own groups (for instance, the Violet Quill, whose members included White, Felice Picano, and George Whitmore). Gay bars, bookstores, and clubs became sites for readings and performances (such as the famed production of Doric Wilson's *The West Street Gang* at the Spike in New York). Editors like Michael Denneny, founder of the Stonewall series at St. Martin's Press, and critic-columnists such as Richard Hall, Michael Bronski, and Vito Russo encouraged more creative work, higher standards, and a more involved audience. Business, politics, and art came together in the late 1970s in a proliferation of gay theater collectives and film festivals, bookstores and small presses.

As a significant body of gay work makes its way into college classrooms, fears are sometimes voiced about the way in which the academizing of any burning social issue tends to drain the topic of its relevance to the rest of the world, situating it in a context different from that in which nonacademics live and perceive it. In some forms, "queer theory" in the 1990s is particularly vulnerable on this point. But it is worth remembering that a foothold in the university is the only sure way today of keeping a subject before a public that counts for a great deal: the educated young, whose values often determine the political and cultural agenda of the future. At its inception, that process was tempestuous. In *Christopher Street* in 1984, Richard D. Mohr recounted his experience of introducing a gay studies course at the University of Illinois in Urbana and the barrage of criticism he took from all sides. On the first day of the class, the football players were aggressive in their statements about sick "fags" who were always trying to "rub on them"; the gay students had complaints about Mohr's "clone outfit" and monolithic representations of gay life. The course included the optional viewing of gay pornography. Long gone was the gentility of the ONE Institute seminars, replaced by the more politically aggressive style of the professor-activists. In the same article, Mohr summarized his view, shared by many who would later teach Gay Studies, of the decline of Stonewall-era militarism: "The gay rights movement does not need to be clean, respectable, or unified as much as it needs to be up front. The gay movement would do well to take up as its Motto of Political Life a bit of advice Rhett gives to Scarlett: 'If you had enough courage, you wouldn't need a reputation.' "

But up-frontness was the order of the day in several contexts beyond the literary and artistic. Specifically, gay bonds were being forged that approached gay identity issues from diametrically opposite points. The founding of the Gay Games in 1982 and the rise of gay Republican clubs in the late 1970s irked some gay men who saw these enterprises as aping the oppressor. Tom Waddel's version of the Olympics, like the gay wrestling clubs or the gay rodeo tournaments that followed, was antithetical to the Radical Faerie attack on muscle and competition; the Republican Log Cabin Clubs were accused of supporting the party of institutional homophobia. Those criticisms ignored the fact that proponents of radical effeminacy and left-wing politics had never spoken for the majority of homosexuals in America. Long before 1980 it was clear that they were leaders without a growing constituency, of more importance for the ideas they raised than any large-scale changes they were going to effect. Plenty of gay men and lesbians were genuinely interested in athletic competition and wanted to undermine the stereotypes about gays hating sports. Many more were mainstream or even conservative in their politics on all issues save those concerning sexual rights. There was no reason they shouldn't promote themselves as "gay athletes" or "gay Republicans." They argued that their efforts publicized the diversity of gay America more effectively than previous organizations ever had.

A group like Black and White Men Together, started by John Teamer and Michael Smith in 1980, implied a different approach to this search for a constructed meaning at the heart of modern homosexuality. Though it had its own difficulties to face from both a black separatist perspective and those men who wanted to see it largely as a sexual forum, BWMT, as it was known, attracted several hundred members and assumed varied forms in different states, from the purely social and low-key (picnics, potluck suppers, and discussion groups) to the more pointedly activist. In a few cities, discrimination at gay bars and discos met with public protest in the form of interracial picket lines and the filing of complaints to human rights commissions. As the first national convention in San Francisco in 1981 affirmed, the fundamental goal of its membership went beyond gay rights to a commitment "to fostering supportive environments wherein racial and cultural barriers can be overcome." The Gay Games or the Log Cabin Club implied one message: as gays, we are not fundamentally different from other Americans, but we do require our own well-defined space—for now—as we work our way into a system that continues to exclude us. This outlook, they maintained, was not to be confused with a retreat from pride in homosexual identity and a sense of gay fraternity. But Black and White Men Together offered a more challenging premise: we are like everyone else in our essential humanity, but having been cast in the role of the ultimate outsider, we have no desire to be integrated into a system that perpetuates racial divisions as well. On that front, BWMT suggested, gay men and lesbians are—or should be willing to see themselves as—uniquely situated to help undermine archaic social attitudes that dominate life in twentieth-century America despite Supreme Court rulings and the death of Jim Crow. BWMT proffered a variation on Harry Hay's answer to the question, "What are we for?" by answering that we are *about* embracing differences, *about* questioning and enlarging on the values we grew up with, or we are about nothing meaningful at all.

In this view, then, a community might not have to be a group with a single-focus identity; the sexual identity questions could continue to evolve at their own pace, never quite the same in every region, for every racial group or social class. But a community originating in same-sex erotic love did have to want to chart some kind of limited future as a group. It did have to know something about its fragmented past, did need to see the point to exploring and pondering the multiple meanings of that past—and to disseminating that information beyond the academic world. It had to be willing to search for common ground, while avoiding a false homogenization. It had to acknowledge its elders, which the founding of an organization like SAGE (Senior Action in a Gay Environment) in 1977 looked to do, and demand fair depictions in the media of its experiences, which became the cause of GLAAD (Gay and Lesbian Alliance Against Defamation) in the 1980s. As would soon become apparent, a community would also need, in tragic times, to care for its sick and give voice to its grief and fear. The extent to which gay men in America could do that would determine a great deal about gay life in the United States in the last two decades of the twentieth century.

VII. CRISIS

24

THE BOTTOM LINE

Words and phrases overheard, again and again. Diagnosis. Ward 86.
KS. AZT.
　　And canes. Young men with canes.

　　　　　　　　　　　　　　　—Laurence Tate, "The Epidemic:
　　　　　　　　　　　　　　　A San Francisco Diary," 1986

In the autumn of 1980 and throughout the first weeks of 1981, physicians—first in Los Angeles, then in San Francisco and New York City—
began to observe the startling phenomenon of a massive immunological
breakdown in some of their gay male patients. Two of the most virulent
manifestations of that breakdown were the onset of pneumocystis carinii
pneumonia and Kaposi's sarcoma, illnesses labeled "highly unusual" in previously healthy young men by the Center for Disease Control in Atlanta. In
May 1981, the CDC formed a task force to study the reports, and by the
end of the summer, its *Morbidity and Mortality Weekly Report* carried two
two-page articles on the rapidly declining patients, who at that point numbered just over one hundred. Members of the task force were puzzled that
journalists covering medical issues for the networks and the major newspapers expressed so little interest in what was obviously an impending
crisis. Reflecting on the press blackout a few years later, gay men were a
good deal less surprised.

Everything about the timing of AIDS in America conspired to make a bad situation worse. The deadliest of venereal diseases common among gay men, hepatitis B, appeared on the verge of eradication that year because a vaccine had been developed, thanks in part to the thousands of gay men who had participated in the CDC's research study and blood-testing programs. A modicum of complacency about sexually transmitted diseases in 1981 seemed justified to the layman. The "Reagan Revolution" in November 1980 had completed the shift to the right heralded by Anita Bryant and the Moral Majority, ending even the lip service paid to the cause of gay rights by the Carter administration. The ramifications of that development were understood soon enough by the politically astute in the medical establishment. An illness concentrated among sexually active homosexual men was going to be a very low funding and public relations priority in the new decade. Anyone who missed the first *Newsweek* and *Time* stories in December 1981 about the strange opportunistic diseases attacking gay men was not likely to read much more about GRID, or Gay-Related Immune Deficiency, until well into the new year.

Though the best evidence (lucidly detailed in Mirko Grmek's 1990 *History of AIDS*) now suggests that the immune-destructive HIV virus has been around for some time—documented cases in the United States include a twenty-eight-year-old man in Tennessee in 1952 and a homosexually active St. Louis teenager in 1968—its appearance as a detectable agent precipitating a syndrome of crippling illnesses seemed new and unbelievable in more ways than one. Middle-class Americans born after World War II had been conditioned to think of modern medicine as an engine of inexhaustible powers. Yet confronted with men in their twenties and thirties wasting away before their eyes, physicians had little to offer but their own perplexity and despair. Even more disturbing, the manner of death was singularly brutal. By the time a patient expired, often within several months of his diagnosis, as his pneumonia-ravaged lungs filled with fluid or cancerous lesions spread across and through his body, he might also experience, simultaneously, a barrage of other maladies: eruptions of herpes zoster, a thick coating of yeastlike candidiasis in the mouth and throat, cryptococcal meningitis, dementia, uncontrollable diarrhea, painful neuropathy, loss of muscle control, and blindness caused by cytomegalovirus retinitis. Two hundred cases of Kaposi's sarcoma or pneumocystis pneumonia, or both in the same patient, were reported by the end of the year. Close to five hundred cases were reported six months later. Yet the figures, and the incipient drama they imply when recited years after the fact, are misleading. The tragic actuality of 1981 and 1982 was that, if one didn't know any of these individuals or live in a city where the panic was growing, it was easy to ignore the rumors or assume that the full story of cause and cure had yet to be told. It seemed far-fetched to link sex or sexual orientation with disfiguring cancers, and many gay men—like all Americans—found it hard to believe in a tragedy that was not a product of frequent media scrutiny and alarm.

The laxness of the mainstream media in reporting on the outbreak and spread of AIDS, as the syndrome was renamed in 1982, is one of the most amply studied aspects of gay life in late-twentieth-century America. The 1976 death of thirty-four people from Legionnaires' disease and the 1979–1980 deaths of eighty-four women from toxic shock syndrome were covered in dire tones by all the network news programs and made front-page headlines across the country, as did the poison Tylenol scare in the fall of 1982. The *New York Times* even found the death of the famed Austrian Lipizzaner stallions from an unknown virus to be worthy of a front-page story in 1983. But that kind of urgent attention to a crisis among gay men was not forthcoming. "We have a family newspaper here," the managing editor of the *Amsterdam News* commented when asked about the Harlem-based newspaper's poor record on AIDS reporting among men of color in New York City. But William Egyir might just as well have been speaking for the *New York Times*, ABC, CBS, NBC, and the large-circulation news weeklies and monthlies. Only when it became apparent by degrees in 1982 that heterosexuals were at risk, and especially when doctors began reporting incidents of AIDS infection in children and hemophiliacs, did the publishers, editors, and producers responsible for those decisions make room for coverage of the topic. The stories behind the first *Wall Street Journal* article, the April 1983 *Newsweek* cover article, or the probing reports of NBC medical correspondent Robert Bazell all involve the same elements: the curiosity or passion of a few journalists set against indifferent or skeptical bosses, fear of reader or viewer antagonism, a widespread sense in the profession that this was a risky or marginal subject. By the end of 1982, according to Edward Alwood in *Straight News*, the three major networks had devoted a combined total of thirteen minutes' airtime to the epidemic.

The record of the government agencies and individuals charged by law with safeguarding the health of the citizenry was no better; the Center for Disease Control found its funding needs thwarted at every turn, even when Congress was willing to appropriate the money. But the problem went beyond the conservative cast of the new administration. If it took President Reagan until 1987 to deliver his first speech about AIDS, by which time it had claimed over 20,000 lives, the commitment of liberal Democratic politicians such as New York's Governor Mario Cuomo or Massachusetts's Governor Michael Dukakis was almost as reluctant. Jesse Helms might speculate about the need for quarantine and William F. Buckley could argue the benefits of tattooing HIV-positive men, but in New York City, Mayor Ed Koch, a middle-aged bachelor assumed by many to be a closet gay himself, made no secret of his displeasure at being identified with the fight against AIDS. Ultimately, the politicians were simply the most visible symbols of society's ongoing antagonism toward gay life. AIDS rent the illusion of a certain kind of progress. The diseased child molesters of the 1940s became the disease-spreading debauchees of the 1980s.

This climate affected the healthy as well as the infirm. Wresting control away from medical and psychiatric authorities of the terms in which homosexuality was discussed had been an important gay political goal since the 1950s, and by the end of the 1970s, doctors had been relegated to a minor role in the public commentary. Overnight that situation changed. Heterosexual medical experts once again had plenty to say about "the gay lifestyle" and, once the virus was identified, could now talk openly about the price to be paid for engaging in anal sex. The source didn't have to be as crude as Pat Buchanan ("The poor homosexuals. They have declared war on nature and nature is exacting an awful retribution") or the October 1982 Saturday Evening Post ("Being Gay Is a Health Hazard"); sophisticated urban physicians lectured gay patients about celibacy or monogamy—with scant attention to variations in gay male sexual practices—in a manner they would not have with their heterosexual patients. Their illnesses, gay men were told in different ways, had to do with more than infectious agents. The implicit, unscientific message was that their illnesses were part and parcel of the gay refusal to accept straight opinions about erogenous zones, an appropriate number of partners, and the personal relationship to those partners. Heterosexual venereal diseases are caused by the spreading of infection, which can be linked to a failure to use condoms—and not, everyone agrees, by vaginal intercourse itself, not by the failure to have sex with the right number of people whose names one knows. Accordingly, generations of straight men were not told by their doctors to abstain from intercourse as a necessarily disease-begetting act, but rather to abstain from *unprotected* intercourse. That crucial distinction did not, until much later, carry over into male same-sex intimacy. AIDS played too neatly into preexisting prejudices.

The remedicalization of homosexuality triggered a pervasive psychological assault on gay men, its intentions reflected in every aspect of the language employed in the AIDS discourse from the early 1980s into the 1990s. A rise in breast cancer cases signaled an "epidemic," but AIDS announced a "plague," even something as scientifically anomalous as a "gay plague." People with cancer were cancer "patients"; people with AIDS were AIDS "victims." There were "innocent" contractors of the virus (children, hemophiliacs, the spouses of IV drug users and bisexual men) and, by extension, those who were guilty of courting the disease (IV drug users who shared needles and men who were sexually active with other men) for whom too much sympathy would be misplaced. A gay man now was universally taken to be, *as a gay man*, part of a "risk group," whether or not his practices included anal intercourse or exchange of semen. The inclusion of Haitians in this taxonomy for a brief period in 1982 and early 1983 should have been the telltale sign of its sloppiness, as any student of biology knows that viruses do not distinguish among nationalities. In time, that categorization was dropped, but "gay male" continued to be the phrase of choice for the leading risk group.

Seldom in the 1980s was the focus purely on the virus or what was known of its transmission. Metaphors and moral lessons abounded—"The lifestyle of some male homosexuals has triggered an epidemic," NBC News informed the nation in June 1982, and the attribution of blame was never far from the heart of the story. ("GAY PLAGUE" SHOWING UP AMONG HAITIAN REFUGEES, a *Miami Herald* headline ran that same summer.) Even three years later, Secretary of Health and Human Services Margaret Heckler had no qualms about voicing the common hope that a cure would be found before AIDS reached "the heterosexual population." She would, presumably, have hesitated to refer to a disease among black Americans that had to be stopped before endangering the white population. But members of the nonheterosexual population were reminded many times throughout the decade that medical, media, and government concern could be expected only insofar as the crisis threatened the "normal," consequential majority. The others were expendable, and a decade and a half of marches, speeches, and lobbying had not altered that fact.

THE RESPONSE OF gay men themselves was not swift, nor did it reflect well on any such amorphous concept as "the gay community." En masse, heads went into the sand, and editors at *The Advocate* and other publications (with three or four key exceptions) adopted a wait-and-see approach. When Dr. Lawrence Mass, a gay New York physician, provided the first mention in a gay periodical of an "exotic new disease" afflicting male homosexuals, there wasn't much to say, in truth; his May 18, 1981, article for the *New York Native* was a simple, sensible acknowledgment that something odd was afoot. He kept writing, as there was more to report in the following months, and alerted other gay doctors to the new developments. But the capacity of gay men for ignoring that which they didn't want to hear shocked those who had a clearer awareness of the situation.

Bobbi Campbell, a San Francisco nurse, came out as a Kaposi's sarcoma patient in the pages of one of that city's gay papers, the *Sentinel*, and proclaimed himself a "KS poster boy." "The purpose of a poster boy," he wrote, "is to raise interest and money in a particular cause, and I have aspirations of doing that regarding gay cancer. I'm writing because I have a determination to live." Enough hiding, enough shame, Campbell insisted. He persuaded a pharmacy in the Castro to place bulletins in its window about Kaposi's sarcoma, with explicit photos, a tactic that grabbed attention faster than any number of articles. Several months later, New Yorkers Michael Callen and Richard Berkowitz published their landmark article, "We Know Who We Are," in the *Native*, announcing their own health status and decrying fast-lane sex.

An equally decisive action was precipitated by the irascible author of *Faggots*, Larry Kramer, who brought together a crowd of gay men in his Washington Square apartment in the summer of 1981 to hear from a doctor at NYU about the KS patients he had seen and to initiate a campaign to raise funds for research. The assembled guests came up with $6,000 that night. The card table that Kramer, Lawrence Mass, Paul Popham, and others set up at Fire Island over Labor Day Weekend, beneath a banner reading "Give to Gay Cancer," met with less approbation. "No one took it kindly," novelist Andrew Holleran observed, in an understatement. The take that weekend was $124. Part of the problem had to do with the setting: gay men went to Fire Island to get away from it all. Another factor had to do with Kramer's reputation as a blistering critic of the baths and back-room bars—many of his Manhattan and Fire Island friends had never forgiven him for the tone of his novel—and with his perpetually aggressive style. Playwright Robert Chesley advised readers of the *Native*, when Kramer began publishing in that forum, not to accept the jeremiads uncritically. The medical evidence was unclear and the source of the alarm was suspect. "The concealed meaning of Kramer's emotionalism," Chesley argued, "is the triumph of guilt: that gay men deserve to die for their promiscuity. . . . Read anything by Kramer closely. I think you'll find that the subtext is always: the wages of gay sin is death." Another acquaintance of Kramer's from the theater world commented in the 1990s, "It was possible to be worried about these strange medical problems cropping up among gay men and still be put off by [Kramer's] attitude. He was just a little too happy to be proved right."

Yet Kramer's ego and anger, coupled with his prominence in the gay world and his willingness to be "out" in any public circumstance, were the qualities needed to begin the next wave of gay activism and empowerment. A man constitutionally unable to keep from alienating his closest friends,

Kramer knew how to nurse his grievances into visionary labor. He also understood from the outset that there wasn't time to be polite, restrained, or dependent on a gradual education of those not intimately affected by the virus. An episode of the Phil Donahue show in October 1982 at which Kramer, a doctor, and an AIDS patient appeared—the first lengthy television discussion of "A-I-D-S" (pronounced then as four distinct letters, not as a name)—illustrated what activists were up against. At his most articulate and informed (certainly his least hostile), Kramer outlined what was known and not known about the illness and the impact it was having on his life. The three men spoke wisely about "defusing" words like *promiscuity*, and Donahue did a yeoman's work on the theme of homophobia. But many of the questions from the studio audience quickly situated the problem in the context of that general population who determined media and government responses to emergencies: Why do we have to hear about this unpleasant topic? Do the numbers of sick people justify any big expenditure of funds? Does A-I-D-S really have anything to do with discrimination? Why must homosexuals talk about their sexuality all the time, when heterosexuals do not?

Against this backdrop, the sense that gay men would have to take care of their own, in a manner and to an extent they never had before, took shape. It was obvious in 1982 that the consequences of infection went beyond the medical and were nothing short of catastrophic. Debilitated with frightening speed by their illnesses, men lost their jobs and health insurance and were evicted from their apartments before other arrangements could be made. Coping with the disability and health care bureaucracy, stressful even for those who had all their faculties, was an insurmountable obstacle to many who were weakened and confused by what was happening to them. Treatment of AIDS patients by hospital workers was not unlike that accorded lepers in previous centuries, and stories of food trays left outside the door and standoffish or disdainful orderlies were common. Questions about symptoms and prevention went unanswered as many straight doctors admitted to having less concrete information than some of their patients and none about such gay-specific matters as the potential risks involved with poppers, sex toys, or oral sex. With the national gay rights organizations still focused on congressional lobbying and a legislative agenda, no clear-cut means existed for pursuing local, state, or federal funds or for monitoring the way in which scientists unfamiliar with gay male sexuality conducted their research.

The founding of the not-for-profit Gay Men's Health Crisis, Inc., in January 1982 by Nathan Fain, Larry Kramer, Lawrence Mass, Paul Popham, Paul Rapoport, and Edmund White was one answer. Taking up residence in a ramshackle brownstone on West Twenty-second Street in New York City, the group sent out news of its intentions by word of mouth, mailings, and notices in the gay press and enlisted the support of men and women from every profession and background. That GMHC, as it was called, was going to fill a grave need was immediately evident. The Client Services Committee developed by Diego Lopez and Rodger McFarlane set up a hotline, using McFarlane's own phone service, and took one hundred nervous calls on its first day in operation and 5,000 by the end of the year. In what became GMHC's best publicized function, the Volunteer Training Program brought together a small army of dedicated "buddies"— 300 by the end of the year, several hundred more by the end of the decade—to offer emotional support and practical help to men in various stages of illness and bereavement counseling for those who had lost lovers and friends. The 200 first "clients" of GMHC grew within twelve months to five times that number, a group that soon also included IV drug users, many of whom were not gay.

Another part of this attempt to take control of a chaotic situation was demonstrated by GMHC's AIDS Scientific Review Committee, which existed to put the medical establishment on notice. As gay epidemiologist Alan Kristol wrote, members of his profession had to be told they could no longer "barge in and study us unprepared," displaying their usual "unfamiliarity or discomfort with important elements of the way gay men live." That approach was unscientific, wasted time, and cost lives, and knowledgeable GMHC staffers began to demand consultation on study protocols. The allocation of funds and the dissemination of information played a part here, too. In its first year, GMHC painstakingly raised over $150,000, a third of which was given away as research grants to three hospitals and two private practitioners. The organization's newsletters, first published in July 1982 and January 1983, were voraciously read in dozens of cities. Twenty-five thousand of the first were printed, and 100,000 of the second. Combining pragmatism with propaganda, they listed the names and numbers of over fifty New York City doctors who were familiar with the care of AIDS patients, reports from the Center for Disease Control, opportunities for free lymph gland surveys, bibliographies, a question-and-answer guide by Dr. Mass, and appeals for volunteer help.

The urgent need for money to pay for these good works put to the test both the image of gay men as particularly affluent and the brotherhood the 1970s had supposedly engendered. In a put-up-or-shut-up moment, most men shut up. Artist Larry Rivers donated his Long Island home for a fundraiser and other gay cultural notables—Edward Albee, Nestor Almendros, Richard Howard, Robert Mapplethorpe—lent their names to a benefit committee, but the response (compared to what might have been expected in a city with a fair number of gay stockbrokers, bankers, and corporate lawyers) was feeble. Not until the sold-out benefit performance of the Ringling Brothers Barnum & Bailey Circus at Madison Square Garden in 1983, which netted $250,000 in one night, did gay men begin to show what they were capable of. The days of million-dollar gifts from men like David Geffen were more than a decade in the future. Coupled with this tightfistedness was the usual professional-class reluctance to be identified with any group known to be gay. That was a touchy subject even within the ranks of GMHC. To Larry Kramer's fury, Paul Popham, an Irving Trust vice president, was fearful that his employer would find out that he was the president of a homosexual organization and refused to make television appearances on behalf of GMHC. The toll taken by the "conspiracy of silence," from Harry Hay to Harvey Milk, is a theme that echoes down the corridor of the years. The difference in 1982 was that the stakes were much higher.

To many gay men involved with GMHC, the value of its multifaceted program reached beyond its original intentions. Benefits extended not only to those who used the services, but to those who provided them. Like all six founders, who had steered clear of the movement in the 1970s, many staff members and buddies were making their first commitment to gay life in a nonsexual or nonsocial context. Some were also HIV-positive and would later become clients themselves. Despite the inevitable strain and burn-out, the bonds that could develop between a GMHC client and his buddy or other caregiving volunteer were often described by the latter as transforming; they allowed for new friendships and an altered self-image. "There was a feeling," remarked Harry Adler, a psychotherapist in his sixties when he began as a volunteer support-group facilitator, "that this was a fight you *had* to be a part of. What did your life mean if you didn't get involved with something like this?" For fifty years, since frequenting the *"faygeleh"* coffee shops of the Williamsburgh section of Brooklyn in the 1930s, Adler had been actively gay, but kept the professional and the private separate: "GMHC changed that. That made a difference in my life." Other men, just out of college or on the verge of retirement, cleaned apartments and changed soiled sheets for men too weak to do it themselves, dealt with recalcitrant health care workers and disbelieving next-of-kin, made doctor's appointments, waited in emergency rooms, or held bedside vigils for people they hadn't known a few months before. If a group is judged by how it treats its weakest members, an editorial in the *Washington Blade* observed, "the compassion that gays are showing to those afflicted with AIDS is a wonderful sign of strength." For the first time since the Anita Bryant attack, gay men also worked side by side with lesbians, who responded to AIDS suffering with more energy and alacrity than gay men had ever shown to the women's causes.

The problematic aspect of volunteerism, especially of an elaborate community-based caring system, was equally evident. Government, brought into being in part to minister to the collective needs of its people in moments of crisis, is falsely absolved of responsibility. What private citizens can do, governments generally will not do. The point becomes moot when government indicates that it has no intention of providing the necessary help, but that does not alter the fact that charitable deeds and political agitation for reform are sometimes mutually exclusive. There was, apparently, some ambiguity on this point at the inception of GMHC. Kramer left the organization in 1983, surprised and frustrated that his friends did not share his vision of an activist body that would *demand*, to the point of rudeness and finally civil disobedience, an appropriate government commitment of public resources. He was right that this area of AIDS work needed more time and muscle; the GMHC board let the Koch administration get away with murder—a statement that does not have to be taken as metaphorical. By 1982, San Francisco's city government had allocated $300,000 in emergency grants to the newly formed Kaposi's Sarcoma Foundation, the Shanti Project for patient counseling, San Francisco General Hospital's KS clinic, and city health department lab screening. Gay men and lesbians there knew how to lean on Mayor Feinstein and would continue to do so. However, they also had an "in" at City Hall, by way of a gay presence on the Board of Supervisors, and a history of influence. In New York, the gay relation to the power structure was almost nonexistent, and GMHC board members felt they had no choice but to devote themselves to what they knew they could do best. The organization's more controllable flaws as it grew (flaws that were not sufficiently addressed) were an increasingly bureaucratic structure, uneasy relations later with smaller organizations viewed as competitors (for example, the PWA Coalition), and an absence of outreach to communities of color. Yet GMHC remained in selective ways a model for the rest of the country.

Elsewhere in the early 1980s, gay mobilization to fight AIDS was slow in proportion to the magnitude of the problem and often attributable to a few impassioned individuals—but it was taking place. Jack Kersey, who had started a gay switchboard in Louisville, read about GMHC and went to New York to talk with Larry Kramer when he decided that an AIDS support group was needed in Kentucky. In southwestern Virginia, Wayne Slusher and a few friends formed the Roanoke AIDS Project at his kitchen table, set up a hotline in his living room, and began tending to client needs for information, social-service help, and at-home care. In Seattle, the Chicken Soup Brigade began a cooking program for housebound patients, while the Philadelphia chapter of Black and White Men Together produced a rap record about AIDS awareness. The men and women who kept the always financially strapped *Gay Community News* going in Boston used the pages of that indefatigable paper to keep their readers informed. In the summer of 1983, drag queens performed at two Charlotte, North Carolina, clubs for "awareness fund-raisers," one of which sent the night's proceeds to GMHC in New York. The Houston KS/AIDS Foundation and the Minneapolis AIDS Project worked with local gay businessmen, particularly bar owners, to initiate safe sex campaigns, though disagreements about the meaning of "safe" and the relevance of condoms to that goal were heard from the start. Gay doctors in several states were in the forefront of the struggle, appearing at lectures and slide shows in their communities and writing columns for the gay newspapers in their area. Gay lawyers and accountants donated their services, and gay psychiatrists and therapists organized support groups. In smaller towns, the local watering hole was often the one and only avenue to consciousness-raising and practical assistance. Lenny Tweedon's gay bar in Fargo, North Dakota, for instance, had to serve as a makeshift health education center, providing condoms and brochures and, in 1984, hosting a fund-raiser for the Minneapolis AIDS Project.

But despite these laudable efforts, infection rates continued to climb, embarrassment and misinformation were rife, and a lingering sense of unreality bedeviled the attempt to control or even publicize AIDS as something more than a New York–California concern. Writing about East Tennessee ("the embodiment of small-town America"), where he treated many gay patients, Dr. Abraham Verghese observed of both homosexuals and heterosexuals, "AIDS simply did not fit into the picture we had of our town. The TV stations and the *Johnson City Press* did a fine job of parroting what the wire services carried about AIDS. But they never succeeded in treating the deaths of Rock Hudson or Liberace as being any more significant to *our* town than famine in the Sahel or a plane crash in Thailand." For tens of thousands of gay men outside the major metropolitan areas, particularly those who were young or those whose sexual lives were divorced from a gay social or political context that might have increased their AIDS awareness, the same lack of connection to the crisis applied. A massive government-sponsored public education effort or a more vigorous, widely read gay press might have made a difference, but neither was in place, or even visible on the horizon, in most of America at mid-decade. By June of 1986, the U.S. Public Health Service was estimating that as many as one million Americans had been infected with HIV. That same month, the U.S. Justice Department upheld the right of employers to fire employees with AIDS, and the U.S. Supreme Court, in the famous *Bowers* v. *Hardwick* case, affirmed the right of states to outlaw private homosexual sex.

To GAY MEN, the Hardwick case, like the Helms Amendment in 1987, which banned the use of federal money for AIDS education that in any way "promoted or encouraged" homosexuality, was proof that heterosexual antipathy toward the way gay men made love had not abated one jot. It wasn't likely that it would at a time when anal sex was equated with purple lesions and movie audiences jeered onscreen kisses (for instance, Christopher Reeve and Michael Caine in *Deathtrap*). But for all the diatribes over the years against soulless gay promiscuity and men's-room sex, a slightly different point was being affirmed with the Hardwick decision and the Helms measure; namely, that the privacy of a gay man's bedroom (which was the scene of Michael Hardwick's arrest in Atlanta in 1982) meant nothing, that the nature of the bond between the men meant nothing, and that even illness and death on a massive scale were preferable to any tacit approval by the state of male-male sex. The open-forum challenge to sex-act prejudices Bob Kunst had called for in Dade County in the 1970s had not gotten off the ground a decade later. Yet something else undertaken in the wake of AIDS was fully as useful and dynamic. Gay men began to debate among themselves the nature of their sexual lives and they did so in public, bravely and explicitly.

Nothing about this debate was easy. And nothing was resolved in a definitive way. Bathhouses were a natural early topic, though the debate about closing them involved, at first, so much invective and rancor that it could scarcely be called a debate. In San Francisco, Larry Littlejohn, Bill Kraus, Harry Britt, Cleve Jones, and others—including *San Francisco Chronicle* reporter Randy Shilts—made no secret of their view that the baths were the site of a considerable amount of dangerous sex that could otherwise be stopped. They urged the Department of Public Health to act, and Littlejohn went so far as to call for a referendum on the question. Despite their credentials as gay leaders, these men and their supporters were vilified as homophobes and "sexual fascists." They were charged with opening a civil liberties Pandora's box. At one demonstration, towel-clad protestors appeared carrying signs that read TODAY THE TUBS, TOMORROW YOUR BEDROOM, a slogan that seemed less hysterical when the details of the Hardwick case became better known two years later, in 1986.

The ensuing battle to keep the state out of gay sex venues was fought on several levels: the disingenuous (bathhouse owners could become AIDS educators to their patron-pupils); the libertarian (personal rights, including the right to self-harm, are sacred); the social-historical (unique, supportive gay environments in a hostile world were about to be lost); and the medical (the virus itself should be everyone's concern, not the rooms in which it might be passed on). Bay Area Physicians for Human Rights, a group of three hundred San Francisco doctors, asserted that the medical data did not support intervention and that bathhouse patrons were probably the members of the population most educated about AIDS and safe-sex practices. Gay attorney Tom Stoddard, soon to be the director of the Lambda Legal Defense and Education Fund, argued that gay picketing of the bathhouses would be an appropriate response on the part of those in favor of closure, but that inviting the state to act would be giving "succor and encouragement to bigots and homophobes throughout the country." In October 1984, the city made its decision and closed all of San Francisco's bathhouses. To some gay men, an air of inevitability surrounded that turn of events; to others, Littlejohn and his allies epitomized the betrayal of the movement.

San Francisco's example did not lead to national clarity or uniformity on the matter, however, either within the gay world or among politicians and health authorities. Bathhouses in Atlanta were raided by police in 1985 and ultimately shut down, while similar establishments in Fort Lauderdale, New Orleans, and Chicago were untouched. In New York, Man's Country closed as business evaporated, the St. Mark's Baths was padlocked by the city in a much-publicized case in 1985, while the East Side Sauna remained open (and, as of 1997, still is). Logic was often thrown to the winds. It made little sense to close bathhouses anywhere—sites where one could at least fully see the body of one's partner, obtain a condom on the spot (at the more socially responsible places), negotiate a level of risk one could accept, and shower after sex—if the state was not going to close all of the X-rated movie houses, video stores with back rooms and booths, and wooded public areas where more furtive and guilt-ridden (hence, theoretically more risk-taking) sex occurred, where condoms were rarely discussed, and where it was impossible to clean up after sex. Indeed, these locations would have made more sense as a primary focus, *if* one wanted to argue for state intervention, and *if* one believed that it was possible to "stamp out" unsafe sex. Yet bathhouses—"AIDS dens," in the parlance of yellow journalism—were a neat, readily identifiable target, and gave the appearance that something was being done. Fewer gay voices were raised in protest over state control as the years went by. That would change in the mid-1990s with the arrival of the group Sex Panic!, but in the 1980s, battles had to be chosen more selectively, and gay men themselves were divided, even self-divided. "I don't know what I thought by 1985," one GMHC buddy and 1970s bathhouse regular remembered. "Reading about [the St. Mark's closing] in the paper, I didn't recognize the experience anymore."

(Rather little attention was given to what might happen to those who would continue to go out for sex anyway or who simply couldn't have sex at home. When he first came out, in Washington, D.C., in the mid-1980s, journalist Wayne Hoffman noted that "the only sex venues left for gay men were crowded near the Navy Yard, in a neighborhood renowned for its astronomical crime rate." Bathhouse manager Bob Kohler observed about his job in the 1970s that "part of our function was to offer gay men something some of them never had before—privacy and safety.")

The new openness cut both ways. Anal intercourse, bathhouses, sex clubs now *existed*, finally, in the mainstream media. But heterosexual America could scarcely believe what it was hearing and that shock served to further stigmatize gay men as the alien Other. The "anti-sex lobby," as Simon Watney termed it, was handed plenty of ammunition long before the overplayed specter of Randy Shilts's Patient Zero sowing death in his path. The more unfortunate aspect of this process was that gay men themselves were vulnerable to being caught up in the characterization. Numbers of partners, anonymity, roles, settings: the attention to certain aspects of gay male sexuality, without a thought to their diverse cultural meanings, was relentless. It was a rare gay man who did not experience AIDS as chastisement, by nature if not by God. Even for men unburdened by notions of external judgment, the psychological baggage was overpowering. Bodies were perceived as time bombs, and a smothering association of sex with death, intimacy with danger, and health with isolation and survivor's guilt took over their lives.

The development of ideas about safe sex, the publicizing of those ideas, and the wish to reinstill gay life with a potent eroticism—especially important as the next generation of gay men came of age in the late 1980s—became a painstaking enterprise, complicated by numbing grief and a lack of agreement about levels of risk. In its early days, GMHC tried to avoid any directive statements about sex, merely advising men to limit their number of partners and to know something about the health of those partners. (The dubiousness of that counsel by 1983—How do you know who is healthy? What good does it do have five partners a year instead of fifty, if all it takes is one to become infected?—was pointed out at the time.) The Sisters of Perpetual Indulgence brought up the use of condoms, a revolutionary suggestion for gay men, in their 1982 safe-sex pamphlet, "Can We Talk?"; by 1984 that was judged by everyone to have been prescient advice. Over the next several years, gay men in every part of the country were inundated with brochures, posters, books, comics, videos, workshops, and articles in the gay and straight press about the need for protection. (The gay pornography industry, which experienced a boom concurrent with the rise of AIDS and the adoption of the new technology of videotape and VCRs, might have involved its actors in the cause, but did not.) Breaking down antipathy to condoms and even dealing with ignorance about their use were not the easy tasks some thought they might be. Few people seriously considered condoms at all for oral sex. But the inroads that were made—statistically immeasurable as they are—seemed worthwhile considering that condoms had played no part whatsoever in gay sex before the epidemic. Various encouraging studies indicated that HIV transmission rates among gay men declined significantly between 1984 and 1987. The problem was that there was no way to be sure if this change was the result of increased condom use or if, as some therapists claimed, gay men were abstaining from sex altogether out of sheer terror. The latter possibility was a troubling one. Mass celibacy would not work for the long run, and AIDS counselors in every city were forced to deal with that possibility. The "Safe Sex = Hot Sex" theme acquired a new urgency, replacing the earlier "Unsafe Sex = AIDS" emphasis.

How this message and these insights or speculations were received had as much to do with tone as it did with fact. Michael Callen—like Bobbi Campbell, an early and articulate "poster boy" for AIDS—is a case in point. Never a convert to the single-factor theory of causation, Callen began his life as an AIDS-education crusader with a four-square attack on promiscuity as a way to avoid the many immune-destroying microbes to which gay men were prey. In the 48-page booklet, *How to Have Sex in an Epidemic* (1983), he and his coauthor, Richard Berkowitz, were testifying, as Callen later wrote, "with the frenzy of recently reformed whores singing gospel." He was associated in the early 1980s with cautious restraint or "sex-negativity," depending on the reader's point of view. He bore the criticism well. By the end of the decade, he was generally perceived as one of the livelier celebrants of a renewed—safer—gay sexuality, though the core of his approach (condom use was important) hadn't changed.

Callen's 1989 essay in the *PWA Coalition Newsline*, "In Defense of Anal Sex," took on the Whitman Walker Clinic's ad campaign in Washington, D.C., which asked gay men simply to give up anal sex for the duration. In 1985 that idea had found numerous adherents. "Some may feel only an asshole would defend the asshole in the age of AIDS," Callen declared with typical bluntness, but that was precisely what he aimed to do. The importance of sexual fulfillment to a complete life was not to be ignored, he maintained, even or especially during an epidemic. The consequences of that were deadly in their own way. Pretending that anal sex was "some exotic, extraneous vice like, say, cigarette smoking" and not at all comparable to vaginal sex (which heterosexuals would never so stigmatize) was wrong in a time of heightened condom awareness. Teach men to withdraw before ejaculation even while wearing a condom, Callen urged. Agitate for stricter standards of condom manufacture. Redouble efforts to educate gay men about condom use. Be truthful about the ambiguities surrounding oral sex. But, he and other critics warned, anything that made gay men feel yet again limited in unnecessary ways and degraded by their urges was counterproductive on all fronts.

Callen's embrace of gay sex and his refusal to trumpet a simulation of straight marital arrangements was important in a period when gay men weren't sure what would turn out to be best, or even workable, for them. Straight media hype about a gay community that had "matured" out of its libido-crazed adolescence often carried with that pat on the back an underlying message: you are now acting as we wanted you to all along, within limits we have set for our own social arrangements (marriage, childrearing), which, however, we have no intention of allowing you to share in. Not surprisingly, speeches and editorials that smacked of the "hetero-imitative" were galling to many. When Larry Kramer demanded to know if gay men were incapable of thinking of anything "beyond their cocks and asses," what most people heard was not his plausible call for a richer, deeper gay culture, but the complaint of a man who was intolerant of safe-sex activity beyond a proscribed limit. There were plenty of men ready to see if a new approach was right for them; the very novelty of "dating" and domestic commitment was part of its appeal. In *Sex Between Men*, Douglas Sadownick quoted African-American novelist Steve Corbin on settling down with a lover in the 1980s: "Serial monogamy had a radical tinge to it." Commitment ceremonies were staged during the Gay March at the nation's capital. But millions of men were not overnight going to find the right person to "marry," even if they wanted to. That was the heterosexual fantasy of what homosexual men should do; that was the gay man's fantasy about what lesbians had always done. Reality demanded more complex possibilities, more options.

The traumas of the 1980s broadened interest in sex pursuits that had been around for ages and introduced new ones. S&M veterans pointed out that the role-playing involved in their ritualistic method of sex did not have to include the exchange of body fluids to be satisfying. A modified version of S&M in the form of spanking parties attracted some men who had never thought of sex as anything but a penetrative activity. Mutual masturbation and oral sex in pornographic movie houses thrived, though the danger of raids and city closings of the theaters varied from city to city. Private masturbation clubs were another, more self-monitored alternative, directly challenging sexual hierarchies (fucking is serious, jerking-off is adolescent) and sometimes addressing racial tensions in gay life. Lidell Jackson started Jacks of Color in New York City in the mid-1980s in response to the all-white makeup of New York Jacks, which had been around since 1979, as a safe, hot space for gay men of color that was also, on occasion, multiracial. Similar private clubs for men of color opened in Los Angeles in 1986 and in Chicago in 1988. They were, Jackson said in an interview with Kendall Thomas, about embracing "freedom of sexual expression as a positive political act."

Phone sex was regularly advertised in the back pages of the gay press by this time and, as Robert Chesley dramatized in his controversial play *Jerker* (1986), could represent its own kind of intense bond, no less real for the physical distance involved. Other philosophies looked beyond ejaculation altogether, though not necessarily beyond erections and sexual energy. The Body Electric School of Massage, founded by Joseph Kramer in 1984, brought men together, in pairs at private sessions or in groups, to reconceptualize sex as "sacred, playful, nonaddictive, noncompulsive, and nonstop." At Body Electric workshops around the country, men were guided into a tantric massage form of giving and taking pleasure that had nothing to do with muscle, stamina, and fluids and everything to do with breathing, nudity, total body touch, communication, and nonorgasmic arousal—with liking and trusting men. "The idea," noted Tim Cooley (a workshop participant and massage therapist), "is that sexual contact between men doesn't have to be driven or competitive. That's a new idea for some men. It can be something sensual and almost spiritual, if you will." Most of these settings—the private clubs, the workshops—and practices were safe in terms of HIV infection, continued the tradition of gay male exploration at odds with heterosexual norms, allowed one to be as multipartnered as one wished, and yet did little to undermine lover relationships previously complicated by the threat of venereal disease or AIDS.

In later years, time and experience allowed for numerous critiques of the approaches to sex, wholeness, and identity gay men had fashioned for themselves in the 1980s. Psychologist Walter Odets wrote about the grave errors made in "undifferentiated education" and that method's failure to tailor safe-sex campaigns to the different psychological needs of HIV-positive and HIV-negative men. Eric Rofes argued that a focus on behavior modification that ignored the fraternal and psychological context of gay life was a mistake. Journalist Gabriel Rotello wrote about the condom as a "technological fix" and the defeat of the condom code itself as a panacea in the real world of inconsistent and haphazard use. He and Michelangelo

Signorile called for a rethinking of the degree of freedom gay men practiced in their sex lives. Others, citing different studies and anecdotal evidence, disputed the mixed messages about the safety of oral sex. These issues still provoke furious responses and too little acknowledgment that the discussions themselves are evidence of health and achievement. If no one prior to 1982 could have imagined the support gay men and lesbians (and their heterosexual friends) would extend to thousands trapped in a medical nightmare, no less unimaginable in the darkness of the early 1980s was the effort to keep gay sexuality alive—alive in the doing, but also in the questioning and reflection that are one mark of mature, undaunted individuals.

25

DIVERGENT PATHS

Over the course of my travels, it began to occur to me that the dogmas of sexual "communities" must necessarily be mercurial, for they do not so much declare any broad commonality among us as answer repression, whose substance and form mutate with each generation and from person to person.

—Darrell Yates Rist, *Heartland:*
A Gay Man's Odyssey Across America, 1992

Hundreds of same-sex couples walk hand in hand through Disney World's Magic Kingdom in an annual June display of gay affection. A suburban Chicago high school institutes policies to protect its gay and lesbian students from discrimination. The Hawaii Supreme Court rules that denying gay men and lesbians the right to marry violates the state's constitution. A rainbow flag is hung in the lobby of the Department of Transportation in Washington, kicking off Gay Pride Week, and the president of the United States warmly greets a contingent of gay and lesbian activists in the Oval Office.

To homosexuals in pre-Stonewall America, any of these events of the early 1990s would have existed in the realm of delightful fantasy and suggest a level of progress that does honor to gay activists' labors over a period of thirty years. Yet contemporaneous with these random examples, a different kind of list could be compiled: in many parts of the country, violence against gay men lesbians not only continues, but is reportedly on the rise. On the Main Streets and in the shopping malls of America, one is no more apt today to see same-sex couples walking with their hands linked, or kissing each other on the cheek when they part, than twenty years ago. Like the high school teacher in New Hampshire summarily fired in 1995 for distributing the novel *Maurice* to her class, elementary and secondary-school teachers across the country could attest that the subject of men falling in love with, and making love to, other men is almost never raised in class, not in discussing the literature of courtship and marriage or in most sex-education programs. The ruling of the Hawaii Supreme Court sent legislatures everywhere scurrying to preempt judicial action on same-sex marriage by the passage of restrictive legislation. The same president who did not hesitate to be photographed with homosexuals and approved the display of the gay pride flag in a government building signed the Defense of Marriage Act, reaffirming the principle that gay relationships were not to be seen, in law or morality, as equivalent to straight unions. His "don't ask, don't tell" policy on gays in the military made a bad situation worse, according to many reports, and his silence on Colorado's anti-gay amendment to its constitution spoke volumes.

AIDS asked large questions of gay men in America. It asked if they were prepared to fight in public as they never had before. It asked them to consider their relations to one another, the depth of their commitment, and what that actually meant to them. It asked them to evaluate afresh what they wanted from the rest of society. Several years into the crisis, the responses were decidedly mixed.

As the end of the century approaches, gay life would appear to be built around a series of paradoxes. A key one concerns the gay understanding of advancement. Access to the circles of power, visibility on television, hearings before sympathetic lower-court judges, and a niche as a consumer market are now attainable. Yet this "virtual equality," in Urvashi Vaid's resonant phrase, has a narcotizing effect. What seemed unfair and unbearable begins to feel bearable even if most of the original injustices—in law, action, or attitude—have not been fully dealt with. Advancements are often gauged by an artificial measure, more concerned with what takes place on the largely symbolic stage of public life than in the day-to-day world of gay citizens. What was progress in the 1960s and 1970s is not necessarily so in the 1990s.

The incongruity is most apparent today for drag queens. *The Birdcage* and *The Adventures of Priscilla, Queen of the Desert* played in suburban movie houses across the country; RuPaul's fans cut across many lines; and the millions of Americans who enjoyed *Midnight in the Garden of Good and Evil* took the egregious Lady Chablis in stride, but that did not mean that cross-dressing (let alone transsexualism) was in any way easier, better understood, or more acceptable in America. In that respect, movies have ceased to be the barometer of social change they used to be; the media can now act as a way of deflecting change by raising thorny issues and enveloping them in an aura that intentionally distances them from mundane reality and the roots of prejudice. The lives that have probably been the least changed since 1969 are those of the very drag queens who played such a significant part in the Stonewall riot, which provided the jump-start for the next phase of the gay movement.

If, on the other hand, one wanted to gauge advancement by what gay men have come to know and decide about themselves, rather than what straight society chooses to know or accept about them, the picture changes somewhat. PWAs refused to accept the victim designation handed to them in the early 1980s and created a self-empowerment movement that led to their participation in AIDS research, drug trials, a medical drug underground, education programs, caregiving management, and public debate. From the pages of *Diseased Pariah News* to the black comedy of David B. Feinberg, the image of the fairy going meekly to his grave was shot to hell. Efforts to reconnect with family were made in the shadow of AIDS, though the lessons there were not always encouraging: as the protagonist of Wayne Corbitt's play *Crying Holy* (1993) acknowledges in the face of his mother's denial, "I could not go home as who I was." Gay men also became more alert to the ways in which it served society's interests to portray them as sex-crazed and immoral, and to the fact that the burden rested on them to differentiate between true morality and ideas about erotic expression that were, in fact, subjective and arbitrary. Compulsive, demeaning promiscuity, masking self-hate or a flight from intimacy, did exist; it was no longer to be mindlessly applauded, if it ever had been. It also had to be distinguished from a free choice not to be monogamous, a decision that could just as easily enhance long-term relationships or an individual's well-being.

Gay men learned, too, that as a group, they were capable of some of the most immediately productive activism ever seen in the United States. The worst shock about AIDS after the severity of its physical toll was what it revealed about the politics of health care in the United States. In four years, only one drug—the highly toxic AZT, costing each user several thousand dollars a year—had been introduced to treat HIV, and the Food and Drug Administration was discouraging about expectations for much more in the near future. Under President Bush, AIDS remained a low priority. In 1987, the year of the second Gay March on Washington, Larry Kramer ended his retirement as an activist to found ACT-UP, the AIDS Coalition to Unleash Power, and channel the fury that animated his popular 1985 play about the disease, *The Normal Heart*, toward the kind of work he had originally hoped the Gay Men's Health Crisis would tackle. What resulted was, at its peak, a controversial, fluctuating force of three hundred or more young gay professionals, many of them HIV-positive, and lesbian-feminists expert at fund-raising, phone zaps, guerrilla theater, visual propaganda, disruption of scientific conferences that ignored their input, and the inventive harassment of politicians and bureaucrats. They stormed the FDA in October 1988. They carried the body of a deceased PWA to the lawn of the White House. They embarrassed Burroughs-Wellcome, manufacturer of AZT, by chaining themselves to the balcony of the New York Stock Exchange to make their case about corporate greed. (Later that week, Burroughs-Wellcome lowered the price of AZT by 20 percent.) They gave away condoms outside high schools and did clean needle exchange in the streets. They distributed mountains of press releases, drug-trial reports, denunciations, and pronouncements.

Derided by cynics as marketing "a sensual anger that became Gay America's new aphrodisiac," ACT-UP did indeed have an aura and an attitude. Within three to four years of its beginning, not unlike the Gay Activist Alliance of the early 1970s, it began to feed on itself. The group's mammoth demonstration in St. Patrick's Cathedral in December 1989 to protest Cardinal O'Connor's opposition to condom distribution and abortion was a serious misfire. Infighting was fierce. Tensions due to the AIDS death rate within the coalition, felling men in their twenties and thirties, were hard to deal with. Members who had become as knowledgeable about HIV and drug trials as any scientist in the country wanted to separate their research committee, the Treatment Action Group, from the body of ACT-UP. Outside New York, local versions (of which there were more than sixty nationwide) started later or lasted longer, but eventually died the same slow, ragged death. Yet what matters about ACT-UP in the long run has nothing to do with its radical chic, ungovernable explosions of rage, the diffusion of its energies amid too many different causes, or Larry Kramer's calls for riots he had no intention of participating in. ACT-UP accomplished what GMHC, the national gay organizations, liberal columnists, and supportive politicians could not do: it intimidated pharmaceutical companies into lowering the astronomical prices they were charging for their drugs, and it coerced the FDA, a department of glacial slowness, into speeding up the approval process for new drugs. The gay men and lesbians of ACT-UP kept the heat on and provided hope.

For some gay men who would never dream of taking to the streets for any reason, just hearing about the new mode of activism was a strong if complacent comfort. Anything was preferable to the psychological malaise of 1982 to 1987. But to others, the sight of Los Angeles's ACT-UP members blocking a float in the New Year's Day Rose Parade in Pasadena with a banner reading EMERGENCY / STOP THE PARADE / 70,000 DEAD OF AIDS, or a contingent from ACT-UP/Atlanta at a sodomy-law protest being arrested in front of the Georgia State Capitol with inflatable same-sex dolls in provocative poses, was unnerving. ACT-UP was best seen as a theatrical alternative "to the natural passivity of people," Frank Sieple, a Chicago participant, explained. But support or appreciation tended to divide along many lines—regional and generational among them. In the Deep South, one gay man in his forties countered, "that is what is known as in-your-face Yankee activism, and it isn't appreciated." Older gay men who were doubtful about the usefulness of gay pride parades found ACT-UP beyond the pale.

To the unfailingly prissy Bruce Bawer, author of *A Place at the Table* (1993), much of the agitation was based on "only doing what feels good" and was "less about achieving specific goals at some future time than losing oneself in the euphoria of the present moment . . . a substitute for self-destructive promiscuous sex." Yet even men with impressive track records working for gay rights, such as the now venerable Harry Hay, found themselves occasionally at odds with the tone of ACT-UP. Hay's complaint was with the group's imitation of the worst qualities of macho straight men, their love of confrontation and tough talk. As he had many times in the past, the Mattachine founder and Radical Faerie put his finger on an important inner change in gay life. AIDS was claiming another victim in gender-role diversity. There was less room than ever in some quarters of the community for attributes that smacked of victimhood: the gentle, the delicate, the campy, or the quietly effeminate.

COMMUNITY ITSELF WAS the basis of the second paradox that came into sharper focus in the late 1980s and early 1990s. Rarely had the words *gay community* been spoken or used in print as frequently—by allies, enemies, and gay men themselves. Compared to pre-Stonewall days, brotherhood and bonding were everywhere to be seen, especially in the tenderness with which men took care of partners, friends, and utter strangers who needed them. Everyone knew, or thought they knew, what they meant when they referred to "the gay community." But standards for the use of that phrase (always criticized by some) were changing, becoming more exacting. Even if one thought in the more specialized terms of Benedict Anderson about "imagined communities," in which groups of people too large to know each other individually live in the mind of each "in the image of their communion," the difficulties became apparent. Among the qualities of an imagined community, Anderson wrote in his study of the rise of nationalism, are its "finite, if elastic, boundaries" and a fraternal attachment or solidarity that may be false or may be genuine but is nonetheless perceived by its members to exist. Gay liberation and AIDS had called forth large-scale representations of a gay community, but the pictures and the spokesmen tended to be achingly uniform. The phrase elicited a measure of disdain. Yet to abandon altogether the possibility of some approximation of community was to court disaster in the face of an increasingly organized opposition. The idea of a gay community was a "useful fiction," Michael Callen observed. That idea, others believed, was crucial to maintaining the involvement that was still needed to push for AIDS funds, to beat back anti-gay referenda, to create safe zones for gay youth and more affirmative self-images for everyone.

But the concept had no future if too many men continued to live their lives as if their sexual orientation was not a central fact of their existence and refused to consider that all freely chosen adult violations of society's sexual proscriptions—two men living together in a gay marriage, homosexual sex outside the home or outside of a relationship, dressing in "gender inappropriate" attire, transgenderism—were linked. "It was hard to accept," Jack Kersey recalled of his gay activism circa 1980 and subsequent AIDS work in Kentucky, "how many men were able to distance themselves from what was happening all around them. They couldn't help, they wouldn't help, if it meant being publicly gay. Or if it meant they would be taken as having anything in common with those 'other types' of gays. Sometimes our enemies aren't our worst enemies." Kersey's statements by no means apply only to Kentucky. The concept of community was also endangered if more vocal groups branded certain styles of gay affirmation as less authentic than others. An understanding of modern gayness that could not encompass the gay rodeo men and the pageantry of Wigstock, Dignity and Jacks of Color, was not worth very much. The left-wing criticism of the Log Cabin Club, the gay Republican group that had been around since the late 1970s but acquired a higher profile in the Bush-Dole years, was as knee-jerk as the huffing and puffing over the short-lived, punk-inspired methods of Queer Nation, which in 1991 sent its adherents into mainstream settings to kiss up a storm and deride the "breeders." In the words of Frank Kameny, éminence grise in Washington, D.C., gay circles decades after his first Mattachine marches, "We forget that all significant political change, and this is going to be the case for gays more than anyone, doesn't just need a wide spectrum of styles and strategies—it *depends* on a wide spectrum of styles and strategies."

Of no less importance, gay community was undermined and mocked if too many men were made to feel marginalized within the larger marginalized group based on the color of their skin. The gulf was similar to that among straight Americans, but it also had causes particular to gay male life. A good deal of African-American commentary directed toward white readers in the gay press over the last fifteen years, for instance, has been concerned with articulating those problem areas in detail—that minority allegiances to gay causes cannot be made as if racial identity were a separate or secondary matter; that certain movement goals over the years never had much, or any, relevance to men of color (government security clearances for jobs they would never occupy; the approval of psychiatrists they would never see); that the relationship of men of color to their own communities, particularly in terms of family and church, were in subtle ways different from those of white gay men; that a tradition of white male organizational leadership in America presented inherent obstacles to trust and cooperation; that sexual objectification had to be owned up to and examined.

Other men of color made related arguments about cultural blindness by way of specific protests. The Asian-American Alliance of San Francisco in the 1980s let discriminatory bar owners know they were not averse to picketing. In the 1990s, Asian-American gays in New York staged a demonstration against a Lambda benefit performance of the Broadway musical *Miss Saigon*, a show that employed a white actor in an Asian role. At the same time, Native American gay men, eager to protect tribal religious heritage, took to task a white AIDS group in the West that had sponsored tours of sweat lodges as part of a health-and-wellness program. At university panels and at gay community-center discussions, the complaint was vehemently reiterated: Where was the sensitivity to less media-visible experience and to cultural diversity that white gays had been asking heterosexuals for all along? On balance, this atmosphere led some gay white men to think more deeply about the intersection of race and sexuality but had others nervously wondering if a fracturing into different communities was going to mean a weakened political movement and social fabric. The answer, of course, was both yes and no, and the louder, less amicable assertions of men who did not want to see their backgrounds lost under the one heading "Gay Man" were responsible for a healthy, prodding tension. No one could be taken for granted anymore. Nuances had to be accepted. Native Americans pressed the point that neither the term *gay*, a white invention, nor the word *berdache*, a European concept, spoke to the reality of their history or their current lives. The introduction of the term *Two-Spirited* to replace *gay* signified a step in a new direction. In *One More River to Cross: Black and Gay in America* (1996), Keith Boykin quoted Cleo Manago, founder of the Black Men's Xchange in California, as wishing to define himself as an activist for "same-gender-loving people," shunning *gay* as a white Eurocentrist creation. "Don't call me a Black Gay Man. Don't call me a Gay Black Man," asserts one voice in the Pomo Afro Homos' satiric *Fierce Love* (1991). "I'm an Afrocentric Homosexual Male. Get it right."

The task of constructing a more public racially centered understanding of gay life has been an ongoing challenge over the last twenty years and it has taken many paths. Spurred by the need to see that the allocation of AIDS funds became more equitable than it had been, dozens of minority service organizations came into existence in the 1980s as political and cultural groups such as the Black Lesbian/Gay Leadership Forum, Gay Men of African Descent, the Latino/a Lesbian and Gay Organization, Colors United Action Coalition, the Caribbean-Identified Lesbian/Gay Alliance, and various Asian and Pacific Islander networks became better known in their communities and on the national stage. The invisibility that had marked all of gay life fifty years earlier was beginning to lift for minorities as well, a process advanced, not surprisingly, by journalists, anthologists, and artists as much as it was by activists.

The loss to AIDS of so many talented men, most in early stages of their careers, gave the arts—as a means of bearing witness—a special urgency. Norman Wong, Han Ong, Dwight Okita, and Chay Yew brought to their writing a much-needed awareness of Asian family life in conflict with open homosexuality, the persistence of stereotypes, the difficulties of interracial romance, and a keen sense of what it was to be, in filmmaker Gregg Araki's words, "a card-carrying . . . member of two, count 'em, two 'oppressed' subcultural groups." The novels and poetry of Reinaldo Arenas and Jaime Manrique excited readers whose sense of Latino literature had been exclusively heterosexual and certainly not explicit in its depictions of men coupling with other men. Michael Nava's detective fiction introduced the first gay Latino sleuth, the ever-charming Henry Rios, in stories that showed a protagonist living and working comfortably in and out of the subculture—a situation that probably corresponds to the reality of most gay men's lives. In response to the medical tragedy engulfing their world (both homosexual and heterosexual) and mainstream theater's depiction of AIDS as a largely white gay male problem—*As Is*, *Falsettoland*, *Jeffrey*, *The Destiny of Me*—Latino playwrights (Edwin Sánchez, Louis Delgado, Alberto Sandoval) were especially vigorous in seeking productions for their plays and performance pieces on that subject. *"Tell my story,"* Rane Arroyo's transvestite uncle told his gay writer-nephew before he died of AIDS, and that spirit of remembrance and education inspires many authors and actors. Teatro Viva, for example, administered by a Latino gay and lesbian arts organization in Los Angeles, presented the agit-prop theater skits of the "Divas from Viva" to tens of thousands of southern Californians in the early 1990s.

For black men, the literary anthologies of Joseph Beam and Essex Hemphill, *In the Life* (1986) and *Brother to Brother* (1991), were milestones, giving participants in African-American writing collectives a forum and proving that a market was there to be reached, making it easier in the years to come for popular novelists like Steven Corbin, Larry Duplechan, E. Lynn Harris, and James Earl Hardy. Beam's books were created, he said shortly before his death, out of frustration at the futile search for images of black gay life in the novels and magazine fiction that dominated the gay world. A "white, middle-class, youthful, nautilized, and probably butch" scene was a cramped space. Where did that leave Assotto Saint, David Frechette, Blackberri, or Beam and Hemphill themselves? White gay fiction had never been especially attentive to working-class characters and settings and had grown skittish about queenly gestures and flamboyant rebellion.

Director-writer Isaac Julien took on the censorship mentality of some African-Americans, including the irate Langston Hughes estate executors who would not own up to Hughes's ambiguous sexuality. Julien's 1989 film *Looking for Langston* was a lavish, stylized attempt to tease into being the merger of a black icon and a gay icon, without ever suggesting that all distinctions had to be clear-cut. ("Talking about black gay identity is very difficult," Julien acknowledged. "The cultural gatekeepers around black history can't stand the context of *Looking for Langston*.") In *Tongues Untied* the next year, Marlon Riggs made a landmark gay independent film, brought congressional wrath down on the public broadcasting system, and gave the "SNAP! queen" a place in cultural lore. In excoriating the film from the floor of the U.S. Senate, Jesse Helms not ineptly referred to Riggs's movie as *Tongues United*.

As the two best-known examples of what cultural critic Kobena Mercer has called the "wildly creative upsurge in black queer cultural politics" in our day, these postmodernist films not only broke with white narrative structures and bald documentary intentions, but also highlighted important unresolved issues within the black gay male audience itself. Julien's meditation on Langston Hughes is peopled with men of a certain class and temperament. The film too blithely situates itself, critics charged (Riggs among them), in a world of tuxedos, private dance clubs, and evocations of the

Harlem Renaissance with only a glimpse at other urban black gay realities. Julien was accused of trapping black men all over again in a context that white America has long since appropriated as acceptable middle-class cultural history. In contrast, the less dainty here and now is very much present in Riggs's work, even to its attack on Eddie Murphy and homophobic black ministers. Yet publicity around Riggs's private life, focusing on his long-term relationship with his white lover, stirred a firestorm of its own that was played out in the pages of Boston's *Gay Community News*. Black men loving other black men, at least at this moment in history, had to preclude interracial love and sex, Riggs's critics insisted. The whole purpose of *Tongues Untied*—a separatist validation, a poetic examination and celebration of bonds that had nothing to do with gay white America—was undermined, they felt, by learning that its creator went outside his race to find a life partner and elected not to bring that fact into a movie with many autobiographical elements. Issues of class and context, allegiance and betrayal, authorship and aesthetic intention, were hotly contested in the gay press, but this time the principals and the mediators were not the usual white postmodernist academics, but African-American homosexual men.

THESE ANTHOLOGIES, NOVELS, plays, and films also pointed to a third paradox at the beginning of the last decade of the century, but one that pertained to gay men of all colors. Heterosexual society now readily discussed what "gay" meant. Gay men discussed the subject at exhaustive length in the pages of glossy magazines and the most abstruse journals. But the meaning of gay identity proved elusive, less open to summary all the time.

Between the inadvertent stigmatizers always ready to announce that homosexuals are "born that way," as if with an infirmity that only the heartless would persecute, and the students of "queer theory" who urged the dissolution of all socially constructed categories, many gay men were left to flounder. These were men who spent their lives assuming that they had played a role in their own postnatal sexual evolution (albeit not always a conscious one) and paid scant attention to the search for a gay gene. They also could not quite locate the "fluidity" queer theorists touted, though it was easy to respect an urge to make emotional and erotic choices that transcended labels. But the break with a recent past constructed on the heartiness of "Gay Is Good," an identity foundation that suddenly was made to feel rather tenuous, was difficult. It was obvious to the middle-aged that the generation following them had no more interest in their lives and experiences than they had displayed for the generation before them. Continuity was wishful thinking. Moreover, the adoption starting in 1990 of the terms *queer* and *lesbigay* by those who sought, with good reason, a word that would include bisexual and transgendered people was another wedge. ("I am *not* a 'queer of color,' " an older African-American man interviewed for this book announced, after seeing his picture on the cover of the *Village Voice* under the heading "Queers of Color." Proud of having been featured in the article, proud of his experiences in gay life, he—like a vast number of gay men—felt at odds with the new language, if not its intent. But how to separate the two?) With the 1990s, the term *gay* itself came under aggressive scrutiny from several angles. The success of the gay movement is burdened by contradictions in this regard, as a word and an identity intended to be liberating was rejected by many younger men as smothering, almost as narrow in ideology and dress code as 1950s heterosexual culture had been.

The most troubling and, ironically, the most subversive perspective arose from what appeared to be the least radical viewpoint: how much homosexuals have in common with heterosexuals. An emphasis on gay-straight commonality had been widening and deepening for over a decade. The opinion is today repeated in every imaginable forum. But for their choice of sexual partners, homosexuals in this society are on the whole no different from heterosexuals. There is a banal truth to the argument. The need for love, sex, companionship, creature comforts, professional satisfaction, and intellectual stimulation is universal. No group has a monopoly on goodness or stupidity. But another motivation lurks behind an insistence on the point: the fear that in late-twentieth-century America, difference beyond certain limits is anathema. Success is about fitting in. Acceptance is about similarity. In the late 1970s, Dennis Altman studied the "homosexualization" of Western culture; in the 1990s, one might more properly write about the grinding homogenization of that world for everyone. AIDS understandably exacerbated the perception that difference comes at too high a cost. Money and sympathy were forthcoming when it appeared that "normal" citizens were threatened and when the gay sufferers became the Aidan Quinns of *An Early Frost* rather than the sexual outlaws of the first frightening *Newsweek* reports. Marshall Kirk and Hunter Madsen's 1990 book, *After the Ball*, went so far as to call for a national advertising campaign to stress the ordinariness, the wholesomeness, of American homosexuals.

Yet one does not have to subscribe to the notion of gay men as "a people" to feel ill at ease with the denial of all meaningful inner differences. If gay identity does not represent the same or unchanging thing, or any *one* thing, to all men who describe themselves as gay or queer, it does not follow that gay identities do not exist or should not be further explored, reinvented, and debated. The contention of a difference-denying straight-gay sameness overlooks the truth that such was not the case for many men when they were six or twelve or sixteen. If before puberty they did not know what to make of the masculine codes their fathers anxiously pressed upon them, if they knew in their teens that they longed for the touch of another boy and fantasized about a forbidden companionship and love of the sort their male peers found with girls, then they also knew that they had to keep a secret whose enormity other children and adolescents could not imagine. They felt *touched* by a profound difference. And it is unfathomable that so grave—so complex, so enveloping—a dilemma would not have meaning, if only as a source of a certain kind of potential later in life. A better part of a gay man's adolescence and adulthood may be spent in purging himself of the dangerous mannerisms that felt right in childhood and in erasing, or mitigating, the marks of alienation, deception, and assaults, both physical and spiritual. But the marks are there, not merely to be cultivated as a grievance or contemplated as a painful scar (as they no doubt are for thousands of gay men), but to be the basis for a life more attuned to other ways of seeing the world, more critical of unquestioning conformity, more open to doubt and change than might otherwise have been the case.

Like most potential, this goes untapped in the main, and to know that one has suffered, to acknowledge that one has confronted an injustice before there was even a consciousness of its roots and meaning, is never quite enough, anyway. It can be worse than not enough. The cult of the victim beckons and promises more closed doors and lost opportunities. But when others validate a particular form of suffering that has been experienced in private but, as it turns out, was widely shared, when men of talent dramatize individual struggles to move beyond that wrong, when they explore all the interesting paths that having been thus treated will offer—in political or imaginative terms, in an earnest, erotic, or even a comic spirit— that potential stands ready to be tapped. Gay men have not always been heroic in this area. Securing the same rights as their straight relatives and neighbors, essential as it is, will not be enough. Neither have they been as timid or self-centered as some would have it. Whether one chooses to decide what gay is based on observing updated versions of the Castro clone who lives at the gym, the couple next door behind the picket fence, the queen in heels at the parade, the black poet writing about his lover, or the men who devote their evenings to supporting other men troubled by relationships and health concerns will depend on moment and mood. Some make easy targets for glib critics. Others, no less gay, are harder to reduce and caricature.

"Chicanos did not know we were a people," Gloria Anzaldua has written, "until 1965 when Cesar Chavez and the farmworkers united and *I Am*

Joaquin was published and La Raza Unidad party was formed in Texas. With that recognition we became a distinct people." Gay men are not likely to become "a distinct people" in the same way. Economic and racial divisions are too important. They existed in that capacity in the minds of homophobic writers and witch-hunting politicians but were always too motley, less neatly categorizable than their adversaries recognized. But Anzaldua's point about the impact of history making, political struggle, and culture on the formation of identity is not without relevance to the looser—but still real—ties that unite men who love other men in a predominantly heterosexual world.

For thirty years, gay scholars have been working to delineate to varied audiences a history of persecution and resistance. Its emergence from pockets of PBS airtime and specialized sections of bookstores is a crucial next step. For forty years, gay men have been waging a gritty political fight in America, and they ultimately made of a medical catastrophe a moral example of caring for others. They have long had their own culture, which flourishes in spite of right-wing attacks and the decimation of AIDS. It has immediate roots—bold, passionate, sly, elegiac, or adversarial—in Whitman, Wilde, Cocteau, Auden, Isherwood, Genet, Mishima, James Baldwin, Joe Orton, and Manuel Puig, in Charles Demuth and Marsden Hartley, in John Rechy and Kenneth Anger, in three generations of drag performers. It is experienced today in the books of Edmund White, Andrew Holleran, Rafael Campo, Melvin Dixon, James Merrill, Thom Gunn, Mark Doty, Edward Swift, Lev Raphael, Christopher Bram, Randall Kenan, Jaime Manrique, Shyam Selvadurai, David Leavitt, and Alan Hollinghurst; in the films of R. W. Fassbinder, Todd Haynes, Gus Van Sant, Derek Jarman, Marlon Riggs, and Isaac Julien; in the plays of Martin Sherman, William Hoffman, Harvey Fierstein, Robert Patrick, Doric Wilson, Tony Kushner, Chay Yew, and Edwin Sánchez; in the restless and sometimes shocking creativity of Peter Hujar, David Wojnarowicz, Essex Hemphill, Assotto Saint, Bruce Benderson, Larry Kramer, Dennis Cooper, Samuel Delany, Everett Quinn, Lyle Ashton Harris, Glenn Ligon, David Hockney, Robert Mapplethorpe, Guillermo Reyes, Felix Pire, Ian McKellen, Dan Butler, Luis Alfaro, Justin Chin, Douglas Sadownick, Harry Kondoleon, Brian Freeman, Bill T. Jones, Tim Miller, and hundreds of others, some living and a large number gone before their time. Their work suggests different ways of looking at the forms of love, lust, and self-knowledge gay men have evolved and sustained through the years, only occasionally overlapping. Their labors reflect gay life—a past in which little has come easy, a vital and contentious present, and a future that is anything but clear.

Sources

Brevity was my intention, but it eluded me on all counts. In the interests of ensuring that a long book is not made any longer, I have restricted my source notes to a few concise paragraphs per chapter. In many instances, the book or individual quoted or paraphrased is named in the text; when that isn't the case, the reader should be able to learn that information from these intentionally abbreviated source notes. The libraries and archives that house gay materials and were consulted in my research are listed in the Acknowledgments, as are the names of those people I interviewed who were willing to be identified.

When I embarked on this project, I did not anticipate that so many people, most of whom were over the age of seventy, would be happy to speak to me only on the condition that their anonymity be preserved (probably an equal number to the two hundred or so listed in the Acknowledgments). One of the interesting surprises for me in studying gay history was to learn that more older gay men than I realized were married in their younger days, have children and grandchildren, and necessarily prefer that those ex-spouses and grandchildren not know the details of this aspect of their lives—even when they are today openly a part of gay organizations for older men like SAGE (Senior Action in a Gay Environment) and Primetimers.

So in all cases I have been guided by the wishes of the men who shared their memories and trusted their interviewer: some people are listed by name in the Acknowledgments but not in the episodes concerning them in the text; some are simply not named, as they requested; some are referred to in the text by a pseudonym. With only one unavoidable exception, no pseudonyms are included in the Acknowledgments, but I am grateful to one and all. My conversations with these individuals are really the heart and soul of this book.

1. SCANDAL IN NEWPORT

Lawrence Murphy's posthumously published *Perverts by Official Order: The Campaign Against Homosexuals by the United States Navy* (New York: Harrington Park Press, 1988), is the one full-length examination of the Navy's anti-gay campaign in Newport. The episode is discussed in recent biographies of Franklin Delano Roosevelt, though earlier ones tended to say little about what was thought to be too unsavory a subject for a presidential biography. Ted Morgan's *FDR* (New York: Simon & Schuster, 1985) devoted a good chapter to the events of 1919 and 1920. Frank Freidel's *Franklin Delano Roosevelt: The Ordeal* (Boston: Little, Brown, 1954) was the first to deal with the subject. George Chauncey's essay "Christian Brotherhood or Sexual Perversion? Homosexual Identities and the Construction of Sexual Boundaries in the World War I Era," which is reprinted in *Hidden from History: Reclaiming the Gay & Lesbian Past* (New York: Meridian, 1990), edited by Martin Duberman, Martha Vicinus, and George Chauncey, offered the first suggestion that the clergy of Newport might have been further alarmed by the investigation because they feared that their own ministering homosocial instincts—caring for and fraternizing with the male servicemen—would be mistaken for homosexual intentions. The fact that there was a precedent for that concern, a 1912 scandal involving a highly placed Philadelphia clergyman, was brought to my attention by archivist Tom Cook of Portland, Oregon. Many Philadelphia newspapers recounted the Alfred Garnett Mortimer episode throughout the last days of 1912 and the first weeks of 1913.

The references at the beginning of the chapter to pre–World War I gay life are from Jonathan Ned Katz, *Gay American History* (New York: Harper Colophon edition, 1985) pp. 40–43, 48–52, and Havelock Ellis, *Studies in the Psychology of Sex: Sexual Inversion* (Philadelphia: F. A. Davis, 1915) pp. 63 and 351. The quotation about Mardi Gras is from the *Times-Picayune* (24 February 1895); the reference was supplied by Karen Leathem of the Louisiana State Museum, author of a fascinating dissertation on gender roles and Mardi Gras, 1870–1941. The quotation about the St. Louis incident is from Charles Hughes, "Homosexual Complexion Perverts in St. Louis," *The Alienist and Neurologist* (November 1907) pp. 487–88. The Portland, Oregon, scandal was covered extensively (and hysterically) in the area tabloid, the *Portland News*, through the fall of 1912 and winter of 1913. (A front-page article, "Exposé Involves the East," alludes to the Philadelphia scandal then unfolding as well.) See also Peter Boag, "Peeping Toms and Tearooms in 1920s Boise" in *Northwest Gay and Lesbian Historian* (Summer/Fall 1996) pp. 4–5; Allan Bérubé, "The History of the Gay Bathhouse," *Coming Up!* (December 1984) p. 17, on the Baker Street Club; and Sharon Ullman, "'The Twentieth-Century Way': Female Impersonation and Sexual Practice in Turn-of-the-Century America," *Journal of the History of Sexuality* (vol. 5, no. 4, 1995) pp. 573–600.

The conclusions concerning an active gay life in Louisville and New Haven are based on my interviews, one anonymous and one not, with two older gay men who knew individuals living in those cities earlier in the century. Curtis Dewees, onetime president of the Mattachine Society in New York, grew up in Louisville and in the late 1940s was friends with a man in his fifties who had come out there in 1915. He shared his memories with Dewees of a welcoming prewar gay subculture. My other source reported his much older lover's account of a similar circle of gay friends who met regularly in New Haven circa 1918.

2. IMAGINING THE TWENTIES

The quotation about baptizing the Jazz Age is from Jeffrey Myers, *Fitzgerald* (New York: HarperCollins, 1994) p. 59. Early fiction by gay writers or including gay characters is the subject of Roger Austen's landmark *Playing the Game* (Indianapolis: Bobbs-Merrill, 1976). Other informative studies include David Bergman, *Gaiety Transfigured* (Madison: University of Wisconsin Press, 1991); Byrne S. Fone, *The Road to Stonewall* (New York: Twayne, 1995); James Gifford, *Daynesford's Library: American Homosexual Writing, 1900–1913* (Amherst: University of Massachusetts Press, 1995); James Levin, *The Gay Novel* (New York: Irvington, 1983); Georges-Michel Sarotte, *Like a Brother, Like a Lover* (New York: Doubleday, 1978).

Kaier Curtin's *We Can Always Call Them Bulgarians* (Boston: Alyson, 1987) is the essential guide to the history of gay and lesbian drama in America before the 1970s; he devotes a full chapter to *The Captive*. The censorship saga of Radclyffe Hall's novel is recounted in Michael Baker, *Our Three Selves: The Life of Radclyffe Hall* (New York: William Morrow, 1985), and Edward DeGrazia, *Girls Lean Back Everywhere: The Law of Obscenity and the Assault on Genius* (New York: Random House, 1992) pp. 165–208. On early twentieth-century gay life in Tampa and Long Beach: gay archivist Dorr Legg spoke many times of his encounters with a gay community in Tampa circa 1927, and Sharon Ullman's "The Twentieth-Century Way" (see notes for chapter 1) discusses the gay scene in Long Beach. Bill Tilden's homosexuality and the public awareness of it are covered in Frank Deford, *Big Bill Tilden* (New York: Simon and Schuster, 1976). The Richard Cowan diaries are in the collection of the Boston Atheneum. The experiences of Jeb Alexander in Washington, D.C., are preserved by means of his niece's vital work in editing his diary, *Jeb and Dash: A Diary of Gay Life, 1918–1945* (New York: Faber & Faber, 1994).

Samuel Steward narrates his adventures in *Chapters from an Autobiography* (San Francisco: Grey Fox Press, 1981), one of the great gay memoirs of all time. Richmond Morrell Purinton's diary was recently donated by his lover, Donald Vining, to the National Gay and Lesbian Museum at New York City's Community Center. Paul Phillips's experiences are taken from his interview with Eric Marcus in *Making History* (New York: HarperCollins, 1992) pp. 80–87. On Inge's experiences recorded in his autobiographical fiction, see Ralph F. Voss, *A Life of William Inge: The Strains of Triumph* (Lawrence: University of Kansas Press, 1989) pp. 6, 24, 26 ff. On Julian Green's years in Virginia, see Julian Green, *Love in America* (New York: Marion Boyars, 1994). Stuart Timmons recorded Harry Hay's initiation in *The Trouble with Harry Hay* (Boston: Alyson, 1990) pp. 35–36. The Gene Berton anecdote is from Ralph Berton, *Remembering Bix* (New York: Harper & Row, 1974) pp. 216–18. On Philip Johnson's experience, see Franz Schule, *Philip Johnson* (New York: Knopf, 1994) p. 35. All other quotations are from my own interviews.

For a sampling of the popularized medical views of the time, see Joseph Collins, *The Doctor Looks at Love and Life* (Garden City, N.Y.: Garden City Publishing, 1926) pp. 64–103; Don Cabot McCowan, *Love and Life: The Sex Urge and Its Consequences* (Chicago: Covici, 1928) pp. 128–33; and William Sadler, *Piloting*

Modern Youth (New York: Funk and Wagnalls, 1931) p. 291. The medical sex books of the late 1920s suggest that the topic was neither brand-new on the national scene nor exclusively governed by an "invert" (fairy)–normal man dichotomy. In 1928, Dr. McCowan took it for granted that "most everyone is familiar with at least a few persons who are sexually unbalanced" (sissy men, butch women), but defined homosexuality simply as "sexual attraction between persons of the same sex." In another context that was anything but arcane, Dr. Joseph Collins's 1926 observation that all homosexuals were not immediately identifiable by their effeminacy might be taken as telling Americans something new, but could just as well be read as a statement of a conclusion that many alert people had already come to on their own.

Samuel Kahn's dissertation was published as *Mentality and Homosexuality* (Boston: Meador, 1937). Vern Bullough's assessment of the profession is from his book *Science in the Bedroom: A History of Sex Research* (New York: HarperCollins, 1994) p. 18. Ruth Benedict and Joseph Fishman are discussed in chapters 4 and 5, respectively. In *The Hobo* (Chicago: University of Chicago Press, 1923), Nels Anderson was unusually explicit and realistic in his treatment of the subject compared to other sociologists of the day: "Homosexual attachments [among vagrant men and boys] are short-lived, but they are real while they last" (p. 148). Kenneth Alsop, *Hard Travellin'* (New York: New American Library, 1967) p. 220, makes reference to the homosexuality in California's lumber camps.

3. DEFIANCE, PAGEANTRY, POLITICS

Information about Mae West and her plays of the 1920s is taken from Kaier Curtin's *We Can Always Call Them Bulgarians* (see the notes for chapter 2); West's memoirs; two biographies, Maurice Leonard, *Mae West: Empress of Sex* (New York: HarperCollins, 1991) pp. 61–85, and George Ellis and Stanley Musgrove, *Mae West: A Biography* (New York: William Morrow, 1982) pp. 58–95; and Marybeth Hamilton's thoughtful critical study, *When I'm Bad, I'm Better: Mae West, Sex, and American Entertainment* (New York: HarperCollins, 1995). The only known copy of the infamous *The Drag* can be read in the Special Collections room of the Library of Congress. George Chauncey gives a full account of the pansy craze and Greenwich Village gay life in *Gay New York* (New York: Basic Books, 1994), pp. 227–44, 312–39. See also Chauncey, "The Way We Were: Gay Male Society in the Jazz Age," *Village Voice* (1 July, 1986) pp. 29–30, 34. C. J. Bulliet's *Venus Castina* (New York: Covici-Friede, 1928) is an impressionistic and utterly delightful account of female impersonation through the ages. It is also one of the first books to acknowledge openly a link between that practice and homosexual desire.

Information about Harlem nightlife, the drag balls, and the gay men of the Harlem Renaissance is taken from Eric Garber, "Tain't Nobody's Business: Homosexuality in Harlem in the 1920s," *The Advocate* (May 1982) pp. 39–43, 53; Garber, "Gladys Bentley: The Bulldagger Who Sang the Blues," *Out/Look* (Spring 1988) pp. 52–61; Garber, "Spectacle in Color: The Lesbian and Gay Subculture in Jazz Age Harlem," reprinted in *Hidden from History*; Chauncey, *Gay New York*, pp. 244–267; Wayne F. Cooper, *Claude McKay: Rebel Sojourner in the Harlem Renaissance* (Baton Rouge: Louisiana State University Press, 1987); Taylor Gordon, *Born to Be* (New York: Covici-Friede, 1929); Jeff Kisseloff, *You Must Remember This: An Oral History of Manhattan from the 1890s to World War II* (New York: Harcourt Brace

Jovanovich, 1989) p. 189, for the Richard Bruce Nugent remark about "no closets"; David Levering Lewis, *When Harlem Was in Vogue* (New York: Oxford University Press, 1981); Arnold Rampersad, *The Life of Langston Hughes: Volume I, 1902–1941, I, Too, Sing America,* vol. 1 (New York: Oxford University Press, 1986) and *1941–1967, I Dream a World,* vol. 2 (New York: Oxford University Press, 1988); Charles Michael Smith's interview with Richard Bruce Nugent in Joseph Beam, *In the Life: A Black Gay Anthology* (Boston: Alyson, 1986) pp. 209–20; Eleonore van Notte, *Wallace Thurman's Harlem Renaissance* (University of Leiden, 1994); and Steven Watson, *The Harlem Renaissance* (New York: Pantheon, 1995). My conversations with Tom Wirth, Richard Bruce Nugent's literary executor, were helpful; he also allowed me to look through the Alexander Gumby scrapbooks in his possession, which contained some useful leads. Gumby's non-gay scrapbooks at Columbia University are an unusual form of chronicle in themselves.

The comment about Mrs. Locke's odd wake is from Leonard Harris, ed., *The Philosophy of Alain Locke* (Philadelphia: Temple University Press, 1989) p. 5. Locke's unpublished essay about psychological disturbances and homosexuals is discussed in Johnny Washington, *A Journey into the Philosophy of Alain Locke* (Westport: Greenwood Press, 1994), pp. 126, 131. Jeffrey Stewart's unpublished doctoral dissertation on Alain Locke's life and career to 1930 (Yale University, 1979) is a particularly thoughtful account of the man and one of the few studies to address his homosexuality as pertinent to his work and outlook.

The account of the founding of the Society for Human Rights is Henry Gerber's, published in *ONE* (September 1962). See also Gregory Sprague, "Sixty Years Ago—America's First Gay Rights Group," *Gay Life* (12/6/84) pp. 1, 6; and Jim Coughenour, "The Life and Times of an Ordinary Hero," *Windy City Times* (6/22/89) pp. 60, 62. The contents of Gerber's publication were described by a French contemporary; see Gilles Barbedette and Michel Carassou, *Gay Paris 1925* (Paris: Presses de la Renaissance, 1981).

4. DAYS OF THE CODE

On the raid on the Lafayette Baths, see Jonathan Ned Katz, *Gay/Lesbian Almanac* (New York: Harper & Row, 1983) pp. 452–53. On Mike Gold's attack on Thornton Wilder, see Michael Kimmel, *Manhood in America: A Cultural History* (New York: Free Press, 1996) p. 218. On Adam Clayton Powell's sermons against homosexuality, see Powell, *Against the Tide: An Autobiography* (New York: Richard R. Smith, 1938) pp. 57–59. The antipansy crusades in Atlantic City, San Francisco, etc., are discussed in Chauncey, *Gay New York,* pp. 321 and 353. Julian Eltinge's swansong is recounted in F. Michael Moore, *Drag!: Male and Female Impersonators on Stage, Screen, and Television* (Jefferson, N.C.: McFarland, 1994) p. 108, and Lester Strong with David Hanna, "Hollywood Watering Holes, '30s Style," *Harvard Gay and Lesbian Review* (Summer 1996) p. 31. The letter about the Chicago mayoral campaign is in the Leo Adams Papers (Merle McBain file, 3/3/31) at the New York Public Library. The Paul Cadmus scandal is reviewed in Jonathan Weinberg, "Cruising with Cadmus," *Art in America* (November 1992) pp. 102–9 and in Weinberg's book *Speaking for Vice: Homosexuality in the Art of Charles Demuth, Marsden Hartley, and the First American Avant Garde* (New Haven: Yale University Press, 1994) pp. 34–41.

Information about gay content in films and film censorship is from Vito Russo, *The Celluloid Closet* (Harper & Row, 1979); Rob Epstein and Jeffrey Friedman's movie of the same title; Parker Tyler, *Screening the Sexes: Homosexuality in the Movies* (Reprint, New York: DaCapo Press, 1993); my own viewing of the films; and assorted clippings from *Variety* and *The Hollywood Reporter* provided by Cole Gagne. Also useful were Leonard J. Leff and Jerold L. Simmons, *The Dame in the Kimono: Hollywood, Censorship, and the Production Code from the 1920s to the 1960s* (Grove Weidenfeld, 1990); Frank Walsh, *Sin and Censorship: The Catholic Church and the Motion Picture Industry* (New Haven: Yale University Press, 1995); Paul W. Facey, *The Legion of Decency: A Sociological Analysis of the Emergence and Development of a Social Pressure Group* (New York: Arno Press, 1974).

On Ernest Burgess's study of urban ecology and his students' field work, see David K. Johnson, "The Kids of Fairytown: Gay Male Culture on Chicago's Near North Side in the 1930s" in Brett Beemyn, ed., *Creating a Place of Our Own* (New York: Routledge, 1997). On Ruth Benedict, her relationship with Margaret Mead, her pioneering work in anthropology and views on homosexuality, see Margaret M. Caffrey, *Ruth Benedict: Stranger in This Land* (Austin: University of Texas Press, 1989) pp. 188, 206, 212, 253–54.

"They are a tribe with incantations and grapevines of their own," in Ted Le Berthon, "Night Court—The Homosexuals," *Los Angeles Evening News* (4/13/37) quoted in *Sexology* (August 1937), p. 796. The list of 1930s gay slang referred to is G. Legman's "The Language of Homosexuality: An American Glossary," published as an appendix in vol. 2 of George W. Henry's *Sex Variants* (Hoeber, 1941) pp. 1149–79. Several of the men I interviewed who were active in gay circles in the 1930s (outside of New York and California) also discussed their recollections of the more commonly used slang at the time.

On gay life in Cherry Grove, see Esther Newton, *Cherry Grove, Fire Island* (Boston: Beacon Press, 1993). On Willard Huntington Wright's assault on Witter Bynner, see John Loughery, *Alias S. S. Van Dine* (Scribners, 1992) p. 112. The books about gay life and gay individuals in pre–World War II Hollywood fill entire shelves of their own, but the following are notable: Hector Arce, *The Secret Life of Tyrone Power* (New York: Morrow, 1979); Mark Gatiss, *James Whale* (New York: Cassell, 1995); Charles Higham and Walter Moseley, *Cary Grant: The Lonely Heart* (New York: Harcourt Brace Jovanovich, 1989); Emmanuel Levy, *George Cukor: Master of Elegance* (New York: Morrow, 1995); Judith Mayne, *Directed by Dorothy Arzner* (Bloomington: University of Indiana Press, 1995); Patrick McGilligan, *George Cukor: A Double Life* (New York: St. Martin's Press, 1991). Axel Madsen and Boze Hadleigh have provided gossip aplenty in their writings, and many academics and journalists are now turning their attention to the gender issues implicit in such disparate work as Laurel and Hardy's films and Warner Bros. cartoons; see Hank Sartin, "Bugs Bunny: Queer as a Three-Dollar Bill," *Windy City Times* (6/24/93) sec. 2, p. 79. Best of all, the biographical practice of ignoring any but the most veiled hints about an actor's homosexuality began to give way in the 1970s to a wider sense of reality and honesty (see Arce's book on Tyrone Power). Higham and Moseley's 1989 biography of Cary Grant is a fine example: well researched and unexploitative, it deals sensitively with Grant's feelings for Randolph Scott and his need for homosexual sex (his arrest during World

War II) within the context of his era and his quite genuine, if troubled, interest in women. It does not reduce the man or sensationalize his experience.

Information on gay activity at the University of Colorado, Texas Christian University, the University of Nebraska, etc., comes from my interviews with the individuals mentioned in those paragraphs. See also Donald Vining, *A Gay Diary: 1933–1946* (New York: Pepys Press, 1979) pp. 116–17. It should be noted that David L. Leavitt's photograph albums, which include pictures of those immortal Nebraska party-givers, Walter and Emmett, are among the most extensive visual chronicles of a gay love life I have ever encountered, and I can only hope David has heeded my pleas by now and arranged for their future preservation in an appropriate archive. On professor-student relationships, a surprising number of the men interviewed for this book who had been in college in the 1930s commented on friendships—or relationships that were, to one degree or another, more than merely friendly—with gay teachers who seemed unconcerned with the threat of discovery. See also Will Fellows's interview with Cornelius Utz of Missouri in *Farm Boys: Lives of Gay Men from the Rural Midwest* (Madison: University of Wisconsin Press, 1996) pp. 140–41: "[My biology professor] really introduced me to what it can mean to have gay sex. It was an idyllic experience."

On the party circuit and bar scene, interviews with David L. Leavitt and Stuart Loomis (on Omaha and Lincoln); Gean Harwood (on the Nucleus Club); Bob Basker (on JUGGS). Bill Walker and the late Eric Garber compiled a decade-by-decade annotated listing of "Resorts for Sex Perverts: Gay Bars, Bathhouses, Restaurants, and Other Social Places in San Francisco," now in the collection of the Gay and Lesbian Historical Society of Northern California, which I found very helpful; two of that organization's newsletters, June 1988 and Spring 1989, discuss area bars as well. Tommy's of San Jose, mentioned earlier in the chapter, and Stella's of Pittsburgh are described in notes from oral histories in that archive provided by Bill Walker. Havilland Ferris's "Lions and Lambs: An Extract from Washington Gay History," the *Blade* (9/11/80) p. A5, describes Carroll's. New York's bar scene is discussed at length in George Chauncey, *Gay New York*. A note about a Broadway theater's use as an after-hours club appeared in *The Hollywood Reporter* (6/3/35) p. 2. Various essays in Brett Beemyn's anthology, *Creating A Place for Ourselves: Lesbian, Gay, and Bisexual Community Histories* (New York: Routledge, 1997) discuss or allude to gay social life in the 1930s, especially in Chicago. Also of interest in this regard are the papers of Gregory Sprague at the Chicago Historical Society—his notes, correspondence, and unpublished doctoral dissertation, "Homosexuality in Urban America: The Development of the Gay Male Subculture, 1890–1950." Other men spoke to me about all- or largely gay bars they went to in the time of their coming out in the late 1930s— Bernard O'Shie, Buffalo; George Dale, Milwaukee—but they were not able to recall the names of those bars.

In coming to realize that, grim as the 1930s could be, gay life was far from desolate for many enterprising men, I am especially grateful for my conversations with Elver Barker, Bob Basker, Floyd Clement, Lawrence Freeman, John Halbach, Gean Harwood, Morris Kight, David L. Leavitt, Stuart Loomis, Arthur Maule, George McNabb, John Moore, William Reynard, Robert Rothschild, Dr. Bertram Schaffner, Howard Sosnicki, Fred Stevens, and Donald Vining.

5. A LITERATURE OF SEXUALITY: I

Aside from the novels and plays themselves, the principal sources for this chapter are Roger Austen, *Playing the Game*; Donald Spoto, *Laurence Olivier* (New York: HarperCollins, 1992); Anthony Holden, *Olivier* (London: Weidenfeld-Nicolson, 1988); and several interviews with men who were in one way or another involved in gay life in the early 1930s (Forman Brown, Floyd Clement). The remark about *The Well of Loneliness* was made by Clarkson Crane to Elsa Gidlow (Gidlow Papers at the Gay and Lesbian Historical Society of Northern California). Byrne Fone offers insightful observations about the much-maligned *A Scarlet Pansy* in *The Road to Stonewall*. On the same subject, I am grateful to Hugh Hagius for the opportunity to read his privately published essay, "The Mystery of *A Scarlet Pansy*," the 1990 reprint of which makes the best case for considering Robert McAlmon as the novel's pseudonymous author. The California writer Lou Rand Hogan has also been discussed as a possibility, though clues in the plot suggest otherwise. (A copy of Hagius's essay is in the collection of the National Museum of Gay and Lesbian History at New York City's Gay and Lesbian Community Center.) The quotation about *The Green Bay Tree* ("The gay bars must all be empty tonight . . .") is from Curtin's *We Can Always Call Them Bulgarians*, p. 188. Information about Parker Tyler and Charles Henri Ford comes from Steven Watson's introduction to the 1988 Sea Horse Book reprint of *The Young and Evil*. Alyson Press provided copies of the 1933 review clippings for *Better Angel*.

6. FROM PANSY TO PUBLIC MENACE

The Walter Ward trial occurred during a newspaper strike in New York City, but the major dailies joined together to bring out a composite issue each day. Coverage extended over a period of weeks. The *New York Times* for 9/28/23, p. 1 noted, "Family Secret Remains Safe." "The Sex Criminal" appeared in *The Christian Century* (11/10/37) pp. 1391–96. The Wayne Lonergan case (discussed in chapter 8) involved a good-looking, athletic airman who in 1943 murdered his wife and turned out to have been involved with his wife's father. Many of the men in different parts of the country interviewed for this book, who were teenagers or older at the time, commented on the notoriety of the Lonergan case and the discussion it raised about homosexuals as surprisingly masculine, even married men. George W. Henry's *Sex Variants* (New York: Hoeber, 1941, two vols.) contains his interview notes with the dozens of gay men and lesbians he interviewed in the 1930s. Henry's work is discussed in chapter 7.

On homosexuality in the Marine Cooks and Stewards Union, Allan Bérubé's lectures for a book-in-progress and the author's interview with a member of the union, Stephen Blair of Seattle. On homosexuality in the hobo camps during the Depression, William Manchester, *The Glory and the Dream* (Boston: Little, Brown, 1974) p. 19; and Eric Sevareid, *Not So Wild a Ride* (New York: Knopf, 1946) pp. 42–47. On homosexuality in the C.C.C. camps, Martin Duberman's essay "The New Deal: Sex in the C.C.C. Camps" is included in his anthology, *About Time: Exploring the Gay Past* (New York: Meridian, 1991) pp. 149–54, and the author's interviews with three men who lived and worked in the camps. To reiterate, the point here is not that young men in C.C.C. camps might have been sexually active with one another, but that in the recollection of at least a few participants, some of those men—an uneffeminate, often nonurban group—self-consciously identified themselves, to themselves, as homosexuals.

On public hints about J. Edgar Hoover's sexuality before it became common knowledge at the end of his life, see Ray Tucker, "Hist! Who's That?" in *Collier's* (8/19/33) pp. 15, 49. Cartha DeLoach's remarks are from *Hoover's FBI* (Washington, D.C.: Regenery, 1995) p. 163. On Edith Gwynne's remarks (among others) about Cary Grant's image at the time, see Charles Higham, *Cary Grant*, pp. 72, 60. The Glenn Carrington Papers are part of the Schomburg Center for Black Culture in New York City; the letter quoted is from the William Dilforth file in the Carrington Papers.

On the 1930s concern with homosexual sex and relationships behind bars, see Joseph F. Fishman, *Sex in Prison: Revealing Sex Conditions in American Prisons* (National Library Press, 1934) pp. 58, 73–74; Victor Nelson, *Prison Days and Nights* (Boston: Little, Brown, 1933) pp. 149–53; and F. A. Wylie, "Reform By Surgery?" *Louisville Herald Post* (2/15/36). The January 1934 raid is discussed in George Chauncey, *Gay New York*, pp. 92–95. The James Day trial juror is quoted in Hal Higdon, *The Crime of the Century* (New York: Putnam, 1975) p. 301.

On the view of Hitler and the Nazis as homosexuals—pansies or otherwise—see Neal Gabler, *Walter Winchell: Gossip, Power, and the Culture of Celebrity* (New York: Knopf, 1994) pp. 195–196; Kaier Curtin, *We Can Always Call Them Bulgarians*, pp. 234–37; *Americana* (April 1933) p. 3 and (July 1933) p. 22; and *Broadway Tattler* (January 1934), unnumbered clipping at the New York Public Library. Gay men also made fun of this widespread notion of the Nazis as homosexuals; the Gregory Sprague Papers at the Chicago Historical Society contain a mock certificate for a group called the "Nawsty Nazis." The certificate reads: "——— is now a member of the Nawsty Nazis with privilege to lick any Jew he comes into contact with." Yet the Nazis themselves used the charge of homosexuality as a forceful weapon against their own enemies, a fact which did nothing to mitigate the mudslinging against Hitler on the same grounds. See the *New York Times* (4/30/37) p. 1, for report on a very public Nazis purge of thousands of Catholic priests and monks accused of sodomy. As a character in Noel Grieg's play *As Times Goes By* observes to Magnus Hirschfeld in the early 1930s, how ironic it would be if the label "homosexual" stuck to the Nazis and the Nazi aggression toward homosexuals was overlooked by history. And, of course, that is exactly what happened for the next four decades.

Henry Wadsworth Longfellow Dana's arrest is noted in the *Boston Herald* (4/5/35) p. 10, and in Dana's letter to Glenn Carrington (Schomburg Center) of 10/8/35. The arrest of George Bartholemew, a physical education teacher at Washington and Jefferson College and a Boy Scout leader, for the murder of George "Mitzi" Manis, a female impersonator at Pittsburgh's Rhythm Club, was the headline story in the *Pittsburgh Press* (6/19/34). The sex crimes panic of the late 1930s and its homosexual dimension crops up in many newspapers. See, for example, *New York Times* (3/25/37) p. 15; *New York Post* (4/2/37) p. 1; *Detroit Free Press* (4/2/37) p. 1; *Philadelphia Inquirer* (4/11/37) p. 2; *New York Times* (9/5/37) p. 5; *New York Times* (9/8/37) p. 16; *New York World-Telegram* (11/29/37). The Claude Kendall murder was reported in most New York papers on November 27, 1937. The Charles Mattson kidnapping and murder was covered in many major papers throughout late December 1936 and early 1937. See also Frances Strain, *New Patterns in Sex Teaching* (New York: D. Appleton Century, 1938) p. 168.

The William Haines attack was reported in the *San Francisco Examiner* (MOB BEATS FILM STAR FRIEND, 6/3/36), p. 1; the *New York Daily Mirror* (6/3/36), p. 2; and many other papers across the country.

Interviews with approximately thirty gay men over the age of seventy, some named in the chapter and many others not, were important in directing my research and thinking about this era.

7. FREUDIAN AMERICA

Freud's influence in America and the evolving and conflicting responses to his work within the American medical community are traced in fascinating detail in Nathan G. Hale, Jr., *Freud and the Americans: The Beginnings of Psychoanalysis in the United States, 1876–1917* (New York: Oxford University Press, 1971); and *The Rise and Crisis of Psychoanalysis in the United States: Freud and the Americans, 1917–1985* (New York: Oxford University Press, 1995). See also Vern Bullough, *Science in the Bedroom: A History of Sex Research* (New York: HarperCollins, 1994); J. E. Carney, "The Freudians Come to Kansas," *Kansas History* (Summer 1993) pp. 78–93; John D'Emilio and Estelle Freedman, *Intimate Matters* (New York: Harper & Row, 1988); Peter Gay, *Freud: A Life for Our Time* (New York: Norton, 1988); Kenneth Lewes, *The Psychoanalytic Theory of Male Homosexuality* (New York: Simon & Schuster, 1988); and Hendrick Ruitenbeek, *Freud and America* (New York: Macmillan, 1966). Freud's 1935 letter to the mother of a homosexual is reprinted in Ronald Bayer, *Homosexuality and American Psychiatry* (Princeton: Princeton University Press edition, 1987) p. 27.

On the popularized understanding of Freud, see Dorothy Bromley and F. H. Britten, *Youth and Sex: A Survey of 1,300 College Students* (New York: Harper & Bros., 1938) p. 210; Floyd Dell, "Speaking of Psychoanalysis, the New Boon for Dinner Table Conversationalists," *Vanity Fair* (December 1915) p. 53; and Peter McFarlane, "Diagnosis by Dreams," *Good Housekeeping* (February 1915) pp. 125–33.

The medical/professional beliefs and biases circa 1930–1950, both specialized and crudely popularized, can be sampled in Edmund Bergler, *The Basic Neurosis* (New York: Grune & Stratton) pp. 213–42 and *Selected Papers, 1993–1961* (New York: Grune & Stratton, 1961) pp. 537–67, 614–22; G. V. Hamilton, *A Research in Marriage* (New York: Boni, 1929) pp. 478–98; George W. Henry, "Psychogenic Factors in Overt Homosexuality," *American Journal of Psychiatry* (January 1937) pp. 889–908 and *Sex Variants* (New York; Hoeber, 1941); Karen Horney, "The Dread of Women," *The International Journal of Psychoanalysis* (July 1932) pp. 348–60; Samuel Kahn, *Mentality and Homosexuality* (Boston: Meador, 1937); Robert P. Knight, "The Relationship of Latent Homosexuality to the Mechanism of Paranoid Delusions," paper presented to Chicago Psychoanalytic Society, 5/10/40, in the *Bulletin of the Menninger Clinic* (vol. 4, September 1940) pp. 149–59; William C. Menninger, "An Evaluation of Metrazol Treatment," *Bulletin of the Menninger Clinic* (vol. 4, July 1940) pp. 95–104; Newdigate Owensby, "Treatment with Metrazol," *Journal of Nervous and Mental Disease* (July 1940) pp. 65–66 and "The Correction of Homosexuality," *Urologic and Cutaneous Review* (August 1941) pp. 494–96; LaForrest Potter, *Strange Loves: A Study in Sexual Abnormalities* (New York: Robert Dodsley, 1933); Sandor Rado, "A Critical Examination of the Concept of Bisexuality," *Psychosomatic Medicine* (October 1940) pp. 459–67; Bernard S. Robbins, "Psychological Implications of the Male Homosexual 'Marriage,' " *Psychoanalytic Review* (1943) pp. 428–37; William V. Silverberg, "The Personal and Social Significance of Passive Male Homosexuality," *Psychiatry* (February 1938) pp. 41–53; Wilhelm Stekel, "Is Homosexuality Curable?" *Psychoanalytic Review* (October 1930) pp. 443, 447–48; Ervin Wexberg, *The Psychology of Sex* (New York: Farrar & Rinehart, 1931) pp. 191–93; Joseph Wortis, "A Note on the Body Build of the Male Homosexual," *American Journal of Psychiatry* (March 1937) pp. 1121–25. Kinsey's implicit call for a wider view of the subject is expressed in Alfred C. Kinsey, "Homosexuality: Criteria for a Hormonal Explanation of the Homosexual," *Journal of Clinical Endocrinology* 1 (5 May 1941) pp. 424–28.

Michael Kimmel's *Manhood in America: A Cultural History* (New York: Free Press, 1995) and Kevin White's *The First Sexual Revolution* (New York: New York University Press, 1993) are among the rare examples of books concerned with the history of gender issues that are both instructive for scholars in the field and for more general readers. Claude Hartland's *The Story of a Life* (1901) was reissued by Grey Fox Press in 1985 with a foreword by Dr. C. A. Tripp. An interesting interpretation of it is to be found in James Gifford's excellent *Daynesford's Library* (see notes for chapter 2), though to this reader, Hartland appears a much less subtle or subversive commentator on gay life than Gifford makes him out to be. Earl Lind's *Autobiography of an Androgyne* was reissued by Arno Press in 1975, as was that book's fascinating sequel, *The Female-Impersonators* (1922). The passage from Somerset Maugham is quoted in Ted Morgan, *Maugham* (New York: Simon & Schuster, 1980) p. 40. Information about the individuals involved in George W. Henry's study is from Henry L. Minton's absorbing essay, "Community Empowerment and the Medicalization of Homosexuality: Constructing Sexual Identities in the 1930s," *Journal of Sexuality* (January 1996) pp. 435–58.

On Henry Stack Sullivan, see A. H. Chapman, *Harry Stack Sullivan: His Life and Work* (New York: Putnam, 1976); Helen Swick Perry, *Psychiatrist of America: The Life of Harry Stack Sullivan* (Cambridge: Belknap Press, 1982); Patrick Mullahy, *The Beginnings of Modern American Psychiatry: The Ideas of Harry Stack Sullivan* (Boston: Houghton Mifflin, 1973); and David McK. Rioch, "Recollections of Harry Stack Sullivan and of the Development of His Interpersonal Psychiatry," *Psychiatry* (May 1985) pp. 141–58. Michael S. Allen's essay "Sullivan's Closet: A Reappraisal of Harry Stack Sullivan's Life and His Pioneering Role in American Psychiatry" in *Journal of Homosexuality* 29 (1995) pp. 1–18, is central to an understanding of the man. The quotations from his lectures are from "The Study of Psychiatry: Three Orienting Lectures by Henry Stack Sullivan," William Alanson White Foundation (September 1947), copies at the New York Academy of Medicine Library.

My conversations with Dr. Bertram Schaffner and Dr. C. A. Tripp, who worked for George W. Henry and Alfred Kinsey, and with several men who were in psychoanalysis or psychotherapy circa 1935–1950 were especially helpful.

8. ON THE HOMEFRONT

Allen Bérubé's *Coming Out Under Fire: The History of Gay Men and Women in World War II* (New York: Free Press, 1990) is the definitive account of the subject and one of the great works of American social history of the last twenty years. Bérubé's book is a key source for this chapter, though my own interviews with thirty-odd veterans and several men who were classified as 4-F during World War II were helpful to me. (All direct quotations in this chapter are from my own interviews, with the following exceptions: Buse, Basker, Driberg, Hall, Liebman, Peters, Johnnie Phelps, Vining). John Nichols's "The Way It Was: Gay Life in World War II America," *QQ Magazine* 7 (August 1975) pp. 9–11, 51, 54, provides some detailed listings of social and sexual opportunities at the time; and John Costello's *Virtue Under Fire* (Boston: Little, Brown, 1985) contains a good chapter on homosexuality in the armed forces from 1941 to 1945, pp. 101–19. Keith Vach's oral history, *Quiet Fire: Memoirs of Older Gay Men* (Trumansburg, N.Y.: The Crossing Press, 1985) includes the interviews with ex-servicemen Bob Basker and John Hall of which I made use. Arthur Dong's film, *Coming Out Under Fire*, based on Bérubé's book, has a few interviews not in his book.

The quotation from William Menninger at the beginning of the chapter is from his *Psychiatry in a Troubled World: Yesterday's War and Today's Challenge* (New York: Macmillan, 1948), as are some of the statistics, pp. vii, 4, 227, 229. Donald Vining's induction experience is recorded in *A Gay Diary, 1933–1946* (New York: Pepys Press, 1979), p. 227. The quotation from Vining later in the chapter about life in wartime Manhattan is from the same volume, p. 274. The reminiscences of George Buse, Chuck Rowland, and Johnnie Phelps are taken from Andrea Weiss and Greta Schiller's Emmy Award–winning 1986 film *Before Stonewall*, and Marvin Liebman's discharge ordeal is described in his book *Coming Out Conservative* (San Francisco: Chronicle Books, 1992) pp. 49–66. My own conversations with Buse and Liebman were beneficial in amplifying their published or recorded memories. Other evocative autobiographies dealing with homosexuality in the service are Robert Peters, *For You, Lili Marlene* (Madison: University of Wisconsin Press, 1995) pp. 19–22; and Tyler Carrington with Edward Yeates, *Stars Without Garters: Gay G.I.s in World War II* (San Francisco: Alamo Square Press, 1996).

Tom Driberg describes the male brothel he visited in wartime San Francisco in *Ruling Passions* (London: Jonathan Cape, 1977), p. 123. The Cardinal Spellman episode is from my interview with Dr. C. A. Tripp and the revised edition of his *The Homosexual Matrix* (New York: Meridian, 1987) pp. 277–80. On the Senator Walsh scandal, see *New York Post* (5/4/42) p. 2, and *New York Post* (5/6/42) p. 3. The Sumner Welles situation is verified in Irwin F. Gellman, *Secret Affairs: Franklin Roosevelt, Cordell Hull, and Sumner Welles* (Baltimore: John Hopkins University Press, 1995) pp. 234–36, 306, 208, 371, and 392. The Wayne Lonergan murder case was reported on in the *New York Post* (10/29/43) p. 3, and in *Time* (4/3/44) pp. 68–69. Two biographies of James Baldwin refer to the sensational homosexual murders of the time as material that interested the young writer, though the books point to different events. James Campbell in *Talking at the Gates: A Life of James Baldwin* (New York: Viking, 1991) p. 101, refers to the Carr-Kammerer case as a germ for the later *Giovanni's Room*. David Leeming in *James Baldwin: A Biography* (New York: Knopf, 1994) pp. 52–53, discusses the aborted manuscript *Ignorant Armies* as based on the Wayne Lonergan case. On the Carr-Kammerer murder, see the *New York Post* (10/6/44) p. 4.

The Athletic Model Guild is discussed in Randy Shilts, "Plain Brown Wrappers,"

The Advocate (6/30/76) pp. 15–17, and in John Burger, *One-Handed Histories: The Eroto-Politics of Gay Male Video Pornography* (New York: Harrington Park Press, 1995) pp. 7–9.

9. THE POSTWAR SCENE

The Stammler murder-suicide was reported in many newspapers; see, for example, *Washington Post* (3/5/46) p. 1B. In fact, numerous murders were covered by the press in this period that had an unstated, but nonetheless evident, homosexual element (the murder of prominent Los Angeles attorney William Bonsall, whose nude body was found outside his house in February 1946, was reported in many California papers in a manner that allowed readers to fill in the blanks without too much difficulty). The Alan Helms quotation about "going straight" is from his book *Young Man from the Provinces: A Gay Life Before Stonewall* (New York: Faber & Faber, 1995) p. 61. The Leo Adams letters are in the New York Public Library's IGIC Collection, but I have not named the correspondent in this instance as it is impossible to know if the man did in fact marry or ever "came out." On Gladys Bentley's "conversion," see *Ebony* (August 1952) pp. 92–98. On Owen Dodson, see *Ebony* (May 1948) p. 54, and James V. Hatch, *Sorrow is the Only Faithful One: The Life of Owen Dodson* (Urbana: University of Illinois Press, 1993) p. 150. On Jimmie Daniels, see *Ebony* (November 1949) p. 80.

The second Alan Helms quotation, about "seeing a shrink," is from page 74 of his book. The paragraphs on George Weinberg are based on my interviews with him. See also the newsletter of the Mattachine Society of Washington, D.C., *The Homosexual Citizen* (March 1966) p. 5. On "therapeutic castration," see Katz, *Gay American History*, p. 182. On "Homo-Anonymous," see Katz, pp. 183–84. Howard Brown recounts his experiences in therapy in *Familiar Faces, Hidden Lives* (New York: Harcourt Brace Jovanovich, 1976) p. 212. The quotations from Edmund Bergler's books in this chapter are, in order, from *The Basic Neurosis* (New York: Grune & Stratton, 1949) pp. 219 and 216; *Homosexuality: Disease or Way of Life?* (New York: Hill & Wang, 1956) pp. 228 and 28–29; and *1,000 Homosexuals* (Paterson, N.J.: Pageant Books, 1959) pp. 108–9. Interviews with Rick Colantino and George Handler were among the twenty or so of my interviews with gay men who saw psychiatrists in the late 1940s through the early 1960s.

On the postwar sex crimes panic, see George Chauncey, "The Postwar Sex Crimes Panic," reprinted in William Graebner, ed., *True Stories from the American Past* (New York: McGraw-Hill, 1993) pp. 160–78; Estelle Freedman, "'Uncontrolled Desires': The Response to the Sexual Psychopath, 1920–1960," *The Journal of American History* 74 (June 1987) pp. 83–106. Quotations are from Howard Whitman, "The Biggest Taboo," *Collier's* (2/15/47) p. 24, and "Queer People," the *Newsweek* review of *The Sexual Criminal* (10/10/49) p. 52. See also the *Philadelphia Inquirer* (2/9/49) p. 3, among many other newspapers, on the arrest of Bill Tilden on a morals charge. Adam Clayton Powell's worries about homosexuality are expressed in his article in *Ebony* (November 1951) pp. 27–36. "The Man Who Lived as a Woman" appeared in *Ebony* (October 1951) pp. 23–26. Perhaps the point about black journalists keeping a balanced perspective on sexual issues at the time is overstated—*New York Age* printed some anti-gay articles in the 1950s and *Jet* (see the February 1954 issue) was not above milking the lesbian-as-seducer-of-good-women cliché, but to this writer's knowledge, the extent of the anti-gay coverage is not the same, and it is inconceivable that an article as humane as "The Man Who Lived as a Woman" would have appeared in *Life, Time, Collier's,* or any one of a hundred other white mainstream publications.

Harassment of gays in Philadelphia, Denver, and San Francisco is discussed in Marc Stein's 1994 doctoral dissertation, "The City of Sisterly and Brotherly Loves: The Making of Lesbian and Gay Movements in Greater Philadelphia, 1948–1972" (copy in the Philadelphia Gay Archives); the *Denver Post* of 5/31/49, quoted in Thomas Jacob Noel, "Gay Bars and the Emergence of the Denver Homosexual Community," *Social Science Journal* 15 (April 1978) pp. 59–74; and the *San Francisco Chronicle* (6/15/49), from the clippings file of the Gay and Lesbian Historical Project of Northern California.

On college life in the late 1940s and 1950s, the author's interviews with approximately thirty gay men were critical, especially those with James Baird, George Buse, Jack Campbell, Tom Conner, Peter Conway, Bill Cotter, Albert Friedman, Paul Gallo, Ronald Gold, Harris Kimball, Seymour Kleinberg, John LeRoy, Michael Rumaker, George Shaw, Henry Van Dyke, Randy Wicker, and Edward Weber. On Robert Frost, see Katz, *Gay American History*, pp. 74–76. On James Beard, see Robert Clark, *James Beard: A Biography* (New York: HarperCollins, 1993) p. 66. One of my interviewees lived in Austin at the time of the University of Texas scandal, which made the national news in 1943. Jim Duggins's "Uncles" oral history project in San Francisco brought to light the University of Missouri scandal involving E. K. Johnson, though George Buse of Chicago, who was there at the time, also sketched in for me some of the events of this period in Missouri. Benjamin Glover's article, "Observations on Homosexuality Among University Students" from the 1951 *Journal of Nervous and Mental Disease* was reprinted in A. M. Krich, ed., *The Homosexuals as Seen by Themselves and Thirty Authorities* (New York: Citadel Press, 1962) pp. 141–53.

The quotation from Laud Humphreys is from *Tearoom Trade* (Chicago: Aldine Publications, 1970) p. 5. Judge Crumlish's remarks are from *The Legal Intelligencer* (12/11/50), pp. 1, 6. Bob Basker is quoted in Keith Vach, *Quiet Fire*, pp. 46–47. The experiences of Arthur Maule and John Handler are recounted based on my interviews with them in New York and California.

Quotations in the last part of this chapter are from Don Paulson, *An Evening at the Garden of Allah* (New York: Columbia University Press, 1996) p. 70; Donald Vining, *A Gay Diary, 1946–1954* (New York: Pepys Press, 1980) p. 44; John Kelsey, "The Cleveland Bar Scene in the Forties" from Karla Jay and Allen Young, eds., *Lavender Culture* (Reprint, New York: New York University Press 1994) pp. 146–49; Jim Jackman, "Missing the Ports O' Call," also from *Lavender Culture*, pp. 150–54; and interviews with James Baird, Rick Colantino, Keith Hall, Morris Kight, George Flemister, Frank Kameny, Dick Leitsch, Arthur Maule, and many others who first began going to gay bars in the years 1945 to 1955. See also George Buse, "The Way We Were, Life Before Stonewall: Fear, Furtiveness—and Fun," *Windy City Times* (6/2/94) pp. 51–52; David Olson, "The Wonder Years: Chicago Gay Life Before Stonewall," *Windy City Times* (6/27/96) pp. 44–47; Ginger Snapp, "Little Codes: The New Orleans Bar Scene in the 1950s and 1960s," *Southern Exposure* (Fall 1988) p. 32; and Bob Swisher, "One Big Community: Gay Life in Richmond After 1944," *Southern Exposure* (Fall

1988) p. 29. Particular thanks to Hugh Hagius for opening his private collection for my study: the two editions of *The Gay Girl's Guide* he owns, from 1949 and 1950, include invaluable lists of the bars of the period.

10. A LITERATURE OF SEXUALITY: II

Aside from the texts named in the chapter, I have made use of those literary studies cited earlier in the notes for chapter 5: Austen, Bergman, Fone, Levin, Sarotte. The results of the survey by Barry M. Dank were published in his essay "Coming Out in the Gay World" in *Gay Men: The Sociology of Male Homosexuality* (New York: Harper & Row, 1979), edited by Martin P. Levine. Frank Beach of the Department of Psychology at Yale wrote "a comment on the second [Socratic] dialogue" for the Farrar, Straus edition of Gide's *Corydon* in 1950. James Baldwin's essay "Preservation of Innocence" is discussed in Jonathan Ned Katz, *The Invention of Heterosexuality* (New York: Dutton, 1994) pp. 99–105. Gore Vidal reminisced about John Horne Burns in an essay about his fellow expatriate in *Homage to Daniel Shays* (New York: Random House, 1972) pp. 181–85 and about *The City and the Pillar* in an afterword to the 1965 revised edition of the novel. My interviews with several people who knew Donald Webster Cory were helpful: Dr. Albert Ellis, Curtis Dewees, and especially Barry Sheer (a.k.a. John LeRoy). See also Martin Duberman, "Dr. Sagarin and Mr. Cory," *Harvard Gay and Lesbian Review* (Winter 1997) pp. 7–14. William B. Kelley, interviewed in Chicago, is the source of the Lafayette Square anecdote.

11. "PURGE OF THE PERVERTS"

On the State Department and homosexuals in the federal government, *New York Times* (22 May 1950) p. 8; *New York Times* (15 June 1950) p. 6; Harold Stone correspondence in the Leo Adams Papers (IGIC Collection); Irwin Gellman, *Secret Affairs*, p. 371, on Nelson Rockefeller's efforts to ferret out the homosexuals at Foggy Bottom; John D'Emilio, "The Homosexual Menace: The Politics of Sexuality in Cold War America" in his collection of essays, *Making Trouble* (New York: Routledge, 1992) pp. 57–73 and his book *Sexual Politics, Sexual Communities* (Chicago: University of Chicago Press, 1983) pp. 40–53; *Time* (9 April 1951) p. 22. Allan Bérubé documents the cause of the blue discharge veterans in chapter 9 of *Coming Out Under Fire*. The Max Lerner series in the *New York Post* (10–23 July 1950) is still worth reading as an incisive piece of journalism. James Barr Fugate wrote about his discharge in "Release from the Navy: Under Honorable Conditions" in *The Mattachine Review* (May/June 1955) pp. 6–9, 39–42. On Pensacola in the 1950s, see Bill Rushton, "The Killing of Emma Jones," *The Advocate* (1/15/75) p. 10. The Paul Clarke interview is from the film *Before Stonewall*. All other direct quotations in this section are from my interviews. See also Robert Goldston, *Nightmare: Senator Joseph R. McCarthy and the Politics of Hate* (Indianapolis: Bobbs-Merrill, 1973), and Thomas C. Reeves, *The Life and Times of Joe McCarthy* (New York; Stein and Day, 1982).

On gender anxiety in the 1950s, see Paul Monette, *Becoming a Man* (New York: HarperCollins, 1992) p. 68. Michael Kimmel in *Manhood in America* is especially good on this topic in the chapter entitled "'Temporary About Myself': White-Collar Conformists and Suburban Playboys, 1945–1960," pp. 223–58; as is Barbara Ehrenreich in *The Hearts of Men: American Dreams and the Flight from Commitment*

(New York: Anchor, 1983) pp. 14–98. On Joe Alsop, see Robert W. Merry, *Taking on the World: Joseph and Stewart Alsop—Guardians of the American Century* (New York: Viking, 1996) pp. 361–362. On Roy Cohn, see Nicholas von Hoffman, *Citizen Cohn* (New York: Doubleday, 1988).

On the postwar gay male interest in masculine rituals and in putting an end to the image of fairies, see Donald Webster Cory and John LeRoy, *The Homosexual and His Society* (New York: Citadel Press, 1963) p. 4. Many of the essays in Mark Thompson's anthology *Leatherfolk: Radical Sex, People, Politics, and Practice* (Boston: Alyson, 1991) deal with the history and development of the leather and S&M scene. A tape, "Sadomasochism in the 1950s," (#A00492) in the IGIC Collection at the New York Public Library recorded a panel discussion in the 1970s in which members of the leather scene in New York in the 1950s shared their memories. For this section, conversations with Bob Milne, Chuck Renslow, Doric Wilson, Rich Colantino, "Benjamin Walker," Laurie Chilcote, and Jose Sarria were helpful.

12. VISIONARIES

John D'Emilio's *Sexual Politics, Sexual Communities* (Chicago: University of Chicago Press, 1983) is the best guide to the origin and later history of the Mattachine Society; Stuart Timmons's biography *The Trouble with Harry Hay* (Boston: Alyson, 1990) is the principal source on Hay's life. A bibliography of the articles mentioning Hay, Chuck Rowland, Dorr Legg, etc., would be quite extensive, but Hay's own "Birth of a Consciousness" in the *Harvard Gay and Lesbian Review* (Winter 1995) pp. 11–14, is especially interesting. An anthology of Hay's writings, *Radically Gay* (Boston: Beacon, 1996), edited by Will Roscoe, provides a detailed portrait of Hay's personality and philosophy.

In studying the roots of the modern gay movement, I was aided by conversations with approximately twenty former Mattachine Society members in New York, California, Colorado, and elsewhere and a few members of the lesbian Daughters of Bilitis. John D'Emilio's tape-recorded interviews with Gerard Brissette, Ken Burns, Hal Call, James Gruber, Harry Hay, Donald Jones, Jim Kepner, Dorr Legg, Don Olson, George Shipley, and Konrad Stevens (all in the IGIC Collection at the New York Public Library) were also extremely helpful. Jim Kepner answered several important questions for me about Chuck Rowland, Dorr Legg, and other activists he knew in the 1950s and 1960s.

13. HUNTED

Interviews in 1995 and 1996 with Elver Barker, Hal Call, Curtis Dewees, Frank Kameny, Rolland Karcher, Morris Kight, Harris Kimball, Dick Leitsch, John LeRoy, Arthur Maule, Bob Milne, Jack Nichols, William Reynard, Arthur Warner, Randy Wicker, and Doric Wilson are the central sources for this chapter (as well as for the preceding and the following chapters). Dudley Clendinen wrote an account of Kimball's arrest nineteen years after the fact for the *St. Petersburg Times*, "The Lake, the Bar and the Gay Crusader," (9/16/74). John Gerassi's *The Boys of Boise: Furor, Vice, and Folly in an American City* (New York: Macmillan, 1966) is the definitive record of the madness in Boise, though Eric Marcus's interview with Morris Foote in *Making History*, pp. 314–18, and Jonathan Ned Katz's interview with an anonymous participant in *Gay American History*, pp. 110–19, add to our knowledge of the era and the atmosphere. The librarians at the Florida State Archives in Tallahassee were helpful in my 1995 study of the papers of the infamous Johns Committee, and I thank Robert Cassanello for pointing me in that direction. James T. Sears's account of the Johns Committee in *Lonely Hunters: An Oral History of Lesbian and Gay Southern Life, 1948–1968* (Boulder: Westview, 1997) pp. 48–84, provides a thorough study of the subject—"must" reading for anyone who wants to understand social and political life in 1950s America. Jim Kepner's terse monthly reports in his "Tangents" column in *ONE Magazine* concerning harassment of gay men and lesbians across the country (based on information provided by his far-flung correspondents) are an invaluable record of gay life under attack in the 1950s. The note about the Proctor Hotel in Greenville, North Carolina, appeared in a letter to the editor ("Greenville, N.C.'s Gay Scene in the 1950s") in *The Front Page* (6/7/83) pp. 14–15, and an account of the Walt Whitman Bridge controversy can be found in Marc Stein's 1994 doctoral dissertation, to be published by the University of Chicago Press, "The City of Sisterly and Brotherly Loves: The Making of Lesbian and Gay Movements in Greater Philadelphia, 1948–1972" (Philadelphia Gay Archives). See also *New York Times* (12/17/55).

14. QUEER IN CAMELOT

The less hagiographic biographies of JFK and the less idealizing views of the early 1960s were a long time in coming, but one that is particularly unsensationalistic and thorough in its research (and alert to the sexual-political undercurrent of Camelot mythology) is Richard Reeves, *President Kennedy: Profile in Power* (New York: Simon & Schuster, 1993). Most of the anti-gay episodes of this period are mentioned in Jim Kepner's "Tangents" column in *ONE* (May 1960, p. 18; July 1961, p. 18; August 1961, pp. 24–25). See also Jack Nichols's vivid memoir, "Miami: The Summer of '62," *TWN*, (9/6/85). The Jack Adair raid was recounted to me by one of the men arrested that night, Al de Dion. Other key articles referred to in this chapter are Jack O'Brian's column in *New York Journal-American* (7/9/62) p. 18; "Radio: Taboo is Broken," *New York Times* (7/16/62) p. 47; Robert Doty, "Growth of Overt Homosexualty Provokes Wide Concern," *New York Times* (12/17/63) pp. 1, 33. The latter is reprinted in Martin Duberman's anthology *About Time*.

Also helpful were my conversations with Hal Call, Ken Doss, Lee Glaze, Burt Gerrits, Dorr Jones, Michael Lavery, Bob Linton, Jerry Mitchell, and Jose Sarria; John D'Emilio's interviews with Larry Littlejohn and George Mendenhall in the New York Public Library's IGIC Collection; the Craig Rodwell Papers in the IGIC Collection; and the files of the Northern California Gay and Lesbian Historical Society in San Francisco. *Gay by the Bay* (San Francisco: Chronicle Books, 1996), edited by Susan Stryker and Jim Van Buskirk, is an informative pictorial history of San Francisco gay life that contains a good summary of the activities of the 1960s. The quotation from William Plath is from John D'Emilio's interview with him.

Information about Frank Kameny, Jack Nichols, and the Mattachine Society of Washington, D.C., comes from my interviews with Wayne Dynes, Barbara Gittings, Frank Kameny, Jim Kepner, Dick Leitsch, Jack Nichols, Kay Tobin, Otto Ulrich, Lilli Vincenz, Arthur Warner, George Weinberg, and Randy Wicker, as well as John D'Emilio, *Sexual Politics, Sexual Communities*, pp. 150–57; David K. Johnson,

"'Homosexual Citizens': Washington's Gay Community Confronts the Civil Service," *Washington History* (Fall/Winter 1994–1995) pp. 45–63; Eric Marcus, *Making History*, pp. 93–103; Toby Marotta, *The Politics of Homosexuality* (Boston: Houghton Mifflin, 1980) pp. 22–68; Jack Nichols's unpublished autobiography, *Friend*; Kay Tobin, *The Gay Crusaders*, pp. 89–134; and the Washington Mattachine newsletter *The Homosexual Citizen*. Randy Wicker, Craig Rodwell, Dick Leitsch, and New York Mattachine in the mid-1960s are also discussed at length in D'Emilio and Marotta as well as in Martin Duberman, *Stonewall* (New York: Dutton, 1994). The first White House picket is summarized in Jack Nichols, *Friend*, pp. 68–70, and Lilli Vincenz, "Marching for Gay Rights, 1965–1993," *Newsletter Program for Creative Self-Development* (Spring 1993) pp. 1–2. Nichols and Vincenz were participants. My interviews with Renee Cafiero, Leitsch, Nichols, Vincenz, and Wicker were illuminating on many aspects of 1960s gay life and contrasting styles of activism.

The gay publications of the 1960s are covered in detail in Rodger Streitmatter, *Unspeakable: The Rise of the Gay and Lesbian Press in America* (New York: Faber & Faber, 1995). The reaction of the establishment press to the early activists is an important topic in Edward Alwood's study, *Straight News: Gays, Lesbians, and the News Media* (New York: Columbia University Press, 1996).

15. THE FRIENDS OF EMMA JONES

This chapter is largely based on interviews I conducted in Florida, Alabama, Louisiana, California, and New York in 1994 and 1995, with particular thanks for information provided by Michael Adams, Roberts Batson, the late Thom Bean, Al de Dion, Ronald Hall, William B. Kelley, Jim Kepner, Karen Leathem, Dick Leitsch, Martin Palmer, Wayne Phillips, Duncan Teague, and Burke Williams. A taped interview with Robert Hecht at the SAGE Heritage Foundation discusses a dance at the Corduroy Club in the 1960s. Darrel Yates Rist's account of the Club and his observations about black-white dynamics in *Heartlands: A Gay Man's Odyssey Across America* (New York: Dutton, 1988) pp. 464–70, are similarly interesting. On Dick Leitsch and the Mattachine Society's efforts to end police abuse at Cherry Grove, see Esther Newman, *Cherry Grove*, pp. 196–99. A videotape of the 1966 Richard Inman interview debacle was shown to me by Jack Nichols. Inman's political philosophy and contributions to the movement are discussed at length in James T. Sears, *Lonely Hunters*.

Information about SIR comes from the organization's newsletter, later a magazine, *Vector*; the clippings file of the Gay and Lesbian Historical Society of Northern California; John D'Emilio's interviews with Bill Beardemphl, Marc Forrester, Larry Littlejohn, and William Plath (IGIC Collection); Eric Marcus's interview with Nancy May in *Making History*, pp. 136–46; and my interviews with Dorr Jones, William Plath, and several other Bay Area residents.

Information about Clark Polak comes from numerous interviews with those who knew him in the homophile movement and from John D'Emilio, *Sexual Politics, Sexual Communities*, pp. 197–98. Marc Stein wrote at length about Polak and the Janus Society in his dissertation, "City of Brotherly and Sisterly Loves." *Drum* is discussed in many contexts in Streitmatter, *Unspeakable*. The opening of the Oscar Wilde Memorial Bookshop is recounted in Martin Duberman, *Stonewall*, pp. 163–66.

On the Council on Religion and the Homosexual and the New Year's Day contretemps, see John D'Emilio, *Sexual Politics, Sexual Communities*, pp. 193–95, 202, 214; Eric Marcus's interview with Herb Donaldson and Evander Smith in *Making History*, pp. 147–65; Del Martin, "The Church and the Homosexual," *The Ladder* (September 1964) pp. 9–13; and Mary Ann Swissler, "San Francisco's Pre-Stonewall Stonewall," *Bay Area Reporter* (12/29/94) p. 13. Troy Perry's autobiography, written with Thomas Spicegood, *Don't Be Afraid Anymore* (New York: St. Martin's Press, 1990), describes the founding and growth of the Metropolitan Community Church, pp. 28–43, and Kay Tobin's first chapter in *The Gay Crusaders*, pp. 13–27, gives a lively portrait of the man. My own interview with Rev. Perry in 1995 was also helpful, and I am grateful to the late Stephen Donaldson for arranging that.

16. THE BOYS IN THE BAND

The information about the genesis of *The Boys in the Band* comes from my interview with Mart Crowley in 1994. The clippings files of the Lincoln Center for the Performing Arts Theater Collection and the Hartford Stage Company are the sources for the reviews quoted in this chapter. The notable articles on gay dramatists—one by Howard Taubman and two by Stanley Kauffman—referred to in the text appeared in the *New York Times* (11/5/61) section 2, p. 1; (1/23/66) sec. 2, p. 1; and (2/6/66) sec. 2, p. 1, respectively. "Why Do Homosexual Playwrights Hide Their Identity?" by Lee Barton appeared in the *New York Times* (1/23/72) sec. 2, p. 1. Martin Sherman's description of *Passing By* and observations about the difficulty of finding actors to play certain kinds of affirming gay roles is quoted in Michael Wilcox, ed., *Gay Plays: Volume One* (London: Metheun Theatrefile, 1985) p. 101. Doric Wilson provided information about TOSOS and other aspects of gay theater in the 1960s and 1970s.

17. 1968–1969: MAELSTROM

Information about the police raid at Patch comes from " 'Patch' Raids Police Station," *The Advocate* (September 1968) pp. 5–6, and my interviews with the bar's manager, Lee Glaze, and Rev. Troy Perry, a patron of the bar that evening.

On the Chicago convention, see Stephen Donaldson, "NACHO Debates National Structure, Chooses Offices," *The Advocate* (October 1968) pp. 2, 6; John D'Emilio, *Sexual Politics, Sexual Communities*, pp. 195–97; Martin Duberman, *Stonewall*, p. 22. I interviewed several delegates: Barbara Gittings, William B. Kelley, Jim Kepner, Bob Martin/Stephen Donaldson, Arthur Warner.

On Perry Watkins's experiences in the military in 1968, see Gary Adkins, "Sgt. Perry Watkins: 'Little Black Nellie Queen' Takes on the United States Army—and Wins," *BLK* (December 1989) pp. 7–16; and Randy Shilts, *Conduct Unbecoming* (New York: St. Martin's Press, 1993) pp. 60–71, 79, 83.

On Clay Shaw, Roberts Batson, "Claiming the Past," *Impact* (pt. 4 and 5 of Batson series on Louisiana gay history), clippings generously provided by Batson; the *Times-Picayune* and *States-Item* for January and February 1969; Rosemary James and Jack Wardlaw, *Plot or Politics?: The Garrison Case and Its Cast* (New Orleans: Pelican Books, 1967); James Kirkwood, *American Grotesque: An Account of the Clay Shaw–Jim Garrison Affair in the City of New Orleans* (New York: Simon & Schuster, 1970); Fred Powledge, "Is Garrison Faking?" *New Republic* (6/17/67) pp. 13–18; Warren Rogers, "The Persecution of Clay Shaw," *Look* (8/26/69) pp. 53–60, and my interviews with Martin Palmer (now of Anchorage, Alaska), who knew Shaw and resided in New Orleans in the 1960s. (James DiEugenio's 1992 book *JFK, Cuba, and the Garrison Case* and William Davy's 1995 privately printed manuscript *Through the Looking Glass: The Mysterious World of Clay Shaw* are a few of the works that argue Garrison's side and believe that Shaw was guilty. Neither text, however, deals forthrightly with Shaw's homosexuality and Garrison's anti-gay stance, and the role that prejudice may have played in Garrison's actions toward Shaw. Most important, neither text makes much of the idea that it is possible to dismiss the Warren Report as a suspiciously sloppy piece of work and to believe that Oswald was *not* the lone assassin—views this writer shares—and yet still think that Garrison never had any compelling evidence against Clay Shaw. Neither do Shaw's earlier ties with the CIA, if D'Eugenio and Davy are right, prove that he was involved with killing Kennedy.

On the murder of Howard Efland, "Death at the Dover," *The Advocate* (April 1969) pp. 1–2; "Beating Death of Handcuffed Man Ruled 'Excusable Homicide,' " *The Advocate* (May 1969) pp. 1–2; and my interviews with Jim Kepner and Troy Perry.

On the James Allen Stitt trial, *Columbus Post Dispatch* (28–31 May 1969) p. 1.

On the Stonewall riot, Martin Duberman, *Stonewall* (New York: Dutton, 1994), pp. 181–211; Toby Marotta, *The Politics of Homosexuality*, pp. 71–76; Donn Teal, *The Gay Militants* (New York: St. Martin's Press, 1994 paperback reprint) pp. 8–13; Charles Kaiser, *Gay Metropolis* (Boston: Houghton Mifflin, 1997) pp. 197–201; and my interviews with various participants and spectators (Jerry Hoose, Bob Kohler, Sylvia Rivera, Doric Wilson) and more than a few alleged participants. In *Becoming a Man* (New York: HarperCollins, 1992) pp. 198–199, Paul Monette wrote with terse clarity about the way in which the fact and the meaning of Stonewall passed most gay men by at the time. The chapter entitled "Covering Stonewall" in Edward Alwood's *Straight News* reviews the press reaction to the riot. See also (among many other good articles) Dick Leitsch, "The Hairpin Drop Heard Around the World," *New York Mattachine Society Newsletter* (6/28–7/3/69) pp. 21–22; Lige Clarke and Jack Nichols, "Pampered Perverts," *Screw* (7/25/69) p. 16; Donn Teal, "Stonewall Anniversary: The Riots Recalled," *Village Voice* (7/12/79) pp. 29–36; Robert L. Pela, "Stonewall's Eyewitnesses," *The Advocate* (5/3/94) pp. 50–55; Christopher Guly, "The Judy Connection," *The Advocate* (6/28/94) pp. 49–55; Rick Bragg, "From Nights of Rage, Seeds of Liberation," *New York Times* (6/23/94) pp. 1 and B6.

18. THE NEW ACTIVISM

This chapter is based on a reading of Arthur Bell, *Dancing the Gay Lib Blues: A Year in the Homosexual Liberation Movement* (New York: Simon & Schuster, 1971); the last section of Martin Duberman, *Stonewall*, pp. 216–280; Arthur Evans, "A Response to Arthur Bell" (unpublished essay, 12/20/93); Arnie Kantrowitz, *Under the Rainbow: Growing Up Gay* (New York: Morrow, 1977); Joe Kennedy, *Summer of '77: Last Hurrah of the Gay Activists Alliance* (Westport, Conn.: PPC Books, 1994); Toby Marotta, *The Politics of Homosexuality*; Rodger Streitmatter, *Unspeakable*; Donn Teal, *The Gay Militants*; Kay Tobin, *The Gay Crusaders*; newsletters and periodicals of the individual organizations mentioned; general coverage of the movement provided in *The Advocate* and *Gay*; Eric Marcus's interviews with Morty Manford and Martha

Shelley in *Making History*; and conversations with more than forty gay activists. Particularly informative were my interviews with Stephen Donaldson, Barbara Gittings, Ronald Gold, Fred Goldhaber, Jerry Hoose, William B. Kelley, Joe Kennedy, Jim Kepner, Morris Kight, Bob Kohler, Kiyoshi Kuromiya, Michael Lavery, Jack Nichols, Troy Perry, Phil Raia, Sylvia Rivera, Kay Tobin, Rich Wandel, Randy Wicker, Doric Wilson, and Allen Young. The Rudy Grillo, Ted Rauch, and Marty Robinson Papers at the National Museum of Gay and Lesbian History in New York City contained useful clippings, as did the Craig Rodwell Papers in the IGIC Collection at the New York Public Library.

19. CREATING A SCENE

References at the beginning of this chapter include Ken Ross, "Gay Rights: The Coming Battle," *Nation* (11/19/77) p. 528; Paul Robinson, "Invisible Men," *New Republic* (6/3/78) p. 10; and Ransdel Pierson, "Uptight on Gay News," *Columbia Journalism Review* (March/April 1982) pp. 25–26. Doug Ireland, "Open Season on Gays," *Nation* (9/15/79) p. 207, recounts some of the anti-gay "liberal" sentiment mentioned here. (Edward Alwood in *Straight News* notes that throughout the 1970s the *New York Times* supported a bill before the New York City Council barring discrimination against gays, though the paper's management refused to adopt a nondiscrimination employment clause of its own.) On the *Los Angeles Times* protests, see Alwood, p. 133. Accounts of the September 1970 *Harper's* essay by Joseph Epstein and the October 1970 GAA zap can be found in Arthur Bell, *Dancing the Gay Lib Blues*, pp. 131–37, and Donn Teal, *The Gay Militants*, pp. 247–52. The Fordham University episode took place during my time as a student there in 1973. The *Marcus Welby, M.D.* story and the gay lobbying campaign are analyzed in Kathryn C. Montgomery, *Target: Prime Time* (New York: Oxford University Press, 1989) pp. 74–100; and Joseph Turow, *Playing Doctor: Television, Storytelling, and Medical Power* (New York: Oxford University Press, 1989) pp. 127–28, 146, 162. See also Richard Levinson and William Link, *Stay Tuned: An Inside Look at the Making of Prime-Time Television* (New York: St. Martin's Press); S. Robert Lichter et al., *Prime Time* (New York: Regnery, 1994); and Richard M. Levine, "How the Gay Lobby Has Changed Television," *TV Guide* (5/30/81).

Conversations with Martin Duberman, Wayne Dynes, Barbara Gittings, Ronald Gold, John C. Graves, Jim Kepner, and Morris Kight, among others, provided background information for this chapter.

20. THE PLEASURE PRINCIPLE

On the baths, interviews with owners Jack Campbell in Miami and Chuck Renslow in Chicago and onetime Club manager Bob Kohler in New York, as well as with several 1970s bathhouse employees in different cities and bathhouse patrons from the 1930s to the 1990s, were important to the research for this chapter. Useful readings include Joe Barker's 1983–1984 columns in *Dallas Gay News*; Arthur Bell, "The Bath Life Gets Respectability," reprinted in Karla Jay and Allen Young, *Lavender Culture* (New York: New York University Press, 1994 paperback) pp. 77–84; Allen Bérubé, "A History of Gay Bathhouses," *Coming Up!* (December 1984) pp. 16–19; Joel I. Brodsky, "The Mineshaft: A Retrospective Ethnography," *The Journal of Homosexuality* 24 (1993) pp. 233–51; Rita Mae Brown, "Queen for a Day: Stranger in Paradise," reprinted in *Lavender Culture*, pp. 69–76; George Chauncey, *Gay New York*, pp. 207–25; Samuel R. Delany, *The Motion of Light in Water* (New York: Arbor House, 1988) pp. 172–76; Richard Goldstein, "A Night at the Continental Baths," *New York* (1/8/73) pp. 51–55; Karla Jay and Allen Young, eds., *The Gay Report* (New York: Summit Books, 1979) pp. 496–508; John LeRoy, "The Bathhouse Boom," *Gay* (9/28/70) p. 15; and "Rub A Dub Dub/3,000 Men in a Tub," *Gay* (2/7/72) p 4; John J. O'Connor's review of the *Pat Collins Show* filmed at the Continental Baths, *New York Times* (2/20/74) p. 75; Michael Rumaker, *A Day and a Night at the Baths* (San Francisco: Grey Fox Press, 1979); Randy Shilts, "Big Business: Gay Bars and Baths Come Out of the Bush Leagues," *The Advocate* (6/2/76) pp. 37–38, 45; and Ira Tattleman, "The Rise and Fall of the Gay Bathhouse," *Harvard Gay and Lesbian Review* (Spring 1995) pp. 28–30. The second chapter, "Sex and the Bathhouses: The Politics of Privacy," in Ronald Baker's book *Private Acts, Social Consequences: AIDS and the Politics of Public Health* (New York: Free Press, 1989) is a good account of the 1980s debate over the baths in the age of AIDS. Douglas Sadownick's *Sex Between Men* (San Francisco: HarperSan Francisco, 1996) considers many aspects of gay male sexuality from the 1940s to the 1990s, including the baths.

On this and related topics, a wise, well-written, and highly opinionated book is Ian Young's *The Stonewall Experiment* (London: Cassell, 1995). I disagree with some of Young's conclusions, but he treats the issues of bathhouses, back-room bars, and gay drug use of the 1970s with the analytical and even spiritual seriousness they deserve. Dennis Altman's *The Homosexualization of America* (New York: St. Martin's Press, 1982) is a similarly important account of the same decade. Young writes as a poet interested in "psychohistory"; Altman writes as a historian/activist. Arthur Bell wrote about the lack of gay romance in "Looking for Mr. Gaybar," *Village Voice* (1/24/77) p. 19; for a contrasting view of 1970s sex modes, see Arnie Kantrowitz, "The Boys in the Backroom," *The Advocate* (5/31/78) pp. 40–41, and David Reed's survey of popper use in "The Multi-Million-Dollar High," *Christopher Street* (February 1979) pp. 21–28. Young's book contains an informative section on poppers, pp. 102–12.

On the rise of gay pornographic magazines and films, see Michael Bronski, "Gay Publishing: Pornography," in *Culture Clash: The Making of Gay Sensibility* (Boston: South End Press, 1984) pp. 160–74; George De Stefano, "A Wank Through History," *OutWeek* (5/9/90) pp. 38–42; *New York Times* (7/13/76) p. 55; and Randy Shilts, "Plain Brown Wrappers," *The Advocate* (6/30/76) pp. 15–17. On gays becoming a definable consumer market, see "Homosexuals: America's Most Affluent Minority," reprinted from *Business Week* in *Impact* (October 1979) p. 13. Interestingly, in the early 1970s the opposite view was taken to be the conventional wisdom; see Lorraine Balters, "No Gay Market Yet, Admen, Gays Agree," *Advertising Age* (8/28/72) p. 43.

21. DADE COUNTY AND BEYOND

I consulted the usual sources for this chapter: accounts in Florida newspapers, national newspapers, national news magazines, and the gay press, and I am grateful for the many clippings provided by friends in Florida. "Bryant/Kunst: Caught in the Middle" by Bill Hutchinson and James Kukar in *Miami Magazine* (May 1977) pp. 38–65, is a good profile of two of the principal combatants. Charles Ortleb's interview with Ethan Geto in *Christopher Street* (August 1977) pp. 21–33, is a key source, if a highly opinionated one, and "The Battle for Gay Rights," *Newsweek* (6/6/77) pp. 16–26, illustrates the positive and negative aspects of the mainstream press response to the subject as effectively as any other article. Of greater value, however, were interviews with Bob Basker, Jack Campbell, Bob Kunst, Cassandra Langer, and several other longtime residents of Miami from both sides of the line. The chapter's epigraph about Anita Bryant—vintage Gore Vidal—is quoted in John Mitzel's *The Boston Sex Scandal* (Boston: Glad Books, 1980) p. 55.

A detailed account of the impact of the Bryant crusade on New Orleans gay life is provided by Roberts Batson's "Anything But Orange Juice" (4/14/95) pp. 14–15, and other articles in his "Claiming Our Past" series in *Impact*. Batson and Alan Robinson were informative in their differing perspectives. See also "St. Paul Falls to Fear," *San Francisco Gazette* (5/2/78) p. 1; "The Story of Gay Rights in Wichita," *San Francisco Gazette* (5/9/78) p. 3; "Hartford Mayor Vetoes Gay Rights Ordinance," *New York Times* (7/26/78) p. 22; "New York Governor Hugh Carey Opposes Banning Discrimination Against Homosexuals in State Government," *New York Times* (1/24/78) p. 1; and "Anita Bryant's Successful Campaign Encourages Other Cities to Oppose Gay Rights," *Newsweek* (3/13/78) pp. 14–16.

On John Briggs and Proposition 6, see Randy Shilts, *The Mayor of Castro Street* (New York: St. Martin's Press, 1982) pp. 221–50.

On Initiative 13 and gay infighting in Seattle, see *Seattle Weekly* (July 29–July 5, 1977); the 1977–78 issues of *Seattle Gay News*; and Eric Marcus, *Making History*, pp. 305–13. Charles Brydon of Seattle helpfully answered several questions for me on this topic.

22. CALIFORNIA FERVOR

Conversations with dozens of longtime and former residents of the Bay Area were central to this chapter, though a reading of San Francisco's many gay periodicals of the 1960s and 1970s, especially *Vector*, the *Bay Area Reporter*, and the *San Francisco Sentinel*, was also crucial. (Thanks to Bill Walker for making my visits to the Gay and Lesbian Historical Society of Northern California productive in this regard and in showing me the informative newsletters of that organization.) Peter L. Stein's television documentary, *The Castro*, part of KQED's *Neighborhoods: The Hidden Cities of San Francisco* series, which was first broadcast in March 1997, and Rob Epstein's film *The Life and Times of Harvey Milk* (1984) were helpful in providing new information and confirming some earlier impressions from my own interviews.

Books and essays consulted for this chapter include Nan Alamilla Boyd, " 'Homos Invade S.F.!': San Francisco's History as a Wide-Open Town," in Brett Beemyn, ed., *Creating a Place for Ourselves* (New York: Routledge, 1997) pp. 73–95; John D'Emilio, "Gay Politics, Gay Community: San Francisco's Experience," *Socialist Review* (January–February 1981) pp. 77–104; Frances Fitzgerald, *Cities on a Hill* (New York: Simon & Schuster, 1986); Herbert Gold, "A Walk on San Francisco's Gay Side," *New York Times Magazine* (11/6/77) pp. 67–69, 96–114; Stephen O. Murray, "Ethnic and Temporal Differences in Coming Out and in Moving to San Francisco" in his book *American Gay* (Chicago: University of Chicago Press, 1996); Randy Shilts, *The Mayor of Castro Street: The Life and Times of Harvey Milk* (New York: St. Martin's Press, 1982); and Susan Stryker and James Van Buskirk, *Gay by the Bay: A History of Queer Culture in the San Francisco Bay Area* (San Francisco: Chronicle Books, 1996). I am grateful to the late Thom Bean for calling my attention to his essay "Racism from a Black Perspective" in Michael J. Smith's anthology *Black Men/White Men* (San Francisco; Gay Sunshine Press, 1983).

On the lack of gay awareness outside California about Milk and the vibrancy of San Francisco gay politics, random interviews in the early 1990s with gay men, who were in their thirties, forties, or fifties in the 1970s, included a (to me) staggering number who said they had no knowledge of Harvey Milk prior to his death. Larry Kramer reprinted his December 13, 1978, *New York Times* Op-Ed article comparing San Francisco's commitment to gay politics and New York's backwardness in *Notes from the Holocaust* (New York: St. Martin's Press, 1994) pp. 3–7. Darrell Yates Rist wrote in *Heartlands: A Gay Man's Odyssey Across America* (New York: Dutton, 1992) p. 24: "I knew little of the burgeoning gayness of San Francisco then and paid Milk's election no attention. Few in the heartlands did, I think. There was little public display of homosexuality in [Chicago]. At U of C, though the school had a long, liberal history— pinko and defiant of red-baiting—I had professors who glibly referred to 'faggots' in class. No one protested. Homosexuals hid."

23. HISTORY MAKING

Edward Alwood treats the production of the CBS documentary "Gay Power, Gay Politics" in engrossing detail in *Straight News*, pp. 181–91; I thank Rich Wandel for passing a transcript of the program on to me. In this chapter, I was also helped by some lengthy conversations with Doric Wilson about the history of drama by gay writers in the 1970s and with Allen Young about the editing of *The Gay Report*.

Among the notable expressions of social constructionism are David F. Greenberg, *The Construction of Homosexuality* (Chicago: University of Chicago Press, 1988); David Halperin, *One Hundred Years of Homosexuality* (London: Routledge, 1990); and Jeffrey Weeks, *Coming Out* (London: Quartet Books, 1977). Those skeptical of the social constructionist approach, or at least of the all-consuming character it assumed by the 1990s, include (aside from the late John Boswell) Stephen O. Murray in *American Gay* (Chicago: University of Chicago Press, 1996) and Richard D. Mohr in *Gay Ideas: Outing and Other Controversies* (Boston: Beacon Press, 1992) pp. 221–42. Mohr argues convincingly that some social constructionists define the modern homosexual in a way that intentionally negates any possible connection to the past or to other cultures. In that narrow sense, the modern homosexual didn't even come into being in 1892 when the word first appears in the medical literature; he came into being in midsummer 1969.

Also relevant to this topic of locating "gay" life in the past are John Boswell's review of Greenberg's *The Construction of Homosexuality* in *The Atlantic* (February 1989) pp. 74–78, and Michel Rey's essay "Parisian Homosexuals Create a Lifestyle, 1700–1750: The Police Archives" ("Police archives of the eighteenth century indicate, at the heart of the Parisian population, a transformation which had perhaps begun earlier at court: male homosexuality becomes a taste that sets one apart from other men, being seen as both as a refinement and a source of particular identity.")

On John Boswell, though it could be said that his use of "same-sex" in preference to "gay" in his later book, *Same-Sex Unions in Premodern Europe* (New York: Villard, 1994), is backtracking a bit from the premise of *Christianity, Social Tolerance, and Homosexuality* (Chicago: University of Chicago Press, 1980), that is not the case. In the 1980 book, he was writing about homosexuality itself and arguing that the Church's opposition to that specific form of nonprocreative sex was not a significant part of its teachings until the late Middle Ages; in the 1994 book, he was analyzing same-sex unions that might sometimes, but not always, have been erotically based and in any case were not seen as "a parallel alternative" (that is, a gay marriage) to what we now define as heterosexual marriage (p. 191).

The questions on page 412 are obviously rhetorical; many writers note the homosexual bonds between men of the same age and class in Greco-Roman literature. See Boswell, *Same-Sex Unions*, p. 60, on Philolaus and Dioclese in Aristotle's *Politics* or, p. 66, on the love relationships in the *Satyricon*. Michael Rocke's social constructionist study of sodomy in Renaissance Florence, *Forbidden Friendships* (New York: Oxford University Press, 1996), focuses on widespread homosexual acts that did not imply an identity radically different from the norm and did not preclude marriage and respectability, yet also describes in passing a few relationships that clearly did. Similarly, to nine readers out of ten, Walt Whitman's concept of "adhesiveness" and "adhesive love" will sound close enough to modern notions of gayness for a spiritual bond—an ancestry—to be fairly claimed, no matter what nervous disavowals the elderly Whitman made to John Addington Symonds. As Boswell observes in a footnote, p. 15 of *Same-Sex Unions*, this whole debate has become something of an inquisitorial ordeal for those who do not want to abandon essentialism altogether: "I do not, however, *recant* my many published opinions on this subject."

On the new expressions of more diverse gay male interests in the late 1970s and 1980s: several early members of the Log Cabin Club (special thanks to James Baird) and Black and White Men Together shared their recollections. The newsletters of both organizations are informative. See also Thom Bean's interview with BWMT cofounder Michael Smith in Smith's anthology *Black Men/White Men* (San Francisco: Gay Sunshine Press, 1983) pp. 187–95; and on the founding of the Gay Games, Tom Waddell and Dick Schaap, *Gay Olympian: The Life and Death of Dr. Tom Waddell* (New York: Knopf, 1996).

24. THE BOTTOM LINE

Bibliographic information on the articles consulted as background for this chapter would be too extensive to list, as would the interviews and conversations that helped me, but the key books can be readily cited: Dennis Altman, *AIDS in the Mind of America* (New York: Doubleday, 1986); Ronald Bayer, *Private Acts, Social Consequences: AIDS and the Politics of Public Health* (New York: Free Press, 1989); Elinor Burkett, *The Gravest Show on Earth: America in the Age of AIDS* (New York: Picador, 1995 paperback); Michael Callen, *Surviving AIDS* (New York: Harper Perennial, 1990); David B. Feinberg, *Queer and Loathing: Rants and Raves of a Raging AIDS Clone* (New York: Viking, 1994); Mirko D. Grmek, *History of AIDS* (Princeton: Princeton University Press, 1990); Philip M. Kayal, *Bearing Witness: Gay Men's*

Health Crisis and the Politics of AIDS (Boulder: Westview Press, 1993); James Kinsella, *Covering the Plague: AIDS and the American Media* (New Brunswick, N.J.: Rutgers University Press, 1989); Larry Kramer, *Report from the Holocaust: Notes of an AIDS Activist* (New York: St. Martin's Press, 1989); Bruce Nussbaum, *Good Intentions* (New York: Atlantic Monthly Press, 1990); Cindy Patton, *Sex and Germs: The Politics of AIDS* (Boston: South End Press, 1985); John Preston, *Personal Dispatches: Writers Confront AIDS* (New York: St. Martin's Press, 1988); Paul A. Sergios, *One Boy at War: My Life in the AIDS Underground* (New York: Knopf, 1993); Benjamin Heim Shepard, *White Nights and Ascending Shadows* (London: Cassell, 1997); Randy Shilts, *And the Band Played On* (New York: St. Martin's Press, 1987); Abraham Verghese, *My Own Country: A Doctor's Story of a Town and Its People in the Age of AIDS* (New York: Simon & Schuster, 1994); Simon Watney, *Policing Desire: Pornography, AIDS, and the Media* (Minneapolis: University of Minnesota Press, 1987), and Ian Young, *The Stonewall Experiment* (London: Cassell, 1995).

Gabriel Rotello's controversial *Sexual Ecology: AIDS and the Destiny of Gay Men* (New York: Dutton, 1997) reviews the history of AIDS in the wider context of the gay sexual revolution. Cindy Patton's *Inventing AIDS* (New York: Routledge, 1990) includes a thoughtful account of changes in the AIDS service industry throughout the 1980s and the problems of AIDS education. More recent perspectives on gay male sex in the time of AIDS are an important part of Walter Odets, *In the Shadow of the Epidemic* (Durham: Duke University Press, 1995) and Eric Rofes, *Reinventing the Tribe* (New York: Haworth Press, 1996). "AIDS and Transformation," the third chapter of Urvashi Vaid's *Virtual Equality*, examines the epidemic's impact on the gay political movement. The fiction, film, and drama about AIDS is voluminous, but Larry Kramer's play *The Normal Heart* (1985) still stands out as among the most informationally and historically important. (For a scrupulously balanced consideration of Kramer's prose and the tone of AIDS writing in general, see "Larry Kramer and the Rhetoric of AIDS," chapter 7 of Daniel Bergman's *Gaiety Transfigured*.) Rodger Streitmatter's review of AIDS coverage in the gay press (in *Unspeakable*) and Edward Alwood's on AIDS coverage in the establishment press (in *Straight News*) are also essential reading. The Museum of Radio and Television in New York City has in its holdings many hours of news broadcasts and documentary coverage of the epidemic from the Phil Donahue show in 1982 mentioned in this chapter as well as many similar programs of the mid-1990s.

Several chapters in Frank Browning's *The Culture of Desire* (New York: Crown, 1993) and Douglas Sadownick's *Sex Between Men* (San Francisco: HarperSan Francisco, 1996) include the best accounts to date of gay men's efforts to deal with their sexuality and identity as gay men in a time of epidemic. Lidell Jackson speaks about Jacks of Color in Kendall Thomas's interview with him, "Going Public," in Strange Bedfellows, ed., *Policing Public Sex* (Boston: South End Press, 1997) pp. 53–71. The Wayne Hoffman quotation is from his essay (p. 338), "Skipping the Life Fantastic" from the same book. That anthology is an invaluable guide to the debate about gay male sexual rights and practices in the 1990s. The Robert Kohler quotation is from my interview with him. See also Don Shewey's superb article on the Body Electric, "Sexual Healing," in the *Village Voice* (4/21/92) pp. 37–39.

25. DIVERGENT PATHS

My impressions of ACT-UP were formed during my participation in the demonstrations and attendance at the weekly meetings in New York City over a two-year period (1990–1992) and through conversations with participants whose involvement pre-dated and was more extensive than mine. It was also helpful to me to review the files of Marty Robinson and Bill Bahlman in the collection of the National Museum and Archive of Lesbian and Gay History at the Lesbian and Gay Community Services Center in New York.

Articles from the gay press (especially in *BLK*, *The Advocate*, and *Outweek*) about interracial understanding, or the lack of it, among gay men would fill several folders; most recently novelist James Earl Hardy has written some strong editorials on that theme. On Marlon Riggs and Isaac Julien, see Kobena Mercer, "Dark and Lovely Too: Black Gay Men in Independent Film," pp. 238–56, and B. Ruby Rich, "When Difference Is (More Than) Skin Deep," pp. 318–39, both in Martha Gever, ed., *Queer Looks* (New York: Routledge, 1993). See also Russell Leong, ed., *Asian-American Sexualities* (New York: Routledge, 1996); William G. Hawkeswood, *One of the Children: Gay Black Men in Harlem* (Berkeley: University of California Press, 1996); and Keith Boykin, *One More River to Cross: Black and Gay in America* (New York: Pantheon, 1997). Among its other important qualities, Boykin's book offers a wake-up call to anyone who believes that images of modern gay diversity are ubiquitous in this society; as recently as the late 1980s, Boykin (who attended Harvard Law School and worked in the Clinton White House) assumed that he was not gay because he did not fit the gender-role stereotype. Daneel Buring's "Gay Activism Behind the Magnolia Curtain: The Memphis Gay Coalition, 1979–1991" in the *Journal of Homosexuality* 32, 1996, pp. 113–135, chronicled a particularly depressing example of the failure of interracial cooperation in a gay group.

Though this book ends in the early 1990s, several anthologies published later in the decade deal with conflicts among gay men that were already percolating in the 1980s. Even a glance comparing any two of the following books provides a sense of vast disagreements and tensions: Bruce Bawer, ed., *Beyond Queer* (New York: Free Press, 1994); Michael Bronski, ed., *Taking Liberties* (New York: Richard Kasak, 1996); Michael Lowenthal, ed., *Gay Men at the Millenium* (New York: Putnam, 1997); Mark Thompson, ed., *Gay Soul* (San Francisco: HarperSanFrancisco, 1994); Lawrence Schimel and Carol Queen, eds., *PoMoSexuals* (San Francisco: Cleis Press, 1997).

The zaniest of all the 1990s publications that touched on the issues of a divided community is Mark Simpson, ed., *Anti-Gay* (London: Freedom Editions/Cassell, 1996), which, despite the implications of its title, is not a right-wing "family values" collection, but an anthology devoted to a gay critique of subculture conformity and trendiness. The book includes valid criticisms and a fair amount of hyperbole. (When a fine gay novelist and journalist like John Weir writes in his contribution to *Anti-Gay* that he isn't gay anymore because he can't afford the gym membership, he is being pointed and funny. When he writes in the same essay that the next time he sees a carload of New Jersey dudes gay-bashing a guy in the Village, he will cheer them on, he is anything but.) Daniel Harris's *The Rise and Fall of Gay Culture* (New York: Hyperion, 1997) is another landmark of the-glass-is-half-empty spirit of the moment. In a book of interesting insights about camp and pornography and unmerciful grumpiness about everything else, Harris belittles the oldtime Mattachine line, the Gay Liberation Front approach, and 1980s identity politics as equally ineffective, while deriding as foolish and inauthentic gay ventures such as Alyson Publications, the sermons of Troy Perry, and even the Names Project Quilt ("the pinnacle of AIDS kitsch . . . [which] exudes a spurious aura of artsy-craftsyness, of kindly grannies in bifocals and bonnets stitching up a storm").

Other useful readings that illustrate the widening gap in perceptions of gay life and identity circa 1990 include Marshall Kirk and Hunter Madsen's call for a more decorous middle-class public image, *After the Ball* (New York: Doubleday, 1990); Darrell Yates Rist's account of his travels, *Heartlands: A Gay Man's Odyssey Across America* (New York: Dutton, 1992); Michelangelo Signorile's cogent defense of selective "outing," *Queer in America* (New York: Random House, 1993); and Bruce Bawer's critique of gay subcultural values in *A Place at the Table* (New York: Poseidon, 1994).

Acknowledgments

First and foremost, my thanks to the many individuals who took the time for conversations and interviews or the sharing of information, research suggestions, and insights that have shaped this book and educated me about gay life in America: Michael Adams, the late Harry Adler, the late Nestor Almendros, James Baird, Thomas Baker, Elver Barker, Joseph Bauer, Bruce Bawer, the late Thom Bean, Nick Bianco, George Black, Stephen Blair, Doug Blanchard, George Bohot, the late Forman Brown, Charles Brummer, Charles Brydon, George Buse, Renee Cafiero, Hal Call, Jack Campbell, Laurie Chilcote, Floyd Clement, Rich Colantino, Tom Conner, Tim Cooley, Thomas Copeland, Bill Cotter, Quentin Crisp, Mart Crowley, Don Dade, Bob Davis, Al de Dion, Curtis Dewees, Dan Dickerson, Ken Doss, Jim Duggins, Wayne Dynes, Marvin Edwards, Gene Elder, Dr. Albert Ellis, Jules Elphant, Will Fellows, Alexander Fenn, George Ferencz, Thomas Ferrara, George Flemister, Michael Foo, Albert Friedman, Tom Galbraith, Paul Gallo, Sam Garrison, Thomas Gatch, Burt Gerrits, Laurette Giardano, Jim Gillespie, Lee Glaze, Ronald Gold, Fred Goldhaber, Paul Goldman, Hal Gomeau, Eric Gonzalez, Don Goodwin, Charles Greunberger, Barbara Grier, Keith Hall, Jerry Hoose, Duke Howze, Robert James, Warren James, Gary Jerolman, David K. Johnson, Robert Johnson, Dorr Jones, Frank Kameny, Rolland Karcher, Jonathan Ned Katz, William B. Kelley, Joe Kennedy, Jack Kersey, Harris Kimball, Seymour Kleinberg, Bob Kohler, Bob Kunst, Kiyoshi Kuromiya, Cassandra Langer, Michale Lavery, Dick Leitsch, the late Marvin Liebman, Bob Linton, Ace Lundon, Clark Marlor, Abner Mason, Arthur Maule, Joe McGrath, George McNabb, Robert Milne, Jerry Mitchell, Jesse Monteagudo, Dan Murphy, Bob Newcomb, James Ng, Terry Olsen, Bernard O'Shie, Wayne Owen, Martin Palmer, Don Paulson, George Perez, Rev. Troy Perry, William Plath, Phil Raia, Chuck Renslow, William Reynard, Ray Rigor, Sylvia Rivera, Alan Robinson, Rich Rogers, Robert Rothschild, Michael Rumaker, Jose Sarria, Dr. Bertram Schaffner, Lawrence Schimel, James T. Sears,

J. R. Seymour, Barry Sheer (a.k.a. John LeRoy), Mark Silber, David Silver, Alan Silverman, the late Don Slater, Howard Sosnicki, William Starkie, Fred Stevens, Duncan Teague, Ed Torrero, Dr. C. A. Tripp, Otto Ulrich, Henry Van Dyke, Geno Vezina, Donald Vining, Robert Vinson, Skip Ward, Joseph Washington, Steven Watson, Edward Weber, Dr. George Weinberg, Katherine Wilkins, John Wilkinson, Burke Williams, Thomas Williams, Edward Willis, Tom Wirth, Adam Wright, and Allen Young.

Special thanks to the late Jim Kepner, founding father of gay archival studies, who answered many obscure questions; to archivists Richard Wandel, Bill Walker, Tom Cook, John C. Graves, David Williams, Stephen Nonack, Wayne Phillips, and Steven Capsuto; to Jack Nichols, activist, journalist, and generous host; to Randy Wicker, a spirited man of vivid memories and an ample (if dissheveled) Rolodex; to Robert Cassanello for sharing his Florida oral-history tapes with me and alerting me to the opening of the Johns Committee files; to Lilli Vincenz for her clippings, copies of *The Homosexual Citizen*, and films of the early gay marches; to Bob Manners for all those wonderful books and good contacts; to Eric Marcus for his interview suggestions; to Martin Duberman for generously sharing many files, letters, and research leads; to Bob Batson for pointing the way in Louisiana from Clay Shaw to gay Mardi Gras; to Kevin Lally for answering all of my film-history questions and for the use of his well-stocked video library; to Hugh Hagius for the chance to peruse his collection of gay literature spanning the centuries; and to James Hill, Michael Blakenship, Wayne Slusher, David Williams, Peter Conway, Paul Brazeau, and Lawrence Rolla, for acting as my guides and/or hosts in Pensacola, Mobile, Roanoke, Louisville, Boston, New Orleans, and Chicago, respectively.

I count it a good day when I met Ed Sedarbaum and the men of SAGE in Astoria, Queens, who took the time to talk about their diverse memories—watching Gladys Bentley perform in Harlem and seeing Laurence Olivier in *The Green Bay Tree*; personal experiences of the McCarthy-era purge in Washington, D.C.; membership in the early homophile groups; firsthand knowledge of the methods of anti-gay psychiatry in the bad old days; and the trials and tribulations (and good times) of being gay in the military. Vincent Fagan of SAGE Queens was a tireless scout for more and older interview prospects. My thanks as well to Hal Gomeau and Donald Vining for telling me about the New York SAGE Heritage Foundation oral-history collection, which was a treasure trove in and of itself.

Several people gave of themselves to an extent that grew into daylong interviews or numerous visits in order to provide information on a range of subjects and to convey the flavor of the times as they saw it, and for that level of interest I am grateful to Bob Basker, Peter Conway, the late Stephen Donaldson (a.k.a. Bob Martin), Barbara Gittings, Gean Harwood, Morris Kight, Kay "Tobin" Lahusen, David Leavitt (the architect, not to be confused with the novelist of the same name), Stuart Loomis, Jack Nichols, Arthur Warner, and Doric Wilson. Doric Wilson also provided the title of this book; The Other Side of Silence was the name of his pioneering theater company in the 1970s.

I also appreciate the help I received from the staff at the New York Public Library and its International Gay Information Center (IGIC); the Library of the New York Academy of Medicine; the National Museum of Lesbian and Gay History at the Community Services Center in New York City; the Boston Atheneum; the Stonewall Library and Archives in Fort Lauderdale; the Williams-Nichols Institute in Louisville;

the New Jersey Gay and Lesbian Archives at Rutgers University; the Gender and Diversity Issues Collection at Central Connecticut State University; the Philadelphia Gay and Lesbian Archives; the Gerber-Hart Library in Chicago; the Happy Foundation in San Antonio; the Washington D.C. Historical Society; and the excellent public libraries of Boston, Chicago, Louisville, Philadelphia, San Francisco, and Tallahassee. For a writer like myself not regularly affiliated with an academic institution, access to the stacks of the libraries of Fordham University, New York University, and Tulane University made an enormous difference as well.

Mention should be made, particularly for anyone studying gay social life in America before the 1960s, of the Leo Adams Papers at the New York Public Library; the Glenn Carrington Papers at the Schomburg Center for the Study of Black Culture in Harlem; the Richard Cowan diaries and the Stewart Mitchell Papers at the Boston Atheneum; the Henry Gerber–Manuel Boyfrank correspondence at the International Gay and Lesbian Archives in Los Angeles; Jim Duggins's "Uncles Project" transcripts and the Ralph Green Scrapbooks at the Gay and Lesbian Historical Society of Northern California in San Francisco; the "J. H." World War II correspondence at the Howard-Tilton Memorial Library at Tulane University; the Johns Committee files at the Florida State Archives in Tallahassee; the Gregory Sprague Papers at the Chicago Historical Society; the Carl Van Vechten Collection at the Beinecke Library at Yale University; and the typescripts of Mae West's plays from the 1920s at the Library of Congress. All of these sources proved to be rich, vital, idiosyncratic windows on the past, and they are only some of the resources available to contemporary scholars. I regret that time and funding prevented even wider explorations.

I am grateful for the help provided by my literary agent, Faith Hamlin of Sanford J. Greenburger Associates, and by Jack Macrae of Henry Holt, both of whom showed from the outset the requisite faith in this project. I was well served by the editorial work of Rachel Klauber-Speiden, Kenn Russell, Erin Clermont, and the entire staff at Henry Holt.

The interest and enthusiasm of Mary Allen, Gerald Anders, Bruce Castellano, Tim Cooley, Ty and Ange Florie, Ross French, Stewart Galanor, Ron Koury, Kevin Lally, and Maria Soares were important to me. They are ideal readers just as they are ideal friends. Many members of the Loughery and the Orefice family have shown an interest in the progress of this book, which I appreciate.

The help provided by Joseph K. Youngerman is impossible to summarize beyond noting that he is a man of keen perceptions and boundless compassion.

Finally, I am grateful to my lover and best friend. Without Thomas Orefice, whom I have lived with and learned from over the last two decades, I would not have completed this or any other book I have written. He is one of the reasons that I know it is—no other word for it—a blessing to be gay.

John Loughery
October 1997

Index

506 • *Index*

Waddel, Tom, 416
Wade, Austin, 66
Wahl, Loren, 148
Wakefield, Dan, 268
Wales Padlock Bill (1926), 37, 155
Walker, A'lelia, 45
Walker, Benjamin, 216
Walker, Bill, 178
Walker, Jimmy, 21, 37
Walker, Mitch, 350–51
Wall Street Journal, 421
Wallace, Henry, 219
Wallace, Mike, 279, 405
Walsh, David I., 152–53
Walsh, Raoul, 63
Walter and Emmett, 77–78
Waltz in Goose Step (Garrett), 107
Wandel, Rich, 332
Wanderer of the West (film), 61, 63
War Department, 60, 137, 144–45, 148
Ward, Walter, 94–95
Wardlaw, Jack, 310
Warhol, Andy, 365
Warren, Earl, 235
Warren Commission Report, 309, 311
Washington, D.C., 79, 151, 181, 202
Washington Afro-American, 270
Washington Blade, 427
Washington Confidential, 198
Washington Gay Activists Alliance, 354
Washington Mattachine, 264–67, 335
Washington Post, 267, 271, 296, 354
Waters, Ethel, 46
Watkins, Perry, 307–8, 354–55
Watney, Simon, 432
Waukesha, Wisc., arrests, 257
Wayne, John, 210
WBAI (radio station), 268
Webb, Clifton, 74
Webster Hall, 48
Weeks, Jeffrey, 407, 411, 412
Weinberg, George, 162–63
Weinberg, Jonathan, 60
"We Know Who We Are" (Callen and Berkowitz), 424
Welch, Joseph, 213
Welcome, The (Creekmore), 186
Welles, Sumner, 12, 100, 153, 200, 210
Wellman, William, 20

Well of Loneliness, The (Hall), 21–22, 42, 82
West, Mae, 36–38, 62, 94, 106
West Chester State Teachers College, 77
Westmoreland, General, 307
West Street Gang, The (Wilson), 415
Wexberg, Ervin, 122
Whale, James, 64, 74
"Where Have All the Sissies Gone?" (Kleinberg), 348
Wherry, Kenneth, 201, 202, 209, 227
White, Dan, 399, 400–402
White, Edmund, 379, 414–15, 425, 449
White, Kevin, 128
White, Dr. William Alanson, 119
White House conference (1977), 404
White Night Riots, 401
Whitehall Induction Center picket, 269
Whitman, Howard, 167–68
Whitman, Walt, 50, 54, 184, 237, 242, 411, 449
Whitman Walker Clinic, 433
Whitmore, George, 415
Whittington, Gale, 313
"Whom Should We Tell?" (Barker), 231–32
Who's Afraid of Virginia Woolf? (Albee), 292
Wichita gay rights ordinance, 384
Wicker, Randy, 250, 267–69, 331
Wilde, Oscar, 25, 29, 31, 50, 54, 77, 86, 184, 409, 449
Wilder, Billy, 155
Wilder, Thornton, 25, 58
Wildmon, Donald, 404–5
Wilkins, Roy, 255
Willer, Shirley, 271
Williams, Al, 47
Williams, Cecil, 286
Williams, David, 333
Williams, Emlyn, 357
Williams, Tennessee, 184, 211–12, 292, 299–300, 301
Willingham, Calder, 186
Wilson, Doric, 250–51, 260, 301, 318, 415, 449
Wilson, Edmund, 39
Wilson, Lanford, 260, 293